A GENERAL HISTORY OF EUROPE

GENERAL EDITOR: DENYS HAY

A GENERAL HISTORY OF EUROPE

General Editor: Denys Hay

For many years the volumes of Denys Hay's distinguished *General History of Europe* have been standard recommendations for university students, sixth formers and general readers. They offer broad surveys of European history, in which the detailed discussion (on a regional or continent-wide basis) of social, economic, administrative and intellectual themes is woven into a clear framework of political events. They set out to combine scholarship with accessibility in texts which are both attractively written and intellectually vigorous. Now the entire sequence is under revision by its original authors – most of the volumes for the first time since they were published – and the books are being redesigned and reset. The revised *General History of Europe*, when complete, will contain twelve volumes, three of them wholly new.

★ *Available in the original edition*

◇ *New edition published in the revised format*

◻ *New title in preparation*

EUROPE

1880–1945

SECOND EDITION

J. M. ROBERTS

LONGMAN
London and New York

Longman Group UK Limited,
Longman House, Burnt Mill, Harlow,
Essex CM20 2JE, England
and Associated Companies throughout the world.

Published in the United States of America
by Longman Inc., New York

First published 1967
Second edition 1989

British Library Cataloguing in Publication Data
Roberts, J. M.
  Europe, 1880–1945 – 2nd ed – (A General history
  of Europe)
  1. Europe – History – 1871–1918
  2. Europe – History – 1918–1945
  I. Title
  940.2'8   D359
  ISBN 0-582-02388-2   CSD
  ISBN 0-582-49414-1   PPR

Library of Congress Cataloging-in-Publication Data
Roberts, J. M. (John Morris), 1928–
  Europe, 1880–1945.

  (A General history of Europe)
  Bibliography: p.
  Includes index.
  1. Europe – History – 1871–1918.   2. Europe –
History – 1918–1945.   I. Title.   II. Series.
D424.R6 1989   940   87–22524
ISBN 0-582-02388-2
ISBN 0-582-49414-1 (pbk.)

Set in 10/12pt Bembo Linotron 202

Produced by Longman Singapore Publishers (Pte) Ltd.
Printed in Singapore

CONTENTS

LIST OF MAPS

LIST OF ABBREVIATIONS

AHR   *The American Historical Review*
AR   *The Annual Register*
CEH   *The Cambridge Economic History of Europe*, vol. VI,
        The Industrial Revolutions and after
CMH   *The Cambridge Modern History*, vol. XII
GDD   *German Diplomatic Documents*, selected and translated
        by E. T. S. Dugdale (4 vols) 1928–31
HJ   *The Historical Journal*
JCH   *The Journal of Contemporary History*
JPE   *The Journal of Political Economy*
NCMH   *The New Cambridge Modern History*
RH   *Revue Historique*
TRHS   *The Transactions of the Royal Historical Society*

PREFACE AND ACKNOWLEDGEMENTS

PREFACE TO THE FIRST EDITION

Many people have helped me with this book. To Professor Hay
I shall always be grateful for suggesting to me that I should lay
aside my interests in an earlier period for a time in order to find
out something about recent history. He made the experiment
much easier and more pleasant than it might have been by his
tolerance in waiting for my manuscript and commenting on it.
Several other friends and colleagues were also good enough to
read parts of this book and answer my questions. For their patience and generous gifts of time and attention I am deeply grateful:
they are too many to thank by name and I hope they will allow
the two whom I laid most heavily under contribution to stand as
representatives of them all – Mr James Joll, who read more than
half the text, and Mr J. R. C. Wright, who read the proofs. I also
owe special thanks to Miss Elizabeth Ratcliff, who typed and
retyped much of the earlier draft with a sharp eye for its inadequacies, and to Miss J. Hetherington, who on several occasions
came to my rescue by typing against a close deadline.

From two other sources I have received help of a different sort,
which has no less deeply marked this book. One is my College.
In a collegiate and tutorial system, the friendship and stimulus of
pupils and colleagues deeply and subtly influence even the
humdrum task of writing a textbook. I cannot believe that such
influences are anything but beneficial and they are only a small
part of the benefits for which I owe thanks to Merton. Finally,
I wish to thank my wife. She helped me greatly by reading,

checking, and commenting on what I had written, but even more by her unflagging encouragement and support.

No one except myself, of course, bears any responsibility for the shortcomings of my final version. It may be that there cannot be a satisfactory general history of these crowded years in one volume; certainly I thought so at several moments while writing it. If this is so, I still do not regret the experiment. Like the other contributors to this series, I have tried to emphasize general patterns. I have also tried not to lose sight of the circumstances in which those patterns appeared and the particular colours these circumstances have sometimes given them. This has meant a long book, though I have tried to keep in view the criteria indicated in the first chapter and to include what is relevant to the main theme, the self-destructiveness shown by Europe in these years.

Some readers will undoubtedly complain of what has been left out. If they only regret the uninformative catalogues of names, dates and titles which often appear in manuals because of a presumed timeless historical 'importance', remote from any particular argument, I shall not mind; the place for such things is an encyclopedia. If, more seriously, they think a major theme has been neglected, I can only apologize for what must be, in the last resort, a personal judgment. I hope they will be forbearing enough to reflect on what would have to be cut out to make room for what they miss. Overall, if this book is thought a useful starting-point, I shall be satisfied.

It is convenient to note here that, in order to save space, conventional abbreviations (e.g. T.U.C., S.P.D.) have been used in the text after the first appearance of the full expression for which they stand. Abbreviations listed above are those used in references. Full names and dates of birth of persons mentioned will be found in the index.

Merton College, Oxford　　　　　　　　　　　　　JOHN ROBERTS
August 1966

The publishers are indebted to the following for permission to reproduce copyright material:

Cambridge University Press for material from *The Cambridge Economic History of Europe, Vol. VI*, and The Twentieth Century Fund, New York, for material from *World Population and Production* by W. S. and E. S. Woytinsky (1953).

PREFACE TO THE SECOND EDITION

After more than twenty years, I still owe great debts to all those who helped me with the original edition of this book and whom I thanked in its preface. If I do not now repeat those thanks specifically it is only because I should now add to their names those of a great many other people, too numerous to record, who have favoured me with comments, suggestions, criticism and notes of errors to be corrected. I hope they will feel that my gratitude is clear from the evidence in these pages of the changes which have followed from what they said to me.

Rereading my original text in preparing this edition did not, though, lead me to think radical reconstruction was desirable. For good or ill, modestly or immodestly, I thought its general approach, plan and proportions seemed to have stood the test of time and the sales seemed to bear out that judgment. I decided therefore to restrict myself to particular and specific amendments of the text. Several were needed because there was recent writing to which attention should be drawn, some because individual statements were out of date, some in the interests of greater brevity and lucidity. Once or twice I have changed a convention adopted in the first edition and in accordance with the imposed scheme of the general editor of the series of which this book is part, the bibliographical notes (Further reading and reference books) have been consolidated at the end.

It may also be useful to emphasize a few points of a more general nature. In the first place, the book's structure was determined by my wish to analyse a continuum in a way which emphasizes the big determinants – population, economic change, ideas. In pursuing a single topic, therefore, the reader should use the index. Not all of what he or she wants to know about a single topic will be likely to be found in one place.

Secondly, although this book is about a period in which a true global history becomes a reality for the first time, and in which no part of the world remains absolutely immune to the great events and influences of the age, it is a book about *European* history, and part of a series on *European* history. Subject to what is said on p. 2 below, it is not about *world* history 1880–1945; had I wished it to be, I should not have written this book in this series. A final point which may need explaining, since some friendly critics have appeared to overlook it, is that I meant to write a history of Europe, not an anthology of national histories (though there are sections in it about the national histories of major countries). Whenever possible I have tried to establish connexions, ties, general influences, without obscuring or disguising the immense particularism of daily life and social tradition in even the most closely developed and closely articulated societies. I should perhaps add that although my closing date, 1945, still requires, for a true historical perspective, that the book closes in sombre tones, the added perspective given by another twenty years has revealed how tenacious was the fire in the ashes, and how much the vitality of European countries, east and west, had survived disaster. But that is best recognized by the decision of a general editor and publisher to prolong the series by another volume by another hand which will tell that splendid story of resurgence.

Merton College, Oxford   JOHN ROBERTS
March, 1987

1

THE SUBJECT-MATTER AND MATERIALS

One big difference between ourselves and our predecessors centuries ago, is our acceptance of historical change. We are no longer surprised by it; it is taking place all the time, and more rapidly and widely than ever before. The growth of population in the last 200 years is enough by itself to make much of previous history seem almost static. Yet this is the sort of change of which comparatively few people, perhaps, are aware; there are others which have been more spectacular. Since the first edition of this book was published, men have gone to the moon and walked about on it. Yet among those who watched them on television screens as they did so were many who had been born before there were aeroplanes, and even before the motor-car had become a familiar object.

Another great change which has come about since 1880 has been the establishment of communications and international relations which have made the whole globe 'one world'. In 1880 the Americas were in large measure still untroubled by political events in other continents. Great tracts of them were, if not undiscovered, still unexplored. The rest of the known world was mainly dominated directly or indirectly by a few European states. Their dominance outside the Americas grew into a world supremacy which reached a climax at the beginning of the first world war and began to crumble before the end of the second. As it crumbled, a new world appeared in which Europe was overshadowed by two super-states and jostled by a throng of new nations. These great innovations, roughly speaking, are what this book is about.

EUROPEAN AND WORLD HISTORY

Because these changes were worldwide, Europe's history is inseparable from world history between 1880 and 1945. Yet we can still distinguish a 'European' history with themes of its own in these years. At least until 1917, and to some extent even until 1945, Europe was the decisive arena of world power, as it had been for centuries. Since the Muslims turned back from Tours in the eighth century, the decisions made in Europe had increasingly been the decisions which altered the history of the world. However many millions it ruled, Akbar's Empire in the end changed history less than the foundation of the East India Company, and the Declaration of the Rights of Man and the Citizen had greater repercussions than the thousand-volume encyclopedias of China. The omission from this book of the history of most of the globe can therefore be defended, because political power was the most important determinant of European history. For all her heritage of shared civilization, Europe was not an economic, nor a social, nor a racial or national entity. Such identity and unity as she possessed in these years was essentially the identity and unity of a system of power, though one beginning to decay. Europe contained, for most of the years between 1880 and 1945, the most important forces in world politics, and was the focus of the arrangements which governed the world: these arrangements left unregulated only the western hemisphere (and even there the British Royal Navy tacitly provided the under-writing of power needed by the Monroe Doctrine). The nature of these arrangements was determined mainly by events in Europe itself, and not outside it. So, European history is a distinguishable topic in these years.

At some time after 1880 came a turning point in world history. By 1945 the decisions taken in Washington and Tokyo were already as important as those taken in London, Moscow or Berlin (a little later, the decisions made in Peking would be important too). But this book includes only such non-European history as is necessary to explain the shattering of the European preponderance of power. Traditionally, historians of Europe write about Russia and this principle covers that country: she was a European before she was a world power. The history of the United States, on the other hand, has to be left out. Important as it is to the understanding of the world today, it was in these years only occasionally decisive for Europe. For most of the time the United States played little part in the organization of world power except in the Far East. At the same time, while Europe has the limelight, the stage of this history must be worldwide. The steamship and the railway, the legacy of the colonial past and the expansive power of commerce make this inevitable.

If one theme of this book is the ebbing of Europe's pre-eminence in the system of world power, another must be the passing of an epoch in European civilization. It is not easy to characterize the cultural and mental style of civilizations. They contain contradictory elements, importations and survivals from other cultures, and it is very difficult to delimit them geographically or chronologically. Yet a civilization existed between 1880 and 1945, reaching its greatest coherence and strength just before 1914, which was European in its origins although already transplanted to North and South America and the British white colonies and although unevenly spread among European countries themselves. Its essential features had few clear and unqualified expressions, but it was a civilization which had come to be distinguished from others by the emphasis it placed on the individual, by its increasing separation of social and political institutions, by its material wellbeing, and by its growing rationality. Another way of characterizing it is to describe its fundamental institutions, such as the sovereign state, the self-regulating market and the scientific method.[1] We can call it liberal bourgeois civilization, and a fuller picture of its nature will emerge later in this book. All we need do here is to remark that by 1914 it had carried the control of violence and unreason in national and international life further than ever before, and brought Europeans to a previously unmatched level of material and mental achievement. But this success was followed by a decline in the vitality of this civilization. It was also followed by an intensification of a process which had already begun, the adoption of European institutions and standards in other parts of the world. European civilization was the first to impose itself on the whole surface of the globe. In 1880, some of its greatest successes in diffusing its institutions and

---

1 Another choice of fundamental institutions can be found in K. Polanyi, *Origins of Our Time* (London, 1945), p. 13 and a more extended and informal discussion in my own book *The Triumph of the West* (London, 1985).

ideas were still to come. When they did, the clarity of outline of European civilization gradually blurred into a world culture and in this way, too, its distinction was increasingly lost.

This cultural change is the second major theme of this book, but it is not easy to separate it from the political story. This book is not, therefore, divided on traditional lines and a mixture of analytical and narrative chapters has been adopted in order to bring out, whenever possible, the general rather than the local and particular, characteristics of European history in this period. Wherever possible, statistics have been cited to condense general changes which cover long periods. The criteria of relevance to the central themes of European history have led me to set aside some topics often included in textbooks of this kind. The history of the Ottoman Empire, for example, is only dealt with here in so far as it immediately affects non-Turkish Europe. The smaller nations get short shrift on somewhat different grounds: in so far as they are affected by general trends, their history recapitulates that of the major states. The criterion of historical effectiveness must almost always mean that their history has to be ignored to give space to explain that of bigger and more effective nations. This is not mere deification of success; many of the most important facts of European history have been its great failures. They have, none the less, been failures which have affected large numbers of people, and this is the only standard of importance which, in the long run, the historian can discover within the confines of his own subject.

International relations pose special difficulties. There is much more to them than diplomatic negotiation. Yet the diplomacy itself must be adequately rendered, and it is its nature to be very detailed and complicated. Mr Kennan, who has written one of the major works of diplomatic history of this century, noted this. 'The more I saw of . . . the doings of an official generation slightly older than my own', he writes, 'the more it was borne in upon me that the genuine image of the diplomatic process is hardly to be recaptured in historical narrative unless the lens through which it is viewed is a sharp one and the human texture of which it consists becomes visible in considerable detail.'[2] Coming as it does from a historian who spent many years as a

2 George F. Kennan, *Soviet-American Relations, 1917–1920*, vol. I, *Russia leaves the War* (Princeton, 1956), p. vii.

professional diplomatic officer, this judgment must command respect. But narrative on the scale which it demands is impossible in a book like this. Accepting, therefore, that selection must falsify, I have adopted the compromise of treating diplomacy only within a general context of international relations. The main concern of the chapters on international relations is with facts revealing the changes of states' attitudes. I have tried to confine diplomatic narrative to major episodes to which diplomacy was central. At such points, quotation and a slightly closer narrative attempt to give the reader some idea of the reality behind the colourless abstractions of 'England', 'Germany' or 'Russia'.

THE PROBLEM OF SOURCES

The series of which this book is a part was intended to go beyond the conventional textbook by introducing its readers to sources and methods. Recent history raises no fundamental or peculiar questions of historical criteria. There is no reason to re-fight battles over history and moral judgment in this book. Perhaps it may now be accepted that so long as a historian is acting as a historian, his criteria must arise from his own study and must not be imported from some other autonomous field. He must make decisions about what was historically important, not about, let us say, what was theologically or aesthetically important, significant though that might be to a believer or an artist. This means he must look for what had the most far-reaching effects. History is not the story of success, but the story of what was effective, for good or ill, in modifying men's behaviour. (This is one reason for giving more attention to economic movements and social structure than our predecessors would have done.) In this book, that means more analytical and less narrative material than there would have been in a book written half a century ago.

Problems of content nonetheless go beyond questions about criteria. In the first place, the historian of recent times has a subject-matter different in kind from that studied by some of his colleagues. Recent history has, for example, a mass character more marked than the history of earlier times. The historian has to concern himself more and more with the disentangling of mass trends and less and less with the exploration of the work of individuals. This does not mean that individual men do not count. The twentieth century would have been very different without the decisions taken by Hilter and Stalin, the speculations of Freud and Einstein. But we have become more aware of the web of necessity in which even exceptional men must move, especially if they are men of action (as, indeed, recent discussion of the role of Hitler abundantly makes clear). We are more aware, too, of how much greater, usually, is the influence of social and economic institutions – the strategic factors shaping society – than that of conscious policy. Now, we realize, do statesmen operate in a private mental world; climates of opinion, received ideas, even intellectual crazes and failures, all influence them, sometimes unconsciously. One way in which modern history is distinctive is that it deals with societies which are increasingly aware of such facts as these, and therefore try to come to terms with them.

The self-consciousness of modern Europe raises another problem. Some of the emphasis which is placed on general and mass trends in modern history arises from a sort of optical illusion, because we have so much more information about the general nature and working of recent societies than we have for earlier periods. This is one of the difficulties posed by the evidence available to the modern historian. The ancient historian or the medievalist has often to wring his conclusions from fragmentary and inadequate sources. At best, his work is defined by what is known to be available as source material. His characteristic attitude is one of close scrutiny and interrogation; he puts his documents on the rack, as it were. Where evidence is thin, individual men seem to stand out heroically, taking decisions which drastically and simply shape historical events. The modern historian, on the other hand, tends to see individuals in conflict with the inertia of history and society. The concentration and technical improvement of the apparatus of power have been perfected, but our awareness of limits on the exercise of power has also increased.

THE PROBLEM OF EVIDENCE

Copious information is far from being an unmixed blessing to the recent historian. The abundance of his sources is, in fact, his central problem. They are, quite simply, unmanageable. There is no simple answer to the question 'What are the sources of the modern historian?' because the only defensible one would be the logical but nonsensical 'everything'. And although this may conceivably be an acceptable answer for an earlier period, it is now useless because of the weight of evidence about the recent past. More documentation is generated by the modern world than by its predecessors, and more of what is generated is preserved.

Spreading literacy has meant more printed materials of all kinds, whether books, pamphlets or periodicals. This has been obvious since the seventeenth century. But the output of 'papers' which form the conventional primary materials of the historian has also risen. In part the reasons are technical (the typewriter and camera – and now the computer tape – have made the keeping of records easier), but it is also a result of the increasing complexity of social organization. All social and economic organisms now produce documents on a vast scale. The greatest of them is the state, which has everywhere taken on more and more tasks in recent decades which have swollen its administrative archives. Nor is that the whole story. Speedier communications and the existence of more sovereign states and international bodies have swollen diplomatic records. Legislation has not only so multiplied that it is now the characteristic activity of the modern state, but it has been addressed to complicated matters which have increased the complexity and bulk of individual statutes so that they often go unread even by the legislators who pass them. Most European countries, too, have had parliamentary institutions during at least some part of this period and the debates and proceedings of these bodies have usually been printed.

The result has been intimidating. A few instances quickly convey an impression of it. When, for example, historians began to prepare the official civil histories of Great Britain in the second world war, the records of twenty departments, some of which contained 2 million files, confronted them.[3] When Germany was defeated in 1945, 400 *tons* of material from the German foreign office alone were seized by the Allied authorities. A comparative example provides another good illustration; in 1959, we are told, French archives of diplomacy already held more documents for

3 W. K. Hancock and M. M. Gowing, *British War Economy* (London, 1949), p.x.

the years since 1914 than for the whole history of French diplomacy backwards from that date to its foundation under Richelieu.[4] Once the line between the conventional primary source and the secondary study is crossed, the flood is even worse. In Russia, something like 20,000 books have already appeared about the second world war.[5]

This mass of paper is the most obvious difference between the problems facing the recent historian and those facing his colleague who studies earlier periods. Yet it is not the only abundance which confronts him. Industrial society has multiplied not only written documents, but artifacts of all kinds. This material abundance gives the modern historian a quite different range of experience from that of his classical or medieval colleagues. We do not have to go far to see the houses of the men of 1880; many of us are still living in them. For the historian of modern urbanization, scores of cities are available for direct inspection, while the ancient historian has to make do with a few fortuitous survivals. Of course, the historian may find irritating gaps even in this abundance. Collections of aircraft, for instance, are few, and far from complete. But a historian of modern transport can go to an enormous mass of recorded and photographed information when he cannot find a surviving model of an early bombing aeroplane; the historian of, say, medieval navies has infinitely smaller resources. The photographic record alone, indeed, has still to be exploited fully by historians. Our collections of still photographs take us back to the Crimean War, but for this century we have millions of feet of movie record, much of it unexplored. Other means of recording have received even less attention, but there are signs that this is beginning to change.

Conscious preservation has also done much to prevent these copious records from undergoing erosion by destruction and loss on the scale which might have occurred in other centuries. Rats are fewer, buildings drier and fire precautions more effective than in the past. Occasionally, a bombing raid or a battle does something to reduce the mass, but such incidents are hardly significant. French foreign office records were destroyed in great quantity in

4 Examples from Daniel H. Thomas and Lynn M. Case, *Guide to the Diplomatic Archives of Western Europe* (Philadelphia, 1959).
5 Information kindly provided by Professor John Erickson.

Paris in May 1940 to prevent their capture, and even more were accidentally burnt in fighting four years later, but most of the lost material has been reconstructed from duplicates in embassies and missions abroad. Germany was the scene of some of the heaviest fighting of the last war, yet its records, by and large, survived. The typewriter, carbon-paper and the camera have made duplicates of important papers readily available. Archivists and curators are devoted to preserving what might otherwise perish. Their position reveals another source of the difficulties of the recent historian. This is a cultural fact, the obsession with the past which has marked European civilization more and more strongly since the romantic era. It has led not only to the preservation and publication of documents – in the narrow and conventional sense of the term – on a colossal scale, in an age when they are more plentiful than ever before, but also to the reverential preservation of monuments from the more distant past by learned societies, governments and interested private persons. Indeed, mere preservation is no longer thought to require justification; every local history society thinks it has an unanswerable case when it seeks to protect what is left of the past. Even living statesmen are now encouraged to record on tape their comments on events which they have observed for the benefit of archives of sound-recording. Much of this is pointless. Like the reverential preservation of every scrap of paper written on by secondrate men of letters, it is an example of a flight from discrimination. But it is also an example of the dangers inherent in the assumption of positivist historians that, if enough facts are piled up, a changeless, timeless historical 'truth' will emerge. A false historical-mindedness in this way enslaves the historian to the fetish of the Facts.

Of course, not all concern to record and preserve evidence is like this. Consciously accumulated record has always given the historian evidence of enormous value; inscriptions are an example. One recent instance was an *enquête orale* into the French Resistance which interrogated 2,000 witnesses in a standard manner under central direction.[6] Nor, for all the abundance, is the evidence of recent history without its gaps: historians can still argue about the nature and origin of Hitler's decisions on policy. Some destruction has been effective, papers still private conceal the sources of some

6 See H. Michel, 'Le Comité d'Histoire de la deuxième guerre mondiale', *RH*, 1965, p. 132.

important decisions, and few states permit access to their most recent archives. Only the defeat of Germany in 1945 made it possible for a satisfactory study of German war aims in the *first* world war to be undertaken. None the less, such a mass of available material has made nonsense of the old dream that historical judgment might, in principle, be preceded by a complete survey of every available piece of evidence. This ambition always had its logical weaknesses; its impracticability is now manifest. In so far as the historian must now ask himself rigorously when confronted with new evidence, 'evidence for *what*?', this is an excellent thing. But it presents a major difficulty at the outset to the writer of general history. There is just too much to read, or even to scan. Nor does it seem that systems of information retrieval will come to his help for a long time, if ever.

Something has been done to help the historian to make sense of this abundance by publishing selections of material on certain important topics. The influence of growing literacy and the competition of rival claims to belief and allegiance have increasingly driven states to abandon the assumptions of privacy which governed their relations in more aristocratic ages, and this has provided more published material for the historian to study. Unfortunately this is by no means always unambiguously helpful. Governments interested in publicity and propaganda have published much under the impulse of the urge to justify themselves and vilify their opponents.[7] Even when such a selection of documents for publication is reasonably impartial, a historian must consult other materials in order to evaluate it properly. This can be obvious in an instance like that of the huge mass of evidence assembled for the trial of war criminals at Nuremberg; revealing though it was, it is hardly the whole story about Germany after 1933. Collections of diplomatic documents concerned with the origins of the Great War have also had their built-in weaknesses. The big German series, *Die grosse Politik der europäischen Kabinette*, was begun in the 1920s and reflects the contemporary preoccupation with 'war guilt'. Nor was this the only subtle and half-conscious bias which shaped this great collec-

7 There has also, of course, been systematic destruction of materials in order to bury the past; an example is the destruction or falsification of much of the record of German concentration camps (see Michel, pp. 133–4).

tion. When it became possible to study the German foreign office records after 1945, says an American scholar, 'tests did not reveal essential documents . . . that were not printed by the editors of *Die grosse Politik*, [but] they did reveal that the editors, in making their selection, were influenced by a desire not to make the task of the rulers of the Weimar Republic more difficult, and not to injure the reputation of foreign statesmen who were still active after World War I and who were sympathetic to Germany'.[8] Other collections have been more conspicuously tendentious than this. The Russian *Livre Noir* was a collection of documents published by the Bolsheviks to discredit Tsarist policy.[9] The 'Nye Report' of the American Committee investigating the munitions industry in 1935 printed a mass of documents on the entry of the United States to the Great War with the intention of influencing American policy. Other publications emanating from official enquiries, such as the French National Assembly's postwar investigation of the events of the 1930s, may without being corrupt, nevertheless reflect special interests and be to that extent unrepresentative.

Collections of this sort often cut across the old distinction between primary and secondary sources. But, so, oddly enough, does much of the statistical and purely 'factual' material which has become more abundant as the state extends its role. Where policy has to be settled over such matters as public health or education, statistical and factual material is needed. It is put together in accordance with criteria of relevance which are those of a certain group of interested persons. From this point of view, the resulting surveys are sometimes like historical studies. Reports such as those of British Royal Commissions or the Italian agricultural enquiries are both primary evidence for the historian of policy and sometimes secondary monographs on the background of their own recommendations. There are many available from non-governmental sources, too, for it was an important achievement of European culture to invent the social survey and social studies and they have proliferated since 1880. Such ambiguities, of course, are not peculiar to recent history. But they may be more

8 Sontag, in Thomas and Case, pp. 87–8.
9 The instance of diplomatic documents is admirably discussed in the valuable bibliographical essay at the end of A. J. P. Taylor, *The Struggle for Mastery in Europe* (London, 1954), pp. 569–601.

dangerous there, because of the great bulk of official paper which sometimes supplies tempting shortcuts.

Yet in spite of the enormous output of historical books and articles on modern subjects, the general historian does not always have good secondary studies by specialists to cut a path for him through material which he has not time to study at first hand. Often this is because the materials are not available, whether because they have been destroyed or not yet revealed. Even in such circumstances, none the less, much can be found out by the judicious interrogation of the sources and witnesses which are available, as the history of the Suez crisis shows. Gaps may well be there because no one has yet troubled to fill them. When this book was first written, for example, no comprehensive study existed of the effects of land reform in eastern Europe after 1918 although many states then embarked upon schemes for the break-up of the great estates which had been the framework of economy and society in the east since the seventeenth century. The changes must have been as great as those in western Europe after 1789, but their impact could only be traced piecemeal.

Undoubtedly, some of the missing studies would prove very difficult to carry out. If we think about Freud and his influence it is not hard to find out what he wrote and said, and it is easy to guess that it must have been important. But how important? What part, for example, did his teaching play in the increasing secularization of modern society? Was it more important than, say, anticlerical propaganda or urbanization? Such questions cannot be answered without many more secondary studies. We can assess roughly the impact of Freud's teaching and doctrine on the academic and clinical mind, but it is an immense task to document the slow, informal irrigation of society at large by new ideas. Yet millions of Europeans who may never have heard of Freud's name are now affected by his work, even when this is grotesquely misinterpreted. Further, when his influence on educated people is considered, there remain huge problems of discrimination. It seems likely, for instance, that some of Freud's work affected widely held views on sexual matters. Most educated people in this country now believe, in a vague sort of way, that we ought to be less sexually prudish than the Victorians are alleged to have been, and that sexual morality should be guarded rather by example and exhortation than by penal sanctions. The change is revolutionary, and it is difficult to believe that Freud had nothing to do with it (though, possibly, through misunderstandings of what he said). Yet it may also owe much to John Stuart Mill, to the decline of religious discipline, or to the invention of cheap and efficient contraceptives. When intellectual influences of this sort have to be considered by the general historian, he cannot go far for himself. Yet he must make a tentative judgment on inadequate evidence, for such a matter is of fundamental importance. Modern communications make the diffusion of ideas in a largely literate population so rapid that Freud was undoubtedly a name more widely known in his own lifetime than was Newton's a hundred years after his death. Moreover, ideas and assumptions circulate in disguised and concealed forms, once they have achieved a certain currency. Novels, newspapers and films feed the public with the ideas of a Freud without ever invoking his name.[10]

This suggests another difficulty. Mass literacy has meant, in most countries, a mass press whose output is enormous in bulk and difficult to assess.[11] Newspapers no longer serve the historian mainly as a chronicle of reported fact, but also provide material which may illuminate that culture of the majority previously so hard to observe. The reactions of an educated élite, the study of whose reading matter has so often given social and cultural historians their main access to the past, no longer remains the only documentation by which we can get at the culture of 'the common man'. The medievalist has had to accept the limitations, as well as the advantages, of having as his subject matter a culture with only a small literary élite. An age of mass literacy similarly presents advantages and limitations. The crucial question about a mass press – 'who read it?' – is often hard to answer. Yet, if we can answer it, we can understand the twentieth-century city-dweller as we can never hope to understand his medieval counterpart. And that is very important in an age whose cultural life

10 The example of Freud, raw evidence of whose impact surrounds us, should make us cautious about assertions about the influence of intellectuals in more remote ages.
11 The British Museum Newspaper Library at Colindale increases annually by roughly 5,500 English and 800 overseas parcels. In addition, it also acquires over 12,500 reels of microfilm each year (over 200,000 reels are already held by the Library). 1984 acquisitions, require more than 750 feet of shelving. I am grateful to the staff of the Library for this information.

is divided between 'high', minority, activity and 'low', mass, activity as never before.

AIDS TO STUDY

This brings us back, uncomfortably, to the problem of over-abundant evidence. Acton's vision of a final version of history became impossible long ago simply for practical reasons, even had it remained intellectually acceptable. But there have also been compensations. The modern historian can use works of reference written after the lessons of scholarship had been learned and while respect for accurate learning was at its height. Whatever gaps may remain, scholarly investigations have gone forward since 1880 as never before. This has been partially a result of literate Europe's historical-mindedness; one of its first manifestations was the rapid appearance of a number of new historical journals at the end of the nineteenth century.[12] It is also in part a result of the demands of modern life which have made access to ordered information more and more necessary. The rest of this chapter will describe some of the resultant advantages for the historian of recent times.

Indispensable help can be found in many unspectacular but invaluable summaries of factual information. Besides the obvious encyclopedias, most countries produce several annual or periodical repertories of useful information; a well-known British example is *The Statesman's Yearbook*, which began to appear in 1864. There also exist many handbooks containing valuable data on more specialized subjects, such as the League of Nations economic reports. They can be supplemented by biographical dictionaries. Many of these have been published as national biographical repertories, but not all are complete (that for France, for example, had reached the letter D when the first edition of this book appeared and has now, nineteen years later, almost completed G; Italy, in the same time, has got from B to C. Works for reference

---

12 In one decade, for example, there appeared the *Mittheilungen des Instituts für oesterreichische Geschichtsforschung* (1880), *Rivista storica italiana* (1884), *English Historical Review* (1886), *Deutsche Zeitschrift für Geschichtswissenschaft* (1889). At roughly the same time, there was a great acceleration in the publication of sources in series started long before, such as the British *State Papers*.

such as these form the scholarly end of a spectrum of contemporary works which runs at its other extreme into straightforward journalism. Between the two extremes stand intermediate classes of books, such as the Chatham House series of annual surveys of international affairs, *The Annual Register*, the American *United States in World Affairs*, or the French *L'Année politique* (which was published only from 1874 to 1905). One valuable series of hybrid books is the Carnegie Foundation's 200 volumes of *Economic and Social History of the World War*, directed by J. T. Shotwell; many of these were written by participants about processes they had witnessed. The factual content is high, yet these books are neither simple repertories of data, nor objective scientific studies. Such publications must be treated critically; Namier provided a good example of the deflation of a quasi-official authoritativeness in his review of the *Survey of International Affairs, 1938* published by the authoritative Royal Institute of International Affairs (Chatham House).[13] The dangers of overlooking the admixture of interpretative comment and factual information is much less in more frankly individual reporting like that of *The Annual Register*; the comments on the Prime Minister and Archbishop of Canterbury in the 1938 volume, for example, readily disclose the writer's sympathies.[14] Nevertheless, whatever their weaknesses, and although such books must be read critically, they contain an immense amount of information, and enormously simplify the task of the student.

Many of these works contain important statistical material, but there exist also many purely statistical digests and collections. Few of them, however, go back as far as 1880, though historical reconstruction can often supplement them.[15] But over most of the period covered in this book there are continuous records of some sets of figures, even if they are not always reliable.[16] In all countries, governments and businessmen have become aware of the importance of statistics. Where there are gaps (for instance in the

13 Reprinted in *Conflicts* (London, 1942), pp. 102–20.

14 e.g. pp. 9–10, 35.

15 e.g. B. R. Mitchell and Phyllis Deane, *Abstract of British Historical Statistics* (Cambridge, 1962).

16 'Some statistics are nearly true, some are approximate guesses disguised as exact knowledge, some are merely the shortest kind of short story; and some in all three categories are meaningless': W. Ashworth, *An Economic History of England 1870–1939* (London, 1960), p. 3.

15

Russian population statistics for the second world war), skilled statisticians can sometimes carry out very elaborate reconstructions of the missing data by using what is known. Unfortunately, the flood of statistics is very large; nothing more can be done here than to indicate some of the most useful summaries available. For population figures, the U.N. *Demographic Yearbook* is the best starting point. It began to appear only in 1949, but has some retrospective material. Most countries have periodic censuses and also publish such other demographic material as is available in publications like the British *Annual Abstract of Statistics*, the *Annuaire statistique de la France* or the *Annuario statistico Italiano*. These publications are very valuable, even when they require correction, but they only make up a tiny part of the huge body of statistical information now available in print. Much other statistical and record material also appears from time to time in major newspapers and economic commercial and industrial periodicals.

So far, this has indicated the most elementary sort of raw evidence which the historian needs to use, but it is rarely satisfactory to describe it as 'primary material' in the old sense of 'sources'. It has already been 'processed' and digested. Primary sources also exist in their traditional form, and they are, inevitably, the crucial material in the investigation of many diplomatic or political questions. A great deal of documentary primary material is now quickly published because it is needed for reference. Many diplomatic documents, for example, appeared in the *Staatsarchiv* (published from 1861 to 1919, with a last volume in 1928), in the annual documentary collections of Chatham House, and in similar collections published in other countries. More selective collections on specific topics are likely to be the student's most convenient first references in searching this class of material. The diplomatic collections referred to above are only one example of them; others are such convenient scholarly compilations as the Chatham House collection of documents on the Comintern.[17] Such collections are listed in the main historical bibliographies and there is no point in trying to list them here. But it is worthwhile to reiterate that, in a sense, every book published about recent history is of value as a source[18] and the conventional 'official'

---

17 J. Degras, ed., *The Communist International 1919–1943. Documents* (Oxford, 1956–65).

18 For example, three books by outstanding journalists: H. Wickham

documentation does not necessarily occupy in recent history the commanding place which its comparative isolation in a sea of illiteracy gives it in earlier epochs. Some memoirs, too, take us much further than official material; those of de Gaulle are a case in point, while British official documents which in their original form remained hidden from the historian by the thirty-year rule were printed in the books of Winston Churchill and Eden, or have been unearthed in private collections by scholars able to disregard the consequences of publication.

Where sources are unpublished and accessible, there are usually official guidebooks available. Private collections also simplify research in some topics; Moscow may be closed, but there are the Trotsky papers at Harvard. A collection for the study of socialist history exists at Amsterdam. Specialization has often assembled both primary and secondary material for a specific area or topic in a centre such as the Hoover library at Stanford in California, and there has been a plenteous growth of specialist periodicals and learned societies. If the historian is lucky enough to be working on a topic falling within the scope of one of them, his task is greatly simplified. Even when no such help exists, many bibliographical handbooks simplify the initial labour of research. The indispensable starting point is the annual *International Bibliography of Historical Sciences* which began to appear in 1930 and is now published at Paris with the assistance of UNESCO. Of many other periodical bibliographical guides, only one needs to be mentioned here as a useful first quarry for the student: the American *Foreign Affairs Bibliography* published by the Council on Foreign Relations, whose first volume appeared in 1933. It has a brief description and critical comment on each item listed.

Steed, *Through Thirty Years 1892–1922* (London, 1924), G. E. R. Gedye, *Fallen Bastions. The Central European Tragedy* (London, 1939) and Alexander Werth, *The destiny of France* (London, 1937).

2

EUROPE IN 1880

STATES AND PEOPLES

Europe's political structure in 1880 had been given its shape by the Congress of Vienna, the wars of the middle decades of the century and the Congress of Berlin.[1] The states which made it up can be classified in several ways, but there is much to be said for distinguishing European states which had already existed in 1815 from those which had come into existence later. Such a division into 'old' and 'new' states is useful and not merely chronological; it draws attention to a great difference between the Europe of Bismarck and that of Metternich. The new states were all organized on the basis of nationality.

It was coming to be generally accepted by 1880 that the state was the proper political expression of the nation. Europe, of course, still contained many nations which had no state to express, far less to guarantee, their political existence; the Poles were the glaring example. There were also two great monarchies, Austria-Hungary and the Ottoman Empire,[2] which, whatever

1 The first, meeting 1814–15, closed the era of the war of the French Revolution and the military dominance of France. The second made possible the unification of Italy and Germany, and the appearance of what was to be Rumania. For the third, see below, pp. 89–90.

2 The Ottoman Turks ruled a large area of Africa and the Near East, inhabited by many non-Turkish peoples. 'Turkey' was not the official name of the Turkish state until after the Great War, although it was often used by Europeans as a way of referring to the Ottoman Empire. See B. Lewis, *The Emergence of Modern Turkey* (2nd edn, London, 1968), esp. pp. 323–61.

concessions they might have to make to nationality in practice, could not accept that statehood went with nationhood. Russia, on the other hand, accepted the principle while denying its application to its own subject peoples. Nevertheless, in spite of such qualifications, Europe was by 1880 mainly organized as a collection of nation states.

Nationality is the key not only to the structure but also to the sources of change in European politics between 1880 and 1914. It had already produced great wars and upheavals; even greater ones were to come. The separation of one nationality from another, virtually achieved in the west by 1880, was to be much harder in eastern Europe. There, a mosaic of national and racial groups and the sensitivity of great powers made it impossible to find either simple or peaceful geographical solutions to political problems. Explosions of some sort were almost unavoidable if the principle of nationality was to be extended beyond the states which embodied it in 1880.

Such states were a majority of the twenty or so units making up political Europe. They divided between them about one-fourteenth of the land surface of the globe (if we exclude Asiatic Russia). Not all of them enjoyed full sovereignty nor were very united or coherent in structure. But they all counted as pieces on the diplomatic chessboard and enjoyed some sort of self-government; it is convenient to regard them at this point as comparable entities.

The Atlantic states, Portugal, Spain, France and Great Britain, had centuries of national unity behind them. Also, whatever their dissimilarities, they all had the advantage of good geographical definition (the only exception being France, whose eastern frontier had been carried to the Alps by Napoleon III, but which had lost Alsace and Lorraine to Germany in 1871). Except in Ireland, barely recognized yet as a national problem, and, less importantly, in Catalonia and Wales, none of these nations contained any large national ethnic minorities likely to disturb their political life. All of them still possessed big overseas empires, in spite of the losses sustained by Spain and Portugal, and they were all heirs to traditions of worldwide enterprise. One of them, Great Britain, far outran the others in colonial possessions, though the partition of Africa and the final absorption of south-east Asia were still to come. These nations shared another characteristic: they were all in form constitutional states (see below, Ch. 5). Moreover, in spite of nineteenth-century changes in their constitutions – and Great Britain's had changed none the less radically because it had not changed violently – all these states were old, their consolidation achieved well before 1815.

To the north and east, from the Rhine valley to the western boundaries of Russia, great changes had taken place since 1815. Belgium and Holland may be considered together; both were 'new nations' created by splitting the kingdom of the Netherlands set up in 1815. Holland had both a tradition of national independence to which it could look back, and important colonial possessions, but, like Belgium, was formally 'new'.[3] Both, also, were constitutional monarchies. A difference between them was the existence in Belgium of two racial groups, the Flemings and the Walloons. Their neighbour, Germany, was the greatest of the new nations. The German Empire had been constituted only in 1871 and formally it was a federal structure of twenty-six kingdoms, duchies, free cities and other units. Supremacy among them and the effective direction of imperial policy belonged to Prussia; the king of Prussia was Emperor. His Empire contained big national minorities, of which the most important was a population of 2,500,000 Poles in Prussia itself; 250,000 Frenchmen lived in Alsace and there were also substantial numbers of Wends, Danes and Lithuanians within the Empire. The kingdom of Italy, the second big new state to emerge from the wars of the mid-century, had only to deal with a few French-speaking communities and some Germans in Venetia; it did not yet have to face a minorities problem. Italy's boundaries also enclosed a tiny anomaly – the republic of San Marino.[4] To her north lay Switzerland, a republican confederation of anciently-rooted cantons long protected by geography. There were old traditions of Swiss independence, but the new cohesion given to the Confederation by constitutional changes in 1848 and 1874 almost made it a new nation. The three other small states of Europe, the Scandinavian countries, had before 1815 been two, but in 1815 Denmark surrendered Norway to Sweden, and the two northern countries were united in a personal union under the same king, although

3 Strictly speaking, Holland was the name only of one province of the reduced 'Kingdom of the Netherlands', but the word was conventionally used in England for the whole country.
4 France had a similar one, the principality of Monaco, and shared another with a Spanish bishop – Andorra.

each had its own representative institutions. Each of the three was a constitutional monarchy. Alone among them, Denmark had substantial overseas possessions in Iceland and Greenland but these territories hardly strengthened her hand in Europe. There was little likelihood of Denmark being able to regain control over the Danish populations lost to Germany in 1864, nor of Sweden regaining Finland, a Russian province, where there were still large numbers of Swedes.

It was in eastern and south-eastern Europe, the area of the dynastic empires, that the national minorities problem was most intractable. The Russian Empire was the colossus of European politics. Of uncertain extent, population and resources, economically backward, she could not always exercise her full weight in international affairs. Within her boundaries were 4,500,000 Poles; among her important non-Slav minorities were 4,500,000 Finns, 2,750,000 Lithuanians and 750,000 Germans. There were also the Ukrainians or Ruthenes, a distinct Slav group. As a predominantly Slav power, Russia positively influenced racial problems elsewhere, too. Other Slav peoples tended to look to her, especially if they shared her Orthodox religion. One other peculiarity she shared with the four Atlantic states: she had great extra-European interests, though they lay across land frontiers in Asia rather than across the sea.

Strictly speaking, the Dual Monarchy of Austria-Hungary was a new state, yet most of its components were ancient and had long been ruled by the same family. The dual system was an anomaly based on the *Ausgleich* or 'Compromise' of 1867 which guaranteed the independence of both Austria and Hungary except in certain matters of common concern (see p. 202). This was a concession to the Magyars at the expense of other peoples within the borders of the Dual Monarchy; Germans, Slovaks, Serbs, Croats, Ruthenes, Rumanians, Poles and Czechs were among the most numerous. The Dual Monarchy also ruled Bosnia and Herzegovina although they remained formally under Ottoman sovereignty.

The crumbling of the Ottoman Empire had already produced a number of new states in the Balkans. Three principalities, Serbia, Montenegro and Rumania, obtained their formal independence at the Congress of Berlin, where each was bound to maintain certain constitutional safeguards. The kingdom of Greece had a longer history; the Greeks had been the first subject people to break free from Ottoman rule after 1815. Bulgaria was an autonomous though tributary principality under the suzerainty of the sultan; it may be regarded as an independent state although a weak one. Finally, there was the Ottoman Empire itself, still in 1880 formally suzerain also over Bosnia and Herzegovina, and still administering the Sanjak of Novi Bazar (between Montenegro and Serbia) although Austro-Hungarian troops occupied it. The Turks still held Macedonia (Rumelia) and in eastern Rumelia exercised authority through a Christian governor, appointed by the sultan; Turkish troops might be maintained there and forts garrisoned, but the province was officially ruled under 'conditions of administrative autonomy'. Over Crete, Turkish control was firmer. All these complicated arrangements of status and privilege contained plenty of combustible material. Most of the new Balkan governments were irritable, ambitious and anxious to exploit the rivalry of great powers for their own ends. Large numbers of Greeks, Albanians, Bulgars and Serbs still under Turkish rule could provide the new states with pretexts for making trouble. If they did, then because of her strategic position, because of her great extra-European interests and because of the problem of filling the vacuum left by her withdrawal from the Balkans, the fate of Turkey would once again involve the interests of all the great powers.

This political framework filled a continent whose physical characteristics were a long and indented coast, few very high mountains, moderate rainfall and temperature and much fertile land. Over the centuries, these conditions had built up a large population with a high level of energy. Population history ignores political or military chronology; it requires a long view and it will be helpful to take one at the outset by considering the years between 1880 and 1945 as a whole.

The population of Europe, including Russia, had grown steadily since the seventeenth century, and continued to do so after 1880. As a result, Europe's share of the total world population does not vary greatly between then and 1945: it fell slightly, but continued to provide about a quarter of the world's people.[5] Moreover, during those years, Europe sent great numbers of

5 Rough totals of European population:

1880	320 m
1900	390 m
1940	570 m (including U.S.S.R.)

people to other continents, above all to the Americas. This means that its power of reproduction was greater than its growth in numbers suggests. This is all the more surprising because almost from the start of this period the birthrates of many European countries began to go down. What is more, they continued to go down. Whether we take as our measurement the crude birth rate or the net reproduction rate (N.R.R.), this tendency is marked and continuous in most countries since the late 1880s.[6]

This simple picture requires elaboration. The reproduction rates of some countries, regions and classes dropped more steeply than others. Some achieved peak rates even after 1880. East and south-east Europe show declines much less sharp than the industrialized north and west. An estimated German N.R.R. of 1.48 between 1907–12, for example, had sunk to 0.98 in 1940, while Poland, whose N.R.R. in 1927 was 1.30, still enjoyed a rate of 1.11 in 1934. Most east European countries seem to have had N.R.R.s of above unity for most of the years covered by this book. An example of regional differentiation within a country was Italy, where a strikingly sharper drop in fertility appeared in the north than in the south in these years.[7] England already showed evidence of significant differences of fertility between classes in the 1880s. The trend towards slower population growth appeared more and more in wealthier countries and regions. An inverse relation appears between natality and economic wellbeing.[8] Why was this? It may be that growing wealth meant that more people came to have access to modern contraceptive techniques. Nonetheless, different social and religious traditions make the influence of this very difficult to assess. The details of the change form too

6 The measurement of natality is a complicated matter. A good introduction can be found in *The Cambridge Economic History of Europe*, vol. VI, *The Industrial Revolutions and after*, ed. H. J. Habbakuk and M. Postan, Cambridge, 1965 (hereafter *CEH*), pp. 90–103. The criteria used here are two of the most common. *Common birth rate* states the number of births p.a. per thousand of a given population. *Net reproduction rate* states, with corrections for anticipated mortality, the ratio of the number of girls born to the number of women passing through the child-bearing age in a given population; an N.R.R. of 1 shows a tendency to long-term demographic equilibrium, an N.R.R. of below 1 to an eventual decline, though it may not appear for some time.

7 See table in S. B. Clough, *The Economic History of Modern Italy* (New York, 1964), p. 134.

8 See tables in *CEH*, p. 106.

complicated a problem for discussion here. What is not in doubt is that in spite of huge emigration, steadily dropping natality and enormous wartime losses, the European population as a whole still went up throughout this period (see also pp. 367–68). Why did it not go down?

The main reason was that mortality rates dropped very sharply. This can be illustrated easily by taking figures which show extreme cases at the beginning and end of our period.

Mortality per thousand; annual averages

		1881–90		1941–50
Highest rate	Hungary	32.5	Rumania	19.4
Lowest rate	Sweden	16.9	Netherlands } Denmark	9.4
English rate	England	19.1	England	12.5

(Figures from table in W. S. and E. S. Woytinsky, *World Population and Production* (New York, 1953), p. 165)

The first and most striking thing about these figures is the sharp fall which they show. The next is the disparity between different countries. Roughly speaking, the country with the highest mortality rate in the 1940s had achieved a level comparable with that of England, but not as good as the lowest rate, in 1880. Its mortality was still at the end of the period about double that of the countries with the best (that is, lowest) mortality rates. The geography of this gap is striking, too, and reflects a division between north and west European countries and those of the south and east which will appear in other matters.

This drop in mortality was above all a drop in infant mortality.[8] More babies were surviving their precarious first twelve months. This is the fundamental explanation of the continuous growth of population and its full effects were not to be felt in some countries until the 1930s. Although the number of births might fall, there was throughout this period an excess of births over deaths – and, indeed, an excess over deaths *plus* the loss by emigration.

In explaining the fall in mortality, some weight must be given to the increasing wealth of Europe which made possible better

8 Some examples: deaths within one year of birth, per thousand births.

	England	Switzerland	France	Italy	Austria
1880–90	142	165	166	195	256
1931–38	52	43	65	104	80

feeding and better housing – however slight the improvements may have seemed to the poor. But more is due to medical and sanitary science. Without these, the dense urban populations of the twentieth century would not have been possible. The greatest achievements were obtained in the fight against communicable disease. Many of the great killers were mastered, either by reducing their prevalence or by cutting down their case-fatality rates. Spectacular victories were won over children's diseases. Diphtheria, whooping-cough and scarlet fever rapidly declined in advanced countries. In England the death rate from scarlet fever was reduced almost to nothing. This was largely done by driving down the case-fatality rate (as was done also with diphtheria) but by cutting the prevalence of diseases even greater successes were won. Germany between 1901 and 1931 cut her diphtheria rate from 39.1 to 6.4 per 100,000 inhabitants. Typhoid and paratyphoid death rate fell similarly, although there were great contrasts between, for example, England, where it fell from 15.5 in 1901 to 0.4 in 1941, and Spain, whose rate dropped only from 51.3 to 16.1 in the same period.[9] In spite of such differences, the general advance was enormous. Some diseases were virtually wiped out. There was no plague after slight outbreaks in Spain and south Russia in 1899. Though fever and diarrhoea still linger as killing diseases in parts of southern and south-eastern Europe, and malaria was only beginning to give way before D.D.T. in 1945 these diseases now linger on only in backward districts. Between 1880 and 1945 European society succeeded in mastering its health environment in a way which was historically unprecedented. The huge growth of its towns and cities would have been impossible without the medical advances of these years and the action by governments, singly and in concert, which supplied new health and welfare services, and imposed new standards of health, sanitation and accommodation.[10]

Declining mortality rates meant people lived longer. Again, the improvement was uneven. An Englishman's expectation of life at birth in the 1880s was 43.7 years, a Frenchman's a little over 40, and a German's a little under. By 1940 the first two might

9 See the table of Controlled Diseases, Woytinsky, pp. 204–8.
10 In 1907 an International Office of Public Health was set up. For the international organization of measures against epidemics, see F. S. L. Lyons, *Internationalism in Europe 1815–1914* (Leyden, 1963), pp. 237–45.

expect to live 60.2 and 55.9 years. These figures may be compared with those for India; in 1881 male life-expectancy at birth was 23.6 years there, and in 1931 this figure had risen to 26.9. It is worth recalling that on the eve of the French Revolution the French peasant's expectancy is thought to have been rather below that of the Indian in 1881; so far had Europe already come in the ninety years before 1880. Such an increase meant, of course, a much older population (and this tendency may have been exaggerated by the emigration of young people), and that more people were going to die of the diseases of old age. Medical science did not make the progress in mastering cancer, heart ailments and mental and nervous disorders which it had made in dealing with communicable diseases. On the other hand, its considerable success in controlling tuberculosis, pneumonia and influenza benefited the old. When human life could be expected to last two or three times as long as it had done in the Middle Ages, great changes were bound to occur in the way men thought about themselves. Such changes are hard to describe and this is not the place to discuss them. But it is important to see that the great European population changes which are almost entirely the work of the last century and a half are not just of statistical interest. Europeans were consuming more in these years, they were dying of different diseases at later periods of life, their physique (taking rough measures such as those of height) was improving. It is difficult not to infer that they grew to suffer deprivations more impatiently and to believe more strongly that earthly happiness was attainable. That belief, in the last resort, is one which separates modern from medieval man.

Europeans were divided in 1880 into states as small as Montenegro, with less than a quarter of a million inhabitants, and as large as Russia, with between 90 and 100 million. But four-fifths of Europe's population was to be found in six states. Russia, Germany, Austria-Hungary, England and France were the 'great powers' (or their lineal descendants) which had made the Vienna settlement. The sixth, Italy, was to prove something of a lame duck in their company, because of her lack of resources. Being a 'great power' meant being able to conduct a big war. Several factors came into this equation, but population was fundamental.[11] The rates at which populations grew were therefore

11 For national populations in 1880, see statistical table in appendix.

very important. All six powers were getting bigger, but at very different speeds. Russia grew fastest between 1880 and 1910, increasing her population by between 50 and 60 per cent. Germany was next, going up by 43 per cent and her ally Austria-Hungary came in third place with an increase of 35 per cent. Great Britain was rising more slowly; she added over 26 per cent to her population, and Italy added 24 per cent.[12] A long way behind everyone else came France, with an increase of only a little more than 5 per cent. This registered a very important change in France's international position. Once the wealthiest and most populous of the great powers, in 1880 she had 15.7 per cent of the European population. In 1900 the fraction was 9.7 per cent and it was shrinking fast. This accounts for some of the hopefulness with which France was to look to her African possessions for military manpower in the twentieth century.

In some countries, national and racial minorities meant that total population figures do not tell the whole story about military strength. Russia's Poles were not necessarily a military asset. On the other hand, Irish recruiting to the British army provided it with some of its finest soldiers. The worst problems were those of the Dual Monarchy. In each half of it, the dominant race was itself a minority. In Austria the Germans made up 36.8 per cent of the population. In historic Hungary itself, the Magyars provided 41.2 per cent of the total, but they were much thinner on the ground in the Croatian provinces which were also part of their half of the Monarchy. In 1910, all the other minorities, to which had been added the Muslim Serbo-Croats of Bosnia-Herzegovina (annexed in 1909), outnumbered Germans and Magyars combined and provided about 58 per cent of the subjects of the house of Habsburg.[13]

12 Figures for Great Britain and Italy may be misleading; they were the two countries which sent abroad the highest number of emigrants in these years (U.K.: 8.5 m; Italy: 6.1 m). These people *and their children* are missing from the 1910 totals.

13 Minorities of the Dual Monarchy in 1880: distribution per cent:

Hungary:			Austria:		
	Rumanians	15.4		Czechs	23.8
	Germans	12.5		Poles	14.9
	Slovaks	11.9		Ruthenes	12.8
	Croats	8.0		Slovenes	5.2
	Serbs	5.0		Italians	3.1
				Serbo-Croats	2.6

Besides its political and racial distribution, population density varied greatly. Europe as a whole was thickly populated but the mass was unevenly distributed. In Scandinavia, the more mountainous south, and the plains of the east it was thinly scattered; the north-west was thickly populated and more urbanized. The most densely populated countries in 1880 were Belgium (481 per square mile), Holland (304) and the United Kingdom (279). But there are difficulties in speaking of national averages, because such figures hide differences as great, say, as those between Lancashire and Inverness-shire, or between the Ruhr and Posnan.

Urbanization is another index which may be misleading if unqualified. There are difficulties in deciding exactly what constitutes a town. Some states counted administrative areas as urban units, and some counted agglomerations of a certain number of people. Nor is it easy to say whether the number of towns or the size of the biggest is the better index of urban development. Great Britain and Russia, for example, led in numbers of towns, but were very different societies. None the less, some features of the urban pattern of 1880 are fairly clear.

In the first place, the number of very big cities was growing rapidly, as it had been since about the middle of the century. In 1880 only London, Berlin and Paris had more than a million inhabitants. By 1910, four more cities had been added to this list – Glasgow, Vienna, Moscow and St Petersburg.[14] The new big cities tended to accumulate in a comparatively small number of countries. If we count cities of over 500,000 inhabitants as 'big', fourteen out of twenty-three of them were to be found in five countries, the United Kingdom (6), Germany (3), France (3), Belgium (1) and Holland (1). The other nine were shared between Spain (2), the Dual Monarchy (2), Italy (2), Russia (2) and Poland (1). The existence of one big city in so small a country as Belgium or Holland was, of course, of far greater significance than, say, the existence of one in Poland.

Great Britain and Germany led the rush to the cities. (The French population tended to shift to the towns much more slowly; we are told the rate was about 3 per cent per decade down to 1911, and this had been true for a century.) Some general stimuli seem to have been the persistence of higher birth rates in

14 Istanbul is left out, although we may regard Turkey as partially a European power.

rural areas (which meant pressure on land), the attractions of city life, better public transport, which made it easier for cities to recruit labour from a wider area, and, above all, the creation of employment as industry grew up near supplies of raw materials and important transport centres. Later technical changes in transport were to make it possible for the city to change its nature by spreading out great suburban dormitories, and electrification would help to decentralize industry. But at first the cities simply increased in number, grew in population and became more densely packed. As they did so, they created new service industries for their feeding, lighting, cleaning and maintenance and so offered yet more chances of employment. Sometimes these clustered around an old governmental or cultural centre, but in most cases, the character of the new cities was dominated by industry. We can add to our knowledge of the European from 1880 onwards the fact that he is more and more likely to be a city-dweller, and to live in an industrial city.[15] Millions of Europeans still worked on the land, and the absolute numbers of those dependent on agriculture for a livelihood did not begin to fall until very recently, yet the tendency for population to increase and to accumulate in a few densely populated and highly urbanized regions had already begun to alter the patterns of earlier centuries. To understand the sources of the new ways of life, we must turn to economic history.

THE ECONOMY BEFORE 1914

Although there are great contrasts between the countries and regions in which they live, most Europeans enjoy moderate temperatures and good rainfall. Very roughly, about one-third of the 2,500 million acres of the world's land which are naturally suitable for cultivation are in Europe. Most of them were growing food or timber in 1880, although not all of them were as productive as they were later to become. Underground lay huge mineral resources and abundant supplies of energy in the great coal belt which runs across the northern hemisphere and is richest and most accessible in Europe. From 1880 to 1945 coal was the

15 Some implications of this are discussed in Ch. 3.

greatest single source of energy for her industry. Coal gave Europe the industrial supremacy which enabled her to commandeer petroleum supplies when she later needed them, but even in 1939 coal was still her fundamental source of power. Her vast deposits were in 1880 still largely unexplored; those of Silesia alone were believed to be even greater than the huge fields already opened in Great Britain. Iron, too, was abundant; only Ireland, Switzerland and Denmark had no ore, and Europe's deposits were supplemented in the 1890s by huge discoveries in north Sweden, whose ore was twice as rich as that of Lorraine. Later, when the development of ferro-alloys made new minerals necessary, tungsten, chrome, manganese and bauxite could be found in Europe, although more and more rare metals had to be imported.

To exploit these resources there was a large labour force, recruited from the rising population and rich in experience and technical skills. However backward in some respects, its educational level was high, and it was certainly better adapted in 1880 to the demands and discipline of industrial life than the population of any other part of the world except North America. Such human resources were soon to be available elsewhere – notably in Japan – but for some decades they guaranteed to Europe and North America a monopoly of technical invention and discovery. Not one important industrial process was produced by Asia or Africa during the period covered by this book.

Almost as important as her mineral and human resources, was Europe's physical position. A long, indented coastline, with many harbours on both the Atlantic and the Mediterranean, gave her easy access to the oceans and had made her the economic centre of the world. Transport costs were low because of the cheapness of water carriage. It cost 60 francs to send a ton of freight from London to Braila, on the Black Sea, by ship; to take it the much shorter distance from Vienna to Bucarest by rail cost 160 francs. Grain went from Rumania to Danzig by sea, all the way round Europe, and still cost 30 per cent less than overland by rail. The accessibility of the seas led the maritime countries of Europe to build up huge fleets of ships, amounting to about six times as much tonnage as the rest of the world (most of whose ships belonged to the United States) and this predominance was to increase later. In 1880, even on the British register, most of these ships were still under sail but steamships were common. Fishing, which centuries of experience had made into a great food-supplying industry, and which was blessed by the exceptionally rich fishing grounds of the North Sea and the North Atlantic, also employed ships and provided a livelihood for thousands of men.

These were the foundations of Europe's wealth. They were exploited by an economic system which was in 1880 increasingly characterized by capitalist organization, large-scale production for the market and specialization. These tendencies had gone furthest in industry, but had also changed Europe's agriculture very deeply. The superseding of medieval forms of agricultural exploitation had taken centuries (and was still going on in some parts of Europe in 1880), but the decisive changes were over; the worker had been freed from indissoluble ties with the land, that land itself was increasingly treated as a commodity like any other, and it absorbed more and more capital to make higher and higher production possible. Without this slow agricultural revolution, which still had a long way to go in many European countries in 1880, food production would not have been able to keep up with population growth. As it was, Europe had not been able to supply herself with all her needs since the middle of the nineteenth century. Even France was not self-supporting in wheat after 1880. Germany's supplies of rye, barley and oats usually had to be augmented from outside. The most dramatic dependence on imports was that of the United Kingdom, which imported four-fifths of her grain on the eve of the first world war. But all the more advanced European countries tended to increase their dependence on imported food between 1880 and 1914. Not all of it, of course, came from outside Europe; some went from one European country to another. But self-sufficiency was becoming rarer. Germany, for example, saw the cost of her food imports multiply roughly four times in this period, when prices were not, on the whole, rising very much.

Imported food was needed not only because populations were growing, but because some Europeans were eating more and better. The differences between what is eaten in the richer countries of the northern hemisphere and what is eaten in much of Asia and Africa is now a commonplace; it was already becoming visible. Most food imports went to comparatively few countries. The western European had by 1880 begun to eat more wheaten bread, and more meat (it was in 1878 that the first cargo of frozen meat was successfully landed in Europe) and he was beginning, also, to consume more agricultural produce indirectly through industrial products which depended on animal or vegetable supplies. In spite of spectacular increases in productivity, Europe's farmers would be able to supply less and less of the needs of her growing populations. By 1939 Europe could meet her own needs of agricultural products only in olive oil and wine; in 1880 she could still do much better than this. Only after 1945 would Europe move back towards self-sufficiency again.

Agricultural productivity varied from country to country with its structure. It is impossible to generalize about so complicated a subject. At one extreme was the highly capitalized and special-ized agricultural industry of Denmark, and at the other the huge *latifundia* of Andalusia or south Italy, with their poverty-stricken swarms of landless peasants working for day wages when they could. The properties farmed by tenants or owners in the United Kingdom and some parts of west Germany also used wage labour, but it was better paid, better housed, technically more skilled, and less of it was needed. This produced different social patterns from those of, say, south-eastern Europe, where there were still peasants who remembered *Robot*, the servile labour service surviving from the feudal era, and who lived in a poverty like that of Calabria or the Guadalquivir valley.[16] Some of them supplemented wages from the great estates with tiny holdings, where they were lucky enough to have them. But even among peasants, there were distinctions. In east Germany and Prussia, for example, the peasant was not quite so poor as elsewhere, but he was disciplined to the estate by legal devices which seem to have been as powerful a stimulus to rural emigration as poverty. On the other hand, the land was less crowded: migrant foreign labour was needed on the Prussian estates at some seasons. Still other patterns of agricultural life could be found in western Germany, France and Switzerland, where a high degree of subdivision of the land among peasant proprietors was already in 1880 the rule, and was to increase. The holdings varied greatly in size: some were almost small farms while others were plots too small to support their owners. In 1892 in France there were

16 For some Hungarian figures, see O. Jászi, *The Dissolution of the Habs-burg Monarchy* (Chicago, new edn, 1961) pp. 222–3. Conditions in Rumania produced the worst *jacquerie* of modern European history, in 1907; see P. G. Eidelberg *The Great Roumanian Peasant Revolt of 1907* (Leiden, 1977).

2,250,000 peasants with less than 2.5 acres each. (The average British holding of the same date was 66 acres.) In 1907 about 2,250,000 German peasants had from 5 to 250 acres apiece, most of them less than 50. And in this varied picture there were even some share-croppers still to be found, though everywhere they were dwindling in importance. Generally, peasant proprietorship or sharecropping meant low productivity. The production of grain was highest on the big, well-capitalized estates of east Germany. Peasants tended to be conservative in technical matters. Even in 1939 there could still be found peasant holdings in eastern Europe where the old pattern of division of open fields into scattered strips survived, and it was commoner still in 1880. Individual proprietorship was to show great powers of survival and was even to spread further before 1939.[17]

Land-holding affected demographic trends. Everywhere in Europe there was a drift to the towns, but it was less marked in areas with large numbers of peasant proprietors and tenants – in France and west Germany, for example – than elsewhere. In southern and eastern countries a high rural birth rate and pressure on land was driving the masses either to the towns or abroad, although in 1880 legal restraints still hampered the Russian who wished to leave his village. In France, where more peasants owned land, the rural population between 1886 and 1896 fell only from 64 to 60 per cent of the whole. In Germany, the drift was more rapid: whereas 35.8 per cent of the population of 1895 was connected directly with agriculture, in 1907 this figure had sunk to 28.6 per cent. Substantial though such rural populations were, both France and Germany had to call on immigrant agricultural labour. Such movement from the land caused alarm. There were frequent attempts to check it. In England, Radicals claimed that the establishment of a smallholding peasantry would provide 'the only natural barrier against socialism'[18]; both Conservative and Liberal governments brought in legislation to create smallholdings in England and Ireland. Stolypin had much more success in Russia (see Ch. 6). In Prussia, too, there was legislation to encourage the smallholder, but the motive was in that case a different one:

17 See F. Dovring, *Land and Labour in Europe 1900–1950* (The Hague, 1956), and his chapter in *CEH*.
18 Jesse Collings, see R. B. McDowell, *British Conservatism, 1832–1914* (London, 1959), p. 146.

peasants were supposed to make better soldiers. The drift from the land still went on.

Great though improvements in European agriculture had been and were to be, it was industry which gave Europe world leadership, as it was later to give it to the United States. It was the single great strategic factor which shaped Europe's economic and social life and, through her, that of the world. For nearly two centuries a political framework had existed which had made it increasingly easy to tap Europe's resources and savings. By 1880 the result was already a highly concentrated and mechanized industrial system. Its modernity is so impressive that it is important to remember just how much of an older ecónomic world was still interlocked with it. South and south-east Europe, for example, was still covered with primitive peasant industries. In both France and Germany, too, there were little pockets of old-fashioned methods and organization, for example, in the cutlery trade. Even the factory system, the characteristic form of production of the new industrialized Europe, must be understood in a special sense: in 1898 there were 8,500 power-using 'factories' in London, and they employed an average of only forty-one workers each. In 1896 France had 575,000 manufacturing *établissements*; they had an average of 5.5 workers each and only 151 of them employed more than a thousand people.

With all these qualifications, the industrial Europe of 1940 can be seen in that of 1880. Its key elements were the 'heavy' industries: steel, and its supporters, coal and iron. For practical purposes, the Europe of these industries was a Europe of four states: the United Kingdom, Belgium, Germany and France (Russia's contribution would later become significant, but was not in 1880). In each of these products, Europe accounted for more than half of the world's output; most of the rest came from the United States.[19]

The location of European industry was dictated partly by the availability of capital and markets, which meant that countries which were rich before industrialization tended to become richer, and partly by the deposits of the raw materials, coal and iron.

19 Averages of annual production 1881–5 in millions of tons:

	Coal	Pig-iron	Steel
World	374	18.5	4.4
Europe	264	13.4	2.5

These materials had not always been associated; it was only in the nineteenth century that iron smelting came to the coalfields because of technological and economic convenience. England first showed the pattern and with this juxtaposition the ground-plan of industrial Europe was settled. France, Germany and Belgium were the main places outside England where coal was raised in 1880. Germany predominating, they also shared the iron ore deposits of the Saar basin and Lorraine (these last had only just come into use, because of the discovery by an English chemist, Thomas, of a way of making steel from iron ore with a high content of phosphorous).[20] France and Belgium were the two lesser industrial powers[21] and although France had been a big eighteenth-century producer of coal, her resources were unable to provide her with the fuel she needed for industry on the German scale. Germany's coal reserves were huge and were concentrated in a few large fields. Nearly all of them lay in the Ruhr and Silesia; those in the latter area were to become more and more important because of the ease with which they could be worked and the quality of Lower Silesian coking coal. But although these advantages soon overcame the early handicap of Silesia's remoteness from markets, in 1900 the Ruhr still produced nine-tenths of Germany's coal.

It was in the United Kingdom and Germany that the mature industrial complex was furthest developed. Russia was later to exploit her mineral advantages and other countries were to be linked to this mass of industrial power as was, for example, Sweden as a supplier of iron ore, but heavy industry was in 1880 mainly concentrated in western Europe. Most of it lay in Great Britain, in a northern belt running from Lens and Lys in France across Belgium to the Ruhr, and in the Lorraine-Saar-Luxembourg region.[22] This was only slightly less true of the industries unconnected with coal and iron. In bulk output, Great

20 By 1916 about 65 per cent of French and German steel was made by the Thomas process: N. J. G. Pounds and W. N. Parker, *Coal and Steel in Western Europe* (Bloomington, Indiana, 1957), p. 120.
21 'Lesser', of course, in terms of total output; if this is related to size and population, Belgium rightly appears much more heavily 'industrialized' than France.
22 There are useful maps of steel and coal production in Pounds and Parker, pp. 78–9, 124–5.

Britain was outstandingly the biggest producer of textiles, for example.

Between 1880 and 1914 the economy based on these industrial elements expanded enormously. Nevertheless, the era opened in despondency. Since the middle of the 1870s a world monetary depression had thrown trade into confusion. A long deflation lasted until about 1896. During this period, most commodity prices fell about a third, rates of interest dwindled to vanishing point (as it appeared to those who remembered the inflationary middle decades of the century), and banking and commercial disasters multiplied. The roots of this deflation are too complicated for discussion here.[23] That there were many factors to be considered is shown by the fact that in 1880 the depression was only just beginning to be felt by industry, while it had already hit agriculture badly.

All over Europe, the flood of transatlantic grain in the 1870s had brought grain prices tumbling down. In addition, there had been several successive bad harvests, and a phylloxera epidemic which devastated the vineyards. The impact of the slump was felt most heavily where costs of grain production were highest, in England, but all countries suffered. Emigration overseas shot up, and most countries clapped on tariffs to protect their farmers. The French duties on wheat, for example, rose steadily from 1881 to 1897 and behind them French agriculture improved its methods and cultivated new products as specialities for urban and foreign markets. Although her wheat area decreased, the crop France took from it grew. The wine industry recovered from the phylloxera by 1905. This policy meant a sacrifice of agricultural exports, since French grain prices could not compete with American, but France preserved her farming industry. From 1906 to 1912 France had to import only one-thirteenth of the grain she needed.

The German grain-growers had felt the transatlantic threat, but also wished to protect themselves against Russian grain, cheaply produced and easily distributed by rail. The tariff which came into operation in 1880 was a direct response. There was also an important element of war insurance in German thinking about agricultural duties: not only was food important, but so was peasant manpower for the army. The duties gradually rose. Germany had to import more of her food than did France but her

23 See D. S. Landes, *CEH*, pp. 458–76 for an assessment.

landowners were saved as the French peasants had been. A high social price was paid in a lower standard of living for the industrial worker and the economic and social power of the Junker class. This was hard on other Germans, yet something of value was preserved with the maintenance of a substantial agricultural sector in the German economy. Production rose with population, too: between 1880 and 1912 4 million more acres came under the main food crops.

British arable farming was the hardest hit by the slump.[24] Exposed to the same hazards as the continent – but with some bad bouts of livestock disease instead of phylloxera – England, because of her political and social structure, had to do without tariffs. The results were revolutionary. Almost at once a rapid shrinkage of the arable area began. By 1885 the area under wheat was already 30 per cent smaller than it had been in the previous decade. It went on falling steadily, although not so rapidly as this. Between 1897 and 1912, the wheat crop of the United Kingdom fell by 6 per cent while that of Germany rose by 38 per cent. The area of cultivated land in Great Britain also dropped by 9 per cent. The repercussions of such a decline were far-reaching. Movement from the land faster than in any other country helps to explain the United Kingdom's high rate of emigration in the last two decades of the nineteenth century. The agricultural industry had ceased to be the greatest employer; in 1914 about 43 per cent of the occupied population was working in agriculture in France, 35 per cent in Germany, 22 per cent in Belgium and only 8 per cent in Great Britain.[25] This is a striking change. Its first effects fell on the landowners, the tenant-farmer and the Irish peasant rather than the agricultural labourer, who, like his urban contemporary, benefited from lower food prices. The level of British farming declined sharply and it was only in the first decade of the twentieth century that it began to get on its feet again by shifting its emphasis to specialities like beef-fattening and vegetable-growing. A strategical handicap of increased dependence on imported

24 The bad summer of 1875 had been the beginning; although there was little English corn to be had, the price it commanded was lower than in 1874.
25 These figures also reflected the early industrialization of England, of course, and the earlier shift of her labour force to rapidly growing and high-yielding industries. For other comparisons, see *CEH*, pp. 46–7.

food[26] and the incalculable cultural loss involved in commitment to an overwhelmingly industrial society were other results to be set against a higher standard of living for the majority. England's response – or lack of one – to the problem of overseas competition was, none the less, unique. Other countries used protection to promote specialization and increasingly intensive production for urban markets. Denmark, for example, was quick to turn her farmers into industrial agriculturists, processing imported grains and concentrates into bacon and dairy products which kept her fully competitive in a specialized market.[27] Fertilizer consumption shot up. Such changes partially offset the increasing dependence of Europe on imported food. In 1914 Europe including Russia still took only 6 per cent of her grain from outside.

Industrial growth, too, suffered from depression, but when a new period of inflation began in the 1890s, it was soon clear that the European economy as a whole was expanding at a rate unsurpassed except in the United States – an exception which must be remembered. Although Europe was growing, she was falling behind relatively; her share of world manufacturing output was decreasing and until 1914 most of the rest of that output came from the United States. In 1880 Europe produced 63 per cent of the world's steel; in 1910 48 per cent. Meanwhile, the United States increased its share of the world production of steel from 29 to 43 per cent. By 1913 the United States was producing about one-third of the total manufacturing output of the whole world: this was as much as Great Britain, France and Germany together.

It has also to be remembered that although in the early years of the twentieth century, the advanced countries of the western European industrial 'base' (Great Britain, Germany, France, Belgium and Luxembourg) still provided the bulk of European production, industry was growing in other countries. Russian output was still small, but had grown quickly; the Russian rate of growth, indeed, was very high. The Russia of 1880 lifted less than 1.5 per cent of Europe's coal; to the greatly enlarged production of 1900 she contributed 3.6 per cent – about four and a half times as much. She made 2.9 per cent of Europe's pig-iron in 1880, and 11.4 per cent in 1900. When it is remembered that

26 In 1912, with only two-thirds of Germany's population, Great Britain spent £260 m and Germany £160 m on imported food.
27 *CEH*, p. 28.

at the same time the beginnings of large-scale industry could be discerned in Japan, it can be seen that a big absolute growth in this period masks a significant change in Europe's relative position. It must not be exaggerated; the growth of the United States was enormous, but even that giant's stride did not deprive Europe of the economic leadership of the world by 1914. The United States was too busy exploiting the possibilities of her own vast domestic market. In 1914 Europe still dominated international trade, and Europe, richer than ever before, was still growing fast.

The expansion of productive capacity already existing in 1880, especially of the heavy industries, was one sign of her growing wealth. By 1914 Great Britain alone was producing as much coal as the whole of Europe had done in 1880. In the thirty years before 1910, Europe's pig-iron output trebled; even more spectacular was the expansion in steel, whose production increased tenfold. There were no new fundamental discoveries after 1880 to explain this. This great expansion is to be explained by newly available resources – available in Lorraine because of the Thomas process, in Scandinavia because of railway-building – a fall in costs thanks to a better transport network, the development of integrated plants and improvements in fuel technology. Above all, the heavy industries, growing faster than other sections of the economy, benefited from a growing demand. Ship-building was a great consumer of steel; by 1914 Great Britain alone had as much steam tonnage as had the whole of Europe in 1880 and was launching another 2 million tons a year. The production of textiles was still going up; in 1913 two-thirds of the whole world's imports of cotton goods still came from Great Britain. Factory expansion kept up the demand for machines and power which fed the heavy industries.

Just as significant for the future were new industries springing up beside the old. Some of them were closely connected with those already in existence but they also sprang from advances in science and technology. The rapidity of expansion in the last quarter of the nineteenth century makes it possible to treat the chemical industry, for instance, as virtually a new creation. Previously, her raw materials and industrial demand for heavy chemicals – especially alkalis, bleaches and sulphuric acid – had made Great Britain the main chemical producer of the world. After 1880 she was displaced in Europe by Germany. The explanation lies partly in German access to certain patents, partly in a heavy commitment of capital in England to obsolete plant, partly in better business management, but, above all, in Germany's superior level of education and technical instruction. The chemical revolution was based on fundamental research in organic chemistry and, later, in electrochemical processes. Germans did more of this work and did it better than the British. Yet it is ironical that the most startling changes in industrial chemistry came in dyestuffs, because the fundamental discoveries in this field had been made as far back as 1857 by an Englishman, and England and France dominated aniline dye production until 1870. Ten years later the Germans had taken the lead.[28] Besides meeting a potentially huge demand for cheap, fast colouring, the chemistry of dyestuffs opened the way to innumerable new synthetics. By 1914 they already included drugs, plastics, explosives, anaesthetics, rubber. This huge industry was dominated by Germany.[29] The expansion of heavy chemical production was also enormous, and in this business, too, the Germans excelled, although the fundamental achievement here was Belgian: the ammonia process of soda manufacture. Electrolytic production of alkalis and improved methods of making sulphuric acid soon followed. The resulting increase in heavy chemical output mainly took place in Germany although some smaller producers, such as Austria-Hungary and Russia, made their appearance. A rough but convenient index of heavy chemical production is provided by sulphuric acid, because it was used to make dyestuffs, fertilizers, and many other chemicals. Between 1900 and 1913 production in Europe rose from 2.5 to 6.3 million tons annually (but here too, United States production meant that the later figure represented a smaller proportion of total world output than the earlier).

New metal industries also appeared which were based on scientific research, but the most revolutionary result of the

28 The decisive step in the development of the new industry was the discovery of synthetic alizarin in 1869: Perkins filed his patent application the day after German chemists had filed theirs! See L. F. Haber, *The Chemical Industry during the 19th century* (Oxford, 1958), p. 84, a book throwing light on many topics not indicated by its title.

29 Basle was the only important centre of the new dyestuffs not in Germany. On the basis of the production of small quantities of highly priced specialized dyes the Swiss built there a prosperous and growing export industry.

marriage of science and technology was the spread of electricity. It was to change the life of the human race as much as had steam. Its first two major applications were as light and motive power and they are still the most familiar; both can be conveniently dated in 1879, when Edison perfected the incandescent lamp and Siemens made his electric tram. The names are significant; from the start Germany and the United States dominated the new industry and the invention in 1882 of Edison's system of generating power in a central power station launched electricity in both countries on an enormous wave of growth. Factories no longer had to generate their own electricity; more of them were willing to invest in electrical machinery when they could draw on central power supplies. Europe began to equip itself with electrical power stations; London's first was the Edison Holborn Viaduct station of 1882. This meant much greater freedom in the siting of industry; small workshops could now equip themselves with power tools. The worker was eventually to benefit from better conditions of work; for the moment, electricity probably affected him most by providing transport for travel to his work from greater distances. Electricity was not taken up everywhere with the same rapidity; central European cities were ahead of Great Britain, for example, with their electric trams. But it was everywhere beginning to change life before 1900. It was to be of great importance to countries like France and Switzerland where a shortage of mineral fuels could be offset by an abundance of hydroelectric power.

One other conspicuous feature of the modern scene also appeared in these years. This is the motor-car. The first internal combustion driven machine appeared in 1885, and the recognizable ancestor of the modern car is first to be seen in the 1894 Panhard. By 1914, France and Germany were already producing a fair number of motor-cars. England lagged behind. But in Europe as a whole the car was still a rich man's toy. A lead in volume of unit production was soon established by the United States and it has been maintained ever since.

Not all the new industries – and there were others – seriously affected the European economy before 1914. None the less they were at once a part and a symptom of a great expansion of European wealth. The world trade in manufactured goods doubled between 1900 and 1913, and Europe still produced the bulk of what was sold. Not all of Europe shared equally in this expansion. Its benefits were felt most strongly in a small number of advanced countries in northern and western Europe. In 1913 a half of the total trade of the world was made up of the exports and imports of seven European countries which enjoyed the advantages of a highly developed science and technology, well-established basic industries, and access to capital for investment. Expansion fed the imbalance in Europe which these conditions implied. These countries became more specialized as they became richer, interchanging more and more products with one another and the world. Yet some of their wealth spread to their more backward neighbours. Industrial nations needed more primary materials as their consumption rose and they could provide the capital for investment in poorer countries.

The relations of the advanced countries to one another were also changing. The United Kingdom's economy continued to expand, but more slowly than other nations. Foreign competition alarmed English manufacturers, who thought it the explanation of their difficulties. There were deeper causes.[30] The outcry over declining profit margins seems to show that British commercial enterprise had been sapped by decades of trading on advantageous terms as the only great exporter of manufactured goods. It is also significant that the steam turbine and the pneumatic tyre were the only major British innovations of this period; in the new industries she was a long way behind Germany and the United States and by 1914 was falling behind even in the older industries in which she had first established her supremacy. Germany had by then passed her in pig-iron and steel production and the United States could out-produce her in coal and iron ore as well. Yet the British standard of living was maintained and, indeed, went on rising. Great Britain still had great industrial resources: there were specialized skills available among her workers, she still had huge supplies of her excellent coal, she had opened up new markets as fast as she had been pursued into her old ones by her competitors, and she had an enormous income from investments overseas and from the services which she supplied – in transport, banking and insurance, for example – to the rest of the world. All these kept her rising with the tide, even if she rode lower in the water than Germany.

30 There is an excellent discussion of the complicated question of explaining the difference between British and German performance in these years by D. S. Landes, *CEH*, pp. 533–84.

Germany's was the great industrial achievement of these years and her metals industry was the basis of her strength. About three-quarters of it was concentrated in the Ruhr and Saar-Lorraine area and by 1913 she could meet all her own metal needs except in tinplate. Between 1880 and 1910 her steel production grew twentyfold. She dominated Europe's electrical engineering. In 1900 she made between 80 and 90 per cent of the world's dye and had quintupled her sulphuric acid production since 1880.[31] The pace of her expansion was matched only by Russia's, but Russia's was on a much smaller scale and depended on foreign capital, some of it German.

French industrialization had been slower than German or Belgian. An early start had been checked by a lack of cheap fuel and she fell further behind by 1914. The loss of Alsace and Lorraine had taken away not only the greater part of the French iron industry but also some of her oldest-established textile mills; this cut into the market for France's own dyestuffs industry which, after a good start in the 1860s, dwindled away, and French textile manufacturers soon met their dyestuff needs from Germany or Switzerland. By 1914 France's main industrial exports were textiles and iron ore. The pig-iron, crude steel and semi-finished metal products from the *minette* area went to other parts of France. Her average manufacturing establishment of 1912 used only 53 h.p.: her investment in hydroelectric plant had not by then compensated for her lack of fuel. In 1914 France still imported most of the coal she needed for smelting, together with machinery and transport equipment. She had begun to export alkalis but had to import other chemicals.[32] A better balance than elsewhere between industry and agriculture was the advantage she derived from slower industrial growth; she also owed to it some of her resilience and powers of recovery after two world wars.

Almost everywhere, industrial growth, like agricultural recovery, took place behind the protection of tariffs.[33] This was

31 Haber, pp. 122, 128.
32 Haber, p. 221.
33 Major tariff measures were introduced as follows: 1879, Germany; 1881, Russia; 1882, Russia, France, Austria-Hungary; 1884, Russia, Switzerland; 1885, Germany; 1887, Russia, Austria-Hungary; 1888, Italy, Sweden; 1890, U.S.A.; 1892, France; 1897, U.S.A. The industrial duties usually followed agricultural duties; this is an interesting fact since we are often told this was the age when Big Business dominated government. Only Great Britain had no tariff.

encouraged by the long depression of prices. Protection usually began at fairly low rates. The French manufacturers had to wait until 1892 for the Méline tariff, which meant an average duty of about 34 per cent on British goods. The Germans, too, began with tariffs more favourable to farming than industry, and it took the McKinley tariff in the U.S.A. and the enormous Russian protective duties to convert the German rulers to protection for their manufacturers. After 1902 the duties on British manufactured imports to Germany were on the average about 25 per cent. Such tariffs undoubtedly made the lot of the British manufacturer much harder and the American tariffs hurt him most of all.

One way of summarizing the results of European economic progress before 1914 is to group nations roughly according to their increase in wealth. They can be arranged in three classes. The first and smallest was that of true industrial nations, committed above all else to sharing the fate of their manufacturing industries. They differed greatly in size and structure, but Great Britain, Belgium and Germany fell into this group. Then there were mixed economies which enjoyed a fairly high standard of living and whose diversified resources included some heavy industry, but where no one branch of the economy predominated. Into this group fall France, the Netherlands and Sweden. The third group was still in 1914 the largest. It embraced all the other European nations and in them, however its preponderance might vary, agriculture was dominant. *Per capita* distribution of wealth roughly followed this division, the industrial countries having the highest standard of living and the agricultural nations of the south and east the lowest, but the figures do not exist for precise comparisons. Roughly speaking, too, this tripartite division would reflect a division between capital-exporting and capital-importing countries. The richest nation in the world, in any case, was the United States, a mixed economy on a continental scale, and a capital-importer.

It is impossible to confine a discussion of Europe's economy solely to Europe; it was already by 1880 a part – the dominant part – of a world economy whose organization was to be elaborated even more before 1914. The last prewar years have been called 'the golden age of international economic specialization and exchange',[34] and the organization which made this golden age possible, an intricate and massive structure tying, for the first time, every continent into one economic process, was completed between 1880 and 1914. Its indispensable framework was the machinery of communication which now united the globe. The problems of bulk transport had been solved before 1880, with the coming of the steamship and the railway, and it only remained to spread and perfect them. The railway systems of Europe, outside Russia, were all complete by 1910. In the 1880s there had begun to run on them the transcontinental luxury expresses which were to dominate long-distance land travel until the second world war. In 1888 it was for the first time possible to go by train the whole way from Constantinople to Calais, and the Trans-Siberian railway was completed in 1904.[35]

Water transport also improved. The gradual replacement on ocean routes of sail by steam increased the volume of traffic faster than the number of ships; steamships could make more journeys in the same time.[36] The Panama canal was not opened until after the outbreak of war in 1914, but may stand for the completion of the world sea communications system. Hamburg and Bremen had become great oceanic ports, and France and Germany began to compete in the ocean liner traffic; soon there were regular services to every part of the world. Germany's progress in oceanic commerce was especially rapid, but Great Britain remained the greatest international carrier. France and Germany also drew economic benefit from the use of their internal waterways for heavy industrial goods. Both countries carried out improvement schemes to take advantage of their rivers. About one-fifth of French and German domestic freight went by water in this period. In each country, politics complicated development, but German interests finally obtained an east–west canal to link Berlin with the Ruhr and by 1905 ships of 2,000 tons could go up the Rhine as far as Mannheim, a very important change since the Ruhr by then needed more than German ore. These improvements lowered costs and extended markets. It was equally important to

34 *The New Cambridge Modern History*, XII, *The Era of Violence*, ed. D. Thomson (Cambridge, 1960), p. 502.
35 New railway mileage built 1890–1910: Germany, 18,000; Russia, 16,000; France, 13,000; Spain, 5,000; Italy, 4,000.
36 The 'clippers' had been very fast, of course. But they were a special case, racehorses for valuable prizes. Even their supremacy was only a short one and lasted little longer than the 1860s, when the fastest Atlantic crossing by a sailing ship was made. Many of the clippers were still sailing between 1880 and 1914.

a world economy that information could move as freely as commodities. The cable system which united the world was already almost complete by 1880; its completion made world prices a reality.[37] The market economy which had been exported by western Europe was now worldwide. Locally, the telephone was also speeding up business. Transport and communications could soon after 1880 meet most needs of European commerce.

This was not quite all that was required for the smooth working of the world economy which was at its height in 1914. It assumed also an absence of political interference. On the whole, in spite of governmental interest in some special areas and in some kinds of investment, and in spite of tariffs, economic life was more free from interference and more completely self-regulating than at any other time, before or since. Capital could flow about freely to seek investment, and labour could migrate to look for work. Property and persons enjoyed almost complete security throughout Europe. World prices might be distorted by tariffs, but a world market existed. The gyroscope of this system was the world's financial capital, London. Organization and expertise were available there for the financing of increasingly complicated business. The medium of world commerce was often the sterling bill of exchange, which provided something like an international currency. Behind it stood the international gold standard.

Europe had rapidly adopted the institutions of developed capitalism, and spread them through the world. The joint stock company, the characteristic device for the mobilization of capital, became more and more the usual pattern of business organization and the freely transferable share a more and more common form of property. Commodity and stock exchanges multiplied as dealing by sample became easier thanks to technical improvements and standardization. Older trading institutions such as the Fairs which had served Europe since the Middle Ages, were disappearing, at least in their old forms. Legal reforms were everywhere taking account of the new needs of international society; patent protection was improved.[38] There were also signs of new industrial developments, for which the theory of classical

37 In 1900, three-quarters of the world's cables were, like the bulk of the world's carrying trade, in British hands. In 1905, more than 82 m international telegrams were sent (Lyons, p. 41).
38 See Lyons, pp. 127–31.

capitalist political economy had no place; cartels and trusts began to interfere with the process of unrestricted competition.[39] By 1914 there were known to be 114 of them. Industrial firms in the heavy industries tended to grow in size as the integration of manufacturing processes made further economies possible. Capitalism was getting bigger, and changing its nature as it did so. Bureaucratic skills were becoming as important to it as commercial flair, and the change of scale was introducing economists and businessmen to the idea of centralized planning. New forms of quasi-public enterprise began to appear; town corporations appointed directors to boards of German companies and 'municipal socialism' appeared in England. The increased scale of industry meant, too, that management was increasingly separated both from labour and from capital. The old-fashioned owner-manager was rarer and specialized management techniques were beginning to be studied. All these things were signs of the elaboration and growth of the economic order of which Europe was the centre in 1880.

Expansion and elaboration more and more justifies our consideration of Europe as an economic whole before 1914. It was a discernible unity, embedded though that unity might be in the economic order of the rest of the world. In spite of their tariffs, European nations were interdependent. In 1914 only the United Kingdom sent more of its manufactures to non-European nations than to European; yet she was also Germany's best customer, and Germany came second only to India as a buyer of British goods. British coal and tinplate went to Germany, and German sheet steel to the shipyards of the Tyne and Clyde. Almost 60 per cent of the ore smelted in the Ruhr came from abroad (mainly from Sweden and France, but some from Spain, too) and some minerals crossed frontiers in both directions, German ore going to France, Belgium, Switzerland, Holland and Austria, while Welsh steam coal went to Hamburg and Bremen. In 1906 a fifth of the coal burnt in the Berlin area was British. More specialized exports such

39 Cartels were, strictly, price-fixing agreements entered upon for a fixed term, but the term is often used more loosely to cover other sorts of association. One of the biggest combines, The [British] United Alkali Company, was an unsuccessful attempt to save a mortally wounded industry. See Lyons, pp. 112–17, and *CEH*, pp. 472–5, where Professor Landes happily characterizes them as a 'new, commercial version of the enclosure movement'.

as French woollens, German chemicals, Belgian locomotives or British machinery formed still more complicated patterns of exchange. Ownership and control also crossed frontiers. The tradition of foreign investment was an old one and the spread of shareholding in joint stock companies and the practice of floating foreign loans in London, Berlin or Paris, all tied the economic affairs of one European country closely to those of others. Even tariffs may have helped by making it better business to own factories inside a market than to try to break into it from outside: the Germans and Swiss supplied the French textile industry in 1900 from eight factories inside France, Germans made chemicals in Russia, and other Germans invested heavily in the coal mines of French Lorraine. In 1914 the building of blast furnaces in Normandy with German capital was going forward; Norman ore was to have been smelted there with Ruhr coal, transported cheaply by sea. Some international trading agreements began, like cartels, to regulate markets and production regionally as well as nationally. Professional journals and institutions quickened the international flow of information. Innovations crossed frontiers more quickly in an age of easy communication, and processes could be exported by the entrepreneur to the place where they would find the resources and markets they needed. As an economic system, Europe, in spite of its internal contrasts and competition, remained a unity down to 1914.

EUROPE AND THE WORLD

In 1880, 'the civilized world' was a phrase readily understood. It meant Europe and those countries which inherited European traditions and values. The Europe-centredness of civilization was easier to distinguish then than it is today, but Europe's relations with the rest of the world were already complicated. In those relations European nations as units, European civilization as a whole, and elements of the same civilization mediated by agents not geographically European all played their parts. The result was an informal, sometimes unrecognized, domination of the world by European culture and institutions.

This cultural and institutional hegemony must always be distinguished from the more transient political and economic supremacy of European nations. It showed most obviously in certain political institutions, above all the sovereign state and representative government, in some central ideas, of which the most potent were ultimately drawn from Christianity or the Enlightenment, and in a powerful technology, based on experimental science. The civilization founded on these existed in mature form in the United States of America in 1880, and had just been extended, at last, to the whole of Europe itself outside the extreme south-eastern corner. Elsewhere, after three centuries' growth only one big geographical region was still untouched by it: the mass of Central Africa. Soon this was to be entered and then only Tibet and Ethiopia would remain for a time unresponsive to European politics, ideas and technology.

Everywhere else, European civilization was already predominant although there were important differences in the forms it took. The United States, Central and South America (with a few small exceptions), Liberia and Japan were politically independent of Europe. Other nations stood in ambiguous or changing political relationships to Europe; they were invalids, infants or fossils, like the Ottoman Empire, Persia, Morocco, Egypt, China or Korea. A British viceroy of India spoke of them as 'those countries which must inevitably have attracted the attention of Europe, partly from increasing infirmity, but still more from the opportunities suggested by their latent though neglected sources of strength'.[40] They could either become clients of European nations, or resist them by adopting European ideas and methods; in either case the cultural dominance of Europe was implied. A third class of territories was ruled by European countries as colonies. Some of them were disputable cases, such as the British colonies which were really independent nations of European stock – an illustration that Europe's world supremacy had many different forms and many different agents.

Colonies were the most obvious expression of European political supremacy. Africa and south-east Asia had still not been completely apportioned into outright possessions or spheres of

40 Curzon, see G. P. Gooch, *History of Modern Europe, 1878–1919* (London, 1923), p. 369. This was wordier, but more exact than Salisbury's better-known formulation in a speech to the Conservative Primrose League, 4 May 1898, dividing the nations of the world into the 'living and the dying.'

influence, but great European empires already existed. The world's leading colonial power was Great Britain, ruling not only the biggest non-European population gathered under one sovereign government of Europeans, in India, but, formally at least, the largest colonies in area also. In 1880, Queen Victoria's dominions fell roughly into three groups. First were the self-governing colonies with large white settler populations which can almost be regarded as independent: Cape Colony, Natal, Australia, New Zealand and Canada. India was a second class by itself, unique in size and in the complexity of its problems, and governed by a special department of state. Then there was a large number of Crown Colonies, ruled by governors with or without local advice, and subordinate to the colonial office in London. Some of them were strategic harbours, coaling stations or communications centres, like Gibraltar, Malta and Aden. Others had grown up around old-established trading posts, such as those on the Gold Coast or in Sierra Leone. Still others were old plantation colonies in the West Indies and the Caribbean. In the Far East there were the Straits Settlements and Hong Kong. British rule was even being extended again (under pressure from Australia and New Zealand) into the South Pacific, where Fiji had recently been acquired. The next colonial power in size was France. She still had Caribbean colonies but the bulk of her possessions were in Africa, where she ruled Algeria, part of Gambia, the French Congo and French Somaliland and was about to acquire (in 1881) a protectorate over Tunis. In the Far East she had protectorates in Cambodia and Indo-China and ruled Cochin directly; further south and east were her numerous South Pacific stations. Another important power in southeast Asia was the Netherlands. Java and Sumatra were the core of the Dutch empire which still had colonies in the West Indies as well. In 1880, Spain still held Cuba and Puerto Rico; in Africa she had Rio do Oro and in the Far East the Philippines. The only other great colonial power was Portugal, ruling a huge area in Angola, Portuguese Guinea and Mozambique, and oriental footholds in Maçao and Goa. This is not a full list but it shows the extent and solidity of Europe's direct political control. All these colonies belonged to powers whose empire-building had begun in the age of the great discoveries; Germany and Italy had not yet entered the picture. The only really important nineteenth-century extension of European rule before 1880 had been the acquisition of a new African empire by France after the losses of the eighteenth century and the revolutionary wars. In most of the other colonies, Europeans had ruled for a long time.

Direct rule was not the only way Europeans exercised political power overseas. Besides the intermediate stage of setting up protectorates over local political units, there was considerable open interference in the affairs of some formally independent countries. Extraterritorial privileges, which removed Europeans from the operation of the local judiciary, existed in Japan, China and parts of the Ottoman Empire. In Egypt a European commission administered the Egyptian national debt – which was largely owed to Europeans – and therefore played a big part in the financial policy of the khedive's government. In this case, the interference helped to stimulate a nationalist movement, but this in turn led to further European control after 1880. Even more drastic intervention was to take place in China; its roots went back to the control of the Chinese government's revenue by foreign supervision of the Customs from 1858 onwards. Intervention of this sort occurred in most areas where European powers showed interest. Korea and Persia were both to have foreign 'advisers' and officials. China is perhaps the best example of the way in which European influences operated in many forms because political power, both direct and indirect, was mingled there with economic exploitation (for Egyptian and Chinese affairs; see below, pp. 107, 124).

The world's economic relation to Europe has already been touched on; it was not simply a matter of one-way domination. The United States was too important for this to be true. Especially in South America, American economic weight was to count more and more. Gradually, American exports of manufactured goods grew; the exploitation of their own domestic market by Americans, too, was bound to affect the outlets for European goods. Yet in one sense even the United States might be said to have been part of an economic system controlled by Europe down to 1914 in that she remained a capital-importing nation, and that capital came from Europe. International commerce was more than just an exchange or European manufactures for primary produce from the rest of the world. The trading pre-eminence of the United Kingdom, the only European nation which in 1914 was selling more outside Europe than inside it, made possible a more flexible and roughly triangular system. British purchases of European manufactures and other products were paid for with cash, with British manufactures, and with overseas produce. To the rest of the world Great Britain exported capital and manufactures, and provided services. Some of her earnings she took in food and raw materials, some in cash. Because of this, Europe's economic relationships with the rest of the world were complex. But if, remembering this qualification, we consider Europe as a unit – as it often appeared to the rest of the world – then Europe's *main* economic role in the world economy was to be a supplier of capital and manufactured goods; the rest of the world absorbed that capital and those manufactures and supplied Europe with primary materials.

The influence of this economic system on the non-European world was, in the end, revolutionary. Some of its effects were to be much condemned. Expropriations in Indo-China, forced labour in the Congo and ruthless exploitation of resources in Java and Sumatra all left behind them hatred and bitterness. But unrealized potential was exploited as well as people and European economic intervention was not always at the expense of the non-European. He benefited from the creation of new industries and new chances of employment. European companies provided the managerial and entrepreneurial services needed to make the best use of existing resources. Europe provided a huge and growing market for primary produce. The needs of commerce and government created a native middle class (from which were later to come the leaders of nationalist movements). But the most important resource Europe offered to the rest of the world was capital. From 1900 to 1913 European investment abroad ran at an average of £350 million a year, to the real benefit of the receiving countries. European investment tended to follow the flag. Great Britain exported capital to the Far East, India, the Middle East and North and South America. The Dutch put their money into Indonesia, the French into West Africa, Indo-China – and Russia. Germany was less keen on overseas investment; she preferred eastern Europe and, increasingly, the Ottoman Empire. There was some rivalry between nations in this process, as there was in all economic penetration. But, as the case of China showed, there were plenty of opportunities for both trade and investment. European nations had a common interest in opening the world to commerce. Even their colonies were not always reserved to the sovereign nation: the French imposed a close protective system on theirs, but those of Great Britain were good markets for the Germans. Furthermore, so many traders were involved in non-European countries independently of their governments that it is misleading to think of world trade only in national terms.

The growth of the European economy had also some more subtle and pervasive long-term effects. Migration followed the establishment of a world economic system: Indians spread all over the British Empire; Chinese went to Singapore and Indonesia. Crops appeared where they had not grown before: rubber was carried from Brazil to become the staple of the Malayan economy, and soon to be very important in Indonesia and Ceylon. Steamboats, railways and telegraphs broke down geographical isolation. Together with drugs and drainage they checked the effects of disease and famine, while the imposition of order and the creation of new employment began the slow demographic revolution which long prevented many countries from cashing their new wealth in the form of a higher standard of living. Sometimes traditional economies were broken up by European competition: the cultivation of indigo, for example, collapsed with the discovery of synthetic dyestuffs. Such effects emphasize that the immediate economic dominion which Europe appeared to enjoy in 1880 was really less important for the future than the gradual integration of the whole world with the European industrial and commercial system. The institutions of manufacturing capitalism gradually spread worldwide. Banks, factories, joint stock companies began slowly to replace the traditional economic machinery of Asia and Africa, as they had already replaced that of pre-industrial Europe.

This was part of the cultural revolution which has gone on ever since. Non-European countries were more and more to take up the methods and manners of Europe. It was not merely a matter of European machines or European clothes (though the adoption of such uncomfortable dress in tropical countries is certainly a testimony to the prestige of European civilization). What was important was the sometimes unconscious assimilation or half-assimilation of the mental furniture of the European. In some cases this happened by the direct emigration of European ideas and institutions. In North America, Australia, New Zealand and South Africa there were already in 1880 'civilized countries' cut from the European stock. In South America the same thing had happened; even the continuing presence of a large native population and wars of liberation had not much differentiated their institutions from European models. At least formally, the Roman Catholic Church and the State were the dominant institutions of that continent. Algeria and Tunisia attracted immigrants from France and Italy so that a fringe of European society already existed on the southern shore of the Mediterranean. Emigration to all these areas – except the United States – had been defined by strong national preferences and traditions, but emigration everywhere meant the emigration of the ideas and assumptions of Christian, legalistic Europe.

After 1880 there was still a great wave of emigration to come. Its distribution was uneven. In the 1890s about 60 per cent of European emigrants went to the United States, but this proportion tended to drop while South America's share grew steadily. Australia and New Zealand did best between 1900 and 1914. Such figures as we have need careful scrutiny, because they rarely take account of those who came back. Nevertheless, it seems justifiable to call the period 'the Great Resettlement' of European stocks. The main reason for the flow of emigrants was the farm crisis in Europe, and the circumstance that made it possible was the availability of cheap steamers. In round figures, about 26 million people emigrated from Europe between 1880 and 1910. To this figure should be added another, uncertain, number (perhaps $3\frac{1}{2}$ million?) who went to Asiatic Russia. Such a dispersion was enormously important. Whatever the 'frontier' might do to emigrant traditions on the ranchlands of Uruguay, in the island of Sakhalin, or the mines of the Rand, the institutions and ideas which were being adapted there were European.

European languages were spread by this emigration, and by colonial rule and economic intercourse. English was the most far-flung language in 1880; not only in new nations, but in British colonies where it was the language of official life and therefore a language of record and social advancement for the native. French was widely used over North Africa, the Middle East and southeast Asia, and had the additional advantage of being the language of diplomacy. Spanish and Portuguese dominated South America (leaving a tiny island of Welsh-speakers in Patagonia), and Italian was a widely understood *lingua franca* in the eastern Mediterranean. However mangled they might be – in pidgin, for example – European languages took with them European concepts.

One of the major influences in this diffusion of European ideas was the missionary movement. The nineteenth was the greatest century since the first for the spread of Christianity. What the missionaries spread was not merely the doctrine and practice of Christianity. Their schools, hospitals and dispensaries also brought with them secular ideas and techniques. Their quarrels with one another did not really compromise these benefits, any more than quarrels between European nations prevented colonial administrators from giving much of the world the framework of European law and order. But here generalizations are especially dangerous. Where direct rule had been established a long time – in India, for example – it provided a framework in which there could grow an acceptance of European ideas of political organization. In an extreme case such as Algeria, there might even be an almost complete formal assimilation of administration and government to the metropolitan structure. Elsewhere, only a sector of administration, such as the Chinese Customs or the Egyptian judiciary, would disseminate European influence. Sometimes such influence was exercised by invitation. A British captain at one time ran the Chinese navy and the Persian government tried to get an American to run its finances. Colonial forces such as African *askaris*, Indian *sepoys*, or Algerian *goumiers* were another channel through which European ideas reached non-Europeans. There were also western schools and universities. The British government organized universities in India; Americans helped to found schools and colleges in the Far East. The Lycée of Galata Serai had been founded by Frenchmen in Turkey and English public schools were imitated on the Gold Coast.

In the long run, the most durable achievements of the age in which Europe dominated the world may seem to have been brought about less by political dominion than by such impalpable but irresistible influences as these, by the corrosive effect of its economic institutions, or even by the simple desire to imitate. The world paid Europe the flattery of imitation because of Europe's success. Some nations, faced with the European political, economic and cultural offensive, drew the conclusion that they must adopt Europe's weapons if they were to resist. Almost everywhere, westernization was advocated by reformers and resisted by conservatives. Many nationalist movements were to appear before 1914. The Egyptian nationalists were crushed in 1882, but their cause survived and was even helped by the improvement of

Egyptian life under Cromer's proconsulate.[41] In 1907 the first Egyptian Nationalist Congress met. In Persia, the nationalist movement was anti-European and by 1906 it produced the first *Majlis* and a liberal constitution. Indonesia's first nationalist movement appeared in 1908. India's first Nationalist Congress met in 1886 and Indian M.P.s were even elected to the Imperial parliament.[42] In China the dying Tso Tsung-t'ang's memorandum of 1885 pointed the way to reform on western lines but nothing important was achieved until the Hundred Days of reform in 1898. The Boxer rebellion was a reactionary, xenophobic movement, but the adoption of a western instrument, the boycott, against American trade in 1904 is more significant. By 1908 China had a draft constitution and in 1912 she was a republic. In this process of adaptation, what was really wanted was European power: the demands of the Hundred Days had been for arms, railways and shools. Even firmly traditionalist states could not resist this. Turkey seriously set about reform under Abdul Hamid and at last the sultan of Zanzibar abolished slavery in 1897. Only a few states held out against Europe as staunchly as did Ethiopia. Of all the westernizing nations, Japan had the greatest success in adopting European institutions and technology. The Meiji period (1868–1912) began with the surrender of feudal fiefs to the Emperor; 'thus the country will be able to rank equally with the other nations of the world', concluded the memorial of the lords who initiated this step.[43] The last important resistance to modernization was crushed in the Satsuma rebellion of 1877. After that, European ideas and instruments flooded into Japanese life. The Gregorian calendar; European officers to train her armed forces; steam power for her industry; central banking; a new peerage specially created so as to make orthodox bicameral governmnent possible by providing the material for an Upper House; the codification of her law; a representative system: these were all pieces of the structure of a new Japan which was at last crowned by alliance with one European power and victory in war over another (see below, Ch. 8).

Such borrowing from European civilization had only just begun in 1880. It went ahead later on such a scale and at such a pace that

41 1883–1907.
42 One was as a follower of Lord Salisbury, one of Gladstone.
43 See R. Storry, *A History of Modern Japan* (London, 1960), p. 105.

it can now be seen as one of the most important facts of modern history. Taken with others, it explains the displacement of Europe from world hegemony. It cannot be the subject of this book, which has to be about what happened in Europe. But it must never be forgotten that the political, economic, cultural transformation of the world by European influences went on right down to 1945 and beyond. Of those influences incomparably the most important was the spread of nationalism; it is ironic that this European idea was eventually to be the most powerful force undermining Europe's colonial supremacy. Yet it, too, was a registration of the triumph of European culture; down to our own day the political life of the world has increasingly been debated in the terms forged by European history and in a European idiom. Whether the voice is Mazzini's, or that of Marx, the ideas those of 1789, or those of 1848, they are always European. But that triumph can be seen in small things, just as in great.[44]

The final testimony to the vitality of European civilization in this period is the small concession which it made to reciprocal influences from the world outside. Diplomatically and politically non-Europeans could be ignored by Europe down to 1914, except in the western hemisphere, where United States influence was paramount, and in the Far East, where Japan became increasingly important and the Americans had interests which might require respect. Apart from this, the non-European world was, diplomatically speaking, simply that area of the world where European powers could quarrel with one another less dangerously than at home. Economically, Europe had conceded more than she knew; she was already dependent on products from certain areas and would become more dependent in the age of the internal combustion engine. Culturally, too, there were signs that Europe was beginning to be receptive again, as she had not since the sixteenth century. Anthropology had begun the slow erosion of certainty of the absolute superiority of European civilization, although only a few were aware of what was happening. The artists began to hint at change; Japanese prints were re-educating the European

---

44 Games are one example; the implications of the spread of cricket and football alone deserve a chapter to themselves. Another is holidays. Once an exported European feast, sustained by a foreign power, Christmas has had often to give way, in new states, to anniversaries of national significance which, by happy coincidence, happen to fall on 25 December.

eye and African masks attracted the attention of the sculptor and painter.[45] Yet though the reciprocal interplay of European civilization and the world was to continue, Europe remained, on balance, an exporter of culture. When non-Europeans revolted against colonial rule, they would do so with the slogans of the Rights of Man and national self-determination on their lips. They would seek to liberate themselves with European machinery and European techniques. Eventually, they would even turn for expression to European artistic forms like the novel, or abstract painting. But this could hardly have been foreseen in 1880.

45 See John Golding's analysis of 'The "Demoiselles d'Avignon"', *The Burlington Magazine*, 1958, pp. 155–63 for a crucial instance, a painting marking Picasso's transition to Cubism.

3

THE ANCIEN RÉGIME

Ideas and institutions were just as much a part of the 'given' facts of European society between 1880 and 1914 as were geography, or political and economic structure, but they are much harder to measure. What has to be described is the sort of thing which Europeans took for granted as they went about their daily lives. But things taken for granted attract less attention than the striking and untypical. The early feminists make more of an impression on us than the overwhelming mass of their contemporary sisters who took it for granted that their place in society would be one of legal and social inequality to men. The nobility of the *ancien régime* from which twentieth-century Europeans emerged was one of deeply entrenched attitudes which were often hardly made explicit – because they did not need to be. It was republicans who argued their case, not those who took monarchy for granted.

Moreover, which Europeans? Given the racial, regional and economic diversity surveyed in the last chapter, how can there be such a thing as 'European' assumptions? One answer to this could be that articulate Europeans, however much they differed, were formed by a common educational heritage and thought of themselves as Europeans when they looked at the rest of the world. Even the 'civilized world' meant, effectively, the world of nations of European stock. Another answer would be that economic or racial diversity could not mask a common drift in all countries towards similar economic arrangements. Cartels, churches and the Scandinavian and Latin monetary unions straddled political frontiers. A few Europeans even cherished federal dreams. But the strongest argument for attempting to identify, however arbitrarily, some general assumptions in so complicated a structure, is Europe's success: she imposed a pattern of civilization on the rest of the world. Some, at least, of the fundamentals of this pattern were accepted throughout almost all Europe, whatever qualifications have to be made. That pattern can also be called liberal, or bourgeois, civilization and it was most developed in the industrialized countries, least in the agrarian east and south. It profoundly shaped European society, politics and religion.

SOCIETY

Social institutions – property arrangements, for example – could be very different in agrarian south-east and the industrialized north-west of Europe; nonetheless, common economic tendencies were already producing common ways of conceiving society. The German Empire might be the extreme case of industrialization but even Russia was beginning to produce a recognizable capitalist industrial structure. In a traditional Spain Catalonia had long been an industrial region. As there was a rough, though by no means exact, correlation of social power with wealth, this meant that the élites of European society tended to be more and more permeated by members of the financial, industrial and professional bourgeoisie which had emerged increasingly as the dominant class in progressive societies since the seventeenth century.

Nevertheless, however blurred the lines between them, two roughly defined but distinct models of society can be discovered in Europe before 1914. For convenience, one can be called 'market' society, and one 'status' society; the crucial distinction between them is that in one privileges and obligations were increasingly distributed through competition in the market, and in the other by the operation of an acknowledged and traditional hierarchy of status. In one, rewards and influence went to wealth and enterprise, in the other to rank and birth. Of course, no society in 1880 perfectly embodied either principle, but this division is a useful rough guide. Some societies straddled it; others fell obviously on one side or the other of it. This distinction was roughly mirrored in a major division in Europe's economic geography (which was also, outside England, one between those directly affected or not by the French Revolution and the changes it brought). In the agrarian south and east of the continent, the character of society was dominated by two classes of very different size: a body of wealthy landowners, still often enjoying the prestige and privilege and sometimes the legal and noble status of its feudal forebears, and a huge mass of subordinate peasants, some of whom might be freeholders, but by and large economically dependent on the landowners. In such countries, city-dwellers were not very important in setting the style and tone of life which reflected instead the old-fashioned, patriarchal assumptions of a long-established way of doing things. Authority, in such countries, was drawn from tradition and prescription and was usually buttressed by religious belief and practice.

In the economically more advanced countries of northern and north-western Europe, things were already very different. The most important social division ran between a dominant class based on the legal ownership of industrial and commercial capital (and sometimes having little to do with either management or labour) and a population most of which worked for wages. This was in its organization and principles an increasingly 'bureaucratic' pattern of society, in which authority was usually legitimized by results.[1] Class, in such societies, more and more bore an economic connotation and left behind the older ideas of timeless social 'orders' or 'estates of the realm'. Nonetheless, for all these differences, it was taken for granted in both agrarian and industrial Europe that society was split for its practical working into a small élite which ran things, and a large mass which was subordinate. The economic significance of this division was that it made possible a very high rate of saving.[2]

Although standards of living rose in the advanced countries, the economic gap between élite and mass remained everywhere enormous. Both eastern and western Europe accepted such a gap, though some people regretted and some hated it. The two parts of society lived different sorts of lives. This could be seen in standards of literacy and taste. It could be seen, also, in the localized life of the masses, in the residue of superstition in their thinking,

1 'Bureaucratic' is a classification invented by the German sociologist Max Weber.
2 See, on this, J. M. Keynes, *The Economic Consequences of the Peace* (London 1919), pp. 16–19.

in the size of their families, and in their health. It appears most vividly in dress. Because photography was already well established in 1880, this is easy to see. In city or countryside in 1880, dress was an almost infallible denominator of social class. The Colonel's Lady and Judy O'Grady might be sisters under their skins, but they went to different shops.[3] The poor workman's clothes might well be better than those of earlier centuries, but they were badly cut, ill-fitting and drab. The Rumanian or Andalusian peasant went in rags.

Yet the social élites of different countries could differ dramatically from one another. Some were outright extensions of traditional hierarchies, while others were predominantly recruited from the new plutocracy and professions. This sometimes made for superficial complication; the Third Republic conferred no titles of nobility, yet more were used than ever before in France, thanks to the inflation and confusion of aristocracies which had flowed from the creations of Bourbon, Orleanist and two Imperial régimes. Proust's Faubourg St Germain was acutely aware of differences between them, but they tell us little about the distribution of power in France. Such distinctions mattered more in Russia or the Dual Monarchy, where the capitalist and professional classes had still a long way to go before winning social acceptance by the old nobility. Even in Germany, the social disqualification of middle-class origins might still have to be purged by a reserve officer's commission – hence, in part, the wide acceptance of the military tone of German society. Medieval hierarchies survived into an epoch of industrial capitalism; feudal military castes presided over national states and industrial societies whose needs they did not understand. The result was confusion about ends and policy (as in Russia or Germany) and the survival of aristocratic assumptions in political life.

Formal distinctions of rank can sometimes provide a very rough index of the resistance of status society to market society in the Europe of 1880, but the line between them was already blurred.

3 That is, if they shopped for clothes at all. There are no figures, but it seems at least probable that in 1880, and perhaps even in 1914, upper-class women had most of their clothes made privately for them, as did middle-class women, serving-women were often provided with clothes as a part of their wages, and women in the countryside made their own clothes or wore cast-offs. The influence of the shop as an agent of social and educational change was in 1880 almost confined to townswomen.

In the United Kingdom, for example, the peerage began seriously to take up directorships of commercial companies in the 1880s: by 1896 directorships were held by 167 members of the House of Lords. The enormous Spanish nobility, luxuriant with the growth of centuries, absorbed in the nineteenth century still larger additions of yet newer nobles drawn from the army, banking and politics. But constitutional states had left few of the old privileges of rank untouched; elsewhere, even when their formal legal status was beginning to be challenged, concessions to aristocratic tradition were still expected in practice.[4] Some were even embodied in law, as well as in custom. Duelling, one index of the survival of the values of barbarism, had been forbidden in the British Army since 1844, but the Russian officer corps was specially exempted from the laws prohibiting it.[5] In certain circumstances German officers, too, were allowed to duel and membership of a good duelling club as a student was to a large degree a *sine qua non* for promotion in the higher German civil service. Much of the past, indeed, survived in the special traditions and interests of soldiers and although the outstanding example was Germany, as the Zabern incident was to show (below, p. 212), it was recognized even in Great Britain that the Guards had the privilege of avoiding the duller overseas stations. In the Curragh Affair of 1914 some British officers appeared to claim to stand for a special national interest above that asserted by civilian politicians and their attitude would have been understood by professional soldiers in other countries. The French army before Dreyfus appealed especially as a career in which it was possible to offer patriotic service untainted by compromise with the Republic.

Such survivals in attitude and custom, however, cannot obscure the fact that the fundamental direction of European society had

4 The extraordinary goings-on of the Magyar nobility (many of whom, oddly, thought they were imitating English country gentlemen) are recalled in O. Jászi, *The Dissolution of the Habsburg Monarchy*, pp. 234–5; and, startlingly, in the *Memoirs of Michael Karolyi* (London, 1956), pp. 31–2. A more amusing example of a privileged attitude can be found in V. Sackville-West, *Pepita* (London, 1937), pp. 248–9.

5 Even without legal sanction, it was often connived at, of course, and not only in the autocracies. The Third Republic produced many political duels; Clemenceau's political opponents feared his pistol as well as his tongue. Cavalotti, the Italian politician, was killed in 1898 fighting his thirty-third duel against an opponent fighting his fifteenth.

been for decades moving increasingly into the hands of a bourgeoisie whose assumptions were at bottom not those of aristocratic society, even if it aped aristocratic style. Bourgeois society
took for granted the sanctity of property, the supremacy of the
market as a social regulator, the propriety of individual self-
improvement and self-advancement, the abandonment of the
traditional and irrational where they stood in the way of utility,
and a belief in progress. This last was not merely material; progress had a moral and ethical content, which spelt hope for
mankind.[6] Bourgeois society traded on the intellectual capital of
optimism inherited from the Enlightenment; science and moral
values were not yet in conflict. And if some of these assumptions
were harsh in their operation they were tempered by a humanitarianism which stemmed from the same eighteenth-century
roots. Violence was believed to be declining; the last war
involving more than two great powers had been fought in the
Crimea, far away, and the assumptions which governed fighting
were more humane than ever before.[7]

Another expression of humanitarianism was a growing concern
with the poor. Nineteenth-century philanthropic endeavour, if
inadequate and ill-coordinated, was nevertheless conducted on a
large scale. It did something to spread awareness of the way the
majority lived, and therefore to spread dissatisfaction and alarm
about a potentially destructive force. Yet, except for their
poverty, it is not easy to generalize about the poor: their attitudes
and assumptions are harder to disinter than those of the dominant
and vocal élites. Economic and political change has now blurred
differences between ways of life then distinct. Variations of economic pattern were then more striking; rural society was a matrix
much more localized and resistant to change than it is today. And

6 Many instances could be given, but for two which embody this
confident and important element in liberal culture, see Carducci's ode to
Victor Hugo, written for his seventy-ninth birthday, in 1881, and
Acton's inaugural lecture at Cambridge in which he identifies 'progress
in the direction of organized and assured freedom' as 'the characteristic
fact of Modern History' (*Lectures on Modern History*) (London, 1906),
p. 11.
7 As late as 1911, for example, five years before the beginning of unrestricted submarine warfare, a British authority expressed the view that
'No Power will incur the odium of sinking a prize with all hands.' J. S.
Corbett, *Some Principles of Maritime Strategy* (London, 1911), p. 166.

many of the town-dwellers of 1880 were recent immigrants from the countryside.

Nevertheless, the trend towards standardization could be discerned in countries where industrialization had gone furthest. In spite of local differences, modern mass society was beginning to appear. Conscription and working-class political movements supplemented the factory and the city as homogenizing and disciplining agents. Nor do terrible exceptions offset the generally standardizing effect already achieved in 1914 by rising real wages, cheaper consumer goods, big stores and central markets. Hours of work were falling – by 1900 most western European countries were down to about sixty per week for adult men – and social services and welfare legislation were becoming more usual.[8] Reciprocal arrangements to promote similar labour legislation were more frequent. Sweating remained, child labour survived, and reformers could still find terrible poverty to expose, but improving conditions meant rising expectations, even though these were at first limited to a few. Greater wellbeing showed itself in new pleasures; the appetite for holidays grew with cheap transport. Savings banks and cooperatives spread new ideals about independence and thrift. A new literacy and cheap newsprint spawned the monster newspapers which were the first cultural artifact of mass society.[9] France had *Le Journal* from 1892, and the *Daily Mail* appeared in 1896. Finally, and most important, came the great spread of popular education which, though it might destroy old habits, also created a new discipline.

All these things helped to diffuse common ideas and assumptions. As selfconsciousness and literacy grew, so did the permeation of the mass society by bourgeois standards. The process was bound to be self-accelerating, as new cities provided new opportunities for greater cultural contact. It has been simply expressed in a mathematical form. A population density of 35 per square mile gives less than 1,000 possible contacts within three miles to any individual: a density of 10,000 per square mile gives him 280,000 possible contacts in the same radius. This makes clear the

8 Workmen's compensation, for example, was introduced in Germany in 1879, Great Britain in 1880, Austria-Hungary in 1887 and in France in 1899. By 1914 Great Britain, France, Belgium, Holland, Italy, Denmark, Austria, Norway, Sweden and Switzerland all had systems of social insurance.
9 Linotype was the decisive invention.

importance of urbanization in disrupting attitudes rooted in a highly localized culture. In the great cities, people had to make more choices for themselves as traditional social institutions like the family and the church lost their grip on the individual. Bismarck was right to distrust the cities as breeders of socialism, but wrong to exaggerate the danger. New disciplining agents were at work in them, and a new kind of politics was to give outlet to their grievances.

POLITICS

Few Europeans would have contested the view that they should be organized politically in sovereign states. They felt, that is to say, that within a given territory, there should be one authority with an ultimate monopoly of coercive power. There were still people who resisted the idea of a sovereign law-maker with the right to invade any vested interest and set aside any restraining principle, but, by and large, the supremacy of the State was acknowledged after centuries of dispute. Political argument was usually about particular forms of the State, about the grounds of its legitimacy, and about the way its power was used.

Some European nations still gave much weight to traditional authority, but most of them also showed a growing tendency to seek to legitimize such authority on other grounds.[10] This was a part of the general movement of progressive societies towards replacing non-rational by reasoned arrangements, a movement which goes beyond politics. The family, for example, was at the same time tending to lose some of its authority and responsibilities. By the end of the nineteenth century, the political side of this process was far advanced. More precisely, it meant that discussion about the organization and use of state power turned

10 Max Weber, the German sociologist, usefully distinguished *traditional* authority (resting on historical transmission, often by inheritance) which is irrationally based, from *legal-rational* authority which separates persons and offices, is organized bureaucratically around the performance of defined tasks through impersonal institutions, and is usually justified by appeals to the reasonableness of its arrangements. Of course, like such terms as 'market' and 'status' society, these terms are only useful working categories, not historically pure forms.

more on means and less on ends. This did not mean there were not still big divergences of belief about ends. Views held widely, but by no means universally, about monarchy, nationalism and democracy were questioned because of this, just as much as because of their results.

Monarchy was almost the rule in Europe, which had many republicans, but few republics. France and Switzerland were the only two which mattered in 1880; Portugal joined them in 1910. New states, as they appeared, were given kings; Albania came last, getting hers in 1914. This kept alive the nineteenth-century export trade in cadets of major ruling houses. As late as 1915 Masaryk could only envisage a monarchical future for a Bohemian state. Monarchy was as widely taken for granted at the end of the nineteenth century as is universal suffrage today.

Some of its appeal undoubtedly lay in its ritual and spectacular trappings; in an age when pageantry was declining elsewhere and when a new mass public was appearing, royal marriages, funerals and coronations were welcome as stirring displays. Monarchy became itinerant as it had not been since the Middle Ages, but the reason for this was not administrative but political and diplomatic. State visits had become easier in the age of the railway; photography, cheap prints and ceramics diffused the human images of rulers more widely than ever before. Monarchy also appealed because it was the logical development of a hierarchical view of the universe which might be waning but which was still immensely strong and very widely understood.[11] The monarch stood at the top of a pyramid of aristocracy in a period when most people still assumed society must be run by élites. To many people, monarchy seemed to offer greater stability than other political forms; the record of republics was not very impressive. This accounted for the distrust felt for Great Britain in more autocratic states. The British crown lacked power; Alexander III of Russia described it as 'hardly to be counted as a monarchy, but rather as a Crown by election'.[12] Because of this, British policy

---

11 Jászi, p. 44, tells us that in Transylvania he found the Rumanian peasants regarding the Emperor 'with almost a kind of religious sacredness', and for years after his death the Crown Prince Rudolph was believed by the peasants of Galicia to be travelling among them in disguise, preparing to share their sufferings.

12 *German Diplomatic Documents*, selected and translated by E. T. S. Dugdale (4 vols., 1928–31, hereafter *GDD*), 1, p. 131.

was constantly a source of apprehension, and the democratic overthrow of British society was sometimes foretold abroad.

Fears of revolution and subversion were widely held in 1880. The French Revolution had begun less than a hundred years before; the Paris Commune was only nine years away. Political assassination was frequent. Both Spain and Italy had near-revolutionary crises at the end of the century. Even in England there were riots which needed cavalry charges to contain them and when the period opened Fenians were letting off bombs. Law and order seemed fragile when opposed to the growing danger of the huge new slums whose populations were feared as *classes dangereuses*. In these circumstances, conservatives clung to monarchy as a tried institution, and monarchs clung to one another. They did not all put it quite as bluntly as William II,[13] but there existed a European society of kings which had real importance for its members. Expressed in the *Dreikaiserbund* and in the hands of a Bismarck, the self-interest of monarchs could be of European significance as a force for peace. When William I was to meet Alexander III in 1887, Bismarck provided him with notes which included the words '*Au temps où nous vivons plus qu'à aucune autre époque de l'histoire, il est de l'intérêt des grandes monarchies d'éviter la guerre . . . même en Allemagne – si contre toute attente nous venions à être vaincus – les chances de la république démocratique ou sociale gagneraient considérablement par notre défaite.*'[14]

The self-interest of monarchs, however, could also operate in a more provocative way. Dynasticism was not dead; for some rulers, promoting family interests was as important as it had been to a Tudor or a Valois. The outstanding example was the Habsburg monarchy, forever subordinating all the practical and sentimental realities of its components to the interests of the dynasty. In the middle of the Great War, the Emperor Charles told his foreign minister Czernin that he wanted neither a military nor an economic agreement with his ally, Germany, because that might fit the Hohenzollern design to make of Austria a second Bavaria. But there were milder examples. Queen Victoria pressed upon her

13 'The democratic countries governed by Parliamentary majorities, against the Imperial Monarchies.' *The Kaiser's letters to the Tsar. The Willy-Nicky Correspondence*, ed. N. F. Grant (London, 1920), p. 99, 19 November 1903.
14 *Die grosse Politik*, v, p. 323.

government her sympathies for Alexander of Battenberg in Bulgaria. Prussia had a dynastic interest in the same question, as Bismarck recognized when he opposed Alexander's marriage to a Prussian princess: 'English policy', he said, 'has an interest in our being on bad terms with Russia, and a Prussian princess on the Bulgarian throne would be a fairly sure way of achieving this.'[15] He also blamed the English family connexion of the crown princess for opposition to his politics at court.

The institution of monarchy at the end of the nineteenth century provides some of the best illustrations of the overlapping, or the incapsulation within one another, of ideas drawn from different ages. Dynasticism still operated in societies governed increasingly by nationalism, and both were challenged by other ideological influences. It was an age when Russian soldiers still carried into battle and jealously guarded the picture of the tsar, when Englishmen could still respond emotionally to the title 'king-emperor'; yet it was also one in which assassination had become an occupational hazard of royalty. Family and proprietary considerations still loomed so large that the Kaiser could in 1891 give orders for a mobilization to be carried out if his mother was insulted in Paris, yet it was also an age in which monarchs had more and more to personify national and even democratic causes.

Nationalism enjoyed enormous prestige. Politically, it was the master idea of the nineteenth century, drawing on the need of men to feel linked to other men at a time when market society tended to make them feel isolated beings. It thrived on the irrational, almost magical, appeal of kinship, on the rubbish talked about international struggle by men like Treitschke, on the intensification of economic rivalries, on the need for myth and colour. Its prestige also had a basis, as a political doctrine, in the liberal idea of self-determination. Nationalism had been primarily supported by liberals, because the emergence of self-governing nations had seemed to be a final step towards the effective protection of individual rights. Gladstone saw nationalism in this light, and it was the same impulse which led, for example, Menotti Garibaldi, the great hero's son, to try to raise an Italian legion to help Arabi Pasha in Egypt.

15 Letters of *Queen Victoria*, 2nd series, vol. III, pp. 26–7, and N. Rich and H. Fisher, *The Holstein Papers* (4 vols. Cambridge, 1955–63; hereafter *Holstein*), 1, p. 136. See also Ch. 4, below.

It was assumed that Europe (outside the Dual Monarchy and Russia) ought to be organized on national lines. From the Treaty of Berlin onwards, the states emerging from the Ottoman Empire were theoretically, though not very successfully, demarcated by nationality. In 1905 Norway separated from Sweden peacefully, a step of great interest to Magyars who considered the Dual Monarchy too constricting a framework. The Magyar example itself much impressed the Irish; in 1904 a Sinn Fein leader published a book on *The Resurrection of Hungary*. Frustrated national movements like those of the Irish, or south Slavs of the Dual Monarchy, of the Armenians in Turkey or the Poles in Russia, could usually rely upon a reflex of ready sympathy in at least some foreign countries. Sometimes the struggle for political autonomy stimulated a search for cultural identity; the great achievements of the Irish literary revival of the end of the century are its monuments (they are, of course, written in English).

Nationalism also produced degenerate offshoots and analogies in various forms of racialism. A literature of white supremacy appeared between 1880 and 1914. The vogue for this owed much to a bastard Darwinism; Latin nations were less taken in by it than were Slavs and Teutons. Perhaps its most coherent exposition was a book called *The Foundations of the Nineteenth Century*, published in 1899 by Houston Stewart Chamberlain, an Englishman naturalized as a German. Racial doctrine was far more influential in German official thinking than in that of any other country: even the 'White Book' published by the German government to justify its acts of 1914 invoked racialist arguments. In England, Joseph Chamberlain dreamed of an Anglo-Saxon-German alliance and scholarships founded by Cecil Rhodes expressed the same aspiration. The Slav version of this sort of thing was the complicated bundle of phenomena lumped together as panslavism.[16] By 1880 this was more and more a matter of Great Russian chauvinism within the boundaries of the Russian Empire, and tsarist imperialism abroad, but it had great sentimental appeal among Slavs living under non-Slav rulers who were encouraged by it to look to this 'big brother'. Its ideological origins were complex. Darwinism entered into the panslavism of Danilevsky as it did into panteutonism. But panslavism had little practical effect on

16 For an excellent brief discussion, see the Historical Association pamphlet *Panslavism* by John Erickson, 1964.

policy: it was a matter of popular mood rather than of official ideology.

One other form of racialism, a negative one, must be mentioned. Antisemitism was not the creation of the nineteenth century but it revived in intensity about 1880. This was the beginning of a great revival; it followed decades during which the legal position of Jews had, on the whole, steadily improved. In the Treaty of Berlin, for example, almost every Balkan country was obliged to legislate for their protection. Yet in 1880 a German antisemitic league was founded and an antisemitic meeting was held under Christian Socialist auspices at Berlin. In the following year, the police stood by and did nothing when students rioted against Jews. By 1914, antisemitism was strong and widespread in Germany. Its first political use had been by extreme conservatives against Bismarck; during his struggle against the socialists antisemitism spread to all parties on the Right. It found support in the professional and middle classes, and Treitschke gave it intellectual respectability. The Germans of the Dual Monarchy, too, were particularly susceptible to political antisemitism. This is partially to be explained by the influx to Vienna, the heart of German Austria, of Jewish immigrants from the east. By 1911 two-thirds of the German votes in Austrian elections went to anti-semitic parties. Middle-class people and intellectuals, as in Germany, were greatly attracted; student organizations at the universities were quick to exclude Jews, forbidding their members to take cycling or walking trips with them. (Another of their bans, on duelling with Jews, may seem less deplorable because of its practical results, but it must have been even more humili-ating.) Antisemitism also drew support in both countries from working-class people disturbed by the impact of industrialism and large-scale capitalism, and possibly because of the success of big business houses with Jewish names. This helps to explain why such figures as Stöcker, the court chaplain in Berlin, or Karl Lueger, the demagogic Christian Socialist mayor of Vienna, were able to couple antisemitism and social reform in anticipation of the Nazis. The new antisemitism bit less deeply in France, but even there Drumont's best-seller *La France juive* had over a hundred printings in the 1880s, and antisemitic journals prolifer-ated. Ruined Catholic investors blamed Jewish (and Protestant) financiers for the collapse of *L'Union Générale*, a great Catholic bank, in 1882, and Jewish names were prominent in the Panama scandal. The Dreyfus case produced grave excesses, when Frenchmen were urged to '*arroser du sang des Juifs l'arbre de la liberté*'[17] and a Papal Nuncio reminded a French diplomat that '*la religion catholique avait en reserve des indulgences spéciales pour ceux qui, lorsque la bonne cause le réclame, versent le sang des juifs et des paiens*'.[18]

Whatever justifications were invoked, sentiments of this sort show a new violence in antisemitic feeling quite different from the traditional popular dislike of Jews exploited, for example, by a Russian government looking for scapegoats which led in 1881 to a terrible series of anti-Jewish riots, followed by legislation creating new ghettoes.[19] This was condemned in western countries, but feeling against Jews was common everywhere: Freud's father had his hat knocked off by a Gentile who shouted at him 'Jew, get off the pavement', and Jewish shops were smashed by miners in Tredegar in 1911. A bill to legalize the marriage of Jews and Christians was thrown out by the Hungarian Diet in 1883. Yet the new antisemitism went further. It was often a lower middle-class phenomenon, and was always fiercest in central and eastern Europe where the great mass of the population had little commitment to capitalist society or to the liberal values it generated.

Much disillusionment has followed the discovery that formal democracy, as the case of antisemitism shows, has no necessary connexion with tolerance and freedom, the liberal ideals. In 1880, this had already been discerned, but most men gave a growing acceptance to democratic institutions because they seemed to provide not a threat to, but a guarantee of, liberal standards. This may seem surprising in view of the widespread acceptance of monarchy. Yet, as Sir Henry Maine, no friend of democracy, pointed out in 1885, 'Russia and Turkey are the only European states which completely reject the theory that governments hold their power by delegation from the community'.[20] In 1900 only

17 See A. Debidour, *L'église catholique et l'Etat sous la troisième République* (Paris, 1901), vol. II, p. 193.
18 See *Studies in Diplomatic History . . . in honour of G. P. Gooch*, ed. A. O. Sarkissian (London, 1961), p. 28.
19 Russia contained 5 million of about 8 million European Jews in 1880. There is a good map of Russian pogroms in M. Gilbert, *Jewish History Atlas* (London, 1969), p. 71.
20 *Popular Government* (1885), p. 8.

these two states and Montenegro did not have parliamentary
institutions of some kind. Further formal evidence can be found
in the spread of wider suffrage qualifications. In 1880 both the
German Empire and France had universal adult male suffrage (in
Germany, over the age of twenty-five). In Britain, the rural
worker got the vote in 1884, and Holland extended her franchise
in 1887 and 1896. Spain adopted universal male suffrage in 1890
and Norway in 1898. In the Dual Monarchy, Austrian men
obtained the vote in 1907. The movement towards a democratic
franchise was clearly under way everywhere by 1914. With this
went other liberal innovations such as the limitation of the power
of the House of Lords in the United Kingdom and the initiation
of parliamentary government in Russia. In 1908 the Ottoman
Empire acquired a parliament, and even where such institutions
were a sham (for example, in Austria) lip service was paid to the
spread of democratic and liberal ideals.

The century had also brought the acceptance of other liberal
assumptions. One of these was that the state should make laws
as required. 'It is not often recognized', said Maine in 1885 'how
excessively rare in the world was sustained legislative activity till
rather more than fifty years ago',[21] but law-making had by 1880
already become the characteristic activity of the modern state.
Legislative vigour was still tempered in many countries by vested
interest, the rule of law and respect for individual rights, but
traditional limits on state activity were weakening as the state
took on more and more duties. One obvious symptom was the
growth of bureaucracy. Comparisons are not easy, but Germany's
civil service, for example, grew from 450,000 to 1,180,000
between 1881 and 1911, and Great Britain's from 81,000 to
644,000.[22] These employees not only ran new economic, welfare
and educational services, they also cost money, and the burden
of government expenditure had by 1880 already risen to heights
undreamed of in 1800. Until the 1890s income tax was virtually
unknown outside Great Britain; indirect taxes still bore much of

21 *Popular Government*, p. 128. See also *Early History of Institutions*
(London, 1875), Lecture XIII.
22 These figures are from the useful table in H. Finer, *Theory and Practice
of Modern Government* (4th edn., London, 1961), p. 710. They should,
however, be read in the light of the careful qualifications included in
Professor Finer's footnotes.

the burden in other states in 1900, but by then Germany, Italy, Austria and Spain all had some form of income tax, and Russia and Great Britain had taxes on inherited wealth. This change in the nature of the state's role did not go unresisted, but it was more often deplored than checked.

The widening of electorates, the spread of parliamentary institutions and the making of new demands on the state brought the appearance of a democratic political style. In many states, the political framework could be described as 'constitutional monarchy', but only Spain and Sweden shared the two-party conflict with which Great Britain seemed to make the system work. Elsewhere, multi-party systems proliferated, though in some states the technique of organizing mass parties was beginning to be seen as the key to political power. The first systematic studies of political parties belong to the end of the nineteenth century. Wider suffrages, urbanism and growing literacy were forcing new techniques and new institutions on the politicians.

RELIGION

Much of what matters most in religious experience and belief is personal and private. So, it is inaccessible to the historian. Even such observable facts as churchgoing are hard to interpret. The study of religious behaviour must, inevitably, be largely the study of the records of organized groups, the Churches. Yet these define their 'membership' in such different ways that it is hard to draw conclusions from their figures. Figures of religious observance are harder to come by. England's only census of churchgoers was taken in 1851 and there was no systematic enumeration of religious practice in France until a survey of attendance at mass in one area in 1903. They are harder still to interpret: what does a large attendance at Easter communion imply? Which is more significant, a drop in regular churchgoing or the enormous efforts of the Churches in the nineteenth century in the mission field? Occasional statistics sometimes throw light on the problem; in 1875 Gladstone's pamphlet on the Vatican Decrees sold 100,000 copies and it is difficult not to see in this a level of religious interest which later declined. Statistics of baptism, civil marriage and civil funerals, too, in some countries, may help, but they can only be used with difficulty.[23] Moreover, traditional and historical factors can do much to localize the significance of even such evidence as seems firm. Gladstone's pamphlet was published in a country where anti-popery was the religion of many people. It was also a country which consciously rejected the 'continental Sunday' and whose Grand Lodge of Freemasons severed contact with the French *Grand Orient* when French freemasonry no longer required of its members a belief in the Grand Architect of the Universe. Liberalism in most European countries meant anticlericalism, while in England it was a movement led by a High Churchman with the devoted support of many Nonconformists.

1880, moreover, is not a date in religious history, even if the French abolished military chaplains and the British parliament opened parish churchyards to nonconformist burial services in that year. Almost every European country still had an Established Church. But religion had long been losing its power to shape and control behaviour and external forces had long sapped the traditional theocentric views of Europeans, even if it was only in 1882 that Nietzsche pronounced the notorious words: 'God is dead'. Yet it is easier to sense the swing of history against traditional religion than to measure it. It was helped by the *de facto* secularizing of the state since the Reformation, by the growth of towns, by the rise of positivism, materialism and a belief in natural science, some of whose exponents were militantly and bitterly anticlerical. A rising standard of living may have weakened the tendency to turn to religion for explanation or comfort. More self-knowledge meant that it was easier to see man as one natural object among many. The English Free Church Year Book of 1911 probably spoke for many communions when it said 'the truth is – and we must face its startling reality – the educated middle class, especially the young people, are losing touch altogether with the House of God'.[24]

23 In the case of France, civil funerals at first look promising, but on examination do not seem to provide a very good indicator of religious belief. See Isambert, *Arch. Soc. Rel.*, 1960, p. 31. And in Saxony, a strongly Socialist area, nine out of ten children were baptized in 1896.
24 Compare the interestingly similar language of the Bishop of Cremona, in his letter to the Pope of Christmas 1886 (see A. C. Jemolo, *Church and State in Italy 1880–1950*, (Oxford, 1960), p. 72): 'intellectual Youth, which one day will be the mainstay of society, is steadily detaching itself from the Church'. H. McLeod, *Religion and the People of Western Europe* (Oxford, 1981) pp. 98–117 is helpful on this topic.

Intellectual revolt was one source of militant anticlericalism. It also grew from the old rivalry of Church and State which had brought a life-giving tension to European history since the days of Hildebrand.[25] This quarrel had been renewed and intensified as the modern state emerged and is easier to narrate than the shifting of the foundations of belief. In the eighteenth and nineteenth centuries, enlightened despotism, secularism, nationalism and liberalism had all fanned the flames. And apart from this exacerbation of old quarrels at the level of official and formal relations, religion lost some of its hold on the masses as it did less and less to provide channels for social protest. The new popular movements of revolt, anarchism and socialism, were not only as anticlerical as any enlightened despot, they were often antireligious as well.[26] The growth of liberal assumptions of free speech and tolerance meant that the anticlerical challenge came just when religion had been deprived of much of its legal protection. Religious liberty was cherished in the nineteenth century, but it implied toleration of religious debate.[27]

Different traditions experienced this change in different ways. Roman Catholics have grown in numbers in modern times, but it is not easy to use figures to compare the Roman Church's position in 1880 with that of say, a century before. Nineteenth-century concordats had improved the legal position of Roman Catholicism in many countries and often left the clergy considerable powers over such matters as education, yet Papal Infallibility, the Syllabus of Errors and the Church's resistance to the conclusions of biblical criticism alienated intellectuals. Ecclesiastical institutions were still, in countries such as Spain, outstanding examples of corporate privilege. No Roman Catholic movement of the left had appeared to help Rome in its political

25 See C. Brooke, *Europe in the central Middle Ages* (London, 1964) e.g. pp. 265–7.
26 Cf. Bebel, the German Socialist leader: 'Our revolution differs from all its predecessors in this – it does not seek for new forms of religion, but denies religion altogether.' (see A. L. Drummond, *German Protestantism since Luther* (London, 1951), p. 221).
27 See, e.g. the attention given to religion in the Treaty of Berlin. 'The great modern principle of religious equality has in every civilized nation superseded those antiquated and bigoted ideas of hostility and exclusion,' Ulstermen were reminded by two German professors in 1914 (see A. P. Ryan, *Mutiny at the Curragh* (London, 1956), p. 166).

struggles at a time when the suffrage was spreading; in spite of a few 'Christian socialists', Roman Catholicism still seemed to be tied to social and political conservatism. Finally, in Italy and Germany, it had to live down decades of struggle against the nationalist movements. In Italy in 1880 Catholics were still ordered to abstain from political activity; in Germany, the *Kulturkampf*, a struggle whose origin lay in a quarrel between Bismarck and Catholic Germans opposed to Prussian dominance of the new German Empire, was still under way. Between 1870 and 1880 the Jesuits had been expelled from Germany, religious orders dissolved, the State had interfered with the discipline of the clergy, civil marriage had been made obligatory and Prussia had withdrawn its financial support from Catholic churches. Germany's bishops were in exile when Bismarck, in 1879, began to consider a restoration of relations with the Papacy, a process which took several years (see also below, p. 220).

The *Kulturkampf* was easily the most spectacular quarrel with Rome. Anticlericalism elsewhere was sometimes simply a matter of anti-Roman pinpricks, as in Great Britain, when agitation arose about aristocratic conversions to Rome and the British Reformation Society could protest to the government over the appointment of a Roman Catholic viceroy of India and a Roman Catholic lord chamberlain. But in France, as in Germany, anticlericalism inflamed a confrontation of Church and State at many points, from educational policy to marriage laws, and was to finish in disestablishment. The quarrel of the Italian government with the Papacy nearly led to an anticlerical league of governments around about 1880. Later, the Portuguese revolution of 1910 created a bitterly anticlerical republic which expelled religious orders and, as in France, finished by separating Church and State. The Spanish anticlericals, too, fought stubbornly against the Church, but, as Spain showed, the Roman Church did not always lose. In Belgium the clerical party won the 1880 elections and held power for the next twenty-five years, repealing an earlier secularization of education and making instruction in the Roman Catholic faith obligatory in all publicly maintained schools in 1895. Dutch anticlericalism produced in 1889 a curious coalition of Calvinists and Roman Catholics to defend State support for denominational schools.

As these examples suggest, the pontificate of Leo XIII (1879–1903) saw something of a recovery in the political fortunes of the Papacy. Much of it can be attributed to his astute realization that it was possible to break with the disastrous tradition of Pius IX without compromising on essentials. No State, it was clear, was going to help the Papacy recover the Temporal Power; meanwhile, bad relations with the governments of France, Italy and Germany were endangering the spiritual and material welfare of millions of Roman Catholics. Leo quickly began to apply emollients, abandoning the Catholic separatists who rejected Prussian hegemony in Germany, dropping the French monarchists and urging the loyal acceptance of the Republic by French Catholics (the policy known as *Ralliement*). 'None of the several forms of government is condemned in itself,' said the encyclical *Immortale Dei* (1885), 'in as much as none of them contains anything contrary to Catholic doctrine, and all of them are capable, if wisely and justly managed, of ensuring the welfare of the State.'[28] Even in Italy, though Leo never ceased to assert the Papal claim to the Temporal Power, there seemed a prospect of conciliation between Church and State in the mid-1880s.

Already by 1890 there had been a big improvement in the relations of the Papacy with governments conscious of Roman Catholicism's contribution to social order in a time of revolutionary fears. And Leo had also been taking steps to revivify the influence of religion at other levels. In 1880 St Thomas Aquinas was acknowledged the patron of all Catholic schools and learning, and a great revival of Thomist scholarship began which was to do much to integrate Catholic dogma with the advances of natural science. In 1891 came the publication of the encyclical *Rerum Novarum*. This pronouncement on social policy upheld the institution of private property, but acknowledged that limitations might rightly be laid upon its rights so as to protect the poor and weak. It even approved the formation of trade unions and reminded employers of a moral duty to pay adequate wages. The way was thus cleared for the emergence of a Catholic social policy suited to mass society.

Nevertheless, Leo's pontificate did not realize the hopes it awoke. The dawn of good relations in Italy proved false; under Crispi's first ministry (1887–91) the Pope even considered leaving Rome. In 1898 he repeated his predecessor's injunction that Italian Catholics should abstain from political activity. Although the

28 See also the encyclicals *Diuturnum* (1881) and *Libertas* (1888).

gains in Germany were preserved (the symbol of agreement to end the *Kulturkampf* was the completion and consecration of Cologne Cathedral in 1880, in the presence of the Emperor and all the reigning German princes), those of the *Ralliement* in France were blown to the winds by the Dreyfus Affair. Pius X opened his pontificate (1903–14) amid an uproar which brought about the end of the Napoleonic concordat (1905). He reacted with a revived authoritarianism. New disciplinary measures and recommendations asserted his authority over clerical and lay Catholics.[29] Leo XIII's approach to social and economic questions was qualified and priests were ordered to submit to their bishops on social and political matters. There was a relaxation of the ban on Catholic participation in Italian politics, it is true, for Pius was convinced of the importance of defending the social and moral order and foresaw the possibility of a Catholic majority in the Italian parliament. New confessional political parties emerged in other countries, too. But such acceptance of the possibilities afforded by modern political institutions was opportunist; Pius remained implacably opposed to the assumptions of liberal bourgeois civilization. This became most strikingly clear when the encyclicals *Lamentabili* and *Pascendi* in 1907 condemned the 'modernists'. 'Modernism' was a name which covered the individual efforts of several Catholic clergy, many of them French, to reconcile Catholic dogma with the discoveries of science and scholarship. It owed something to the atmosphere of Leo XIII's innovation (but even in 1893 Loisy, a leading French biblical scholar and modernist, had lost his chair at Paris, and an encyclical had been published affirming the complete inerrancy of the Bible).[30] Pius's encyclicals killed Modernism. Loisy was excommunicated in 1908 and what one scholar has called 'a reign of terror' began in the intellectual life of the Roman Church.[31] A young Italian nobleman had already summed up the dismay felt by liberal Catholics in 1906 when he wrote, in a famous letter, 'Since the death of Pope Leo the Roman Curia has assumed towards the world of thought a reactionary attitude reminiscent

29 For details, see Jemolo, p. 112.
30 A year later the Protestant theologian Harnack's views on the Virgin Birth were condemned by the Lutheran Supreme Council of Germany.
31 A. R. Vidler, *The Church in an Age of Revolution* (London, 1961), p. 188.

of the days of Pius IX, when the Church was at war with every-thing and everybody.'[32]

Protestantism's strength and influence at the end of the nine-teenth century is even harder to assess than that of Roman Cathol-icism, because of its diversity. There were established Protestant churches in the United Kingdom, Scandinavia and Germany as well as millions of Protestants in unestablished denominational connexions. Protestant theology, under German leadership, had more readily accepted the implications of Biblical criticism than had Roman. 'Liberal' protestantism had done much to recreate an accepted image of the 'historical' Jesus, even if its theological validity was soon to be exploded. In both England and Germany, too, the 'social gospel' was preached with increasing vigour. In 1877 Anglicans founded the Guild of St Matthew, the first organ-ization inside the Church of England to address itself to the social implications of Christianity since the 1850s. In 1889 the more academic Christian Social Union was founded and the effect began to be felt in attacks on 'sweated' labour and other social abuses before the end of the century. In Germany a Christian Socialist movement was built up by Stöcker, the court chaplain, and Naumann (later the theoretician of *Mitteleuropa*) publicized the 'social gospel'.

Yet, in spite of these accommodations to the spirit of the times, established and traditional Protestantism does not seem to have been better able than Roman Catholicism to meet the challenge of industry and the big towns. Anglicans were still too heavily committed to an organization suited to a predominantly rural society. German towns were not adequately equipped with clergy or churches (Berlin in 1880 had churches for only 25,000 worship-pers).[33] In Germany, too, the clergy were distrusted still by the workers as 'black police' and the most powerful Socialist move-ment in Europe was avowedly antireligious.[34] Nor did divisions and bickering between Protestants lend prestige to their faith. It was only in 1880, after fierce quarrels, that English dissenters were given the right to burial in the parish churchyard by their

32 See Jemolo, pp. 119–20.
33 For other examples, see Latourette, vol. II, pp. 96–7.
34 Yet in strongly socialist Saxony, for example, 96 per cent of marriages in 1892 were solemnized by pastors – a figure which suggests the diffi-culty of evaluating the statistical evidence (Drummond, p. 222).

own pastors. A proliferation of pentecostal and evangelical sects, and the success of the Salvation Army (founded in 1878) seemed to show that though the masses could still be moved by religious fervour, they could not find it in the established churches.

In Orthodox Europe, mass religion seems to have decayed less than in the west. Enlightened anticlerical views could only spread among a fairly small educated élite and in Russia, in spite of some ultraconservatives, it was the ruling class which was alienated from the church rather than the mass of the people. The church ran primary education, and even among the intellectuals Orthodoxy was not without vigour: the early twentieth century brought remarkable conversions to Christianity among Russian Marxists.

The Jewish faith was affected by liberalizing tendencies, but the most important development it fostered during these years was not theological but political. It is hardly surprising that the Zionist movement should have appeared in the violently antisemitic atmosphere of the Dual Monarchy. In 1896 Theodore Herzl's *Der Judenstaat* proposed the re-establishment of the Jewish people in a national, territorial state as the only workable solution to the Jewish problem. In 1897 the Zionist Congress was founded by Herzl at Basle. The first wave of Jewish reimmigration to Palestine had already taken place and these events marked an epoch in the history of Jewry, the replacement of assimilation by nationalism as an ideal. It was a change by no means welcome to all Jews, but its assertion of the primacy of national ties was characteristic of the age. Some Jews regretted the abandonment of the essentially liberal road of peaceful assimilation by the extension of civil equality to Jews in more and more countries. Zionism, too, was thus in this way a challenge to the assumptions of liberal culture. It fed both on a new nationalism, and a re-vivification of orthodoxy in the face of the challenge of science and materialism.

4

INTERNATIONAL COMPETITION, 1880–1901

THE SETTING OF INTERNATIONAL RELATIONS

An English radical commented in 1887 that 'the present position of the European world is one in which sheer force holds a larger place than it has held in modern times since the fall of Napoleon'.[1] Yet after the end of the Franco-Prussian War (1871), none of the great powers fought one another for more than forty years, although these years were full, if not of wars, at least of rumours of wars. The fundamental reason for this was that between 1880 and 1900 there was coming to an end that Concert of Europe which, in spite of the wars of the mid-century, had avoided a general war since 1815. How this happened is the subject of this chapter. It was known that a change was taking place and perhaps it was felt the more because of the very success of the Concert; humanitarian impulses and liberal assumptions had disguised the fact, axiomatic to professional diplomats, that the interests of states often conflicted. New occasions of conflict were now appearing and would eventually break up the long peace, and as this became clearer so did the essentially competitive nature of the European system. The objects of competition varied: the traditional ones were territory, wealth, prestige and the power which these gave. The competition for them was not bound to result in the use of force, but it kept force in view. Great power status was in the last resort the ability to wage war. As that ability was still,

1 Anon. (C. W. Dilke), *The Present Position of European Politics* (London, 1887), p. 1.

in 1880, much more purely a matter of armies and navies than it was later to become, it is worth while to consider them briefly before turning to the diplomatic story. An approximation of relative strengths can be seen in the following table:

Military and naval strength of the powers, 1880

	Major ironclads[a]	Soldiers[b] Peacetime	Wartime
Austria-Hungary	10	267,000	771,000
France	30 + 29	502,000	740,000
Germany	12	419,000	1,304,000[c]
Great Britain	48 + 19	135,000	392,000
Italy	7	199,000	444,000
Russia	14	765,000	1,213,000[d]

Notes to table:
[a] 'Major ironclads' = those of more than 3,500 tons displacement. Distinctions between first-line ships and others are indicated by the double sets of figures.
[b] To the nearest thousand.
[c] Not counting *Landsturm* and other reserves with the addition of which the wartime total would probably be more than 2 million.
[d] A possible total of 130,000 Cossack irregulars is not included here.

Among the great powers of 1880, only Great Britain was not a land power; armies were more important than navies to continental countries. Land warfare sixty-five years after Waterloo would still have been comprehensible to Napoleon. Brightly-coloured uniforms and gleaming breastplates were not kept for the parade ground, but were meant to be worn in battle. Although breechloading weapons had been generally adopted, the small-bore rifle, the machine-gun, and the quick-firing fieldgun had not yet altered military thinking; they had only increased the range at which fighting would take place. Battles had begun to be much more dispersed affairs, but the internal-combustion engine had not yet scattered them over hundreds of miles. Signals were still largely a matter of horsed despatch-riders and flags; the heliograph and electric telegraph were the only important additions to the repertoire at Napoleon's disposal.[2] Ancillary services such as engineers and field hospitals had become a little more elaborate, but an army was still essentially composed, as was Napoleon's, of the three great arms: artillery, cavalry and

2 The first signalling regulations of the German army were only issued in 1902.

infantry. Artillery was to prepare the way for the infantry assault; the cavalry was to provide reconnaissance, occasional shock intervention in the battle if circumstances were favourable, and, it was hoped, effective pursuit of the defeated enemy.

The strategic and tactical doctrines of 1880 were also recognizably Napoleonic. The aim which obsessed military thinking was the winning of a decisive battle soon after the outbreak of war. Local superiority of numbers was thought to be the key to such a victory. This belief had been reinforced by the experiences of 1866 and 1870; it was assumed that these showed the future pattern of warfare. The fact that the American Civil War had lasted five years was overlooked or discounted. In this vision of rapid warfare there was still a place for great fortresses to provide temporary protection for frontiers and strategically vital areas during the crucial, disorganized days at the beginning of the campaign while the armies were assembling. At this point appeared a major difference from Napoleonic warfare: much more skilled staff work was now required. Organization was the key to successful and rapid mobilization, and the Prussian army had set new standards for all armies by its performances against Austria and France.

'The Moltkean Revolution', as it has been called,[3] led to the adoption everywhere in continental Europe of what were believed to be the secrets of its success – compulsory military service to provide a short-service army with a large trained reserve, and the creation of a permanent, highly-trained general staff. The old long-service, professional army survived only in the United States and Great Britain; everywhere else the 'nation in arms' was the ideal. Effective deployment of the larger reserves which this system made available required intricate staff work. The railway was used to assemble the army as near to the decisive theatre as possible; it was the big contribution of nineteenth-century technology to warfare, because of the strategical mobility it provided. Once away from the railhead, however, the army was back in the age of Napoleon and moved at the pace of horse and man. At this point, planning provided little guidance to what would follow;

3 See T. Ropp, *War in the Modern World* (Durham, N. C., 1959), p. 177. Moltke was chief of the German general staff until 1888. For a near-contemporary view of his machine, see Spenser Wilkinson, *The Brain of an Army* (London, 1891).

the difficulties of extemporizing new manœuvres were enormous and helped to reinforce the prevailing view that the overriding aim must be an early victory obtained essentially by good initial deployment.

Within this general consensus, the armies of individual states made plans for their own circumstances. The strength of each was a function of three variables; the strategic tasks to be carried out, numbers (weapons and equipment did not differ importantly), and the level of organization and training. Great Britain's was a peculiar case. She could do without large conscript armies to defend land frontiers and needed long-service troops who could be employed overseas for long periods.[4] As a result, the small British army had a high degree of expertise in irregular and colonial warfare, could be deployed easily over great distances by sea, and had a rank-and-file which was possibly better trained than that of any other great power. Its corresponding defects were that it was almost insignificant in Europe, retained out-of-date weapons adequate only for colonial use, and paid little attention to training its senior officers for large-scale operations. It had no permanent general staff. The French army, formed of a selected number of conscripts serving five years, was still digesting the lessons of 1870. Its morale had recovered far too well, in that its officers and instructors were turning to a doctrine of offensive warfare at all costs. Yet France's only probable land enemy, Germany, was certain to enjoy numerical superiority. If France remained without an ally who could force Germany to fight on two fronts she would find it impossible to match German numbers because of the difference in the birthrate of the two nations. The German army itself was in theory a composite force of Prussian, Saxon, Bavarian and Württemberger troops; this diversity meant little more than differences of name and uniform, for the Prussian staff controlled the whole apparatus as a unified system and made it the best army in the world. Beside the French and German armies, those of Austria-Hungary, Russia and Italy were second-rate. None of these nations could afford to mobilize its whole strength. Russian organization and training were poor, although her soldiers always showed great hardihood and endurance, and she had to find forces to defend a frontier from the Baltic to the Black Sea, as well as detachments for the Caucasus,

4 In 1880, 62,000 of her 135,000 soldiers were stationed in India.

central Asia and the Far East. The Austro-Hungarian forces were fragmented by the complicated constitutional arrangements of the Dual Monarchy. The Italians were more united, but the traditions of the old army of Sardinia had been diluted by the disgruntled soldiers of other pre-unification states.

Navies had changed much more than armies during the nineteenth century. The Industrial Revolution affected them in many ways, by providing iron and steel for shipbuilding, by applying steam to propelling the ship, by developing more powerful guns and harder armour. Some odd-looking monsters had been produced by designers striving to come to terms with these innovations, but by 1880 warships were already essentially what they were to be for the rest of the century, armoured, steam-driven and screw-propelled, with their main armament in revolving turrets or carried broadside. Signalling was by flag. The main classes of vessel which made up a fleet were first-class armoured ships (which were to hand out and absorb the punishment of a pitched battle), other ironclads used for cruising, coast-defence and the many functions of the old sail frigates, and the 'flotilla' of smaller ships, of which the commonest were gunboats and the newest, torpedo-boats. The British *Collingwood* class of battleships, laid down in 1880, represented the best contemporary design; they displaced 9,500 tons, could steam at a maximum of $16\frac{1}{2}$ knots on coal-fired engines, and carried 18 inches of armour on their sides. Their armament consisted, as did that of almost all battleships for the next two decades, of four big guns (12-inch in this case) mounted in two pairs and a secondary broadside battery of half-a-dozen 6-inch. Battleships would grow bigger after this, but the essential formula of the heavily armoured ship with four big guns making about 16 knots was unchanged until 1906. No other ship could stand up to their guns, but some sailors thought they might be defeated by the new weapon of the torpedo. This self-propelled weapon was not yet a serious threat; it still had an effective range of less than a mile, but the tiny torpedo-boats which were beginning to make their appearance heralded a whole new range of warships for the future.[5] The submarine, which was eventually to provide the best means of delivering the torpedo, was still an infant; only one or two curious submersible craft had been built

5 'No. 10 T.B.' launched in 1880, weighed 28 tons, could make 21.7 knots, and carried one torpedo.

and they had not yet affected naval thinking. That thinking was still cast in the mould of a hundred years before; the methods of conducting war at sea were still those of blockade, commerce-destroying and protection, and still depended ultimately on the ability to win a pitched gun-battle with the enemy fleet.

In numbers, the Royal Navy was the strongest in the world, although its superiority was not so great as it was later to become. Its weakness was its technical conservatism; although in 1880 the Admiralty agreed to reintroduce breechloading guns on heavy ships, the armoured cruisers *Impérieuse* and *Warspite*, which were laid down in the same year, were still designed to carry a full spread of sail. Moreover, the tasks of the Royal Navy were greater than those of other navies. While it was stretched over the whole length of imperial communications, its most dangerous possible rival was the more easily concentrated French fleet; the prospect of a descent on the Channel ports still preoccupied the Admiralty. But even the French navy had to divide itself between the Mediterranean and the Atlantic coasts and the Russians had to maintain a small separate fleet in the Black Sea.[6] The Austrian, Italian and the German navies could be ignored in 1880.

Although armed force lay in the background of every statesman's consciousness, it was not the normal instrument of competition between states. Governments had many other weapons; some were economic. Statesmen were rarely the tools of business in this period; sometimes they made businessmen do their work for them and they were alive to the possibility of political influence being spread through such economic channels as chartered companies. In other circumstances, commercial agreements, tariffs and loans might give diplomatic leverage. There is no simple and general pattern to be discerned in the interplay of politics and economics in the eighties. It would be unreasonable to expect one, given the complexity of the national interests involved in the competition of international relations. Moreover, not only are national interests complex, but they change. At the end of the nineteenth century, dynastic influence could still cut across them. Yet certain facts tended to dominate the making of foreign policy in each country.

British foreign policy started from the incontestable and appar-

6 Twenty-seven out of a total twenty-nine Russian ironclads of all classes in 1880 were stationed in the Baltic.

ently unchanging facts that the United Kingdom was an island, depended on sea-borne commerce and communications, and had large overseas possessions. As Lord Salisbury once put it to a German, '*nous sommes des poissons*'.[7] The consequences of this often seemed to be a neglect of Europe, but the impression was misleading. It was true that many British interests, lying overseas, were not affected by events in Europe. But it was also true that Great Britain could only view events in Europe with detachment or indifference if the balance of power there remained undisturbed. British interests demanded peace and prescribed respect for the independence of all other countries because that was the best insurance against disturbance of the peace. The classical British attitude towards Europe was to intervene decisively there only when there was a danger of one Power threatening the independence of others. That this had always been in the interest of Great Britain did not alter the fact that such interventions had tended since 1815 to favour liberal and nationalist causes. Apart from this, a few more specific British interests touched other European powers; they usually concerned three important regions, the Mediterranean, the Straits of Constantinople and central Asia. The last two made her suspicious of Russia, and even ready to fight her in the 1870s.[8] The navy was the guarantee that Great Britain's interests elsewhere could be looked after and gave her enormous strategical advantages outside Europe. To these facts has to be added the special susceptibility of British public opinion to liberal and humanitarian appeals. This might hamstring the government and its operation was sometimes confusing to foreign observers. The empiricism and opportunism of British foreign policy, its reluctance to embark on long-range plans, its dislike of large commitments and its responsiveness to public opinion all gave it a deceptive appearance of unprincipledness.

German foreign policy in 1880 had very different sources. Great Britain and Germany were only alike in one respect; they were both at that time contented powers. As Bismarck put it, Germany was 'saturated'. Her population, geographical position, army and industrial strength made her the leading continental nation. The Empire had been made by the wars of the mid-century, and

7 *GDD* I, 249.
8 See H. Hearder, *Europe in the Nineteenth Century 1830–1880* (London, 1966), pp. 160–3.

Bismarck wanted peace to consolidate it. His method, however, was to preserve peace by keeping Europe in a state of discord and alarm. Whether a man of his temperament, faced by the threat of French recovery, could maintain peace indefinitely was another matter. But it was clear that the isolation of France was in the interest of Germany. This meant the maintenance of good relations with Russia and Austria-Hungary, who might again come into conflict in the Balkans. So, for German foreign policy, the over-riding concern was not the French question, but the Balkan. Bismarck wanted Germany to maintain the conservative alliance with Vienna and St Petersburg whose roots went back to 1815. He could make concessions to his allies and all would be well so long as they did not come into conflict with one another. This suited the prejudice which he shared with ruling circles in Germany against liberal, constitutional, and above all, republican states. Even Great Britain was, in Bismarck's eyes, a nuisance because her foreign policy might change with each general election; reliable agreements with her were impossible.

French policy was dominated by Germany's demographic and military superiority. '*Nous ne faisons plus d'enfants et nous n'avons pas de frontière, comment voulez-vous que nous vivions?*' enquired one French diplomat of a German colleague.[9] The disparity of the two countries provoked a rough division of French politicians into two schools of thought. One school clung to the dream of *revanche*, the recovery of the lost provinces of 1871 and a Rhine frontier. If the dream were to become reality, France must be militarily strong and find an ally so that she need not face Germany alone. The other school drew a different conclusion. Believing *revanche* to be either unrealizable, or not worth the price to be paid, it looked to colonies, social progress and economic expansion for French achievement. These alternatives weaved in and out of French policy until 1902. Both were compatible with the repub-lican-radical ideals which made up the official ideology of the Third Republic and which in 1880 meant in the main a deep distrust of Russia, the oppressor of the Poles.

Austro-Hungarian foreign policy was both simplified and complicated by her forcible exclusion from Germany in 1866–7; this ended a struggle opened by Frederick the Great's seizure of

9 *Holstein*, II, p. 297.

Silesia. Her exclusion from Italy was less important, but had also tidied up a dangling thread of history. From this time she was a south-eastern power. But by the *Ausgleich* the Habsburgs took into partnership one of the racial groups of which the empire was composed. Hungarian influence on foreign policy meant, in effect, subordinating foreign policy to the maintenance of the racial settlement of 1867. It meant that no more Slavs should be taken into the Dual Empire, because that would distort the balance of races there. It meant also that the consideration which more and more came to dominate the Dual Monarchy's foreign policy was the need to check Russian influence over the Slavs of the Balkans. This might have been less dangerous had the Ottoman Empire held together, but it was crumbling fast and something was bound to take its place. Whether it would be Russian or Habsburg influence was in 1880 still uncertain. No one in authority in Vienna wished to have the question posed. The Dual Monarchy's best hope, if she could not solve her internal racial problems, was that no further changes should take place in the Balkans.

Russian interests are harder to assess. The autocracy counted for something; personal friendship between the Romanoff and Hohenzollern dynasties was important under Alexander II.[10] Traditionally, her rulers had pressed towards the Straits. Traditionally, they exploited their special relationship with the Christian subjects of the Sultan. Traditionally, they looked to the preservation of a conservative alliance against revolution in Europe for the continued enjoyment of their Polish booty. This alliance had always embraced Prussia, and had lately reincorporated Austria-Hungary, in the *Dreikaiserbund*. Across all this now fell the force of panslavism, a force hard to define, but increasingly expressing purely nationalist feeling, hostility towards Austria-Hungary and readiness to abandon the *entente* with Berlin. Panslavists felt aggrieved and humiliated by the settlement of the Congress of Berlin. Another factor which made Russian foreign policy different in kind from that of the other Great Powers in 1880 was that, like Great Britain (with whom she often came into

10 'The foreign policy of Russia was to a special degree the Tsar's policy', B. H. Sumner, *Russia and the Balkans 1870–1880* (Oxford, 1937), p. 19. The whole first chapter, 'The Russian background', is still valuable for this period.

conflict over them), she had great extra-European interests, both in the Far East and central Asia, where her territories, influence and commerce had been growing steadily for twenty years. In defending these interests, other forces, uncontrollable by the ministry of foreign affairs, such as the soldiers and provincial governors, were often decisive. In 1880 Russia remained what she had often been, the least predictable of the great powers.

The least important of them in 1880 was Italy. Poor, lacking cohesion, she could not pursue a vigorous foreign policy. The cardinal points of her compass card were friendship with Great Britain (partly because of traditional and sentimental reasons and partly because of a long coastline) and watchfulness towards her neighbours, Austria-Hungary and France. The Habsburgs were the traditional enemy and still ruled 'unredeemed' Italians. Nevertheless no Italian government envisaged war or subversion to obtain Trent or Trieste.

It was an important fundamental assumption of international life in 1880 that no great power contemplated the use of revolutionary methods to break up its rivals. All of them, it was presumed, would continue to exist, adjusting their claims against one another from time to time, and extending their influence, sometimes, into areas where, as yet, no equilibrium of forces existed. The most important such area was the Balkans. The eclipse of a great power by another was conceivable. But the total collapse or disappearance of one was never seen as an appropriate goal of foreign policy. One other characteristic of the 1880 system is also remarkable. Although the speculations of a few Italian statesmen about the African shores of the Mediterranean hinted at the patterns of future international rivalry, the powers for the most part displayed in 1880 an almost complete preoccupation with European interests and lack of sensitivity about the rest of the world.

While the interests which ruled the foreign policies of European states might differ, the machinery which put them into effect did not. Since the Congress of Vienna, a general diplomatic system had provided the accepted channels of international relations. The professional diplomatists had the duties of representing their own states, of negotiating for them, of observing, and of keeping their governments informed. They represented sovereign states; no international authority existed which was superior to these states[11] and the governing assumption of their conduct was that their primary aim was the promotion of their own national interests. On the whole the professional diplomatists ran this machinery themselves. The participation of heads of states, and even meetings of foreign ministers, were rare, though their personal susceptibilities might influence policy. Only an occasional great congress or conference – such as that of Berlin in 1878 – brought momentarily into existence something palely anticipating the 'summit' diplomacy of the twentieth century, and even then the major decisions tended to be made before the great men met. Even the freemasonry of European royalty could not displace the professional machine in the transaction of international business.

This was just as well. Not only did professionalism provide an efficient conduct of business, but it may also have tended, by its nature, to some mitigation of the competitiveness of international life. The facts that diplomatists were all drawn from similar levels of society and, by training and by experience, developed a professional sense, helped to strengthen common assumptions, confidence and agreement on common interests. They even spoke a common language – French. Although they were the servants of governments whose interests it was their duty to uphold unreservedly, it was easier in such a setting than it is today to recognize certain common interests. The balance of power was one of these, the Concert of Europe another. In varying forms, at one time strong and another weak, the assertion of these principles was the history of nineteenth-century diplomacy. They were distinct, and might conflict, but at the core of the idea of the Concert lay the idea of community of European nations. The fear of the effects of war had been diminished by the quick struggles of the mid-century decades, but warfare was still known to be expensive and the Paris Commune had revived old fears that war might bring revolution. There were, therefore, powerful tendencies resisting unrestrained international competition at work inside the machinery of the system itself.

Unfortunately, other forces were at work outside which

---

11 This is true in all except one or two marginal instances where governments accepted limitation on their freedom in narrowly-defined fields. The most important before 1914 was the 'Sugar Union' of 1902. See Lyons, pp. 103 ff.

increased the danger of conflict. One of them was the influence of 'public opinion' on policy. In part, this was because of the spread of liberal ideas and institutions since 1815; governments were tending to be less the oppressors of the governed than identified with them, though this process had still far to go in 1880. The appearance of mass electorates, the idea of the 'nation in arms' which underlay military service, and the growth of literacy all made statesmen give more thought to public opinion. Liberals might welcome this; yet the effects, as they varied from state to state, were by no means reassuring. In constitutional states, the need to placate electorates cramped the officials; a British diplomatist's freedom of action was diminished, for example, if a problem involved national self-determination. Even in more authoritarian states public opinion could be a real force. Governments had to live up to the mythical images of themselves which were part of their acceptability. 'The power of Russia is wielded by a single man', said Dilke, but went on, 'or should I say, by two – the Emperor and the Moscow newspaper emperor, Katkoff.'[12] Russian statesmen had increasingly to take account of panslavist agitation, and no French statesman could directly affront the ideal of *revanche*. Questions of prestige, irrational though they might be, received new emphasis when more people identified themselves with the nation. 'Nowadays', said Bismarck in 1884, 'no Government is strong enough to stand the reproach of having sacrificed its own national interests as a favour to a friendly Power.'[13]

Increasingly conscious use would be made of public opinion on international affairs. Gladstone did so in his electioneering, Bismarck in his use of the press. Together with improvements in communication, above all in the use of the telegraph, this meant closer control of professional diplomatists by their governments. International relations were therefore changing in 1880,

12 Dilke, p. 19. For Katkov, see Summer, pp. 78–9.
13 His remark has the more significance because the context in which he made it – a colonial dispute with Great Britain – was one which had no intrinsic interest for him. He was writing to a diplomat (1 June 1884, *GDD*, I, p. 177) who had himself remarked in 1878 that Great Britain was then in danger of going to war 'merely for the establishment of power and of what is involved by "prestige", a word existing only in the French language' (*ibid.*, p. 90). The original Latin verb, *praestigiare*, means 'to deceive by juggling tricks' (Lewis and Short).

but the extent of the change must not be exaggerated. It was Canning, after all, who had been the first virtuoso of diplomacy by public opinion. A more obvious change in diplomatic activity, perhaps, was the increasing assumption by foreign offices of responsibility for commercial and economic business.[14] This hints at changes which were eventually to destroy the balance of power itself (the two most important were industrialization and imperialism), though their bearing on international affairs was not yet discerned in 1880.

BISMARCK'S EUROPE

Between 1880 and 1890 international relations were dominated by the system which Bismarck built on the Berlin settlement of 1878. The equilibrium of this system lived after it; its remnants were only finally blown away in 1914 although it had begun to disintegrate long before. It roots lay far back, in the rise of Prussia to the position of leading power in Germay, but there is no need to go back beyond the Congress of Berlin. It had dealt successfully with yet another of the many crises arising from the slow dissolution of the Ottoman Empire. Like all the others since the beginning of the century that crisis involved two separate problems: the interests of great powers and the claims of Balkan nationalists. The Treaty of Berlin partially settled the first by handing out bits of Turkish territory to the powers mainly concerned; Russia was allowed Bessarabia and some of Asian Turkey, Great Britain obtained a lease of Cyprus,[15] and the Dual Monarchy was allowed to occupy and administer the Turkish provinces of Bosnia and Herzegovina and to garrison the Sanjak of Novi Bazar. To Great Britain and Austria-Hungary it was more important to check the expansion of Russia than to win territory. The attempt in the Treaty to reorganize the Balkans as a stable structure of national states appealed to them for this

14 The British foreign office appointed Commercial Attachés to Paris in 1880 and to St Petersburg in 1887.
15 In return, Turkey was given a British engagement to defend Turkish territory in Asia against future Russian encroachment. The island was finally annexed by Great Britain on Guy Fawkes Day, 1914.

reason. Rumania, Montenegro and Serbia all therefore had their national independence recognized. In addition, Bulgaria, though left formally under the suzerainty of the sultan, became an 'autonomous and tributary principality' with a Christian government and a national militia of its own. Its prince was to be elected by the Bulgarians, confirmed by Turkey with the assent of the powers, and was to belong to none of the great reigning houses of Europe. Further south, eastern Roumelia was left within the Turkish Empire but with a Christian governor and in 'conditions of administrative autonomy'. Except for the Albanians, each of the main nationalities of the Balkans had now, therefore, a territorial core of its own. Finally, the aspirations of the Greeks of Crete were met by a Turkish promise at last to put into force constitutional reforms announced ten years before. This comprehensive settlement was to be buttressed by reforms in those parts of European Turkey not otherwise dealt with. The Turkish government was to uphold religious liberty and equality; the recognition of the governments of Serbia and Bulgaria was made conditional upon their doing the same. Special reforms were promised to the Armenians. Two commissions were set up to regulate the Danube, on which no warships were to be allowed below the Iron Gates. The signatories could congratulate themselves in not forgetting important details in their concern over large aims.

Yet the Berlin settlement was less stable than it looked. It had three defects: it left the Balkan states disgruntled, it annoyed the Ottoman government, and it had, in the long run, a bad effect on the relationship of Germany and Russia.

Most of the Balkan states were irritated about territory. Greece had hoped for a more favourable frontier with Turkey; she got some of what she wanted in 1881. Rumania, too, improved her frontier in the Dobrudja in 1880, but still regretted the loss of Bessarabia and her obligation under the Treaty to grant citizenship to Jews. Serbia had done well out of the Congress, but disliked the Austro-Hungarian occupation of Bosnia and Herzegovina (resistance to which was suppressed by force). Montenegro and Bulgaria were aggrieved to obtain less at Berlin than they had won earlier by fighting. Montenegro had to make do with about three-fifths of her earlier gains but Bulgaria with less still. Macedonia and an outlet to the Aegean were taken from her, and other territory went to Serbia and Rumania. A further grievance was that eastern Roumelia remained under the Turks. Most Balkan states could not afford to disturb the general peace, but Bulgaria was a Russian satellite and might be tempted, therefore, to make trouble, under Russian protection. Moreover, a violent irredentist movement in Eastern Roumelia was ready to struggle for union with Bulgaria. Austria-Hungary and Great Britain opposed this. They thought the division of the two provinces a check on Russian influence. When the question of union was next raised, therefore, the interests of the great powers were again likely to be involved.

The second defect of the Treaty was its humiliation of the Ottoman Empire. Certainly the Turks would have lost more without it, but the Berlin settlement added the sting of interference in their internal affairs. The British, supposedly their friends, not only took Cyprus, but obtained the appointment of Englishmen as military consuls in Asia Minor, to work under an English Inspector-General of Reforms.[16] The guarantees of the safety of the Armenians were humiliating, too. Moreover, the Austro-Hungarian occupation of Bosnia and Herzegovina was in the end blamed on Great Britain. Soon there were to be further strains on the Anglo-Turkish relationship in Egypt. This was ironical. Internal reform, which only Great Britain took very seriously, was probably the only way in which the Ottoman Empire could have been kept on its feet. If it went on crumbling, its instability was bound to endanger the good relations of the great powers.

Finally, the Berlin settlement had damaged Russo-German friendship. The traditional sympathy between Berlin and St Petersburg went back to the partitions of Poland. Strengthened in the revolutionary crises of the nineteenth century, it was central to Bismarck's policy. But its implicit premise, since Prussia's defeat of Austria, had been the avoidance of collision between Habsburg and Romanov interests in the Balkans. At the Congress of Berlin the 'honest broker' avoided a Balkan conflict, but only, Russians thought, at the cost of letting down his friends. As early as 1877, the tsar had begun to complain about a lack of German

---

16 On Salisbury's attempts to promote a 'pacific invasion of Englishmen', see Lady Gwendoline Cecil, *Life of Salisbury* (4 vols., London, 1921–33), vol. II, pp. 304–26. One of these consuls was H. H. Kitchener.

support. Panslavists were soon talking of the Congress as a conspiracy against the Russian people. Russo–German relations did not, of course, change overnight. Too many forces were still in favour of the traditional link. Alexander II's nationalism was outweighed by his successor's fear of revolution. Nevertheless, the first crack in the Bismarckian structure had appeared.

Bismarck's overriding aim was peace; he was a conservative who feared the revolutionary effects of war. When the Congress of Berlin met, the German Empire was barely seven years old. This made an alliance with Vienna seem attractive. It could provide additional security against France and underwrite the *Dreikaiserbund* (the latest form of the Holy Alliance). So, in October 1879 the Dual Alliance was signed.[17] Its terms, secret at the time, have seemed odd: if one of the signatories were to be attacked by Russia, the other was to come to her support. Yet Germany was in no conceivable danger from Russia, unless already at war with France. Nor would Germany, if she were attacked by France alone, obtain more than the benevolent neutrality of Austria-Hungary. This has led to the view that Bismarck's real aim was to stifle Austro-Russian conflict by attaching Austria-Hungary to Germany, so that he could hold her back and prevent the two autocracies from mutual destruction. The overriding aim of peace would thus be achieved. If the alliance is to be understood as a means to that end, it was also an announcement that the *kleindeutsch* solution of the German problem had come to stay; the Habsburgs had no more to fear from Prussia and the corpses of Königgrätz were buried at last.[18]

The tsar was personally reassured by the kaiser but by adding to the shadowy *Dreikaiserbund* a special relationship with Austria-Hungary, Bismarck had begun the slow elaboration of alliances which were to divide Europe more and more down to 1914. 'He had made a deadlock and called it peace'.[19] Moreover, alliances bind both parties; the kaiser properly reminded Bismarck that he had in the past 'always opposed tieing our hands through alliances'.[20] It was the first long-term peace-time alliance for many

17 It was renewed in 1883.
18 For *kleindeutsch* and *grossdeutsch* themes in German unification, see Hearder, p. 213).
19 W. N. Medlicott, *Bismarck, Gladstone and the Concert of Europe* (London, 1956), p. 337.
20 E. Eyck, *Bismarck* (3 vols., Eulenbach, 1941–4), vol. III, p. 329.

years. Nevertheless, although its terms were unknown, Europe welcomed it. Bismarck followed it up by putting out a feeler to Great Britain, but nothing came of it. In 1881 and 1884 he renewed the *Dreikaiserbund* and the Russians were assured of German and Austro-Hungarian help if they needed to coerce Turkey into keeping the Straits open in wartime. The Russians for their part promised to recognize the annexation of Bosnia and Herzegovina by Austria-Hungary when it seemed appropriate and Austria agreed not to oppose the union of Bulgaria and eastern Roumelia, if circumstances brought it about.

In 1882, this elaborate system was extended further. The French gave Bismarck the opportunity for this. With British and German encouragement a French protectorate had been established over Tunis (Treaty of Bardo, 12 May 1881). The Italians, their own African ambitions stimulated by the fact that 20,000 Italian settlers were already in Tunisia, could do nothing. Popular outcry only revealed how powerless the Italian government was against France. It looked round for an ally, and found one in the old hereditary enemy, Austria-Hungary. Bismarck pushed the Dual Monarchy towards Italy – he was momentarily upset by a burst of panslavism which made him worry about a Franco-Russian *rapprochement* – and the result was the Triple Alliance (20 May 1882). Germany and Austria-Hungary promised to help Italy against a French attack, and Italy promised Germany help against the same danger. The advantage was Italy's; unless France was involved, she would not be pulled into a conflict with Russia; she obtained a special declaration that the treaty was not directed against England; finally, the association proved that Italy was a great power. Other buttresses to Bismarck's system were an alliance between Austria-Hungary and Serbia, which virtually made the smaller country a Habsburg satellite during the reign of King Milan, and the accession of Rumania to the Triple Alliance,[21] which guaranteed that country against Russian attack. Bismarck had in fact increased the likelihood of Russo-German conflict by these elaborate commitments. The peace of Europe now rested more heavily than ever upon his ability to control his allies. Yet Europe appeared much more stable because Germany's

21 Rumania and Austria-Hungary became allies on 30 October 1883. Germany acceded the same day, Italy not till 15 May 1888. The alliance was steadily renewed down to 1914.

one likely enemy, France, was more effectively isolated than ever and therefore presented, for the moment, no danger.

There were also reasons why tension between France and Germany might decline in the early eighties. As Tunis showed, French interest was turning overseas and there she was likely to come into conflict with Great Britain. The first place where this happened was Egypt. The French had invested money there, had built the Suez canal and recalled Napoleon's expedition of 1798. The British also had financial interests, were the principal users of the canal, and remembered Napoleon's threat to India. Both countries were entangled with one another willy-nilly because of the lack of sound government in Egypt, which was nominally under the suzerainty of the sultan, ruling through the khedive. This had led to the setting up of a joint system of financial control. But this in turn helped to stimulate an Egyptian nationalism which threatened the security of European residents, their investments, and the canal. The French and British could not agree about what to do and the situation drifted; the one thing which the French were determined not to have was a permanent British occupation.[22]

Yet this was the outcome. In June 1882 riots at Alexandria killed many Europeans. The British hoped that the Turks would restore order and break the nationalist movement; the French were more ready to come to terms with its leaders. The nationalists strengthened their position until the British admiral commanding the naval force at Alexandria decided that he must destroy its fortifications if his ships were to be safe. When his French colleague refused help and sailed away, he bombarded the forts of Alexandria (11 July). More riots followed and more diplomatic pressure on the Turks to assert their authority. The French Chamber of Deputies killed the chance of Anglo-French cooperation by refusing to vote money for a joint expedition. The results were momentous; a British force landed by itself, defeated the nationalists and began an occupation which was to last seventy years. The crumbling of Turkish rule produced no alternative which seemed likely to guarantee the security of the canal and the good management of the Egyptian debt. Nevertheless, the British occupation, once it had begun, obsessed French statesmen and

22 The French government, that is, French holders of Egyptian bonds, would have been happy with the security of a British occupation.

destroyed the chance of Anglo-French cooperation for twenty years.

This suited Bismarck. He could enjoy good relations with a France at odds with Great Britain. Of course, French demands for *revanche* had not ceased. Some deputies had voted against an Anglo-French expedition because they thought that Egypt was a distraction from the proper concern of a French government over the lost provinces; other Frenchmen already envisaged an understanding with Russia. But the 'line to St Petersburg' from Berlin was still open, the tsar detested the French Republic as a nest of revolutionaries and French radicals detested the tsar as the oppressor of the Poles. Tunis had driven Italy into Bismarck's arms. There was, therefore, no reason for him to be worried about France, still isolated in the first half of the decade. Danger to the stability of his Europe appeared, instead, for the first time in the Balkans, where it was impossible to muffle forever the basic clash of interest between Austria-Hungary and Russia. The *Dreikaiserbund* was again renewed in 1884, but panslavism was becoming more strident. The first crises came over Bulgaria. After 1880, Russian behaviour towards her satellite quickly destroyed Bulgarian goodwill. As relations deteriorated, Russia ceased to favour the eventual union of Bulgaria and Roumelia, and forced Prince Alexander of Bulgaria, nominally an autocrat, to accept Russian generals as ministers. In 1883 he decided to shake off his controllers by restoring a more liberal constitution. This made him popular at home, but enraged Alexander III. Russian illwill grew when the Prince wanted to marry a Prussian princess, a granddaughter of the kaiser. In spite of Queen Victoria's sympathy, the match fell through; Bismarck would not permit it because he was not going to risk offending the tsar (see above, p. 69). Angry though the prince was about this, he was still trying to repair the damage which had been done to Russo-Bulgarian relations when Roumelian irredentists took the game out of his hands. Their secret organizations had long planned a revolution; it took place on 18 September 1885, when the Turkish governor-general was expelled, and a telegram sent to Prince Alexander welcomed him to his new realm. Anxious not to offend the tsar further, he hesitated; after three days he gave way, went to Philippopolis and the union of the southern and northern Bulgars was proclaimed.

The Turks cautiously did nothing except invite the powers to maintain the Berlin settlement. The British ordered their consuls to recognize the new régime *de facto*; conflicts with the Russians in Asia had just reawoken a Russophobia which reinforced Salisbury's desire to strengthen Balkan nations against Russian pressure. This may well have saved the new Bulgaria. Russian objections led the *Dreikaiserbund* to ask for a conference of ambassadors at Constantinople to summon the prince to withdraw. Bismarck hoped this would enable him to avoid an Austro-Russian quarrel by showing that the implicit assignment of Bulgaria to a Russian sphere of influence still held good. The Austrians joined in because it seemed to them the best way to avoid a resuscitation of 'big Bulgaria'. But the idea came to nothing because the British would not cooperate.

The next stage of the crisis was precipitated by the Serbians, who declared war on Bulgaria to get compensating advantages (14 November 1885). They were heavily defeated; Bulgarian soldiers were about to enter Belgrade when they were halted by the threat of Austrian intervention. Peace was patched up on the basis of the *status quo* but military victory made it impossible to destroy the new Bulgarian union. In April 1886 the powers recognized the prince as governor-general of eastern Roumelia for five years; this 'personal union' was a face-saving recognition of the new state. The crisis should now have been over except for a brief and unwise Greek sally against Turkey which produced a spasm of concerted action by the powers, pleased to find themselves able to agree in holding Greece back.[23]

A dangerous corner seemed to have been passed. But the Concert of Europe had been undermined. Everyone, it seemed, was doing well out of the erosion of the 1878 settlement except the Russians, for whom that settlement had been a defeat in the first place. The tsar expressed his annoyance by a gesture; he repudiated the free-port status which had been given to Batum by the Treaty of Berlin. But his animosity was above all directed against Prince Alexander. In August he was kidnapped by Russian officers, hurried out of the country and bullied into abdicating. Bulgaria's effective government was from this time in the hands of a Regency under Stambouloff. A newly elected Bulgarian

---

23 A joint note (26 April 1886) from Britain, Austria, Germany and Russia led to a blockade of Greece and the fall of her government. This averted open fighting between Greece and Turkey.

assembly turned out to be very anti-Russian. It enthusiastically supported Stambouloff in opposing a Russian who had been sent to rule them. It became clear that nothing had been gained by removing the prince, especially as another ruler had now to be found.

With each provocation it seemed that the next step would be an outright Russian invasion. This was a grave danger, for anti-Russian counsels were beginning to be heard in Vienna, where the *Dreikaiserbund* was attacked as a sacrifice of Magyar interests. It was obvious that Austria-Hungary would not allow the Russians to invade Bulgaria; a year before she had disliked the possibility of a united and strengthened Bulgaria, even if it were on bad terms with Russia, and the prospect of one under Russia's thumb was even worse. Bismarck was alarmed; he did not want to have to choose between his allies in a Balkan quarrel.[24] He hoped Great Britain would support Austria-Hungary against Russia and that Germany could remain on the fence. The British position was simpler; Russia was to be kept away from the Straits and Austria-Hungary was to ensure this, if possible. The British did not want to act themselves if they could avoid it. The panslav-ists fanned the flames in Russia, and in Bulgaria the search for a new ruler went on throughout the winter.

The outlook remained gloomy well into 1887. Bismarck stayed uncommitted as long as possible. He used a tiff with France as an excuse for military preparations he might need in the east.[25] But the kaiser pleased the tsar by vetoing Prince Alexander's return to the Bulgarian throne. Giers, the Russian foreign minister, was still anxious to keep the line to Berlin open and responded, in spite of the attacks of the panslavists. Even so, the renewal of the *Dreikaiserbund* was impossible. Its successor was another dual arrangement, the Reinsurance Treaty between Russia and Germany (18 June 1887). Germany promised to support a Russian seizure of the Straits and to be neutral unless Russia launched an attack on Austria-Hungary; Russia promised to remain neutral unless Germany attacked France. Meanwhile, the

24 His criticisms cut both ways: 'the idea that we are expected to do Russia's work for her in Vienna and elsewhere, as the avowed agents of her policy, is on a par with that which inspires the Hungarian conception of Germany's relations towards Austria' (10 December 1886, *GDD*, I, p. 279).
25 On the Boulanger episode, see p. 158.

British edged closer to the Triple Alliance and might still be persuaded to take the strain of direct opposition to Russia, if Russia moved. When the Bulgarians chose the Coburg Prince Ferdinand as their ruler (7 July 1887), it was Salisbury who warned the powers not to eject him unless they had an agreed successor ready. The Bulgarian succession problem, indeed, was gradually settling itself under the noses of the mighty opposites, because each day made joint action on Bulgaria less likely. The Austrians would not accept an eviction; the Russians could only remove Ferdinand, if he did not resign, at the cost of a general war. Russia was in the last resort not prepared to fight and the crisis fizzled out; no one paid any attention to the Turkish contention that Ferdinand's title was illegal.

The two years' Bulgarian crisis had complicated results. In the Balkans it meant that for the next few years Bulgaria under Stambouloff would look to Austria-Hungary (and even, a little, to Turkey), for fear of Russia. A Bulgaria which was a client of the Habsburg monarchy was a convincing refutation of the old view that independent Balkan nations would automatically look to Russia. In a longer perspective Austro-Russian rivalry in the Balkans had superseded the old Straits question as a detonator of European explosives. Here was the real importance of Bulgaria's troubles. Furthermore, that rivalry clearly arose from Hungarian fears of any extension of Slav influence in the Balkans. Finally, the crisis killed the already enfeebled *Dreikaiserbund*. The Reinsurance Treaty was not a good enough substitute, and Bismarck knew it.[26]

The Russian panslavist press had long been advocating a Franco-Russian alliance and in November 1887 Bismarck had forbidden the Reichsbank to float a Russian loan. It was also true that the renewed Triple Alliance of the same year was soon buttressed so as to isolate France and Russia still more. The first Mediterranean Agreement (February 1887) promised to Italy the support of Germany in a war with France over Mediterranean questions, while Great Britain exchanged with Italy mutual guarantees of the Mediterranean *status quo* and support. In other words, the British fleet would defend Italy against the French

26 For Bismarck's own scepticism about the future see his son's correspondence, recently edited by W. Bussman, *Staatssekretär Graf Herbert von Bismarck* (Göttingen, 1964).

navy while Italy would support Britain in Egypt. Further agreements in December 1887 and May 1888 extended the guarantee of the *status quo* to the integrity of the Ottoman Empire and Turkish rights over Bulgaria, while Spain agreed not to support France against the Triple Alliance. Both Russia and France were thus made more and more aware of their loneliness. Yet although the hardening of lines seems ominous in retrospect and the thin tie of Reinsurance could hardly have linked Russia and Germany for long, it could be argued that in 1888 Bismarck's system was still successful. It had weathered the storms of the Bulgarian crisis. Germany was still in touch with both Russia and Austria-Hungary; France was still isolated and still embroiled with Great Britain over Egypt. Great Britain had been associated with the stabilizing system by a skilful use of her Mediterranean fears, although Bismarck failed to turn association into alliance in 1889.

The danger for the future lay in the fact that the conflict between Austria-Hungary and Russia in the Balkans was still there. And for how long could France be kept isolated? This became a more and more pressing problem in Bismarck's last years. Earlier French governments had not felt drawn to Russia. In 1885 the two countries had even been on bad enough terms to recall their respective ambassadors. But colonial troubles, Franco-German tension and the Bulgarian crisis began to change this. Common cause against Great Britain was the first step. When an Anglo-Turkish convention over Egypt was concluded in May 1887, the Russians and French cooperated in bullying the sultan into rejecting the draft. A change of atmosphere was noticeable; *'l'empire des Tsars est à la mode'* wrote the Belgian *chargé* from Paris in 1888.[27] When a Russian loan was oversubscribed in Paris in the following December, a bigger change was implied than was recognized at the time.

Yet when Bismarck left office in 1890, Franco-German relations seemed to improve. From a distance this looks paradoxical, because although Bismarck's fall was not in itself decisive in changing the course of German foreign policy, it removed the most important restraint upon it. It opened the way for the transformation of the European system which Germany had dominated since 1871. But other forces were necessary to bring that

27 See G. P. Gooch, *History of Modern Europe, 1878–1919* (London, 1923), p. 164.

system to an end. One of them, spreading across both the decade of Bismarck and that of his successor, was important in bringing about a Franco-Russian alliance. This was the new concern of European states with other parts of the world which is usually called imperialism, a concern which had meant almost nothing to Bismarck.

THE BEGINNING OF IMPERIAL RIVALRY, 1880–90

By 1890 diplomatists were already paying more attention to business which arose outside Europe than they had done ten years before. By the end of the century, people had become used to talking about 'imperialism' as a new factor in international relations. They did not mean by this the centuries-old quarrels of the Atlantic states about the colonies and trade, but something new. Between 1870 and 1900 (and especially after 1885), a sudden and striking change occurred in Europe's political relations with the rest of the world. The British Empire increased its territory by a half and its population by a third in those three decades. In fifteen years after 1884 Germany acquired 1 million square miles of territory and the French $3\frac{1}{2}$ million between 1880 and 1900.[28] Italy did not do so well, but took part in the competition; both Belgium and Portugal added to their possessions. Russian expansion was unique in being conducted overland, but was also very large. Even the United States won colonies in the 1890s, mainly at the expense of Spain, the only European power involved as a loser.

One feature of the new imperialism was that most of these acquisitions were in areas unsuitable for white settlement. Many of them could only be entered with a fair chance of survival because of recent medical discoveries. Most of them lay in tropical Africa, south-east Asia and the Pacific; the old colonial movement to Central and South America was over. This often put large

28 These are rough figures and not all territory 'acquired' had the same status. J. A. Hobson, *Imperialism: a Study* (London, 1902), from which these examples are taken (pp. 18–21) lumps protectorates with true colonies. But this does not distort the scale and rapidity of what was going on.

native populations under European rule. Many ideological tributaries were tapped to provide the justification this seemed to require. A Darwinian belief in the prosperity of the fittest and technical assurance sometimes ran in harness with racialism; there was more moral responsibility in the Anglo-Saxon attitude which Kipling summed up as 'the white man's burden'.[29] The French saw themselves as the bearers and transmitters of European culture. Sometimes economic justifications were put forward: 'undeveloped estates' was a famous phrase of Joseph Chamberlain. Missionary zeal also came into play. Some of these currents had long histories, but their appeal was stronger than ever at the end of the nineteenth century and there were others fed by the most up-to-date *idées reçues*. The impact of imperialism on European culture, indeed, is as important a topic as its impact on the new colonies and has been neglected.[30] In part it appealed because people were ready to be influenced along certain ideological lines, in part because cheaper newspapers and increasing literacy made it easier to awaken a response. Colonial societies and pressure groups suddenly proliferated. Books of travel and adventure sold well because they fed the same new interest in the overseas world which nearly all countries showed. Sometimes the new climate of opinion broke out in jingoist hysteria; but jingoism was not new, it only had new outlets, and the violent phase of the new imperialism was in most countries shortlived. As a mass 'craze' it was only one among many.

In retrospect, for all the widespread and rapid changes which it brought about, and for all the enthusiasm it evoked, imperialism does not seem novel. It was only an episode, even though a unique one, in the expansion of European civilization to the achievement of world supremacy. It was the last and most spectacular of Europe's assaults on the world and in such a perspective, the 'causes' of late nineteenth-century imperialism seem more complicated than they did at the time. Explanations offered for it at the end of the century tended to fall into one of two classes: either they said that imperialism was inevitable at that particular stage of history, or that it succeeded because it offered

29 The phrase occurs in a poem about the American occupation of the Philippines.
30 For a start, see V. G. Kiernan, *The Lords of Human Kind* (London, 1969).

remedies for important problems. (These could be combined.) The determinists were divided in explaining why imperialism was inevitable. Some pointed to racial differences, their views ranging from assertion of the white races' physiological superiority in a Darwinian struggle between species to quasitheological dogmas about the historical mission – and, therefore, eventual triumph – of European civilization. Some used other biological analogies to prove imperialism an inevitable form of increasing competition between growing populations for food and space. Others appealed to economics, saying that competition for trade led inescapably to competition for territory outside Europe. Similar arguments were used by the other school of thought, that of the remedialists, some of whom thought empire was an answer to domestic over-population and the ills of industrialism. It might even avert the threat of civil war. In any case it would almost certainly provide encouragement to trade and manufacture; it could therefore do something about the waves of depression which were so marked a feature of contemporary capitalism.

Most of these theories now seem inadequate. This should be a warning against too ready an acceptance of any one overriding explanation of imperialism for all these theories, in their day, seemed to have something to be said for them. To whatever still seems acceptable in them there must be added other things: the weight of missionary impulse, of the effect on national policy of the simple spur of emulation, of the countless tiny, but sometimes decisive pressures exercised by adventurous individuals, their ambitions and cupidity. There is no simple 'cause' which 'explains' nineteenth-century imperialism. It is better to approach the events of the 1880s simply with the recognition that circumstances then made European expansion easier than ever before. Greater wealth was mobilized more effectively; communications, medicine and arms were all improved; almost everywhere in the imperialist nations big slum-dwelling populations were appearing which were semi-literate and found the feeling of racial superiority enjoyable; finally, the atmosphere in which the European middle and upper classes moved was soaked in a vulgarized and diluted romanticism which made people receptive to the exotic and sensational.

Egypt provides a good example of the complexities of imperialism. The British occupation, once launched, ended for the time being both Dual Control and the nationalist movement.

England's problem was henceforth to find a way of leaving Egypt while at the same time safeguarding her interests there; this meant finding a guarantee of the security of the Suez canal. Until this could be done, bad relations with France and Turkey were likely, and the French could express their annoyance by using the tangled financial agreements which governed the Egyptian debt as a means of encumbering British reform plans. Yet the longer reform was delayed, the likelier was nationalism to be a danger, and so long as it was a danger, the British occupation could not come to an end. Moreover, the situation tempted other powers to dabble. At first Germany tended to support Great Britain and Russia supported France. When Bismarck changed his tack Great Britain was isolated. The Russians used their opportunity to make trouble in central Asia. Two years later the French were still trying to deprive Great Britain of any advantage she might gain from the Egyptian occupation by wrecking British attempts to regularize the position by negotiating with the Turks. But the more insecure British governments felt their interests in the eastern Mediterranean to be, the more firmly they clung to control of the Suez canal.

Egypt would have been a more manageable problem had it not been affected by wider rivalries. That with France was world-wide. 'It is not that I suppose that France has any deliberate intentions of going to war with us', wrote the British Ambassador in Paris to his chief in June 1883, 'but the two nations come into contact in every part of the world. In every part of it questions arise which, in the present state of feeling, excite mutual suspicion and irritation. Who can say, when and where, in this state of things, some local events may not produce a serious quarrel, or some high-handed proceedings of hot-headed officials occasion an actual collision?'[31] At that moment France seemed Great Britain's most likely enemy thanks, not only to Bismarck, but to Ferry's adoption of a forward colonial policy. The British disliked French colonial expansion because it was accompanied by protectionism; nevertheless, they were not disposed to be difficult except in some special areas. But there were enough of these to cause trouble. One was in south-east Asia, where France had won an empire. China was obliged in 1885 to recognize a French protectorate over Tonkin. An administrative union of Cambodia, Annam, Cochin

31 Lord Newton, *Lord Lyons* (London, 1913), vol. II, p. 332.

and Tonkin followed in 1887. The India Office in London was always sensitive to any change in the balance of influence in south-east Asia and when it became known that French diplomacy was making headway in Burma, a settlement of British relations with that kingdom seemed necessary, if a strategical threat was to be avoided. On New Year's Day 1886, therefore, it was annexed to the British Empire. This closed down the south-east Asia question until it revived in the 1890s. Meanwhile, disputes arose in the Pacific. A French occupation of the New Hebrides (1886) led to a mixed commission of French and British officers there which was prolific of trouble for the future. But the most serious troubles were in Africa.

What was called the 'scramble for Africa' began when Leopold of Belgium invited geographers from all over the world to come to Brussels to talk about Africa in 1876. The meeting which followed set up an 'International Association for the Exploration and Civilization of Africa' (the double aim is interesting) under Leopold's presidency; it then dispersed. Soon after this, the results of Stanley's explorations became known; Leopold sent him out again in 1879, and in the next five years Stanley made hundreds of treaties with native chiefs and established many stations in the Congo basin. Meanwhile, a French explorer, de Brazza, had entered the region from the north; he, too, made treaties. This reminded the Portuguese of ancient claims. They were supported by the British with whom they signed a convention in February 1884, by which both banks of the mouth of the Congo and some surrounding territory were recognized to be Portuguese. In return, the Portuguese promised to uphold the free navigation of the Congo and Zambezi. France and Germany at once refused to recognize this agreement. When, almost at the same moment, the United States recognized the territorial sovereignty of Leopold's International Association, it was obvious that the convention could not last.

A conference met at Berlin to consider Africa in November 1884. Not only was this the last time the great powers met in congress to regulate a matter of common interest and, to that extent, the last use of one of the institutions which had maintained the Concert of Europe,[32] but it also created what became the Belgian Congo and began the process by which Central Africa

32 The United States also attended.

was peacefully divided up between the Powers. It delimited the Congo basin and granted virtual sovereignty to the International Association. It also appointed an international commission to maintain freedom of trade on the Congo and its tributaries, to suppress slavery and to look after the natives' welfare. Leopold obtained from the Belgian parliament authorization to accept the position of sovereign over what was now called 'the Independent State of the Congo'. Although the connexion was, in theory, purely personal, the new state soon lost its independent character. Belgian officials ran it and Belgian money was invested in it, especially when the publication of Leopold's will in 1889 revealed that he left the Congo State to his countrymen after his death. The other powers lost interest as soon as their own disputes had been regulated; they had other problems.

Among them was the first quarrel on a colonial issue between Germany and Britain. Normally, relations between the two countries were good, but they were violently disturbed in 1884 and, even given Bismarck's well-known dislike of Gladstone, it is not at first easy to see why. Certainly no simple conflict of imperial ambitions was involved; trouble broke out in the very year in which the Prime Minister said: 'If Germany is to be a colonizing Power, all I say is, God speed her! She becomes our ally and partner in the execution of the great purposes of Providence for the advantage of mankind'.[33] At worst, the British government can be accused only of some failure of appreciation; it did not understand German feelings and it was maladroit in handling them. Opinion in the British colonies was always much more anti-German than in London. On Bismarck's side, weight must be given to his readiness to fall out with a Liberal government, to his contempt for and lack of understanding of Gladstone, to his general distrust of constitutional States, and to suspicion of what he believed to be pro-French tendencies in the English cabinet. But this was no more than contributory. It was more important that public opinion in Germany was beginning to be excited by colonial affairs. Previously Heligoland had counted for more than colonies in Bismarck's view of Anglo-German relations; he could still speak in 1884 of 'our colonial jingoes'.[34] But for the autumn elections, he had to take notice of public

33 See Gooch, p. 108.
34 *GDD*, vol. I, p. 227.

opinion. Germany's inoculation by colonialist propaganda had begun to take by the time Bismarck made his remark about public opinion.[35] This was unfortunate, because Germany and Great Britain came into conflict over three African and two Pacific questions in the mid-eighties.[36] The territories concerned were in South-west Africa, the Cameroons, Zanzibar, New Guinea and Samoa. The African questions were the most troublesome.

South-west Africa is a 700-mile long area between the Orange river in the south (in 1880 the border of Cape Colony) and the Kunone river in the north, on the other side of which lies Angola. Roughly halfway along its coast is Walfisch bay, just north of the tropic of Capricorn, where German missionaries had been established since the sixties. In 1880 Bismarck was told that protection would be given to Germans within the Walfisch bay area, which had been declared under British sovereignty only two years before, but also that the British government specifically disclaimed responsibility for any other part of the coast. In 1882 the German Colonial Society began to show interest in South-west Africa and Bismarck again enquired whether Great Britain claimed sovereignty or would offer protection to German subjects in other spots, such as the little settlement of Angra Pequena, nearly 300 miles south of Walfisch bay. The British response was dilatory, partly because of Granville's temperamental disinclination to take prompt action, and partly because it was felt that the government of Cape Colony should be consulted. While this was being done, a German landed at Angra Pequena and signed a treaty with a local chief under which he claimed ten miles of coast. When he hoisted the German flag (1 May 1883), a German gunboat was sent to back him up. In November Granville at last replied that *any* territorial claim between Angola and Cape Colony was an infringement of British rights. To a German enquiry about the title of these rights no answer was given; the foreign office was still waiting to hear from Cape Colony. When the colonial government finally spoke, it recommended the annexation of all the territory between Walfisch bay and the Orange river; by then Bismarck had lost his temper and had annexed all the coast from Angra Pequena to Orange river (24

35 Above, p. 89. See also A. J. P. Taylor, *Bismarck* (London, 1955), pp. 215–16 for a more elaborate sketch of his domestic preoccupations.
36 As well as over the Anglo-Portuguese convention already mentioned.

April 1884). He talked of a league of neutrals against Great Britain and his bitter denunciations were only slightly checked by British recognition of German sovereignty over Angra Pequena. When the wishes of Cape Colony were known, a new outburst followed. In August Germany annexed the whole coast from the Orange river to Angola, except for Walfisch bay. The British cabinet soon acquiesced; it was dissatisfied and divided over Granville's handling of the matter and, in any case, it wanted German support in Egypt. So Germany got her first colony, Anglo-German relations were badly strained, and the British foreign and colonial offices had been embroiled with one another.

The other African quarrels were less complicated. One blew up when, after a promise of British assistance in his visit to West Africa, a German explorer suddenly in July 1884, declared a German protectorate over Togoland and hoisted the German flag on the Cameroon river. The British consul in the Cameroons promptly declared a British protectorate over the mouths of the Niger, but Germany was subsequently allowed to annex all of the Cameroons for herself. Even in Zanzibar, where British influence had long been paramount and where German interests had long received British support, there was trouble. The suzerainty over the interior of Africa adjacent to his territories claimed by the sultan of Zanzibar attracted the attention of Karl Peters, who went inland and made a claim to 60,000 square miles of what became Tanganyika. The British supported the restriction of the sultan's suzerainty to a ten-mile-deep strip of coast and in 1886 recognized German rights over Uganda and the Kilimanjaro region. Yet Bismarck took every opportunity of quarrelling over the frontier commission and the conduct of the British agents on the spot. It was a revealing case of his purely diplomatic and domestic approach to colonial questions. To him they were moves in an essentially European game; East Africa gave him a chance to show he could be a nuisance to Great Britain, even when Lord Salisbury was Prime Minister, and to win support from German public opinion.

Bismarck treated the New Guinea matter in a similar way. A British New Guinea Company had been chartered in 1881. In 1883, the colony of Queensland annexed the eastern half of the island but was overridden by London. The gap between colonial views and those of the home government was again emphasized when the Australian Intercolonial Conference of 1883 asked for the annexation of the whole of New Guinea. Nothing was done, however, and in the following year, a German New Guinea company was formed and sent out an officially protected expedition. Once again, Gladstone's cabinet was divided and there were delays and fumblings. Once again Bismarck huffed and puffed. In the end, New Guinea was partitioned between Germany and Great Britain, and the colonies again thought London too pro-German. The German annexation of Samoa a little later laid up more trouble for the future.

These disputes encumbered England and weakened her diplomatic standing. Gladstone's ministry had been effusively conciliatory to Germany because German support was needed in Egypt, where Bismarck turned his goodwill on and off as if with a tap. Other diplomatic questions were also involved; when Anglo-Russian relations were bad Bismarck's lack of cordiality hampered Great Britain (see below, p. 113). At Constantinople, too, where British influence had waned since 1880, German support would have been useful. When the Bulgarian crisis suddenly burst, Great Britain was isolated and, to make matters worse, was in the middle of new Irish troubles. All this makes the colonial successes of Bismarck between 1884 and 1886 easy to understand, as it also makes understandable the British wish to resume good relations. By 1889 things were so much better that Bismarck went so far as to offer an alliance to Great Britain.

No alliance was concluded, but Salisbury's government took the chance of making a comprehensive settlement (17 July 1890) with Bismarck's successors. So far as the two countries were concerned, it completed the partition of Africa. Germany recognized a British protectorate over Witu, the Somali coast, and Zanzibar; more important, Uganda and the basin of the Upper Nile were to be a British sphere of influence. The British were awakening to the importance of the Sudan and its hinterland. The Germans were in return to be allowed to expand inland to the region of the Great Lakes, to acquire a corridor to the Zambezi, and were promised support in buying the coastal territory of the sultan of Zanzibar. In Germans' eyes, their greatest acquisition in this negotiation was the North Sea island of Heligoland. The German colonialists strongly disapproved; a German government did not, after all, have to take account of them on questions where their sentimentality could be balanced by that of other Germans.

Down to this moment, the partition of Africa had gone remarkably smoothly. This was a great diplomatic achievement; the American continents had been partitioned only by two centuries of conflict and Turkey-in-Europe had been causing quarrels between European states for almost as long. Central Asia looked as if it, too, might start a war between Russia and Great Britain. Their antagonism had much deeper roots than the British disputes with France or Germany. Russian imperial expansion, except into Alaska and California, had been almost entirely overland and was bound up with the advance of a frontier of settlement similar to that in North America in the nineteenth century. This movement was gradually to spread through Siberia. Another force shaping it was a struggle to subdue the troublesome frontier peoples which had led to the steady extension of Russian political authority towards the south-east. It had brought the Russians into conflict with Turkey in the Caucasus and had begun to press increasingly upon Persia. As Russian communications improved, Afghanistan began to be affected and, 300 or 400 miles away across the Pamirs, even the ill-defined hinterland of China. By 1885 the most important oases of central Asia were in Russian hands. In 1879 the trans-Caspian railway had been started; it was to run along the northern frontier of Persia, which had already shown itself incapable of resisting Russian influence. There was no reason to suppose that Afghanistan would do any better. Although Russian movements towards the Chinese province of Sinkiang alarmed British diplomatists, it was to the north-west that the government of India and the India Office in London began to look with growing alarm in the seventies and eighties.

That alarm was not so unjustifiable as is sometimes said. The appearance of even a small force of invaders, it was felt, might precipitate a new Indian mutiny; whatever might be the reassurances offered by the Russian foreign office in St Petersburg, it was certain that the Russian government was not completely in control of its soldiers and provincial governors in Asia, and some of them might cherish schemes of Indian conquest. They acted with small regard for relations between London and St Petersburg and they had a tempting encouragement to do so in Afghanistan, with which British relations had been unhappy. When Gladstone's government took office in 1880 it was determined to liquidate its commitments and (as Disraeli's government had already decided) to withdraw the British force there. This took time and more fighting but eventually led to the appearance of a friendly amir at Kabul and, apparently, the recovery of British prestige there. Afghan foreign policy, it was agreed, should be controlled by Great Britain in return for protection and a subsidy. This should have secured the Indian frontier by creating a buffer state. But alarm revived in Calcutta, when, in 1884, the Russians occupied the Turcoman centre of Merv, only 200 miles from Herat.

Both the Russians and the British had for years underestimated the obstacles which terrain and distance would put in the way of any invasion of India *via* the Hindu Kush. Herat was still 400 miles from Kabul, the Afghan capital, over a single mountain road. But when frontier disputes finally exploded in a Russian attack on Afghan forces at Pendjeh (30 March 1885), Gladstone's government reacted more rapidly than in any of its other imperial crises. A special credit for preparations for war was voted by parliament, and it did not seem that a clash could be avoided. Jingoism ran high on both sides. But Russia was not prepared to fight. Salisbury's government made a compromise territorial agreement with Russia which was not the end of Anglo-Russian rivalry in central Asia, but closed a phase. There was no other comparable crisis for some time. What was important about Pendjeh was that the first crisis which brought two of the great powers to the verge of war since 1878 was over a non-European question. It was not, moreover, provoked by the new 'imperialism'. It was easier to divide Africa and the South Seas than to stabilize central Asia.

The most obvious common factor in all these quarrels which disturbed international life in the 1880s is that they all involved Great Britain. (The only other real tension outside Europe between two of the European powers was that between France and Italy, and even there what was at stake was as much a matter of Mediterranean strategy as of colonialism.) But Great Britain's attitude was flexible. She sought the cooperation of France in Egypt and did not contest French expansion in Central Africa; nearer India, on the other hand, French influence was opposed. German colonization took Great Britain by surprise but in most cases met with British cooperation; it was the British colonial governments which opposed it, not London. In central Asia, the outlines of the problem had been familiar for longer; British policy was correspondingly tougher. To see matters simply as the resistance of an old colonial power to new rivals is too simple. Indeed, imperial concerns may have simplified and even eased relations between great powers. They provided a safety-valve for emotions in France and Russia which might otherwise have been dangerous. They made it possible for Bismarck to give France a friendly hand over Egypt and to help Russia by ostentatiously not supporting Great Britain during the Pendjeh crisis. Finally, these years showed that the peaceful partition of the new colonial regions was at least possible.

In other ways, too, the imperialist wave was more complicated than is sometimes thought. The role of popular opinion and agitation, for instance, was by no means always simple. French parliamentary and public opinion was only half-interested in Empire and that interest collapsed with defeat in Indo-China; the issue of prestige in Egypt was a different affair. Even when German opinion seemed to be strongly imperialist, it was not always decisive. Bismarck could ignore it, once he had used it for his own purposes. Gladstone's government ignored British jingoism after Majuba. Imperialism was therefore not just a response to mass enthusiasm. Nor were the statesmen at the head of affairs in 1880 usually very sympathetic to imperialist pressure for they had been trained in pre-imperialist ways. Few of them were interested in imperialism as such; they responded to more traditional claims of interest and prestige. Soldiers and colonial officials often complained of neglect and of a lack of vision in their political leaders. Statesmen were not even really very interested, except in France, in mixing up politics and economic expansion. They might talk about the commercial bearings of foreign policy but there was no constant connexion between imperialism and needs of trade. The only government which was perhaps ahead of imperialist feeling at home was the Italian, yearning already for Tripoli and the proof that Italy was a great power like France.

The most acute of the early critics of imperialism, J. A. Hobson, recognized this and produced a more elaborate analysis of its economic roots. The core of his argument was that the taproot of imperialism was to be sought not in trade, because the acquisition of colonies could be shown to bring no considerable commercial benefit, but in investment. In his view, new colonies meant new outlets for capital, offering a higher yield than could be obtained at home. The true explanation of imperialism, there-fore, was to be sought in the special interest of the capitalist; since his interest was not the national interest but a minority one, the capitalist also favoured conservatism and opposed social reform at home. Hobson accompanied this argument with much supporting fire to show how this special interest worked. Since this view allowed that many statesmen were unaware of the operation of the capitalist factor behind their policies, it was not easy to refute. Yet it will not do. There are too many examples of the origin of expansion in wholly non-economic facts. Hobson did not understand even the British example; his description hardly fits the French or German. Russia, indeed, was a capital-importing country. Even from Great Britain, the proportion of overseas investment which went either to the old pre-1880 colonies or to the United States or South America, continued to increase after 1885. Not much capital went to the new possessions, except South Africa.[37] Important as the provision of new outlets for capital may have been in some instances, the explanation in fact seems as unsatisfactory as any other based on one supposed cause. If, in speaking of imperialism, we are trying to account for the acts of governments, then very different influences can be seen at work. In France, the defeat of 1870; in Russia, the setback of 1878; in Germany, Bismarck's views on the crown prince; in Italy, the pressure of population – all these, and many others came into play.

One other comment may be made. Besides affecting the relations of the powers with one another, imperialism also changed their relationship with the rest of the world. The major changes were to come later, with the entry of Japan and the United States into world politics, and on a lesser scale, that of the British self-governing colonies. It was foreshadowed by the beginnings of French and Russian pressure on China. The need for resistance, which was to take the form of commandeering the ideas and techniques of Europe, had already produced a transformation in Japan and the rest of Egyptian nationalism, but little else by the eighties. Nor had Europe's access to new sources of wealth yet begun to affect the international balance of power. All that could be described by 1890 was that the final stage had begun in the evolution of a worldwide system of international compe-

37 See A. K. Cairncross, *Home and Foreign Investment 1870–1913* (Cambridge, 1953), pp. 183–6. If we say that the export of capital is always imperialism and that German investment in Rumania, or French in Russia, should be treated on the same basis as the partition of Africa, then it is impossible to see the acquisition of territory as having anything new in it at all.

tition. What made this evolution fatal to Europe was the break-down of the balance of power in Europe which followed the reshaping of German policy into a struggle for hegemony by all means, including, if necessary, force of arms.

REALIGNMENTS IN THE 1890s

Bismarck kept France isolated, and averted an Austro-Russian collision. His brief unpleasantness towards Britain had not endangered Anglo-German relations in the long term. Above all, in 1890 his line to St Petersburg was still open, even if it was less likely than ten years before that Austro-Russian conflicts could be avoided for ever. These achievements were thrown away in the next decade. France emerged from her isolation, German relations with Great Britain became worse (although British statesmen went on trying to believe that an alliance of the two powers was possible) and nothing was done to keep alive the embers of the Holy Alliance. Only in the Far East did the Russo-German connexion still matter. A settling-down of relations between Russia and the Dual Monarchy into a sort of Balkan *entente* and the rise of disputes outside Europe (notably in China) concealed the crumbling of Bismarck's system and Great Britain appeared to be so isolated that there was little danger in treading on her toes. Nevertheless, by 1901 that system had gone; France and Russia were allies and Great Britain had begun her slow re-orientation away from benevolence to the Triple Alliance and towards practical arrangements about common interests with France and Russia. However it might be disguised, the safeguards against the division of Europe into two camps had gone; the occasion was still required for the division to become explicit. Thus, the crucial facts of international life in the last decade of the century were the making of the Franco-Russian alliance, the avoidance of a clash in the Balkans and the deterioration of Anglo-German relations.

A Franco-Russian alliance was not a new idea. It had been advocated by both the panslavists and French nationalists like Déroulède.[38] The idea remained insignificant so long as Bismarck

38 See p. 157.

nursed Russia and encouraged France to efforts overseas where she would need German goodwill. As late as 1866 France declined Russian offers of help. The Russian overtures, on the other hand, were a sign that already both the tsarist government's distaste for republics and the traditional connexion with Berlin were being weakened. In 1887 the Boulanger episode excited *revanche* feelings in France only to leave a sudden and unpleasant awareness of isolation and weakness. Flourens saw the opportunity for a gesture when a deputation of anti-Russian Bulgarians turned up in Paris; to their surprise they were advised not to thwart Russia's aims. Soon after this came a joint Franco-Russian protest on a convention concluded between England and Turkey about Egypt. Bismarck's use of financial pressure against Russia now turned to the advantage of France; at the end of 1888 the first Russian loan was floated in Paris and the dependence of Russia on the French capital market began.[39] The Russian army began to buy French weapons.

Changes in Germany after the accession of William II also helped France and Russia to come together. The new emperor was, in the first place, disposed to listen to soldiers biased against Russia, but this was less important than the friction with Bismarck which led to the Chancellor's resignation in 1890. German foreign policy was from that time a confusion of influences. One of the most important was to be the instability of William's own character, which greatly reinforced the impatient, histrionic style of German diplomacy at a time when it responded as it had not done under Bismarck to gusts of pressure from special interests. Inside the foreign ministry, too, new influences were felt; in 1886 one of its officials had confided to his diary his belief that the time for a Russo-German alliance was past.[40] Such changes did not necessarily mean friction with Great Britain. William, although he had reacted strongly against his father's views, respected his grandmother, Queen Victoria, and Caprivi, Bismarck's successor, was delighted to be able to make the colonial agreement of 1890. British policy did not discourage the extension of German economic and political interest in the Near East and the British ambassador at Constantinople spoke of his

39 See H. Feis, *Europe the World's Banker 1870–1914* (New Haven, 1930), pp. 212–15.
40 *Holstein*, II, p. 315.

country acquiring 'a powerful ally in her agelong guard against the Russians on the Bosphorus'.[41] The new tendencies first appeared to affect only German relations with Russia, and expressed themselves in the non-renewal of the Reinsurance Treaty.

This did not cause Russia to turn suddenly to France. Russian conservatives, especially Giers, were distressed by the lapsing of the Reinsurance Treaty but still too distrustful of radicalism to welcome an *entente* with France, let alone an alliance. But arms purchases were followed by technical and military exchanges. The French government obligingly arrested some Russian nihilists in 1890, and there were more French loans. The influence on both powers of their dislike for Great Britain was finally decisive. The renewal of the Triple Alliance made Russia and France fear that the good-will of Great Britain towards Germany and Italy could lead to the Alliance being used against their interests. France wanted help against Great Britain over Egypt, Russia over the Straits. Their cooperation began to seem logical even to Giers. In July 1891 the French fleet paid a symbolic visit to Kronstadt and diplomatic notes were then exchanged promising cooperation and 'concerted' measures if one of them were menaced by aggression. The French wanted more: they wanted a guarantee that Russia would go to war if France were attacked by Germany alone, an event which might follow from British and Italian hostility. This assurance was obtained in August 1892 and in return France promised to come to Russia's help if she were attacked by Germany; there was no obligation to assist Russia if she were attacked only by Austria-Hungary. This agreement was decisive. Their quarrels with Great Britain were still preoccupying the new allies, but a corner had been turned. From this time the road led to a Europe organized in two camps: 'the system by which Germany directed the affairs of Europe came to an end'.[42] An important change in German military thinking also occurred. Although the convention's terms were unknown, the German general staff believed that it must defeat France first in any future war. Russia was not necessarily a stronger power, but it was

41 See E. L. Woodward, *Great Britain and the German Navy* (Oxford, 1935), p. 144.
42 A. J. P. Taylor, *The Struggle for Mastery, in Europe, 1848–1919* (Oxford, 1954), p. 339.

believed that her numbers and geography made her less easy to destroy in one quick campaign. This decision made it impossible to avoid a war becoming a two-front one against both France and Russia, even if Germany were only to want to support Austria against Russia.

The formal conclusion of the alliance was still delayed by the Russians' reluctance to recognize the significance of what had been done. A Russian fleet visited Toulon before a diplomatic convention was signed to reinforce the military one at the end of 1893. The kaiser, two years later, was still appealing to the new tsar, Nicholas II, to refrain, in the interests of monarchical solidarity, from supporting the French republic.[43] But a few months later Nicholas became the first European monarch to pay Paris the compliment of a state visit. French money continued to flow to Russia. The Germans need not in fact have been alarmed. The Franco-Russian allies could by 1897 concentrate their attention on their troubles with England, because Russian relations with Austria-Hungary had by then much improved, and the danger of a European war was therefore slight.

The fundamental cause of this improvement was that Russian attention had turned away from the Balkans to the Far East. Other changes also helped. When the Bulgarian crisis spluttered out in 1887, the Russians were left feeling angry and resentful towards both Bulgaria and Austria-Hungary. The Austrians at that time emphasized their patronage of Bulgaria and strove to attach Great Britain to the Triple Alliance. The death of Alexander III removed an obstacle to Russian acceptance of the new régime in Bulgaria; the murder of Stambouloff removed another. Russia soon announced her recognition of Prince Ferdinand and it became known that the prince's son would be baptized into the Orthodox Church, the tsar acting as godfather. The re-establishment of Russian influence in Bulgaria removed the sting of 1887. Another Balkan crisis seemed to be looming up in October 1895, when a series of officially instigated massacres of Armenians took place in Turkey. Public opinion was greatly agitated in England,

43 *The Kaiser's Letters to the Tsar*, p. 24, 25 October 1895 – 'The constant appearance of Princes, Grand-dukes, statesmen, Generals in "full fig" at reviews, burials, dinners, races, with the head of the Republic or in his entourage makes Republicans – as such – believe that they are quite honest excellent people, with whom Princes can consort and feel at home!'

though nowhere else.[44] None the less, there seemed to be a danger that Russia would use the massacres of Christians as a pretext to act against Turkey. The British government, harassed by agitaion of its electorate, strove to show that it was doing something to make the Turks behave, but its real concern was only that the Russians should not act first. Convinced of the impossibility of Ottoman reform, the British sought safety in collective action, hoping to persuade the Concert to intervene. The Austrians were willing to go as far as naval action at Constantinople (which would forestall Russian plans for a land intervention and would mainly have to be carried out by the British fleet), but no further. The Germans would not endanger their growing influence at Constantinople.[45] Agreement on a partition of Turkey was impossible. The Russians, too, were inhibited, because the French would not allow them to act on their own. In the end, the crisis had an admirably clarifying effect on British policy. The massacres had made the defence of Turkey against Russia by British arms morally impossible just when the Admiralty said the Straits could no longer be defended successfully against the combined Franco-Russian fleets. The artery to the east could be better protected by the occupation of Egypt. Virtue was made of necessity and the danger was over.

An agreement between Austria-Hungary and Russia to put Balkan problems 'on ice' was nonetheless desirable. Franz Joseph visited St Petersburg and on 5 May 1897 the two states agreed to cooperate to maintain the *status quo* in the Balkans and the Straits. Furthermore, they agreed that if changes took place in the Balkans, they should include the foundation of an Albanian state. This understanding restrained their satellites. Revolutionaries in Macedonia would continue to find support in Bulgaria, but neither Serbia nor Bulgaria came to the help of Greece when that country fought a brief and unsuccessful war against the Turks in 1897.

44 See Lord Salisbury, C. J. Lowe, *Salisbury and the Mediterranean 1886–1896* (1965), pp. 100–1. 'It is curious that two psychological climates can exist side by side so utterly different as those of England and Continental Europe. I do not believe that from Archangel to Cadiz there is a soul who cares whether the Armenians are exterminated or not. Here the sympathy for them . . . approaches to frenzy in its intensity'.
45 In 1898 William II was to proclaim himself 'friend of 300 million Muslims' in a speech he made in Turkey.

Together with Russian activity in the Far East and French pressure in Africa, this agreement made Great Britain seem peculiarly isolated. From time to time at the end of the century there was talk of a 'continental league' from which Great Britain was to be excluded. New difficulties with Germany reinforced this impression. Their roots did not lie in imperial or naval rivalry; the British Naval Defence Act of 1889, which had begun a new era in British maritime history, was aimed at France and Russia, not Germany.[46] The good relations of 1890 had been only slowly undermined. The first sign had been British protests over German railway building in Asia Minor in 1893. Another step in the process may have been taken when Gladstone's last government withdrew from the Mediterranean Agreements and Salisbury did not renew them; the German response to this was to assume that Great Britain could be blackmailed back into her ties with the Triple Alliance by showing her the value of Germany's support. Another Anglo-French crisis in 1893, over Siam, fed this mistaken assumption and, together with William's temperamental bent, made Germany's bearing disagreeably truculent. A series of snubs and affronts followed. Germany supported France over the Congo Free State treaty in 1894. Shortly afterwards, two German warships were sent to Delagoa Bay as a demonstration against British pressure on Portugal. In 1895 William II paid a visit to Cowes which was disastrous both socially and diplomatically. Not only did the emperor annoy his uncle, the Prince of Wales, but he had a conversation with Salisbury in which a clash of views on the future of the Ottoman Empire was revealed (worse still, Salisbury failed to appear for a second meeting which William believed to have been arranged). When, the crisis over, the Armenian massacres blew up, Great Britain received no help from Germany.

This background helps to explain William's sympathy for President Kruger when Great Britain quarrelled with the Transvaal Republic. On 2 January news of an incursion into the Transvaal by a party of freebooters operating from British territory – the 'Jameson raid' – reached Berlin. On the following day the kaiser sent a telegram to Kruger congratulating him on its suppression; though is not easy to establish precise responsibility for the

46 A. J. Marder, *The Anatomy of British Sea Power* (New York, 1940), esp. pp. 105–209.

sending of the telegram, he wanted to show the British how inconvenient his displeasure could be. But the effects of his gesture had been underestimated; it touched a sensitive nerve. British public opinion was outraged; imperial emotions were roused.[47] Conciliatory gestures afterwards did not wholly mend matters. However much statesmen might in future hope for an understanding with Germany, public opinion in the United Kingdom was alert for further signs of German hostility. Several were soon to appear. In July 1897 Bülow became secretary of state and Von Tirpitz went to the German admiralty; an era of *Weltpolitik*, with implications of hostility to England, now began. The satisfied Germany of Bismarck had been replaced by a new one, dissatisfied and restless that her power seemed unmatched by appropriate influence in world affairs. Almost at the same time, British opinion was beginning to be worked up by newspapers over goods 'Made in Germany' and economic rivalry seemed to be added to diplomatic friction. A visit by William II to Abdul Hamid in 1898 was followed by a Turkish concession to Germany of the right to build a railway to Basra. Events in the Far East further added to the materials for Anglo-German disagreement.

Ever since 1887 Russia had been showing more and more interest in the Far East. The influence of Witte, pressing for commercial and economic advances into Asia, dominated the early 1890s. The Trans-Siberian Railway, begun in 1891, reached Lake Baikal four years later. Inevitably, this brought to a head the question of another decaying empire, the Chinese, already threatened by the French from the South. Witte wanted commercial domination, not military occupation. Manchuria was the richest target and lay on the direct route for a railway to Vladivostok. Pressure on China was bound to alarm the Japanese; they were uncertain of what the real aims of the Russians might be and aware that China was unlikely to be able to resist. Japan therefore went to war with China to secure her special position in Korea before Russia was established strongly enough to threaten it. The war ended with the victorious Japanese imposing peace in 1895 in the treaty of Shimonoseki. It gave Japan the Chinese territories of Formosa (Taiwan), the Liaotung peninsula and the important harbour of Port Arthur. In this oriental San Stefano, an 'inde-

---

47 See E. Pakenham, *Jameson's Raid* (London, 1960), for further information.

pendent' Korea was cast as Japan's big Bulgaria; it ensured Japanese control of the sea communications of Manchuria. France, Russia and Germany at once acted to overthrow this settlement. Witte wanted the Japanese out of Port Arthur and the French wanted to support their ally. The Germans were moved by a variety of forces. Among them were willingness to help Russia where they could do so without compromising their own European interests, William's personal excitement over the 'Yellow Peril',[48] and the admiralty's wish for a coaling-station on Chinese soil for prestige purposes (it was unlikely to have any strategic value). The British stood aside, but Japan had to give back Port Arthur.

The damage to Japanese national pride was considerable. Japanese fears were heightened when a Russo-Chinese Bank was set up, and a Russian-controlled Chinese Eastern Railway began to build a line across Manchuria to Vladivostok. Russia had clearly won the primacy in Manchuria which Witte had sought. There was also a secret Russo-Chinese alliance. More militarist advice was, in fact, also being taken at St Petersburg; the possession of Port Arthur became an object of Russian policy in spite of Witte's opposition. In 1897 the Russian eastern fleet was allowed to winter at Port Arthur. A minor 'scramble' for Chinese ports followed. The Germans began by taking Kiao-chou, formally ceded to them in 1898. Surprised, the Russians leased from the Chinese Port Arthur which, unlike Vladivostok, was not ice-bound in winter. Great Britain joined in by taking Wei-hai-wei and the French Kwangchow. Salisbury was alarmed for Great Britain's traditional commercial pre-eminence and proposed to the Russians a partition into spheres of influence. When this failed British policy began to turn towards cooperation with the United States to maintain an 'open door' for trade into China. It was a poor riposte to her rivals' successes. Elsewhere in Asia, too, traditional points of friction with Russia were beginning again to cause alarm. But other events in the Far East were needed to bring

48 A recurring theme in his letters to Nicholas (e.g. pp. 10, 13, 19). Its most famous embodiment was the much-reproduced engraving made from his sketch: in his words 'it shows the powers of Europe represented by their respective Genii called together by the Arch-Angel Michael – sent from Heaven – to *unite* in resisting the inroad of Buddhism, heathenism and barbarism for the Defence of the Cross'. Letter of 26 September, 1895.

about a decisive change in Britain's position there.

The unfriendliness of France was less alarming than the new developments in the Yellow Sea area. It was brought, none the less, to a new pitch, first by the quarrel over Siam in 1893 and then in Africa, where the crucial zone of conflict was the Upper Nile valley. In 1884 the British government had decided that Egypt could be secured without occupying the Sudan, the area which covered the Upper Nile from the north, and had withdrawn the Egyptian garrisons from the region; successive British governments persisted in this decision for a decade. Then the French detonated a new quarrel. French opinion was annoyed by the Anglo-Congolese treaty and by the British government's assumption in 1894 of administrative responsibility for Uganda. Once the Anglo-Congolese treaty was overthrown, the French started what became a race to establish incontrovertible claims to the Upper Nile. The British decided to re-enter the Sudan. They were prompted not only by fears of a French advance into the Sudan, but by popular clamour over revelations of the cruelties of the régime established by the fanatical Muslim ruler, the Mahdi (he had died in 1885), and by encouragement from Berlin to do something which might help the Italians, who had become entangled in Ethiopia. The French protested; they saw the British move as a mere preliminary to the conquest of the whole Sudan and the adjournment *sine die* of any settlement of the Egyptian question. Marchand, an army officer of exceptional ability and leadership, was given instructions on 24 February 1896 to establish French claims by occupation. Soon, other disputes between the two nations arose in Madagascar and on the lower Niger. Fortunately they were adjusted before the next crisis. After the battle of Omdurman destroyed the dervish forces (2 September 1898), British troops were sent on up the Nile. At Fashoda, they found Marchand's force, with the French flag flying; he had marched right across Africa. In the crisis which followed the British government refused discussion until Marchand had withdrawn; it was obviously prepared to go to war. France, troubled at home by the Dreyfus affair (see p. 161), faced the almost certain loss of her colonies if she fought. Cambon and Delcassé wanted better relations with Great Britain. In the end the French gave way; this greatly inflamed popular Anglophobia in France.

William II, too, was annoyed by the French withdrawal. But Anglo-German relations seemed better after a colonial agreement in 1898, although the Samoa question embittered negotiations. During the Boer War, Germany's diplomatic behaviour was correct, in spite of the popularity of the Boers in Germany. But no such alliance with Germany as Chamberlain still dreamed of was possible. Yet without such an alliance, Great Britain seemed far from 'splendidly' isolated by 1900. At loggerheads with France and Russia, she was soon also condemned by world opinion for the Boer War, a conflict whose roots lay deep in British determination to permit no threat to the security of the Cape area. Nevertheless, her position was in fact stronger than twenty years before. Fashoda and the Boer War both rubbed home a comforting truth, that Great Britain could ignore foreign disapproval wherever sea-power could isolate the decisive theatre in which her interests were involved. Only when she could not do this had she to come to terms. Now unchallenged as a naval power, she could ride out diplomatic hostility. The era when extra-European quarrels might have entailed a war was, because of this, over. The focus of diplomatic attention was once more to be the relations of the powers in Europe.

5

BEFORE 1914:
CONSTITUTIONAL STATES

One way of categorizing European states before 1914 is to separate them according to the way their public affairs were run. On one side can be grouped countries which can be called 'constitutional': the United Kingdom, France, Italy and Spain were the largest, but Portugal, Belgium, the Netherlands, Switzerland, Denmark, Sweden and (after separation from her in 1905) Norway should also be remembered. Two of these countries were republics (France and Switzerland), the rest monarchies, but monarchies whose crowned rulers had limited powers (some, very limited). Most of them had written constitutions, and in them final authority rested for the most part in law-making parliaments made up of elected representatives of wide electorates. Such bodies sometimes existed in other countries, but, for varying reasons, they did not have the power in them which they had in the constitutional states (sometimes they were quite formally excluded from it). This was the major characteristic of the constitutional States. It was also true (and not unconnected with this) that these were states which at least paid lip-service to, and often really respected, the rights of individuals, and freedom of expression and association in a way which was not usual elsewhere in Europe. There were, nonetheless, many differences in practice between them arising from tradition, circumstance, religion and culture.

Two of these states – Great Britain and France – were indisputably great powers; Italy sought to become one and Spain had once held that rank. Italy was a new nation, founded in 1861; the other three were long established though France and Spain had undergone important changes to their state structure in the nineteenth century. The three were very different from one another, very unalike in the levels of opportunity and welfare they could provide (or thought they should provide) for their citizens. Nonetheless, for all the injustices and inequalities which persisted within them, these States were upholders of liberal values and practice, as the great monarchies of eastern Europe could never be. It was a tribute to the constitutional principles they embodied that new nations emerging in south-eastern Europe during the nineteenth century were almost always given the formal apparatus of constitutional government, even when it was unsuited to their needs and beyond their powers to maintain. It was also true, too, that in these major constitutional States there could be detected before 1914 alarming signs of new forces which threatened the maintenance of liberal standards in all of them.

THE UNITED KINGDOM

With no conscription for military service, an established Church and religious freedom existing side by side, a still largely hereditary caste of rulers accepting high taxation and a Press restrained only by the law of libel and blasphemy, England was as distinct from other European countries in 1880 as she had ever been. She had known nothing of the direct impact of the French Revolution, which had transformed European institutions within the lifetime of many men still living, and she had also been almost untouched by later excitements. She was also a rich country, in which industrial capitalism had matured further than in any of her neighbours, and was yet still ruled by landlords.

This *ancien régime* was to be transformed in the next thirty-five years. It had sustained decades of rearguard action against middle-class money by a brilliant combination of timely concession and resistance. The mental habits of a deferential society and the cumulative prestige of continuous peaceful change still left great power in the hands of the aristocracy in 1880. Gladstone's cabinet of that year was full of representatives of the old aristocratic Whig tradition; there sat in it only two radicals, John Bright, an exhausted volcano left over from the age of improvement, and Joseph Chamberlain, in the disregarded office of president of the

Board of Trade. Yet by 1914, although the Whig tradition was still represented in a Liberal cabinet by Winston Churchill, the prime minister, Asquith, was a sometime Congregationalist who had made his own way as a successful barrister, the chancellor of the exchequer was a small-town Welsh solicitor, and a socialist agitator who had left school at ten presided over local government. On the opposition bench, Bonar Law, the Conservative leader, was the son of a Canadian Presbyterian parson, but this was a less striking change, the Conservative party having always been tolerant of those whom Mrs Asquith called 'hired bravos or wandering minstrels'.[1]

Changes in the personnel of politics registered the passing of the old order. Industry and the growth of cities had for decades undermined its social and economic supports while the triumph of democratic principles had thrown down is legal and institutional protection. Even the habit of deference was sapped. Ironically, there was also dying with the older England one of the forces which had done most to weaken it: the orthodox political economy of *laissez-faire* and free trade.

Nevertheless, during this period the outward appearance of institutions remained much what it was in 1880. Their formal centre was the monarchy, an institution much misunderstood by foreigners and sometimes by the occupant of the throne herself. Bagehot had distinguished the incalculable symbolic importance of the Crown from its real constitutional rights to be consulted, to encourage, and to warn,[2] powers of which prime ministers were very conscious. Gladstone had, if anything, an exaggerated respect for the Crown (perhaps it owed something to the fact that after Disraeli's death, Victoria was the only political figure whose experience went back far enough to begin to rival Gladstone's own) but the Queen gave him no credit for it; he promoted measures she disliked and lacked the power over her feelings which the insinuating grace of his predecessor had won. Yet Victoria's increasing cantankerousness and fears of the destructive onrush of democracy were not, in the last resort, significant. She might not like radicals, but they were ministers just the same. Only in 1894

1 Margot Asquith, *Autobiography* (Penguin edn London, 1936), vol. 1, p. 118.
2 W. Bagehot, *The English Constitution* (Oxford, World's Classics edn), p. 69.

was she able to exercise a decisive power by choosing between candidates of the same party for her prime minister. Except at such a juncture, Victoria's power was limited to those important but subsidiary issues on which she could bring to bear the impalpable influences of age, experience and her position at the head of the European clan of royalties, great and small.

The royal veto might be dead, but the House of Commons did not exercise the powers it possesses today. Parliament was still truly bicameral; there was no doubt that the House of Lords had the right to amend or reject Bills sent up from the Lower House, other than financial measures. Clashes between the Lords and Commons seemed unlikely to be severe in 1880, because the peers were still the true leaders of the ruling class. The landed interest and the landowners still provided the bulk of the House of Commons; only just over 100 of its 658 members were engaged in manufacturing or mercantile operations. Many M.P.s were the sons or close relatives of peers and the distribution of the constituencies still favoured rural rather than urban England. But old corruption was gone and a democratic electorate in the towns, voting by secret ballot, had already ended close aristocratic control of the House of Commons, whatever influences might linger.

The queen in parliament was the legal sovereign.[3] No fundamental law, no written constitution, no antique statute could resist the legislature. Legislatively, Great Britain was already as she has remained, one of the most highly centralized states in the world. So long as the cabinet could maintain control of the House of Commons and secure the acquiescence of the Lords, its word could become law. This is why so much British history is parliamentary history. Administration was less coherent; the anthology of institutions which administered the business of the Empire could be justified historically, but not logically. Their centre was the Treasury, jealously watching the other departments and thus informally embodying in the constitution a powerful bias against departmental initiative – if it cost money. Most new business of state for which the historic departments had no obvious responsibility tended to go to the Home Office or to a new cutting from the venerable tree of the Privy Council. This incoherent structure

3 A. V. Dicey, *The Law of the Constitution* (9th edn, London, 1939), pp. 39–40.

was increasingly staffed by a·non-political civil service of high quality selected by competitive examination. The increasing elaboration of its grades and its growth in size is as good an index as any of the increasing scope of government down to 1914.[4] Yet civil servants exercised very little direct authority over British subjects. Local government was elective in the towns; in the countryside the quarterly sessions of the county bench of justices of the peace ruled England as they had ruled it since the Tudors.

There was a remarkable implicit agreement between Englishmen who operated this constitution and little demand for fundamental constitutional change. Republicanism had petered out after a few sparks in the seventies; socialism was unimportant. Most Englishmen paid constitutional monarchy the compliment of recommending it whole-heartedly for export to other states. To them it meant first and foremost the rule of law and settled, regular, procedures for legislative change. It also meant a loyal acceptance of constitutional conventions and for most Englishmen an acceptance of the trend, a half-century old, which combined the assertion of individual liberties with the application of Benthamite principles. This had proved a powerful enemy of privilege. Yet although Englishmen accepted the Hobbesian sovereign under which they lived, they distrusted centralization and administrative authority with a passion which has now disappeared.[5] Above all, they disliked political violence; there were still to be deaths in riots and demonstrations after 1880, but the English people had already achieved an orderly freedom in their public life which may be considered their chief contribution to civilized living. Distrust of armed forces went with this; it was emphasized that the soldier was only a citizen armed in a particular manner. In this instance, as in all others, the ultimate safeguard of Englishmen's liberties lay in parliament. The English solution to the problem of liberty in modern times has usually been to ensure that government was in hands acceptable to the majority, rather than to limit its powers. If civilians controlled the army, then the army would not be a danger. The application of

4 See p. 73, for an estimate. Another, on a different basis, is given in K. B. Smellie, *A Hundred Years of English Government* (2nd edn, London, 1950).

5 An interesting example of this is the English antipathy to French 'centralization'. See, for example, the continuous attempts to reassure the English reader in J. E. C. Bodley, *France* (1898).

the principle was theoretically incomplete, because the House of Lords could thwart a majority in the House of Commons; but the principle of democratic government, that of majority rule, was already recognized, however doubtful some people might be of its consequences.

English politics had to deal with a growing, ever more tightly packed population, whose rate of natural increase was not to fall much until after 1918.[6] But fewer children were being born and middle-class families, at least, were getting smaller; the population was growing older, although the vast majority of its members were still of working age. Fear of overpopulation in part accounts for the enthusiasm for emigration in the eighties and nineties. England was visibly crowded; her towns showed it. In 1880 the great shift to suburban areas had not yet taken place and the larger cities were tightly packed warrens of noise and dirt. Englishmen were thicker on the ground than Scots or Irishmen, roughly a third of them living in seven great conurbations,[7] often in miserable poverty; in 1886 it was calculated that about a third of the people lived in a state 'incompatible with physical health and industrial efficiency'.[8]

There were dangers in this. Life in the slums of a great nineteenth-century industrial city was brutal, violent and criminal. Drunkenness was the great symptom and one aggravation of these evils.[9] It was the dangers of a brutalized population that made people strive to improve England's schools. In 1880 attendance at primary school was made compulsory, but it was only in 1899 that the Board of Education was thought important enough to be separated from the Privy Council. It has been calculated that in 1896 only four or five children in every thousand reached a

6 A continuance of the late nineteenth-century rate would have created a population of about 100 million today.
7 London, Birmingham, Liverpool, Leeds, Bradford, Manchester, Newcastle-on-Tyne.
8 See Smellie, p. 95.
9 The annual consumption of beer dropped by nearly half from 27.5 standard gallons per head in 1913–14 to 14.6 in 1939–40 and the beer got weaker. Spirit consumption fell by two-thirds. See A. M. Carr-Saunders, *World Population, Past Growth and Present Trends* (London, 1936), pp. 250–1 (where the author also remarks that 'the figures for a century ago are not very different from those relating to 1913–14'). This registers one of the most important changes in English behaviour in this century, and one since reversed.

grammar school.[10] With such feeble attempts to civilize them it is surprising that the town population remained as docile as they did. They were not much restrained by religion, for England's slums were to all intents and purposes pagan. Although nineteenth-century England was religious to a degree now hardly imaginable, it was the middle and lower-middle classes who made it so. The Salvation Army might reach the industrial worker for a moment, but the nonconformist conscience was a middle-class phenomenon. It was not religion which restrained the working-class. The simplest explanation of its docility may be that the safety-valve of trade union activity and the vote reconciled the workers' leaders, and that although progress might be slow, standards of living had steadily risen.

The political parties were still much more parliamentary than national, although they had begun to set up national organizations. Their leaders were still mainly drawn from the traditional ruling class. Both Liberals and Conservatives were broadly committed to the maintenance of free trade and *laissez-faire*, but there were differences between them. To Lord Beaconsfield, who led them in 1880 but was to survive only a year, the Conservatives owed much. He had associated his party with the monarchy and the Empire so that ever since it has enjoyed the incalculable advantage of a patriotic haze which softens its image in the eyes of many voters. Though the Conservatives lost the general election of 1880 in spite of this, the fact that after Beaconsfield they could accept social reform was central to their subsequent survival as a national party; by positive action they managed to avoid the dangerous doctrines of some European conservatives. But the danger of their empiricism was that they sometimes appeared to have no ideas at all. The Liberals of 1880, on the other hand, made great play with principle. Gladstone's resolute presentation of his struggles as moral rather than political appealed both to the traditional reforming radical and to the nonconformist; the practical politicians knew that he was a vote-catcher. His retirement from the Liberal leadership had been shown to be difficult; he dominated the coalition which was the Liberal party as no one else could. Apart from him, its basic elements were old Whigs and middle-class radicals. Gladstone's own politics in 1880 were dominated by Ireland, which provided the third important group

10 i.e. secondary education, in effect.

in the House of Commons, sixty-nine M.P.s who wanted Home Rule. There was also the so-called 'Fourth Party' of four members, the most brilliant of whom was the young Lord Randolph Churchill; they embarrassed their own conservative leaders almost as much as the government. They had plenty of opportunity, for Gladstone's ministry (1880–85) was dogged with troubles.

Economic depression was one of the most intractable, not only because of nineteenth-century ideas about the ineffectiveness of conscious attempts to affect the operation of economic laws but also because no one was really sure what was happening. By 1886 a Royal Commission felt able to assert that trade and industry *were* depressed, but economists, of course, could still disagree. Foreign competition was blamed and a 'fair trade' agitation began for industrial protection. But by 1887 the advance to still greater prosperity seemed to have been resumed by industry, although no one could solve the troubles of agriculture; a Royal Commission of 1882, like Beaconsfield, still blamed the weather and, when the effects of foreign competition were at last recognized, protection was inconceivable. Yet the depression only gave a *coup de grâce* to a declining supremacy. The integration of agriculture with the capitalist economy had begun before 1880 and the traditional squire had already had to adopt the methods of the business-man. Changes in land law allowing land to be treated as a commodity like any other and exposing it to the operation of the laws of the market brought an end to many of the non-economic conventions which rural society had respected. Landlords and tenants were opposed in a new way; and the labourer was opposed to them both. The tenant wanted security and low rent and the labourer wanted high wages. The erosion of the overpraised but sometimes real community of interest in the countryside had begun long before 1880.[11]

With the traditional rural order was to go the old landowning ruling class. The Ground Game Act of 1880 (which gave English tenants rights obtained by French peasants in 1789) is a good symbol of the change. A big extension of the rural suffrage in

11 The best access to English rural life in the late nineteenth century is the magnificent book by M. K. Ashby, *Joseph Ashby of Tysoe 1859–1919* (Cambridge, 1961), a biography which contains much more than one man's life-story.

1884 was followed in 1888 by the most dramatic change of all, when the justices of the peace lost to elected County Councils the administrative functions given them by the Tudors. In 1804 parish councils were made elective, and democracy's triumph seemed complete. The landlord was no longer the dominant figure of English politics. Both political parties had accepted the change; the Act of 1888 was passed by a Conservative government. In society, it was registered by the growing acceptance of rentier wealth; plutocracy was beginning to displace aristocracy. But the best evidence of the end of the old order was that although agriculture might have Royal Commissions and a Board of Agriculture set up to look after it, no one dared to reintroduce protection. The main interests to which politicians would have to listen in the future were capital and labour; the old 'landed interest' had ceased to command.[12]

The politicians responded. The electorate of 1880 was well over 2 million; after 1884 over $4\frac{1}{2}$ million, organized in roughly equal constituencies mostly with one member each. Large-scale permanent organization had become necessary in the constituencies even before 1880, and Joseph Chamberlain's Birmingham 'Caucus' had shown the way (though many observers thought it the wrong one). It seemed to mean the domination of parliamentary life by electoral considerations and the displacement of statesmanship by what Lord Salisbury called 'wire-pulling'. It is true that electoral programmes, the strengthening of central party organization, and the gradual submission of the individual M.P. to the whips, were all to follow. Yet this change to democratic mass politics inside the parties did not overthrow the authority of the leaders. Lord Randolph Churchill urged the Conservatives to 'trust the people' and sought power through the party organization, but was checked by Salisbury; meanwhile Chamberlain had broken with the Liberals and sacrificed an almost certain succession to Gladstone as their leader. This rupture was immeasurably important; it was the worst consequence of Gladstone's preoccupation – some said obsession – with Ireland.

To some Irishmen, Ireland was as oppressed as Poland, and

12 See, for the origins and effects of many of these changes, F. M. L. Thompson, *English Landed Society in the Nineteenth Century* (1963). For the immediate impact of the County Councils, see J. P. D. Dunbabin in *HJ*, 1965, pp. 353 ff.

they were not to be argued out of this view by appeals to any merely factual difference between the Royal Irish Constabulary and the cossacks of the tsar. A long tradition of racial and religious bitterness led them to grasp eagerly at the ideas of Mazzini and the financial and moral help offered to them by Irishmen in the United States. Ireland also had economic trouble. She did not have enough good land to satisfy her peasants and what land she had was in the wrong hands. Its owners – sometimes English and often absentee – applied to Ireland the unacceptable principles of English landholding. Worse still, they wanted to exploit their lands economically just when the agricultural depression was cutting at the slender profit which the Irish tenant needed to pay his rent. It did not need a political genius to entangle these two questions, since the landlord was so often racially and religiously an alien, but, as it happened, the Irish M.P.s were led by one. With the single-mindedness of the fanatic, Parnell was willing to sabotage English parliamentary life if he could get Home Rule for Ireland by doing so. And he knew that in the Land League (of which he was president) he had the machinery for co-ordinating disorder in Ireland with struggles in the House.

Two parliamentary battles over Ireland each culminated in a Bill to give Ireland a measure of self-government. When Gladstone took office in 1880 the Irish countryside was already gravely disturbed. Evictions for failure to pay rent had been followed by rick-burning, cattle-maiming and intimidation. Gladstone accompanied a Land Act (1881) to meet the peasants' needs with firm measures of coercion to restore order, imprisoning Parnell and banning the League. An attempt to resume a policy of clemency by releasing Parnell was wrecked at the outset by the murder of the Irish secretary in 1882 by a band of terrorists. Their action horrified Parnell; he at once condemned the assassins, but an English government could not drop coercion after this. In fact, coercion was successful and Ireland was quiet again when the 1884 Act gave the Irish peasant the vote on the same terms as the English country-dweller. This guaranteed Parnell a solid Home Rule party in the next Parliament. Before a general election could take place, Gladstone was defeated; the Irish M.P.s voted against him because he wanted to renew the Crimes Act for Ireland, and his followers were at loggerheads with one another. A minority Conservative government under Lord Salisbury took office in

June 1885. Coercion was not resumed and, from both the Irish viceroy and Churchill, Parnell gained the impression that Salisbury was willing to give Ireland some kind of autonomy. With no equivalent hope held out to him by Gladstone, Parnell decided to trust the Conservatives and instructed the Irish in England to vote for Conservative candidates in the general election of 1885. The Irish M.P.s returned were solidly committed to Home Rule. There were eighty-six of them. But the Liberal majority over the Conservatives was also exactly eighty-six.

This meant that Parnell was able to prevent effective Liberal government, but could not impose Home Rule on either party. The uncertainties of the situation were dissipated when it was learned that Gladstone had in fact decided that Ireland must have Home Rule. Any hope of Conservative support for the idea at once vanished. Parnell helped turn out Salisbury's government and Gladstone took office for the third time in February 1886. But he had not overcome the divisions inside his party. Indeed, they had deepened. The most important deterioration had been in his own relations with Chamberlain. Chamberlain was the acknowledged leader of the radicals in the party and already felt slighted by Gladstone's coolness to his schemes for political and social reform; now he said that he had been deceived by his leader over Ireland and left the cabinet. Some important Whigs had already left, so that from this time the Liberal party was also badly underrepresented in the House of Lords. Gladstone went on to present his first Home Rule Bill. Not surprisingly, it failed to pass the House of Commons. A general election quickly followed, returning nearly 400 Conservative and 'Liberal Unionist' members, and Lord Salisbury again took office in July.

The significance of this schism in the Liberal party was not at once seen. In fact, it meant the end of the Liberal coalition which had ruled England almost continuously since 1859. The Whigs had begun to leave Gladstone in the early eighties, over his Irish land policy.[13] Chamberlain had taken the radicals from the party's other wing. This helped the party to grow more and more out of touch with radical opinion and working-class demands. Radicalism had lost its leader; Gladstone, fascinated by Ireland, was, as he was to show in 1892, only interested in radicalism as

13 They later swallowed much more radical land legislation from Conservative governments.

window-dressing to catch the voters for a Home Rule majority. The working class would therefore look elsewhere for leaders, and soon the foundation of the Scottish Labour Party (1888) and the Independent Labour Party (1893) showed the result. In the more class-conscious nineties the nature of English politics was to begin to be changed by a new political movement wholly based on class. The Conservative party was also to change. The desertion of the Whigs left the Liberals with hardly a foot-hold in the fashionable world; the Conservative party was from this time the party of the 'classes' (though it did not forget jingoism and social concessions for the working man). Gladstone, always a great traditionalist, was grieved by the change and alarmed for the House of Lords; 'the Tories have no hope, no faith, . . . and only class-interest remains', he told a young lady, sadly.[14] The truth of this was clearer than ever in the second phase of the Irish question.

The Conservative government confronted a new wave of distress in Ireland. Parnell did his best to use this; it was met by a combination of severity and remedial legislation by A. J. Balfour, the new Irish Secretary. The prescription seemed to work, especially when Parnell's appearance as the co-respondent in a divorce suit turned him into a liability to his cause. Many Irishmen thought his leadership was too expensive if it cost the support of English nonconformity – which meant, in large measure, that of the Liberal party. The Irish parliamentary party split; Parnell died soon afterwards (October 1891). Shortly before, Chamberlain had dashed the last hope of Liberal reunion and the party divisions were clear for the next round of the Home Rule struggle. It came when the general election of 1892 returned a Home Rule majority, though one which depended on the Irish members. The Liberals were fewer than the Conservatives and Liberal Unionists together, but had a majority of forty with Irish support. The second Home Rule Bill was introduced by Gladstone, prime minister for the fourth time, and passed the House of Commons only to be overwhelmingly rejected by the House of Lords in September 1893. Gladstone wished to resign on this issue, but did not; when he left office for the last time six months

14 Margot Asquith, *Autobiography*, vol. I, p. 130. See also the memorandum sent by Gladstone to the Queen (*Letters of Queen Victoria, Third Series*, vol. II, p. 172), which she found 'very curious'.

later, his party was again in the doldrums and so was the Irish question. The Conservatives again formed a government and took up the policy of killing Home Rule by kindness.

The defeat of the second Home Rule Bill closed one great question temporarily, but brought forward another, that of the House of Lords. The landlords had already shown their ability to use the Upper House to defeat plans for Irish reform if they were put forward by Liberal governments; now the peers were increasingly acting in a generally anti-Liberal sense. Since the Liberals had lost most of their support in the Upper House, the Lords seemed to show a new consciousness of the dangers presented to the traditional ordering of society by a mass electorate. Home Rule was only one of many Liberal measures they had rejected. Some Liberals – including Gladstone – believed that a general elections could be fought successfully on the improper use of its powers by the House of Lords. Salisbury, too, had misgivings, but thought that so long as he was in the Lords, nothing serious would happen. He was right; Gladstone was wrong in thinking that the issue had come to a head in 1893. The conflict of peers and people was put off by the weakness of the Liberal party and by the passage through a grumbling House of Lords by Conservative governments of some of the social legislation which the period demanded.

This legislation was then often called 'collectivist', a term applied not only to 'welfare' legislation, but to government interventions of all kinds. State action seemed alarming but there were powerful forces behind the 'collectivist' trend and respectable precedents.[15] Politicians were more and more convinced that there were votes in it; the formidable structure built by Chamberlain on the bedrock of his Birmingham 'municipal socialism' seemed to prove the point. Men as different as Cardinal Manning and General Booth believed that in social improvement lay a hope of stopping socialism, a powerful consideration for a generation so close to the Paris Commune. And there was also a perfectly clear and continuing tradition of radical protest against injustice. In the

15 As John Morley wrote in 1881, 'in the country where Socialism has been less talked about than any other country in Europe, its principles have been most extensively applied'. *Life of Richard Cobden* (1908 edn), vol. 1, p. 326. 'Collectivist' became a popular term after A. V. Dicey extended its meaning (see *Law and Public Opinion in England*, p. 64).

eighties, Chamberlain had been its outstanding spokesman. 'It is not our duty, it is not our wish, to pull down and abase the rich', he had said, 'although I do not think that the excessive aggregation of wealth in a few hands is any advantage to anybody. But our object is to elevate the poor, to raise the general conditions of the people. . . . I am in favour of accompanying the protection which we afford to property, with a large and stringent interpretation of the obligations of property.'[16] Chamberlain's language was sometimes more violent, and he could make society shiver by his references to ransoms to be paid by property and to the obligations of 'those that toil not, neither do they spin', yet he voiced a tradition not inconsistent with Tory paternalism. There was really nothing surprising about Salisbury's acceptance of the fact that 'We have got, as far as we can, to make this country more pleasant to live in for the vast majority of those who live in it.'[17] Conservatives who remembered Oastler, Shaftesbury and Disraeli could often swallow social legislation more easily than many Liberals, who looked back on a half-century of struggle by the business classes to cast off the power of landed aristocracy. When Herbert Spencer attacked reforming Liberals in 1884, he condemned their plans as 'the new Toryism'.[18]

A mass of legislation was enacted in the last two decades of the century. Local authorities were empowered to provide housing, baths and libraries. The central government regulated conditions of work, interfering further with hours of employment and introducing schemes of accident insurance and arbitration services for use in industrial disputes. Old age pensions did not reach the statute book, but were being considered in the late nineties. Education long remained a Cinderella, but Balfour's great Act of 1902 provided England belatedly with an ordered scheme for elementary and secondary schools administered by local authorities.

Increasing wealth provided the money for this, though Gladstone had already discerned troubles ahead if international competition also increased the cost of armaments. The naval estimates led a Conservative chancellor in 1889 to introduce death duties. A Liberal chancellor increased them in 1894. This inno-

16 5 August, 1885. See *AR*, pp. 139–40.
17 See H. Ausubel, *The Late Victorians* (New York, 1955), p. 84. See also H. Cecil, *Conservatism* (London, 1912).
18 The title of an article later reprinted in *The Man versus the State*, 1885.

vation pointed a way to the redistribution of wealth by taxation which was to be the announced policy of some twentieth-century governments. Yet by later standards, government expenditure on social services was still tiny. In the last two decades of the century, the wage-earner probably benefited more from rising real wages and shortening hours of work. Bigger trade unions extended the bargaining power of the man in work.[19] Working-class life was improving. But as it did so, distinctions between classes grew in some ways sharper. Middle-class families tended to be smaller, with, therefore, substantially higher incomes *per capita*. There were obvious differences of physique between the well-to-do and the wage-earning class. Education was gradually making such differences less tolerable. Above all, at the bottom of the heap, as great social investigations of the 1890s showed, poverty meant appalling destitution.[20] Even those in work could be dreadfully ill-used, as the House of Lords Select Committee on Sweating revealed in 1890. Local government, brave though its efforts might be, could do little more than remedy some of the obvious symptoms of such ills. And no one seemed to be able to do anything about the blight of unemployment.

It is not really surprising, therefore, that these years were spotted by disturbance and violence. The Riot Act was read in Trafalgar Square and the Life Guards called out on 'Bloody Sunday', 13 November 1887. Two people died later of their injuries.[21] Five years later, soldiers opened fire in Yorkshire to protect property and there were two more deaths.[22] The 'new unionism' of the unskilled workers erupted in stoppages, the greatest of which, the Dockers' Strike of 1889, brought the strikers much sympathy and, more important, victory: a standard wage of sixpence an hour. Socialist societies were also trying to organize the workers. But the old 'Lib-Lab' alliance was still alive and working, though the constituency organizations of the Liberal party were more and more dominated by middle-class men

19 The biggest Union in 1881 was the Durham Miners' Association, with 35,000 members. In 1891, the Amalgamated Engineers had 72,000.
20 Two outstanding examples are Charles Booth, *Life and Labour of the People in London* (3rd edn, 17 vols, London, 1902–3), and B. S. Rowntree *Poverty: a study of Town Life* (London, 1901).
21 The actual occasion of the riot was a demonstration about Ireland, but it followed weeks of agitation by the unemployed.
22 The Featherstone riots (7 September 1893).

unwilling to select working-class candidates for parliament and, on the other side, the older generation of labour leaders was passing. In 1899 the Trades Union Congress (T.U.C.) agreed to call a special conference on Labour political representation and in the following year the Labour Representation Committee (L.R.C.) was founded to put up Labour candidates for parliament.

This was alarming but, as some statesmen could see, almost unavoidable, given the extension of the franchise and the Liberal collapse. Some employers tried to resist by using lock-outs and the law against trade unions. Their successes in court only hardened opinion against them and the government. A truly radical response to industrial unrest by the Conservatives was in fact impossible given the gradual transformation of the English ruling class from one based on land to one based on industrial wealth; the one man who might have provided it was effectively muzzled by his preoccupation after 1895 with the Empire. Chamberlain's gift to the Conservatives of electoral victory in the 'Khaki Election' of 1900 only made it less likely that he could draw them away from a defence of property which sapped Tory paternalism for the next twenty years.

The death of Queen Victoria altered no fundamental trend, yet brought an important change in atmosphere. A great weight was lifted at court and some of the new levity of 'society' touched the nation as a whole. Edwardian England seems, in retrospect, a nervous, febrile organism, swept by gusts of sentiment and anger, unstable and insecure. Some of this insecurity stemmed from a growing awareness, driven home by the Boer War, of England's international isolation. The war had sprung from a determination to allow no threat to England's strategical supremacy in South Africa. It began in October 1899 with a series of humiliating defeats. No doubt these contributed to the excitement and bellicosity shown by the British public, but there was more than this to the howls of Mafeking night. Besides providing an opportunity for the exploitation of the new mass readership (educated by compulsory primary education) by newspapermen, the war's strident patriotism released other tensions.

The imperialism of the late nineties was in some ways a psychological compensation. It was in part a response to real and imagined economic threats; so were the 'made in Germany' uproar and Tariff Reform agitation. Political leaders did not share the crudest delusions of their followers, but both Rosebery and

Balfour were alive to a new conception of 'national efficiency'; Disraeli and Gladstone had not bothered with such things. But most Englishmen were harassed, though they might not know why, when real wages ceased to rise; moreover, down to 1914 between 3 and 8 per cent of the working population was usually unemployed. Great Britain still dominated the world market, and her capital exports every year equalled her current receipts and dividends from overseas investment but the benefits were no longer so obvious as they had been. The changing ideas which went with growing uncertainty are harder to identify. England was growing less Christian decade by decade and the replacement of aristocracy by plutocracy gave a flaunting quality to wealth which robbed it of much of its power to dazzle the masses.

Some of these tendencies helped to undermine the Conservative electoral victory of 1900. But some of the old certainties helped, too. Balfour's Education Act, for example, revived the old fears of a bigoted nonconformity that public money would be used to buttress the Established Church. Meanwhile, the war came to an end. The Boers sued for peace in March 1902 after 10,000 men on both sides had been killed in action and 16,000 British had died of disease. The army benefited from investigations of what had gone wrong in South Africa (though it had to wait for the arrival of Haldane at the War Office in 1905 to get both a General Staff and the reforms that made the British Expeditionary Force of 1914 the finest army ever sent abroad from this country) but the Conservatives got no credit for this. The humanitarians forgot the magnanimity of the Peace of Vereeniging (31 May) and recalled only the 'methods of barbarism' which ended the Boer guerrilla campaign, mild though they now may seem.

But it was the disruption of Conservative unity which destroyed the government. Chamberlain, disappointed in earlier attempts to promote the confederation of the self-governing colonies in a more united Empire, came to the conclusion that 'Reciprocal preference' over tariffs would help. This made it very difficult for Balfour to keep his cabinet together. The Liberals, pleasantly surprised to find their own divisions resolved by their defensive reflex over the Free Trade dogma, enjoyed the Unionist split as the foundation of a Tariff Reform League was matched by Unionist Free Food League. Balfour pressed on as best he could until he resigned in December 1905.

The election which followed was an overwhelming triumph for the Liberal party. They had been helped not only by the emotional reaction from the Boer War and the Unionists' agonizing over tariff reform, but by an alliance with the new Labour political movement. 'We are keenly in sympathy with the representatives of Labour', said Campbell-Bannerman in January; 'we have too few of them in the House of Commons.'[23] In September a 'pact' was arranged to provide for more – and more Liberals, too – by ensuring straight fights where a Labour or Liberal candidate had a good chance. There were difficulties, but the arrangement was successful. For the first time since 1885, the Liberals had a majority in the House of Commons without counting Welsh or Scottish seats. The 377 Liberal M.P.s were a majority, moreover, over all other parties combined, and depended neither on Labour nor on Irish M.P.s. The L.R.C. won twenty-nine seats and there were twenty-four other 'Labour' members of one sort or another; the L.R.C. decided to call itself the Labour party. Radicalism seemed firmly in the saddle at last. Young Liberals like Lloyd George and Winston Churchill interpreted the victory as a demand for social reform. It has rightly been called 'a landmark in our social history'.[24] Hardships taken for granted were now to be questioned, as a literate working class began to be able to envisage a different social order: 1906 voiced their new demands.

Conservatives took comfort from the thought that the House of Lords was still a barrier to revolutionary change. From this conviction came constitutional crisis. The House of Lords selectively purged the Bills sent up to it by the new House of Commons. Careful not to attack measures clearly in the interests of the working class, the peers nevertheless made a mockery of the Liberals' majority. They finally blundered by using their veto where its use was not sanctioned by constitutional convention, in rejecting a financial measure, the Budget of 1909. Their motive appears to have been that the measure went beyond normal financial provision; the vested interests behind the Conservative party

23 2 January 1903. See H. Pelling and F. Bealey, *Labour and Politics 1900–06* (London, 1958)
24 E. H. Phelps Brown, *The Growth of British Industrial Relations* (London, 1959), p. xxxviii; a book of much wider interest than its title suggests.

were to be protected from Lloyd George's attack.[25] It seemed, too, that the Lords might have popular support in rejecting 'beer and baccy' taxes which were disliked by the working man. In the background was the desire to anticipate the Irish danger by showing the Lords' power was unblunted.

Unfortunately, the chosen ground could hardly have been worse. Such class selfishness could easily be represented as unconstitutional. The Budget question was quickly overtaken by that of the House of Lords. The Parliament Bill proposed by Asquith's government[26] provided that the Lords could not hold up a Bill from the Commons for more than two years, that the Lords should neither amend nor reject a money Bill, and that the life of parliament should be reduced to five years. A general election (which was virtually a referendum on the issue) took place in January 1910 and another in December. They had the result of equalizing the Liberal and Conservative members in the Commons, but the Irish and Labour M.P.s provided a substantial majority for the reform. With much violence of language, personal and social bitterness, and amid forebodings of disaster, the Parliament Bill passed the Lords, a majority of whom failed to appear, aware that to vote against it would mean the creation of enough new peers to swamp them, but too angry to associate the aristocracy with the cause of reform. Such bitterness and exaggerated fears require explanation. Some weight can be given to Lloyd George's speeches on the budget, which deliberately whipped up class feeling against the Lords; some peers were only paying the Liberals back in the chancellor's own coin. But greater principles were involved. On one side was the firm conviction that it was too late to admit any qualification to the principle that the United Kingdom was governed by an elected majority of her members of parliament; on the other was a belief that this principle was only a specious covering for revolution – for that was what Home Rule would be, in the eyes of many Unionists.[27] The

25 We should perhaps also recall that the weight of taxation imposed by the wish to finance social services and to build battleships was unprecedented; 'almost revolutionary' is one description (Woodward, *Great Britain and the German Navy*, p. 13).
26 Asquith in 1908 succeeded Campbell-Bannerman, who died soon afterwards.
27 See, e.g. L. S. Amery, *My Political Life* (3 vols, London, 1953), vol. 1, p. 376.

two convictions were irreconcilable; either the Liberals had to accept that their governments would be tied down in their legislative work as no Conservative government would be, or the Conservatives had to accept what they saw as the subversion of the constitution under cover of the parliamentary process. Some Conservatives were not prepared to accept defeat in 1911 and were prepared to risk civil war to resist Home Rule.

With the Parliament Act out of the way, the government could turn again to founding the modern welfare state. The budgets of 1908 and 1909 had been big steps towards providing the financial means; old age pensions were introduced and in 1911 the greatest Act among the social reforms of this ministry instituted national insurance for all weekly workers against ill-health and for those in some trades against unemployment. Labour exchanges had been set up and other measures, such as the Shops Act, improved conditions of work. The government also redeemed its promises to trade unions by removing legal handicaps on their activity. That the civil estimates doubled between 1905 and 1914 (the fighting services' estimates rose by less than a third at the same time) is a telling indicator of the direction of Liberal government. But Labour pressure grew, and after 1910 the Liberals needed the Irish and Labour vote if they were to stay in power. One concession made to the new party was that M.P.s should be paid £400 a year. Yet this could not stop a wave of strikes prompted by a new militancy owing something to the example of continental syndicalism, something to disappointment with the achievements of Labour M.P.s and something to a drop in real wages for two or three years after 1909. It mainly affected unskilled labour, but also all workers in mining and railways. The industrial unrest which followed had several distinctive features. Unlike that before 1900, it was the unrest of employed, not unemployed men. It was marked by local leadership acting sometimes in defiance of national trade unions. It was also violent: two men were killed in riots at Liverpool in 1911, and two at Llanelly. The strikers achieved little, but they hampered a government entangled in international affairs and over Ireland.

One more difficulty facing the government was that of the advocates of female suffrage, the 'suffragettes'. England had just seen a series of rapid changes in the social and economic role of women. More offices and shops employed them, higher education had produced its first generations of women graduates, and middle-class girls were beginning to use their independent means to obtain the freedom Ibsen and Shaw taught them to covet. Many of them supported the 'suffragettes', whose more extreme antics endangered life and property and presented a hard problem to the government (see p. 250). Like industrial strife, suffragette violence was a significant symptom; like the syndicalists, the suffragettes rejected legality in favour of disorder and political blackmail. They rejected parliament once it seemed not to favour their cause, and to that extent shared the widespread anti-parliamentarianism which was a political expression of the rejection of liberal civilization before 1914.

The gravest challenge to parliament, none the less, came from Ireland. The Irish situation had been transformed since the mid-1890s. Until its financial basis began to break down, in about 1909, the policy of land purchase and sponsored improvements seemed to have solved Ireland's economic difficulties. But new problems were appearing. The Irish town-labourer, the slum-dweller of Dublin, was now turning to unionism and strikes. He might be exploited by the extreme nationalists just when the 1910 general election had reopened the Home Rule question by forcing the Liberal government to depend on the Irish vote in the Commons. Yet Home Rule itself had changed. Parnell once confessed he had never thought of Ulster, whose inhabitants, exploited by Conservative politicians from Randolph Churchill onwards, were now fiercely resisting any grant of Home Rule which would place them under a Dublin government. Yet Redmond, who led the Irish M.P.s, could not, because of the extremists in Ireland, accept anything else than a united, self-governing Ireland from the Liberals.

One result of the Parliament Act crisis had been that Bonar Law replaced Balfour as the leader of the Unionist party. Law decided to destroy Home Rule by threatening revolution in Ulster. The Ulster leader, Carson, prepared, in his own words, 'the morning Home Rule passes, to become responsible for the government of the Protestant Province of Ulster'.[28] In January 1912 a volunteer force was formed in Ulster and was soon drilling with real and dummy rifles; it was soon matched by a similar nationalist force in the south. The third Home Rule Bill was introduced to the House of Commons on 11 April 1912. If Asquith had accepted

28 R. C. K. Ensor, *England 1870–1914* (Oxford, 1936), p. 453.

clearly the fact that he did not intend to coerce Ulster – which meant subduing the volunteers by force of arms – then he could firmly have insisted that the best terms he could offer would be Ireland without Ulster. He was not forthright, and both sides were encouraged to play for higher stakes. Bonar Law's violence was inexcusable; it was not usual for the leader of the Opposition to encourage subjects of the Crown to armed rebellion. Redmond's attitude is more forgivable; he was driven by the extremists of Sinn Fein and the Irish Republican Brotherhood who might capture the movement for independence if he compromised. Gradually, Home Rule had turned into the Ulster question. For two years, the Bill steadily went ahead through the machinery of the Parliament Act and provoked increasingly wild opposition; it was said that the King should dismiss his ministers and appeals were made to the Lords to refuse to pass the Annual Army Act and thus dissolve the forces of the Crown. The Liberal government was, indeed, unsure of some of its officers; the director of military operations was dishonourable enough to communicate its military plans to the Unionists, and many regimental officers were unwilling to take part in operations against the Ulster volunteers. In March 1914 a cavalry brigade commander said that his officers would rather leave the army than carry out orders to coerce Ulster. The government seemed unable to depend on its soldiers. When it failed to stop gun-running to the Ulster volunteers, it gave its weakness the appearance of partiality, by attempting to stop the southern volunteers from getting rifles in the same way. On 26 July troops returning from this duty opened fire on a crowd and killed some civilians; the government's reputation in Ireland was in ruins. It was only rescued from its embarrassments by the outbreak of the Great War.

FRANCE

In 1880 France was the only republic among the great powers. This sometimes alarmed the autocrats of eastern Europe, where the Republic was thought of as revolution incarnate. This was not just because of dim memories of 1789, 1848, or the bloody fighting of the Commune of 1871. The Republic also seemed fragile.

Yet the impression of fragility was misleading. By 1880 the Third Republic had already outlived its two predecessors; it was to last until 1940 and then only to succumb to military defeat. And, far from being revolutionary, it proved very resistant to social and political change. Many of its institutions were older than those of other Great Powers. The public executions of the *ancien régime* continued into the twentieth century in Paris, the *Loi le Chapelier* of 1791 still regulated labour in 1880 and the Napoleonic *livret* which recorded a workman's employment did not disappear until 1890. The Concordat of 1801 still determined the boundary between Church and State and was, like the administrative armature of France, a legacy of the first Napoleon. The turbulence of political life obscured such conservative influences, to say nothing of others rooted in economics and culture. France changed less than England or Germany between 1880 and 1914.

Such changes as occurred stood out clearly. Few Frenchmen emigrated, the population was ageing and France's share of the total European population steadily fell.[29] Alarm led to study; researches showed that, as in England, natality fell more quickly among the better-off than among the poorer families. This tempted some thinkers to equate national decadence with wealth. It is clear that the lot of Frenchmen was improving; life expectancy rose steadily and was still in 1914 higher than in Germany. This was not because of rapid urbanization. More than half the French in 1914 lived in communes whose chief centre contained fewer than 2,000 inhabitants. The number of very small (under two-and-a-half acres) holdings of land seems actually to have increased after 1880 and millions of Frenchmen were landowners; large-scale farming was less common than in England. The drift from the land might worry Frenchmen but it was not very fast, although the 1880s began in France, as they did everywhere, with an agricultural slump[30] whose effects lasted until the 1890s.

In spite of this, and in spite of the ending of a commercial boom when the *Union Générale* bank collapsed in 1881, French economic life in the twenty-five years before the Great War showed expan-

---

29 See p. 27.
30 An additional blow in the wine-growing districts after the recent ravages of phylloxera. Wine-making was the section of the agricultural economy hardest hit by foreign competition, too. Importation began about 1880, and the lean years lasted well into the twentieth century.

sion and growing prosperity. In retrospect, it was *la belle époque*. The number of new joint stock companies formed each year doubled in the 1890s. It has been suggested that an 'industrial revolution' at last began then.[31] Heavy industry was less important than in Germany or Belgium, but grew fast enough for the iron industry of the nineteenth century to be replaced by steel mills turning out 4 million tons a year in 1914. By then, France was also the biggest European exporter of iron ore. Communications were improved, although some of the investment in railways proved to be uneconomical. The Panhard car (the first of the basic modern design, with a vertical engine in front), showed that French inventiveness and technology could still make important contributions to engineering.

Even if some industries – such as hydroelectric power – appeared to lag, the overall advance was more rapid than ever before. Some expansion can be attributed to reserve colonial markets. Some of it was undoubtedly due to protection. The *Société des Agriculteurs de France* began the agitation for tariffs; duties on agricultural imports steadily rose as prices fell. Food exports stagnated, but the farmers were saved. In 1892 came the heavy Méline tariff, one of the stiffest in the world, imposing, for example, a duty of roughly a third on British goods. Meanwhile, the growth of France's investment abroad showed the essential prosperity of its economy.

Such progress implied the growth of an industrial proletariat, but one smaller than those of Germany or Britain. (This partly explains the slow growth of trade unions.) Distributive and service occupations absorbed a lot of labour, and a numerous bourgeoisie drew from its investments a larger share of the national income in 1913 than the corresponding class in Germany. With the mass of peasant proprietors, it provided a solid conservative core to French society. Beside it, the old *noblesse* was economically and politically insignificant, though, as Proust's pages show, snobbishness flourished under the Third Republic. But a deeper distinction between Frenchmen than rank, and politically a more important one than occupation or income, was that of belief. For some people, atheism was the touchstone of Republicanism; others felt that Catholicism and acceptable society were

31 J. H. Clapham, *The Economic Development of France and Germany 1815–1914* (Cambridge, 1921). p. 240.

coterminous. Protestants and Jews had their own distinctions and were both, at times, accused of enjoying influence disproportionate to their numbers.

These social forces were deployed inside political arrangements which were 'republican' in rejecting the hereditary principle in favour of an elected head of state, but the formally irresponsible president and a Second Chamber which could thwart an elected Chamber of Deputies suggest, rather, constitutional monarchy. Unlike earlier French republics, too, the Third had no unified written constitution and no declaration of rights. Her institutions were created by a body of laws passed piece-meal between 1871 and 1879,[32] and amended over the next sixty years. Some of these laws could only be changed by a special legislative procedure and in that sense were raised a little above the swirl of everyday politics.

The President, elected by the two Chambers, was the choice of the politicians, not the people. He could not be a member of any family which had ever sat on the French throne, had no veto on legislation, nominally possessed the power of appointment to all offices, exercised the prerogative of pardon and could dissolve the lower Chamber on the advice of the upper or prorogue Parliament for a month. The upper Chamber, the Senate, heavily over-represented the small communes and justified Gambetta's description of it as the 'Grand Council of the Communes of France'.[33] It was a conservative counter-weight to democratic extremism. But its powers were limited and uncertain. Ministers did not regard themselves as responsible to the Senate, but to the Chamber of Deputies, elected in 1880 by direct universal adult male suffrage in single-member constituencies. Deputies were very powerful. The lack of firm party discipline forced governments to woo them with patronage and the support of the deputy was vital to persons anxious to influence the administration.

That administration was highly centralized. Each of the eighty-six Departments was directed by a prefect, the representative and agent of central government. He exercised great powers. (Paris alone stood outside this structure, governed both by the prefect of the Seine and the prefect of police.)[34] The local representative

---

32 See Duguit, Monnier and Bonnard, *Les constitutions et les principales lois politiques de la France depuis 1789* (7th edn, Paris, 1952).
33 There were also, until 1884, some life senators.
34 Lyons had also had a special regime which, however, lapsed in 1881.

bodies had strictly limited attributes and little power. Furthermore, the coming and going of ministers left the civil servants with little control from above. At law, they were shielded by an administrative jurisprudence which protected the official in the execution of his duties. English and American observers[35] were often struck by the arbitrariness of the Third Republic and by its interference with the individual. In their eyes, Frenchmen lacked liberty. No association of more than twenty persons could be formed, except for purely commercial or professional purposes, without the permission of the minister of the interior or the prefect. Trade unions were still not legal in 1880. No liberty of assembly or procession existed. Government could hold prisoners without trial and had even more stringent powers in a state of siege. In many ways, the citizen was no more free than he had been under the Second Empire. Yet there was a press which, by English standards, was irresponsibly licentious, being unhindered by the English law of libel. Nor were such restraints as existed felt to be irksome by the mass of Frenchmen. Political life was less a matter of doing what one wanted than of preventing your opponents from doing what they wanted and the political machine was meant to do this while the civil servants went on running the country. People might feel scepticism about the parliamentary system but, noted a shrewd observer, 'no one has a substitute to propose',[36] and so the Republic went on.

The political forces which struggled inside this framework look very confusing. The governments of the Third Republic suceeded one another with startling rapidity. Yet changes did not always mean significant differences of policy or principle. No strong parties existed to provide clear alternatives to the existing government; instead, alliances were formed by arrangements between groups of deputies for particular purposes, which did not usually go far beyond turning out the incumbents of the day. Nevertheless, two tendencies, moods or, as they have been called, *tempéraments politiques*,[37] can be distinguished in France, dividing the country more fundamentally than the evanescent slogans of the professional politicians. On the one hand stood those

35 e.g. Dicey and Lowell.
36 Bodley, p. 38.
37 F. Goguel, *La polique des partie sous la IIIe république* (Paris, 1946), pp. 25–31.

Frenchmen who distrusted the use which might be made of politics by democracy: this was the side of Order. On the other stood those Frenchmen who wished to press further the implications of the Republican régime, the side of Movement.

Just before 1880 these tendencies had corresponded more exactly than was usual to the divisions among the cliques of politicians. The politicians of the left had combined to defend the republican form of government, which they believed to be threatened. But this unity soon began to crack. Many republican labels were invented in the next few years but, broadly speaking, only two mattered, the Opportunists and the radicals. The Opportunists grouped in 1880 about Gambetta, whose leadership they had tended to follow in the seventies, stood for the stabilization of the Republic on the basis of the 1880 institutions, making only such fresh concessions to 'movement' as were absolutely necessary. One consequence was a peaceful foreign policy. 'Think of it always, speak of it never', was Gambetta's advice about *revanche*; some people thought this just a device for quietly abandoning the lost provinces. The radicals violently opposed such opportunism. They still sought to carry out the whole programme of the republican opposition of the Second Empire, with some added features intended to 'republicanize the republic', notably by abolishing the Senate and the Presidency, which they thought monarchical survivals, and by obtaining freedom of public meeting. Unlike the Opportunists, they were wholeheartedly committed to *revanche* and the return of Alsace and Lorraine. But both factions had common ground in anticlericalism. Much history lay buried in it. The alliance of Church and royalism went back to 1791 and memories of the Vendée; catholics remembered that when the archbishop of Paris was shot as a hostage by the Communards in 1871, he was wearing the pectoral cross of a predecessor killed in 1848. The Second Empire's official catholicism had confirmed the hatred of many republicans for the Church, and the hierarchy had repaid the hatred.

The religious issue was one demonstration that the fundamental divisions of the Third Republic went back to the lack of a general will, which sprang from the Great Revolution. The myths and language of 1789 were still alive. When in 1892 the Municipality of Paris celebrated the centenary of the overthrow of royalism and put up a statue of Danton, everybody knew it was really crowing over the September Massacres. (The legitimists replied a year later by turning masses for the soul of Louis XVI into political demonstrations.) Such attachment to symbols helps to explain the ludicrous intolerance of upholders of *libre pensée* who imposed their views with such success that the tradition grew up that the President of the Republic might not pronounce the name of God in any public utterance.

Royalism was alienated from the national community and legitimists and *Orléanistes*[38] lived in a state of political schism. At the other extreme of the political spectrum was another alienated group, the Paris working class, distrustful of the bourgeoisie ever since the June Days of 1848, and bitterly so since the Commune.[39] Their old leaders in the *enragé* tradition were going; Blanqui died in 1881. Socialism was slow in taking root; in the seventies it had been a penal offence to belong to the International. Given the rural preponderance in French society, the class struggle was as much a sentimental appeal to French history as a Marxist confrontation of proletariat and capitalists. But the extreme left began slowly to organize itself outside the framework of republican assumptions. The *Parti Ouvrier Français* which appeared in 1879 was specifically non-parliamentary. Its first split occurred in 1882 and others were to follow: French socialism was not to produce a solid, broadly based parliamentary party like the German. In 1900, though there were thirty-odd deputies calling themselves 'socialists', the movement to which they belonged was a chaos of quarrelling fragments.

The lack of broad political consensus was one cause of governmental weakness in the Third Republic. It increased the bargaining power of deputies because the easiest way for a government to resist extremists was by promising not to do things disliked by people near the centre who would support it. Consequently, little was done. This is why the detailed parliamentary history of the Third Republic is not worth much atten-

---

38 Orleanists supported the claims of the cadet branch of the Bourbon family to the French throne and aspired to a parliamentary and constitutional monarchy. But the distinction had little more than social significance after 1880.

39 Language and mythology are linked in French politics as in no other country. Consequently it is worth noting, in passing, two semantic confusions which the events of 1871 made possible: those between *capitaliste* and *capitulard*, and between *communiste* and *communard*.

tion in a book of European history. It was only in a negative sense decisive in shaping French life.

In 1880 the republicans could feel complacent, in spite of the economic slump. For the first time under the Republic the *quatorze juillet* was an official holiday. A year earlier, they had at last taken possession of the Republic by installing a Republican majority in the Senate and the first Republican President, Jules Grévy. He was known to favour the renunciation of Alsace and to dislike and distrust Gambetta, whom, except for one short ministry, he kept from being prime minister. Gambetta, too, was already suspect to the radicals. Anticlericalism seemed to be all that was left of the 'Belleville programme',[40] although he managed to obtain an amnesty for the Communards still in exile. The elections of 1881, however, showed that the radicals were determined to go their own way. Their electoral programme included social reform, the reintroduction of divorce, the separation of Church and State, and an income tax. Few republicans were willing to go so far, and a split inside the republican bloc which was to dominate the next twenty years was thus established. The moderate coalition won the elections, though Gambetta was himself defeated in Paris. His government lasted until the beginning of 1882 and he died soon after its fall.

The field was open to the Opportunists whom Grévy favoured. They could get on with the purging of the administrative apparatus. The most successful of them was Jules Ferry, prime minister in 1880–81 and again from 1883 to 1885. While minister of education he had carried in the Chamber a law which excluded members of certain religious orders from teaching in schools. The Senate emasculated it, but the Opportunists proceeded to dissolve the Society of Jesus and attack teaching by other Orders. In 1882, primary education was made compulsory and secularized; it had been made free in the previous year. In 1884 divorce was reintroduced. The climax came in 1886 with a law laicizing all schoolteaching. But no attack was made on the Concordat itself. Ferry, like many others, claimed to be anticlerical, not antireligious, and to seek only the prevention of improper clerical interference with civil society.

40 The programme put to the electors of Belleville, a working-class quarter of Paris, in 1869, had become the touchstone of radical republicanism.

His other great field of activity was outside Europe. In seeking territory and influence overseas, Ferry was deliberately, and with Bismarck's support, swinging French policy away from *revanche*. Colonial enterprise not only lessened the danger of European conflict but promised to supply France with markets. Other motives also had a part in French Imperialism; in Madagascar it was religion; the theory of 'assimilation', of cultural integration, also had an idealistic element in it. Apart from the Tunis protectorate, the greatest single achievement of French imperialism in the early eighties was in south-east Asia, where France occupied Annam in 1884, although this was followed by war with China and the defeat at Langson (1885). Unfortunately, by this time Ferry was losing control of the Chamber. French opinion was never really gripped by the colonial idea. Anticlericalism had gone so far that many Frenchmen were ready to vote for right-wing candidates again. Economic conditions were still bad. Meanwhile, the left remained dissatisfied. In spite of freedom of press and assembly being extended as a result of their efforts, the radicals wanted more constitutional reform; the Senate had been modified in 1882 and 1884, but the rural communes were still over-represented in it. In 1885 the radicals managed to amend the electoral system of the Chamber by instituting *scrutin de liste*. They also wanted an end to the Concordat and to colonial adventures. Obviously Anglo-French hostility and the diversion of Frenchmen from *revanche* suited Bismarck, but many Frenchmen were not to be diverted. In 1882 a nationalist journalist, Paul Déroulède, had founded a 'League of Patriots'; he was famous for a book of patriotic verse, the *Chants du Soldat*, which was so great a success that Ferry even had it distributed to schools. Déroulède's followers stood behind the parliamentary opposition to Ferry. Clemenceau, the only deputy who had voted against the Tunis annexation, led it to the attack.

Ferry's fall in 1885 was part of general swing of feeling against the opportunists. In the teeth of administrative pressure, France voted against them. The candidates of 'order', most of whom stood in lists labelled *union conservatrice*, won 201 seats. The traditional dynastic right (unified since the death of Chambord in 1883) had many of its representatives elected. When it became clear how the elections were going, the republicans hastily buried their disagreements. To meet the threat, a republication coalition of moderates and radicals was formed under De Freycinet. The minister of war in this government was a soldier, General Boulanger. For the next three years he dominated the politics of the Republic and came near to overthrowing it. He was the man of the left, put into office as the representative of the radicals, to guarantee the 'republicanizing' of the army. This alarmed Conservatives, who became even more agitated when Boulanger openly sympathized with the workers in a strike his troops had been called in to control. Their alarm grew again when Déroulède's league publicized him as the general of *revanche* and Bismarck denounced him in the *Reichstag*. At the Bastille Day review in 1886, Boulanger was cheered far more than the president of the Republic.

The prolonged crisis which followed began over the German arrest of a French customs official, Schnaebelé, for spying. Boulanger did all he could to fan the flames and demanded that an ultimatum should be sent to Germany. Grévy refused and the moderates, alarmed by this adventurous approach to foreign policy, overthrew the ministry. As no government without the General could obtain radical support, the moderates turned to cooperation with the Right and Rouvier formed a government based on the exclusion of Boulanger and the abandonment of anti-clericalism. Boulanger had now to look outside Parliament for support; he could not expect office while the coalition of moderates and the Right held together. The second phase of the crisis was therefore dominated by his anti-parliamentary campaign. He was presented as the symbol of a pure patriotism which rose above the sordid struggles of the politicians. His popularity was great; when the government posted him to duty in the provinces in order to remove him from Paris, a huge demonstration took place at the railway station (8 July). It shocked the radicals into their senses. They suddenly realized that their *protégé* might have Napoleonic ambitions. But they could not destroy his popularity, which rose to even greater heights when a scandal brought him back into the public eye. The president's son-in-law, Wilson, had been trafficking in honours and favours under his father-in-law's protection. Grévy was forced to resign by a strike of deputies which left him without a government. Carnot was elected president as the compromise candidate of the radicals and moderates. More than ever, Boulanger seemed to represent republican purity and patriotism in contrast to the politicians who had closed ranks against him. He was so obviously a vote-winner that some of the legitimists, disappointed at their failure to obtain relaxation of anticlerical laws, and dissatisfied with their exclusion from patronage, now began to think of him as a man who might stage-manage the restoration of the monarchy. Boulanger may not have been sincere with them (or the Bonapartists) but used their money in a spectacular series of by-elections in 1888. He stood as the candidate of the discontented; all kinds of opposition to the régime could be found behind him, even socialist. The system of *scrutin de liste* gave him the opportunity of holding what was in effect a continuous plebiscite in one department after another because the whole Department voted to fill one vacant seat. His programme was the vague – and therefore attractive – slogan '*Dissolution, Constituante, Revision*'. His dismissal from the army only made him a martyr. A series of electoral victories came to a climax in January 1889, when, after a sensational win in the Nord, a major industrial Department, he swept the boards in a by-election at Paris. Had he wished, Boulanger could have led a wildly enthusiastic mob to the Chamber of the Elysée and over-thrown the Republic. His nerve failed him; he was not Bonaparte after all. His chance was now gone; the government had been frightened enough to act decisively against him at last.

The legislature hastily abolished *scrutin de liste* and prohibited multiple candidacies, to stop Boulanger from standing in every constituency in a general election. The Senate was given powers to act as a special court for the trial of crimes against the state. The minister of the interior set about the collection of evidence for the prosecution of the Boulangist leaders. Boulanger fled to Belgium to avoid arrest, and the heterogeneous alliance of his followers was soon falling apart in mutual recrimination. It failed completely in the 1889 elections and Boulangism was dead. Frenchmen were more interested in the great exhibition held in Paris that year to mark the centenary of the Revolution.

But it had been a close thing. Because of this, in the long run the crisis strengthened the Republic. Important constitutional changes had been made and the radicals were forced at last to recognize the danger of shaking the foundations of the Republic. There was a broadening of the central mass of opinion which supported the régime. The royalists were thoroughly discredited and the old legitimist party never again presented a serious political threat. The Bonapartists virtually disappeared (there were only six in the Chamber of 1893). Antirepublican feeling was, in fact, diverted from its traditional channels and reaction began its evolution towards new forms; the possibility of a monarchical restoration by Parliament had gone.

With radicals becoming men of Order, a new republican consolidation sustained a ministry under Freycinet for two years; it was mainly preoccupied with tariff and economic questions. Nationalists were pleased by the *entente* with Russia, while, outside Parliament, the catholics were being reconciled to the Republic by the *Ralliement*. Leo XIII had been struck by the folly of the royalists' alliance with Boulangism, many of whose adherents were violently anticlerical. He was also aware that the United States had shown the possibilities of clerical influence in a republic. The *Ralliement* was therefore in essence the abandonment by the Church of legitimism and its acceptance of the Republic. Many Frenchmen who were tired of anticlericalism were ready for such an initiative. Even Ferry said the real peril lay on the left. Others thought that, so long as anticlericalism obsessed them, the politicians would put off necessary social reforms. The first formal expression of the *Ralliement* came in November 1890, when Cardinal Lavigerie toasted the Republic at a banquet for the officers of the French Mediterranean fleet. Hostile though the majority of French bishops remained, the Papal Encyclical *Inter Innumeras* (1892) confirmed the acceptance of the Republic by the Church. 'Who now speaks of it?' said Waldeck-Rousseau when the question of separating Church and State was again raised.[41] By 1897 there were 16,000 religious schools against 11,750 ten years before.[42]

A great scandal also helped the *Ralliement*. The financial failure of the Panama Canal company revealed that money had been paid to deputies and journalists to keep their mouths shut when the company had to raise more capital. Six former ministers were among those prosecuted. In the 1893 election the rallied conservatives and the moderates were triumphant; there were 311 'representatives of government' in the new Chamber. Thanks to the *Ralliement*, the monarchists were overwhelmed. But it was significant also that 8 per cent of the votes were cast for 'socialists', some of whose eighteen deputies were only disguised Bonapartists. The vote for them was as much a negative protest as an

41 See Debidour (*cit.* above, p. 72).
42 *Ibid.*, p. 165.

ideological affirmation, but it was a grave portent. Panama had discredited the older generation of opportunists and radicals alike. The conservative majority in any case meant that the days of republican 'concentration' were over. There was no need for concessions to the radicals now. For a while France was to be governed by conservative republicans who continued to pass social legislation but were bitterly attacked by socialists and radicals for the way they dealt with a wave of anarchist violence. When the president was murdered by an anarchist in 1894, Casimir-Perier was elected to his place, but he retired in disgust after a few months to be succeeded by President Faure, a moderate. Meanwhile, the conservative majority staggered on, crumbling gradually. In the end, in 1895, after a freak defeat of the government, the first exclusively left-wing government of the Republic took office under Bourgeois. It was pledged to the introduction of a progressive income tax but was soon replaced by Méline's government of 'capitalist defence'. Public opinion had been frightened by tax reform, anarchism and strikes; the Chamber approved Méline's policy of dropping the income tax proposal two days after it had voted for the Bourgeois resolutions in favour of it. Although Méline's government was soon being attacked for favouring the clericals and for the complacency with which it observed the impossibility of real fiscal reform, the country was not dissatisfied. The government only fell when there broke on it the full weight of the Dreyfus affair.

The cultural and social importance of the Affair is huge and, apart from reopening the clerical issue, it is hard to delimit its political importance. Its essentials were that a Jewish officer, Alfred Dreyfus, had been convicted of espionage on false evidence by a court martial in 1894. Although in 1896 evidence that he had been improperly condemned was already coming to light, the army and the government resisted attempts to reopen the case and find the real culprit. There were many reasons for this. Anti-semitism made people unsympathetic to the victim. It was alleged that diplomacy and security might be compromised by stirring up the matter. Patriots found it difficult to believe that French officers would willingly connive at injustice or forgery and accepted complacently the assertions of the generals that nothing need be done. Many politicians, once the affair was under way, found themselves committed to the *chose jugée*. But after 1898, when the publicity-seeking Zola published a notorious article entitled *J'accuse*, it was impossible to quiet the uproar. The radicals discovered, belatedly, that injustice had been done and began to make political profit out of the affair.[43] At the height of the affair the president died suddenly and his successor, Loubet, was believed to be in favour of reopening the case. Déroulède tried to persuade the soldiers at the presidential funeral to turn the occasion into a *coup d'état*. Clashes were by now occurring in the streets between the nationalists, supported by royalists and Catholics, and the republicans who had identified the cause of Dreyfus with that of the régime itself. An anti-Dreyfusard assaulted the president, and the appearance of old Boulangists in the anti-Dreyfus ranks reminded people of the dangers which menaced the republic ten years previously from demagogic reactionaries. Another court martial was held and passed the ludicrous verdict that Dreyfus was guilty with 'extenuating circumstances'; Loubet followed this with a presidential pardon and Dreyfus at this point passed out of history until in 1906 the judgment of the second court martial was quashed as erroneous.

But the Affair rolled on, embittering the national life. The soldiers were divided from the civilians; the religious from the tolerant and free-thinking. The politicians were so obviously fishing in troubled waters that many Frenchmen, like Georges Sorel, lost faith in politics.[44] The republican politicians were again forced to consolidate – in the camp of the Dreyfusards – against the enemies of the Republic and in defence of the supremacy of tolerance, law and civil society over prejudice, privilege and the soldiers. The recognition of their new unity was the formation in June 1899 of the ministry of Waldeck-Rousseau, the first to contain a socialist. Its function was to defend republican institutions and restore discipline. Many of the religious associations had irretrievably compromised themselves by the violence of their political interventions during the Affair and their enemies were determined to use the chance this gave them. In 1901 a law ordered the dissolution of all religious congregations not authorized by the government. Most of them applied for authorization

43 The Radical Socialist deputies had at first attacked Méline for leniency to Dreyfus; the socialists had ostentatiously washed their hands of a bourgeois quarrel.
44 'On aurait pu croire, parfois, que deux troupes de charlatans se disputaient une clientèle de voyous', *La révolution dreyfusienne*, pp. 63–4.

but the victory of the left in the general election of 1902 showed they could expect little sympathy. The Chamber, indeed, was more extreme than the prime minister, who resigned. He was replaced by the violently anticlerical Combes, who fell upon the catholic schools and congregations with enthusiasm and without scruple. By 1904 the *Ralliement* was in ruins; the president's state visit to Italy, the despoiler of the Pope, made things worse. Finally, in 1905, under Combes's successor, Briand, the Concordat itself was swept away and the separation of Church and State effected. The symbolic disruption and spoliation weighed more heavily with Catholics than the advantages. Apart from this spectacular legal change, the Dreyfus Affair had other important but negative effects. It prevented the consolidation either of a party of order committed to the Republic or of a powerful Catholic left. Worse still, by reviving old quarrels, it distracted politicians from new issues for another decade.

The inevitable, if slow, dissolution of the Dreyfusard coalition revealed that the major facts of French life were changing almost unnoticed by the politicians. One symptom of this was the renovation of the old revolutionary tradition by socialism. A law of 1884 had removed from trade unions the restrictions on associations. Clemenceau observed after the May Day celebrations of 1891 (in which ten people, including children, were killed at Fourmies), '*C'est le quatrième état qui arrive au pouvoir*',[45] and he was right. But the proletariat did not, as in England and Germany, turn to the existing political apparatus for its instruments. The French trade unionists made up in militancy what they lacked in numbers.[46] Incidents like that at Fourmies helped; the anarchist tradition of direct action appealed to them more than Marxism. Their unions, mainly grouped in the *Confédération Générale du Travail* (C.G.T.), held aloof equally from peaceful negotiations with the employers and from parliament; in 1895 they formally committed themselves to industrial action – that is, to winning reform by striking. Parliamentary socialism was limited to a few deputies who were, in any case, a very divided group until 1904. Then, the decision of the Second International to abandon the

45 *Journal Officiel*, May 1891.
46 The *syndicats* had about a half-million members in 1900. In 1911 they had just over a million – only about two-fifths of the British trade unions' numbers.

policy of cooperation with governments of *bourgeois* politicians ended socialist participation in the left-wing republican *bloc* which had been constituted by the Dreyfus Affair. Marxist socialism in France was now cut off from pragmatic socialists like Briand on its right, and from the institutionalized violence of the syndicalist movement committed to the ideal of strike action on its left.

Violence had also come to play a more important theoretical role in the politics of the right. Here, the Affair was very important. The first number of a new periodical, *Action Française*, appeared in 1899, advocating a new sort of royalism, not based on the old legitimist doctrine of prescriptive right, but on the argument that only the monarchy could pull France together and restore her national greatness. The irrationalism of this new doctrine of integral nationalism,[47] associated especially with the writings of Maurras and Barrès, was the right-wing counterpart of the syndicalist rejection of parliamentary republicanism on the left. Nationalist, antisemitic and anti-parliamentarian, relying heavily on street gangs, the movement foreshadowed some of the feaures of Fascism. It was fundamentally anti-parliamentary and drew on a widespread disillusionment with the Chamber as a mere arena in which the representatives of the peasants and bourgeoisie pursued their private interests. The radicals, increasingly the representatives of the small *fonctionnaires* and proprietors, had lost touch with the worker, who was becoming restive as the cost of living rose steadily because of protection. In 1906 it looked as if the radicals might be able to regain the initiative, with a radical ministry led at first by Sarrien, then by Clemenceau; 250 radical or 'radical socialist' deputies, seemed to provide a solid base for reform. Briand was in the cabinet, and the post of minister of labour was created for the labour leader Viviani. A programme was announced which included – once more – the introduction of income tax. Yet what should have been a great reforming ministry petered out miserably. One cause was a wave of strikes. The twentieth-century price rise had started wage agitation everywhere. In 1906 the C.G.T. congress at Amiens formally adhered to the doctrines of revolutionary syndicalism. There had already been a stroke of bad luck in the weather of 1907 which had provoked rioting among the peasant wine-growers of the Midi. In two years, fifteen people were killed and nearly five hundred

47 The word 'nationalism' was invented about this time.

wounded in industrial disturbances. Even civil servants struck in 1909. The only result of Clemenceau's ministry in the end was the confirmation of the disunity of the left. A series of weak governments followed down to 1914. The first, headed by Briand, called out troops to defeat the general strike of 1910. But domestic issues were being dwarfed by international affairs in these years. The major issue in domestic politics was the passing of a three years' military service law in 1913, in the teeth of bitter socialist opposition, led by Jaurès.

Politics had disappointed and disillusioned many Frenchmen. They were proving inadequate to express the new issues emerging after the Affair; *Action Française* and the C.G.T. were the result. Only on the eve of war did the government succeed in carrying an income tax law; much of the year was taken up with financial scandals and the murder of a newspaper editor by a prime minister's wife. 'We are neither defended nor governed', said Clemenceau in a gloomy debate on the state of the army.[48] The *immobilisme* of France's political system was also paralleled by that of an economy which, in spite of its prosperity, was still anchored firmly in the preponderance of agriculture and small-scale production which, behind the walls of the tariff, preserved so much of the past. This ossification explained the tenacity with which Frenchmen conducted their politics in terms of a dead mythology. Frenchmen were still impressed with the grandeur of their history and the role France ought to play in Europe (as both Boulanger and Maurras showed). They admired their cultural monuments, while they neglected scientific education.[49] Yet there is something to go on the other side of the account, too; it was a rich culture which could match Cézanne with the Curies. French diplomacy had been brilliantly successful and the country was no longer isolated as she had been in 1880; the army had recovered its prestige after the doldrums of the Dreyfus Affair. French resistance to change, moreover, showed a fundamental stability. The political and economic structure had great reserves of strength. The Republic had assimilated many of its opponents and universal education had made most Frenchmen republicans. Popular anti-parliamentarianism had subsided. If the C.G.T.

48 See AR (1914), p. 281.
49 Lille's *Institut Industriel du Nord* was the only French institution approximating to a German *Techniiische Hochschule*.

espoused violence, it represented only a minority; less than half a million people took part in the general strike. Foreign observers might have their doubts; but France was still a great power in 1914 and was to show it by her survival of the next four years.

SPAIN AND ITALY

The monarchies of Spain and Italy ranked next in importance to Great Britain and France among constitutional states, but neither was taken very seriously by other nations. In 1880 each had pretensions to major status as a power, Spain because of her past, Italy because of her strategic position, but by 1914 Spanish pretensions had been exploded and Italy's only survived because they had not been tested. Geographically both countries had long Mediterranean coasts and each was broken into regions differing greatly in climate and topography. Lombardy was as different from Calabria as the *huerta* of Valencia from Estremadura. This variety was repeated in social structure; in each country there were many small peasant properties but each was also cursed with *latifundia* and their accompanying rural slums. The peasant was the typical figure in each society, and he was usually poor, illiterate, ridden by superstition and disease,[50] and liable to express his politics in secret societies or a sudden *jacquerie*. Emigration was a safety-valve for Spaniards and Italians alike because neither country could industrialize fast enough to absorb its surplus labour; Italy did not produce a million tons of steel a year until after the first world war nor Spain until after the second. Yet, in spite of social and economic backwardness, the politicians of both countries tried to work the machinery of constitutional monarchy. In both countries this was impossible without an effective, though informal, restriction of the real political nation. In each case, too, politicians had to take account of a spiritual crisis, if so intangible a thing can be identified. In Spain this arose from the disasters of 1898, in Italy from the fading of the dreams of the *Risorgimento*. Finally, each country was overwhelmingly Catholic.

50 The last important outbreak of plague in western Europe was in Spain in 1899. Andalusia was devastated by cholera and over 100,000 deaths occurred in 1885. There were epidemics only slightly less severe in Italy at the same time, but malaria was a greater scourge there.

Their contrasts are just as important. Italy was wealthier than Spain, and the gap between them in 1880 had widened further by 1914. The Italian population grew faster than the Spanish, and Spain's enormous territory was a source not of strength but of weakness. With an area 85,000 square miles bigger, she had only 9,000 miles of railway to Italy's 10,000 in 1907, and a long coastline was less help to her communications because of the difficulty of reaching the interior from the sea. Nearly three-quarters of Spain was classified as 'arid',[51] and most of the centre was only rocky steppe; much more of Italy was fertile. Italy, too, for all her backwardness, could draw on an industrial tradition; outside Catalonia and Biscay, Spain had hardly any.

Such structural differences help to explain the contrast in the energy which the two states displayed in international affairs. Spain had lost most of her empire in the early nineteenth century; in 1898 thirty years of smouldering rebellion in Cuba at last involved her in war with the United States and the loss not only of Cuba and Puerto Rico, but of Guam and the Philippines, followed. After four centuries Spain ceased to claim to be an oceanic power.[52] All that was left was a straggle of bits of African coast and a nasty entanglement in Morocco, which was not successfully wound up until the 1920s. Spain took no effective part in the 'imperialist wave'. Italy, on the other hand, pursued a vigorous policy of expansion abroad, disregarding unprofitability and disaster on the way, and the result in 1914 was an African empire based on Eritrea in the east and Tripolitania in the north. Insubstantial it might be, but it was a striking registration of the difference between the two countries.

This exemplifies the difference between the ways in which Spain and Italy adapted themselves in this age. Spain moved much more slowly than Italy towards the pattern of advanced societies which characterizes twentieth-century Europe and this demands an explanation which goes beyond her inferior social and economic resources. It can begin with her politics.

Paradoxically, Spain, an older country than the newly united Italy, was worse divided. The constitutional ideals of the French Revolution were resisted in Spain more bitterly than anywhere

---

51 i.e. where mean rainfall is less than 20 inches a year.
52 Her sale of the Marianas and the Carolines to Germany in 1899 liquidated her last Pacific commitments.

else in western Europe. Since 1808, liberals and conservatives had fought doggedly to control the Spanish state.[53] The result was a legacy of traditional hatreds; the Church committed itself to the conservative side and this further divided Spaniards. The monarchy was twice interrupted before its last restoration, when Alfonso XII was proclaimed king in 1874, and a family of pretenders had ravaged the country with the Carlist wars.

The constitution of 1876, it was hoped, would put an end to this turbulent era and reintegrate Spain. It set up the usual forms of constitutional monarchy. Conservatives were reassured because the electorate was small and liberals because the *Cortes* (parliament) could control the monarch. These forms, in fact, were less important than the realities which underlay them. The essentials of Spanish politics were oligarchy and corruption. As in eighteenth-century England, there were good arguments for both. The political nation consisted of those who wanted peace and stability. They were recruited both from old conservatives and from new rich who had bought Church lands and shared the enormous nineteenth-century creations of new noble titles. These men sought to buy off opposition to the compromises of the Restoration by sharing the spoils, but not all their politicians were without ideals. Some of them held moderate, middle views, and sought above all else to hold things together peacefully so that a healthy and decent political life could at last develop around parliamentary institutions. But in the Spain of 1880 the means they had to use to stay in power made sound growth almost impossible. Bribery and intimidation were needed to obtain a docile *Cortes*. In many parts of Spain, this was the golden age of the *cacique*, or local boss, who organized elections and was the retail distributor of the patronage sold wholesale in Madrid. With the local commander of the civil guard and the provincial governor, he shared an authority against which the individual Spaniard was often helpless, and the courts, an elementary safeguard of rights, powerless. The result was that the formal triumph of liberalism in the constitution of 1876 opened an era of disillusionment for many liberals. Meanwhile, two great historical institutions stood to some degree apart from the oligarchy and, potentially, challenged it. The Church was one; it tended subsequently to rally to the régime. The army

---

53 There were at least eight *successful* revolutions or counter-revolutions before 1880.

was the other, and it was increasingly conscious of its distinct standing. Both embodied important ideals, but ideals from the past, and each was profoundly divided from the new forces which were to emerge in the Spain of the Restoration. Beside them, Carlism and Republicanism, the movements of the unreconciled, were unimportant. The Carlists (whose origin lay in support of Don Carlos, the Bourbon pretender of 1833) were an anachronism, poorly led and dependent on a few areas for support. They were soon finished as a political and dynastic movement, partly because the papacy withdrew its support. Republicanism was too divided to matter.

The Restoration began promisingly. Governments were decently stable: there were only twelve between 1880 and 1901, and nine of them were formed by one or other of two men, Cánovas del Castillo and Sagasta. Cánovas was a conservative; he was a celebrated historian of his country and (perhaps for this reason) sceptical and pessimistic. Sagasta was a liberal, just as sceptical as his opponent, but gregarious, debonair and a more likable figure. He was the son of a grocer and himself a civil engineer. Both men had greater integrity than many of their followers and agreed that the country needed quiet for constitutionalism to take root. Both accepted the 1876 settlement as a viable framework, although one of Sagasta's governments restored universal male suffrage in 1890. Only the formal anticlericalism of the liberals differentiated them significantly. An essentially complementary relationship was symbolized by the 'pact of El Pardo' in 1886 when, faced with the birth of a posthumous heir to the throne and the dangers of a long regency, Cánovas advised Maria Cristina, the regent for the infant Alfonso XIII, to call Sagasta as prime minister and agreed with him that liberal reforms should only be introduced slowly, so that the regime should not be shaken by fundamental debate. The new government managed the general elections which followed in the usual way and the new *Cortes* was as 'ministerial' as its predecessors, although a few extremists were allowed in to show that the liberals took their principles seriously.

Unfortunately the Restoration was not stable but stagnant. Change within the constitutional framework usually meant no change at all. Universal suffrage made small difference; the elections continued to be made by the time-honoured means of purging municipalities, cooking electoral registers, and even by

169

polling the dead. Sometimes the votes cast were ignored and the returns filled in with figures thought suitable in Madrid. The only change was that more force had to be used as time went on. This debasement of the representative system spread a deep scepticism about politics itself as a means of achieving social purposes. Public opinion could not form itself on the artificial polarization of the two-party system and its corruption.

Practically, government undertook little in Spain except the management of elections and national finances and the preservation of order. An underpaid bureaucracy demoralized by the spoils system made more than this difficult, and the *débâcle* of 1898 showed that it could not even maintain the interests of the nation abroad. The humiliation of the Spanish-American War was the more crushing because the facts had for so long been kept hidden. Those who had advocated Home Rule for Cuba had been unable to get a hearing. Now the inefficiency of the armed services was also suddenly revealed. Two Spanish squadrons, at Manila and Santiago, were wiped out without the loss of a single United States ship; in the entire war only seventeen American sailors were killed. Nor was this because the poorly armed and equipped Spanish fleet lacked courage.

This was really the end of the illusions of the Restoration. With the 'generation of 1898' began a spiritual and cultural revival. Radicalism had a disaster to exploit. The loss of colonies was not, in itself, wholly disastrous; a big drain on the budget was removed. The new century brought a new vigour, but also a new turbulence into Spanish history. The disappearance of the two great statesmen of the oligarchy sharpens the impression of a break. Cánovas was assassinated in 1897 and Sagasta died in 1903. Their followers soon began to fall out, parties disintegrated and governments succeeded one another rapidly; there were fifteen between 1901 and 1914. Alfonso XIII, officially of age in 1902, was in part to blame; he combined consciousness of his prerogative with a taste for intrigue, a combination often fatal. His caprice seemed to make the political system even less responsive to public need. As abortive attempts to deal with *caciquismo* showed, reform was becoming more, not less difficult, just when new problems were beginning to demand new remedies.

In the 1890s there had been a wave of strikes and rioting in town and country alike: sheer misery did more to produce it than agitation. Industry could not absorb the flood of peasant labour;

emigration shot up, continuing to climb until the 1920s. But this did not remove poverty. Wages were low, conditions of work bad. Such social legislation as the factory acts of 1900–02 was rarely enforced. Discontent had always found spokesmen outside the political class. There was a tradition of revolutionary extremism going back to Bakunin; in the last decade of the century it produced bomb-throwing and the murder of Cánovas. The popular agitators were handicapped by rivalry between anarchists and socialists, but anarchism, originally strongest in the country-side, conquered Catalonia by 1911. The province became the stronghold of the anarcho-syndicalist *Confederación Nacional de Trabajo* (C.N.T.). The socialists, directed from Madrid, had their own trade union organization, the *Unión General de Trabajadores* (U.G.T.), and elected the first socialist deputy to the *Cortes* in 1910. By 1914 modern ideology thus embittered the old division of rich and poor in rural Spain.

The divergence between C.N.T. and U.G.T. reflected in part the rebirth of Catalan nationalism. Rich Catalans were the first to rediscover the oppressiveness of government from Castille; Spanish liberalism had meant more centralization, not less. Carlist survivors and industrialists seeking tariff protection and a reduction of the share of national taxes paid by Catalonia were the founders of the new regionalism. All classes coalesced about the 1892 *Bases de Manresa*, a regionalist programme, and the Catalan movement emerged as a crusade of progress and prosperity against the backwardness which stemmed from Castilian hegemony. The disaster of 1898 seemed the culmination of incompetence. In 1901 a newly formed regional league fought and won the general election in Catalonia, in the teeth of governmental pressure. This opened a period of great confusion, when governments in Madrid struck back by paying terrorists to let off bombs in the homes and factories of Barcelona manufacturers, and encouraged radicals to run against candidates of the Catalan *Lliga*. One conservative prime minister, Maura, deplored these methods. He had sought in 1893 to conciliate Cuba and still strove to follow the ideals of 1876; 'Either we make the revolution from above,' he said, 'or it will be made for us from below.'[54] Unfortunately, circumstances were changing too rapidly. When he

54 See *Historia Social y Economica de España y America*, ed. J. Vicens de Vives (Barcelona, 1959), iv, pt.ii, p. 396.

temporarily abandoned the unscrupulous methods of his colleagues in 1905, the government again lost the elections. It became clear that the political system could no longer be made to work in Catalonia except by force. But force only reunited Catalans against the army, and in 1907 a new coalition, *Solidaritat Catalana*, again won an easy electoral victory. An outburst of excitement and exploding bombs followed in Barcelona. At the height of tension the government called up the Catalan reserves for service in Morocco. The result was the orgy of destruction in Barcelona which began on 25 July 1909, called the *Semana Tragica*. A general strike turned into an attack on class enemies. Significantly, but, to the wealthy, shockingly, the Church was the main sufferer. Twenty-two churches and thirty-four convents were burnt down. Even the republicans were frightened, because they had clearly lost control of their supporters; the middle-class Catalan nationalists suddenly became aware of the tensions within their own movement. *Solidaritat* broke up; the Anarchists set to work organizing the C.N.T. and the industrialists settled down, satisfied temporarily with a new tariff.

This was not the end of Catalan nationalism, but began a lull. 1914 is not a significant date in Spanish history and none of the problems which emerged under the Restoration was removed by the temporary prosperity of the Great War. All that had happened by 1914 was that the first phase of a new historical epoch had been passed. In that phase, the Church and army appeared in new roles. The strong anticlerical movement of the seventies had waned under the Regency. The church had been cosseted and favoured by the Court. There were signs of an intellectual and spiritual revival within it. Its schools and universities were able to starve the state educational system. After the French anticlerical laws, its clergy was reinforced by *émigré* monks and nuns. The last attempts of traditional liberalism to limit the power of the Church came under Canalejas, whose government passed the so-called Padlock Law in 1910, forbidding the establishment of more religious houses without the consent of the government and attempted to enforce the toleration of the public worship of non-Catholics. This had little effect, but it consummated the alienation of the Church from such progressive elements as existed in Spain. The *Semana Tragica* showed already that the Church had lost the loyalty of the town masses. By 1914 it was firmly allied with

Crown and army in looking to authority for the solution to Spain's problems. The army, for its own part, had undergone an ideological and social transformation since the great days of the political generals half a century before, when it had often been a liberal force. Catalan nationalism had reawakened the army's allegiance to Castilian centralism and its awareness of itself as the guardian of Spanish tradition and unity. The 1905 electoral success of the Catalans led directly to the 1907 Law of Jurisdiction, which submitted press offences against the army and nation to trial by court martial. This was the first major concession to the new officer class. The *Semana Tragica* was followed by a military repression so severe (175 workers were shot in the streets) that the government fell, but the independence shown by the *juntas* in which the officers organized themselves was a symptom of future trouble.

The political system symbolized by the pact of El Pardo had, in fact, almost worn itself out by 1914, and the forces that were to dispute its legacies had already appeared. After the fall of Maura's government in 1909, Canalejas, the only other distinguished statesman of the prewar years, managed to hold the system together a little longer, at the price of concessions to the Church. But the oligarchy could no longer assume the indifference and quiescence of town or country. 'A sense of wrong, a wish to escape, and a tendency to revolt are spreading', wrote a British observer in 1910.[55] Not only internal order, but even external interests seemed to be jeopardized. The Catalan problem had not been solved, the colonies had been lost and the Moroccan ulcer ran on. Force, not will, was the basis of the Spanish State.

It is less easy to see what might be said in defence of the régime, but it should be remembered that the oligarchs had to govern a country which had had no general will since it lost the unity of religious faith. Against this background, to introduce universal male suffrage at all was a bold step, and the constitutionalism of the régime was at least a symbol which kept liberal hopes alive. Any Spanish government would have had to meet economic backwardness with the same lack of natural resources, and protection, even if it meant high prices, meant some economic advance

55 *CMH*, vol. xii, p. 267.

too.[56] The army was a big financial burden, yet if it were not paid it would certainly present a danger to the state. Indiscipline in the government service made efficient administration difficult. Finally, no régime could have shaken off the paralysis of political life caused by the ideological divisions which made Spaniards unwilling to use constitutional methods for fear of helping their opponents. In this setting, wire-pulling was not enough, as the long periods of martial law showed. The fundamental achievement of the oligarchic régime in the conditions was survival: its predecessors and successors did no better.

Italy's trials were almost as great as those of Spain. As a new nation, she had to carry the psychological burden of disappointment that the hopes and myths of the *Risorgimento* had not been fulfilled.[57] Not only were there still Italians living under Austrian rule, but the new state had many opponents inside Italy. Too many Italians felt excluded from the benefits of unity which seemed to be monopolized by a small class. New taxes and new laws kept local resentment of central government alive. Old radicals like Garibaldi still talked about revolution. Some Italians, the Catholics who obeyed the Pope (and the qualification is important) in taking no part in politics, deliberately excluded themselves from the *Risorgimento* legacy. Athough this did not impede cooperation by officials behind the scenes, it kept alive an obsession with Church and State problems which prevented Catholics from exercising their due weight in public life. It also fed the petty anticlericalism of the *Risorgimento*; pinpricks such as the erection of a statue to Giordano Bruno in Rome, or salacious gossip about clerical scandals, only indulged an already overdeveloped taste among politicians for words rather than deeds. The Church responded just as ostentatiously; until 1888 the Pope's 'imprisonment' in the Vatican was publicized by his refusal even to go so far abroad as St Peter's.

Such divisions cut across a country already deeply divided in other ways. In part this was because of policy; in part it arose

---

56 As late as 1882 duties were being reduced. But the protectionists – a combination of Biscayan ironmasters, Catalan manufacturers and Castilian cereal-growers – gained a great victory with the 1891 tariff. Thereafter tariffs rose steadily.

57 The *Risorgimento* is the name given to the process of unification which was completed by the occupation of Rome in 1870.

from Italy's geographic and demographic structure. Unification had meant a huge national debt – now to be shared by regions not previously saddled with the burdens of trying to be a great power – and the pursuit of balanced budgets. The result was heavy taxation. The most hated tax was the grist tax, the 'tax on bread', which fell heaviest on the poor, but there were plenty of indirect taxes on other commodities. Municipal authorities also raised revenue by local *octrois* which fell mainly on the poor. Although revenue had by 1880 more than doubled since unification, this was at a heavy cost. Many of the tasks of local government – for example, in education – could not be carried out in the poorer regions because of their poverty. Worse still, such surpluses as the peasantry might be able to make were soaked up by taxes and could not go into the improvement of agriculture.

The fundamental social fact was peasant poverty. A census in 1881 showed that only one in ten peasants either owned land or held it by share-cropping (*mezzadria*). The rest were day-labourers, working when they could and competing for work in a time of agricultural slump and rapid population growth. Between 1880 and 1900 the population rose by nearly 4 million: at the same time the annual value of the national agricultural product was declining; only once before 1901 did it regain the level of 1880. The peasant became poorer and poorer. Unfortunately, few politicians were interested in his plight, in spite of a great investigation of agriculture by a parliamentary commission between 1877 and 1885. The result was that poverty more and more could only find an outlet in violence. Forcible occupation of uncultivated land was one manifestation; jacqueries against landlords, brigandage, and secret societies were others. They all put up the cost of government still more by requiring military intervention on behalf of the landlords. And this, in its turn, sharpened the class conflict and led to the identification of the rich and powerful as the cause of all the peasants' ills, from malaria to hunger.

The worst effects were found in the south. The economic and social gap between what lay above and what lay below Rome, long familiar, had widened terrifyingly by 1914. Such industry as the south had possessed was wiped out by foreign and north Italian competition when unification imposed free trade. Overpopulation, undercapitalization, poor soil and a lack of technical skill blighted agriculture in the south more than elsewhere. Even

the temporary fillip given to Italian wine-growers by the phylloxera in France was followed by the spread of the disease to
Sicily and Italy. Disorder and brigandage were worst in the south.
Large areas of Sicily escaped from government control altogether
and were ruled in semi-independence by an alliance of landlords,
corrupt officials and the *Mafia*. Emigrants came overwhelmingly
from Sicily and the south by 1900. And as the industrial growth
of the north accelerated in the twentieth century, the south simply
sank farther behind. In 1901 the illiteracy rate in the Basilicata was
75 per cent – nearly five times that of Piedmont. This meant,
amongst other things, that the south was under-represented in
Parliament because the franchise was based on literacy. The
borough-mongers in Rome easily manipulated southern constituencies whose social backwardness therefore provided a built-in
obstacle to its own removal by ensuring that the south sent
unrepresentative deputies to Rome. When the socialists, the
candidates of the poor, polled 300,000 votes in the election of
1904, only a tenth of them came from the south. Only two years
before had an Italian prime minister for the first time thought the
south worth even a visit.

The political aspect of the southern problem looks back to the
Risorgimento. The constitutional and political machinery of Piedmont had been extended to the whole peninsula in a way which
took no account of regional needs. The fundamental instrument
was the *Statuto* granted by the king of Sardinia to his subjects in
1848. Italy was ruled by the king and his ministers, who were
chosen from a bicameral legislature. The Chamber was chosen by
a restricted electorate. Providing the ministers could control the
Chamber, the initiative and preponderant power lay with the
king's government. The most important weapon of the king was
the granting or witholding of dissolutions. As governments had
the power to 'make' majorities by pressure during elections, they
were not changed by elections – which never went against the
government in power – but, like English eighteenth-century
ministries, only when they lost the support of the Crown or the
politicians in the Chamber.

The power to win elections was based on a highly centralized
administrative machine. Italy was divided into sixty-nine provinces, each under a prefect responsible to Rome. As effective
public opinion was non-existent, as the courts did not protect the
individual and as the Italian official tradition was arbitrary and

irresponsible, the prefect was very powerful. He could negotiate with the local wire-pullers about the favours available from Rome. The deputy, once elected, took over the running responsibility for looking after local interests at the centre, and gave or withheld his support in return for patronage. The underpaid ranks of the lower civil service were swollen to provide more spoils. Means tests and the literacy qualification produced such small electorates in many areas (further diminished, too, by Catholic abstentions) that the average constituency in 1900 had less than 5,000 voters. This political structure assured governmental victory in elections providing that the prefects did their job; to encourage them in 1892, two-thirds of them were dismissed or moved before the elections. The result was representative of little except professional politicians; in 1900 only eight deputies called themselves agriculturists. Cynicism and distrust for parliamentary methods inevitably resulted. Parliamentary activity was unreal because it ignored the real issues around which parties could have formed.

Although its professional nature meant that the political class did not always represent traditional ruling-class interests, as its anticlericalism showed, it was, broadly speaking, the mouthpiece of the rich who, as landlords, controlled the politics of the constituencies, or, as financiers and industrialists, bribed deputies who received no salary. The patterns of the old status society did not signify much in this; the picturesque debris of the Italian nobilities[58] was already confused with the capitalist bourgeoisie of Lombardy and Piedmont. The old aristocratic order had really given up its hold on power in the 1870s. There was also a change of generation; the younger participants in the *Risorgimento* were coming to the top. Victor Emmanuel and Pio Nono both died in 1878; Garibaldi followed them four years later. A change of political mood can therefore be detected about 1880. What happened, in essence, was that the radicals themselves had become part of the establishment. By 1880 they accepted the régime. In doing so they fell to pieces as a party of principle. With the right in a minority, no serious competition on the left, and the Cath-

---

58 The plural is important. Each pre-unification state had its own highly self-conscious nobility. And there were two layers of 'Italian' nobility, one created by Napoleon I, and one by the new kingdom, imposed on top of them.

olics out of politics, there was no need for progressives to hold together. An era of cliques began. Names concealed the fact that true parties did not exist. Principles were attenuated into slogans. Parliamentary *condottieri* hung about the flanks of governments hoping to worry them into the granting of a portfolio. As in Spain, politics resembled a formal game played for local and personal ends against a background of fear. The dangerous political forces – revolutionary republicanism, intransigent Catholicism, socialism, anarchism – built up their strength outside the pale of parliamentary constitutionalism and were to show no wish to preserve it. There was just a little more reality in Italian politics than in Spanish, but it was not enough to save Italian constitutionalism in the long run.

The dangers facing it can be seen in all three of the political phases which can be discerned between 1880 and 1914. In the first, from 1880 in 1896, parliamentary government was increasingly unable to meet the nation's needs. From 1896 to 1900 a near-revolutionary crisis occurred. From 1900 onwards, there was a period of recovery, though dangers were still present in 1914.

The first period is dominated by two men, Depretis and Crispi. Both were old *Risorgimento* hands. Depretis was a Piedmontese with a radical past who formed the first government of the left in 1876 and was serving in 1880 as minister of the interior in the government of the man who had overthrown him. He became prime minister again after the French occupation of Tunis. By this time Depretis was of the left only in name: 'we . . . will accept the help of all honest and loyal men' he said later,[59] and he presided for six years over Italian politics like a Piedmontese Walpole, doing nothing whenever possible (because doing anything might antagonize potential support) and using his talents to construct foolproof majorities. His buying-in of opposition produced four cabinets of increasingly incoherent and varied membership. The system was not new; it was called *trasformismo* from its effectiveness in transforming men of widely different views into colleagues in the same government, but Depretis used it more skilfully than his predecessors.

As more and more men of the right joined those of the centre in Depretis's later cabinets, the reforms urgently demanded by the radicals of the previous decade were forgotten. Only the *estrema*,

59 D. Mack Smith, *Italy* (London, 1959), p. 112.

as the twenty-odd deputies of the far left were called, were outside this system. So little was done. The most important change was the extension of the electorate in 1882 from about 600,000 to 2 million. This admitted the literate artisan and small shopkeeper, but made little difference to the conduct of politics. In 1884 the grist tax was at last abolished; but this was followed almost at once by higher prices because of new grain duties (they were to rise even more sharply after the lapsing of the commercial treaty with France in 1888). Outside the parliamentary class, dissatisfaction mounted. Nationalists disliked the foreign policy of alliance with Austria, the traditional enemy. Violence and disorder increased from 1885 onwards. The election of the first socialist in 1882 had been an ominous sign, but Depretis's only response to disorder was to suspend the right of association. Meanwhile he was dabbling in colonial adventures. Shortly before he died in 1887, a colonial disaster forced him to form his eighth and last cabinet. This last essay in *trasformismo* showed he was again going over to a radical tack; one of the portfolios was given to his old rival Crispi, who succeeded him as prime minister.

The change was less significant than it seemed. Once a critic of *trasformismo*, Crispi had condoned it by entering the government. He was no longer the old Garibaldian who had ostentatiously led the left in abstaining from applause when King Humbert opened his first parliament in 1880. He was now a republican reconciled to monarchy and a Sicilian loyal to the House of Savoy. What was left of his past was anticlericalism, an obsession with plots, and a love of conspiracy. Yet even his attitude to the Church had evolved; he had come round to the Law of Guarantees, and although he was a freemason and a materialist, two cardinals officiated at his daughter's wedding. Crispi was more flexible than he liked to appear. He knew what he sought: that Italy should be a great power. He idolized Bismarck (and, like him, was a bitter enemy of socialism) but he was far more impetuous and therefore less effective. He held both the portfolios of foreign affairs in his own government and more and more bypassed Parliament, governing by decree; politicians accelerated the drift towards dictatorship by acquiescing in his measures. In retrospect, he achieved as little as had done Depretis. His foreign policy overstrained Italy, and his assertion of energy at all costs caused confusion. The change he brought was essentially only one of *tempo*.

His first government enacted local government, penal and sanitary reform, but also a severe law on public order. In spite of this, disorder continued; Crispi in fact made it worse by encouraging a tariff war with France, which led to yet higher prices. Anticlericalism was represented by a law on charitable associations which enraged Catholics. When his first government fell in 1891 – largely because of the withdrawal of right-wing support – Crispi had not solved the major problem of the mounting crisis of the parliamentary régime. The governments which followed were soon facing near-rebellion in Sicily. The south suffered most from the tariff war; when higher taxation was imposed, leagues of peasants and townsmen (*Fasci*) spontaneously appeared in Sicily, demanding fiscal and municipal reform. Socialism was blamed, but longstanding class hatreds lay behind them. Crispi resumed office in 1893 (when an unsavoury financial scandal brought down a government under Giolitti and further discredited the parliamentary régime) and vigorously began to restore order by attacking symptoms rather than causes. The electoral rolls were purged of 100,000 'malcontents'. The socialist party was dissolved. The prefect of Palermo lost his job for allowing a socialist deputy to be elected. Fifty thousand troops were sent to Sicily and martial law was proclaimed there. But nothing was done about basic reforms, the unrest smouldered on and an attempt was made to assassinate the prime minister. In his frustration he behaved more and more dictatorially, at one point suspending parliament for six months. Authoritarianism had become a substitute for domestic reform.

His foreign policy made success at home impossible. So long as France was antagonized by Crispi's attempts to make the Triple Alliance tighter, the tariff war would continue, and it would hurt Italy more than France. So long as he continued a forward policy in Africa, higher taxes were inevitable. Italians suffered from the delusion that colonies were a way to easy wealth; economically, their acquisition by Italy was indefensible. Crispi's colonialism could only be defended psychologically: after the disappointments of the Congress of Berlin[60] and the Convention of Bardo, Italy's morale needed a fillip. At the end of the nineteenth century viol-

60 Cairoli had said, in a famous sentence, that 'Italy will go to Berlin with her hands free, and wishes to leave it with them clean': they were also to be empty.

ence was in fashion and there was much talk of 'national virility'; England's position in Egypt was misunderstood and much envied. The first outcome of these pressures had been under Depretis in the Red Sea area. Crispi went further by proclaiming the colony of Eritrea and a 'protectorate' over Ethiopia in 1890. By this time, population pressure in the south was adding emigration to the arguments for imperialism and did much to overcome the greater scepticism felt in the north for colonial ventures. But Crispi, like Ferry, was brought down by colonial disaster in the end. Even those who had once supported him as a strong man to deal with social disorder had belatedly come round to regret parliamentary government and orthodox finance and a cabal overthrew him when an Italian army was wiped out at Adowa in 1896. This ended Crispi's government and, for the time, Italian colonialism in Africa.[61]

Crispi was not regretted. It was at last realized that he had achieved little and had exacerbated the class war. But he had been energetic and courageous. The next government, another transformist hodge-podge, was unable to agree on anything except inaction; it drifted towards the near-revolutionary crisis which marked the end of the century. The whole parliamentary régime, not just one group of politicians, was challenged. The basic problem was hunger: some regions experienced near-famine conditions between 1896 and 1900. The socialist movement, which had survived Crispi, provided leadership in many places. In contrast to parliamentary Italy, it made a strong appeal to the intellectual élite but it also appealed to revolutionary traditions and had by 1901 acquired a syndicalist wing, which looked to direct action by strikes and not to legislative change.

In 1896 there were riots by starving and unemployed workmen as far apart as Sicily and Piedmont. People in Sicily were said to be living on grass. Brigandage revived on the mainland; the fashionable world was startled to hear of highwaymen robbing a German Grand Duke and his retinue near Frascati. The following year, Roman peasants were seizing uncultivated land, and an attempt was made to kill the king. The harvest that year was bad. In January 1898 corn duties were temporarily reduced, but the country was by now almost uncontrollable. In May there were bread riots in all the big cities; strikers at Milan threw up barri-

61 By 1899 Italy was again dabbling in overseas expansion, but in China.

cades. In the street fighting which followed, gunfire was heard in Milan for the first time since 1848; eighty-two civilians and one soldier were officially said to have been killed. Four hundred thousand soldiers were under arms, thirty provinces under martial law and the greatest cities of Italy in a state of siege. The opportunity was taken to arrest Socialist deputies and suppress Catholic charity organizations. This did little good. Rudini resigned when the king refused him a dissolution and was succeeded by General Pelloux at the head of a very military government. Parliament was paralysed by obstruction to the government's assumption of special powers to govern by decree: the Italian liberals were not frightened into reaction by the danger of socialism. For the first time in decades, a government entered an electoral campaign in 1900 with a broad and fairly coherent coalition against it. The result was a moral defeat; the government's majority could not be destroyed, but 200 of its opponents were elected. Pelloux resigned and it was clear that under his successor the policy of repression would end.

The crisis had in fact almost blown itself out although there were still riots in 1900 and an anarchist assassinated King Humbert to avenge the dead of Milan. The new king, Victor Emmanuel III, appointed Zanardelli prime minister, a liberal choice which meant the restoration of parliamentary politics. Socialists, even, were soon supporting the new government in the Chamber. But Zanardelli did not overcome the weaknesses of coalition government; his successor, Giolitti, who became prime minister in 1903, (and was, with only brief exceptions, to remain in office until 1914), was more successful. Under him, it seemed that Italy had somehow turned the corner. Prosperity began to appear at last. Italy underwent an 'industrial revolution'. Between 1901 and 1913 industrial production nearly, and foreign trade more than, doubled.[62] In electricity and chemicals, Italy's advances were especially marked, and the standard of living rose for the first time since the 1860s. Politics for a time seemed quieter. How real this appearance was, and how much of it can be attributed to Giolitti remains to be examined.

In the first place, it is clear that he was a great conciliator. Personally, he was well equipped; he had the excellent mental

---

62 The increases were, respectively, 87 and 118 per cent. *Breve storia della grande industria in Italia* (Bologna, 1961), Romeo, pp. 82–3.

habits of the Piedmontese bureaucrats, he knew how to work the machine of patronage, and he had an infallible instinct for leaving sinking ships. He was also a liberal, with a sense of proportion and a real belief in parliamentary government. He was humane: 'I deplore as much as anyone the struggle between classes', he once said, 'but at least let us be fair and ask who started it.'[63] As an approach to the problem of social disorder this was very novel. Earlier, as minister of the interior, Giolitti already welcomed the organization of trade unions and refused to intervene officially as a strike-breaker, unless essential services were in danger. The result was a great wave of stoppages and a general strike in 1904, but Giolitti's response was only to use the mood thus created to hold elections which slightly reduced the representation of the extreme left. Helped by a temporary 'reformist' ascendancy in the *Partito Socialista Italiano* (P.S.I.) he even offered portfolios to socialist leaders. Cooperatives and other working-class organizations continued to have his support and encouragement, legislation was passed which improved working conditions, and food taxes were reduced. The climax of Giolitti's conciliation of democracy was the introduction of universal male suffrage for those over thirty in 1912.

His conciliatory efforts also extended to the Catholics. The fierce anticlericalism of *Risorgimento* liberalism was ebbing, and the revolutionary crisis had made many Catholics more frightened of socialism than of Victor Emmanuel. In 1905 a Papal Bull allowed each bishop to decide for his own flock whether they might take part in politics. Clerical cooperation against the extreme left had already shown itself in 1904 and it persisted although Giolitti did nothing to weaken the official secularism of the State: the only place of worship ever opened by Victor Emmanuel was a synagogue.

When to social conciliation and economic buoyancy is added an improvement in government finance which at last produced budget surpluses, reduced taxes and allowed a spectacular debt conversion in 1906 without shaking the *lira*, Giolitti's title to admiration seems very strong. Yet his achievements must be qualified. Much of the new industry, protected by tariffs, was uncompetitive. Its overheads were high in spite of the advantage of low wages. Moreover, economic improvement began before Giolitti.

63 See Mack Smith, p. 215.

In 1899 investment for the first time got back to its 1880 level; other signs of economic recovery were also appearing, thanks to a commercial treaty ending the tariff war with France, the only substantial achievement of Pelloux's government.

There is also a positive case against Giolitti. Many of his projects, like railway nationalization in 1905, were failures. The problem of the south remained unsolved although emigration helped to export its poverty to other countries and regions. Industrialization only tilted the internal balance more than ever, as the failure to get manufacturers to invest in the south showed. Nor was the class war ended. Intransigence revived in the still-growing P.S.I. The Socialist Congress of 1912 turned on the reformist leader, Bissolati, and two years later, at Ancona, a young syndicalist called Mussolini led the demand for the expulsion of freemasons from socialist ranks. Many socialists had been made more, and not less, suspicious of the bourgeoisie by Giolitti; his concessions to the Church alarmed them. Finally, he conceded too much to the new nationalists, led by men like Corradini, the strident disciple of Crispi, and d'Annunzio, whose repute was an important symptom of the pathological state of Italian culture. Their political aims reflected the obsession with force so prevalent before the first world war. One result of the clamour was that Giolitti undertook a war in 1911 against Turkey (the syndicalists also approved it as a means to revolution). The reality was disillusioning: a huge budgetary deficit and bitter resentment among the families of conscript soldiers. The same lack of grip in foreign policy was eventually to take Italy into the first world war.

The gist of the case against Giolitti can be boiled down to this: that it was *trasformismo* all over again. Even the 'liberal' reforms can be interpreted as mere tactical expedients. Elections were fought as before and Italy was ruled by the benevolent parliamentary despotism of 'this tight-rope walker', as Mussolini called him.[64] Renewed troubles in 1914 showed that the system was becoming harder to work. The elections of 1913 had been the most violent ever and many moderates had been outraged by an electoral pact with the Church. Once more, Giolitti stepped off the bridge and left his successors to face disorder almost on the scale of 1898. Moderate socialism, it was clear, had not ousted the

---

64 C. J. S. Sprigge, *The development of modern Italy* (London, 1943), p. 91.

extremists: in the 'Red Week' of June, government officials had to go into hiding, several towns declared themselves independent communes and a republic was set up in the Romagna. Italy's ills had not been healed and in this may lie Giolitti's best defence. He did not make the conditions which rendered real parliamentary government and true parties impossible, he only inherited them. Italy, like Spain, lacked the substructure of constitutional government in fundamental social unity and healthy political *moeurs*. It was not accidental that Italy, before Giolitti, produced apostles of dictatorship like Turiello, or acute analysts of the shams and inadequacies of democratic institutions like Mosca and Pareto. The roots of Fascism in prewar Italy can be detected not in the political work of one man, but in the failure of a whole political class to resist authoritarianism, remove social grievances and organize parties which expressed significant interests. In the long run, both Spanish and Italian constitutionalism were to fail because the ideological and social presuppositions of liberal democracy were lacking.

6

AUTOCRACY AND CONSERVATISM

Three great dynastic empires dominated central and eastern Europe. Only one of them (the Russian) was in 1880 formally an autocracy, but all three were, in different ways, resistant to the liberal and constitutional ideas so widely accepted in western Europe and diffused by the French Revolution. Russia, Austria-Hungary and Germany all also shared in varying degree a common problem: the existence of alien nationalities within their borders which, it was believed, might endanger the unity of the state. Their domination of Poland since the eighteenth century was a vivid example. All three states were also ruled by monarchs who still saw them in the old dynastic way as, in a sense, personal and family estates whose function was to support the dignity and standing of the ruling house. Hohenzollerns had ruled Prussia, Habsburgs Austria and Romanovs Russia longer than the Hanoverians had ruled England. Furthermore, though Germany had already shown remarkable industrial dynamism, social power in each of the three empires was still closely tied to land. Over much of eastern Europe, there lived in 1880 men and women who had been born serfs, *adscripti glebae*, committed to bond-labour in some form or other. More of the European Middle Ages survived in the three great empires than any other part of Europe in the late nineteenth century and this explains many of the paradoxes to be observed in them.

IMPERIAL RUSSIA

In 1880 Russia was no longer the awe-inspiring giant of 1815 or 1848. Her masses of hardy peasant soldiers no longer guaranteed military superiority; war increasingly needed technical and economic resources which were always growing more costly and Russia was poor. The gap between her and advanced countries was widening and it posed a problem to Russia's rulers from Alexander II to Stalin: how could so backward a society generate the strength needed by a great power? Much, in fact, was done by 1914 to give her that strength again. Russia under its last two tsars showed great powers of self-adaptation and provided herself with the foundations of an industrial economy and a constitutional system of government as well as renewed military strength. It took three years of war to destroy the empire. It is wrong to assume that collapse in revolution was the inevitable fate of Imperial Russia. Yet in 1880 she had been almost completely without the prerequisites of change. Russian society lacked the values and ideas which were the common-places of western capitalism. Most Russians were poverty-stricken peasants, still subject to the medieval scourges of famine and plague, their misery increasing year by year as their numbers grew. From 1800 the Russian population grew for a century and a half at more than 1 per cent per annum, a rate substantially higher than the European average: the 97 million subjects of the tsar in 1880 had become 165 million in 1914, and the ratio of rural to urban population had remained constant at about seven to one. There were great national, economic and religious differences among them but most of them lived in squalor, misery and ignorance. In 1881 only 9 per cent of the children of school age were getting an elementary education; the odds were six to one against a boy, and thirty-two to one against a girl. Outside the cities, only one man in four and one woman in ten were believed to be literate in 1897. This huge mass remained an enigma, a vaguely threatening background to the activities of a highly civilized and westernized élite. The peasants seemed inaccessible to progressive influences (because of this, they were idealized by some members of the intelligentsia); they lived in a tradition of subjection and exploitation from which the only escape was the hope of owning land. This inevitably led to the reduction of their political thinking to one ambition: the seizure of the gentry's estates.

Paradoxically, poverty seemed to have been made worse by the greatest single reform of Russian history, the emancipation of the serfs in 1861. This had been a bitter disappointment. It had not brought the distribution of land, and a legend quickly grew up that the tsar's terms had been falsified by the landlords. Some of the peasants' communal rights, too, disappeared with their servile status. Russian peasants, like those of many other countries in the previous half-century, discovered that the transition from a feudal to a market economy was by no means an unmixed blessing. Not that the change was complete or the severance with the past clean-cut. Emancipation left the peasant burdened by heavy redemption dues which were to compensate former serf-owners for the loss of their property. These dues were almost everywhere already in arrears in 1880 and were a crushing burden on top of heavy taxes.[1]

Such burdens might have been bearable if Russian agriculture had been more efficient. But although peasants owned nearly a third of the land in European Russia, they did not produce enough to satisfy their families, the tax collector and the redemption dues. In the Black Earth area, most peasant holdings of arable were smaller than those of the old serf allotments. Lack of capital and inefficient techniques complete the picture. The conservatism of the peasants kept the strip system of holdings going in the interests of equality, and productivity remained low. Even on land belonging to nobles the wheat crop per acre was less than a quarter of the contemporary British average.

This structure could not improve the lot of a growing population. The Russian peasant was not only caught in the Malthusian trap but his grain had to be exported to pay for the manufacturers which Russia needed. Protection to him simply meant high prices. Nor, until 1906, could he easily leave the village to look for work; idle manpower was tied up in the communal structure. In its turn, a backward peasant economy meant that demand for industrial products was low and this held back still further the development of industry. The peasants, in fact, were getting the unpleasant effects of the transformation from feudal to market society

---

1 As two-thirds of Russian revenue came from indirect taxes, and poll tax and land tax were also levied, the bulk of taxes came from the peasants in the end, although there was income tax. The population did not double between 1860 and 1900, but the yield of indirect taxation went up four-and-a-half times, while that of direct taxes was only doubled.

without its advantages in alternative employment. Emancipation had not relieved them of an inferior status nor offered them work. The phrase 'people and individuals' summed up Russian society: individuals, who counted, stood apart from the vast, anonymous peasant majority of 'the people'.

The autocracy could not grapple with this problem consistently, because of its own structure and its nineteenth-century tradition of resistance to change. Any change was dangerous; government was the maintenance of the *status quo*. This tradition had been challenged by Alexander II, the 'Tsar Liberator', but Alexander III (1881–94) was, like his successor Nicholas II (1894–1917), rigidly conservative and devoted to autocracy, Russian nationalism and Orthodoxy. They were also both unimaginative, but there the resemblance ends. Alexander was more conscientious, honest and straightforward than Nicholas who, as William II pointed out, was weak, obsessed with his family life and much under his wife's influence. Her repeated urgings that he be 'strong' produced only vacillation and wilfulness in a man lacking self-assurance, and rendered him even more inaccessible than his predecessor to intelligent advice.

This was the more dangerous since anything, in the last resort, might turn on the tsar's approval. As he dealt directly with each important minister and the looseness of the 'ministerial committee' prevented any cabinet solidarity from emerging, the only coordinating power in government was his. There was no prime minister until after the 1905 revolution and informal advisers and *éminences grises* played a great part in the making of policy. One of the most important was Constantine Pobedonostsev, procurator of the Holy Synod[2] from 1880 to 1895 and tutor to both Alexander III and Nicholas II. He does not fit the categories of western conservatism. Not much concerned with the interests of the ruling class, he was genuinely devoted to the Russian people whom he believed still to regard the tsar with affection and awe. Representative parliamentary institutions, he thought, would, as in the west, lead only to the exploitation and manipulation of the masses by wire-pullers. Capitalism he disliked because it meant the break-up of the peasant community and the family. Pobedonostsev rejected western Europe and all its works. His influence made it hard for Alexander and Nicholas to listen

2 Roughly, chairman of the committee directing the Orthodox Church.

to modernizing conservatives, even if they were aristocrats devoted to autocracy.

Nevertheless, the autocracy was immensely strong. It rested on the historic focus of secular and spiritual authority in the tsar. There existed no counter-tradition of representation or protest. Russia's landowners knew that the autocracy was, in the last resort, committed to the *status quo* at home while the peasants still looked to the tsar as the source from which relief might come. So long as Russia remained a largely agrarian society, in fact, the social basis for constitutional change was narrow. Consequently, the autocracy had no incentive to placate progressive and liberal-minded members of the traditional dominant class and so made such concessions as it made to reform both too grudgingly and too late.

Alexander II had begun to do something to change the picture of administrative tutelage by a huge (and not very efficient) bureaucracy, above all by setting up *Zemstvos* (local councils), but their independence had quickly been restrained. Law itself was handed down from on high and was hardly distinguishable from administrative decisions. Its operation, too, might be arbitrary in individual instances and although Alexander II made the courts more independent of the administration, it was impossible to bring a public official to book for abusing his powers. Not that it was often a question of abuse, so wide, usually, were they. In 1881 a decree on public order removed certain cases from the ordinary courts, gave administrative officials judicial powers and provided for action by military tribunals; it was renewed every three years down to 1917. The census of 1897 revealed that there were over 100,000 policemen, and 50,000 men in the security gendarmerie. They deployed a formidable apparatus of informers and spies which confused as well as enlightened the Ministry of the Interior and increased the tendency of the régime to meet social needs by repression rather than by reform. In 1880 there were 8,000 people in 'administrative exile' in Siberia, in addition to those who were actually undergoing imprisonment; the number was tiny by comparison with Stalin's later achievements, but it appalled liberal opinion outside Russia.

Opposition, though violent, was in 1880 still a matter of an alienated minority of intellectuals. The only other possible dangers were to be found in national minorities, and these, since the Polish Revolution of 1863, were quiet. Disappointed with the popular response, some of the intelligentsia had come to accept terrorism as the best means of advertising their cause. The murder of civil servants and officers of the gendarmerie became more common in the late 1870s and, finally, in 1881, the secret society 'The People's Will' assassinated Alexander II with bombs. This ended a brief experiment with benevolent autocracy; a great police offensive took advantage of the public revulsion against a terrorism which had killed the 'Tsar Liberator'. By 1884 People's Will was in ruins and terrorism was at an end for a decade. The new emergency provisions were improved, the censorship tightened up and Russia seemed to have returned to the ice-age of Nicholas I.

Simple repression was accompanied by an assault on what had already been achieved. Alexander III's accession manifesto, an uncompromising reassertion of autocratic principles, was followed by the resignation of all moderately conservative ministers.[3] One civil servant defined the aim of the new men as the restoration of what had been destroyed by Alexander II. The educational system was an early target. The autonomy of the universities was ended and steps were taken to exclude poor boys from the *gymnasia*. Church schools were encouraged because they were believed to inculcate more suitable attitudes than the state schools and for the same reason classics were preferred to the sciences in secondary schools – an odd interpretation of the influence of the curriculum which formed Robespierre and the English Whigs. The independence of the courts was sapped and the institutions of municipal self-government set up in the previous reign were undermined. In 1889 the *Zemstvos* were remodelled. Civil servants were given new powers to override their decisions and control their officials. 'Land captains' replaced the J. P.s in the countryside and combined judicial and administrative functions. They were supposed to be chosen, where possible, from the hereditary nobility, in order to link the natural social institutions of the countryside to the autocracy. The townships were to remain purely peasant bodies. It was a poor idea. Far from being benevolent patriarchs enjoying the loyal deference of their former serfs, the land captains were bureaucratic jacks-in-office, whose stupidity and brutality meant that the peasant would now begin to hate the representative of the tsar as well as his landlord.

3 They included the Grand Duke Constantine, uncle to the tsar.

The land captains illustrate the ideological bent of the reaction; it attempted to build upon and reinforce existing conservative elements in Russian society. A great fuss was made over the nobility, for example, in 1885 when the centenary of Catherine's Charter came round. But the nobility themselves did not have their hearts in it. They had not asked for the government's conservative efforts but passively endured them while the economic position of the smaller landowners steadily worsened. Similarly, attempts to stabilize rural society by such measures as the 1886 law prohibiting the break-up of households only meant further hindrance to economic improvement in the interests of social dogma. As late as 1893 the sale of communal lands by the village community without official approval was forbidden.

A more sinister side of the reaction was the persecution of minorities. Dissenters within Orthodoxy were treated more harshly: already in 1880 an archbishop and two bishops of the old Believers had been in prison for twenty-six, twenty-two and seventeen years respectively. The egalitarian Dukhobors finally emigrated to escape persecution. In some instances national and religious questions were mixed up. Catholicism was central to Polish nationality and was harried because of it; Lutheranism was pursued in part because it was the religion of the Baltic Germans. Russification really began in earnest with Alexander III, and was pressed on every front, religious, educational and administrative.

The Jews were notoriously the worst-treated victims. They suffered special legal disabilities and underwent sporadic pogroms connived at by the authorities. In 1880 most of them (about 4 million) lived in the Pale, the tract of Poland and western Russia to which they were confined by law; 700,000 more were driven into it in the next ten years and this left another 300,000 or so living illegally outside it. Successive restrictions drove Jews out of the legal profession, the *Zemstvos* and the municipalities. Quotas restricted their entrance to secondary schools. In 1893 it even became a criminal offence for a Jew to use a Christian name. True, the roots of Russian persecution were not racial but religious and social: all disabilities vanished if a Jew consented to conversion and they might not matter much in practice if he were a member of the professional classes and not the focus of peasant resentment in a Ukrainian village. Russian antisemitism was nonetheless seen abroad as a disgrace, even by those peoples who had their own discriminations against Jews. It also cost the regime dearly, both through the loss of human resources (over 2 million Jews left the Pale for other countries after 1880) and through the alienation of young Jewish intellectuals from the regime. There were to be many Jewish names in the forefront of the Russian revolutionary and opposition movements of the early twentieth century.

The autocracy never silenced criticism or destroyed opposition. Instead it found new sources, not only among the nationalities but among the growing numbers of industrial workers. Wages were low because of cheap rural labour; factory legislation – which was in any case ineffective through the lack of an adequate inspectorate – could not touch this. The policy of the régime was confused. Legislation against strikes was followed by the extraordinary invention of the Zubatov unions of 1900, labour organizations sponsored and protected by the police to enable the workers to stand up to their employers. The experiment was not very successful.

Industrial unrest, nevertheless, had its roots in an indisputable achievement of the tsarist régime, an enormous economic expansion. The turning-point was the famine of 1891 and the arrival of Witte at the Ministry of Finance next year. At great cost – but 'a great power cannot wait', he said – he abandoned liberal economics for direct state intervention in the economy. The state was to prime the pump of industrialization by intervention in key sectors, such as railway-building. Heavy indirect taxes took up all the peasants' surpluses and between 1894 and 1902 two-thirds of government expenditure went into economic development. Forty per cent of all industry existing in 1900 had been founded since 1891. The long-term effects were enormous. The Russian industrial economy grew in the 1890s at a faster rate than any other in Europe. After a pause, growth was resumed at the slightly lower, but still astonishing, rate of 6 per cent per annum after 1906. By 1914 Russia was producing ten times as much iron ore and steel as in 1880; in 1910 her steel output was equal to that of France and was half that of the United Kingdom. Coal output quadrupled between 1890 and 1914 (although this was not enough to meet the needs of manufacturing industries, which were expanding even faster). Productive units were increasing in size, too, so that Russia had more of her industry organized in big plants than was the case in other countries. By 1914 40 per cent of her manufacturing workers were in factories of over 1,000 people. Moscow and St Petersburg doubled between 1880 and 1910 and the growth of Polish cities was even faster.

Witte had shown that revolution from below was not needed to industrialize Russia. Traditionally, of course, the state had always been a very positive force in Russian economic life. Government ensured the building of the railways which linked coal and iron together in the Donetz basin.[4] The reform of commercial law, the encouragement of private banks and the stabilization of the currency by basing it on gold (1893–7) were all directed towards the modernization of the economy. Protection, adopted originally for fiscal reasons, encouraged industrial investment. Much of it came from abroad. In 1900 one-third of the capital of private industry in Russia was in foreign hands. Government borrowing, too, absorbed much foreign money, most of it belonging to French investors who, by 1914, held 80 per cent of Russian foreign debt securities.[5] British investment, on the other hand, was marked in mining and the new oilfields. In spite of the drain of interest payments abroad this absorption of capital brought growth.

Yet most Russians grew poorer. In spite of famine in 1891–2 and crop failures in 1897 and 1898, some 15 per cent of Russia's grain had to be exported in 1900. Agrarian disorder was still turned as much against landlord as against government; the peasant still saw salvation in getting hold of the gentry's land. In the growing cities, the plight of the workers was producing a more revolutionary frame of mind as the suppression of strikes became more and more a preoccupation of the government. The police and Cossacks were the schoolmasters of revolution.

Fiercer repressive measures confirmed the bias of opposition towards radical and revolutionary solutions. There was no indigenous liberal tradition in Russia and nothing to encourage one. The chance of winning back the loyalty of the *intelligentsia* was long past by 1900. This helps to explain the appeal of Marxism, which more or less replaced Populism (which idealized the peasant commune) as the dominant intellectual trend in the 1890s. But even this happened slowly. A Social Democrat organ-

4 In 1881 Russia had 14,000 m of track, in 1917 52,000 m.
5 Between 1892 and 1914 there were fifteen big flotations of Russian government or railway loans on European markets: ten in Paris, four in Berlin, one in London.

ization was founded in exile in 1883, and there were a few other centres of Marxist influence (such as the circle joined by the young Lenin at Kazan university in 1887), but they had little contact with industrial workers. In the more frequent strikes of the 1890s, working-class leaders favoured direct action to achieve immediate benefits in pay and conditions of work, and distrusted the intellectuals.[6] Only nine delegates came to the first Social Democrat Congress in 1898. Nevertheless the movement now began to take a more coherent and disciplined form. Significantly, a Jewish Social Democrat party, the *Bund*, was organized. In 1900 a party newspaper, *Iskra*, appeared, and in 1902 Lenin published '*What is to be done?*'[7] A congress in Brussels in 1903 was attended by forty-three delegates and produced a division between 'Bolsheviks' and 'Mensheviks' which was to cripple the party for the next two years.

Another new trend towards opposition to the régime, more important at first than Marxism, was the slow crystallization of liberal hopes around the personnel of the *Zemstvo* organizations. Handicapped as these bodies were, they became a rallying point for professional men who through them came into touch with the realities of government and society. The result was the creation of a mood and a set of aspirations much more liberal than anything previously known in Russia. Many *Zemstvo* were first aware of the possibility of joint action on their own initiative during the famine of 1891–2. In 1896 *Zemstvo* leaders decided to hold regular congresses to discuss matters of common interest.

Finally, there also reappeared by 1900 the older populist tradition, many of whose adherents still looked to terrorism as the main weapon against the regime. The most important group was the Socialist Revolutionary party founded in 1900, which both achieved some spectacular murders and was quickly infiltrated by the police. Looking more to the peasants than did the Marxists, the S.R.s contributed importantly to mounting disorder after 1901.

Those years brought a remarkable, if shortlived, consolidation of opposition. Neopopulists and Marxists had come round to the view that the first step must be the winning of political freedom and constitutional government. Consequently, cooperation

6 R. Pipes, *Social Democracy and the St Petersburg Labour Movement 1885–1897* (Cambridge, Mass., 1963).
7 See p. 232.

between them and the *Zemstvo* liberals was possible and a short-lived Union of Liberation (1902) was the symbol of an opposition coalition. It deliberately encouraged all tendencies within its ranks. Yet it could not by itself shake the régime, even when supported by agrarian disturbance, student outbursts, strikes and new national opposition groups. The crisis of the régime was only brought on by war.

The Russo-Japanese war (which began in January 1904) produced disasters for the opposition to denounce and shook the régime sufficiently for it to make concessions. Because they were so often accompanied by inconsistent attempts to reassert autocratic power, these exasperated rather than satisfied their recipients. But they gave opposition the chance to organize more openly and gain a better hearing. In September a congress of radical and revolutionary groups other than the Social Democrats was held in Paris and in November a great congress of constitutional government. The autocracy drifted, unable to control events. By the end of the year, for example, so important a region as Georgia had already been virtually autonomous for nearly nine months. When professional organizations began to hold banquets and passed resolutions demanding specific reforms, all the government did was to pursue rather feebly the proprietor of the restaurant concerned. It attempted to regain the initiative by promising wider functions to the *Zemstvos* and other reforms but nothing was said about an elected representative assembly, the main demand of the united opposition groups. Moreover reform edicts were followed by a ban on public meetings and stiffer censorship. Now came the news of the fall of Port Arthur.

In January 1905 the cities at last became involved. A strike in St Petersburg over the dismissal of three workmen led to a plan to present a petition to the tsar asking for political as well as economic reform. Ironically, this was organized by unions patronized by the police: it is still uncertain whether Father Gapon, the priest who led the demonstration on 9 January, was or was not an *agent provocateur*. The upshot was, in any case, tragic. The security forces lost their heads and opened fire on a loyal and pacific crowd; official figures said that 130 people were killed, certainly many more were injured. The result of 'Bloody Sunday' was that people lost faith in the tsar. A wave of riots and strikes followed throughout the country. They were mainly spontaneous, owing little or nothing to revolutionary leadership, but they pushed the régime into concessions; even liberal politicians hastily moved to the left, taking up more extreme positions than before, in order to retain popular support. By May the *Zemstvo* liberals were proposing not only constitutional government but the expropriation of great estates. The Social Democrats, handicapped though they were by divisions, began to be more prominent.

The government was still reluctant to run before the storm. The minister of the interior resigned after Bloody Sunday, but even the murder of a grand duke could not drive Nicholas further than to assent to a *consultative* assembly, which would not have been a concession of principle; such a *Duma* would be in the Russian tradition which afforded the people access to their tsar – it was far removed from the constituent assembly, elected by universal suffrage and secret ballot, which the liberals now demanded. Agrarian risings had been going on since February; there were jacqueries in the Baltic provinces; the armed forces were unreliable and a famous mutiny occurred aboard the *Potemkin* in June. Many officials were now coming round to the view that expropriation was inevitable if the countryside was to be pacified. In July a congress of *Zemstvo* and municipality representatives in Moscow successfully defied police orders to disperse.

In August an expressly consultative *Duma* was conceded. It was not enough. After further agitation a general strike began in October which paralysed the railways and St Petersburg became the effective focus of the industrial movement. In the middle of the uproar, the Constitutional Democratic party, or 'Cadets', the liberal political party which Russia had taken so long to form, met for the first time. At last Nicholas gave way. Pobedonóstsev was dismissed and, unwilling to trust the unknown liberals, Nicholas turned to a critic within the bureaucracy. Just back from negotiating peace with Japan, Witte was by temperament authoritarian rather than a traditionalist. Ideally, he should have served an enlightened despot, but this was not a part Nicholas could play. But Witte was prepared to recognize that autocracy had failed and to try to work within a constitutional framework. On 17 October, accordingly an Imperial Manifesto announced a *Duma* with real legislative powers, the extension of the franchise and the granting of real civil liberties.[8] But it came too late. There was

8 English text in B. Pares, *The Fall of the Russian Monarchy* (London, 1939), p. 503.

almost none in the opposition who did not now demand, at least by implication, the destruction of autocracy. True, divisions appeared almost at once in the opposition; 'Octobrists' proposed to accept the tsar's gift while the Cadets asked for expropriation of large estates. The Social Democrats rejected 'the police whip wrapped in the parchment of the constitution', as Trotsky put it and the Mensheviks began to suspect the Cadets as a 'bourgeois' party. The St Petersburg *Soviet* of workers which the Mensheviks dominated urged preparation for the final stage of the struggle. This was dangerous. Not only had some middle-class liberals been alarmed by the *Soviet*, but it did not coordinate its action with that of the peasants and armed forces. The 1905 revolutionary movement had been irresistible because it mobilized so many kinds of dissent: this now ceased to be true. Moreover, extremism increased the conservatives' influence in the government and weakened Witte's position.

The breathing space produced by the manifesto gave the government time to pull the army together and get back troops from Asia. A showdown with the *Soviet* was provoked which led to the imprisonment of its members. In Moscow, some hundreds of workmen took part in a strike on 10 December, and there was sporadic fighting for a week. At the same time ultra-nationalist conservative groups in the provinces conducted with official connivance, a series of brutal pogroms against Jews and revolutionaries. In the middle of this, Witte still felt strong enough to make a sweeping franchise concession which went far towards meeting Cadet demands. But his moment had passed. Like the liberals, Witte depended finally on the tsar being frightened and his plans, too, depended on revolutionary pressure. At the beginning of 1906 autocracy had regained its nerve.

As the years which followed brought the frustration of many liberal hopes, it is important not to forget that the principle of constitutionalism had been conceded; whatever its real effect, the *Duma* was enormously important as a symbol. A prime minister and a council of ministers had been created. Parties had appeared which were to mean a great deal for the political education of Russians. Some of the intelligentsia had been frightened by revolution into joining the Cadets and abandoned their old intransigent rejection of the entire régime to take advantage of the practical opportunities which the *Dumas* and *Zemstvos* offered. Even if the police retained exceptional powers, there was greater respect for civil liberties and speech was freer. Religious toleration had come for gentiles and the autonomy of Finland had been restored. Even the workers had won shorter hours.

More might have been done had Witte been given time. His early achievements as finance minister had been overset by the war, but he managed to take precautions against the forthcoming *Duma* by setting up a State Council to serve as a second chamber. He removed control over part of the budget from the *Duma* and negotiated a foreign loan to make the government financially independent. Laws were passed strengthening the apparatus of public order. Finally, on the eve of the opening of the *Duma*, a set of 'Fundamental Laws' were issued which codified the main constitutional enactments of the preceding months and, by implication, placed them beyond revision. A week before this, Witte had tendered his resignation, tired of the hostility of conservatives who could not understand what he was doing. Nicholas was pleased to accept it; in the government which followed, the outstanding figure was that of the minister of the interior, Stolypin.

The elections to the first *Duma* were boycotted by the S.R.s and the Bolsheviks, though ten Mensheviks were elected. This abstention produced an assembly dominated by the Cadets, with no conservatives and only thirty or forty moderate liberals to do service on the right. Two hundred peasants sat in it; contrary to conservative predictions, they all turned out to be very radical. One other identifiable group was supplied by the Ukrainians, who organized themselves as a national *bloc*. When the *Duma* met (on 27 April), demands for more constitutional reform were contemptuously rejected by the government. But adverse votes did not make the ministers resign and there was no way of forcing them to do so. Nicholas II might have tried to form a Cadet government, but preferred to dissolve the *Duma* on 9 July. Some of the Cadets retired to Finland and issued a 'Viborg manifesto' which urged passive resistance. The revolutionary tide had already ebbed too far and they were locked up.

On the day the *Duma* was dissolved, Stolypin formed a government. He shared with Witte a flexible conservatism; he negotiated with the liberals to see if they could be got into his government at the outset. But Stolypin was a landowner while Witte had been a businessman, and he was a militant nationalist. The result was a remarkable period of vigorous government;

whatever Russia did under Stolypin, it did not drift. As a policeman he was unsurpassed, using the whole range of exceptional procedures open to him from courts martial to the proclamation of states of emergency. *Agents provocateurs* flourished. Some 1,500 people were executed in 1906 and 1907; this was less savage than it appears since over 4,000 officials were killed or wounded by terrorists in the same period.

This helped to produce a second *Duma* much more radical than the first. About 100 S.R.s and Social Democrats sat in it, but the government had also managed to elect about ninety supporters. The Cadets, though still in a majority, were thus squeezed much more by the extremists. It is not surprising that after three and a half months of life, this *Duma* was dissolved in June 1907 on the excuse that a great conspiracy had been discovered. Most of the Social Democrats were arrested and exiled. At the same time, the Fundamental Laws were modified; a system of indirect election was set up, and national representation was reduced in favour of Russians (the Poles, for example, losing twenty-two of their thirty-six seats).

The last two *Dumas* (1907–12 and 1912–17) were consequently more docile and more conservative. In part this was fortuitous; the *Zemstvos* tended to pass under conservative control and their representatives moved more and more to the right in each successive *Duma*. The ultra-conservative Union of the Russian People organized pogroms which could still command enthusiastic popular support, and revelations of police penetration threw the S.R.s into confusion. The national minorities were harried as their representation in the *Dumas* shrank.[9] Jews were deprived again of the franchise in *Zemstvo* elections in the western provinces. The Russian language was forced on Ukrainian schools and Polish town councils. In 1910 the Finnish constitution was again attacked.

This did not make traditionalists like Stolypin more. He was frequently opposed and criticized at court and the State Council tried to reject his law on the western *Zemstvos*. In part this was due to the personal intrigues which always flourished around Nicholas. In part it must also have stemmed from Stolypin's greatest achievement, the agrarian reform which probably changed Russia even more than had the events of 1905. He sought

9 Over one-third of the members of the first *Duma* were non-Russians.

to liberate the peasant finally from the commune, breaking completely with the traditional policy of seeing in the commune protection for the peasant and an institution making for social stability. Since 1898 much preparatory work had been done which provided information to justify reform, above all in Witte's great agricultural enquiry of 1902–3. 1905 made a change possible by shaking the whole country with agrarian disturbances. One of Stolypin's first steps was to cancel all arrears of redemption payments. There then followed a series of measures which by 1911 had abolished joint family holdings, made possible individual ownership and the consolidation of strips and gave assistance to peasants who wished to buy their own land (though a completely unregulated market in land was not established). By 1917 a big transference to individual ownership had taken place. Regional variations make generalizations difficult but probably 3 million peasants had obtained proprietary rights over their strips and emancipation from the commune. Although much remained to be done, this was a great achievement. Finally, Stolypin's reform removed the legal hindrances which prevented the peasant from moving to the cities.

Like Witte, Stolypin was disliked by those whom he served. He was assassinated in 1912 and the tsarina said, 'He is gone, let us hear no more of him'. Yet he had broken the back of the worst problem facing the country; as a result of what he had done, grain production at last began to rise more quickly than population. He had mastered the left and restored order, but it would probably not have recommended him to the court that he had also spent more on primary education (or that literacy had dramatically improved since the 1890s). He was succeeded by an unremarkable bureaucrat under whom strikes again became frequent. In 1913 even the fourth *Duma* censured the government for continuing the state of exceptional law. On the eve of war an isolated court, open to corrupt and damaging influences ruled a country which had begun, slowly, to change its institutions after one great crisis had shaken them. Still very backward in some ways, with an enormous gap separating its rulers from a country which now distrusted them, in 1914 Russia was at last beginning to move into modern history. Unhappily, it also faced its greatest test – the ordeal of war – under a regime which may already have squandered its last opportunities for the peaceful management of constitutional change.

THE HABSBURG MONARCHY

The Habsburg Monarchy made much of historic rights and traditions, yet it was based on a compromise made as recently as 1867. This compromise created four entities: 'Austria'[10] and Hungary were distinct constitutional monarchies, an economic union also existed between them which bound them for ten years at a time, and there was a 'common monarchy' which was the great power recognized by Europe as the heir of the old Habsburg Empire and often called the Dual Monarchy. Its apparatus of government was small. There were three ministries (for war, finance and foreign affairs), two bodies called 'Delegations' which met to authorize the estimates of the ministries, and the ruler himself and his court. Even Franz Joseph, emperor since 1848, only gave a personal union to two distinct offices. In Vienna an emperor, he was in Budapest a king; when some of his Hungarian subjects appealed to him at Vienna for protection from their Magyar rulers, they were told that the emperor could not entertain petitions from subjects of the king of Hungary. A constitutional crisis occurred when the particle was omitted from the title *Kaiser und König*, so determined were the Magyars that the two roles should remain distinct.

Inside this odd structure there survived a tradition of divine right and dynasticism. The Dual Monarchy was the dynastic state *par excellence*, indeed it existed only to serve the interests of the dynasty. The only link between its provinces was the personal sovereignty of the ruler. They had no social, racial or geographical cohesion. Their function, in the eyes of Franz Joseph, was to supply the necessary backing for the dynasty's historic role as a great power. Foreign policy was the justification of the Monarchy; almost every important change within Habsburg lands for a century or more had been the result of a need to meet a new crisis in foreign affairs. This was all the more ominous in 1880 because the shape of the Empire made it an immediately interested party in two major problems, the control of the mouths of the Danube and the nature of the régimes which were to replace Turkish rule in the Balkans. Because the emperor strove to

10 Which, strictly speaking, did not exist. The official designation of the part of the Monarchy which we call 'Austria' was 'the kingdoms and lands represented in the *Reichsrath*'.

subordinate the internal affairs of the Monarchy to foreign policy, the domestic problems of the Monarchy mattered to Europe. In the end Europe went to war over the most intractable of them, the nationalities question. Between 1880 and 1914 the politics of the Monarchy were above all the politics of national rivalry. Dualism itself was a recognition of this; it was an attempt to accommodate the national principle in a supernational structure. The dynasty had agreed in 1867 to share power with the Magyars who ruled Hungary. Almost at once, other nationalities had begun to press for recognition. But it always proved impossible to meet their demands without disturbing the balance set up in 1867.

National problems differed in the two parts of the Monarchy.[11] 'Austria' curved like a great bow to form the northern borders of the Monarchy and ran from Illyria, up through the Tyrol and Austria proper to Bohemia and, far in the east, to Galicia, Lodomeria and the Bukovina. It had no unity except that of history. Its major selfconscious peoples were Germans, Czechs and Poles. The Germans regarded themselves as peculiarly identified with the dynasty and a superior culture; they felt endangered by Slav numbers and pretensions. They had often tried to exploit their favourable position in the civil service and towns in order to Germanize the other races. In this they conflicted with the Czechs of the old kingdom of Bohemia, the only Slav people in the Monarchy which was urbanized, industrialized and advanced. Essentially their quarrel with the Germans was one of language: was German or Czech to be the language of administration – and therefore the test for government jobs? The Czechs had been the first people to claim, immediately after the Compromise, a status analogous to that of Hungary within the Empire. The Polish landowners of Galicia did not seek the same recognition because they enjoyed a high degree of *de facto* Home Rule. They were a long way across the mountains and they were Roman Catholics, unlike their Ruthene peasants who were also Slavs, but mainly Orthodox. The Ruthenes might look to Russia for support. This fact, and the memory of the risings of 1846 in Galicia against the Polish gentry, was usually enough to keep the Poles loyal. In Illyria, Italians, Croats and Slovenes balanced one another and propaganda for unity of Croats and Serbs in a South Slav movement had not yet begun really to be effective.

11 See p. 27 for some figures.

Hungary consisted of the lands of the Crown of St Stephen, enlarged by the addition of Croatia-Slavonia and the military frontiers. Here racial divisions were more embittered. In the old Hungarian kingdom, the Magyars ruled big minorities of Rumanians, Ruthenes, Slovaks and Germans. The Magyars simply disregarded other races and regarded Hungary as a purely Magyar concern, combining political and social and economic hegemony in what has been described as 'four Irelands instead of one'.[12] But at least Magyars were there the biggest single group, and by 1914 over half the total. Across the Drave, in Croatia-Slavonia, the situation was very different. There the Magyars were an insignificant one-tenth of the Croat and Serb population. This demanded some formal recognition and a subordinate 'Compromise' had in fact been negotiated between Budapest and Zagreb. None the less, Magyars dreaded the prospect of Slav consolidation. They encouraged rivalry between Serb and Croat and wanted no more Slavs in the Monarchy. Magyars were especially opposed to the further integration of Bosnia and Herzegovina, whose population was completely Slav although divided confessionally into Muslims and Orthodox Christians.[13]

It was the strength and weakness of the Dual Monarchy in 1880 that no nationality was identified with the *status quo* except the Magyars. All the others had something to hope for from the dynasty; none of them rejected the dynastic framework in 1880. This expectancy justified the dynasty's policy of never identifying itself irrevocably with one nationality but of maintaining an 'equilibrium of discontent'.[14] In this it was supported by the great nobles who had weak ties with the localities and strong ones with the court, by the bureaucrats, and by the army. As the Great War was to show, the army was reliable, multinational though it was. Precisely because of this, of course, it was (except in the eyes of the Magyars) above the national struggle. All nationalities could expect good careers in it; though German was the language of command, this meant in practice a vocabulary of only about sixty words. In training, the language of those being instructed was employed. Because of this, the army did not suffer from quarrels

12 A. J. P. Taylor, in *Memoirs of Michael Karolyi* (London, 1956), p. 7.
13 For the sake of completeness, it may be added that Fiume too, was a separate 'associated body' of the Hungarian state.
14 H. Wickham Steed, *The Habsburg Monarchy* (London, 1913) p. 124.

such as those in local administration over the control of schools. Language was the usual issue about which the nationalities fought; in Hungary and Galicia the social oppression of an alien class of landlords was added to this.

In those areas the Dual Monarchy was an agrarian society almost as backward as Russia.[15] Even in the western provinces of the Monarchy there were still at the beginning of this century villages virtually untouched by the market economy, where families still span and wove to meet their own needs. Further east, what has been described as 'age-old tribal communism' could still be found.[16] The gap between these regions and urban Bohemia or the cultural élite of Vienna or Budapest was enormous. Violent contrasts of wealth intensified the bitterness of racial conflicts in Hungary. The emigrants who poured out of the Monarchy at the end of the nineteenth century came, for the most part, from Transylvania and the east, where wealth and poverty contrasted with an Asiatic sharpness. Small landowners were relatively few and poor. Less than a third of Hungary was owned by those cultivating their own land and most of these had less than the twenty acres necessary for a family's livelihood. Most peasants were wage-labourers on the great *latifundia*, over 300 of which averaged more than 40,000 acres each. One monster, the Esterhazy estate, had more than half a million acres and one bishopric possessed more than a quarter of a million. The lack of land of their own or the chance of obtaining it (even if money had been available, a great proportion of the land was entailed) combined with the lack of industrial employment to keep the peasants in crushing poverty. Landlords exploited this, exacting what was virtually forced labour and levies on draught animals in a manner barely distinguishable from the old days of serfdom. The social division even cut across racial ones; Magyar landlords were willing enough to use Ruthenian labour to force down the wages of their Magyar labourers. In such conditions, illiteracy was normal and infant mortality was higher even than in Spain. These conditions were defended by the political apparatus which controlled Hungary and Galicia.

An Austrian socialist leader once described the Dual Monarchy

15 In 1910 48.5 per cent of 'Austrians' and 64.5 per cent of Hungarians were engaged in agriculture.
16 Jászi, *The Dissolution of the Habsburg Monarchy*, p. 193.

as 'despotism tempered by slovenliness' and this gives a fair impression of the tone of its political life. Its institutions did not at once appear to be illiberal. Both halves of the Monarchy were, on paper, constitutional monarchies. But this was not how things worked. In the first place, Hungary had disproportionate influence in joint affairs; in the second, within Hungary the Magyars ruled non-Magyars who had no political influence. Finally, in the Austrian half of the Monarchy there survived a large element of unchecked executive power.

Hungary had disproportionate power because each part of the Monarchy elected equal numbers to the Delegations and they voted in joint session. The Hungarian Delegation was almost totally Magyar, while that from Austria consisted of deputies elected by provinces where different nationalities were preponderant. In consequence, if there were a common session, the Magyars would not have to do more than win the support of one of the minority groups within the Austrian Delegation to obtain a majority. In fact, the Delegations never *did* meet together (though they could have done) and ministers could therefore always rely on them if they took the trouble to square the Magyars first; this gave Hungary a virtual veto on all common affairs.[17]

As for Magyar domination of non-Magyars, within Hungary, only the Croats had some autonomy in local affairs and a provincial Diet of their own, but even in Croatia, Magyar influence maintained itself by exploiting quarrels between Croat and Serb. Elsewhere in Hungary in 1914 only 6.5 per cent of the population had the vote; almost all of these were Magyar since the Magyar language was a qualification. A high illiteracy rate excluded even the poorer Magyars, so that elections were in fact controlled by the gentry. They elected a bewildering number of groups and factions, often called 'liberal' and they had a running quarrel with the magnates, but this threatened the Magyar hegemony no more than the bickering of gentry and great borough-mongers threatened the eighteenth-century Whig oligarchy in England.[18] In this situation the party leaders had great power;

17 True though this was, of course, it was not enough for the Magyar left, who sought to overthrow the 1867 Compromise.
18 The parallel is worth pressing a little because of the identification in each case of class and national interests. Hungary, too, was very anglophile in its tastes; English tailors and hunters were much esteemed.

they could bully the crown with the threat to refuse to renew the economic union or to vote money for the common army. Their followers drew the benefit of this in many ways. In 1913 less than half the total Hungarian population was Magyar, but over 80 per cent of all students graduating from high school in Hungary were Magyars, and over 95 per cent of government officials.

Many foreign observers were deceived by the parliamentary hubbub of Hungary into thinking it a true constitutional monarchy. They usually thought less well of Austria: the police were more obvious there (though they hardly seem very tyrannical in retrospect). An officious bureaucracy left the rights of the individual not ill-respected in practice, though without real security. There was no savage persecution, but the freedom of the press was curtailed by bribery and menace. The right of association was conceded in principle, but restricted in practice. Judges were not independent of the executive and after 1886 juries were not used in political trials. Parliament is normally expected to attend to the defence of liberty in a constitutional state and the *Reichsrath* had, apparently, the powers needed to check the executive. But it did not do so. In their actual working, its powers were significantly limited. Ministers regarded themselves as the servants not of parliament but of the crown and were disciplined by the emperor if they did not. The provincial Diets could prevent the execution of the legislation by failing to make necessary consequential provisions. A complicated system of election produced a preponderance of landowners in the *Reichsrath*, too, which represented a broadly conservative influence favourable to the crown. Also, the national divisions of the *Reichsrath* meant that ministers were usually able to buy support by jobs or economic improvements; liberals would almost always sell out their liberalism in return for national advantages. Finally, even if the *Reichsrath* did resist, there was always the legal possibility of ruling by emergency decree.

Because of this, no force in either half of the Monarchy could carry the reforms needed if it were to continue to be a great power. Its finances were weak (in 1880 it had to raise loans at 70 per cent of par). A tariff which reflected the interests of Hungarian landlords hindered commercial and industrial progress. Progressive forces were held back by national divisions; even the Social Democratic movement spent its time quarrelling over the national distribution of jobs in its own bureaucracy. The monarch, perhaps, had the power to change things. Nor would this have accorded ill with Habsburg tradition: the dynasty had imposed brutal change in the past. Franz Joseph, hard-working and conscientious though he was, was not the man for this. He had grown up in the legitimist atmosphere of the Restoration and took the throne in the revolutionary year of 1848. The disasters of his reign had left him feeling that anything was justifiable if it were expedient for the dynasty. He had no hestitation about using all his power and told his advisers that the Empire could not be ruled in a constitutional manner. He clung to no principle, no policy, no adviser (the ingratitude of the Habsburgs was proverbial) a moment longer than he believed it suited the dynasty for him to do so. The potentially revolutionary will of the monarch was at the service only of a stiff, mechanical view of the Empire in which a concern for its peoples played no part. The nearest Franz Joseph came to affection for them was his respect for the dash and bearing of the Magyar aristocrats, whom he admired even when they opposed him. Unfortunately, also, he grew old in office and increasingly out of touch with realities; in his last years, unfavourable news was kept from him by his entourage.

The most successful of his ministers was Taaffe, who governed from 1879 to 1893. Taaffe came to power when the Germans had forfeited Franz Joseph's favour by opposing the incorporation of Bosnia and Herzegovina in the Monarchy. Imperial influence, aided by clerical and antisemitic prejudice against the German liberals, produced a *Reichsrath* of national groups. Taaffe saw himself first and foremost as the emperor's man, and controlled the *Reichsrath* through jobbery and concessions. His cabinets were all based on the 'iron ring' of Poles, German Roman Catholics, Czechs and Slovenes, whose nationalism he consciously attempted to hold in check by conciliation. The immediate danger came from the Czechs who were placated with administrative decentralization, a wider franchise and, above all, by making Czech as well as German an official administrative language in Bohemia.

Taaffe thus turned the Old Czechs into a constitutional party by showing them that the constitution they despised could be of use to them. The Polish landowners were complaisant so long as they were left free to dominate their Ruthenian peasants. Parliamentary life became a matter of deals and concessions, of *fortwursteln*, or 'bumbling along in the old grooves'. But there were other, younger nationalists coming along who were not so easily satisfied. A new extremism began to appear in Bohemia, where German and Czech had most to dispute. Alarm over concessions to the Czechs led to the alliance of Bohemian Germans with those of Syria and Carinthia. This found expression in the 'Linz programme' of 1882, which demanded guarantees for the Germans, the breaking of all but the personal link with Hungary, and a radical approach to social reform. This lower middle-class, Slavophobe radical nationalism found expression also in the Christian socialism of Karl Lueger, a protest against Jews, capitalists and protestants from which Hitler was to learn much. Pan-German attempts to get the sympathy of Bismarck, none the less, were unsuccessful.[19]

Radical nationalism also produced 'Young Czechs' unsatisfied with Taaffe's concessions in Bohemia. In 1891 they won all the Bohemian seats in the *Reichsrath*, routing the 'Old Czechs' of the Iron Ring. This was the beginning of the end of Taaffe's system. When he began to consider universal suffrage as a way of checking middle-class nationalism, other groups of the Iron Ring also became alarmed and his parliamentary majority crumbled. Franz Joseph now deserted him and Taaffe resigned in October 1893. Under his rule, Czech nationality had become an entrenched reality which could not from this time be ignored.

Parliamentary confusion followed. Meanwhile the bureaucracy went on ruling the country and showing that the *Reichsrath* was really irrelevant. The attempt to find a parliamentary majority only produced another great row, the most serious yet, between Germans and Slovenes over the grammar school at Celje. When the government granted money for Slovene classes there, the Germans in the *Reichsrath* withdrew from the coalition and it broke up. Franz Joseph called to office Badeni, the Polish governor of Galicia, who carried an electoral reform to satisfy radicals and made a head-on attack on the German-Czech problem.[20] The crucial issue was still that of language. In 1897 Badeni decreed that Czech and German should be the languages of the 'inner service' in Bohemia: since all educated Czechs learnt German and few educated Germans learnt Czech, a near-

19 Nor did they prosper under Wilhelm II. Imperial Germany showed no interest in irredentists.
20 The electoral reform of 1896 added 5.5 m voters who elected 72 representatives. 1.7 m voters in the other four electoral *curia* elected 353.

monopoly of administrative employment was assured to the Czechs. The result was an outburst of German rioting which made the *Reichsrath* unworkable and led Franz Joseph to dismiss Badeni. Non-parliamentary government now began in earnest. The budget and the new economic compromise with Hungary were promulgated by decree. Between 1897 and 1904 the special powers of legislation were used ninety-seven times. But the national struggle remained deadlocked. In 1899 Badeni's ordinances were withdrawn and it was the turn of the Czechs to riot.

In this disorder the Monarchy moved towards its greatest crisis since 1867. The extremists were encouraged by the Austro-Russian *entente* which allowed them to feel that the Monarchy could be attacked without risk, since its primary purpose, protection against Russia, was in abeyance. In the Austrian half of the Monarchy, from 1901 to 1904, government could not pass any major business through the *Reichsrath*. No budget was voted in 1903, 1904 or 1905. Outside parliament, radical forces were growing in strength. The emperor had at last to accept Lueger as mayor of Vienna. But 'Christian Socialism' was itself under pressure from the Austrian Social Democrats, who pressed for political reforms. They already had eleven seats in the *Reichsrath*. Increasingly the scheme rejected under Taaffe came to seem more attractive to government: a franchise reform might get parliament working again and universal suffrage offered a way for the dynasty to escape from the middle-class politicians. A crisis in Hungary led to the threat that universal suffrage would be imposed there; after this, Austria had to wait only until 1907 for the same recipe to be applied. In that year a new *Reichsrath* was elected by universal suffrage. It was still unfairly biased against some nationalities, but Ruthenians, Polish radicals, Czechs and Slovenes all won more seats, while the Pan-Germans and German radicals lost heavily. The two largest parties in the new Chamber were the Christian Socialists and the Social Democrats. Lueger's party carried rural Austria, while the Social Democrats defeated nationalists in Bohemia. Unfortunately, the Socialists were themselves more and more divided internally on national lines and in 1910 a Czech Social Democrat Party broke away from the German-dominated Austrian Socialists.

The passing of the Austrian budget closed the constitutional crisis. It had already ended in Hungary, where it had been much fiercer. Dominated still in the 1880s by the ever-fascinating and distracting topic of reforming or preserving the Compromise, Magyar politics had been diverted in the 1890s by the question of civil marriage. Meanwhile Magyarization had gone on in the world of administration and business. This concealed the growth of a yet more extreme Magyar nationalism, deplored by the old leaders, which made it difficult to renew the economic union of 1897. In 1902 the extremists, rallying around the young Kossuth, whose name was the symbol of patriotism, refused to pass the estimates unless their demands for the further Magyarization of the army were met. In the resulting deadlock, the army bill was withdrawn. Another Magyar with a great name, the son of Tisza, formed a government and failed to overcome the violence and obstruction of the parliamentary opposition. His defeat in the elections of January 1905 brought the crown and Hungarian parliament into outright conflict. In the crisis, the Monarchy suddenly showed what powerful resources it possessed. The Hungarian parliament was dispersed by a troop of soldiers, the new commercial treaty was put into effect by decree and the introduction of universal suffrage was proposed. The last threat terrified the Magyars. The lack of public protest against the Monarchy's coup showed the impossibility of their obtaining more support. They had to come to heel if they were to keep the support of the dynasty against the subject races. A new coalition was formed and the Compromise was renewed. The cynicism of this pact revealed how little the subject nationalities had to hope for from the crown. In 1908 a suffrage bill for Hungary became law. It did not concede universal suffrage but by means of literacy tests and plural votes kept political power firmly in the hands of the better-off Magyars.

From the emperor's point of view, nevertheless, the corner had been turned. The old alliance of dynasty and Magyars had been renewed. But the national struggle went on in Bohemia, the danger of social democracy was only held back by national rivalries inside the movement and a new problem, with far-reaching international implications, was coming to overshadow all others. When the cultural unity of the south Slavs had been first stressed in the 1870s, the effects had not been great. The Croats, predominantly Roman Catholic, continued to dislike and distrust the Orthodox Serbs, and their divisions were exploited by the Magyars. This tactic, combined with the concessions made to the Croats (see above) proved adequate until the twentieth century.

Europe 1880–1945

In 1903 there were serious disorders in Croatia and great discontent was caused by the emperor's refusal to receive a deputation from Istria and Dalmatia which wished to represent the grievances of their fellow-Slavs in Croatia. Then in 1905 a conference of Croat politicians at Fiume asked for reforms and the uniting of the Croat provinces in both halves of the Monarchy. They won support among some Serbs who were prepared to envisage an autonomous South Slav state within the Monarchy.

Serbs and Croats were at this time together supporting the Magyars in the Budapest parliament against the government of the day, expecting, in return, concessions if the Magyars were successful. This illusion was dispelled by the new Compromise between the Magyars and the dynasty. The Croatian Diet was dissolved by royal decree. The possibility of a sympathetic hearing for the South Slavs in Vienna had already vanished; the reason is to be found in foreign affairs and the mounting fears of German Austrians.

Serbia, in 1881 virtually a Habsburg satellite, had in the twentieth century come to be viewed very differently in Vienna.[21] In 1903 a change of dynasty coincided with a new Russophile trend in Serbian foreign policy. A new awareness appeared among Slavs that Serbia might be the core around which the eventual unity of the South Slavs could be built. The Dual Monarchy reacted with alarm and treated the new Serbian dynasty with hostility. In 1906, in the interests of the landlords, a 'Pig War' began over the renegotiation of tariff agreements between Serbia and the Monarchy; Serbian agricultural produce was excluded and pressure was brought to bear upon the Serbs to buy arms from the Austrian Skoda works, The tariff war was not ended until 1908 and by that time the repression in Croatia and disillusionment with the renewed Compromise was drawing the attention of some of the South Slav subjects of the Monarchy to the possibility of making common cause with their fellow-Slavs in Serbia. Unfortunately the statesmen of the Monarchy (especially the Magyars), thought things were worse than they really were and detected in Serbia a 'Piedmont of the South Slavs'. Such a belief led to talk of a preventive war against Serbia, to crush her independence (though not to absorb her, because that would add more racial problems to the existing ones).

21 On what follows, see also pp. 266–8.

This was the context of the Austrian annexation of Bosnia-Herzegovina, which transformed the South Slav question because it appeared to Serbia as a deliberate attempt to erect another barrier between her and the sea. And Russia now stood, ultimately, behind Serbia. The atmosphere worsened. In 1909 two notorious episodes occurred. The first was the trial at Zagreb of Serbo-Croat leaders accused of plotting with Serbia. Convicted on forged evidence, they were acquitted on appeal. The next was the discrediting of the evidence (supplied by the Austrian foreign office) on which the historian Friedjung had based an article attacking the Serbo-Croat leaders for intriguing with Serbia. When he was sued for libel and lost, the Austrian foreign office made matters worse by saying it had never been influenced by a belief in a Serbo-Croat conspiracy. In this tense atmosphere, the myth became a reality. Especially in Bosnia, terrorist organizations began to carry out attacks on Habsburg officials. The most famous organization was the Black Hand; founded in 1911, it marked the beginning of an intensive phase of Serbian terrorism, connived at by the Serbian government. The Balkan Wars opened a new stage of the South Slav problem. Serbia, a victor, appealed more than ever to South Slavs inside the Dual Monarchy and Austrian diplomacy encouraged Bulgaria to attack Serbia in the second war. The visits of Croat students to Belgrade, and further assassination attempts, led to renewed demands in the Dual Monarchy for a preventive war against Serbia. Almost the last opposition to be overcome was that of Tisza; he at last agreed because of the violence of the Serbian press. At Sarajevo, Princip and his superiors would take only the final step.

The South Slavs were not the only irredentists in 1914. Ruthene nationalism had developed in a more Russophile direction. Turned first against the Poles (the Polish governor of Galicia was murdered in 1898 by a Ruthene), Ruthenian nationalism became more pro-Russian and Orthodox as there emerged in Galicia and the Bukovina an anti-Russian Ukrainian nationalist movement. Universal suffrage increased Ukrainian representation and the Austrian government showed the Ukrainians some benevolence. This only made the Ruthenes more susceptible to irredentist influence, and led to the familiar sight of new, more radical leaders supplanting the loyalist old Ruthene nationalists. The Russians were aware of this, although they did little to encourage it. Their activity in famine relief in Galicia in 1913–14 alarmed the authorities, none the less, as did the missionary activities of Orthodox clergy. Ruthenes were punished for pro-Russian activity in Hungary, where another problem had appeared by 1914 because of Rumanian anger at ruthless Magyarization in Transylvania. In 1910, nearly 3 million Rumanians had only five deputies in the Hungarian parliament. By 1913 the Austrian chief of staff already reckoned that Rumania had been lost to the Triple Alliance by the Magyars. Such a tangling of domestic and foreign affairs was by 1914 too elaborate for there to be an easy way out. True, few among the subject nationalities had given up the hope of solving their problems within the Dual Monarchy and it was not in danger of immediate collapse. But to some only violence seemed available as a solution.

IMPERIAL GERMANY

The energy of Imperial Germany impressed contemporaries; nowhere else were an industrial revolution and a surge of population so swiftly and evidently followed by diplomatic preeminence and social progress. This dynamism persisted right down to 1914. In some ways it even grew more marked: the foreign trade figures show their fastest advance after the 1890s.[22] By 1914 Germany had to import more industrial raw material for her factories than did Great Britain. She produced a third of the world's electrical goods and her domination of this new industry had already in 1881 given her electric trams before anyone else and a telephone system more advanced than that of any other country. Though the birth rate began to fall in 1904 (as it had done elsewhere), this did not endanger Germany's military superiority over France and the population still grew. Moreover, it was young; over a third of Germans were under fifteen in 1914. The great flow to the cities produced a huge industrial proletariat, yet

22 Germany's foreign trade (in millions of marks):

	Exports	Imports
1880	2.977	2.844
1890	3.410	4.273
1900	4.753	6.043
1910	7.475	8.934
1913	10.097	10.770

standards of living rose. Food imports quadrupled between 1880 and 1912 and in 1914 imports met one-fifth of Germany's needs. Although about a third of the labour force than worked in agriculture, immigrant labour was still needed in the east, where protective tariffs encouraged the cultivation of bigger areas. In the countryside, society did not greatly change, but in the towns the increase in the labour force of the service industries, the rise in material wellbeing and a growing middle class showed that Germany was acquiring the social structure of a mature industrial economy. The scientific and technical skills which sustained it were based on a superb educational machine. The traditions of German scholarly pre-eminence had been transmitted to new studies. Between 1870 and 1900 expenditure on the Prussian polytechnic institutions quintupled, but education was cheap to the student. Study for a scientific degree at Berlin at the end of the century cost the student only £22 a year, all laboratory fees included. Educational opportunities of this sort not only produced men like Röntgen, Planck, Einstein and Wundt, but also a big literate population. The weekly *Berliner Illustrierte Zeitung* already sold nearly 2 million copies of each issue by 1914.

Such impressive vitality might have produced the social and economic base for a highly self-confident, *laissez-faire* and middle-class state run on constitutional and parliamentary lines. History seemed to point in this direction. Germany was a new nation, united only since 1871, and without a strong autocratic tradition focused on one well-established dynasty. Adult male suffrage elected the *Reichstag*; opposition candidates often polled huge numbers of votes cast by secret ballot and could campaign freely. The government could be outvoted in the *Reichstag* which shared the legislative power with a Federal Council (Bundesrat). The rule of law was upheld by the courts. The structure of the Empire was federal not unitary; it consisted of four kingdoms, five grand-duchies, six duchies, six principalities, three free cities and the Imperial territory (*Reichsland*) of Alsace-Lorraine. The adoption of the title 'German Emperor' in preference to 'Emperor of Germany' emphasized the strength of local attachments. Finally, the beneficiary of this constitution seemed to be the common man: the welfare legislation of Imperial Germany was the admiration of the world.

Yet for all that, and although she appeared liberal by comparison with the tsarist autocracy, Imperial Germany cannot be reckoned a constitutional state in any but a formal sense. There was a conflict of appearance and reality; German political life was based on a sham constitutionalism. This was mainly because of Prussian predominance inside the Empire. Geography (Prussia made up five-eighths of the total area of the new state), population and economic strength all told in the same direction. So did prestige; Prussian arms had excluded Austria from Germany and had won the victories which created the Empire in 1871, so realizing at last the liberal hopes of 1848. But those victories had been won for particularism and predominance, too; old-fashioned Prussians only tolerated a united Germany because it was to be managed by the house of Hohenzollern. Prussian officials ran the imperial bureaucracy and the railways. The armies of the other states were integrated with the Prussian even if they wore different uniforms. The chancellor of the Empire, Bismarck, was also prime minister of Prussia. He presided over the *Bundesrat* of representatives of each state and was its spokesman. The position of Prussia in the constitution gave its rulers a built-in veto on change in the federal structure.

Secondly, German constitutionalism was a sham because social and political life were shot through with institutions and assumptions suited to an autocratic government. The *Reichstag*, for example, was certainly free to debate, and could even reject, the budget; but could not coerce the imperial government so long as the Prussian parliament stood behind the Prussian army. The ministers themselves were not responsible to the *Reichstag*, but to the emperor. Nationalists, too, were willing to justify the special position of the Prussian army because a German state surrounded by jealous neighbours supposedly depended upon force for its survival. The practical consequence was that effective power in the last resort rested with the Prussian ruling class, the Junker aristocracy, its position safeguarded by a restricted electoral system in Prussia. This conservative class tied Germany's destiny to its own special agrarian and military interests.

The crucial factor was the Prussian army. The prestige of the officer corps was high and it succeeded in stamping the middle-class material and aristocratic *Weltanschauung*.[23] Their oath of loyalty gave officers a special relationship with the emperor and

23 In 1913 70 per cent of the officers were non-nobles, but only 48 per cent of the generals and colonels.

they violently rejected control by 'civilians' through a war minister who could be questioned in the *Reichstag*. The power of the purse was never an effective instrument of control because, in the first place, Bismarck succeeded in 1880 and 1887 in having a military budget passed to cover seven years, and secondly because, as the international situation became more tense, and as the taste for world power spread through all classes of society, no politician, even those on the far left, was prepared to jeopardize the security of the nation by impairing the army's efficiency. In the end, this was disastrous, because it led to irresponsible military interference in the making of policy. Even under Bismarck, though the army could be controlled, its preeminence fostered the spread of military attitudes and discipline which suffocated liberalism at its roots. True parliamentary government was impossible.

Although there were always protests about militarism, these forces in part explain why the German middle class never sought to control the state as did its English equivalent. This was not only because it could not; it was also because many of its members did not want to. Although criticism never died out completely, the abdication of German liberalism after unification is still curious. In part it is explained by the immense diplomatic and economic success of the new state; a culture impressed by the concept of efficiency could not be expected to resist them completely. Other cultural forces also made for acceptance of the Empire's sham constitutionalism; the cult of monarchy had often been pressed to ludicrous extremes in Germany; religious pluralism had led German clerics to emphasize their dependence on secular power; and there had never been a strong native liberal tradition based on respect for individual rights (which were not guaranteed in the constitution). It was also important that many members of the middle class feared revolution and were not themselves likely to be personal victims of authoritarianism. Finally, international tension emphasized the importance of safeguarding unity before liberty and also helps to explain the traditional distrust of political parties – divergence of political aims within a consensus about ends was not part of the tradition of German political thinking.

Whatever its origins, the results of the failure of middle-class liberalism in Germany were obvious. The government was always ready to turn excitedly to special repressive measures. In

1880, for example, Hamburg and other towns were placed in a state of siege, and the Berlin police were rummaging booksellers' shops for copies of works written by Heine forty years before. There is therefore a deep paradox in the history of Imperial Germany. On the one hand, the state was deeply conservative, and sometimes even brutally illiberal. On the other, it managed to contain dynamic forces which in other states caused huge social changes, yet did so while offering material benefits to its subjects which went far beyond those possible in constitutional states. The architect of this success was the first imperial chancellor.

Bismarck was a Prussian country gentleman, whose whole life, after a few years of youthful aberration, had been spent in the service of the Prussian monarchy. He was sensitive, highly intelligent, and could be charming. Long practical experience of diplomacy and his natural endowments made him the most formidable statesman of his day. He brought these qualities to bear on German political life and by 1880 seemed indispensable. He knew his power and used it; in that year the English *Annual Register* commented drily that 'a resignation of Prince Bismarck must now be apparently accepted as a necessary incident of the year's history'.[24] He had the weaknesses sometimes associated with such talents; his love of sheer virtuosity and confidence sometimes took him to the borders of the irresponsible, he was temperamentally unstable, easily excited and easily wounded in his vanity. But the ship seemed to go steadily ahead so long as he was at the helm.

Bismarck was deeply religious and fervently reactionary; since 1848 he had feared the Revolution. The Commune impressed him with the dangers of the growing cities. The existing order could be threatened, he felt, by a foreign war or a lack of grip at home. The preservation of Prussia was the supreme aim of his politics. He did not believe in parties as a means to this end, because no party, he thought, could represent both Prussia and Germany. Because of the sectional interests behind them, party leaders were bound to be unpatriotic, and to neglect the national interest. This national interest was a reality for Bismarck because a united Germany was for him a way of saving Prussia by putting her at its head. He accepted the social implications of this: the Junkers were to be preserved too, because Prussia could not live without her army. They did not like a united Germany, with its liberal-

24 p. 175.

looking institutions and windy nationalist rhetoric, but Bismarck was able to make them accept it as a means of preserving their power, even if this meant alliances with and concessions to other classes. Bismarck's technique, therefore, was necessarily one of balance. Abroad, everthing was subordinated to the overriding needs of European stability in the interests of the conservative powers. The aim was tranquillity; 'my map of Africa is in Europe' was Bismarck's first response to demands for a forward policy in colonial matters.[25] At home, too, tranquillity was the aim and the chancellor would construct coalitions of startling diversity providing they helped to stem the tide of democracy and to keep Prussia on top. In both foreign and domestic affairs, the balance of power was maintained by a sort of Bismarckian dictatorship, in which he used to the full the irresponsible power which he possessed (under the crown) to make sure that no group got advantages over another which would destroy the balance.

The 'parties' which made the *Reichstag* look like a real parliament were sectional and particular in their nature, rather than national. They were not combinations to form governments, but the exponents of special interests. The 'Conservatives', essentially an agrarian and Prussian party, contained the supporters of throne and authority, old-fashioned, militarist, anticapitalist, and based on the lands east of the Elbe, many of them opposing Bismarck's concessions to nationalism and liberalism. The 'Free Conservatives' (who gradually fused with the Conservatives after the mid-seventies), supported him and represented non-Prussian landlords and, increasingly, industry. The 'National Liberals', losing ground by 1880, had been the admirers of Bismarck's services to nationalism, but disliked his antiliberalism: it was in 1880 the nearest German equivalent to a party of the middle class and it was to become a little more national, and a lot less liberal, as the years went by. It had split in 1879, its left wing melting into the 'progressives', where Bismarck's most determined opponents within the constitutional parties stood up for the principles of 1848 (and even of 1789), opposed socialism and drew support from the commercial middle class and intellectuals. Two other parties stood outside this spectrum. The Centre Party, not originally a confessional party, had come to be the party of Catholicism. The Social Democrats, or S.P.D., were orthodox Marxists,

25 See G. Craig, *From Bismarck to Adenauer* (Baltimore, 1958), p. 24.

drawing support almost entirely from the urban working class. Both were regarded by Bismarck as enemies of the Reich, owing allegiance to other sovereigns, the Papacy and the International. Ideology was joined by Protection as the guiding thread to party politics in Bismarck's last decade. In 1879 an imperial tariff announced the abandonment for free trade in the interests of heavy industry and the grain-growing farmers. Both thereafter enjoyed the protection of high import duties. Soon, the old Prussian landed interest, middle-class industrialists and the Centre Party were able to make common cause in supporting Bismark, who began to close-down the long-running *Kulturkampf* with the Catholics. The agrarians assured his control of the Prussian parliament, and industrialists soon began to withdraw their traditional support from the National Liberals, who were badly defeated in the 1881 elections. From this time, the Progressives more and more represented liberalism, while Bismarck tried to create his own National Liberal party on conservative lines. But he also wanted to avoid dependence on the Centre, which he distrusted because of its non-Prussian roots. Meanwhile two opposition groups were building up their strength outside the conventional political arena. The first of these was a small group of die-hard conservatives, influential at the Prussian court, and led by the court chaplain, Stöcker. The second, and in the long run immeasurably the more important, was the S.P.D.

Recruiting to the S.P.D. was helped both by the higher food prices which followed from protection and by the tradition of state paternalism in Germany. The idea of central control of economy and society was not *eo ipso* objectionable to many Germans. Bismarck's reply to the growth of socialism was repression. Two attempts to assassinate the emperor helped him to persuade the *Reichstag* to pass legislation forbidding socialist meetings and assemblies; socialist newspapers and presses were closed and trade unions banned. Soon afterwards Bismarck moved to the offensive on another front. The poor, he said, 'must be led to look upon the state not as an agency devised solely for the protection of the better-situated classes of society but also as one serving their needs and interests.'[26] The practical expression of this was welfare legislation; before the end of the decade sickness and accident insurance and old age pensions had all been introduced.

26 See Pinson, p. 241.

By 1911 nearly 14 million Germans were insured against sickness or disablement.

Yet the S.P.D. continued to grow; the 300,000 voters of 1881 became a million and a half in 1890. Bismarck's policy was unsuccessful. It seemed that if new social and political forces did not – like the liberal middle class – come to terms with the ruling caste, and satisfy themselves with the scraps thrown to them, they would survive – like the socialists – in quasi-revolutionary opposition to the established order. Part of the cost of Prussian supremacy was that Germany entered the industrial age without the political organization it needed. She was, as one liberal said, an 'industrial nation in the political garb of the agrarian state'.[27] It was a corollary of this that Bismarck had failed to educate Germans politically. 'At that time', the historian Meinecke said later, talking of 1883, 'politics played no role at all in our conversation for Bismarck seemed to do everything well and properly.'[28] Because the *Reichstag* did not offer a road to office, able men neglected politics for business or learning. Bismarck was the only indispensable part of the machine; power had to be concentrated in his hands because only he could achieve the elaborate balancing which was required. He was to blame because, after him, the constitution left a vacuum of power to be filled by William II and because he left a nation accustomed to submit. The Germans were less able to control power after twenty years of Bismarck than they had been in 1871.

Some people hoped that Frederick III (who succeeded to the throne in 1888) would set up a liberal empire. His liberalism remains dubious and his reputation may have been fortunate in the occasion of his tragic death from cancer, after a reign of only 180 days. William II, who followed him, was content to let Bismarck continue, and from the chancellor's point of view a dangerous corner seemed to have been turned. But his relations with the new emperor soon deteriorated. The young man felt neglected and slighted by the old statesman. They disagreed about the way to meet the socialist menace. Bismarck wanted to provoke the socialists to violence and smash them; the emperor cherished vague hopes of more social reform. Bismarck's enemies at court did not miss the opportunity to widen the breach; Stöcker, the chaplain, disliked Bismarck, and Waldersee, the chief

27 Naumann, see Pinson, p. 171.
28 See Meyer, *Mitteleuropa in German thought and action*, p. 47.

of the general staff, saw him as an obstacle to a preventive war with Russia. The crisis came over the emperor's demand that an old order limiting his direct access to his ministers should be rescinded. Bismarck resigned because he had no one to appeal to against the emperor's disfavour; he was the victim of his own creation, the constitutional machine which had to have an irresponsible dictator. No one tried to save him. His technique had been to ensure the survival of the organism he wished to preserve – the Prussian ruling class – not by modifying it, but by modifying the environment in which it lived. In the long run, the *tour de force* could be sustained neither at home nor abroad.

At the time, the change was played down. 'The course remains the same, full steam ahead', said the young emperor, and much of what followed indeed seemed to bear that out. Some euphoria was likely in the first years of a new reign, and understandable, given the continuing dynamism of German society. 800,000 people a year were being added to the population, and economic energy seemed more evident than ever. Nonetheless, there was a new note to be heard, that of *Weltpolitik*. The attitudes which surfaced in Germany in the 1890s were crystallizations of an evolution begun under Bismarck. They made euphoria dangerous. The 'place in the sun' which William had announced as his ambition for Germany made explicit in many Germans' minds their country's claim to a world role. Scholars and publicists began to encourage them to believe that Germany had unjustly been barred from such a role and that if this continued she would have to take her place in a world dominated by Great Britain, the United States, and Russia as a junior and inferior partner. One immediate outcome was a surge of interest in the acquisition of naval power – and, of course, such ideas were welcomed by German industry. The *Flottenverein* which provided propaganda in support of a big navy was founded by industrialists. Colonial expansion was another fashionable craze, supported by well-organized pressure groups and encouraged by the press. Such ideas about world-power status also fitted comfortably alongside a neo-mercantilist, nationalist strain in German economic thinking which looked forward to a *Mitteleuropa* organized under German leadership as a base for world-power status.[29]

29 See, on some of these ideas, the brief discussion of themes in Fischer, *Germany's Aims in the First World War*, pp. 7–11.

The dangers of such ideas only slowly became apparent. As Germany was an autocracy, the worst lay in the person of the emperor himself. Even now, it is not easy to do him justice. William II embodied, disastrously, the contradictions of his nation, torn between the new industrial and technological world of the future, and the feudal and romantic world of the past. He was temperamentally unstable, given to fits of depression and exultation. He preferred the ostentatious brandishing of power to its unobtrusive but effective use. A crowned dilettante, he soon dropped his taste for social reform (though the antisocialist laws were allowed to lapse) and was enraptured by battleships and uniforms. He was a man of phrases – 'the mailed fist', the 'Yellow Peril' – and could not resist a theatrical opportunity. The results were sometimes disastrous. He was tactless, both in his relations with his fellow monarchs (when, for instance, he visited King Victor Emmanuel with an escort of giant grenadiers who dwarfed his host) and in his relations with his subjects. Unfortunately, he was the ruler of the most powerful military state in the world.

His chancellors did not compensate for William's weaknesses. Caprivi (1890–94) was the best of them. Although a Prussian army officer, he sought concession and compromise. Significantly, he gave up the prime ministership of Prussia. He allowed the antisocialist laws to lapse, promoted the more liberal treatment of the Poles in East Prussia, and reduced the period of military service.[30] Above all, he modified the protective system by negotiating commercial treaties; he sought to stimulate industrial exports by conceding lower import duties on grain. When he resigned the Prussian conservatives were glad to see him go. His successors had nothing like such independence. Hohenlohe (1895–1900), a Bavarian, was too old and too tactful successfully to resist the forces seeking to influence the emperor; under him colonialism and 'navalism' established themselves at court, and the soldiers interfered more than ever. Bülow (1900–09) was a slippery flatterer, almost as theatrical as his master, who succeeded in becoming a conservative hero until he asked for death duties; the emperor was willing to let him go. His fall was the high-water mark of German parliamentarianism. Bethmann Hollweg (1909–17), a Prussian bureaucrat, took over when many fatal

---

30 But this was in order to get the *Reichstag* to vote funds for a bigger *total* number of soldiers.

decisions had already been taken, but proceeded to make a tragic outcome inevitable.

Down to 1914, in fact, irresponsibility and lack of central direction continued. 'Who rules in Berlin?' asked an Austrian in 1914, and asked with reason, given the power of special interests, especially the soldiers, to get their way. *Reichstag* votes could not control government: parliamentarianism remained a sham. This would have mattered less had William or his chancellor had clear aims but, said a foreign diplomat, 'In this highly organized nation, when you have ascended to the very top storey you find not only confusion but chaos'.[31]

This state of affairs favoured the *status quo* when, as the growth of socialist votes showed, constitutional reform was more and more urgently needed. The agrarian interest consolidated itself: the *Bund der Landwirte*, founded in 1893, united landlords in the east with peasants in the west and provided the organizational framework for a new, demagogic conservatism. In 1901 agricultural protection was still higher than that enjoyed by industry. The Centre party became more and more conservative because of the growing fear of socialism, and supported the imperial government in the *Reichstag* steadily after 1907. The treatment of Poles deteriorated and an Association of the Eastern Marches appeared in 1894 to promote a cultural 'Germanization'; a rise in the Polish nationalist vote was the result. Industrialists, impressed by the profits to be made by fleet-building, deserted liberalism more readily than ever after Tirpitz's foundation of the bureau of naval publicity in 1897. Meanwhile, the military tone of German life became more and more apparent, a striking example occurring in early 1914. A colonel had arbitrarily arrested and held in custody some civilians in the Alsatian village of Zabern. When the chancellor defended him in the *Reichstag*, the government lost a vote of confidence by 293 votes to 55. None the less, the colonel was acquitted by a court martial in a self-conscious assertion of the army's supreme position in the state.

This sort of thing depended on the acquiescence of many Germans whose culture made them tolerant of authoritarianism. After all, military attitudes seemed appropriate to the age of pan-Germanism, *Weltpolitik* and national self-assertion. Darwinian ideas were in the air, and popular in a Germany very conscious

31 See Viscount Haldane, *Before the War* (London, 1920), p. 71.

of its power to survive in the struggle of nations.[32] Publicists poured out rubbish about the German national mission; this happened elsewhere, but the Germans responded.[33] Racialism had more success than in other countries and a Gobineau society was set up to propagate it. *Völkisch* is a word with no English equivalent, and the ideology of the *Volk* linked Junker farmers and a lower middle class (with which they had nothing really in common) in a new, demagogic nationalism after 1900. The German right was henceforth always susceptible to irrationalism. In Germany the irrationalist currents of the age could draw on a tradition of philosophizing which left Germans less sceptical about high-sounding ideals than other nations. The youth movement was one example of this, but so was the repudiation of liberal values by one of the two cultural giants of Bismarckian Germany, Wagner (the other, Nietzsche, detested the Germany of Bismarck and went insane before he could judge its successor). Even the emperor, thought a British observer, was the 'creation of the Germans themselves. They wanted a sabre-rattling autocrat with theatrical ways, attempting to dominate Europe, sending telegrams and making bombastic speeches, and he did his best to supply them with the superman they required.'[34]

The liberal politicians lacked powerful social support. After losing the capitalists to the Conservatives and the townsmen to the S.P.D. or the Centre, they could provide little more than a journalistic opposition to army and ruling class. Distrust for universal suffrage (which Bismarck had exploited) made many of them unwilling to look to the masses, even if they had not been deterred by the Marxist programme adopted by the S.P.D. at the Erfurt Congress of 1891. Kautsky's ideas and Bebel's leadership made this a 'revolutionary party, but not a party that makes revolutions'.[35] Its growth had gone on steadily since 1891. Inn 1903, 3 million votes were given to socialist candidates and in 1912 4½ million. This was nearly 30 per cent of the electorate; the S.P.D. was the largest single party in the *Reichstag* of which it

---

32 Cf. the remark of Max Weber (who joined the Pan-German League): 'we alone made out of the Poles human beings'. See H. Kohn, *The Mind of Germany* (London, 1961), p. 283.
33 See, for example, some of the material analysed in Laqueur, pp. 43–7, and Fischer, pp. 32–3 for some bizarre comments by William II.
34 F. Ponsonby, *Recollections of Three Reigns* (London, 1951), p. 259.
35 See *NCMH*, XI, p. 281.

almost succeeded in electing Bebel the president. In 1908 it won six seats in the Prussian Diet. The historian Theodor Mommsen was one of the few middle-class figures who saw that hope might lie in the Socialists. In 1902 he said the S.P.D. was 'the only great party which can command political respect'. ('It is not necessary to speak of talent', he went on. 'Everybody in Germany knows that one head like Bebel's divided among a dozen Junkers would be sufficient to make each one of them appear brilliant in his own class.')[36] But its achievements were bound to be small if it would not contemplate revolutionary measures, and it could not. Its revisionist leaders were only too well aware of the hopelessness of mass risings in the teeth of an unshaken army. In 1914 patriotism was to draw the teeth of the party.[37]

The war was to show the Empire's strength and resilience. Yet it entered it with the mass of voters supporting the S.P.D. and the Centre, two parties formally opposed to the Prussian hegemony which was the *raison d'être* of the Empire. On the other hand, success and prosperity were never more apparent than in 1914, and nationalism and culture bound Germany together. The Zabern incident showed how little support public opinion would give to an attack on the soldiers, who, in the end, even treated the emperor with contempt. The war itself was probably more popular in Germany than anywhere else. But there is a qualifying footnote to be added. Imperial Germany was not Nazi Germany. With all its shams, the Empire still had a middle class which had not lost its savings and was not to be panicked into a total abandonment of civilized standards. The aristocrats who conducted government still shared many assumptions with their equals in other countries.[38] Germany was still conscious of herself as part of a European and Christian civilization and the grey-clad infantry who poured into Belgium had on their belt buckles the legend 'Gott mit Uns'. It was left to later generations of Germans to go back to paganism and the forest for their symbols and inspiration.

36 See Kohn, p. 186.
37 See ch. VII.
38 For an admirable dramatization of this, see Jean Renoir's film '*La Grande Illusion*', 1937.

7

ANTI-TRADITIONAL FORCES

INTELLECTUAL AND CULTURAL

In 1880 millions of Europeans still lived in a theocentric universe; whether they could put it clearly or not, they thought they believed in a God, and probably in the God of the Christian or Jewish faith. This was perhaps somewhat less true in 1914, but it was still then an important fact, easily overlooked. One reason it is sometimes overlooked is that we tend to write the history of ideas in terms of the innovators. That is sensible, in that the successful innovators put into circulation ideas which, in the long run, change society. But at the moment of their introduction they are likely to be taken up only by an 'advanced' intellectual elite, while the popular, widely diffused ideas which shape the ideas of many men are still those first noted generations before. This is one reason why it is hard to pin down the intellectual style of an era. What is more, thought about different human concerns changes at different speeds. Political and social thinking may be moving slowly while thinking in the natural sciences is changing very fast (this was, in fact, true in Europe for most of the years covered in this book). Some parts of the intellectual equipment of an age crumble while others are renewed. Each age of European civilization, too, has always carried in itself forces which begin to break it up even before it has worked out its full potential.

This helps to explain the paradox that though millions of traditionally-minded people still clung to their old beliefs and ways, much of educated Europe in 1880 was familiar with, and believed in, a culture whose roots can be sought in the eighteenth-century Enlightenment. It was corrosively sceptical, often materialist, confident in the power of human reason, and self-critical. Some people pressed this culture so far that they had even begun to undermine the critical certainties of the Enlightenment itself. Confident as the Forsytes and Buddenbrooks might be, their society was under unfriendly scrutiny, even in 1880: the challenge to its intellectual foundations had faced them for decades and was now to become more explicit than ever before.[1]

This challenge arose in part from inconsistencies in those foundations. The natural universe of the educated man in 1880 was that of Laplace: it obeyed regular and discoverable laws and consisted essentially of lumps of matter in various combinations and arrangements. It was in principle completely explicable and, therefore, completely subject to manipulation. The explaining and manipulation were the task of Man, the reasonable being, free to choose ends in an otherwise determined material universe. Some thinkers had quickly taken the next step in the argument: man himself was a natural object; he, too, must then be subject to the same determinism which ruled all other combinations of atoms. 'Naturalism' of this sort was to become much more common before 1914 but it was still not very widespread among educated men a generation earlier. Some were, it is true, aware of and impressed by certain special variants of determinist attacks on liberalism which had made themselves felt long before that date. Darwin died in 1882, Marx in the following year, and both had presented a view of history which emphasized the triviality of man's efforts to exercise rational will in resistance to the colossal forces of nature and society. Darwinian – or misrepresentations of Darwinian – ideas were imported into social and political thinking with great effect.

The undermining of this traditional view of the natural order was the great achievement of the natural sciences between 1880 and 1914, though it went almost unrecognized by the educated public until much later. What was much more obvious was the continuation of an older process. Earlier in the nineteenth century, scientists working within the traditional framework had, whether

1 *The Forsyte Saga* (London, 1906–21) is a cycle of novels by John Galsworthy, *Buddenbrooks: Verfall einer Familie* (Berlin, 1901) a novel by Thomas Mann.

they wished to or not, whittled away the foundations of popular religious and moral belief. After 1880 this process continued as the scientific ideas of the early nineteenth century percolated deeper in society. The prestige of science was enormous and understandable. Within a few decades, huge successes had been achieved in mastering and improving man's environment. By 1914, the practical applications of science had become obvious to the man-in-the-street. Electric street lighting and tramcars brought home the significance of electrical discoveries. In 1901 Marconi succeeded in transmitting radio messages across the Atlantic. Five years later, Santos-Dumont made the first man-carrying powered flight in Europe (of sixty-five yards) and aeroplanes were numerous by 1914. Passengers were by then already being carried in the big dirigible airships of von Zeppelin. Even such spectacular and important changes as these may well have done less to change widespread assumptions than the medical advances of these years. It is not too much to say that huge numbers of Europeans began to take for granted for the first time the idea that disease was not inevitable. The work of Pasteur contributed enormously to such a change in attitudes by opening the way to an effective bacteriology. There were many other advances which contributed indirectly to medical improvements – the identification of *Anopheles* in 1897 as the carrier of malaria, for example – and the enormous expansion of the chemical sciences was one source of them. Analgesic and anaesthetic preparations became far more effective and easily procurable. Aspirin was produced in 1897, to be followed shortly by Novocain, and the possibility was at last dimly apparent that pain itself might be rendered obsolete. In 1909 – to select almost arbitrarily from many important discoveries – came the synthesis of Salvarsan, a landmark not merely in the treatment of syphilis, but in the development of substances which make possible the selective destruction of infection.

Such advances as these undoubtedly won the attention of many educated people and led to the spread of an admiration for the natural sciences which was almost religious in its enthusiasm. It has been called 'scientism' and it marked much popular literature, above all the 'scientific' romances of writers from Verne to the young H. G. Wells. To many educated people it made no great difference, because their culture had already absorbed much of the achievements of natural science in the previous decades. But it was immensely important to a wider audience which for the first time became vividly aware of what science could do. This was another of the ways in which the nineteenth-century view of science may be said to come to its culmination between 1880 and 1914.

Yet just as this happened, another change was occurring. At the very moment when the nineteenth-century view of science was most widely acclaimed by a lay public, the shape of the scientists' universe was transformed. This was to lead to the overthrow of the nineteenth-century views and the 'scientism' based on them. The first casualties of the change were the prevailing assumptions that the ultimate constituent of physical reality was ordinary matter interacting with electromagnetic fields and that the task of science was to discover the natural laws which regulated them at both the atomic and the macroscopic levels. This was the background of the layman's world view, but by 1914 the scientist had abandoned it as a comprehensively satisfying scheme. As so frequently happens, a burst of observations and speculations had in a short time rapidly extended the demolition of traditional views. In 1895 Röntgen discovered X-rays and in the following year Becquerel explained the nature of radioactivity. Sir Joseph John Thomson identified the electron as a constituent of the atom in 1897, and the Curies isolated radium a year later. In the twentieth century came crucial experiments by Rutherford and Soddy. A historian of science writing in 1910 in the last volume of the *Cambridge Modern History* was able to present the consequences of these experiments to a non-scientific public in the words: 'it is impossible any longer to say that all chemical atoms are immutable, indestructible, eternal'.[2]

This was an epoch-marking change, though fully appreciated only by scientists. The fundamental assumption of nineteenth-century materialism, that the universe was ultimately made of tiny lumps of matter which might be distributed and rearranged in different patterns but which were themselves unchangeable and indestructible, had to be abandoned. The atom began to be understood as a tiny solar system of 'particles' (the identification and discovery of their variety was to be the main task of atomic physics for a half-century) in a particular arrangement. Moreover, these particles appeared to behave in a way which blurred the

2 *CMH*, XIII, p. 791.

established distinction between the behaviour of lumps of matter and that of electro-magnetic fields.

It was also discovered that these arrangements were not necessarily fixed but that in nature – for example, in radioactivity – elements were changed into other elements in that one arrangement of particles was replaced by another. If it occurred in nature, this process could, given adequate technical skill and resources, be reproduced experimentally. The reshaping of elements into other elements became possible and with it the tapping of an enormous source of energy. On this has been built the whole of modern nuclear engineering, both civil and military. It implied a revolution in the understanding of the natural order. Matter, the very stuff of the regular, manipulatable natural order of the positivists, had been replaced by the almost infinite variability of minute systems of energy.

These great experimental achievements were accompanied by theoretical innovations – above all, those of Relativity and Quantum theory – which were possibly even more radical in their philosophical and cosmological implications. Just as experimental progress had been the work of many men, so was theoretical. Because it depends on mathematical arguments which are highly abstract, it is almost impossible for the layman to grasp its significance and essence. Yet physics had taken its most important theoretical steps since Maxwell.

The new 'relativity' had nothing to do with ethical or moral relativism, but expressed the notion that 'space' and 'time', unexamined concepts of Newtonian physics, were themselves subjective concepts whose validity was related to the standpoints of particular observers. Instead of being words like 'birds' or 'fish', they were words like 'right' and 'left', or 'in front' or 'behind', in that their meaning could only be elucidated if the standpoint of the observer was taken into account. Space and time were to be apprehended by an observer who was himself a part of the world he observed. Only a 'continuum' of 'space-time' could henceforth be said to have objective validity. The same involvement of the observed with the observer also emerged from Quantum theory (whose development was to be mainly the work of the 1920s).[3] It showed that the observer could not observe the

3 In Quantum theory, the outstanding names are those of Planck, Heisenberg and Schrödinger; that of Einstein is better-known in connexion with Relativity.

universe without changing it. Such ideas were easily misapprehended when laymen tried to understand them. Their more ludicrous misrepresentations – such as the idea that light might 'bend' in space-time, or that continuous physical existence might be an illusion – were the features of them which made headlines later. Their philosophical and scientific importance was, however, truly revolutionary. Not only did they open the way to enormous advances in the knowledge of the physical universe, but they shattered the basis of old-fashioned deterministic materialism.

Other sciences than physics were also making great advances between 1880 and 1914 which were to help to damage the conventional world-picture of the nineteenth century. Some, too, were in the boundary areas between accepted fields of study. The discoveries in physics prompted physical chemists to study the molecular structures of their substances in new ways. Biochemistry matured as a subject in its own right. Genetics was transformed by the rediscovery at the turn of the century of Mendel's work.[4] Laymen were only aware of such more obvious applications of new biological knowledge as 'pasteurization', but long-established certainties about man and society were being undermined. The dethronement of humanity itself was under way.

The summarizing of European scientific advance between 1880 and 1914, may, nonetheless, be misunderstood if left in such terms as these. In the first place, to cut up the development of science into periods set by arbitrary dates actually obscures the pace of change and the impact of major discoveries. Science does not move forward on an even front. The identification before 1900 of the nucleic acids DNA and RNA, for instance, made possible in 1928 the transfer of some characteristics of a bacterium to another of a different type, but it was not until 1944 that the medium of exchange was shown to be DNA and not until the 1950s that this was to lead to a revolution in genetic understanding. In contrast, the continuation of work in nuclear physics had completed a huge revolution and brought its first practical applications (to warfare) by 1945. Secondly, to talk of 'European science' is misleading even before 1914. It was already by then also the product of research and technological innovation in North America; its base was western civilization, rather than European.

---

4 He had published an account of his work in 1865 which received little attention at the time.

Symbolically, Marconi's transatlantic messages were sent in the morse code invented by an American and by 1939 Einstein (and many other Europeans) were working in American institutes and laboratories.

One new science in which American enterprise was to be especially important was psychology. The prestige of the biological and physiological sciences directed the efforts of psychologists towards simple experiments with animals and the consolidation of the doctrines of 'behaviourism' (roughly speaking, the explanation of behaviour by changes in environment). The experiments of Pavlov made a great impression on the lay mind in this connexion.[5] The greatest name in the history of psychology, however, is associated with changes going far beyond mechanistic determinism. Sigmund Freud published his most important book, *The Interpretation of Dreams*, in 1899. The public at large did not become familiar with his ideas until after 1918 and even then more often misrepresented than understood them. But from the point of view of the historian of social change the inexactness with which Freud's ideas were understood is only of interest as a symptom. What Freud succeeded in doing – besides founding a new therapeutic technique, psychoanalysis – was to cast doubt on all the certainties of reason itself by providing grounds for believing that the mind was not the proud citadel of rationality that it had been taken to be. Whether this dethronement was itself based on scientific procedures or was logically self-consistent is not something to discuss here; what is clear is that Freud administered a shock to European culture of which literature, education, the arts, philosophy, ethics and medicine were to feel the effects for the next fifty years. A new relativity had been introduced into judgments of human behaviour which was to shake the certainties of liberal civilization more than they had ever been shaken before. Contemporaneously, these certainties were also being undermined by anthropological study and the new awareness of human differences which it brought with it. The discovery of social variety had a cultural effect in the twentieth century comparable to that of the Romantics' rediscovery of the Middle Ages in the early nineteenth.[6]

5 Though this Russian scientist won his Nobel prize for work on digestion.
6 Frazer's great study, *The Golden Bough*, first appeared in 1890; a second edition followed in 1900.

These new intellectual forces began to appear at a moment when an enormous expansion of their potential audience was taking place. In 1914 primary education was free and compulsory almost everywhere in western Europe; in England and Wales alone 6 million children were at school when the Great War began, in Germany over 10 million. The great spread of popular education in the previous half-century had everywhere had very mixed but very important social consequences. On the one hand it helped to create a new social discipline and acted as a steadying force. This was even, in some degree, a conscious achievement. In England it was widely believed that a statesman had said that 'we must educate our masters',[7] and in France the schoolmaster was the standard-bearer of republican ideals and free thought. Even where the ideological content was less blatant than this (and in much of continental Europe, state schooling meant anticlericalism) a new social experience for the children of the poor was at work to produce a new culture and a new discipline. Like urbanization, education helped to break ties with earlier generations and to form a new mentality, which accepted the elementary and standardized social disciplines of mass society.

One ambivalent effect of education was the nearly complete conquest of illiteracy. This made the communication of ideas easier and speeded up the corrosion of old certainties. It created a market for the new mass press which grew rapidly in the 1890s. Monster circulations were to be found in England, but *Le Petit Parisien* printed nearly 800,000 copies by 1900, and the *Berliner Morgenpost* over half a million. The printing of cheap series of books became very profitable and diffused knowledge more widely. There also appeared before 1914 the first movies. Until widespread television broadcasting became common after 1950, the cinema was undoubtedly the most powerful medium of cultural diffusion among the masses. It reached even those who could not read. The key developments all took place at the end of the nineteenth century. Patents for moving-picture apparatus were taken out in England and France in 1895 and on 28 December that year, thirty-three people paid to see the first commercial film show in a Parisian café. In the following year a film of the Derby was shown on the evening of the day of the

---

7 The phrase was attributed to Robert Lowe, but what he said was 'you should prevail on our future masters to learn their letters'.

race in London, where, in 1905, the first European cinema was opened. A great age of cinematic culture was beginning. Among other things, it brought a vast expansion of advertising, which rapidly took advantage of new means of mass communication. Wherever advertising flourished, it subtly raised expectations and encouraged the questioning of established habits; like popular education and the mass newspaper, advertising was both a corrosive and a consolidating social force.

Although the occasional work of a great artist or themes from the visual world of *art nouveau* might leave traces of genuine art in the posters or mass-produced fabrics of the period, the cultural gap between the mass and the élite remained enormous, in spite of the pace of cultural change. This was true even though that élite, once co-extensive with the educated, was now losing its cohesiveness. It is significant that the phrase *avant garde* began to be used of the arts in a new sense in the 1880s. It showed that a growing area of cultural experience was inaccessible, even to educated people, because of its novelty and complexity. It is partly for this reason that developments in the arts which, in retrospect, seem symptoms of important psychological and spiritual changes, were little noticed at the time. In the visual arts, the overthrow of the traditional canons had already begun before 1880. Impressionism had by then produced its greatest achievements. Similarly, literary change had already gone far under the influence of Realism. Such tendencies were to develop still further before 1914, but, in addition, much more radical and eccentric departures from tradition (or over-emphatic reassertions of it) occurred; there was much more conscious and contrived abandonment of accepted forms. The cult of decadence was one of the earliest manifestations of this. Its literary roots went back to Baudelaire; it diffused itself later in the aestheticism of the *fin-de-siècle*. Remote though aestheticism might appear to be from daily life it announced a profound cultural change which became explicit when Oscar Wilde, a fashionable playwright and minor man of letters, became for educated Europe the symbol of rebellion against the whole morality of the liberal age. Nothing since Romanticism so profoundly challenged the pervading order. The old assertion that artistic integrity might entail the rejection of political and social authority was now to expand into a rejection of any authority, even that of moral or artistic principle, in the interests of self-expression. The way was open to artistic adventurers like d'Annunzio and the Futurists.

Pictorial art and music showed the most rapid developments into new and unacceptable forms. The release of music from academicism by Wagner opened a rich period of experiment. It came to its prewar climax with one of the great cultural events of the prewar world, the appearance in Paris of Diaghilev's Russian ballet and the first performance of *Le Sacre du Printemps* in 1913. The break with tradition was too sharp for many people who complained of obscurity and cacophony. Similar charges were brought against the innovators in literature. Although the naturalism of a Zola or a Hauptmann might disgust or shock, it was at least comprehensible. To go further and abandon the convention of normal verbal communication, as did the Symbolists, seemed to throw off the discipline of meaning itself. The word 'Symbolism' was only coined in 1895 by Moréas, but its greatest achievements had already appeared in the works of Rimbaud.

At this point, we begin to touch something quite new in the history of conscious art, the cultivation of irrationalism. In the art of this period there is a new emphasis on will, emotion and instinct. Another expression of the culture which produced it, is the general antipositivist character of much philosophy and sociology of the period. Bergson, who sought deliberately to found his thought on the intuitive perceptions of the irrational and evolutionary elements in life, may seem to the professional philosopher less interesting than Mach, who attempted a restatement of scientific materialism, or F. H. Bradley, who attacked positivism from a rationalistic Hegelian standpoint, but his influence extended far beyond the confines of formal philosophy. 'You have inflicted an irrecoverable deathwound upon intellectualism', Bergson was told by the American, William James,[8] whose own 'Pragmatism', with its blunt dethroning of ethical values and its emphasis on will, was also especially congenial to the European mind at this juncture. Such influences could shape very different sets of conclusions, as Bergson's effect on Georges Sorel, the advocate of political irrationalism, and on Charles Péguy, the only great French writer of the period who abandoned Republican humanism for Catholic nationalism, showed.[9]

8 *The Letters of William James* (London, 1920), vol. II, p. 290.
9 On Sorel, see below, p. 240; on Péguy, D. Halévy, *Péguy et les Cahiers de la Quinzaine* (Paris, 1947).

The European vogue of Nietzsche – like Freud, more often talked about than understood – is one of the clearest indications of these fundamental cultural trends. His works began to be available in translation in the 1890s. Long before Bergson, Nietzsche's insight had been profoundly pessimistic. He saw in the elaboration of the humanistic culture of his day the coming collapse of values, the falsification of reality by a philosophy which postulated unchanging ideas. He sought to escape from these dangers by asserting the need for the re-establishment of values by conscious choice. It was unfortunate that the language in which he couched many of his observations and his introductions of such notions as that of the Superman and the 'master and slave morality' invited misinterpretation. He was really expressing with deep insight many of the dissatisfactions which lay at the heart of the civilization of his day. His cultural and historical pessimism was to feed a widespread mood, later articulated in such works as Spengler's *Decline of the West*, whose title and theme, significantly, were chosen before 1914, though it only became notorious after 1918. But Nietzsche was also ransacked for slogans like 'God is dead' and 'Become what you are', which were torn from their context in his works to justify an unbridled individualism in rebellion against liberal civilization. Similar dissatisfactions were cast into a more conventional form by the playwright Ibsen, although his links with the past were stronger. The central theme of individual self-realization linked him to the Romantics of previous generations, but he was prepared to carry it to new extremes. This theme dominates *A Doll's House*, although the play was sometimes understood as a tract about the narrower question of the position of women. A more violently assertive individualism was expressed in the *Culte du Moi* of Barrès.

Such innovators were neither as noisy nor as celebrated for their rejection of the whole culture in which they lived as the Futurists, who represented at its extreme the tendency to break violently with the past and to celebrate the cult of irrational will.[10] They were of importance in the history of art but also had a more direct popular impact than most of the artists of their age, in spite of their small numbers. This was largely because, in Italy, they were closely connected to the extreme nationalists who were among the

10 Sometimes amusingly, as in concerts for (very noisy) futurist instruments, or the wearing of 'anti-neutralist' clothing in 1914.

precursors of Fascism. The Futurists are also interesting because they embodied, in its most extreme form, the assertion that politics and culture were linked indissolubly and expressed a widely shared dislike of the convention and stuffiness of bourgeois society on the eve of the first world war. '*Le monde étouffe*', wrote a French author. '*Rouvrons les fenêtres, faisons rentrer l'air libre. Respirons le souffle des héros.*'[11] Not all such rejections were violent, and some of the institutions created by this mood were to prove enduring and valuable. The organized youth movements of this period were important in providing a framework for the search for more natural, less artificial values. They by no means rejected outright the culture which produced them. The English Boy Scouts (1908), a movement spread and imitated worldwide, did much to introduce adventure and health into the lives of the young, but remained fundamentally loyal to the ethical standards of the day. Their emphasis on group activity rather than the individual – an emphasis shared by the contemporary German *Wandervogel* movement – was perhaps symptomatic of a less articulate dissatisfaction with the prevailing individualism of liberal society, held in check by recognition of the conventional loyalties.

Some of the other anti-traditional forces at work before 1914 acted less dramatically but not, for that reason, less powerfully than any of these. The slow, steady pressure of town life on the new town-dwellers, for example, inexorably broke down the influence of older social regulators such as church and family. More people were changed by this than by the conscious innovators, as new patterns of consumption, crime, child-rearing and churchgoing all showed in different ways. But such pressures operated gradually and their effect cannot be discerned so clearly in 1914 as in 1939. Only the first signs of change were apparent when the Great War broke out. People could sense a different world in the weakening of such landmarks as the authoritarian and paternalistic family.[12] Religious sanctions could do less to

---

11 Romain Rolland, p. 200. The image crops up throughout the period from Nietzsche (e.g. *Zur Genealogie der Moral*) to Proust, whose Albertine memorably threw open a window in *The Captive*.
12 The evidence of photographs is helpful: the patriarchal beard was already in decline before 1914. As the years have passed, the beard has tended more and more to be the badge of uneasy bachelordom, or of assertive youth.

uphold its authority when civil marriage and divorce were both becoming more common. Education was bound in the end to create a different reference; female emancipation would provide alternative outlets for feminine energies. New economic opportunities and easier communications already made the physical break with the parental home easier. The consequences of such forces were already in sight in 1914, but the war was enormously to accelerate their unrolling.[13] Meanwhile, cultural and intellectual life provided plenty of evidence that liberal assumptions were already under heavy strain by 1914.

POLITICAL AND SOCIAL

The political assumptions of the liberal nineteenth century were as bluntly questioned after 1880 as were its intellectual presuppositions, but by 1914 had suffered no fatal damage. The idea of parliamentary democracy had still enough vitality to have great prestige everywhere in the first decade of this century – as the concession of the Russian Duma of 1905 and the Young Turk successes showed. Many of the traditional conservative criticisms of liberal parliamentarianism, indeed, continued to be made throughout this period (sometimes more loudly after experience of the actual behaviour of representative bodies). In the sense that these criticisms were based on principle, and were 'pre-liberal', they show that political liberalism still had much to accomplish in 1914 and demonstrate that it had still to come to maturity in many countries.

Some more novel criticisms of liberal politics came from sources often vaguely jumbled together as 'social Darwinism'. This was a way of referring to a number of social thinkers who liked to make analogies between the supposed processes of social and biological evolution. They were a very mixed bag. Some of them took up old-fashioned individualist standpoints like that of Spencer, while others ran to a more ferocious and mindless obsession with groups, such as the nationalists Treitschke or Sombart. Such thinkers were 'post-liberal', rather than conservative. Marx had been their forerunner, though he had accepted a

13 See p. 482.

framework of historical determinism. By stripping away the ritual and the camouflaging coverings which, he claimed, hid the existence of an irreconcilable conflict of classes, he cut at the roots of liberalism, its assumption that interests could be harmonized. There were also other, more rational, post-liberal critics who based their arguments on the failure of liberal society to live up to its own ideals. It was also said that liberal assumptions falsified the true nature of man and therefore of society, of which the foundations lay deep in irrationalism, habit, prejudice and myth. Political ideals and institutions, it was claimed, were fictions erected to mask these realities. Such an analysis underlay, for example, the work of the Italian sociologist, Pareto, who argued the decadence of 'pluto-democracy' (as he called parliamentary democracy) from its unwillingness to go behind the shams and sentimentalism of parliamentary rhetoric. Georges Sorel produced a similar quasi-moral, quasi-rationalistic critique of democracy, stressing humanity's dependence upon non-rational stimuli in its greatest achievements.[14]

The other criticism of liberal democracy had some connexions with assertions that it took no account of non-rational reality, but also drew attention to more empirical evidence. It was between 1880 and 1914 that the works of Michels, Mosca and Ostrogorsky began to appear.[15] They all pointed out the reality of the power of relatively small groups behind the façades of the mass political parties which were coming into existence. Pareto made the theory of élites – the idea that in every society, whatever its formal institutions, real power lay in the hands of a small group – central to his sociology and claimed that this was not regrettable but inevitable. 'Elitist' thinking was in the air. In the work of Shaw and Wells there were traces of a vision of society directed by scientific 'supermen'. They admired (as did the Webbs) the ideas

14 On Pareto see S. E. Finer's selection, *Vilifredo Pareto: Sociological Writings* (1966). For Sorel, his *Réflexions sur la Violence* (Paris, 1906). Interest in the irrational foundations of politics did not, of course, always entail anti-liberal conclusions. Graham Wallas, *Human Nature in Politics* (London, 1909), is a book by a liberal who found it possible to remain one while admitting the large part played by prejudice and unreason in contemporary politics.

15 G. Mosca, *Elementi di Scienza Politica* (Rome, 1895); R, Michels, *Zur Soziologie des Parteiwesens in der modernen Demokratie* (Leipzig, 1911); M. Ostrogorsky, *Democracy and the Organisation of Political Parties* (London, 1902).

of Karl Pearson, a 'Darwinian Socialist' who believed socialism was the best way of organizing for international competition and deplored the reduction of the death rate because it meant the survival of the unfit. Lenin provided a revolutionary version of 'elitism' when in his 1902 pamphlet, *What is to be Done?*, he rejected democratic control in favour of leadership by a small, dedicated group. And, of course, similar conclusions could be reached by the alternative route of an aesthetic egocentricity such as that of d'Annunzio.

Some of these speculations had analogies with those of liberals who were discouraged by the reality of democracy. Liberalism had attempted to institutionalize the pursuit of happiness, yet its own institutions seemed to stand in the way of achieving the goal; their ideas were one more example of liberalism's tendency to turn upon itself. The disgust felt by men like Sonnino and Bonghi in Italy, or Milner and Rosebery in England, for the practical shortcomings of democracy contributed to a wave of antiparliamentarianism. Representative institutions had for nearly a century been the shibboleth of liberalism. An Italian sociologist now stigmatized them as 'the greatest superstition of modern times'.[16] There was violent criticism of them, both practical and theoretical. Not surprisingly, this went furthest in constitutional states where parliamentary institutions were the formal framework of power but did not represent social realities. Even where parliaments (as in France or England) had already shown they possessed real power, they were blamed for representing the wrong people and for being hypocritical shams covering self-interest. Professional politicians – a creation of the nineteenth century – were inevitably, it was said, out of touch with real needs.

In constitutional states, conservatives still argued that democratic governments were likely to lose sight of moral principle and long-term interests in their effort to be popular. Even in Great Britain, conservatives could envisage revolutionary action to thwart laws passed by valid majorities. In Spain, such doctrines were institutionalized in the military *pronunciamientos* which the soldiers justified by their self-imposed duty to act as guardians of the enduring national interest. This was extreme, but Boulanger drew on a traditional conservative distrust of parliaments in France, though, it is important to remark, he also drew on the

16 See Mack Smith, *Italy*, p. 209.

plebiscitary Bonapartist tradition. In this respect, he embodies the more modern 'post-liberal' antiparliamentarianism which was to spread more widely before 1914. It reflected in part a general cultural swing to irrationalism and violence and in part the overall rejection of the stuffiness and complacency of mature bourgeois civilization. Europeans were beginning to look to politics for more than the simple adjustment of differences.

Such a tendency can hardly have failed to contribute to the actual physical violence of the age. Yet this violence owed more to the persistence of grievances which the compromises of parliamentary politics seemed to neglect. The most obvious expression of this was industrial strife. Almost everywhere, from the mid-1880s onwards, labour unrest was endemic, though it tended to ebb and flow with the boom and slump of business activity. Economic change was always disturbing; in bad times working-class conditions were depressed brutally, in good times working-class expectations were raised. No country escaped. Belgium in 1886 had a wave of riots, strikes and chateau-burning which simmered on until 1894; there was another from 1901 to 1905, and a general strike for political reasons in 1913. Great Britain had a wave of strikes and unemployment riots from 1886 to the end of the decade and then another outburst from 1911 to 1913. The Netherlands had a severe railway and dock strike in 1903[17] and France a wave of strikes under the Clemenceau government. Even Zurich had severe rioting in 1886. These were all disturbances in relatively advanced and industrialized regions. Among poorer countries, Italy had severe agrarian disturbances in the 1890s, the *Fatti di Maggio* of 1898, and general strikes in 1904 and 1914. In the Iberian peninsula, Spain had a general strike in 1909, and Portugal had one in 1912. Even Russia had one in 1905.

There was also much purely political violence in these years. Besides the street-brawling of *Action Française*, the bombings in Barcelona, or the nationalist atrocities of an organization like the Serbian Black Hand, all of which were the work of small groups, there was a near-revolution in Italy and a real one in Russia. In France there was a sensational wave of anarchist bomb-throwing in the 1890s. Moreover, the intellectual defence, or at least accept-

17 An earlier severe outbreak of 1886 at Amsterdam should also be noted, although its nature was mysteriously cloaked by popular agitation over the suppression of the traditional sport of eel-catching.

ance, of violence became more common in these years. Georges Sorel, the self-appointed theorist of French syndicalism, asserted that violence had a valuable moral and sociological function and urged the workers to have faith in the myth of the General Strike. The Italian nationalists led by Corradini, and later by d'Annunzio, were almost indifferent to the objective of the violence they preached; they valued it for its own sake as an antidote to the enervating boredom of actuality. In the case of Treitschke and Sombart, violence was more explicitly linked to national and racial interest, but even in Germany some people seemed to find the justification of struggle in struggle itself rather than in its outcome. Such obsessive concern with violence seems to show that something had rotted away the assumptions of humanitarianism and reason on which liberal politics had rested. It had analogies with Nietzsche's desperate sense of the need to find a new source of heroic values.

This undoubtedly contributed to the loss of confidence felt by liberals themselves. Economic necessity had begun to drive them away from one of their traditional loyalties, Free Trade, and now political and social dangers tempted them to abandon others. They began to make compromises with former enemies, the Church, for example. At the end of the nineteenth century, liberalism was turning into a conservative, restrictive creed rather than a liberating, progressive one. Yet its vitality was still great. This is shown by the continued spread of its institutions and by its wide formal dominance in 1914.

Nor were the available alternatives successful in winning acceptance. The most spectacular of them was anarchism, much in the public eye because of its causal, indiscriminate style of terrorism, 'propaganda by the deed'. Its activities were most spectacular in France. In two years, eleven bombs were exploded in Paris and the President of the Republic was murdered (this was a great age for assassinations though not all of them were the work of anarchists). Anarchism also had less spectacular but, in the long run, historically more important, manifestations in Italy and Spain. Here Bakunin's influence had been strong and anarchism was a real rival to socialism for the allegiance of the working class. Direct violence was appealing where other means of expressing grievances did not exist. It was always strongest in rural, peasant communities, but in France it had deep influence on the syndicalist movement (to whose doctrines of direct industrial action it contributed), and it Russia it was important in the development of Populism. Its rejection of the existing order went further than that of socialism; it condemned not merely the bourgeois state but the state itself and sought other means of organizing social power. None the less, anarchism did not have the success of socialism in organizing and uniting those who rejected the liberal political order. The two movements were in competition with one another. Socialism had the advantage of being both an ideology which provided a coherent, relevant attitude to the economic and social facts of industrial society, and a great mass movement. Neither of these things was true of anarchism, which was theoretically ill-equipped to meet the needs of an industrial society and was only sporadically in possession of widespread support.

Socialism before 1914 came to mean, almost everywhere, Marxist socialism. Yet although he was still alive in 1880, organised socialism owed little to Marx and the line between anarchism and socialism was long hard to draw. In most countries there were Marxist groups and parties; the German S.P.D. was the oldest. In 1885 the *Parti Ouvrier Belge* was founded, and in 1888 the Austrian Social Democratic party. Marx himself helped Guesde to draft the programme of the French Workers' Party in 1880, and the Russian party was founded in 1883. In Great Britain there was the much less important but well-publicized Marxist Social Democratic Federation. Yet it was not by any of these bodies, but by British trade unionists, that steps were taken to set up a new international working-class organization. There was in 1888 talk of an international congress of socialists to coordinate international action to obtain a reduction of the working day. Following this, in 1889, a significant centenary, the French socialists issued invitations for two congresses in Paris (two because the French Marxists could not agree with another socialist group, the '*Possibilistes*'). From this confused start and the even more confused proceedings at the Marxist congress, plagued by interruption by anarchists, came the Second International. Resolutions were passed in favour of the eight-hour day and the extension of the suffrage, condemning standing armies and advocating the celebration of 1 May by labour demonstrations. It was hard to give practical effect to these. Nor was the problem of the anarchists settled. Two more congresses, in Brussels (1891) and Zurich (1893) discussed their position before a third at London in 1896 finally expelled them. By then it was clear that the Second International was going to last and was going to be Marxist. In 1900 its international bureau was set up in Brussels. A movement had, therefore, appeared by the end of the century which was formally in head-on collision with the existing order at many points. It rejected the market economy and private ownership in favour of social ownership, it assumed that social interests were fundamentally in conflict and that the class war was the basic theme of politics, and it was international, rejecting the claims of the individual sovereign state on its citizens – or so it said.

The most important reason for the triumph of the Marxist version of socialism was that this was the version officially accepted by the biggest and best-organized socialist party in Europe, the S.P.D. In 1891 the German party accepted the Marxist Erfurt programme, adding to the teaching of the master only an assertion of the necessity for continual political struggle for advances in political rights. The prestige of the German movement and the 'scientific' appeal of Marxism was enough to explain its preponderance over the alternatives available. Yet these alternatives had much to offer socialists. The British tradition, for example, owed almost nothing to Marx, but a great deal to trade union experience and the old liberal-radical vein in English politics. The foundation of the L.R.C. in 1900 opened a period of successful parliamentary activity which was to confirm the insularity of British socialism. In France Marxism had not counted for much before the Commune and both the Proudhon anarchist tradition and the Blanqui myth of insurrection made a strong appeal to French workers. The socialist politicians and the C.G.T. remained independent and often distrustful of one another for most of the years covered in this book. Splits and divisions had always weakened socialism in France. They were to trouble the International for years. In 1893 at Zurich the Germans were unable to prevent the Congress admitting some delegates who had been expelled from the German party and Bebel, the German leader, made a violent attack on those who, like the French anarcho-syndicalists, condemned parliamentary action. The May Day dispute was similarly expressive of differences of national tradition. Nor were only the French socialists divided. There was great variety inside Russian Social Democracy before 1898. German pre-eminence inside the International was regrettable because it imposed a single pattern and a single programme in very varied social and economic contexts. One result was to be the exclusion of French socialists from participation in non-socialist governments. The chance of participation in government was never likely to be offered to the S.P.D., yet in France a radical and socialist alliance was essential if reforming policies were to be carried through. The division between French and German traditions was obscured in the interests of dogmatic orthodoxy, although in practice and tactics the Germans were far from inflexible. At the Erfurt convention itself it had already been contended that the party should not take up a formally revolutionary stand.

The issue came to a head at the end of the century over the crisis on 'revisionism'. Two events signalled its opening. In 1898 the German socialist Bernstein published a book called *Postulates of Socialism*.[18] In the following year, the French socialist politician Millerand joined the government of Waldeck-Rousseau as a gesture of solidarity with the defenders of the Republic in the Dreyfus Affair. Soon after, a *rapprochement* of socialists with liberals and radicals was under way in Great Britain and Italy. 'Reformism' and 'revisionism' were the names given to the theoretical positions which Bernstein advanced and which were thought to be implicit in these events. Bernstein had observed that, contrary to Marxist teaching, capitalism was not obviously moving towards economic collapse but seemed to be stronger, more efficient and productive of increasing wealth. He also saw that class struggle did not seem more violent and naked: instead, divisions in society were apparently growing less sharp. Misery was still great, but decreasing. This raised the question whether revolution was, after all, the way ahead. Might it not be that the existing political machinery in many countries would provide opportunities for socialists to conquer power peacefully and transform society without violent struggle? The revisionist case was summed up by Lenin, a hostile critic, in *What is to be Done?*

Bernstein has *stated* and Millerand has *demonstrated*, both with ample precision, what is represented by the 'new trend'. Social Democracy must transform itself from a party of social revolution into a democratic party of social reform. . . . At present . . . the English Fabians, the French Ministerialists, the German Bernsteinians, and the Russian critics – all these belong to the same family, all praise each other, learn from each other, and are rallying against 'dogmatic Marxism'.[19]

18 *Voraussetzungen des Sozialismus und die Aufgaben der Sozialdemokratie.*
19 *What is to be Done?*, pp. 40–1; I have rearranged the order here.

His rejection and condemnation of this trend was uncompromising: 'Any belittling of the Socialist ideology, *any withdrawing from it* means by the same token the strengthening of the *bourgeois* ideology.'[20]

Lenin wrote as a not very distinguished member of a socialist movement notoriously prone to schism. He also wrote for the tactical purpose of asserting the domination of his own views in the Russian party and was much dominated by the intransigent Russian conspirational tradition. Not everyone saw things the same way. For many French critics of Millerand, the crucial fact was that he was serving in the same cabinet as General Gallifet, the victor over the Commune. Millerand, too, was in any case an independent socialist, and the Guesdist's condemnation of him did not impress other French socialists. The Germans, too, although they were to take a firm line, were used to exploiting the possibilities opened to them by the political system in which they lived, especially in the *Land* parliaments of the non-Prussian parts of the Empire. At the Paris Congress of 1900 the ideologist of the S.P.D., Kautsky, while rejecting participation in bourgeois governments as a general practice, was certainly not prepared to rule it out in principle. He, with Bebel, led the majority of the party, the men of the centre who struggled to retain a theoretical intransigence while making accommodations in practice. Theoretical revisionism was condemned at the Hanover Congress of the S.P.D. in 1900 because it was believed that a democratic system would not be conceded without a struggle in Germany. This made revolution inevitable, it was said. Yet the centre was not in practice in agreement with the left in working at once for 'the revolution'.

In 1902 the issue had been crystallized in French socialism by the appearance of a *Parti Socialiste de France*, intransigent, revolutionary and Guesdist, and a *Parti Socialiste Français* which was 'possibilist', non-Marxist and led by Jaurès. At the 1904 Congress of the International at Amsterdam, a debate took place on their unification. The S.P.D. had a great vested interest in the *Land* parliaments, yet it threw its weight against the possibilists, Bebel and Kautsky leading the attack on Jaurès and Bernstein. The Germans were obsessed by their dogma that they could not themselves achieve real political power without revolution. They

20 *Ibid.*, p. 71.

ensured the condemnation by the International of any participation in bourgeois governments, and the Marxist orthodoxy of
the movement. The immediate result was the unification of the
French socialists for the first time in one organization, the *Section
Française de l'Internationale Ouvrière* (S.F.I.O.), and the loyal
acceptance of Guesde's leadership by Jaurès. Some socialists, of
whom Viviani and Briand were the most important, were lost to
the movement, but the party's discipline improved. The price was
the end of the republican unity which had emerged from the
Dreyfus affair and the sterility of French socialism as a political
movement. Internationally the imposition of discipline was
impressive, it is true, but flexibility had been sacrified to the
German view of socialism's future. This view had been formed in
a country without the parliamentary experience in which British,
French and Scandinavian socialism had been born. It was a
tragedy that in countries where the authority of the Second International was taken seriously by socialists (the most important
exception was Great Britain) there should have been a deliberate
rejection of the possibilities of transforming society by
parliamentarianism.

The issue of reformism and revisionism was not dead, but the
climax had been reached in 1904. After this, the International
spent much of its time and energies on the question of socialist
action in the event of a general war. Jaurès was especially active
in trying to devise schemes which would prevent war by cooperation between working-class organizations: Rosa Luxemburg
and Lenin, on the other hand, represented those socialists who
saw in a general war a welcome opportunity for a great revolutionary upheaval. A split was appearing, in fact, between the
revolutionary radicals of eastern European Marxism and the
socialists of the west. Whatever the differences between them,
Bolsheviks, Mensheviks, the German-Polish group around Rosa
Luxemburg, and many of the Austrian socialists were united in
a belief, drawn from their experience of national and class op-
pressions in the dynastic Empires, that a great crash was coming –
and they welcomed the prospect. The S.P.D. reacted very differently. Practically reformist, it had too much to lose in an
upheaval. In 1907 Bebel had the Germans oppose a French resolution at the Stuttgart Congress which asked for socialist opposition to aggressive war by a general strike or insurrection. In the
end, an innocuous, unspecific resolution was passed which only

obliged socialists not to vote for increased armaments. The Congresses at Copenhagen (1910) and Basle (1914) talked about the problem and got no further. The International had two grave weaknesses which made success in dealing with this matter unlikely from the start. In the first place, whatever might be the theoretical internationalism of socialism the movement was in fact riddled by national sentiment. As early as 1891 Bebel had made it clear that the German socialists would willingly help to resist a Russian attack because a Russian victory would mean the defeat of social democracy. In 1913 the socialist deputies in the Reichstag joined in the vote for the largest army estimate in German history. By 1914 some of them were talking of Germany's rightful colonial demands. The French socialists could not say that they would abandon the 'lost provinces' of Alsace and Lorraine. The Social Democrats of Austria were intensely conscious that they were a German party distinct from, say, the Czech Social Democrats. The Polish labour movement was sharply divided into a nationalist Socialist Party led by Pilsudski and Rosa Luxemburg's group which paid no attention to Poland's subjection to Russia. Inside Russia, the most effective socialist group, the Jewish *Bund*, was organized on a racial basis.

In the second place, the German socialist movement had too much to lose to envisage illegal action to stop a war. Within it were many people who felt like the union leader who, on the eve of war, identified the fatherland with 'social insurance, the *Volksschule*, the sanatorium, the wage agreement – indeed, all that organized labour had created; its unions, its press, its union buildings, its secretariats for legal protection, its libraries – and its growing power and its growing hopes'.[21] The growing hopes had been powerfully helped by the electoral landslide of 1912. In 1913, at the Jena Congress, the S.P.D. had renounced the weapon of the general strike and had agreed that its deputies might vote funds for the armed services if they were raised by progressive taxation. This was the eventual position reached by the party which dominated the Second International (it was also the beginning of the split which was eventually to divide it during the war).

21 See Snell, 'Socialist Unions and Socialist Patriotism in Germany, 1914–1918', *AHR*, 1953–4, p. 67. Cf. *The Communist Manifesto*: 'Modern industrial labour . . . in England as in France, in America as in Germany, has stripped him [the worker] of every trace of national character.'

The upshot was disastrous. Only at the end of July 1914 was the Bureau of the International summoned to Brussels. It met and then dispersed to consult the national leaders. The one man who might have pulled things together, Jaurès, was assassinated by a patriotic fanatic on 31 July. By then the Russian mobilization was under way and a wave of patriotic emotion swept Germany, socialist and non-socialist alike. On 2 August the leaders of the forty-eight socialist trade unions of Germany met and decided that national defence was their first duty. Far from calling a general strike, they ended the strikes already in progress; Bethmann Hollweg was confident on 30 July that he would have no trouble through industrial action or sabotage by socialists. On 4 August the Social Democrat deputies voted for war credits in the *Reichstag*, justifying their actions by emphasizing the Russian danger. They said nothing of Belgium. In France, Guesde and Sembat joined the government. Only in Serbia and Great Britain did socialist M.P.s actually stick to their principles and vote in parliament against war credits. There was to be no more convincing demonstration of how little damage had been done to traditional nationalism by the international socialist movement.

In fact, the Second International had few successes. Paralysed by the German stand on participation in bourgeois governments, it was able to effect no social or political reforms from within existing structures; only in a few places could individual socialist parties win concessions by industrial action. It had been unable even to turn May Day into a great labour festival in all countries. National divergences always prevented common action by socialist parties and this fact should have been exploited rather than resisted. The success of socialism before 1914 was its mythical power to frighten the bourgeois and inspire and educate the workers.

The other great political and social challenge to the established order in these years came from a less well-organized and widespread movement. Liberals, socialists and anarchists could disagree among themselves about the identity and nature of the oppressing class: in the eyes of feminists they all belonged to it because they were all men. The slamming of a door in *A Doll's House* had announced the coming of age of the independent woman, but she had still much left to struggle for in 1914. The struggle for her political rights had not gone far and its success was qualified.

Politically, the crucial claim of the feminist movement was the vote. Not all the obstacles which stood in the way of extension of the vote to women rested solely on prejudice. English Liberals feared that the votes of well-to-do women would reinforce the Conservatives and Giolitti opposed female suffrage because, he said, it would be under clerical influence. By 1914 only two European countries had given the vote to women. Finland in 1906 gave the vote to all adults over twenty-four who were not paupers; nineteen women were immediately elected to the Diet. Norway extended the suffrage on a more limited basis but included women in 1907. The nineteenth-century situation in Great Britain had seemed promising: in 1880 a few women – property-holders in the Isle of Man – had actually been given the vote. In 1894 the Local Government Act gave the vote in local elections to women property-holders in England and Wales. Given these precedents, it is hardly surprising that Balfour, a Conservative, was able to say in the 1890s that any further parliamentary reform would have to include female suffrage. Yet the acceptance of this principle by parliament received a sharp setback because of the violence of the 'suffragettes' from 1909 onwards. Feeling ran high against them and it was not until 1913 that the prime minister agreed to accept feminist amendments to a suffrage bill. Only in 1918, after the revolutionary changes in society and politics produced by the war, was the vote given to women over thirty. The immediate results were strikingly different from the Finnish: there was only one successful woman candidate in that year and she never took her seat because she belonged to Sinn Fein.

In spite of the slowness of political advance, it was none the less true that a great revolution had begun in women's lives before 1914, even though its full consequences had still to appear. What was involved was much more than the vote. A whole notion of female personality, a whole psychic and moral atmosphere was being questioned. Ever since the days of Amelia Bloomer dress had been an important – and sometimes irritating – badge of female emancipation. Although still encumbering, clothes were becoming simpler for work and outdoor recreation by 1914. Class differences were important here, as they were in the adoption of effective contraceptive practices. It seems clear from the statistical evidence that middle-class women had benefited from the ability to limit their child-bearing – and therefore to liberate themselves for other activities – far more quickly than working-class women.

The female invasion of employment previously reserved to men was in some ways an index of a growing freedom of choice, but can be misunderstood: it also represents a redeployment rather than an increase in opportunity. There had always been plenty of wage-earning women in the European labour force, whether as olive-pickers in Andalusia, mill girls in Lancashire, farm hands in Hungary or domestic servants everywhere. What now appeared were the new urban occupations of shop assistant and office worker and their appearance was limited at first to advanced countries. The typewriter and the department store created many new jobs by 1914. Yet the overall numbers of the female population working for wages was tending downwards. The total percentage of women in the labouring population has tended to fall, and it fell most rapidly before 1914. It was not balanced by any significant influx of women into the professions, though there were some spectacular appearances by individual women in these traditionally male areas. Madame Curie was the most famous of a growing number of women doctors and scientists. Popular education called for more school-teachers. In 1903 the first woman to plead in a European criminal court was heard at Toulouse.

The expansion of women's education after 1880 was also dramatic, and was to contribute importantly to the acceleration of women's entry to the professions. At the secondary level, the first French *lycée* for girls opened at Montpellier in 1881. German secondary state education for girls began in 1894. Private secondary education for girls already existed in Great Britain before 1880 as did university colleges. In 1880 the Collège de Sévigné began the provision of university education for women in France, and in the following year two Italian girls took doctorates in natural science at Rome. By 1914 there were about 4,000 women at university both in France and Germany. (Oddly, university education for women had long been established in Russia.) But the implications of such changes as these, or the legal changes registered by changes in property law, were only to be observable when decades had passed. They belong, unlike the militancy of the suffragettes, to the class of social changes already described which slowly corroded traditional assumptions and institutions, rather than strove violently to overthrow them.

8

INTERNATIONAL
RELATIONS, 1901–1914

It is misleading to describe international affairs after 1900 as if the only important thing which was going on was the diplomacy which led directly to the Great War. In the first place, there was nothing unavoidable about the war until a comparatively late hour; accidents might have averted disaster at several 'turning points' or 'crucial moments'. Secondly, there were many other developments, hard to relate to the origins of the war, yet important in affecting statesmen's conduct and in changing the historic setting of international affairs. What is more, much had been done to mitigate the disorder of international competition. For all the obvious dangers of militarism and colonial rivalry, the formal willingness of states to accept some restraints on their behaviour was probably greater than in the whole history of modern Europe. War between the great powers had successfully been averted for thirty years. The Concert of Europe was still believed to be important. Africa had been partitioned peacefully. There was more formal international cooperation and organization than ever before. Even before 1880, matters of common interest had begun to be regulated by international agencies and conventions on railways, telegraphs and postage. Technology's implications were recognized by a radiotelegraphy convention in 1906. More important still was the growing acceptance of arbitration to settle disputes between nations. More questions were decided by arbitration in the last twenty years of the nineteenth century than in the previous eighty. It is true that some nations submitted to it more readily than others, that arbitration was usually employed only in a limited class of disputes and that there was no effective sanction available if a nation refused to accept an award against it, yet even a limited resort to this method represented an advance. Matters which had caused conflict in the past were now being settled peacefully. Treaties providing that certain classes of disagreement between two nations should regularly be submitted to arbitration were more and more common; between the Anglo-French Convention of 1904 and the Great War there were over a hundred.[1]

In 1898 the Tsar of Russia, a country alarmed by the increasing strain placed on its economy and finances by the cost of modern arms, proposed a conference on ways to halt competition in armies and navies. The conference met in the following year at the Hague. No agreement on the limitation of armaments was reached but it was decided that a permanent court of arbitration should be set up to which disputes between nations could normally be brought, and this resulted in the appearance of the International Court at the Hague in 1899. Some attempts were made to contain the increasingly horrible nature which modern warfare was likely to assume. Dum-dum bullets, poison gas and the launching of projectiles from 'balloons or by similar new methods' were to be prohibited. A second Hague Conference which renewed and expanded many of the agreements of the first met in 1907, again on Russian invitation. Although a British attempt to obtain some limit on naval building at this conference was thwarted by Germany, it was decided that there should be a third, with more elaborate preparatory study. The movement towards international conciliation which the two Hague conferences represented at its peak was also fed throughout the world by private agencies. During the nineteenth century peace societies had been formed in many nations and the modern pacifist movement appeared. Peace Congresses and a *Bureau International de la Paix* at Berne coordinated their efforts. Other subsidiary organizations which fostered international cooperation and which had no parallel before the nineteenth century were such bodies as the Institute of International Law (1875), the Inter-Parliamentary Union (1887) and, most famous of all, the Nobel Committee and

1 The *Encyclopedia Britannica* (11th edition) 1910, s.v. 'Arbitration, International', provides an interesting reflection of a confidence which would now be lacking: 'With the help of a world-wide press, public opinion can always be brought to bear on any state that seeks to evade its moral duty.'

its peace prizes, first awarded in 1901. More people believed that international cooperation was possible and that peace was the normal condition of relations between states between 1901 and 1914 than ever before.

Another new and important international factor in these years was the emergence of a new world power, the United States. Its full significance was not to be seen until 1917, though American interests were already worldwide. War with Spain in 1898 gave the United States the Philippines, and Hawaii was annexed the same year. The British government already thought it worth while to sound the State Department about the possibility of cooperation over China. Formal agreements were out of the question, but overseas interests were nonetheless beginning to impose upon American policy the need for understandings and arrangements with other great powers. In 1899, British and American ships joined in bombarding a German puppet king in Samoa into submission. A treaty settled the Samoan dispute in 1900. In Caribbean and South American affairs, too, the United States was much more active. A dispute with Great Britain in 1895 over the Venezuela boundary was little more than an affirmation of the Monroe doctrine; the war with Spain in 1898, on the other hand, carried the doctrine into an offensive phase. Continental security now seemed to demand a canal across the isthmus of Panama through which warships could move quickly between the Atlantic and the Pacific; much more American interference with other nations was the result. The legal obstacle to construction and ownership of a canal was removed in negotiation with Great Britain[2]; it then became United States policy to remove the danger of European intervention in the Caribbean area. Since legal and moral claims might arise from the notorious inadequacies of Central and South American governments over such matters as debts to foreign investors, Theodore Roosevelt enunciated a famous 'corollary' to the Monroe Doctrine: that it was proper for the United States to exercise a police power over the affairs of her neighbours if their conduct seemed to invite European intervention. He had already in 1902 persuaded Venezuela to submit her debt disputes with European nations to arbitration, and under his successor, President Taft, American intervention in the affairs of Caribbean states became very direct and considerable. Conversely,

2 The second Hay-Pauncefote treaty, 1901.

by 1914 European interference in the Monroe Doctrine area had come to an end (if an odd eve-of-war cooperation of France and Germany over their demands on the Haitian customs revenues is ignored).

The United States had also taken another step towards a new international role when Roosevelt's mediation brought to an end eighteen months' fighting between Russia and Japan (see below, p. 261) (he won a Nobel prize for it). This war, too, marked the emergence of other world forces; Japan's growing importance and concern over the Asian mainland was already bringing her into conflict with European powers and making her seem menacing to the United States. Her victory over Russia cast longer shadows still, as Asian populations subject to European rule took in the implications: perhaps the whites were not irresistible, after all.

One other new influence on international relations, even if more gentle and indirect, was provided by the self-governing colonies of the British Empire. Well before 1900, they all showed a real national selfconsciousness. Canada achieved the physical reality of national unity when the Canadian Pacific Railway was completed in 1885. Soon she was displaying her independence of the United Kingdom. Canadian troops were sent to South Africa to fight in the Boer War, but they were taken home again before the war ended and Canada led the opposition at colonial conferences in London to any pooling of sovereignty for Imperial defence. Canadian opposition to helping to pay for the Imperial fleet was stronger than that of Australia and New Zealand, more aware of the importance of sea-power in the Pacific, and of the strong Japanese and American fleets there. Nevertheless, Australia, whose national unity was achieved in 1901, was just as irresponsive to appeals to consolidate the Empire as Canada. New Zealand also became an independent Dominion in 1907, but the most striking evidence of the independence of the white self-governing colonies in the British Empire came from South Africa. Conciliation after the Boer War led quickly to the restoration of responsible government there. In 1910 the South Africa Act set up the Union and almost at once a nationalist movement appeared which was eventually to sever completely the connexion with England. These new nations did not change the balance of power in international affairs but even before 1914, if only because of the attention paid to their views in London, they affected European affairs indirectly.

THE CRYSTALLIZING OF THE ENTENTE

An important change took place between 1901 and 1907 in Great Britain's relations with other states. It is not very satisfactory to describe it (as used to be done) as the end of isolation. Certainly, Englishmen felt 'isolated' at the end of the nineteenth century, in the sense that they had no continental allies. But this was still to be true for years to come and Great Britain had never entered alliances since the Crimea. The change is better described as the adoption of different practical arrangements for looking after her interests. The vital decisions were taken piecemeal; they did not form an articulated scheme, though that was how they looked to some critics. One important step was taken when the British government, despairing of the Concert as a safeguard of the Straits, decided in 1896 that British communications with India would have to be safeguarded by a firm hold on the Suez canal rather than by propping up Turkey. Practical arrangements for the defence of British interests in the Nile valley therefore had to be made. There were to be others, over the Far East and Persia. The Boer War probably delayed them a little, but when such arrangements could be made, it gradually began to appear that, willy-nilly, they all tended to move British policy away from its traditional readiness to cooperate with the central powers. This was simply because of the switch in British concern from southeast Europe. The tendency was never anti-German in its origins (as was sometimes said later) and Britain and Germany only became entangled by the consequences of a 'new course' developed piecemeal and almost blindly.[3]

The first adjustments came in the Far East. The Russians profited most from the crumbling of the Chinese Empire. Their gains in Manchuria more than offset Wei-hai-wei and Kiao-Chou. After Fashoda, and during the Boer War, British diplomacy could not hope to get French support against Russia in the Yellow Sea area and attempts to come to practical arrangements with the Germans and Americans were disappointing. The Boxer rebellion made things even worse from the British point of view by making

3 See Marder, *op. cit.*, and Lilian Penson, 'The new course in British Foreign Policy, 1892–1902', *TRHS*, 1943 and 'Obligations by Treaty: Their place in British Foreign Policy, 1898–1914' in A. O. Sarkissian ed., *Studies in Diplomatic History and Historiography* (London, 1961).

foreign intervention in China more likely. The party of violence in Russia found its hand strengthened and Russian troops moved into south Manchuria. Apart from the Americans, who were unwilling to act, Great Britain could find no one else who objected except the Japanese. Still smarting under the resentment of Shimonoseki they watched with alarm the spread of Russian influence to Korea, which the Japanese government had long regarded as its special concern. A Russian company obtained an important timber concession there in 1901. Conscious of the ineffectiveness of British Far Eastern policy since 1895, Salisbury's first attempt to recover was to try to get Germany to agree to holding the ring while Japan and Russia fought it out without French intervention. But Bülow did not feel able to estrange Russia over China, where Germans interests were only secondary.

The common interests of Great Britain and Japan had already begun to appear. In 1898 the two nations had cooperated in a naval show of force to get the Korean government to dismiss its Russian financial agent. In the following year, Great Britain was the first country to pay the Japanese government the compliment of renouncing extraterritorial rights for her citizens; soon, all occidentals were subject to Japanese courts. In 1901 the Japanese took the initiative and asked for an alliance (but made an abortive effort to come to terms with Russia at the same time). The result was the treaty of 1902, the first formal alliance entered by Great Britain in peacetime, and the monument to the failure of the traditional policy of cooperation without alliances.[4] It was confined to the protection of interests in China and the Yellow Sea and was to last for five years. Each government recognized the independence of China and Korea, but agreed that Japan was 'interested in a peculiar degree' in the latter. They agreed that if either government went to war in defence of its interests in the region, the other should be neutral, and that if a third power should enter the struggle against the warring signatory power, the other should come to its assistance. Both powers also agreed to safeguard the special interests of the other. Roughly, that Japan got from the treaty the assurance that she could fight Russia alone, in defence of her Korean interests; Great Britain's Far Eastern interests would in future receive prompt protection from the

4 30 January 1902. G. P. Gooch, and H. Temperley, *British Documents on the Origin of the War* (13 vols, 1927–1938, hereafter *GT*), II, pp. 114 ff.

Japanese and, therefore, the commitments of the Royal Navy were reduced. It seemed at first that the Japanese had the best of the bargain, for the Russians announced their intention of evacuating Manchuria, a prime objective of the Japanese. Anglo-Russian friction, on the other hand, arose over a much wider arc of Asia. In Persia, a Russian had commanded the local Cossack Brigade since 1894 and Russian loans were made to the Persian government, while British proposals to build a railway were resisted. After a reduction in Persian tariff duties on Russian goods in 1902, Lord Curzon, the viceroy of India, thought it wise to make a tour of the Gulf in 1903, to assert British power there. Meanwhile the Russians were again active in Afghanistan and were believed to be at work in Tibet. None of this was touched by the Anglo-Japanese treaty, nor was Great Britain's friendlessness in Europe, where Lansdowne, the foreign secretary, was still fumblingly trying to come to terms with Germany.

The second condition for the precipitation of the *Entente* was the removal of Anglo-French friction. Fashoda had not been a turning point; it merely removed a threat of immediate conflict, although it had embodied an implicit decision on the future of Egypt. Popular anglophobia and francophobia persisted, inflamed by the Boer War and the Dreyfus affair. In 1900, a Franco-Russian military convention still envisaged war with Great Britain. The key figure in changing this state of affairs was Delcassé.

It is still not clear with what intentions he took office as foreign minister in 1898. Clearly, he wanted to improve relations with Italy; Crispi's fall gave him the chance to do so and a treaty of commerce in 1898 was followed in 1900 by secret colonial agreements which promised Italy a free hand in Tripoli and France one in Morocco. The Italian government even promised that under certain circumstances it would not intervene if France attacked Germany. By August 1902, though, Delcassé's eyes were fixed on the Far East and the hope of avoiding Anglo-Russian conflict there. The British liked the prospect of French restraints on Russia and by November 1903 Lansdowne was already talking of France's right to preponderating influence in Morocco. Personal visits between Edward VII and President Loubet had eased the atmosphere when the outbreak of war between Russia and Japan early in 1904 made the matter urgent. An agreement followed whose essentials were that France promised not to hinder British activity in Egypt in return for British goodwill towards French activity in Morocco. To this bargain were added a bundle of deals over West African frontiers, the Newfoundland fisheries, spheres of influence in south-east Asia, Madagascar's tariff, and the New Hebrides. Secret clauses provided that if Morocco collapsed, Spain should receive its northern and Mediterranean coasts. Practically, this settlement was most helpful to France. The bargain on Morocco was advantageous. The British government took it less seriously than the French, seeing it simply as an arrangement which slightly simplified Mediterranean strategy and as an end to some outstanding and tiresome quarrels. It was certainly, but only, an agreement to pursue common policies in certain areas and towards certain problems. Yet the Anglo-French convention of 1904 which registered the agreements was immensely important as a turning-point in diplomatic history. Its nature was soon to be transformed by the first Morocco crisis.

The Far Eastern question, happily, was solved for twenty years. Great Britain had never wanted to fight Russia and was glad to stand aside from the Russo-Japanese conflict which seemed more and more likely after 1902. In April that year the Russians promised to evacuate Manchuria, but the influence of the soldiers and the adventurers like Bezobrazov overrode Witte's caution. In 1903 Bezobrazov became secretary of state and a special committee for Far Eastern Affairs was set up. Negotiations with the Japanese over Manchuria dragged on; in fact Korea was the issue at stake. The Russians were not prepared to forego the chance of expansion and the Japanese were prepared to fight to defend their interests there. Each side sought strategical safeguards; the Japanese wanted somehow to turn the Russians out of Port Arthur and the Russians demanded the neutralization of Korea north of the thirty-ninth parallel. The news that the Russian Far Eastern fleet was to be reinforced was decisive. Negotiations stopped on 6 February 1904, and on the same day Russian troops crossed the Yalu. Two days later the Japanese occupied Seoul and attacked the Russian fleet at Port Arthur. After another two days, Japan declared war.

The course of the struggle was interesting because of land battles of a scale not seen for decades. But command of the sea was decisive. The Japanese won this at the start and thus were able to move troops to Korea without difficulty, and to besiege Port Arthur which fell on 31 December 1904, after a five months' siege. Early in 1905 the main land battles were fought at Mukden.

Russia by this time faced revolutionary troubles at home and in May her fleet from the Baltic was destroyed at the battle of the Tsushima Straits. The president of the United States had begun to arrange peace negotiations and on 29 August Russian and Japanese delegates signed the Peace of Portsmouth. Its core was the recognition of Japan's paramount interest in Korea, where, from this time, she occupied a place like that of Great Britain in Egypt. Soon there was a Japanese resident-general in Seoul and in 1910 the country was annexed. Japan also took over the lease of the Liaotong peninsula and the railway up from Port Arthur beyond Mukden as far as Changchun. The Russians paid no indemnity, but the peace marked the formal abandonment by tsarist Russia of her Far Eastern dreams. The interest of her statesmen, resentful of past German encouragement to oppose Japan, turned back to Europe. Now that Korea was safe for the Japanese, the way was open for a *rapprochement*. A secret agreement on zones of influence in Manchuria was made in 1907. Meanwhile the European balance of power was changed by the damage done to Russia by defeat and revolution. Japan, on the other hand, although almost exhausted by the material and financial demands of the war, had her national confidence and prestige renewed by the mastery she had shown of European techniques of war. The renewal of the Anglo-Japanese treaty just preceded the peace and had been extended to cover India and to operate even in the case of attack by one power alone.

During many of these important events, German policy had remained passive. France had escaped the terrible danger of war between its ally Russia, and Great Britain, but could not look to Russia for help when the first Morocco crisis suddenly blew up in 1905. German interests had not been affected by the Anglo-French agreement on Morocco, nor by that with Spain, but it was felt in Berlin that Germany had been slighted by not being consulted. The moment seemed propitious, given Russia's troubles, for teaching France a lesson: that Germany's views had always to be taken into account. The gesture chosen to announce this was a visit by William II to Tangier in March 1905. A French envoy had been sent to ask for reforms from the Sultan of Morocco. The Kaiser made a public speech emphasizing Germany's commercial interests in Morocco and the importance of maintaining the independence of its Sultan. No one knew quite what this meant but German policy was not moved by economic issues. Holstein had minuted the real motive of the German *démarche* six months before: 'Germany must object to the proposed absorption of Morocco not only on economic grounds, but far more to maintain her prestige.'[5] The German aim was pure diplomatic victory; for all the blunder, neither the Kaiser nor Bülow wanted a war. Their object was to show France that she could not depend on England and that Russia was too weak to help her.

This aim was not achieved. Visits exchanged by the French and British navies, and Edward VII's affable impact on Paris had breached the psychological barriers between the two countries. A step of farreaching significance was taken when Lansdowne and Cambon agreed that the two governments should 'treat one another with the most absolute confidence' should possible difficulties arise in which they might be involved.[6] Delcassé felt confident enough to resist the German demand for an international conference on the Morocco question, though his government did not support him and he resigned in June 1905. But this was the limit of German success. Although William II succeeded in signing a treaty at Björkö with the tsar a month later,[7] it meant nothing; the Russian ministers forced a virtual disavowal of the treaty's obligations by adding to it a declaration that it would not operate against France. Germany had to approach her international conference without the support of any other nation except Austria-Hungary. More important still, Great Britain had been made much more conscious of its association with France. The Algeciras conference was a pyrrhic victory for Germany. It destroyed thoughts of a French reconciliation with Germany. Three and a half months of deadlock solidified the new *Entente* and emphasized Germany's isolation; only Austria-Hungary supported her. In the end, a compromise was reached on the question of police organization in Morocco but Holstein's policy was seen to have failed and he left the foreign office.

5 See Taylor, p. 421. A rough analysis of the value of imports to Morocco, 1899–1901, by Great Britain, France and Germany gives 4 : 2 : 1, in that order. *GT*, II, p. 312.
6 *GT*, III, p. 76.
7 Carried away by his own success, William II wrote to Nicholas (27 July 1905) that it was 'a cornerstone in European Politics and turns over a new leaf in the history of the world'. *The Kaiser's Letters*, p. 191.

A revolution in European affairs had occurred. The imposition of an international agreement on the two-power bargain over Morocco was its least important aspect. The strengthening of the *Entente*, otherwise endangered by Delcassé's fall and Russia's defeat, was crucial. German policy was haunted by envy and distrust of Great Britain and the idea of an Anglo-French military alliance which did not exist, yet it was in fact pushing Great Britain and France together by taking a high and bullying tone. The change of government in England made no difference to this process: Campbell-Bannerman spoke warmly of the *Entente*. More significant still, Anglo-French military conversations began the day after the conference opened. The Germans exaggerated their purport as did Delcassé in French newspapers, after his fall. Grey always insisted, even on the eve of war in 1914, that these discussions had not bound the British government to any course of action. It is true that no written alliance with France existed. Yet these conversations marked a change in the assumptions of British policy. Hitherto, Great Britain had made arrangements to look after her overseas interests; these arrangements had been made with Japan and France because of geography. The Morocco crisis revealed to British statesmen the importance to Great Britain of the independence of France itself; their policy again became concerned with the balance of power in Europe as it had not been for fifty years. This was the real end of 'isolation' for England. The military conversations recognized this; British soldiers took it for granted that France could not survive unaided a German offensive through Belgium.

The international atmosphere had also changed. Not only did the Clemenceau government which took power in 1906 carefully avoid colonial friction with Great Britain, but there was a revival of nationalist feeling in France which helped the popularity of the *Entente Cordiale*, although among intellectuals rather than the masses. Conversely, in Germany the consciousness of danger deepened. A fear of encirclement seemed to be justified by such acts as the exchange of notes between France, Great Britain and Spain in 1907 over the maintenance of the *status quo* in the Mediterranean and an Anglo-Russian convention in 1907. Russian policy towards Great Britain had not become less intransigent only because of the Japanese alliance, important though it was. British resistance in Persia and Tibet and fears that Russia might be squeezed out of the Middle East if the Germans and English came to terms there also helped to make Russia more forth-coming. Discussions had in fact begun in 1903. On the British side, the reform era in Russia which followed the revolution of 1905 (though it was quickly overtaken by other events: see p. 199) made a Liberal government look more favourably on the auto-cratic power. In 1906 British capital participated in a loan to Russia for the first time since the Crimean War. Russian fears of a German-dominated Baghdad railway were in the end decisive. In August 1907 Russia and Britain agreed to regulate affairs in Persia by a partition into spheres of influence. Beyond this, British interests in the Gulf were recognized, Afghanistan's neutrality was to be respected and Tibet was to be a buffer state. The territorial integrity of the Turkish Empire was guaranteed, but nothing else was said about the Middle East, except for a vague promise of British goodwill over the Straits. The emphasis on central Asia and the Gulf showed how the problems of Anglo-Russian relations had shifted since 1887. Difficulties were not so effectively disposed of as in the Anglo-French agreement three years before, but the convention quieted controversies which had embittered relations since 1880. Yet, in spite of its limitations, it became, almost at once, important because of the violence of German reactions to it.

By itself, this response might not have mattered much. After 1906 the Anglo-French military conversations had been allowed to die away. Russia was still weak. A less restless German policy, following more realistic and practical aims, might have restored flexibility to Europe, and even have broken up the *Entente*. The decision to build a great German navy made this impossible. Many Englishmen now began to believe that Germany wished to challenge the Royal Navy's supremacy. This was over-simplified; while a few among Germany's rulers dreamed of outright conflict, most would have been content with simply being able to hold Great Britain in check diplomatically with a potential threat to British power at sea. But for huge numbers of other Germans enthusiasm for a big navy – consciously fanned by the Navy League – soon took on a strain of anglophobia. This fitted well with the claptrap rhetoric of *Weltpolitik* in which England, alongside Russia and the United States, was increasingly seen as the obstacle to Germany's assumption of her proper status. Psychological compensations had always played as big a part in

German 'navalism' as practical policy. The outcome, though, was almost inevitably going to be more alienation of Great Britain and the loss of her government's goodwill.

British policy was slow to swing round. The Kruger Telegram episode had first bought home to Germans the freedom of action sea-power gave Great Britain and the 1898 Navy law announced their intention to build a battle fleet and the 1900 law that this fleet was to be strong enough to challenge the British in the North Sea. If her enlarged yards were not to be idle, this committed Germany to continuing heavy expenditure on warships. Yet British public opinion reacted slowly. Only the decision to build a new naval base at Rosyth and a programme of new ships showed that the British Admiralty saw the strategic tasks of the navy in the future were not likely to be primarily directed against France. In 1904 a powerful new Channel fleet was formed. Other redistributions strengthened the forces available in home waters. Then the Morocco crisis made the British public aware for the first time of the scale of the German naval threat. At the same time, a revolution in naval history took place when H.M.S. *Dreadnought* was launched in February 1906 (See p. 283.). The German navy law of the same year showed that Germany was prepared to continue to build for supremacy in the new class of ship. German public opinion was excited and feared a sudden British attack;[8] there was no response to a British offer to cut down construction at the Hague Conference of 1907. The British estimates for 1908 were, indeed, reduced, but this was as far as British policy could go in spite of a Liberal government's wish to spend money on social reform rather than on battleships. In October an interview of William II with a correspondent of the *Daily Telegraph* caused offence among his own people and alarm in England. The 1909 British estimates were greatly increased, and in the debate on them the British government for the first time justified its programme by the German threat. Although Bülow's successor, Bethmann-Hollweg, had misgivings about antagonizing Great Britain, Germany would only give up her naval plans in return for a British promise of unconditional neutrality in a Franco-German conflict. After Algeciras, such a promise was impossible.

8 See, in this connexion, the very informative article by J. Steinberg, 'The Copenhagen Complex', *JCH*, No. 3, 1966.

THE RE-EMERGENCE OF BALKAN ISSUES

The dividing lines which were beginning to appear in international affairs as a result of the Anglo-Japanese alliance, the *Entente* with France, and Anglo-German naval rivalry, had by 1909 already been given greater importance by the reappearance of Balkan issues. Three things had changed since the Austro-Russian *Entente* of 1897. One was the growth of German economic and political influence in Turkey. Not only did this give another great power a direct interest in what happened in the area, but it tacitly ended the German policy of leaving Russia a free hand in Turkey. The second was the continuing Ottoman misgovernment which kept Macedonia in a state of near-revolution and gave other Balkan states chances to dabble in violence and conspiracy there. Meanwhile, the Sultan Abdul Hamid came to be associated by his native Turkish subjects with a humiliating foreign policy and obstruction of the reforms which Turkey needed to survive as a modern state. In 1908 the 'Young Turks', a nationalist and westernizing group, led a successful revolution. A brief and hopeful cessation of violence in Macedonia followed. But the Young Turks also destroyed the confidence with which European statesmen had watched the slow but seemingly sure decline of the Ottoman Empire into complete decrepitude. If this decline was going to be halted, then the assumptions of diplomacy would have to be revised. This was especially important because of a third important change, the reawakening of Russian interest in the Balkans after the fiasco in the Far East.[9]

In the end, these changes were fatal to the Balkan *status quo* which was the basis of Austro-Russian agreement. The high-water mark of the *Entente* between the two states had been the exchange of visits by Franz Joseph and Nicholas. The two Empires could cooperate against Great Britain over the Armenian massacres and the Macedonian troubles. Non-interference in Macedonia continued to be a bond between them and in 1903 they drew up together a programme of reforms which was accepted by Great Britain and Turkey. The clients of the two great powers were, it is true, becoming restive under this despotism of the

9 Though A. J. P. Taylor goes so far as to say 'China and Persia took up most of the energies of the [Russian] foreign ministry until the very outbreak of the European war in 1914' (*The Struggle for Mastery*, p. 483).

status quo. But Russia still ignored Bulgarian demands that she should help the Macedonian revolutionaries. British pressure on the Turks was successful in obtaining more direct intervention by the powers to maintain order in Macedonia in 1905 (it was significant that Germany was the only power which did not take part in the naval demonstration which brought this about) and Austria and Russia were still working together. Their co-operation was endangered only when Aehrenthal, who became foreign minister in Vienna in 1906, decided that the *status quo* in the Balkans was not, in fact, in the Habsburg interest. His concern was domestic; he wanted to solve the problem of the South Slavs inside the Empire. Because of Hungarian predominance inside the Monarchy, a federalist solution was impossible; foreign policy seemed to offer a way out. The annexation of Bosnia-Herzegovina would stop Slav agitation there and deal a blow to the prestige of Serbia, to which the South Slavs looked for support, by ending her hopes of acquiring those provinces. It might even enable the Monarchy to show that it would govern South Slavs successfully when the Magyars were not involved. The moment seemed a good one; Algeciras had revealed Germany's isolation and Austria-Hungary would therefore be bound, thought Aehrenthal, to have Germany's support. Even a war was not a disastrous prospect; it could be fought with excellent prospects of success against a Serbia without allies. The Young Turk revolution lent urgency to this programme: a regenerated Turkey might reclaim the administration of her provinces.

The last formal cooperation of the two Empires was in 1907, when they sent notes to Greece, Bulgaria and Serbia. After this it became known that Austria was asking the sultan for the right to build a railway through the Sanjak to Salonika. To Russia this seemed a violation of the agreement of 1897; the two powers did not cooperate when the next reform proposals for Turkey were put forward by Grey. None the less, in July 1908 the Russian foreign minister Isvolsky felt able to approach Aehrenthal with a formal proposal for a modification of the *status quo* which would suit both empires; Austria was to be allowed to annex Bosnia and Herzegovina in return for promising to support Russian claims in the Straits. Russian strategic aims were beginning to change; the Straits were no longer just a sally-port for adventures in the Mediterranean, but were now the most sensitive spot on the route by which her grain flowed to the outside world. Russia and

Austria, it appeared, would both be strongly placed to get what they wanted if they agreed with one another before the international conference which would be needed to modify the Treaty of Berlin. In September the bargain was struck. Unfortunately, the two statesmen subsequently disagreed about what had taken place at their meeting. Certainly when they parted Isvolsky did not expect Aehrenthal's next step, the annexation of Bosnia and Herzegovina without warning on 5 October.

The aim of shocking Serbia (and Montenegro) was fully achieved, but Russia, too, was taken by surprise, and this had not been Aehrenthal's wish. The Russian government, anxious for its good name among Slavs, disowned Isvolsky's bargain and protested against the annexation. Because Isvolsky was unable to get as a compensating advantage from Great Britain a promise to reconsider the Straits question, he was obliged to try to bring the question of annexation before an international conference to recover Russia's lost prestige. So Russia, not Serbia, became Austria's principal opponent. At this point the German government, in spite of earlier misgivings, backed up the Dual Monarchy without reserve, abandoning Bismarck's policy of never giving the Habsburgs an unconditional promise of support. This was because of German annoyance over the Anglo-Russian *Entente*; Germany was again, as over Morocco, using a question in which she had no direct interest to win a diplomatic victory over a power she wished to intimidate. Her aim was to force Russia to recognize her inability to stand up to Germany and Austria and thus to teach her the importance of German friendship. Military and economic weakness certainly made the Russian government unwilling to fight. The French were frightened to support their ally. In a war, Serbia would be squashed in any case. In these circumstances the Austrian aim of winning a formal acknowledgment of the annexation from Serbia was eclipsed by the German demand that the Russians provide one too (March 1909). Isvolsky gave in. The Treaty of Berlin was revised without compensating advantages for Russia; Austria made formal amends to the Turks by agreeing to pay for crown property in the provinces and the crisis was over.

The damage was enormous. Open conflict between Russia and Austria-Hungary in the Balkans had reappeared after being hidden for eleven years. Aehrenthal's dream of a revived *Dreikaiserbund* was blown away for ever. A secret Austrian treaty with Bulgaria followed and the chief of the Austrian general staff was soon urging a war to decide who should be master in the Balkans. The South Slav question was not soothed but inflamed. Conditions did not improve in the provinces and Serbian support of the Slav revolutionary movements was now unconcealed. Another territorial blow had been struck at the Turkish Empire (fairly well preserved since 1886); Serbs, Bulgars and Italians noted it with interest. Finally, Russia was not in any final sense intimidated by Germany; she was deeply resentful and began to re-arm in earnest. It was unlikely that she would again allow her prestige among Slav nations to be so far jeopardized.

THE OUTBREAK OF WAR

After the Bosnian crisis, the actions of the central powers did more and more to make the gap between them and the *Entente* powers unbridgeable. The Agadir crisis was the first instance of this. Although (as in the first Morocco crisis) France was Germany's ostensible opponent, its main importance was in Anglo-German relations; in the background was the increased tension over naval programmes since the acceleration of 1909.

French influence in Morocco had grown since 1906. There had been disputes over the help given by the German consul there to German deserters from the Foreign Legion (1908) but Franco-German relations had been good enough for agreement on a French loan to prop up the sultanate. Nevertheless, Morocco was dangerous. It was unstable. Like China and Turkey, Morocco was a crumbling and invalid polity whose decline was bound to pose problems to the great powers. When a Berber rebellion took place in 1911, the French sent an expedition to occupy Fez, the capital. German alarm was natural; the British occupation of Egypt had begun in a not dissimilar way. Since 1905 Germans had begun to believe that Morocco was economically important to them; the German government thought it had better make sure that it obtained compensating advantages for the extension of French influence. On 1 July 1911 the gunboat *Panther* arrived at Agadir and the crisis began.

The excuse was the protection of German nationals in Agadir; there were none. The purpose was to frighten the French into compensations; no such action, in fact, was required. The French government was quite prepared to negotiate an agreement; Caillaux, whose government took office on 1 July, wanted good relations with Germany. Discussions began a few days later, but, fearing to appear weak, the French government had much less freedom to make concessions than it would have had in a negotiation begun less convulsively. Worse still, the *Panther* had stirred up alarm in Great Britain. Although the Admiralty did not mind, the foreign office and British public opinion became very excited about the danger of a German naval base at Agadir. That the Germans did not, in fact, want one was beside the point. The cabinet was less moved but wished to make sure that Great Britain did not lose by any modification of the Algeciras settlement. On 21 July Lloyd George, widely reported, stated publicly that Britain could not be treated as of no account in a question vitally affecting her interests. This was read as a declaration of support for France in a war against Germany. It therefore made compromise much harder, to the distress of the French government, which did not want to find itself going to war as a result of an Anglo-German quarrel. Secret negotiations were begun by Caillaux which led to agreement in November (France gave Germany some territory in the Congo in return for recognition of a free hand for her in Morocco) but the crisis had done a lot of damage.

In the first place, it wrecked Caillaux's hopes of a new atmosphere in Franco-German relations. French colonialists who disliked his underhand methods joined anti-Germans and conservatives who disliked his fiscal policies to overthrow him. Poincaré's government of January 1912 was ostentatiously patriotic and the *Entente* with Great Britain received a great fillip. In Germany, the disappointment of hopes of big territorial gains in Africa was great and anglophobes attributed Germany's 'humiliation' to British threats; Tirpitz got support for yet more dreadnoughts and an enlarged programme was announced in February 1912. This in turn excited the British. Although British naval superiority in absolute terms was not really endangered after 1911 (when the gap between the two fleets was narrowest), a larger British building programme was announced in March 1912 and the British Mediterranean fleet was withdrawn to home waters. In the following September, the French Brest fleet was moved to Toulon. It was clear that British naval strategy now only envisaged one potential enemy and that British governments would not budge on the question of naval superiority, although they were still prepared to make big political concessions to secure this.

Agadir also opened the last stage of the Turkish succession problem. Italy, too, sought 'compensation' for French gains in Morocco – and for the annexation of Bosnia. In September 1911 Italy declared war on Turkey and landed troops in Tripoli, where they soon found themselves in difficulties. Her allies deplored Italy's actions but could not stop her. The war spread to the Dodecanese. An Italian bombardment in April 1912 led the Turks to close the Straits and this alarmed Russia. But Russian attempts to come to an understanding which would guarantee that the Turks would keep the Straits open for Russian commerce came to nothing. Unwittingly the Italians had launched a new Balkan crisis.

This grew out of the Russian failure to agree with Turkey and the need to find other defences for the Straits. One possibility was provided by an alliance between Serbia and Bulgaria in March 1912. It seemed to stand in the way of an Austro-Hungarian drive to the south and also to offset German influence at Constantinople. The two signatories saw it, on the other hand, as a partition treaty; Serbia was to get Turkish territory on the Adriatic, Bulgaria was to get Macedonia. Here was a new set of 'compensations' arising from the Bosnian annexations. Greece joined later, selecting Salonika for her portion. As Russia dare not offend the Balkan states who were to provide the protection for the Straits which she wanted, she was almost certain to find herself in the position of underwriting the risks of a Balkan war. There was no chance of backing out, because of Russian public opinion.

A last-minute attempt to revive the old tradition of joint intervention to force reforms on Turkey achieved nothing and the first Balkan war began when Montenegro declared war on Turkey (8 October), quickly followed by Bulgaria, Serbia and Greece. The Turks hastily made peace with the Italians but could not escape defeat. The new nations of the Balkans were everywhere triumphant. This alarmed both Austria, determined that Serbia should not obtain an Adriatic port, and Russia, frightened that the Bulgarians might seize Constantinople. A conference of ambassadors of the great powers met in London to regulate a new Balkan settlement. In May 1913 the treaty of London ended the first

Balkan war; the Bulgarians had not been able, after all, to take Constantinople and the Austrians had got the powers to agree to the creation of an independent Albania which cut off Serbia from the sea. The danger that the great powers might be dragged into a general war had been averted because both Russian and Austrian interests had been safe-guarded and because the other powers had worked for conciliation and compromise. Great Britain and Germany had seen their own relations improve slightly in the process, though the Kaiser, at least, seems by now to have concluded that conflict was inevitable.[10]

A second Balkan war now began because the Balkan League fell out over the spoils. Serbia wanted both a railway to Salonika and the Macedonian territory she had occupied while the Bulgarians had been busy attacking Adrianople. The Bulgarians attacked both her and Greece at the end of June. Rumania then attacked Bulgaria in order to take the Dobrudja and the Turks seized the chance to recover Adrianople. This time the final settlement (Peace of Bucarest, 10 August) was made between the Balkan states without intervention by the great powers. Bulgaria lost almost everything she had gained in the first war. The Austrians resented this, but the Germans hoped to win the friendship of the new Balkan states and Vienna had to fall into line. Only in October, when the crisis gave its last splutter, did William II promise support to Austria over an ultimatum on a Serbian incursion into Albania. The Serbians withdrew.

These events had a twofold significance. In the first place they symbolized the maturity of the new Balkan states. They were now capable of acting in the peninsula without having to rely on great power backing. Secondly, they further exacerbated the Austro-Serbian conflict. The Serbs were angry about Albania and their exclusion from the Adriatic. On the Austrian side, Serbia's successful aggrandizement (she gained a million and a half inhabitants) was more evidence to feed the fatal myth that Serbia was the 'Piedmont' of the South Slavs.

Meanwhile the arms race had not slackened. In March 1913 the

10 See his comment (reported in Fischer, p. 32): 'England will undoubtedly stand behind France and Russia against Germany out of hatred and envy. The imminent struggle for existence which the Germanic people of Europe (Austria, Germany) will have to fight out against the Slavs (Russians) and their Latin (Gothic) supporters finds the Anglo-Saxons on the side of the Slavs. Reason: petty envy, fear of our growing big.'

German government introduced a new army bill designed to provide superiority over Russia in the following year. In confidence, the party leaders of the *Reichstag* were told the increases were justified by the expectation of 'coming world war' whose first phase would be dominated by the overthrow of France.[11] The unprecedented financial effort was perhaps only possible in the excited atmosphere of the centenary of the *Befreiungskrieg* against the great Napoleon. The French government had more trouble in getting three-year service through its legislature but did so. It urged on its Russian ally the completion of the railways which would enable the Russian army to harry Germany with a two-front war. Despite the misgivings of some members of the government, the British went steadily on with their naval programme, confident of their power to outbuild the Germans decisively by 1920. Yet Anglo-German relations (perhaps because of this) seemed easier. Cooperation over the Balkan crisis was followed by negotiations over the future of the Portuguese colonies, and over the Baghdad railway. Unfortunately, easier relations were interpreted differently in the two countries; the Germans thought it might mean that Great Britain would not stand by France in the event of war.

The Baghdad railway indirectly inflamed a much graver and growing conflict of interests. German economic interests in Turkey for the last time brought Russia and Germany into direct conflict in 1913 because of Russian fears for the control of the Straits. Russia feared above all a Turkey which could not be intimidated. This now began to seem a possibility. The tension became intolerable when a German military mission to reorganize the Turkish armed forces was followed by the appointment of a German general to command at Constantinople. Sazonov, the Russian foreign minister, toyed with the idea of seizing the Straits by force but it was decided that this was militarily not feasible. In the end a face-saving compromise was arranged, but it was clear that a new direct clash of interest between Germany and Russia had been added to the other dangers to peace. The Russians began a huge expansion of their forces (to be completed in 1917) in order to meet the new danger to the Straits. It was the logical end of the road which began with the failure to renew the Reinsurance treaty. For once, one of William II's excited minutes hit

11 Fischer, p. 37.

the nail squarely on the head: 'Russo-Prussian relations are dead once and for all! We have become enemies!'[12]

This helps to explain the willingness of the Germans to encourage Austria in 1914. Because Germany was the preponderant partner in the alliance, this encouragement meant that she was primarily responsible for the outbreak of a world war. No one wanted such a war, of course; the Germans had no wish to find three great powers against them and a naval struggle mixed up with a continental struggle. But they were willing to envisage the land war by itself as an acceptable possibility; the Germans would not seek to fight the Russians, but if they were to have to do so, it would be best to do so while Germany still had a military advantage. It was arguments such as these which were in the background in July and August 1914. The Great War did not, after all, arise as had sometimes seemed likely, from French intransigence over Alsace. Nor did it arise from Anglo-German naval rivalry, or disputes over colonies, important though they were in shaping attitudes in Berlin. It arose from the incapacity of Austria-Hungary to solve its domestic problems.

The background to Sarajevo was the Habsburg fear of Serbia, but by June 1914 there was also alarm over a new irredentist threat to the Monarchy, that from Rumania. In June 1914 Sazonov visited Rumania and, pointedly, crossed the frontier into Transylvania where there were 3 million Rumanians. The government at Vienna could not make concessions which would satisfy Rumania and Serbia because of the Magyars' power in the Monarchy and so had to frighten them. The Germans did not at first like this policy, but were persuaded it was necessary for Austria to show Serbia and Rumania that Russian support could not be depended upon. That meant that Austria must be prepared to face the possibility of war with Russia, if Russia refused to give way. Austria was willing to do this because she was assured of German support and the Germans were willing to support her not only because Austria was their only reliable ally, but because of their new interest in Turkey and their soldiers' calculation that a war if it was to come, was best fought as soon as possible.

The *Entente* powers were involved willy-nilly in this logic. Great Britain and France had some interest in the fate of the only Slav state in the Balkans unfriendly to the Dual Monarchy. But

12 See Taylor, p. 510.

this did not mean that they had to go to war. That was made inevitable by German military planning which required that, if war broke out with Russia, France be attacked first and overthrown, before Russia could come to her aid. Since this attack was to be mounted through Belgium, it risked giving the British grounds for intervention to help France. Thus, for purely European and strategical reasons, the German soldiers accepted the danger of a world war. They had not always done this. The elder Moltke, believing it impossible to overthrow France quickly without an unacceptable infringement of Belgian neutrality, had therefore planned a defensive strategy based on limited offensives against Russia. Schlieffen, chief of staff from 1891 to 1905, had come round to the view that a speedy overthrow of France was desirable and could be achieved. But the German armies would have to pass through Belgium to outflank the French fortresses. From about 1905 the German army staked everything on this strategic concept; the Schlieffen plan was to entail war with England.

The final crisis began on 28 June 1914, when the Archduke Franz Ferdinand and his wife were murdered by a Bosnian Serb, Princip. This was the climax of a South Slav terrorist campaign. The Austrian chief of staff decided that the time had come for a reckoning with Serbia. Tisza, the Hungarian prime minister, was less sure of the advisability of pushing Serbia too far, but was outflanked by assurances from Berlin of German support. This was offered by William II on 5 July; the irresponsible nonchalance with which he and Bethmann took the decision is typical of the governmental processes of Imperial Germany; the foreign minister was not even consulted. Yet this probably made no difference. Germany's rulers welcomed the prospect of a limited Austro-Serbian war which would for ever kill the pan-Slav agitation threatening its ally. They hoped that German support for the Dual Monarchy would force Russia to repeat the humiliation of 1909. If she did not, the German soldiers at least wanted a war before Russia became unbeatable through improvements in her army; they were prepared to fight and defeat both them and their French allies. Egged on from Berlin, the Vienna government presented (23 July) an ultimatum to Serbia which demanded securities against further acts of terrorism; it was so sweeping as to be humiliating. Yet Serbia accepted most of the terms. Encouraged by Berlin, Vienna was unmoved; determined to crush Serbia, Berchthold declared war on 28 July.

Until the presentation of the ultimatum, diplomatic mediation had been impossible. When it arrived, Great Britain tried to act as go-between and the Russians told the Serbians not to resist. Even in Berlin only the soldiers wanted to go ahead even at the risk of war with Russia, but the declaration of war overrode all this. War against Serbia meant that the Russians were bound to support their ally. They began to move, though only slowly; they mobilized only those forces which were to be used in a war with Austria-Hungary even though this was strategically disadvantageous since no plans for such a partial mobilization existed. Yet this was enough. The attitude of the German soldiers hardened. Bethmann sought only to ensure that if war broke out between Austria and Russia, the *Reichstag* would be united against the Slav giant and that the consciences of the S.P.D. leaders would be at rest because the Russians could be made to appear the aggressors. While still seeking to persuade the British that he was trying to mediate between Austria and Serbia, he actually egged his allies on to a showdown. As German hopes of British neutrality in the event of a great-power conflict began to crumble, German mobilization was nonetheless authorized on 31 July. From that moment, Germany's rulers, still hoping that the British could be kept out, set about starting the war against France as soon as possible.

German military planning assumed that France would be the first target of the offensive in a war against her and her ally Russia. When William II asked his generals to redeploy their forces to the east from the west on 1 August, he was told that such an operation was impossible. No machinery existed for such a change. Tied to one strategic plan, Germany's support for her ally meant that she had now to attack France. The soldiers were in command.

On 1 August Germany declared war on Russia, whose mobilization had not been stopped. France was asked for a declaration of neutrality; her reply was insufficiently provocative and an air raid on Nuremberg was therefore invented to justify a declaration of war on France on 3 August. Great Britain's attitude was still uncertain, but it had by now begun to dawn in Berlin that she might support France. Grey had warned Germany on 2 August that naval operations against France in the Channel would not be permitted. As the Germans had no plans for offensive naval operations against France this need have caused no trouble; British opinion, political and public, was still too divided to think war justifiable before 3 August. But on that day the Germans sent an ultimatum to Belgium, demanding transit for their armies attacking France. The British responded on 4 August with a demand that Belgian neutrality be respected. It was ignored and Grey was able to take Great Britain into the war united on a moral issue, the violation of Belgian neutrality. This was the final consequence of the Schlieffen plan. The Anglo-French military conversations had only been given real meaning by the action of the Germans themselves. They meant that when Great Britain was at last able to enter the war, it could do so effectively. But the French had only been at war a day longer; oddly, their alliance with Russia had never come into operation after all, because the Germans had made up their minds for them by attacking them. The final irony of the whole sequence of events was that the original point of the alliance system, the danger of an Austro-Russian conflict, had been lost sight of. It was only on 6 August that the Dual Monarchy at last brought itself to declare war on Russia. That, in a way, was the final evidence of the domination of the 1914 crisis and its unrolling by the decisions made in Berlin.

9

THE GREAT WAR

THE CHARACTER OF THE WAR

Incredibly, many Europeans went to war with little regret in 1914. Some people found it an escape from the unheroic everyday of the bourgeois world, a chance for heroism and self-sacrifice to redeem the materialism in which they lived.[1] Others saw more precise opportunities. German generals, economists and generals thought that the nightmare of encirclement could be ended once and for all; British sailors thought that the chance had come to end German pretensions to sea power; French soldiers saw in victory the only acceptable revenge for Sedan. The Kaiser and many other Germans dreamed of a racial victory over the Slav. Habsburg statesmen dreamed of solving the nationalities problem. So did some of their subjects: the Czech Progressive party manifesto of May 1914 said that 'the Czech question would be solved more justly by war than it has been hitherto solved by peace'.[2]

More than any other force, patriotism mobilized the emotions the war needed. The crowds which heard the kaiser say 'I no longer know anything of parties' accepted the claim of national loyalty as unquestioningly as those which sang 'God save the

---

1 See, for instance, Rupert Brooke, or the *Wandervogel* poetess quoted by W. Laqueur, *Young Germany* (London, 1962), p. 87: 'O holy fortune, to be young today'.
2 See Z.A.B. Zeman, *The Break-up of the Habsburg Empire 1914–1918* (Oxford, 1961), p. 21.

King' outside Buckingham Palace. 'How stupid it is to ask what is our attitude to this war', wrote the newspaper of the German youth movement; 'Anyone who finds time to think about it shows that he does not know how to feel with his people.'[3] The feeling persisted on the battlefield; in November the German student volunteers mown down in *der Kindermord* at Ypres went into action singing their national anthem. Even when experience of the struggle had worn out the front-line soldier, a German sociologist could still say (misleadingly) in 1916, 'This war concerns honour, and not territorial changes or economic gain.'[4] The best evidence of the power of patriotism was provided by Socialists. In England, the Labour party supported the war. The government of 'Sacred Union' in France (28 August) contained two Socialists and a Catholic as the physical embodiments of national unity. The antimilitarism of the *syndicats* did not revive until 1916. Even in Russia, Plekhanov, the *doyen* of Russian Marxism, supported the Allies;[5] the Bolsheviks alone preached 'revolutionary defeatism'. Victor Adler and the Austrian Social Democrats rallied to the Habsburg cause once the war had broken out, though they had denounced the original ultimatum to Serbia. In Germany came the most striking of all identifications of Socialists with the national cause. The German trade unions feared their insurance benefits would be threatened by an *Entente* victory and Social Democrat leaders who saw the war as a struggle against tsarist despotism justified their patriotism with phrases from Marx and Engels. The only *Reichstag* deputy killed in the war was a Jewish Social Democrat, formerly a pacifist.

The war was the greatest of all wars of nationality. Indeed, so long as Russia was part of the *Entente*, there could be no other convincing ideological division between the two sides. Both sides soon recognized this, by appealing to neutrals on grounds of self-interest and to the suppressed nationalities. Before long, Germans were trying to raise a Polish legion to serve against the tsars, were dabbling with insurrection in Ireland, planning independent Finnish and Ukrainian states and envisaging Turkey as the base for a subversion of Great Britain's Moslem subjects.[6] Revol-

3 See Laqueur, p. 87.
4 Max Weber, see Kohn, *The Mind of Germany* p. 285.
5 So did Kropotkin, the Russian anarchist.
6 See Fischer, ch. 4. 'The promotion of revolution' for interesting detail.

utionary nationalism was to be the great gainer from the war; of the political myths of the prewar world liberalism was to be gravely weakened, dynasticism shattered and democracy corrupted, but nationalism was to win its greatest victories.

Yet patriotism suffered terribly. The exaltation of the first months of war could not last. None of the combatant states except Russia and the Dual Monarchy had quite squandered the loyalty of its subjects even by the end of the war, but the idealism of 1914 ebbed and disappeared in 1915 and 1916 with the destruction of the first and best armies on both sides. The French at once lost 300,000 killed and wounded in a month of abortive offensives; the finest of the British volunteer armies had been destroyed by the end of 1916. Russia's losses of officers had by then outrun her total strength of reserve and line officers at the outbreak of the war. In that year, too, the five months' battle of Verdun cost the French and German armies 600,000 casualties, while the British army lost 57,000 men on the first day of the battle of the Somme, 20,000 of them killed.

No one was prepared for such fighting. But no one had prepared for so big a war. It grew until it was worldwide, several wars rolling into one, their purposes often clashing. By 1918 the only European neutrals were the Scandinavian states, Holland, Switzerland and Spain. Formally, at least, eleven American countries went to war. Baluchis from the Indian army and Senegalese from French Africa fought from the start in Europe. The mere geographical spread, nevertheless, had in some sort been foreshadowed in the colonial struggles of the past; in retrospect, it is the technicians' failure to foresee the nature of the war and its demands which is most surprising.

A few of them had glimpsed what was coming. Moltke in 1905 told the kaiser that the next war would 'become a war between peoples which is not to be concluded with a single battle but which will be a long, weary struggle with a country that will not acknowledge defeat until the whole strength of its people is broken; a war that even if we should be the victors will push our own people, too, to the limits of exhaustion'.[7] In 1914 Kitchener spoke of the need to plan three years ahead. Events soon bore them out.

7 See C. Barnett, *The Sword-bearers* (London, 1963), p. 34.

Within a few months the battlefields in the west were largely stabilized. The fighting on them assumed the character it was to have for the whole war. It was dominated by the advances in military technology which had made defensive fighting stronger than ever before. This had not been anticipated by the professionals although the weapons which produced the new conditions had been available for years and used in Manchuria. The new strength of the defence lay in increased fire-power, provided at first by the magazine rifle, and later by the machine-gun. Remington repeaters had been used at Plevna and in 1884 the German army was the first in Europe to adopt a magazine rifle. By 1914 all European armies had them and they had been used with great effect in the Boer War, yet their power was still underrated (partly because continental conscript armies expected a low standard of musketry; in 1914 the twelve aimed rounds per minute of the British professional soldier were exceptional). Nor was the machine-gun new. The Maxim gun, the first true automatic weapon, was patented in 1884; the British army adopted it in 1889, using it with conspicuous success in South Africa and the Sudan. Other armies followed suit, the German taking it up in 1901. Nevertheless, tactical doctrine found it difficult to define its role. It was only in the Great War that it became the master of the battlefield. With the development of light machine-guns the ratio of two guns to a battalion which was laid down for the British army in 1914 grew to over fifty. This was an enormous increase of fire-power. By 1918 tactics both defensive and offensive had been rebuilt around the power of this weapon.

Fire-power and barbed wire had by early 1915 eliminated cavalry from the west European battlefield and made unsupported infantry attacks impossible. The result was increasing reliance on artillery to prepare the attack. This, too, had not been foreseen. Between 1880 and 1914 the major advance in gunnery had been the appearance of the quick-firing field gun after the invention in the 1890s of mechanical means of absorbing a powerful recoil. By 1914 all armies had field guns which could deliver shells of about fifteen pounds weight at a high rate of fire; the most famous of them was the French 75 mm gun. These weapons had been evolved as part of a tactical doctrine which envisaged their main employment to be the firing of shrapnel shell at bodies of troops in the open. They were to 'cover' an attack, rather than to 'prepare' it by smashing defensive works. Yet the stopping-power of even crude entrenchments used in conjunction with up-to-date small arms fire had been shown long before. Field guns needed common shell in huge quantities to incapacitate the defenders of such works and as the war went on the need grew for medium and heavy guns which could pulverize barbed-wire entanglements and well-dug-in machine-gun nests. No army had enough of them in 1914, though the German army had many more than the French as well as a few super-heavy howitzers which quickly smashed the Belgian forts before Liége. Even when the guns were available, the expenditure of ammunition was unprecedented and far outran supply. In 1914 a French battery firing at its maximum rate would use every available round in thirteen minutes, but the bearing of such facts on ammunition supply had not been appreciated.

Failures to anticipate the effect of up-to-date weapons had tragic and ludicrous results. British regimental officers were ordered to get their swords sharpened at the opening of four years' trench warfare. The French army of 1914 went into action in red trousers which were the death of many of their wearers. But the most lethal errors were tactical. In spite of warnings from clear-sighted men, the doctrine of the offensive at all costs dominated the French *École de Guerre* before 1914 and cost thousands of French lives in the first month of the war. The Germans in 1914 also believed in the mass rush of infantry; like the French, they had no experience of the realities of war since 1871.

As soon as the first shock was over, a search began for ways of breaking the deadlock of trench warfare. Some were strategic: a way round the western obstacle was sought. Others were technical or tactical. Out of the search came poison gas (1915) and the tank (1916). Some old weapons, such as the grenade and the mortar, were revived and adapted for trench warfare. But in spite of innovations, tactics did not change much until 1918. Militarily, the first signs of an appreciation of the new conditions of warfare came behind the battle-front, where horse and railway were supplemented by tractor and lorry to make possible the maintenance of bigger armies than ever before with an ease which would have astounded Napoleon. The British army went to war with 100 lorries: it ended the war with 60,000. Advances in food-processing and medicine transformed logistics in another way, too: it was the first war in which the main combatants suffered more casualties by enemy action than by disease.[8]

The war at sea was no better foreseen than the war on land, although technical change had made the fleets of 1914 very different from those of 1880. The torpedo and the mine were available to countries which could not afford a big battle fleet. All major navies had submarines, and the torpedo-boat destroyer had been evolved to deal with the menace of torpedo-boat attack. Guns were bigger – the latest British battleships had 15-inch weapons – improved turbines and oil-firing drove the latest ships, and the armour-plate of the battleships was harder and often thicker. The most conspicuous difference between the navies of 1880 and those of 1914 was the combination of many of these technical advances in a new fighting-machine, which took its name from the revolutionary H.M.S. *Dreadnought*, launched in 1906. She was 1,500 tons heavier than the last pre-dreadnought built for the Royal Navy, and three knots faster. Instead of her predecessors' standard armament of four heavy and some medium guns, she had ten 12-inch guns and nothing else except an anti-torpedo-boat armament of small weapons. At one stroke, she made all existing battleships obsolete, because she could out-gun and out-sail any of them. In the next eight years the new formula for capital ships was adopted by all the major navies; the dreadnoughts grew still bigger, faster, more powerful. They also spawned a subspecies, the battle-cruiser, which sacrificed armour protection to yet higher speed.

Most naval staffs saw technical advances as new facts to be fitted into an older doctrine of naval war. British naval officers understood their wartime task to be the exercise of a general command of the seas which would probably involve one great battle – a Trafalgar of dreadnoughts. Their dispositions provided the major concentration of battleships in the North Sea, where a clash of fleets with the only probable enemy would take place. The Germans had been no more original in their naval thinking and had been less logical. The only point of building the High Seas Fleet at all had been to frighten the Royal Navy with a battlefleet action. Since they could not outbuild the British at the outbreak of the war, they were rarely likely to be in a position

8 In 1870–1, of every 1,000 soldiers mobilized in the French army, 37 were killed by enemy action, and 140 by sickness. In 1914–18, enemy action killed 135 per 1,000, and sickness only 20.

to force a fleet action on favourable terms and for the most part the High Seas Fleet stayed in port. The dreadnought Trafalgar never occurred. Jutland (1916), the only major fleet engagement, was decisive: although the German fleet escaped destruction, it never again risked a challenge to British supremacy in the North Sea. The monsters on which so much care and money had been lavished never performed their intended role. Instead, once isolated German ships and squadrons had been hunted down in the first months of the war, both navies settled down to a war of blockade which neither had envisaged in the form it took. The British had expected to bottle up the enemy's fleet and round up his merchantmen. By the end of the war, this had become a control of supplies of all kinds which disregarded the interest of neutrals and virtually starved the German people.[9] The Germans arrived at a similar strategy by different means. Unrestricted submarine warfare was nearly successful in 1917. Yet the German navy had been slow to see the potentialities of the submarine as a commerce destroyer.

It is less surprising that the possibilities of aircraft were not fully appreciated in 1914. The frail aeroplanes available had only short ranges and low speeds: they carried one, or at most two, people. Dirigible airships and balloons were more advanced. All three types of aircraft were already used for reconnaissance by armies and navies in 1914, and on 22 September the history of strategic bombing began with the dropping of three bombs on Zeppelin sheds at Düsseldorf. As the war went on, aircraft improved in power and reliability and began to be designed for specific duties as scouts, bombers or fighters which would dispute aerial superiority. By 1918 they were indispensable weapons.

Changes in military and naval technology had enormous indirect effects. Their demands revolutionized economics. Before 1914 only one German book had seriously discussed the connexion of the economy with the readiness for war. 'We had prepared no food regulations, did not even consider drafts of wartime industrial regulations', said a German economist; 'Even our ammunition was not planned for a large-scale war.'[10] A month before the war, Germany was still exporting rye she would soon need. In Britain, the first wartime slogan was 'Business as

9 With the help of the German army (see p. 286).
10 Naumann, see Meyer, *Mitteleuropa*, p. 123.

Usual'; it had a century of experience to justify it. Change was slow. This first sign was the disruption of inter-European trade. Governments soon had to undertake the control of foreign exchange and investments. Then, conscription began to affect the labour-force. In some areas, capital equipment was destroyed in the fighting. With shipping more in demand than ever before, the British Empire was unable to replace the ships it lost; it was to finish the war with a total tonnage about two-thirds of that of 1914. Blockade, added to such changes, meant that the United Kingdom, France, Germany and Sweden all produced less pig-iron in 1918 than in 1913. German domestic food production fell further than food imports and at the end of 1916 the area under crops in the United Kingdom was smaller than in 1914. War also had some productive effects: the big German synthetic rubber industry was the creation of wartime needs.

The material demand was unprecedented. In 1914 the British army was still thinking of using 250,000 sandbags a month; in May 1915 it had to ask for 6 million. Expansion on this scale was the greatest blow yet dealt to *laissez-faire* economics. In 1915 a new era opened; governments had to realize that private industry was not able to feed the war machine. Public interference with the economy soon became normal. The high degree of coordination and consolidation which already existed in her industry may explain why Germany preceded other countries in organizational change. Whereas the industrialist Rathenau set up the War Raw Materials Departments to regulate scarce commodities in 1914, the English ministry of munitions did not appear until May 1915, after a scandalous shortage of shells. The turning-point, as in so many things, came in the winter of 1916, when Germany equipped herself fully for economic war. A National Service Law then imposed what was virtually an unlimited conscription for military or industrial service and established compulsory arbitration of labour disputes. The *Oberster Kriegsamt* had already been set up in October to accelerate production. In 1916 the British government, too, set up five new departments of state to run the economy. France moved more slowly, but just as decisively, along the same road.

Everywhere, the key shortage was of manpower. The armies demanded men, but so did industry and agriculture. In Russia, where industry was stripped of workers, the armies could not be supplied. The British government took longer to grasp the nettle than the German but introduced military conscription for the first time in 1916. This made possible a system of exemptions which, in effect, provided administrative direction of labour. In Germany the subordination of all needs to that for soldiers lowered agricultural production and weakened Germany's resistance to blockade. The same thing happened in Italy. By 1918 3.7 million of the French agricultural labour force of 5.2 million had been taken. Labour was never, in fact, allocated perfectly in any country, but the attempts to deal with this problem helped to integrate trade unions with the states they had before the war tended to see as enemies, especially in Germany and France.

To the better-off the financial demands of the war brought new interference with property. During the war the standard rate of income tax in the United Kingdom rose from 1s 2d to 5s in the pound. The Germans started in a less favourable position; they did not have income tax in 1914. Nevertheless, taxes were not enough; the British National Debt rose from £649 million in 1914 to £7,454 million in 1919. Landed property was regulated in Great Britain from 1917 when Orders began to enforce the raising of needed crops. In return, the farmers were guaranteed minimum prices.

Such changes made the war begin to resemble what some observers had always seen in it, a conflict of economic systems which transcended national boundaries. The growth of a siege mentality in Germany and Austria-Hungary helped the welding together of the economies; the dreams of the *Mitteleuropa* enthusiasts seemed on the verge of realization when in 1916 normal rail traffic again ran between Germany and Turkey and the Danube was open. But in 1915 Hungary, the granary of the Dual Monarchy, closed her economic frontiers, with disastrous effects for Austria. The much-praised economic unity of the Dual Monarchy was in ruins long before the creation of new states at Versailles. Economic coordination was more effective on the Allied side. The Paris economic conferences of 1916 which tightened the blockade were one of the first signs of this. In 1917 an Allied Maritime Transport Council was set up to allocate ships and in the next year a series of inter-allied 'programme committees' on scarce materials came into existence. The Inter-Allied Committee of prime ministers had already begun to meet in 1916 to discuss general policies, and in 1917 the Supreme War Council was formally established with a permanent military staff to advise its political members.

The war seemed to move towards an absolute form in which everything was subordinate to the aim of victory (although there were always important limits to what could be achieved in practice). The involvement of the civilian population grew. Noncombatants were the target of economic and psychological warfare; rationing and price controls made their appearance to protect them. The German government was in 1915 the first to ration food; Italy followed in 1917; England only had a comprehensive rationing scheme for sugar, fats and meat in July 1918, but by the end of the war the Ministry of Food had for many commodities abolished the market. Aerial bombing and the confiscation of enemy property also showed the deepening involvement of civilians in the war.

As the war went on, more and more of the ordinary immunities which the civilian had built up over a century of peace were taken away. As morale flagged, liberalism gave ground everywhere. Germany was centralized under military government. In August 1916 Hindenburg and Ludendorff, generals who had won spectacular success on the eastern front, were appointed respectively chief of staff and quartermaster general. From this time both the emperor's authority and civilian influences were increasingly set aside. But the *Reichstag* still met; in Austria, parliament ceased to be called until 1917. In Great Britain and France the civilians continued to govern, but with a difference. When Lloyd George became prime minister in December 1916, a war cabinet of five (later six) members took up the central direction of the war and the big cabinet vanished. In France Clemenceau came to power in November 1917. More of a personal dictatorship than Lloyd George's, his government resembled the British and German in reducing policy to the search for victory.

By the end of 1916 the war had worn out many institutions and assumptions and was generating new ones. This was a revolutionary process. The experience of wartime direction of economic life, as Rathenau hinted, was an education in state socialism. War government meant the suspension of constitutional liberties and parliamentary immunities. Class hatred was exacerbated by food shortages. In the end, as the last eighteen months of the war were to show, the fabric of some states would be unequal to the strain.

THE SPREAD OF THE WAR, 1914–17

Prewar diplomacy had brought together the quarrels between the Dual Monarchy and Russia and between France and Germany; only Germany was interested in both. A contest for world supremacy between Great Britain and Germany had little relevance to either. Consequently, from the beginning, the Great War was a complex of wars, rather than a simple conflict of two sides.

It was soon further complicated by Turkey. Turkish policy had deep roots in fear of Russia. Turkish conviction that Germany would win the war led to an alliance with her against Russia on 2 August 1914. This alliance was limited; it envisaged no conflict with England or France, although the British government had irritated the Turkish by requisitioning two Turkish battleships building in British yards. At this juncture, two powerful German ships, the battle-cruiser *Goeben* and the *Breslau*, settled the fate of the Ottoman Empire by anchoring off the Golden Horn on 11 August. They were officially sold to the Turks by the German government, who thus assumed naval command of the Black Sea.[11] The Turkish attitude now hardened. On 1 October, the Capitulations were abolished (the German Ambassador being among those who protested). Russian efforts to placate the Turks and to secure their neutrality came to nothing. On 28 October Turkish ships bombarded Odessa. The Allies declared war on the Ottoman Empire four days later, and the Caliph proclaimed a Holy War against the infidel.

This completed the teams of combatants for the first eight months of the war. The only other important participating power was Japan, which declared war on Germany on 23 August. Japanese forces captured Tsingtao and a number of German islands in the Pacific, but the main Japanese contribution to the war was to be naval and industrial. Turkey's entry was more important. The first effect was that the Straits were closed to Russia. Supplies could not be passed to her through the Black Sea and by December the Russian army was already forced on to the defensive by shortages. As could be predicted, this effective separation of the two main strategical theatres of the war, the western and eastern fronts, led to great Allied efforts to link them again. The state of Balkan politics and the sprawl of the Ottoman

11 Russia had four dreadnoughts, but they were in the Baltic.

Empire in Asia offered a wide range of strategical possibilities.

It also offered the Allies, too, a revolutionary weapon. Like the Dual Monarchy, the Ottoman Empire, without knowing it, committed suicide by going to war. The nationalist revolts against Turkish rule which had been unfolding for a century in Europe and Africa were now to be repeated in Asia. Although a *Jihad* had been proclaimed, such tribal and medieval figures as the sherif of Mecca or the emir of Nejd turned to nationality rather than religion as the future basis of Arab politics. The negotiations which led to an Arab revolt in 1916 began soon after the war began, and Islamic history entered a new phase, in which its unity was to be shattered by the dynamic of nationalism on the European model. The Turks could do little, because German military aid fell short of what had been hoped. They attempted to cut the Suez canal, but the further spread of the war, until the entry of the United States, was to be the result of allied initiatives.[12]

The strength of the two sides in 1914 can roughly be summed up as follows:[13]

	Population	Armies	Navies
The *Entente* powers in Europe	256 m	199 divns	44 + 71
The central powers and Turkey	137 m	136 divns	27 + 35

The Allied advantage in numbers has to be qualified. The Russian army's numbers were badly backed up by logistical services. Britain and France both had to maintain large forces of white troops outside Europe, and Russia could not denude Siberia of the garrisons which might have to resist Japanese pressure on China. In 1914, the most formidable army in the field was undoubtedly the German, led with great skill and backed by larger numbers of trained reserves than any other. On the other hand, as the war went on, important contributions of men were made by the British Dominions, the Indian army took over more imperial

12 Germany made several diplomatic efforts to get the Japanese to make peace; they were ably exploited by the Japanese to win concessions from her own allies and had no other effect. See F. W. Iklé, 'Japanese-German Peace Negotiations during World War I', *AHR*, 1965.
13 Populations are approximate. The naval figures show capital ship strength (i.e. including battle-cruisers) distinguished as dreadnoughts + pre-dreadnoughts.

duties and released British units for Europe, and France employed large numbers of colonial troops on the western front.[14] Sea power did not seem to matter very much; in 1914 no one guessed how navies would affect the issue of the war because few people had foreseen its length. In immediate economic and industrial strength, there was a rough balance. Germany had a more modern industrial machine, and better scientific and technological preparation. The Allies included one great backward nation, and unlike Austria-Hungary, which was economically something of a burden to Germany, Russia was hard to help. On the other hand, Great Britain's financial resources and sea power made it possible for her to draw upon her empire and on neutrals, as Germany could not. Because of the access which it gave to the United States, the significance of this, too, would grow as the war lasted longer.

Certain non-quantitative facts also mattered. On the Allied side, coordination and communication were difficult; the central powers had the advantage of interior lines. The Allies also found it hard to define their strategical objectives. The early campaigns placed Germany in possession of a big tract of France and nearly all Belgium; by simply staying there, the German generals held the advantage. On the other hand, the central powers had their difficulties, too; Hindenburg was only made commander of the whole eastern front after the defeat of his allies in 1916. And the German High Command soon had to face the spectre which the whole of its planning had been directed to exorcising, that of a drawn-out war on two fronts. The danger was not wholly removed even in 1917, thanks to German ambitions in the east, and by then the cutting of Germany's sea communications in the first months of the war had begun to sap her strength.

Military events slowly revealed that the balance of power was a reality. The story of the war until 1917 is the story of attempts to break a deadlock which existed in essence from the end of 1914. The war was by then virtually confined to Europe; most of the German colonies had been mopped up (although a German army was still in the field in East Africa in 1918 and had successfully invaded Rhodesia). The western front in Europe had been stabilized. The great blow of the Schlieffen plan had failed because

14 'British troops' in this chapter (and chapter 16) usually means 'British and Dominion'.

insufficient forces had been provided to carry it out; the battle of the Marne, in September 1914, forced the Germans to abandon the war of movement and adopt a defensive strategy within an immense citadel of Belgian and French territory.

The first French offensives in Lorraine had been smashed in the bloodiest fighting of the war. After a 'race to the sea' was over, two virtually continuous trench-lines faced one another from Flanders to Switzerland.[15] Fighting in the east had opened with a Russian offensive against Galicia and East Prussia to help the Allies. This drew off German forces badly needed in the west, a strategic success for which the Russians paid with the catastrophic defeats of Tannenberg (26–30 August) and the Masurian Lakes (6–15 September). Enormous but inconclusive battles continued to rage until the end of the year, which found the Russian army still threatening Cracow. On the Serbian front the first Austrian offensive was repulsed. This ended the hope of finishing off Serbia quickly, and in September the Serbian army briefly invaded Austrian territory. An Austrian recovery led to the capture of Belgrade (2 December), but it was retaken a fortnight later.

Although German strategy had failed to achieve the quick over-throw of one of its enemies, and although it was hampered by an incompetent ally, its prospects for 1915 were not unfavourable. The British blockade had not yet begun to hurt. In the west, the German army could sit tight on conquered ground; it would require a major allied effort to displace it, and if it wished to attack it could do so from a favourable position. The Allies were less satisfactorily placed. They had to take the offensive, or they had lost. Broadly speaking, three courses were open to them. They could seek new allies, they could embark upon 'side-shows' which would indirectly weaken their enemies' main fronts, or they could attempt to defeat the German army in the west. These strategies might be combined, and they could all be conducted against the background of the steady pressure of blockade.

A search for new allies inevitably led to the further compli-cation of the already complicated question of war aims. These emerged only slowly and incoherently. Germany's were clear enough, although there has been much argument about responsi-

15 Casualties in the first three months: French 854,000, British 85,000, German 677,000.

bility for them.[16] Adequate securities for Germany meant annexations of Belgian territory, the Longwy area, Luxemburg, the Polish borderlands and Lithuania, and control of satellite régimes in rump Belgium, Poland, Holland and (after 1915) the Ukraine and Finland. The essentials of this programme on which Germany would not compromise were the annexations and control of Belgium. As England had gone to war over this, a deadlock was implied which could only be broken by victory.

On the Allied side, England, France and Russia quickly agreed not to make peace separately, but made formal agreements about a postwar settlement only in March 1915. The Russians were promised Constantinople and the Straits in order to steer them away from dreams they shared with Balkan states about the dissolution of the Dual Monarchy, a war aim which the British government would not accept for another two years. The British *quid pro quo* was to be the formal acquisition of Egypt. While this implied the partition, at last, of the Ottoman Empire, the British route to India could be maintained by holding the Canal Zone. Partition had many times been envisaged as a solution to the Turkish Question; at last Britain accepted the idea.

Meanwhile, Italy had been detached from the Triple Alliance. Instead of joining her Allies in 1914, Italy had used the opportunity to pick up some territory in Albania. The German government pressed the Dual Monarchy to concede territory to Italy, and there was talk of the cession of the Trentino, but Italy, under the leadership of a new foreign minister, held out for more. As they were able to give away other people's territory, the Allies bid higher (in spite of Russian misgivings about the future interests of Serbia) and Italy concluded the secret treaty of London with the Allies (26 April 1915). She was promised the south Tyrol, Trieste and Istria, many of the Dalmatian islands and reversionary rights to Turkish territory if there was a colonial partition. Serbia was to be compensated with southern Dalmatia for the transfer of territories with Slav populations. This was, after all, a step towards the partition of the Dual Monarchy.

16 For the two main views, see F. Fischer (Generals and the Chancellor alike wanted a German-dominated Europe as described above) and G. Ritter, *Staatskunst und Kriegshandwerk: das Problem der 'Militarismus' in Deutschland*, vol. III, *Die Tragödie der Staatskunst: Bethmann Hollweg als Kriegskanzler* (Munich, 1964) (only the generals were to blame).

This bought Italy's entry into the war. On 3 May, she denounced her alliances, and on 23 May declared war on the Dual Monarchy; she did not declare war on Germany until August 1916. For Italy, it was the last war of the *Risorgimento*; she had little interest in the struggle against Germany which preoccupied France and Great Britain. Another complicating subsidiary war had been added to the grand complex, but it is not obvious that the *Entente* had achieved much more than a propaganda success. The new front against Austria-Hungary made her more dependent on Germany and an independent Habsburg policy became more difficult. Croat loyalty to the dynasty revived. South Slav exiles and the Serbian government found out about the secret treaty of London and this led to mistrust among the Allies. Finally, Italy turned out to be a military liability. Perhaps, though, the diversion of Austrian strength helped Russia to stay in the field.

The strategy of seeking new allies also went forward by other means. The central powers could never hope to use the revolutionary weapon of nationalist subversion as effectively as their opponents, because it was in the multi-racial patchwork of the Dual Monarchy that the greatest potential for subversion lay. It is only superficially paradoxical, therefore, that Russia, although herself a multi-national empire, appealed to the Poles with an offer of limited autonomy as early as 14 August 1914, and the tsar received Czech deputations in audience a few days later. A month later, the Slavs of the Dual Monarchy were assured that their national aspirations would be fulfilled through Russia's liberating efforts. Nevertheless, in the end Russia failed to solve the problem a Polish liberation would pose.[17] Yet the central powers could agree about it no more easily. The Germans wanted an independent Russian Poland; the Austrians thought this dangerous for their own Polish territory. Only in November 1916 did the two emperors proclaim Polish independence, after occupying most of Poland, and raising Polish troops against the Russians. This puppet state adopted a constitution (30 January 1917), and was thus the first 'new' nation to emerge from the war. Not surprisingly, France and Great Britain entered the field of revolutionary warfare in Europe more slowly than had Russia; the Dual

17 See *Russian Diplomacy and Eastern Europe 1914–1917*, ed. H. C. Roberts (New York, 1963).

Monarchy was not their main enemy and the British feared for the postwar balance of power. Their exploitation of political subversion was only to begin in 1917.

The second main strategy available to the Allies – that of side-shows – was attractive to many British. Operations against Turkey were needed to defend the Suez canal and the Persian Gulf. It dawned, slowly, that the 'Arab revolt' would have more weight if supported by British operations. It was also desirable to open communications with Russia through the Straits. Finally, a threat to Turkey might lead to the withdrawal of German troops from the western front.

An early Turkish advance on the Suez canal was pushed back, but had alarmed the British government enough to tie down large numbers of British troops in Egypt for the rest of the war. The Turks were pressing hard in the Caucasus by the beginning of 1915, and this, too, played a part in the decision to attack the Dardanelles, the most famous of all the schemes of the 'easterners' (as those British soldiers who favoured action away from the western front were called). The aim was to seize Constantinople by combined naval and land action after forcing the Dardanelles. The operation began in February 1915 and lasted nearly a year before it was abandoned. It failed because of inadequate forces and direction in the early stages, good German and Turkish leadership, the bitter opposition of 'westerners' to the diversion of effort from France, and because of the alarm of the British Admiralty when three battleships were lost. Each side suffered about 250,000 casualties. This great failure convinced the 'westerners' that only the western front could be decisive. It ended the hope of supplying Russia through the Straits, led to a political crisis in Great Britain and may have lengthened the war by another three years.

It was not the end of Allied operations in the eastern Mediterranean where a landing at Salonika grew out of a search for new Balkan allies. Early hopes of a Balkan league had been disappointed. Only Serbia and Montenegro went to war in 1914; Greece, Bulgaria and Rumania all stayed neutral. The Greek government favoured the allies, but the king, Constantine, did not; Venizelos, the prime minister, had to resign in March 1915, and Greek foreign policy developed in a pro-German sense. Meanwhile, both the Russians and the central powers courted Rumania. Her ties with the central powers had deteriorated more since the death in October 1914 of the pro-German king Carol, and the Russians were always more hopeful of winning her over than of constituting a Balkan league. Already in September 1914 they promised Rumania territory in Transylvania and the Bukovina. Unfortunately, the Rumanian government refused to declare itself until there were enough Allied troops in the Balkans to defend it.

By the end of 1914 even Bulgaria had received an Allied offer; her disappointment after the second Balkan War was to be assuaged by Macedonian territory taken from Serbia (who could be paid off with Bosnia, it was thought). This did not attract the Bulgarians; it was far more likely that they could seize at once the Greek and Serbian Lands they coveted than that they could survive the hostility of the central powers and cash their post-dated *Entente* cheque at the end of the war. In consequence, Bulgaria was the first Balkan state to get off the fence. She allied herself with Germany in September 1915. Her obvious target was Serbia, which appealed for assistance to Greece, where the pro-*Entente* Venizelos had returned to power. He obtained the king's consent to the landing of British and French forces at Salonika (although as a blind, an official refusal of their request to land was issued). On 3 October, their disembarkation began. Three days later an Austro-German offensive began which captured Belgrade for the second time, and on 11 October the Bulgarians also attacked Serbia. Unfortunately for the Allies, a crucial piece was suddenly missing. On 5 October, Venizelos resigned when the king refused to join in the war; his successors resisted all Allied efforts to persuade them (even turning down a British offer of Cyprus) and simply proclaimed their benevolent neutrality in return for promises of the restoration of Greek territory at the end of the war. The results were disastrous for the Allies. Serbia collapsed and her army took refuge first in Albania, then in Corfu (where the French installed themselves in spite of Greek objections). In December Montenegro was overrun; in January, Albania. The British and French were bottled up in Salonika after being defeated by the Bulgarians.

This demanded a new Allied effort in the Balkans in 1916. Distrust of the Greek government led in June to an Anglo-French blockade which forced the demobilization of much of the Greek army. At the same time, the Salonika force was recruited by the Serbian divisions from Corfu, by Russians and by Italians. The

British government disliked the Salonika operation but agreed to join in an offensive to relieve German pressure on the armies in France. It was launched, unsuccessfully, in August. What was left of the Greek army was captured by the Germans. This settled the political fate of Greece. At the end of August a pro-Venizelos movement appeared at Salonika under the patronage of the French commander. In September Venizelos formed a provisional government in Crete which crossed to Salonika and declared war on the Germans and Bulgarians. Meanwhile, relations with the Greek government in Athens deteriorated and fighting between Greek and Allied forces had taken place. On 16 December the British government recognized the government of Venizelos.[18]

Before this happened, another disaster overtook the Allies. Russian diplomacy and a successful offensive had at last brought Rumania into the war (28 August). But the Rumanian invasion of Transylvania was stopped almost at once, and soon the Rumanians were falling back. Bucarest fell on 6 December. By the end of January 1917, Rumania's oil and wheat were securely in the hands of the central powers. The Allies' search for new allies and attempts to fight Germany away from the western front seemed unavailing.

During the whole of this time, fighting had gone on fiercely but indecisively in France. Early British and French efforts to break the German line failed because of underestimation of the effort required. In 1915 the French lost 90,000 men in early March in Champagne, 100,000 in Artois in May and June. The autumn campaign cost another 190,000 French casualties; in the battle of Loos the British lost 60,000. More guns, it was concluded, would be needed for 1916. The major German offensive of 1915, at Ypres, achieved some success by using a new weapon produced to beat the trench deadlock, poison gas. Another, the tank, was first used by the British on the Somme in 1916. Before this, fighting of unprecedented fierceness had blazed up before the French fortress of Verdun in a battle deliberately planned to destroy France's will to fight by inflicting unbearable losses; the

---

18 Uncertainty over Greece dragged on a few months more until the failure of further operations in Macedonia led to an Allied ultimatum which obtained the abdication of King Constantine and the accession of Venizelos to the premiership. Greece then entered the war on the Allied side (27 June 1917).

German command believed that the French army would bleed to death there rather than concede ground and the calculation was nearly correct. From 21 February, when 1,400 German guns began their preliminary bombardment, to the French recapture in November of forts they had lost in February, the German army suffered 280,000 casualties and the French 515,000. This ghastly battle strained the French army badly; its morale was seriously weakened. An Allied offensive on the Somme in July had to be undertaken without the large number of French divisions planned. Seven days of unprecedented artillery bombardment preceded the assault on 1 July, to so little effect that the British army lost nearly 60,000 men on that day alone. When the offensive petered out in November, the Allies between them on the Somme had lost 600,000 men, two-thirds of them British; the German army lost 615,000.

Slaughter like this had never been seen before. The eastern front was almost as bad. Advances and retreats of enormous distances differentiated the fighting from the deadlock of France, and the fronts were less continuous, but casualties were almost as heavy. The Russian armies held their ground magnificently in 1914, but an Austro-German offensive in May 1915 shattered them. By December they had lost Warsaw, 300,000 prisoners and 3,000 guns. At one point the forces of the central powers advanced 300 miles, and Russia was only saved from worse by the diversion of her opponents' forces to Serbia in the summer. Yet a vast effort of repair and re-equipment produced another great Russian offensive in 1916. It began in March, in response to appeals from the French, and was at once stopped, losing 110,000 men. In May, however, the 'Brusilov offensive' (named after its army commander) was startlingly successful; it was the last great feat of arms of the Russian Empire.[19] In October Brusilov stopped, after taking 400,000 prisoners and 500 guns. His success led to reluctant Austrian agreement to the appointment of a German to the supreme command on the whole eastern front (30 July).

Such bloodshed made men cast about for other ways to win the war. Some, like the aerial bombing of civilians, were spectacular but not very effective. Propaganda warfare was more important. The most promising alternative was economic

19 One factor in its success was the German army's commitment at Verdun.

blockade. The British blockade tightened steadily and ruthlessly. In 1916 Allied agreements with neutral countries made it almost complete. The German reply was to attempt her own blockade of the *Entente* power vulnerable at sea, Great Britain, by means of submarine attacks. Oddly, this had not been thought practical before the war. When, in February 1915, it was decided to destroy any British ship in a 'war zone' around the United Kingdom, only four or five U-boats could be assembled in the Western Approaches. In April they sank twenty-three ships – but in that month 1,500 entered and left British ports each week. In May the liner *Lusitania* was torpedoed and 1,200 people were drowned; the outcry among neutrals, particularly Americans, was so great that the German government abandoned attacks on merchant shipping. It was only to be resumed a year and a half later, in the crisis of the war.

THE CRISIS OF THE WAR 1916–17

In 1916 the harvests were poor and by Christmas there was famine in the Balkans. Russian cities were short of food and the régime on the verge of collapse. 'The people in the suburbs of Vienna are starving', wrote the German ambassador there in September, and he doubted whether the Dual Monarchy could carry on much longer.[20] In Germany infant mortality in 1917 was nearly one-and-a-half times the 1915 level. Food riots and strikes were more frequent. Meanwhile the fighting had by the end of 1916 cost the French 3,350,000 casualties, the Germans 2,460,000, and the British over 1,000,000. It was hardly surprising that the spirit of the soldiers was no longer that of 1914. The French and Russian armies had suffered most, and both were to prove unreliable in 1917.

Suffering and casualties were beginning to undermine civilian morale. On the Allied side there were some politicians who might rally opposition to the war. Giolitti, who had opposed Italy's entry, was believed to be in touch with Caillaux, the outstanding opponent of the war in France. In Russia, the appointment to ministerial office of the pro-German Sturmer in February 1916,

20 See Zeman, p. 96.

seemed to show a weakening of the régime's will to fight. Even in England, during the last weeks of Asquith's ministry, a member of the war cabinet drew up a memorandum on the possibility of negotiated peace at the suggestion of the prime minister, which suggested that there might really never come an opportunity to bring off the much-desired 'knock-out blow'.

Explicit opposition to the war was less noticeable in the central powers. By 1916, nevertheless, socialist support of the war had begun to crumble.[21] An anti-war socialist party soon appeared in Austria. The first sign of a similar split in Germany came in December 1914 when Karl Liebknecht voted against further war credits in the *Reichstag*. He was the only socialist deputy to do so, but in 1915, Kautsky, Bernstein and many other S.P.D. leaders denounced the war. The old divisions of orthodox and revisionist were being traversed by new ones. In 1916 an Independent Socialist Party appeared. When, after a great antiwar demonstration on 1 May, Liebknecht was arrested, 50,000 Berliners came out on strike. Yet although working-class opposition to the war grew after the November service law, the official trade union leadership still supported the war effort, and those politicians and civil servants who had come to believe that a negotiated peace was desirable, were unable to court the support of antiwar socialists who were formally, and often actually, revolutionaries. Yet without mass support politicians could do nothing if the kaiser did not accept their ideas. Germany stayed at war for the same reason that she entered it, because of the vacuum created by her sham constitutional structure at the centre of policy making.

Attempts had been made to stop the war. A conference of neutral socialists at Lugano in September 1914 was the first; at a second conference at Zimmerwald a year later, unofficial delegates from France and Germany were present. It denounced the war as an interest only of capitalists, and 'official' socialists were condemned for supporting their governments. Other and more important attempts to mediate came from the United States of America. In an immediate sense, no American interest except her maritime rights was likely to be affected by the war, and European quarrels seemed remote and frivolous. British propaganda

---

21 In England, the I.L.P. had consistently opposed the war, but remained affiliated to the Labour movement whose representative, Arthur Henderson, entered the war cabinet in December 1916.

and big Allied purchases of war materials did not much affect the general wish not to take sides. The president of the republic, Woodrow Wilson, was a humanitarian who hated war (he had been brought up in the South during Reconstruction); he could at first discern in the European conflict only a dispute whether Europe should in future be dominated by Germany or Russia. Until November 1916 he was also increasingly preoccupied with the outcome of a presidential election (which he won) and it is not surprising that his earliest messages to the combatant states were mainly assertions of America's maritime rights. This might have led to America being at war with both sides at once, since both sides infringed them. It did not do so because of the difference between the nature of British and German interference; the British merely diverted and delayed them, while the Germans sank American ships and drowned American travellers. Early German submarine attacks produced such tart diplomatic exchanges that American public opinion moved far more decisively against Germany than against the Allies. During 1915, nevertheless, the end of the first phase of German submarine activity led Wilson to try to mediate but only the threat of armed intervention could have made this effective, and this was ruled out by American domestic politics. The November election was won by Wilson on a peace platform: intervention was out of the question.

Wilson's efforts to mediate were stimulated anew in December by a German note suggesting a negotiated peace. It was unspecific and followed hard on German victory in Rumania; the Allies, to whom it was transmitted, rejected it out of hand (30 December). But it led Wilson to appeal to each side to state its terms. The central powers again replied unspecifically, but the Allied governments issued their first publicly avowed war aims (30 January 1917). Not surprisingly, they insisted on the restoration of lost territories and just reparation; they also, for the first time, demanded the application of the principle of nationality as the basis of European reorganization, and the liberation of the subject peoples of the Dual Monarchy. This potentially revolutionary programme seemed unreasonable to Wilson. He sought a clearer statement of German aims. These were communicated secretly (29 January), but further negotiation was made meaningless by the resumption of unrestricted submarine warfare.

Wilson had been working against the grain of events. Attitudes on both sides had hardened. The hope of a separate peace with the Dual Monarchy had faded in London and Paris and no German terms that did not include, as the soldiers insisted, the strategic control of Belgium and big annexations in the east was conceivable. Neutrals had no leverage for mediation. The intransigence of the military predominance in German policy-making had already been shown over Poland. The object of the November proclamation had been to raise a Polish army to fight the Russians, but it made a separate peace with Imperial Russia impossible because no tsarist government could envisage giving up Warsaw. Soon after the proclamation, Sturmer was dismissed.

The most important consequence of the 'silent dictatorship' in Germany was the new strategical departure of 1917, the adoption of unrestricted submarine warfare. The American government had known this was under discussion a year before. Tirpitz had resigned in March 1916 because he had not been allowed to adopt it. The arguments were simple. Submarine warfare offered the only chance of defeating England before the British blockade strangled Germany. England could be starved if every ship, combatant or neutral, sailing to or from her ports were attacked. The price to be paid was America's entry to the war on the Allied side. The decision therefore turned on the probability of the submarines being effective in the months which would pass before the United States could deploy its armies in Europe. As 1916 wore on, the kaiser's civilian advisers grew less and less able to resist the logic of the British blockade: Germany itself was going to starve if the U-boats were not used. At the end of the year, 100 were available for immediate action. The decision was at last taken on 9 January 1917. It was the final capitulation of civilian government in Imperial Germany; Bethmann-Hollweg disagreed, but did not resign.

Thus the German admirals brought about what British propaganda had struggled to achieve. American manpower and money would now reinforce the strained armies and depleted coffers of the Allies. American opinion had been partially prepared by Germany's unresponsiveness to Wilson's overtures in 1916. The Allied declaration of war aims, by taking up the cry of 'national self-determination' after the war, had pleased ethnic groups represented in large numbers in the United States. The decision to sink at sight therefore fell on prepared ground, although on 22 January Wilson was still appealing to the belligerents to make a 'peace without victory'. When the official German notification was received, the United States broke off diplomatic relations (3 February). There quickly followed more evidence of German disregard for America in the 'Zimmermann telegram' from the German foreign office to its minister in Mexico, instructing him to negotiate an alliance with Mexico and Japan against the United States. It had been intercepted in January by British Intelligence, and was not communicated to the American government until 24 February, when German attacks on American ships gave it greater psychological effect. On 15 March, an American ship was sunk without warning. On 6 April, the United States declared war on Germany.

Thus the war was transformed. From a matter between the European great powers, it became one of world powers. To a jumble of wars about the European balance and national rivalries was to be added an ideological crusade. Henceforth the victory of the Allies was certain, if they could only hold on long enough for the Americans to reach the battlefields of France. The age of European domination of world history was beginning to close; the strength of the New World was necessary to contain the most powerful nation of the Old. Immediately, the moral effect of the American entry to the war was enormous; enthusiasm was slowly to dissipate during the weary wait for the American armies to arrive.

Another great event was also to take time to reveal its full significance. The decision on submarine warfare had only been taken by Germany's leaders because, in spite of inflicting grievous wounds on Russia, Germany still had to fight a two-front war. German strategy had turned to the submarine attack on England because of the impossibility of a decisive victory in the west while large German forces were tied down in the east. Russian endurance until 1917 had been the necessary condition of the American intervention, though this went unrecognized at the time. Yet just before the American declaration of war there came the first clear signs that even Russian endurance was not limitless. Riots in Petrograd[22] led to mutiny, the appearance of a provisional government and, on 15 March, to the abdication of the tsar. The

22 The substitution of the Russian form 'Petrograd' for the Germanic 'St Petersburg' was, like the adoption of the name Windsor by the British Royal family, a by-product of wartime patriotism.

first of the dynasties to be victims of the war had fallen: one of the pillars of European conservatism had gone. The prewar balance of power, too, was stricken at its roots; the revolution inaugurated twenty years of virtual isolation for Russia.[23]

At first, it looked as if the Russians would go on fighting (the new government announced its intention of doing so) and the March revolution did much to purge the *Entente* of one of its disqualifications in the eyes of some liberals and Americans. Yet Wilson still tried to distinguish himself from the *Entente* powers, whose aims and assumptions he suspected. America, symbolically, was officially an 'associated power', not an ally; she had no permanent political representative on the Supreme War Council until almost the end of the war. Wilson consciously emphasized his countrymen's idealism; in his War Message to Congress he called on them to fight 'for the things that we have always carried nearest our hearts, for democracy, for the rights and liberties of small nations, for the universal dominion of right by such a concert of free peoples as will bring peace and safety to all nations, and make the world itself at last free'.[24] Vague such a programme might be, but it, too, was revolutionary. It confirmed German fears that a negotiated peace must lead to undesirable social and constitutional changes and it further lessened the chances of prising away the Dual Monarchy to a separate peace, because of its nationalist implications.

A second effect of the Russian revolution was to invigorate the German socialists. For many of them, the thought that they were participating in a struggle against an autocratic Russia had eased their consciences in 1914. Freedom, they could now argue, was no longer threatened from the east. This was a contributory factor, though a minor one, to a political crisis in July which resulted in the overthrow of Bethmann Hollweg and his replacement by a nonentity.[25] It was the consummation of the military takeover begun under Ludendorff and Hindenburg the previous years. The Kaiser was henceforth almost disregarded in Germany's government. Only the breaking of the generals' will by defeat could now bring peace. In these circumstances, a much-

23 See pp. 422 ff.
24 R. Birley, *Speeches and Documents in American History*, IV, *1914–1939* (Oxford, 1942), p. 27.
25 Michaelis, an official of the Prussian ministry of finance and said to have been unknown to the kaiser before his appointment.

discussed 'Peace Resolution' passed by the majority parties (Socialist, Centre and Progressive) of the *Reichstag* was insignificant, worded as it was to exclude only annexations by force; it could, as Michaelis said in accepting it, be used to make any peace the government liked.[26] Compatible with sweeping aims of expansion and hegemony in the east, the Reichstag's only independent action during the war simply eased the consciences of the majority who proceeded at once to vote a huge new instalment of war credits. Germany's rulers seemed more firmly in the saddle than ever, in spite of growing numbers of strikes in favour of peace by trades unionists no longer willing to follow their officials. But there were few signs of weakening in France or Great Britain either. Mutinies in the French army during the summer of 1917 caused alarm, but within a few months Pétain had carefully nursed it back to health and reliability. The socialists left the government, and the *union sacré* was at an end in September, but in November France had a new Prime Minister, Clemenceau. He was a survivor of the Chamber of Deputies which had accepted Germany's terms in 1871, and of all Germany's opponents he was the most implacable and unyielding.

The years when peace might still have been negotiated by agreement were over. Soon after the death of the old Emperor Franz Joseph in November 1916, his successor, the Emperor Charles, had opened indirect negotiations with Britain and France. They had come to nothing because no terms could be agreed upon which would satisfy the Italians, and it was Italy and Russia who were the main opponents of the Dual Monarchy. The only effect was to intensify Germany's distrust of her ally. Another attempt was made to mediate in August 1917 by the Pope, but it soon petered out over the question of Belgium. When Germany announced that Alsace and Lorraine would never be given back to France it only required the British declaration that the return of the provinces was an essential war aim to make the deadlock explicit.

The German soldiers still believed victory was possible. The French had lost 280,000 men in an April offensive. A great British offensive in Flanders, launched at the end of July to relieve the overstrained and temporarily mutinuous French army, took four months and lost 400,000 men to win five miles of mud. The

26 Fischer, p. 404.

German general staff did not know of the French mutinies and its army also suffered severely, but Passchendaele was to remain the bitterest of the British soldiers' memories of the war. The last great Russian offensive had also been halted in July, and a subsequent German advance had taken Riga (3 September). In October the Italians were routed at Caporetto. At that time, more U-boats were in service than ever before and, although the submarine offensive had in fact been mastered, Great Britain had earlier in the year seemed within measurable distance of starvation.[27] The American troops had not yet arrived. On 7 November came a new Russian 'revolution', in which the Bolsheviks, who favoured peace, seized power. In these circumstances, the German generals still believed they had no need to compromise. On 11 November a conference on strategy drew up the outline of German plans for the following spring. Symbolically, no civilian was present. No political preparation was thought necessary for the stroke which was planned to win the war. Victory in the field had become the end in itself, the key to all problems, domestic and external, and to the achievement of the old aims of domination in *Mitteleuropa* and expansion in the east.[28]

THE REVOLUTIONARY WAR OF 1918

The intimate connexions of their foreign and domestic affairs had always made it likely that the Dual Monarchy, Russia and Turkey (and to a lesser extent, Germany) would face upheaval if defeated. By 1918 that had been borne out in Russia. It now became clear that the central powers were fighting to preserve their social and political institutions, and the *Entente* powers to destroy them. Already, the Kaiser had in 1917 conceded in principle that the restricted Prussian franchise should be reformed after peace was made. Authoritarianism and dynasticism were at war with

27 April had been the cruellest month; U-boats then sank over 800,000 tons of allied and neutral shipping (425 ships) and the Western Approaches were, said Churchill, a 'veritable cemetery' of British shipping (*World Crisis*, p. 728). The danger was over by the autumn.
28 On German attitudes at this juncture, see the particularly helpful passages in Fischer, pp. 420–472.

democracy and constitutionalism. This was made explicit during a winter of exceptional severity and growing war-weariness.

The second Russian revolution had sprung from the Provisional government's decision to go on fighting against Germany. Most Russians were sick of the war and disillusioned by the failure of the March Revolution to end it. By November the Bolsheviks felt strong enough to attempt a *coup* and the 'October Revolution' of 6–7 November installed them in power. Almost their first act as a government was (8 November) to denounce Russia's existing treaties, suggest an immediate armistice, and appeal to the workers of the 'three leading world peoples', England, France and Germany. This was a revolutionary document, an appeal over the heads of governments reminiscent of 1792; broadcast by radio, but never officially handed to the *Entente* powers, it signalised the start of what would much later be called 'Cold War'.

Another effect of the October revolution was to speed up still more the disintegration of the Russian state. Almost from the beginning of the war, the Germans had been in touch with Russian revolutionaries and with Ukrainian, Finnish and Estonian separatists to whom they attached more importance than to groups like Lenin's.[29] The March revolution gave separatism its chance. The Provisional government itself recognized Polish independence (30 March), restored to the Finnish Diet its autonomous privileges in July and granted autonomy to Estonia. In May a 'Union of the Peoples of the Northern Caucasus' appeared, and in June the Ukrainians set up a Rada, or constituent assembly, which the Provisional government recognized. A Lithuanian puppet régime set up by the Germans declared its independence. The October revolution further encouraged such movements, both by revealing the weakness of the new order in Petrograd and by its advocacy of self-determination in the decree of 8 November, though Bolshevik Red Guards invaded Finland and preparations were made to attack the Ukraine (which declared itself independent on 20 November). In these circumstances, the decisive factor for the fate of the western borderlands of the old tsarist empire was bound to be the German army.

29 This question has occasioned much controversy. A useful starting point is Z. A. B. Zeman, *Germany and the Revolution in Russia, 1915–1918* (Oxford, 1958), read with G. Bonnin, 'Les Bolchéviques et l'argent allemand', *RH*, 1965.

Weakness deprived Russia of control over territories which the new régime regarded as its own by right, but Russia had to have peace: after its high-flown appeals, the decree of 8 November had gone on to say that the Bolsheviks would consider *any* terms which were offered to them. Recognizing its weak bargaining power, the new Russian government had issued the decree in the hope of not being left alone to make terms with the central powers. The other aim of the peace decree was to appeal to the masses. Trotsky, commissar for foreign affairs, believed that the trench deadlock in the west had made governments and peoples alike responsive to appeals for a general peace. Confident of this, he had even begun to release German and Austro-Hungarian prisoners of war. Yet there was no response, and the Russians had to negotiate alone after all.

Discussions began at Brest-Litovsk on 20 December and continued, with interruptions, until February. The German High Command (who effectively dominated the central powers delegation) was determined to separate Poland and Lithuania from Russia, and to confirm the existence of an independent Ukraine. The Russians resisted these demands and attempted to use the discussions as a forum for revolutionary propaganda (the act of one member of their delegation, Karl Radek, was symbolic: on arriving at Brest he at once began to distribute revolutionary pamphlets to German soldiers at the station).[30] Their hopes were heightened by news from central Europe of antiwar strikes and demonstrations; one issue of *Pravda* headed a report 'On the eve of the Austrian Revolution'. Yet Russia had almost no army with which to continue resistance if the German terms were unacceptable – the soldiers had gone home from the trenches – and the longer the talks continued, the more Russia's position crumbled. On 6 December, Finland declared its independence. On 23 December, a Moldavian Republic appeared in Bessarabia. Latvia declared itself independent on 12 January. On 1 February the central powers recognized the Ukrainian régime and made a peace treaty with it a week later, although it had in fact been overrun by Soviet troops.

One reason for the Russian delay in coming to terms was a conflict within the Bolshevik movement. Roughly speaking, Lenin was for acceptance of German terms at once, for cutting

30 Radek, a Polish Jew, was a subject of the Dual Monarchy.

losses in order to win time to rebuild the Russian state: he recognized that the European revolutionary movements were not yet ripe enough to affect events. On the other side, Bukharin advocated 'revolutionary war'. In the end the sterility of a compromise was adopted: in Trotsky's words, 'We interrupt the war and do not sign the peace – we demobilize the army.'[31] This attempt to avoid both acceptance of German terms and hopeless resistance ended the Brest discussions on 10 February. Almost immediately, the German offensive was resumed and was soon carried to within a hundred miles of Petrograd. In this emergency the Bolsheviks even made enquiries about the possibility of Allied help, but on 3 March Russian delegates signed the peace treaty at Brest. Russia gave up Poland, Lithuania, the Ukraine, the Baltic Provinces and Transcaucasia. The terms had been made harsher by delay: the German High Command was now willing to let the Turks have a slice of the cake too.

Acceptance of these terms was a bitter blow. When Lenin pressed his colleagues to ratify the treaty, he said: 'If you do not know how to adapt yourself, if you are not inclined to crawl on your belly through the mud, then you are not a revolutionary but a chatterbox; and I am asking you to take this course not because it pleases me but because there is no other path, because history has not shaped itself in so pleasant a way that all revolutions ripen simultaneously.'[32] Soviet forces had to withdraw from the Ukraine, which was at once occupied by the Germans, while the Austro-Hungarians occupied Odessa. German troops helped to end a civil war in Finland, crushing the pro-Bolsheviks there. By the end of the war, the Finns had chosen a German prince to rule them, and the Lithuanians a German duke.

To the *Entente* powers this was a severe blow. Not only would Germany derive great economic benefits from the Ukraine,[33] but Russia was now a nullity. The peace took away a quarter of her European territory, two-fifths of its population, three-quarters of her iron and coal. Her government's move to Moscow during the final German offensive had been a withdrawal from Europe, back into the shadows of pre-Petrine Muscovy. No one could be sure

---

31 See I. Deutscher, *The Prophet Armed* (London, 1954), p. 375.
32 See G. F. Kennan, *Soviet Foreign Policy 1917–1941* (London, 1960), pp. 120–1.
33 In fact these benefits turned out to be smaller than anticipated.

how firmly in the saddle the Bolsheviks were. To keep them in power had now become Germany's interest and many *Entente* observers believed them to be German agents. A million soldiers of the central powers stayed in the east, but the peace made it possible for the Germans to move forty divisions to the western front, an enormous strategical gain. In these circumstances, the *Entente* powers' obsession with the strategical threat soon led them, too, to intervention in Russian domestic affairs. (see pp. 332–5.)

Another consequence of the Russian collapse had been Rumania's final defeat; she could not stay in the field without the support of the Russian army and made peace with the central powers by the Treaty of Bucarest (7 May 1918). The 'Moldavian Republic' had joined itself to Rumania (in spite of Russian protests) but Rumania lost territory to Bulgaria and the Dual Monarchy. Germany took a ninety-year lease on Rumania's oil-wells. Brest-Litovsk and Bucarest in fact brought Germany as near as she ever came to the realization of a *Mitteleuropa* which was an economic unity. The organization of eastern Europe had already begun in Poland and the Baltic states before the peace; it was continued by the separate treaty with the Ukraine and, later in the year, by the strengthening of the German grip on the Dual Monarchy. Yet this only strengthened the conviction of the *Entente* powers that no accommodation with so predatory a power as Imperial Germany was possible. It revealed the meaninglessness of the 'peace resolution' of 1917 and convinced Wilson that there was no hope of German civilian opposition to the war aims of 'autocracy'. Brest-Litovsk, like the decisions on Poland and unrestricted submarine warfare, was (as Wilson pointed out on 6 April), the result of the predominance of soldiers in German policy-making. In another way, too, the peace sacrificed Germany's long-term interests to immediate advantages. Germany's real interest in the east was to cut commitments there to the bone, in order to win in the west: a non-punitive peace might have achieved this.

The terms of Brest-Litovsk enraged some Germans, it is true. Feeling against the war broke out in another great wave of strikes in January 1918, when the terms demanded by the High Command were made known. About a million workers were involved; revolutionary leaders appeared who pushed aside the official trades union leaders. The strikes were called off in

February – the government declared Berlin to be in a state of siege and was never in danger of losing control – but they were the most impressive demonstration yet against official policies in Germany. They explain Bolshevik hopes of a German revolution. Nevertheless, only the Independent Socialists voted against the peace terms in the *Reichstag*.

The Habsburg régime faced greater difficulties than did its ally. The death of Franz Josef had removed a moral tie. Then came the Russian Revolution, whose significance Czermin had at once recognized. 'The Russian revolution affects our Slavs far more than the Germans', he wrote to the emperor, 'and the responsibility for the continuance of the war is a far greater one for a monarch whose country is only united through the dynasty than for one where the people themselves are fighting for their national ideals.'[34] In accordance with the emperor's wishes, conciliatory gestures were made. The *Reichsrath* was reopened as a concession to the silenced nationalists of the Austrian half of the Monarchy, an amnesty was offered to political prisoners and Charles promised to rule constitutionally. Unfortunately, nothing could be done about the real obstacles to conciliation, the hegemony of the Magyars within the Monarchy as a whole and the practical supremacy of the Austrian Germans in one half of it. The German government distrusted its ally and wished to uphold the Austrian Germans and the Dual Monarchy was more and more dependent on Germany. It became more difficult still to reform the Monarchy and achieve its withdrawal from the war. It is not surprising that the German ambassador drew his government's attention to rising anti-German feeling at Vienna in 1917.

Peace seemed more and more desirable to the Habsburg government. After the October revolution Czernin wanted to make a conciliatory peace as quickly as possible within the terms of the peace resolution in order, he told the German chancellor, to blunt the revolutionary appeal of the Bolsheviks. The Germans, surer of their grip at home, felt no anxiety to open negotiations; the terms they subsequently imposed showed how little compunction they felt about their ally's problems. Yet, at the beginning of 1918, the Dual Monarchy's food shortage was worse than ever (another reflection of Magyar selfishness, since Hungary was the granary of Austria). A cut in Austrian flour

34 See Zeman, *The Break-up of the Habsburg Empire*, p. 120.

rations in January set off a wave of strikes which turned into antiwar demonstrations parallel to those in Germany. They spread rapidly. Among the industrial areas, only Bohemia remained relatively quiet. In some places, Soviets were elected and troops were urged to refuse to fight. Czernin's assurances that the peace negotiations would not be delayed by demands for annexations led the Social Democrats to call off the strikes. The release of divisions from the eastern front for duty in the disaffected districts brought the greatest disturbance to an end, but the government's control was slipping. On 1 February came a mutiny in the fleet, which, although quickly suppressed, ominously foreshadowed a breakdown of discipline in the forces. Moreover, although the emergency eventually led the Hungarian government to requisition food, shortages were gradually undermining law and order outside the large towns. The situation was similar to that in Russia the year before.

Into this situation there returned the first liberated prisoners of war. The Russians had made great efforts to indoctrinate them with antiwar and revolutionary propaganda; this had some success, especially among the Germans and Hungarians. The corrosive effect was first seen in Styria in May, when a Slovene unit mutinied, shouting 'up with the Bolsheviks, long live bread, down with the war'.[35] It was easily suppressed but other mutinies soon followed, including one in Prague which involved hundreds of men and threatened, for a moment, to win civilian support. By mid-1918, it was clear that social and national revolution were moving hand-in-hand to the destruction of the Monarchy, one of whose traditional supranational supports, the army, could no longer be unquestioningly relied on.

Germany's policy did not help. Charles's attempts to open peace negotiations had led the Germans to disregard their ally's interests again. The peace with the Ukraine antagonized Poles by awarding territory which they regarded as Polish to the Ukrainians. This was the last blow to the Poles of the Monarchy. Galicia was soon in a state of near-revolution and the long-loyal Polish gentry could no longer be relied on. Two Polish ministers offered their resignations (which were refused) to the emperor. The Polish nationalists were now being driven towards radicalism as quickly as the Czechs. Another breach between the nationalists

35 See Zeman, p. 143.

and the dynasty had been widened. Meanwhile, an Austro-German conflict developed over Rumania. The Germans accused the Austrians of encroaching on German economic interests on the lower Danube, and saw Charles's support for the Rumanian dynasty as a part of the old dynastic rivalry of Hohenzollern and Habsburg.

Against this background of distrust and friction, the two emperors met at Spa (12 May) and signed a document which bound the two empires together more closely than ever before. Joint military forces were to be organized, and a customs and economic union. This was a Habsburg abdication, an ironical end to the long Hohenzollern-Habsburg struggle. It revealed to the subject nationalities the final nullity of the dynasty, which now offered them only the strengthening of German hegemony. The Dual Monarchy from this time fell apart more and more quickly, and the 'radicalization' of Slav political life was by now in full swing.

The Allies helped. When Brest-Litovsk ended hopes that Russia would stay in the war, disappointment and fear led to increased eagerness to use all available weapons against the central powers. The revolutionary potential of the Dual Monarchy was one of these. Its use was a slow development. Germany had from the start sought to use the nationalist revolutionaries against Russia (and Muslims and Irish against Britain) but in 1914 France and the United Kingdom had recognized that the continued existence of the Dual Monarchy was necessary to them; they had no revolutionary aims. Wickham Steed, the foreign editor of *The Times*, so annoyed Grey by attacks on the Habsburgs that his correspondents were banned from the Foreign Office in 1914 and early 1915. Only in 1916 did the subject nationalities begin to get a sympathetic hearing in London and only in January 1917 was the disruption of the Dual Monarchy explicitly accepted as a British war aim. Even then, there were qualifications; Allied policy did not change decisively until after the Russian revolutions.

The March revolution gave the Allies a free hand first in Poland. They no longer needed to consider tsarist susceptibilities and soon officially recognized the Polish National Committee in Paris. The central powers had now to match rival bids. The reopening of the *Reichsrath* in Vienna brought demands from Czechs and South Slavs for greater freedom within the Monarchy.

In May the Czechs renounced Dualism, demanding a federal structure, and a Slovene leader called for an autonomous Yugoslav state including all Slovenes, Croats and Serbs. Cooperation between the nationalities in the *Reichsrath* was cordial and productive; it increased German suspiciousness of its ally. From November onwards, demands for complete independence were made which rejected the Habsburg state altogether. Magyar and German pressure had made real concession by the Emperor impossible, while the Allies could encourage the exiled nationalists and thus set the pace for those within the *Reichsrath*.

An early sign of the new possibilities was a meeting of Yugoslav exile groups at Corfu in July 1917 which agreed upon the bases of a future independent Yugoslavia. During this summer, too, Masaryk, the leader of the Czech exiles, was negotiating with the Russians for the transfer to the western front of Czech troops recruited from prisoners – a step likely to strengthen his appeal to the French and British. But the decisive evolution in Allied policy towards the nationalities came only in 1918, and began, not very encouragingly, with the publication of Wilson's Fourteen Points (8 January). It was hoped that a liberal statement of war aims might nerve the Russian negotiators to break off at Brest-Litovsk, and continue the war. They included the withdrawal of all foreign forces from Russian territory, a readjustment of Italian frontiers 'along clearly recognizable lines of nationality', 'the freest opportunity of autonomous development' for the peoples of Austria-Hungary, and an independent Poland. This did not go far enough for some of the radical nationalists. Only Poland was a really revolutionary change; 'autonomy' implied that the prewar structure was still in some measure viable. A month later, Wilson went further, by insisting that self-determination should not be 'a mere phrase' but an 'imperative of action'.[36] This raised greater hopes, but Wilson was running a little ahead of his Allies. The British had reasserted in early January that the 'break-up' of Austria-Hungary was not envisaged and this had greatly dismayed the South Slavs. But by this time the exiled nationalists, more extreme than those in the *Reichsrath*, were beginning to impress the *Entente* as potentially useful instruments, now that Russia had left the war. It was first agreed to

36 See C. A. Macartney, *National States and National Minorities* (London, 1934).

support them with propaganda, without promising them independence; then, at the end of March, the British and French, in response to pressure from Wickham Steed, authorized propaganda to support South Slav demands for independence. A leaflet campaign was begun against the Habsburg army on the Italian front and in April a 'Congress of Oppressed Nationalities' met in Rome. Soon afterwards, the hope of tempting Czech deserters from the army facing Italy won official Allied recognition of Czech independence, too.[37] This was decisive. The Allies were now committed to breaking up the Habsburg Monarchy, for all Czechoslovak territory lay within, and in both halves of, the Monarchy.

Military needs thus shaped policy. When the Rome Congress met, the last great German onslaught had been under way for a fortnight. The resumption of the offensive by the Germans after very successful defensive fighting in 1917 is understandable. Bulgaria, Turkey and the Dual Monarchy were weakening fast. It was now also known that American troops could not be kept away from Europe by the U-boats and would in 1918 begin to arrive in strength. A victorious peace in Russia was not far off and would release large numbers of German soldiers. It was logical to employ them in a final attempt to break the *Entente*'s will to win. Another victory in a secondary theatre (such as Caporetto in 1917) would not do this; the main enemy in France had to be beaten.

The result was the hurricane which broke on the British Fifth Army on the morning of 21 March. A bombardment by 6,000 guns began three months of repeated German attacks, which, in their opening stages, won brilliant successes. Outstanding training, careful planning, good leadership, an imaginative rethinking of tactics, and local superiority of numbers explain them.[38] The crisis of the battle came after a week, when the separation of the French and British armies was narrowly averted, and General Foch was made the Allied commander-in-chief in all but name. A second German attack along the Scarpe then failed

37 The French recognized the Czechoslovak government on 29 June: the British foreign secretary first referred to the Czechs as an 'Allied Nation' in a letter to Benes 9 August.
38 Seventy-one divisions and 2,500 heavy guns faced twenty-six British divisions with 976 heavy guns in the first attack.

to make headway. This was not clear at the time; Haig's anxiety for the Flanders heights, and even the Channel ports, continued throughout April. The French suffered the greatest bombardment of the war on 25 April before a German attack which, by the end of May, carried the German advance-guards to the Marne for the first time since 1914. They were fifty miles from Paris. In June came small-scale Allied counterattacks, and on 15 July the last great German assault. Its left wing, east of Rheims, was stopped almost at once but the western attack crossed the Marne. On 18 July the French counteroffensive began and the second battle of the Marne came to an end. So continuous and so savage had been the three months' fighting, that it was almost impossible to see that the decisive battle of the war was over but the French armies which had held the last German attacks now began to deliver their counterstrokes. The first American divisions to go into battle fought with them; they were few, but fought bravely and suffered terrible casualties through inexperience. Their moral contribution to victory was as important as their material effect. But the heaviest fighting, as the casualty rolls showed, had fallen on the British forces.[39] Their doggedness in defence had saved the Allies in the black days of March and April.

It is no disparagement to the Allied armies and their leaders – or to the bravery and skill of the Germans in defence – to say little of what followed in France. On 8 August a series of limited Allied offensives began. They often cost heavy casualties and bitter fighting, but at a German Crown Council on 14 August there was talk of negotiation; Ludendorff admitted that Germany could not win by offensive warfare. Nevertheless, although some signs of demoralization were beginning to appear even in the German army, it was not in the west that the collapse began.

In June the last Austrian offensive in Italy was stopped and the Bulgarians had begun to take soundings about peace. After Allied offensives in Macedonia in September, they asked for an armistice, granted on 29 September. The Allied forces then pressed forward into Serbia. Bulgaria's collapse gave Turkey an excuse to sue for peace on 14 October (an armistice was granted two weeks later);

---

39 In the first forty days, the British suffered over 300,000 casualties: more than a quarter of the British fighting strength in France on 21 March. For the whole period March–June, the figures are: British, 418,000; French, 433,000; German, 688,341.

she had already suffered a run of defeats in the Near and Middle East. For the Dual Monarchy, too, Bulgaria's collapse was fatal, for it suddenly opened the prospect of an Allied drive into her vitals from the south. In the conditions of 1918, the Monarchy could not face this threat. Disorder in the countryside and disaffection in the forces were growing. Peasant revolts had begun in Hungary. After the June defeat in Italy the Monarchy had already again begun to seek peace. A note from the emperor, sent the day before the Macedonian offensive (14 September) was answered by Wilson, who referred Charles to the terms already enunciated by the *Entente*. The Bulgarian collapse led him to ask at once for an armistice on the basis of the Fourteen Points.

After the war it was sometimes said that the Habsburg Empire was broken up by the peace: this was not true, it had already fallen apart. The nationalist tide was now flooding in everywhere, the Monarchy making half-hearted attempts to keep ahead of it. On 1 October the Yugoslavs were offered national autonomy, and the replacement of dualism by trialism. This might have been the answer a decade before, when the Magyars made it impossible, but now impressed no one. Only the Ruthenes still thought the Monarchy might defend them from the Poles. The Social Democrats demanded a separate German-Austrian state (3 October), and three days later, a National Council of Serbs, Croats and Slovenes began to meet in Zagreb. The last attempt of the dynasty to save itself was an appeal to the National Committees to help reorganize the Austrian territories as a federal state. As this left out Hungary, nobody was impressed. The Magyars themselves were beginning to desert the dynasty, which had now, they claimed, cut away the basis of the 1867 Compromise. Everything was giving way at once. When Wilson said that autonomy was no longer enough for the Yugoslavs and Czechs, who must have self-determination, any lingering hopes of Allied support for the dynasty disappeared. A government was appointed to supervise the division of the Monarchy into national states and a new request was made for an armistice on this basis (27 October). Again, this was too late. The government had no effective control and was losing its will to govern. A Czech National Council had taken over Bohemia and Moravia on 28 October, the day before the armistice request, and the Croatian Diet proclaimed its independence the next day. A German National Council appeared in Vienna (31 October) and an independent Ruthene state the next day. (It was soon fighting Poland, whose independence had been proclaimed at Warsaw in October, thus inaugurating the first war between the successor states of the Monarchy.) The Monarchy was ceasing to exist; only the dynastic myth, like the smile of the Cheshire Cat, lingered a little after the body of the Danubian Empire had dissolved.

In Hungary the Magyar oligarchy clung to power almost to the end. Then a National Committee emerged under Count Karolyi's government took its oath to the crown on the day revolutionary soldiers broke into Tisza's house and murdered him; Charles relieved them of it the next day (1 November). Even Karolyi was too late; he had hoped as a liberal to reconcile the subject national-ities to a new Hungary by autonomy but the Rumanians, Croats and Slovaks had already opted out. Revolution was under way in Yugoslavia. The last governments of the Habsburgs in Vienna and Budapest could hardly hope to control even their armies, so complete had the dissolution been. The cease-fire began at 3 a.m. on 3 November.

The Bulgarian collapse also convinced the German soldiers that the end had come. Under continuous and mounting Allied attack since early August, with no reserves, facing new demands from enfeebled allies and a growing Allied superiority of numbers, they saw by mid-September no prospect of a German victory. Bulgaria was the last straw. On 29 September, Ludendorff reported that a change of government and an armistice were necessary. The link between political change and the diplomatic initiative was twofold; a less military-looking German government would have a chance of getting better terms from the Allies, it was thought, and the military leaders would evade responsibility for the nego-tiations of peace. Prince Max of Baden formed a government which was as widely based as possible (it was the first German government to include Socialists). On 2 October, the *Reichstag* heard, almost with incredulity, that victory was impossible. The next day, on Prince Max's insistence, Hindenburg provided a written request from the High Command for an immediate armistice. An appeal was at once sent to Wilson, who replied that acceptance of the Fourteen Points and evacuation of all occupied territory were essential. These terms were accepted (12 October), but Wilson then announced that the precise terms of the armistice were to be settled by the Allied military commanders. This caused something of a stir in Germany; there were Germans even then, liberals among them, who wished to go on fighting. But the disintegration which the generals feared was already beginning. The fleet had been cooped up in harbour since Jutland; the rumour that it would put to sea for a last mission provoked a mutiny at Kiel (29 October) which rapidly spread to other ports. The sailors shouted 'we want Erzberger' – the deputy who had proposed the Peace Resolution of 1917. On 7 November, Erzberger was sent to negotiate an armistice and a revolution began in Munich. The Socialists demanded the end of the Monarchy, and two days later Prince Max announced the kaiser's abdication. A telegram from Hindenburg that day said that the armistice must be signed, in spite of its onerous terms. Revolution had spread to Berlin. Prince Max handed over the chancellorship of the new German state to Ebert, a Socialist. On 11 November, at 5 a.m., the armistice was signed, and six hours later, at eleven o'clock, the greatest war in history ended, the guns gradually falling silent along the western front.

10

POSTWAR EUROPE

EUROPE IN 1918

The Great War had been unique, both in scale and in the changes it brought about. The slaughter had been unprecedented,[1] the economics of siege warfare had been imposed on whole nations, capital resources had been used up more quickly than ever before, social and political certainties had been swept away in all countries. Three great dynasties had fallen; three great powers had been reduced to nullity by defeat or disintegration. Austria-Hungary, Russia and Germany had been the pillars of order in eastern and central Europe; now, the forces released by the Russian revolution and Allied propaganda threw the area into turmoil. No one could be certain what would emerge from the uproar. Even Germany's existence seemed put in doubt by revolution.

The threat of revolution also lurked in economic chaos. Ill-founded hopes might buoy up the victorious powers but in central Europe, economic structures built up over decades and even centuries had given way. Sapped by destruction and shortage, Europe's fixed capital was overworked and wearing out. Transport and communications had broken down after four years of

---

1 It is impossible to compute precisely the total casualties caused by the Great War; see pp. 351–2. As a *direct* consequence of combat, it is likely that about 10 million men died. This total is roughly made up as follows: Russia 3 m; Germany 3 m; France 1.4 m; British Empire (just under) 1 m; Austria-Hungary 1 m; Italy 0.5 m.

war. Agricultural and industrial production had collapsed since 1914. It was calculated that the coal output of Europe outside Russia and the Balkans was only two-thirds of its prewar level. New boundaries were creating new obstacles to the flow of trade. Above all, Germany, the economic dynamo of central and eastern Europe, was exhausted.

Victory thus presented the *Entente* with an appalling task. It was not made easier because hopes had been raised so high in a 'war to end war'. Unlike the United States, France and the United Kingdom had drawn to breaking-point not only on their capital of blood and wealth but on their moral resources. The results had gone beyond measurement in casualty lists or account books. 'We are at the dead season of our fortunes', wrote a British economist in 1919, almost in despair. 'Our power of feeling or caring beyond the immediate questions of our own material wellbeing is temporarily eclipsed . . . We have been moved already beyond endurance, and need rest. Never in the lifetime of men now living has the universal element in the soul of man burnt so dimly.'[2]

It was difficult to generate new moral energy in the victorious democracies. In 1918 the most widespread mood was one of relief, tempered by fear that such a struggle might come about again. This was especially true in France, where the search for national security dominated thinking about European reconstruction. Germany might be prostrate, but her potential was intact; there had been no complete overthrow of Germany ending with a great occupation by the victorious armies. To France the negotiation of a durable peace meant, above all, the neutralization of this potential by political or economic means. Yet Germany was bound one day to exercise again influence commensurate with her geographical position, her population and her economic power. If this happened, two great European powers would no longer be there to work the traditional balance of power on Germany's eastern and southern frontiers, backward areas riddled with national and social animosities.

This was the heritage of the Great War which confronted the makers of the peace in 1919. One encouraging and positive feature stood out in the tangle – the military and economic strength of the United States, the moral leadership of whose president seemed to

2 J. M. Keynes, *The Economic Consequences of the Peace* (London, 1919), pp. 278–9.

many Europeans an assurance that their problems could and would be solved. In so far as this was a recognition of the new power realities of a world in which England and France had been unable to defeat Germany alone, it was commendable. Unfortunately an appreciation of what should be expected of the United States was often confused by ignorance of American interests, traditions and culture. From this, much disappointment was to flow.

PEACE-MAKING, 1919–23

Although the months following the armistice are often discussed as if all that mattered was the peace treaty with Germany, that was only one part of a general reconstruction of Europe which took five years. This reconstruction can conveniently be separated into three processes: a series of treaties with 'defeated' nations; the cancellation of Brest Litovsk and the stabilization of Russia's relations with her neighbours; and the settlement of the eastern Mediterranean and Aegean. With one exception, all the important treaties were worked out contemporaneously at Paris. They began, five years precisely after the assassination at Sarajevo (28 June 1919), with the treaty of Versailles with Germany and, on the same day, a treaty with Poland. Then came the treaties of St Germain with Austria (10 September) and Neuilly with Bulgaria (27 November). In 1920 the treaty of Sèvres was signed with Turkey (20 April) and that of the Trianon with Hungary (4 June). Other treaties such as those between 'Succession States' of the former Dual Monarchy were also part of the peace settlement. Finally, a renewed treaty with Turkey was signed at Lausanne in 1923 (23 July).

The Peace Conference did not meet until January 1919, two months after the Armistice, largely because of Wilson's wish to be present. This gap coincided with the distraction of a British general election whose result was not known until the end of December. When the statesmen began to assemble in Paris in January, no planning of the Conference had taken place. Membership, representation, and many important procedural and organizational matters had to be decided before the peace itself could be considered. In so far as the Conference had a beginning, it was a meeting of the prime ministers and foreign ministers of Great Britain, France and Italy, with the president and secretary of state of the United States, on 12 January. After a discussion of naval and military matters had gone on for some time, Lloyd George broke in to say that he had expected the meeting 'to discuss questions preliminary to the more formal Conference on peace'.[3] Thus began the discussions of what was to be known as the Supreme Council of the Peace Conference or 'Council of Ten' (when two Japanese delegates joined it). It set the pattern of the domination of the Conference by great powers.

It had at once to decide who should take part. Montenegro was undoubtedly an Allied nation, but the claimants to statehood for the new 'Kingdom of the Serbs, Croats and Slovenes' insisted that Montenegro was now merged in this state.[4] The special claims of Portugal, Siam and Brazil to three representatives each were urged by Great Britain, France and the United States respectively; not unreasonably, Belgium and Greece at once protested and demanded as many (they had been given only two). Great Britain insisted on separate representation for the Dominions and India. Long discussions took place over the possibility of Russian participation. Finally, thirty-two states were invited to attend the inauguration of the Conference on 18 January.[5] The question of the language of the Conference was shelved.

Clemenceau was elected president of the Conference. This, together with the imposition of rules of procedure drawn up by the great powers, kept control firmly in their hands: the Council of Ten thrashed out the basis of the peace, and this made the Plenary sessions largely formal. Some fifty-eight commissions and committees were set up on specific questions; they were to feed

3 See F. S. Marston, *The Peace Conference of 1919* (Oxford, 1944), p. 54. This book may be read in conjunction with Nicolson's *Peacemaking 1919* (London, new edn, 1945) as a guide to the working of the Conference.
4 For convenience, 'Yugoslavia', the name which the new state officially adopted only in 1929, is used hereafter. On Montenegro's position, see Nicolson, pp. 121–4. The Yugoslav contention was finally accepted by an Allied Commission in February 1921.
5 The U.S.A., the U.K., Canada, Australia, South Africa, New Zealand, India, France, Italy, Japan, Belgium, Bolivia, Brazil, China, Cuba, Ecuador, Greece, Guatemala, Haiti, the Hejaz, Honduras, Liberia, Nicaragua, Panama, Peru, Portugal, Rumania, Yugoslavia, Siam, Czechoslovakia, Poland, Uruguay.

the Council of Ten with information. It was the middle of March before all this was settled, but the Conference was well under way by February. The Council of Ten met until 24 March, when it was replaced by the Council of Four.[6] This had become an urgent necessity. The Council of Ten had failed to make headway with the crucial territorial and military questions, and serious leakages of information from it had occurred. The Council of Four consisted of Clemenceau, Wilson, Lloyd George and Orlando (who could not speak English). With some absences by Orlando, this body met over 200 times in the next three months.

In spite of Italian objections and the disastrous state of eastern Europe, it was inevitable that the Council should take as its main task the making of a peace treaty with Germany. German pleni-potentiaries were given the Allied terms on 7 May. The Germans communicated with the Allies and associated powers by written notes; no oral discussion was allowed, but some changes of substance were made in the Treaty. Final, revised terms were presented to the Germans on 16 June: while their reply was awaited, preparations were made to resume fighting and the full rigour of the blockade. After a political crisis in Germany, the treaty was signed on 28 June.

Seven months' peace-making with Germany had given time for important differences to emerge between the victorious great powers (to say nothing of the smaller states). Each had come to Paris with a different view of the peace to be made and against a different back-ground of public and personal influences. Unhappily, the major Allied states were democracies; their plenipoten-tiaries were always aware of their electorates. The mood in Great Britain when the war ended was at first one of almost hysterical relief that so terrible an experience was over and a vengeful anger against the Germans. In the 1918 election, much was made of the justice of 'indemnities' and the personal guilt of German leaders (above all, the kaiser). But the British were also above all anxious to demobilize and end conscription. The surrender of the German fleet and colonies had disposed of Britain's security problem. By the time the Conference opened, Lloyd George, although encum-bered by the expectations he had encouraged and the language his supporters had used, was keen to display his great conciliatory

6 There also appeared a Council of Five – foreign ministers.

and political talents in Paris. He had ample opportunity in the frequent collisions of his colleagues.

American aims were similar to the British in that the president was aware of the relief of Americans that the war was ended and the soldiers could come home, but there was little common ground between him and his colleagues. In July 1918 he had written to House, 'England and France *have not the same views with regard to peace that we have* by any means. When the war is over we can force them to our way of thinking.' Himself a doctrinaire moralist, Wilson distrusted their intentions. He had no sympathy for their secret treaties.[7] He had published and reiterated principles which, he believed, would provide the only viable foundations for future peace, and they were both radical and unrealistic.[8] He was a former professor of political science, formed in the study of a legalistic constitution, and impressed by the power of formulae. Nor was he flexible or imaginative. He would not at first visit the battle zone in France because it might sway his emotions. He was that most difficult of negotiators, the man who does not recognize the emotion he brings to resisting its appeal in others. He was deeply prejudiced in favour of the new Slav nations, especially the Czechs and Poles, but had little appreciation of the terrible experience of France. Her statesmen knew that she could never hope to win a war if she faced Germany alone. Security, above all, was her goal in 1918, and from it there followed logically an implacable determination to wound Germany as deeply and as permanently as possible. There was more fear and fore-thought than mere thirst for vengeance in the ends sought by her prime minister. Clemenceau was fitted perfectly to his task; a cynic about almost everything except France, he believed unemotionally and in an old-fashioned way in the supremacy of material force in history. Nothing was less likely to appeal to the head of the most powerful nation in the world, remote from the issues which had brought war to Europe. Lloyd George sought to bridge the gap between them.

The result was a long document. The printed version of the

7 See Taylor, *Mastery*, pp. 557–8.
8 The 'Four Supplementary Points', of 11 February, the 'Four Additional Points' of 4 July, and the 'Five Additional Points' of 27 September 1918 are printed in S. Bemis, *A Diplomatic History of the United States* (New York, 1950), pp. 641–2.

treaty has over 200 pages, including accompanying and consequential agreements; 440 clauses dealt with a wide range of business, from frontier adjustments to the protection of submarine cables. They provided for the restitution of astronomical instruments to China, of an African chieftain's skull to Great Britain, and of the leaves of a Van Eyck triptych to the University of Louvain. Nevertheless, the most important terms were territorial, military and economic. Territorially, Germany lost Alsace and Lorraine to France, Eupen and Malmédy to Belgium, much of Posen and West Prussia to Poland, Memel to the Allies, and Danzig (which was to be a Free State). Plebiscites were to decide the future of Upper Silesia, Schleswig and the Saar (which was first to have fifteen years of international administration). The French, however, were to receive the coal mines of the Saar in 'full and complete possession'. Germany also lost all her colonies.

The military terms limited the numbers of the German armed forces and the arms they might bear. The east bank of the Rhine was to be 'demilitarized' to 'a depth of fifty kilometres and the Allies were to occupy the Rhineland for fifteen years. The cost of occupation was to be met by Germany, which was also to surrender all merchant ships of more than 1,600 tons, deliver coal free to France, Belgium and Italy for ten years, and 'make compensation for all damage done to the civilian population of the Allied and Associated Powers and to their property'. A Reparations Commission was set up to administer this claim. The sums which would become due were variously estimated, one French minister suggesting a total of £15,000 million; a less sanguine British estimate placed them between £6,400 million and £8,800 million.[9]

This concluded the main work of the Conference. Wilson and Lloyd George left Paris and the heads of delegations took over the management of business. There was still much to be done, and it was nearly a year before the last treaty regulating the affairs of central Europe was signed. This stage concerned Bulgaria, Turkey, and the 'succession states' – states which had not existed in 1914, but which now claimed the divided heritage of Austria-Hungary. They were not all on an equal footing. Poland, Yugoslavia and Czechoslovakia were treated as Allied nations and were

9 Keynes, *Consequences*, pp. 148–9. The discrepancy is less significant than it appears to be; even the smaller estimate was too much.

represented as such at Versailles. Hungary and Austria were treated as defeated enemies, like Germany, in spite of Austrian protests; their frontiers were settled after the new states had *de facto* established theirs, and in the light of commitments made by the Allies during the war.

Peace-making with the new Austria concerned Italy and the succession states more than had the German treaty. Territorially, it was largely a registration of the facts of the Habsburg collapse. The Czechs had by March 1919 occupied the Sudetenland and German Bohemia, the Italians had moved into the south Tyrol, Istria, Gorizia, northern Dalmatia and Fiume, and the Yugoslavs were by May (when an armistice was finally imposed) holding Klagenfurt and southern Styria. The Poles held eastern Galicia. In the end, all Austria got back was Carinthia. She had also to pay reparations to the Allies, and was forbidden to unite herself to Germany without the consent of the League of Nations. Even her chosen name, 'German-Austria', was set aside, the Conference only recognizing the new state as the 'Republic of Austria'.

The treaty with Hungary took much longer. Like Austria, and unlike Germany, the armistice had cost her the occupation of large tracts of her prewar territory by Czechs, Yugoslavs and Rumanians; the French saw in the new states a future reinforcement of French security and connived at this. In March 1919 Karolyi gave up when confronted with an Allied decision to assign Transylvania to Rumania. The promise of Russian support against Rumania was one reason for the brief success of the Bolshevik-trained Bela Kun, who now seized power in Hungary. Unwisely, he alarmed the Allies by revolutionary propaganda; Czech and Rumanian attacks on his regime followed. Bela Kun's forces succeeded in reoccupying Slovakia and setting up a Communist Republic there, but the Rumanians occupied Budapest in August. The Russians were unable to help and Kun's régime collapsed. A confused period led to a stable government emerging under Admiral Horthy (1 March 1920), shortly after a Rumanian withdrawal (under Allied pressure). This government then signed the Trianon treaty, which registered the loss of three-quarters of Hungary's inhabitants. To Czechoslovakia went Slovakia and Ruthenia; to Rumania went Transylvania. Yugoslavia took Croatia-Slavonia and some other strategically desirable areas. Even Austria was given the 1,500 square-mile 'Burgenland'.

Bulgaria had come to a less costly settlement in the treaty of

Neuilly. The reversal of the decision of the second Balkan war which had taken place during the Great War was now itself reversed, and the Dobrudja was handed back to Rumania, western Thrace to Greece and with it Bulgaria's strip of Aegean coast (although she was promised an undefined outlet to the sea). There were also reparations to be paid.

This settlement is very difficult to judge or characterize as a whole. The treaties had certain obvious merits. They regularized and defined the form of two new and revolutionary states, Czechoslovakia and Yugoslavia, and of a resuscitated Poland. They attempted to anchor the new international order to a League of Nations, whose Covenant was embodied in all five treaties negotiated at Paris. Besides setting up the machinery of the League, this document laid down its aims; among them were the reduction of national armaments to 'the lowest point consistent with national safety and the enforcement by common action of international obligations' (Art. 8). A permanent Commission was to implement the League's initiative towards disarmament. Members of the League undertook to submit their disputes to arbitration and provision was made for action against a covenant-breaking state. Other useful objects of the League were the supervision of international agreements on trade in drugs, women and children; labour conditions were given special attention by the creation of another new organization, the International Labour Office. The Covenant even provided for the future revision of the settlement itself.

Besides these attempts to civilize relations between states in the future, the treaties (partly because of Wilson's conscious advocacy, and partly because of the events of the last year of the war) also contained provisions explicitly intended to interest large masses of people in the preservation of the settlement. The democratic principle was followed by holding plebiscites in disputed areas. Even in Eupen and Malmédy, where no plebiscite was to be held, the inhabitants could make written objections to their transfer to Belgium. Minorities were given guarantees of their linguistic, cultural and religious institutions, to be supervised in their working by the League. The principle of nationality ran through the whole settlement. It was taken for granted that it should determine the structure of a new Europe unless strong arguments could be brought against its application in particular cases. Much was said of the failure in 1815 to take account of

nationality, and of the origins of war in 1914 in the national problems of the Dual Monarchy. It was the end of a century-long
struggle between legitimacy and nationalism, which won its
greatest triumph at Versailles.

Unfortunately, nationalism had other, less promising, implications. Although some of the suppressed minorities of former
great powers won their freedom, not all did. Indeed, the problem
they presented was in some ways intensified. Among 'new' states,
only Austria had a fairly homogeneous ethnic composition; the
others were all multinational. The claims of Slovak and Croat
autonomists were ignored at Paris. A new patchwork of national
minorities had been substituted for the old one. New 'unredeemed' lands tempted new states to dabble in one another's
affairs; the post-Versailles national minorities had far greater
opportunities than those of the old Empires to seek encouragement from external sovereign states which now rested not on
dynastic but national foundations. Of Czechoslovakia's population of about 14.3 million, 4.6 million were Poles, Ruthenes,
Magyars and Germans. Of Poland's 32 million, even the Polish
government claimed only that two-thirds spoke Polish as their
mother-tongue. Yugoslavia's 12 million included 1.7 million
Rumanians, Albanians, Magyars and Germans. Rumania was a
prewar state, but had swallowed more than 1½ Magyars. There
were perhaps 25 or 30 million people in national or racial minorities in central and eastern Europe after 1919. There was some
excuse for Wilson's dismay when an Irish delegation recalled his
pronouncements about self-determination. 'When I gave utterance
to these words', he said, 'I said them without the knowledge that
nationalities existed which are coming to us day after day.'[10]

The guarantees of minorities in the peace treaties were an
attempt to avert the danger of this, but had disadvantages. They
were bitterly resisted as an infringement of sovereignty, as the
protests of Paderewski showed when guarantees were imposed on
Poland to safeguard the Jews. Furthermore, guarantees were not
uniformly applied; Italy successfully resisted a minorities treaty
although she had many new German and Slav subjects. There had

10 See E. Holt, *Protest in Arms* (London, 1960), pp. 181–2. The figures
above are approximations drawn from Appendix III, 'The minorities
under Treaty protection', to C. A. Macartney, *National States and
National Minorities* (Oxford, 1934).

been outright bullying of Germans and Slovenes before territory had definitely passed to Italy, just as the Poles had terrorized Ruthenes in east Galicia. Above all, there was danger for the future in the 'new' states which contained large numbers of Germans. Germany, although prostrate in 1918, was potentially a great power, and the only one in central Europe. She was now surrounded by weak states with German *irredenta* whose claims would no longer be ignored in Berlin, as those before 1914 had been in order to preserve Austria-Hungary. This was an instance of a larger problem. Too many people were placed in positions where the rectification of what they regarded as their wrongs was bound to call in question the territorial arrangements of the peace. Italy was one revisionist power; she had gained territory but not so much as she had hoped for in 1915. Hungary had lost enormous tracts and wanted them back. But the greatest revisionist power was Germany.

Much credence has been given to the complaints of Germans and it is mostly forgotten that the final terms were a diplomatic defeat for France. Clemenceau got his way on reparations, but this was a Pyrrhic victory. France had hoped to detach the left bank of the Rhine from Germany; instead she only obtained the Saar coal mines, the demilitarization of the Rhineland, and its occupation for fifteen years. Germany was disarmed, it was true, but the effectiveness of that disarmament as a continuing disability depended on its enforcement. Meanwhile France would have to rely on Anglo-American guarantees, embodied in treaties signed on the same day as the peace itself, of military assistance in the event of a German attack.

Other concessions, too, had been won by Germany at Paris. Lloyd George insisted that Danzig should be a free city protected by the League of Nations, and that plebiscites should be held in districts of East Prussia and Upper Silesia. Nevertheless the Germans found the treaty harsh. Nationalism made some of them peculiarly sensitive to the painfulness of the thought that Germans might anywhere be ruled by inferior peoples, especially if they were Slavs. Others were affronted by the treaty's Article 231, which laid down 'the responsibility of Germany and her allies' for damage inflicted on the Allies 'as a consequence of the war imposed on them by the aggression of Germany and her allies'. This unfortunate clause was to generate an enormous effort of disproof (the German foreign office in 1919 set up a special department to conduct propaganda about it) and its position at the head of the clauses on reparations obscured the fact that the principle of reparation had been accepted by Germany before the armistice. The question of responsibility was, in any case, complex. Moral and factual arguments can easily be mixed together in discussing it. In retrospect, the moral responsibility of some Germans for the outbreak of world war may be thought to have been conclusively established. A general statement in the treaty was, nevertheless, unnecessary and dangerous.

The reparations terms themselves were the heaviest and most unwise penalties inflicted on Germany. Almost at once, the most celebrated criticisms of them were published by J. M. Keynes, who argued that Germany not only did not have the resources to pay reparations on the scale envisaged, but that such resources as she retained should be husbanded and used by Germany not only in her own interests but in those of the European economy as a whole. Moreover, reparations required an intolerable interference with Germany's internal affairs. It seemed that self-determination was not to apply to Germany. This was bound to rouse nationalist feeling in Germany – which was dangerous when Germany was surrounded by small states with big German minorities in them. Lloyd George had seen this before the war ended; he had fought tenaciously at Paris against the creation of a Rhineland state and the outright transfer of Silesia to Poland. Another irritant to German nationalism appeared in the ban on Austrian union with Germany, insisted upon by France. It was significant that when the programme of a new party calling itself 'National Socialist' appeared in 1920, it contained two foreign policy points: the unification of all Germans, and the abolition of the Versailles Treaty.[11] A *Grossdeutsch* programme in the 1920s implied the destruction of a European settlement just as it had done in 1848.

Shortcomings such as these meant that a moral cloud hung over the Versailles settlement from the start. Acceptance of a German surrender on the vague basis of the Fourteen Points also led to difficulty; soon there were Germans saying that Germany had agreed to make peace on terms later set aside by the Allies. This weakened the case of those who sought to resist revision. For this and other defects of the peace, all three major Allies must share

11 The party later to become famous under the abbreviated name 'Nazi'.

responsibility. The anxiety of France to achieve security led to demands which seemed excessive to her fellow allies and alienated their sympathies. But the British, anxious to demobilize quickly, were reluctant to assume obligations which would provide France with security without the crippling of Germany. The American government, above all, fatally weakened the treaty by failing to secure its ratification by Congress and by abandoning the Anglo-American guarantee to France. The British, already disliking French policy in eastern Europe, hastened to make it clear that they would not provide the guarantee single-handed. The French felt that they had been taken in, having given up claims in Germany in return for a postdated cheque for military support which then bounced. Also, they were given even more power to torment Germany because of the extra weight they exercised in the absence of an American representative on the Reparations commission. Finally, the League of Nations began its life linked, in the eyes of revisionists, with the preservation of an unacceptable *status quo* and without the moral authority and the physical force of the most powerful nation in the world behind it.

This was ironic. Wilson had been passionately keen to make the League a part of the settlement. Yet he had helped to bring about this state of affairs. Although a new isolationism was likely to come with the peace, his misjudgments made foreign policy an issue in American domestic politics in 1919. The peace settlement, the League and the Anglo-American guarantees became involved with his political prestige; they need not have been. Wilson was also partly responsible for the Conference's general neglect of economic issues and its frightful repercussions. Above all, his personal contribution to the moral atmosphere in which the peace was made was immense, yet, once it was settled – and it was never faced squarely – that the peace should be imposed, disillusionment was bound to follow. He had raised expectations too high.

It was not that Wilson was unrealistic. Over Russia, he was certainly more realistic than some British and French statesmen. Although Russia's relations with other states were normalized by 1921, her rulers were not much more content with the outcome of these years than were Germany's. Brest-Litovsk had been an imposed peace – a *diktat* – in a far truer sense than Versailles. The defeat of Germany was quickly to make it obsolete, but Russia was to be a revisionist power until 1945. In 1918, she did not alter the facts of Russia's position in the summer of 1918. She was grievously weak, economically, militarily and politically. On her borders had appeared a belt of states which, whatever their size or strength, were not going to submit to the reimposition of Russian rule. Meanwhile, inside Russia opposition to the Bolshevik regime had led to civil war. A revolt of the Don Cossacks in the south produced a counter-revolutionary movement there and a White Russian army was operating (with German connivance) in the Baltic area. An autonomous Siberian government had been proclaimed at Omsk.

Against this background the Allies had had to formulate policy towards Russia in 1918. Their first impulse had been to seek some way of recreating an eastern front against Germany. Brest-Litovsk ruled out cooperation with the Bolsheviks and inevitably led to the consideration of the possibility of finding a pro-Allied government to put in their place. The Allies also wished to keep out of German hands the thousands of tons of Allied munitions and supplies sent to Russia; they lay at Murmansk and Archangel in the north, and Vladivostok in the far east. Another factor was the presence in Russia of one pro-Allied fighting formation which the Bolsheviks agreed should leave for the western front, the 'Czech Legion' of former prisoners of war.

By November 1918 this tangle had already led to the unfortunate and now legendary Allied interventions. Although other motives were to come into play later, their original impulse was defensive: to reduce as far as possible any advantage the Germans had won by their victories. They began with the reinforcement of the small British units already in Russia, at Murmansk and Archangel. The British and French were both short of men, and the Americans were suspicious of projects for intervention on a wider scale. Meanwhile, thousands of miles along the Siberian railway, on the other side of the Urals, the Czech Legion (since February formally attached to the French army) had begun its journey to the east. This came to an end when the Czechs came into conflict with local Bolshevik forces in central Siberia in mid-May. As other Bolsheviks held points along the line to Vladivostok, it was clear that the Czechs would have to fight their way out, and within a few weeks they had seized about 2,500 miles of the trans-Siberian railway. They began to cooperate with anti-Bolshevik forces. They were therefore the first Allied troops to join in the Russian civil war. Other Czechs at Vladivostok now seized that port from the Bolsheviks. Their action led Wilson to concede that an intervention by Japanese and American forces with the limited objective of getting the Czechs out would be necessary. Another American contingent was also authorized to go to Archangel in August. Finally, in October, a British representative at Omsk signed an agreement with the White Russian general on the spot to assure the Czech position.

The Allies were thus well entangled in Russia when the war with Germany ended. But the original point of the Allied intervention had disappeared. The Germans withdrew from the Ukraine and there was no need either to reconstitute an eastern front or to safeguard stores which might fall into German hands. But the Allies in Siberia were by now, willy-nilly, involved in Russia's civil war. Cooperation with the Whites was going on at Omsk and two other interventions of the last month of the war had strengthened Bolshevik belief that the real aim of the Allies was the overthrow of an anticapitalist régime. Like those elsewhere, both grew out of Russian weakness. In March 1918 a successful offensive in the Caucasus looked as if it might rally to the Turkish side the Muslim population of Transcaspia. The prospect horrified the government of India, traditionally sensitive to disturbances in central Asia.[12] When a 'Centro-Caspian Directorate' which had pushed aside the Bolsheviks asked for British help against the Turk, a British battalion was sent to Baku to secure its oilwells and port. It stayed only six weeks and took no action against the Bolsheviks. On the eastern side of the Caspian, the presence of large numbers of former Austrian and German prisoners-of-war, reported to be armed by the Bolsheviks, alarmed the British commander in Persia. In August he responded to an appeal for help from the local anti-Bolsheviks, in order to safeguard Krasnovodsk (the only important port on the eastern side of the Caspian). With this help, the anti-Bolsheviks succeeded in taking Merv. Swift disillusionment followed closer British acquaintance with the anti-Bolsheviks, and this British force was withdrawn early in 1919.

In these interventions Allied forces had only incidentally come into conflict with the Bolsheviks, but the Russians believed interventions were a deliberate attempt to overthrow the first workers'

12 See, e.g., the memorandum in R. H. Ullman, *Intervention and the War* (Princeton 1961), p. 304.

state. There was plausibility in this. The Bolshevik government's repudiation of the debts incurred by its predecessors had alienated big capitalists and small investors alike, especially in France. Bolsheviks never concealed their hopes that revolution would break out in the capitalist countries, and conducted propaganda with this in view. The breakdown of order in the Dual Monarchy in the last months of the war, and revolution in Germany after the armistice, encouraged them to believe that the collapse of capitalism was about to occur. To take advantage of these events the Russians in late 1918 were busy forming in Moscow the first national Communist parties, by recruiting former prisoners-of-war from central Europe. This apparatus of revolution was crowned on 2 March 1919 by the foundation of the Comintern, the Third International. Its hurried assembly was prompted by fears that the Second International might re-establish itself as the organizational centre of world socialism. Only radio invitations could be issued, and few foreign socialists could get to Moscow; the result was an unrepresentative gathering of exiles, dominated by Bolshevik nominees, but an 'International' which would be the instrument of Russian foreign policy now existed. Meanwhile the Red Armies had taken advantage of the German withdrawal to occupy Lithuania and much of Latvia. This gave the anti-Bolshevik Russian and Ukrainian forces a new interest in the eyes of the statesmen at Paris.

Of the leading statesmen, at Paris, only Clemenceau was really anti-Communist; Lloyd George and Wilson both approached the new Russia more flexibly, and even sympathetically. But their advisers and supporters were increasingly hostile to a régime which was trying to organize revolution in their countries. Demands were made for the Allied interventions to be pressed further, with the new aim of overthrowing the Bolshevik government. Such demands in their turn strengthened both the obsessive distrust of the Bolsheviks for the capitalist countries and their conviction that the interventions were and always had been anti-Communist.

This atmosphere made diplomatic relations almost impossible. Discussion of Russian problems had begun in January 1919. The first significant changes only came when the British and Americans decided to withdraw their forces from north Russia. The Archangel and Murmansk troops withdrew in September. The Siberian involvement was harder to liquidate. The main burden was the Americans', but there were also Czech, British and Japanese forces there. Wilson's collapse and paralysis delayed the withdrawal, and the Americans were reluctant to leave while the Japanese were still in the field, but finally they did so in April 1920. The Japanese stayed until 1922. The removal of Allied forces from Russia was an essential preliminary to a settlement in eastern Europe. Another was the ebbing of the danger of revolution in the new states. The final step was the acceptance by the Russians and Poles of a boundary settlement.

Poland was the most important, the most anti-Russian, the most anti-Bolshevik and the most ambitious of the new nations. Distrust of her motives by her Baltic neighbours and the increasing success of the Bolsheviks in the Russian civil war had by the end of 1919 produced a rough equilibrium of forces. The Poles had occupied east Galicia, in spite of British misgivings, and this had weakened the Ukrainians who were trying to resist both Polish claims and Bolshevik pressure. In these circumstances, the Allies now proposed a frontier on a line drawn along the eastern limit of unquestionably Polish population. This 'Curzon line' gave White Russia and the Ukraine to Russia.[13] The Russians offered to negotiate on this basis; the Poles would not. They claimed all the territory lost by them in the eighteenth-century Partitions. In April, they attacked Russia again with the aim of seizing the Ukraine. The effect was to rally Russians in a national resistance symbolized by Brusilov's reappearance under Trotsky's command. By August the Russians were a few miles from Warsaw, where they were at last halted and driven back. Fresh Russian defeats brought to a head a dispute between Lenin, who wished to go on with the war and Trotsky, who wished to make peace. In the end Trotsky had his way, and by the treaty of Riga (18 March 1921) Russia kept the Ukraine, although the Poles gained some of White Russia and obtained a frontier much more favourable than the Curzon line. This defined Russia's western frontiers until 1939 (the Baltic states had obtained recognition from Russia in 1920),[14] and was also the end of the first stage of the Russian Revolution. The civil war was extinguished (the Ukraine had joined in the creation of the Union of Soviet Socialist Republics

13 The line was very like the 1939 German-Russian frontier.
14 Treaties were signed as follows: with Estonia, 2 February; Lithuania, 12 July; Latvia, 11 August; Finland, 14 October.

on 30 December 1920), and so was the danger of European revolution. Symbolically, two days before the treaty of Riga, an Anglo-Soviet agreement reopened trade negotiations between the two countries and led to an unofficial exchange of representatives. In a series of individual settlements, seven years of almost continuous fighting in eastern Europe had at last been brought to a close.

The last area to be settled was that of the former Ottoman Empire. In Asia and Africa the collapse of the Turkish power was before 1939 only of great importance to France and the United Kingdom, the powers given mandates over former Ottoman territory in these areas. They found in them a source of friction. From the Armistice of Mudros itself (30 October 1918), France distrusted the British interpretation of wartime agreements. In the disappointment of Arab nationalism too, there was the seed of future trouble, but European Turkey, the Aegean and the Straits had in 1919 more interest for European statesmen.

One simplification had been the disappearance of Russia's claim to Constantinople. The other Allied states with claims to Turkish territory at the end of the war were Greece and Italy, whose ambitions went back before 1914 and had been encouraged during the war. Consequently, in April 1919 Italians landed at Antalya (Adalia). Soon after, Venizelos (in the absence of the Italian prime minister from Paris) persuaded the Allies to let the Greeks occupy eastern Thrace and Smyrna. The Italians and Greeks subsequently agreed to cooperate, and faced with this incursion the sultan's government (the British were anxious not to depose him in case it had a bad effect on Indian Muslims) signed the treaty of Sèvres, acknowledging the independence of the Hejaz, Syria, Mesopotamia and Palestine. The Kurds were to have autonomy. The Greeks were allowed to occupy Smyrna for five years, after which its future was to be decided by plebiscite. Greece also obtained the Aegean islands, Italy the Dodecanese and Rhodes. The Straits were demilitarized and internationalized. Armenia was given independence and other minorities received guarantees of their future safety.

The main effect of this treaty (never ratified) was to enhance the prestige of the revolutionary Kemalist movement, the first successful attempt to revise a peace treaty. A revolt in Anatolia led by Kemal soon threatened Constantinople, which was thinly garrisoned by British troops. It was soon obvious that if the Allies were not prepared to overthrow him, they would have to come to terms or face the prospect of an indefinite occupation. As the Greek government was the most violently anti-Kemalist among the Allies, the fall of Venizelos (14 November) made things easier. In March 1921 the Italians agreed to withdraw from Anatolia. Kemal made a military agreement with Russia and the Greeks now began to be slowly driven back, losing Smyrna in September. The French came to terms. In 1922 the Greeks were driven from Anatolia and although Lloyd George prevented Kemal from following them into Thrace at Chanak, it was obvious that the dream of a new Greek empire of the Aegean had gone forever. The final settlement was signed at Lausanne 23 July 1923. The new Kemalist Turkey confirmed the abandonment of claims to the Arab states, the Aegean Islands, Cyprus, Rhodes and the Dodecanese. The Straits were to be demilitarized, but under Turkish sovereignty. Turkey recovered eastern Thrace and an exchange of populations and military guarantees were provided for. This was the only negotiated, rather than imposed, peace treaty, and it has lasted longer than any of the other postwar settlements. Thus Turkey began her existence as a modern national state. The Caliphate was abolished in March 1924.

Peace-making between 1918 and 1923 was almost entirely a matter of settling the claims of European states, and European arrangements are the main concern of this book. This emphasis is not artificial. One short-coming of the peace settlement was that it was to a large degree obsessed with European problems. Yet of the thirty-two 'Allied and Associated Powers' which signed the Treaty of Versailles, twenty-three were non-European. There were dangers in the lack of recognition that of the European great powers of 1914, three had been shattered (if, in two cases, temporarily), that another, Italy, had been shown not to be a great power, and that France had only just survived the cost of the effort to remain one. The United States had decided the outcome of the war – yet she withdrew from the peace.

There were other ominous signs for the future. The representation of the Dominions at Paris was an important landmark in the British retreat from Empire. It was already being referred to as the 'Commonwealth' by some. One colonial power, Germany, had lost all her overseas territories, and there were other signs that European colonialism was weakened. More immediately, (see, further, pp. 388–91) the end of the war also exposed a transformation of great power relationships in the Far East which signified a decline in Europe's importance. Germany was now excluded from Asia, and Russia, too, was gravely weakened. The change in the Far East balance of power which had begun with the Russo-Japanese war, was now made explicit. Only Japan, Great Britain and the United States were now great powers in the Far East and the Pacific. The problem of stabilization which this posed was one of balancing the power of Japan.

This was considerable. Japan had by 1918 the third largest navy in the world. During the war she had resumed a forward policy in China which had been checked after Shimonoseki. By the end of the war, the United States was suspicious of Japanese ambitions both in China and Siberia. Unfortunately, Japanese susceptibilities were wounded when the Japanese delegates at Paris failed to obtain an endorsement of the principle of racial equality in the Covenant of the League. The award of a mandate for Germany's former Pacific colonies did not outweigh the irritation of many Japanese.

In 1921 the United States government took the initiative by inviting Great Britain, France, Italy, Belgium, the Netherlands, Portugal, China and Japan to a conference at Washington. At this conference a four-power treaty was agreed between Great Britain, Japan, France and the United States, which established mutual guarantees of one another's Pacific possessions (the special bilateral Anglo-Japanese alliance was allowed to lapse), and a treaty limiting naval armaments between these powers and Italy. A ten-year 'holiday' began during which no new capital ships were to be built, and limits were set to the total tonnages of capital ships which would remain in commission.[15] Other treaties set up a nine-nation guarantee of China's independence and the 'open door', and provided for the return of Kiao-chou to China. On the whole, this arrangement worked well because European powers no longer wanted to take an active role in China. For ten years it was only threatened by Russian activity in China. But the real reason China could be left to stew in her own juice was the change in the comparative strengths of the great powers. In this way, the settlement of world affairs after the Great War already

15 These limits established a ratio between the powers of 5 (Great Britain and the United States): 3 (Japan): 1.67 (France and Italy).

showed, through Japan's independence of action in China, the beginning of the dwarfing of Europe.

There was great reluctance to see this. Trotsky's peace message had been addressed to the working classes of the 'three leading nations' in 1917; he had not thought the United States to be one of them. The illusion of an unshaken European hegemony was going to persist into the 1930s, and, of course, it was to be true that the second world war was to arise from European issues in 1939. But Europe's own exports – democracy, nationalism and industrialism – were already beginning to turn against her. General Smuts, a South African, saw this more easily than many Europeans when he warned his fellow delegates to the 1921 Imperial Conference that

Our temptation is still to look upon the European stage as of the first importance. It is no longer so . . . these are not really first rate events any more . . . Undoubtedly the scene has shifted away from Europe to the Far East and to the Pacific. The problems of the Pacific are to my mind the world problems of the next fifty years or more.[16]

THE SEARCH FOR INTERNATIONAL STABILITY

One new complication in international affairs after 1919 was that there were more sovereign states than in 1914 and that their rulers and diplomats were inexperienced and assertive. These new and smaller states could throw their weight about in a way not possible in 1914, because of the eclipse of Russia and Germany and the disappearance of the Habsburgs. Some of the new states were politically unstable; disappointment with the peace and the irritation of minorities provided material for demagogues given new opportunities by the spread of literacy and the formal apparatus of parliamentary democracy. Almost all of them were economically weak and socially divided. Some of them were still blockaded after the armistice; the weakness of the victorious great powers was thus another disturbing factor. The control of food supplies had to be used as a weapon only because the Allies lacked soldiers to police the new Europe. In July 1919, for example, it

16 See G. M. Gathorne-Hardy, *A Short History of International Affairs 1920–1939* (4th edn, Oxford, 1950), p. 140

was discovered that only two incomplete French divisions would be available to intervene against Bela Kun; the Allies were impotent to enforce their will on a small nation. The peace settlement was only once defended by arms (at Chanak in 1922) and that led to the overthrow of Lloyd George, who was thought to have endangered the peace. No one in Britain wanted to go to war again. The democracies, therefore, could not hope to control by armed force the new 'balkanized' Europe of Versailles.

In this confusion it is hard to discern a pattern. The decade after 1919 is roughly split by the Locarno agreements of 1925, which divided a period of turmoil and danger from one of growing security and optimism. The approach to Locarno can be described about three themes: revisionism, the growth of the new League of Nations and the hopes it aroused, and the constant pursuit of security by France.

The origins of revisionism have already been described. Defeated nations had losses to recover and victorious ones quarrelled over incompatible claims. The fighting of Poles and Czechs over Teschen, or the Yugoslav attempts at a *coup de main* in Carinthia to resist a plebiscite which had gone against them, were unpromising, but not disastrous. Turkey, too, succeeded in rectifying her position without endangering the whole settlement. But the revisionism of Italy and Russia was more dangerous.

It would be superficial to begin the story of Italian revisionism in 1918. Italy's discontents went back to prewar colonial disappointments and *Risorgimento* designs on the Habsburg heritage. The promises of the Treaty of London had been overtaken by Wilson's refusal to be bound by the inter-Allied agreements, and the appearance of a new Yugoslav state in 1918. Wilson was willing to compromise his principles of self-determination so far as to give Italy a strategical frontier on the Brenner; he was not willing to stifle his newly aroused sympathy for Yugoslavia (to which the Allies gave *de jure* recognition on 1 May 1919). American principles and French policy for once walked hand-in-hand, for the French saw in Yugoslavia a future ally and client. Italy saw in her only an obstacle to the satisfaction of Adriatic and Balkan ambitions. Soon the Italians were trying to stop France supplying arms to the Yugoslavs. Thus, acrimonious negotiation with her allies at Paris left Italy disappointed. Although she acquired a million-and-a-half new inhabitants, she was given no more colonial territory and, since Turkey was not partitioned as had been envisaged in 1915, nothing on the Asian mainland. The gravest troubles arose over the Adriatic port of Fiume. This city had not been promised to Italy in 1915, and when the Italians asked for it at Paris (together with southern Dalmatia), they were going beyond the point at which any of the Allies could support them. At Fiume, while discussions went on, the Italian troops who had landed there at the armistice encouraged their local supporters; the French and Serbs who had been part of the Allied army in the Balkans did the same. Violent incidents between their troops soon strained the relations of France and Italy. An apparent deadlock was only broken by an almost comical intervention from the outside, by the poet d'Annunzio. In September, he arrived at Fiume with a few supporters to claim the port for Italy. Foolishly, the Italian commander on the spot accepted his demand and allowed d'Annunzio to take possession of the city, whose annexation to Italy was then proclaimed. This was an open defiance of the Peace Conference which even the Italian government had to disavow. An Italian blockade of sorts was mounted to starve d'Annunzio out.

In 1920, again under Giolitti, the Italian government began to show a more conciliatory spirit. Isolation had become uncomfortable and direct negotiations with Yugoslavia were opened. The result was a treaty which gave Italy much less than she had been promised in the Treaty of London.[17] Italy received Istria, but renounced nearly all her claims to southern Dalmatia, which had been allocated to her in 1915. Fiume was to be an independent city. This was followed by the eviction of d'Annunzio (who had declared war on the Italian government) from Fiume by the Italians at the end of December.

Such a settlement, though moderate (and perhaps because of that), could not be popular in Italy. The rhetoric of d'Annunzio and the Nationalists and resentment against the other Allies combined to weaken the prestige of the government and the parliamentary system. The events at Fiume were presented as part of a process of national retreat evident also in Albania. Greece and Italy, whose forces had roughly divided it at the armistice, had in 1919 made an agreement about their respective interests which gave a protectorate over Albania to Italy. The British and French

17 The treaty was signed at Rapallo 12 November and should not be confused with the Russo-German agreement made there in 1922.

were willing to accept partition if Yugoslavia also could be given a share, but Wilson refused to countenance this. The result was the emergence of an Albanian nationalist movement which soon drove out the Greeks. Giolitti hastened to come to terms and agreed that the Italians too should leave (2 August 1920).

Disappointment with Italy's international standing and the dwindling of her Adriatic visions helped to prepare the way for Mussolini. When he took power in 1922, he quickly began to show a new truculence in foreign affairs which delighted revisionists and nationalists. He put out feelers to Hungary, another revisionist state hostile to Yugoslavia. One of the first Fascist successes was a *coup* at Fiume in March 1922; under considerable pressure, the Yugoslavs now agreed to waive the Treaty of Rapallo and recognized the annexation of Fiume to Italy (January 1924). At home, a policy of violent italianization was adopted in the Alto Adige (the south Tyrol). Soon even kindergarten instruction was given there in Italian, and tombstones were not allowed to bear German inscriptions.

More dramatically, Italy broke with Greece. Hostility to Turkey and Yugoslavia had drawn the two states into something like an *entente*, but the Turkish resurgence undermined this. The Italians came to terms with Ataturk. Then came the Greek collapse of 1922, followed by a revolution which gave Italy the opportunity to disavow the 1919 treaty. At this stage, the Fascists took power in Italy. In August 1923 Mussolini seized a chance to show Italians that they, too, could bully Greece. Three Italian officers on duty with a boundary commission were killed on the Albanian frontier in mysterious circumstances; without investigation, Mussolini demanded satisfaction from Greece with an ultimatum which was at once followed by the bombardment and occupation of Corfu. When Greece appealed to the League of Nations, Mussolini threatened to withdraw from it. The affair was eventually settled; the Italian forces withdrew and the Greeks paid compensation. Italians rejoiced in a great psychological success. It was obvious that Mussolini had no misgivings about threatening the international order set up at Paris; Fiume was the first breach in the European decisions reached by the Conference.

Russian revisionism, unlike Italy's, sprang from a rejection of the whole capitalist world of which the peace settlements were only one expression; it was in principle unappeasable. None the less, the precise nature of the peace shaped the form and tactic of that rejection. The Polish treaty, for example, had been a humiliation forced on Russia by exhaustion; Poland after Riga, whatever her government, was bound to be in Russian eyes a strategical threat. She was part of the lost glacis of the old Tsarist Empire. The shock of the Allied interventions (and their misinterpretation) added to the dislike which the Russians showed to her and to the new Baltic states, henceforth feared in Moscow as dangerous jumping-off points for new attacks on Russia.

An immediate change in this situation was unlikely. In the first place, the central European revolutions from which the Bolsheviks had hoped so much had by 1921 obviously failed. This was above all true in Germany, where the new Communist party staged an abortive attempt to seize power in 1921. Secondly, Russia was exhausted. By 1921 this was beginning to breed political opposition by former supporters of the Bolshevik revolution. In the same year came the damaging further blow of a disastrous famine. The Bolshevik government used a famous writer, Maxim Gorky, as its mouth-piece to appeal to the humanitarian impulses of capitalist states for help. For prestige reasons, it could not make such an appeal itself. The American Relief Administration distributed three-quarters of a million tons of food and saved Russia from complete economic collapse.[18] This was the background to a Russian foreign policy which embodied a persisting basic contradiction. On the one hand, the Russian state ostensibly sought normal relations with the rest of the world, using ordinary diplomatic machinery for this purpose. On the other hand, through the nominally independent organization of the Comintern, Russia sought to overthrow or weaken by revolution the world order which faced her.

Economic weakness pushed Russia's rulers towards normal diplomatic intercourse. By 1921 it was clear to the Bolsheviks that foreign capital was as necessary as it had been before 1914, when Russia's foreign debts were larger than those of any country in the world. But no one trusted a régime which had repudiated the large debts of the tsarist governments and had confiscated foreign properties. By October 1921 the Russian foreign minister, Chicherin,

18 American money (about $60 m) and management fed about 10 million people; an international committee about 1½ million. About a third of the money came from the American government. See also pp. 409–10.

began to hold out the prospect of acknowledging tsarist debts, if further credits were made available. There appeared to be a real hope of better Russian relations with the capitalist world. Already (16 March 1921) an Anglo-Soviet trade agreement had been signed. The normalization of Russian relations with the Baltic states was also going forward. By the end of 1921 there was talk of an international conference on the reintegration of Russia with the rest of the world.

This slow but promising evolution was overtaken by a much more dramatic *rapprochement* with Germany. Need, weakness, and a sense of grievance pulled these two countries together and gave each its first postwar diplomatic success. In December 1920 Lenin had described Germany as 'naturally inclined in the direction of an alliance with Russia'.[19] Allied pressure for reparations and an unpopular League decision over Silesia created in Germany a favourable atmosphere for views already held in some official circles. Poland's existence offended German conservatives as much as Russian Bolsheviks. German soldiers, too, had been quick to see the opportunities which Russia would give for experiment and training impossible in Germany. Secret cooperation over this began in 1922 and lasted about ten years.[20] By the beginning of 1922 the two states had also made an agreement about the exchange of prisoners of war.

Then came the suggestion for an international economic conference at Genoa to repair the damage done by the war. Lloyd George proposed that both Germany and Russia, until now ostracized, should participate. For both states, merely to be at the conference was an achievement. But for all Chicherin's hawking of economic concessions to western capitalists, the Russians distrusted the conference. They feared it would open the way to the economic coercion of Russia under the pretext of assisting reconstruction. The Russians were anxious to carry off Germany from any such potential coalition; they therefore began to hint at the prospect of an agreement with Britain and France over reparations, a still unsettled question for Russia. The Germans were in the middle of a difficult struggle over reparations and under fierce French pressure; when the Russians offered them a bilateral

19 See G. Kennan, *Soviet Foreign Policy*, p. 134.
20 Largely the work of the *Reichswehr*, it was not at first known to the German foreign office.

agreement, they took it. At Rapallo (16 April 1922) the German and Russian governments agreed to exchange ambassadors, mutually renounced claims against one another and set up preferential tariffs. Great alarm was felt in France and Italy. *The Times* called the agreement an 'unholy alliance'. From Russia's point of view it dispersed the cloudy dangers of an anti-Russian 'front' in Europe and gave her the first full diplomatic recognition she obtained. For Germany it banished the dangers of Russian reparation claims, and was an important psychological step and possibly a source of new leverage in her dealings with other powers. The major revisionists had joined hands.

This was a great success for Russian foreign policy, and success continued. The British Labour government which took office in January 1924 was anxious for better relations and gave Russia full diplomatic recognition almost at once without waiting for reassurance on the debt claims which had hitherto bedevilled recognition. Italy soon followed suit, Mussolini having, in fact, anticipated the British in announcing his intention. In these successes, some weight must be given to Chicherin's skill and professional acceptability as an old-fashioned diplomat. He was able, also, to enjoy the advantage that Lenin's illness and incapacity removed some of the close watchfulness of the party on foreign affairs. But Lenin died in January 1924. Stalin was to reassert party control of foreign affairs, and Chicherin's influence was to decline.

Russia's official diplomacy, moreover, had never silenced or replaced the Comintern's revolutionary propaganda. Russia always spoke with two voices and this aroused suspicion and fear in other governments. The Comintern alleged that attempts had been made at Genoa to 'despoil' Soviet Russia. The League of Nations was damned as a 'stinking corpse'. The true meaning of Rapallo, it said, would be revealed with the triumph of the German working class. 'We are the deadly enemies of the bourgeois society', was a reiterated theme. Attempts to back up such views with practice attracted much notice. In 1923 came revelations of Communist intrigue in Norway, and in October an attempted revolution in Germany. In the Middle East the Comintern poured out anti-British propaganda even while the British government was moving towards recognition of the Soviet state. In 1924 came the revelation of the 'Zinoviev letter' on the eve of a British general election. It purported to be an instruction to the British Communists to stir up trouble and sedition. The electoral effect appears to have been slight, if any, though it quickly became a part of British left-wing folklore to believe that it had been important in producing a Conservative victory. Nevertheless, it wrecked the hopes of a general treaty with England and began a period in which Russia lost the diplomatic advantages she had gained between 1921 and 1924. Russia under Stalin began to move back towards isolation. Anglo-Russian relations worsened so quickly that in 1927 diplomatic relations were severed, and were not resumed until the end of 1929. Ideology thus nourished the roots of that continuing distrust of Russia in England which was to be so important in the 1930s.

The League of Nations was the second major new fact in international relations. Many distrusted it and some scoffed, but it seems likely that it made many more people hopeful. The slaughter that grew out of the power struggles of Europe had made men seek a guarantee of future peace in a supranational organization which would provide bloodless resolutions to international conflict. The phrase 'League of Nations' first became familiar during the winter of 1914–15. Later, just before Wilson drew up his Fourteen Points, Lloyd George outlined a scheme for a future international organization. By the end of the war, the idea was widespread and popular. President Wilson was gripped by it, envisaging not only an association of states provided with machinery which would make war unnecessary, but also an association of states which shared democratic forms of government. This was more than could be hoped for, but thanks largely to his urgent advocacy, the Peace Conference approved the principle of a League as early as 25 January 1919.

Anglo-American influences and ideas preponderated in the drafting of the League's Covenant. Wilson devoted much time to it, making important concessions elsewhere in order to see the Covenant in the form he wished. He believed that the League would later put right shortcomings in the peace treaties could it be brought successfully to birth. For Europe, the most important provisions of the Covenant were those which set up safeguards against aggression and renounced the use of force. But neither Italy nor France felt it provided effective safeguards of their postwar position. There were important shortcomings, too (some of them unavoidable) in the form of the League. Russia and Germany were not a part of it, Russia consistently decrying it, and the Germans sulking self-righteously because they were excluded by Wilson and Clemenceau (Lloyd George was willing to admit them). This added to the stigma the League possessed in German eyes as part of an imposed peace. But the most serious defect of the League was the absence of the United States. The decisive vote in the United States Senate was taken in November 1919. A majority voted for ratification of the treaty, but not the two-thirds majority required by the constitution. Although Wilson did not at once give up hope, this was in fact the end of American participatioin. After the election of his successor the official American attitude to the League became even more hostile. The results of this withdrawal of the United States from an organization which might have transformed European affairs are incalculable.

Nevertheless the League came into being on 10 January 1920. Its Council met six days later. Its newly created permanent secretariat established itself at Geneva and during 1920 the Council met in ten sessions before the first session of the League Assembly in November. The Council consisted of representatives of Great Britain, France, Italy, Japan, Belgium, Spain, Greece and Brazil and soon found a large number of items of business before it, many of them tasks thrown on the League by the Peace Conference, other arising from emergency and accident.

The failures of international organizations always attract more attention than their successes because dissatisfaction stimulates propaganda and publicity by interested parties. The League, from the start, worked valuably at such undramatic yet important matters as the refugee problem, the controlling of epidemic disease in eastern Europe, the repatriation of prisoners and the launching of the mandates. It took helpful technical initiatives such as the 1921 Conference on Communications at Barcelona. In a more directly political way, the League, through its high commissioner at Danzig, strove to moderate the differences of Germans and Poles in that city. In 1921, it made a satisfactory settlement of the question of the Aaland islands, disputed between Finland and Sweden. Its intervention in 1922 undoubtedly saved Austria from collapse by providing for foreign funds to be administered under the direction of a commissioner from the League.

All this was very valuable; none the less, when political rivalries were involved in its business, it became clear that there were limits to what the League could do. It was hardly the fault of the League if this disillusioned those who had expected a more startling improvement in international life than was in fact possible.

The Saar provides an instance of this. The assumption by the League of governmental responsibility there did not reconcile Germans to its loss. They were from the start excited that the chairman of the five commissioners who were to govern the area was a Frenchman. The appointment was not unreasonable; the Commission would be constantly in touch with France over economic questions, and it does not seem that the chairman was (as he was alleged to be) violently pro-French or biased, but the choice was unfortunate and made it difficult to win German confidence.[21] This was important in 1923, when a strike took place in the Saar. The chairman of the Commission called in 6,000 French troops, and issued a decree of extraordinary harshness, imposing severe penalties on critics of the Commission or the peace treaties. No one was arrested under this decree, and it was soon withdrawn, but it caused protests. The League Council took the matter up but was divided. The French government was unwilling to allow anything to be done which might appear to disavow the Chairman of the Commission and it was obvious that this fact made his removal impossible, had that been desired. In the end, the Council asserted its authority by summoning the Commission before it and holding an enquiry.

The League also ran into trouble over the city of Vilna, occupied by the Poles during the Russo-Polish war. Both Lithuania and Poland claimed the city. By September 1920, there was a real danger of war between the two new states. Pilsudski, the Polish dictator, himself of Lithuanian descent and particularly touchy on the question; had French support. The Council of the League took the matter up and achieved a limited success in getting a military commission sent to the spot to settle the demarcation question. It had hardly started its work when a Polish army suddenly invaded Lithuania, ostensibly in defiance of the Polish government, but actually as part of a scheme of Pilsudski to present the League with a *fait accompli*. The Council of the League decided to hold a plebiscite in Vilna under the supervision of an international force, but fighting went on. In addition, the Russian govern-

---

21 It was also claimed that of the other four members only the Canadian member was not pro-French, and he resigned in 1923.

ment now complicated the question further by saying that a League force in Lithuania would threaten Russian security. There was a rapid decline in enthusiasm for contributing to such a force. A puppet Lithuanian administration under Polish control also appeared in Vilna. In the end, a solution escaped the League, although Lithuania had joined the League in September 1921. The Conference of Ambassadors awarded Vilna to Poland in 1923, but fighting only ended in 1927. Although the League might have enough authority to command attention, it could only sustain its decisions if member states placed armed force at its disposal.[22]

The League's greatest success was in Upper Silesia. Here, German and Polish territorial claims conflicted. At the Conference, the French supported the Poles, while England and Italy upheld the German case; the area was placed under an Allied Commission until a plebiscite could be taken. This Commission not only found itself bitterly divided, but faced growing disorder as Poles and Germans struggled to prepare for a plebiscite which would favour their own national claims. In some of the troubles Italian troops were killed. The former Allies soon deadlocked on the Silesian question. In the end they passed the dispute to the Council of the League, agreeing to accept its award. A plebiscite was held in March 1921 and was favourable to Germany. The Poles promptly tried to impose their own claims by force but failed. The next task was to draw a boundary inside Silesia between Poland and Germany. This was difficult. A boundary which reflected the results of the plebiscite would run through the middle of the Silesian industrial area, which was an economic unity. The League award drew such a boundary (19 October 1921) but set up elaborate provisions for the continuance of essential services and the movement of labour and materials as before across the political frontier. Germany received roughly two-thirds of the territory and three-fifths of the population of Upper Silesia, while the Poles obtained most of the mineral deposits and industrial plant. The Germans were furious. When the Geneva Convention on Upper Silesia was signed in May 1922, the *Reichstag* marked its ratification by draping itself in black. Nevertheless, the arrangements proved workable, although the mixed Commission which governed the area for the next fifteen years had to deal with

22 Another recognition of a *fait accompli* occurred in 1924 when Lithuania was given sovereign rights over Memel, an autonomous port, after Lithuania had carried out there a *coup* similar to the Polish at Vilna.

a mass of complaints from both Poles and Germans about unjust treatment. But the Silesian settlement worked.

In other ways, the League had disappointed some of its more ardent supporters. It had been unable to act quickly enough to save an Armenian state which had appeared briefly in 1919. It had been silent over a French occupation of Darmstadt and Frankfurt in 1921, and it was ignored by Poincaré in 1923 (see below). These things confirmed popular feeling against the League in Germany. On disarmament, it made no progress. Finally, its authority was flouted by Mussolini over Corfu; even the Greeks took their case to the Conference of Ambassadors. On the credit side stood the interventions mentioned above and the growth of an *esprit de corps* in the League's staff and a habit of consultation at Geneva which would have been inconceivable in 1914. Perhaps more should not have been hoped for in the first five years. Only unreserved confidence on the part of the great powers could have given it the capacity to handle the central problem of Europe in these years, that of French security and the League was too new an idea for that.

French fear for the future was matched for a few years after 1919 by opportunity. The eclipse of Germany and the dissolution of Austria-Hungary gave her a last chance to exercise supremacy in Europe. No land power existed to restrain her; although her relations with Great Britain deteriorated rapidly, this could not affect her behaviour and only confirmed French convictions of the unreliability of her friends. The American failure to ratify the peace or the treaty of guarantee blew away any lingering restraints. In the vacuum of power which existed after 1919, France set out to provide for her own security in a brief Indian summer as a great power.

Three main techniques were open to her: the traditional diplomacy of alliances; the use of the reparations system to strengthen her own resources and bleed those of Germany; and the direct use of military force against Germany. She used all of them.

A substitute for the old Russian alliance was sought in a string of treaties of mutual support between France and Belgium (September 1920), Poland (February 1921) and the 'Little *Entente*' of Czechoslovakia, Rumania and Yugoslavia (1924–7). On the whole, France loyally upheld the interests of these allies (supporting, for example, those of Poland in Upper Silesia), but such alliances had two defects. The first was that in them France

could not oppose the treaty's gradual withering-away under British and German pressure. But it was an unpleasant, violent, and in the end inefficacious, means. It was the supreme example of France's attempt to use direct military action, though not the first. In the occupied Rhineland there had been from the start a notable difference in temper of the British and French occupations. Not only was the civilian population treated more brusquely in the French zone, but it was French policy to encourage separatist movements. In October 1923 France recognized the Palatinate as a separate state, Britain being out-voted on the Rhineland High Commission when this body gave its *de facto* recognition to the new order. Nor did the French government ever hesitate to display its military power when it seemed advantageous. In April 1920 Frankfurt and Darmstadt were occupied because of the movement of German troops to the Ruhr to repress revolutionary disorder and soldiers were freely employed against the Saar miners during the 1923 strike.

Nevertheless, the Ruhr occupation was a turning point. It made it clear that Poincaré's policy had failed; the cost of running the mines could not be met by the deliveries they made, France was still not getting what she wanted from Germany and her own financial stability was suffering. The elections of May 1924 overthrew Poincaré and the effective conduct of French foreign policy passed again into the hands of Briand, who was to retain it until 1932. The first demonstration of a new French attitude was the granting of *de jure* recognition to Russia in October 1924. Passive resistance in the Ruhr had been ended in 1923 by Stresemann, who presided over a shortlived government but who sat in all German governments until his death in 1929. The association of Briand and Stresemann was one of the personal factors sustaining the more hopeful tone of international relations in the later 1920s.

Real improvement began when Britain was able to persuade the United States to concern itself again with a German economic settlement, in order to avoid a worldwide financial crisis. The result was a modified and reduced scheme of reparations annuities, the reorganization of the German state bank under Allied supervision, and the flotation of a loan of 800 million gold marks to Germany with American help. Under this 'Dawes Plan', there began a steady and increasing flow of American investment which gradually restored German prosperity. This was the indispensable preliminary to a change in the political atmosphere.

Signs of such a change were quick to follow. During 1923 the League had discussed a draft treaty of mutual assistance which would provide guarantees against future aggressors. Such a scheme might provide France with the reassurance she had hitherto sought in eastern alliances, reparations and military occupation of Germany. This scheme grew into a proposal officially presented by the British government to the League on 2 October 1924 for a 'Geneva Protocol' on the pacific settlement of international disputes by compulsory arbitration. European countries liked the scheme. But in March, the British Labour government was replaced by a Conservative one more sensitive to the objections of the Dominions. Canada, in particular, felt the protocol to be one-sided, since it was unlikely that Europe would ever be called upon to honour its underwriting of compulsory arbitration in the western hemisphere, while Europe itself contained many danger spots. And there were other reasons. There was the danger of conflict with the United States if Britain should ever have to undertake naval action in support of the Protocol and there was the unwillingness of Britain to guarantee the boundaries of eastern Europe. As the British foreign secretary put it in a conscious reminiscence of Bismarck: 'For the Polish corridor, no British government ever will or ever can risk the bones of a British grenadier.'[23]

None the less, there had been an important change in atmosphere. The next initiative came from Germany, which in February 1925 proposed a pact with France for mutual guarantees of the demilitarized Rhineland. The British supported this promising step; it would mean that Germany would at last freely accept part of the Versailles *diktat*. Briand, for France, added to it the stipulation that such a guarantee should be coupled with Germany's entry to the League; this would be, he thought, at least a partial safeguard against German revisionism in the east. These proposals were the origin of Locarno, where a conference in October worked out a series of treaties (signed 1 December) which together mark the first epoch in postwar European relations. The frontiers of France and Belgium with Germany were guaranteed in treaties signed not only by these states but by Italy and Great Britain. Germany also signed arbitration treaties with France,

23 See F. P. Walters, *History of the League of Nations* (Oxford, 1951), p. 284.

Belgium, Poland and Czechoslovakia. France signed treaties of mutual assistance with Poland and Czechoslovakia in case of German attack.

In many ways, Locarno was a great change. It swept away the old distinction of 'enemy' and 'allied' powers, as the British and Italian guarantees of the Rhineland against attack from *either* side showed. It was also a step towards the psychological dissolution of the Versailles treaty. The Ruhr occupation had already been ended in the spring of 1925; in January 1927, the Inter-Allied Commission of Military Control in Germany came to an end, the control of German armaments being transferred to the League, of which Germany became a member, with a permanent seat on the Council, 8 September 1926.[24] The readmission of Germany to the comity of nations was widely interpreted as an outward and visible sign of an inward and spiritual change. The British foreign secretary saw the agreements 'not as the end of the work of appeasement and reconciliation, but as its beginning'.[25] Stresemann, at the signing, said the new settlement's purpose was 'to introduce a new era of co-operation among nations, a time of real peace'.[26] Briand threw himself into seven years of dedicated activity to make this aim a reality.

Yet some of his countrymen, in spite of his optimism, were right to be sceptical. It is important in judging Locarno not to falsify the historical situation of the time by awareness of the events of the next twenty years. Even in 1925, however, a Frenchman might observe that Britain and Italy were only bound to act if Germany disturbed the Versailles settlement in the west; German aggression in the east, on the other hand, would leave France alone to go to war to defend the new states. If it was objected that this was too cynical, and that Germany had renounced force in the east as well, it would be replied that this did not make the eastern frontiers immune from change. What had happened was that certain sections of the Versailles settlement were given a privileged status: that very fact weakened the rest

24 This led to the resignation from the League of Brazil and Spain, who also claimed the right to a permanent seat. Spain rejoined in 1928.
25 See M. Gilbert, *Britain and Germany between the Wars* (London, 1964), p. 44.
26 G. Stresemann, *Diaries, Letters and Papers* (London, 1935–40), II, p. 239.

of it. Great Britain was encouraged to forget eastern Europe. In these circumstances, it is perhaps understandable that France began in 1930 to build a great defensive work, the 'Maginot line' to free her from strategical anxiety should eastern Europe involve her in a new struggle with Germany. It was in the east that the explosion was to come, but when it did, France was unable to reap the benefits of prudence, because the comforting shelter of her fortresses had diverted her attention from the need to maintain an army capable of offensive action to support her allies.

THE LAST YEARS OF OPTIMISM

Locarno opened a brief era of optimism and confidence in European public affairs. Growing material prosperity contributed to it, but there was also widespread conviction that a major threat to European peace, French fears of Germany, had been removed by the appeasement of German revisionism. Germany seemed to have accepted the loss of Alsace-Lorraine and the demilitarized status of the Rhineland. Her unwillingness to extend the guarantees of Locarno went unremarked.

Another good symptom, it was thought, was the increasing activity of the League. Prime ministers and foreign secretaries now regularly attended its assemblies. This perhaps gave it a more Eurocentric flavour, since it was not so easy for the leaders of non-European nations to be present when air travel was still unusual and over long distances virtually non-existent, but it was also a sign that it was being taken more seriously. It went on trying to achieve disarmament, it had also strengthened its authority by fining Greece for an invasion of Bulgaria in 1925 (a case in which no great power had a significant interest). In 1927, in response to another appeal from Lithuania and after Russian statements that Poland threatened Lithuania's independence, the Council took up again this far more dangerous question, in which France was deeply interested. A notable success was achieved, first in getting Pilsudski to attend the League Council and to announce that he would accept its views and then in persuading Lithuania and Poland to end the state of war which had existed between them since 1921 and to resume normal relations (shortlived and uneasy as they were to prove). There were thus good grounds for optimism about the League. Even those European countries like Russia which did not belong to it took part in some of its activities.

The 'Geneva spirit' and the influence of Locarno were thus potent as the end of the decade approached. The euphoria of the era was symbolized by the Kellogg-Briand pact of 1928 renouncing aggressive war, to which sixty-five nations eventually adhered. And there were also firmer grounds for concluding that international life was healthier than at any time since 1918. Even Italy's foreign policy had become less dramatic (although a sensational discovery of a camouflaged consignment of Italian arms *en route* to Hungary in January 1928 showed both that Mussolini was not neglecting the opportunities presented to him by revisionism in eastern Europe and that disarmament was hardly enforceable). Horthy, the ruler of Hungary, was still convinced that Hungary could not evade a war with a *Little Entente* determined to partition Hungary. But the smaller states of the Baltic enjoyed good relations with one another, and in spite of her bickering with Lithuania, Poland joined with Russia, Rumania, Estonia and Latvia in February 1929 to sign the 'Litvinov Protocol' renouncing war in eastern Europe.

This was one of the few successes of Russia's diplomacy in these years. Her failure to maintain good relations with Great Britain had been followed by a much greater failure in China, where a mistaken intervention on the side of the Kuomintang had led to the creation of an anti-Russian nationalist government at Nanking, and to the near-extinction of the Chinese Communist party.[27] Even formal diplomatic relations with China were not to be restored until 1932. Locarno had also weakened the Rapallo relationship with Germany; Russia's support lost its unique value in German eyes as soon as a friendlier atmosphere obtained in the west. Russia, for her part, was bound to feel uneasy as Germany got together again with the rest of the capitalist world. All these sources of uncertainty undoubtedly accentuated the isolationism of Russian policy under Stalin.

Germany was soon to win further concessions. In 1929 a new body, the Young committee, was set up to make yet another final

27 This foreshadowed the much more complete destruction of the German Communist party which resulted from Russian misreading of pre-Nazi politics in Germany.

settlement of reparations. Its proposals substantially lightened the burdens which Germany had already seemed able to bear under the Dawes scheme and there was confidence that the new ones would therefore be even more easily within Germany's capacity. In return for German acceptance of the Young scheme, the Rhineland occupation was to end by June 1930. As the decade ended, the hopes of continuing world peace were higher than they had ever been since 1918. There had even begun to be indications of a revival of world trade; the new Labour government in Britain produced proposals for a tariff truce and announced its readiness to undertake further obligatory arbitration procedures. It was hard at such a moment for Europeans to detect in America the beginnings of a world economic crisis which was to shatter all their hopes.

11

ECONOMY AND SOCIETY, 1918–1939

ECONOMIC MALADJUSTMENTS

Before 1914 depressions came and went but the fundamental tone of the economy was expansive and optimistic. A steady and often rapid increase of wealth was going on. Between 1918 and 1939 the atmosphere was very different. Rich nations fumbled uncertainly and found it hard to preserve their wealth; poor nations grew poorer. All experienced heavy unemployment. The regularity and generality of prewar movements in the economy was broken up as nations sought to save themselves from common disasters by policies of withdrawal and insulation. The fragmentation of the old economic system is one of the few continuous trends to follow after 1930. Even when the international interdependence of economics is apparent, it is shown by the contagion of economic disaster, rather than by the sharing of growing wealth.

There is an element of exaggeration in this contrast. Some of the economic troubles of the 1920s can be traced back to their roots in developments before 1914. Nevertheless, of the change in mood there can be no doubt; people who remembered the world 'before the war' felt that the hopes of 1918 had been disappointed. Then, there was widespread confidence that peace would restore the prewar economic system. A growing specialization among producers (both at a national and a local level) and complex international exchange arrangements had, for some commodities at least, created a true world market. This market had depended on fully convertible currencies backed by gold, the existence in London of a group of coordinating and lubricating institutions, and on the maintenance of certain assumptions about the autonomy of economics. In spite of tariffs, most statesmen agreed that political interference should be limited to safeguarding the advantages of specialization and the mobility of labour and capital. The system seemed solid and at bottom, unchanging, the ground of an emerging world society.

Yet, in fact, the war had shattered these foundations. 'Very few of us', said Keynes in 1919, 'realize with conviction the intensely unusual, unstable, complicated, unreliable, temporary nature of the economic organization by which western Europe has lived for the last half century.'[1] Everywhere, the war had exposed just this. The advantages of specialization were swept away in the search for self-sufficiency. The sudden thirst of wartime demand led to the growth of industrial and agricultural investment which could not have been justified by pure market criteria. This fixed capital could only be redeployed at great political and social cost. Even where it was still valuable in peace-time, there might well be too much of it. The result was a new wave of protectionist thinking. The Fourteen Points' aspirations towards 'the removal, so far as possible, of all economic barriers' remained unfulfilled over much of Europe. Many new barriers appeared in some areas. One such was the Danube valley.

Not only were the new Danubian states in chaos, but their great supplier of capital and manufactures, Germany, was prostrate. With no raw materials for her industries, no foreign exchange with which to buy them, nor even control over her own coal, she could no longer be the economic dynamo of *Mitteleuropa*. Weakness drove the new states towards protection. None of them except Czechoslovakia had a balanced economic structure. Most of them were overwhelmingly poor and dependent on agriculture. Such industries as they had were often cut off by new frontiers from their old markets or raw materials. Short of resources, distrustful of one another, the succession states were almost bound to impose import and export prohibitions and exchange controls. New currencies were viewed with distrust. Such goods as could be exchanged were laboriously unloaded and reloaded at frontiers because rolling-stock could not be expected to return if it once went abroad. Unemployment spread rapidly and there was

1 Keynes, *Consequences*, p. 1.

at first no capital available to set business on its feet again. Further east, the collapse of the old economy was even more complete. A market for manufactures and capital which had run from Warsaw to Vladivostok and a great source of grain had disappeared almost entirely from the European economic scene. Russia had, virtually, an independent economic history during these years.

Less obvious than the fragmentation of European trade by politics, but no less important, was the damage done to the international monetary system. Its fly-wheel had been London. Even before 1914, there had been signs that a slowing of industrial growth and exports might make it hard for Great Britain to go on being banker to the world. By 1918 she had run down her overseas investments badly, lost ground in old markets to new competitors and had reversed her relationship with the United States; she was now the debtor. The French needed their capital for their own reconstruction and had lost much of their taste for investment abroad after the disappearance of their great stake in Russia. All Germany's foreign investments had gone and she was hamstrung by the obligation to make reparations payments, whose fulfilment other nations demanded as the pre-condition of paying their own debts to the United States, the new world creditor. That country's manufacturing potential made it almost impossible to settle debts with her except in gold. The result was a steady accumulation of gold in the United States which sapped the more evenly spread reserves of the prewar system and thus made currencies more unstable. The elaborate but smooth channels of prewar international payments were disrupted and jammed.

Finally, there was the physical damage of the war. This was not only a matter of the battlefields. Badly as northern France had suffered, direct destruction of resources was less significant than lost production, the depletion of stocks and the erosion of working capital. In 1920 Europe's manufacturing production was nearly a quarter below that of 1913; Russia's was down by 80 per cent. In Hungary, only 27 per cent of the locomotives and 76 per cent of the wagons were fit for service; the figures for Bulgaria were 37 and 56 per cent. Moreover, the most widespread damage was in central and eastern Europe, where fighting and civil disturbance went on longest in economies least able to afford them.

In these circumstances, although men approached the postwar world with hope, they also did so with an unpromising awareness of particular and local interests. However much they wished to return to the prewar economic system, they were psychologically inhibited from doing so, even if the possibility had existed. New habits of thought had been bred by the war years; distrust and fear impeded the cool assessment of economic realities. And, as well as these incalculable psychological tools, the war cost, roughly, the destruction of eight years' production of wealth at the prewar rate.

The outcome can be traced conveniently in four phases. The years from 1918 to 1925 form a period of recovery, those from 1925 to 1929 a period of some prosperity, those from 1929 to 1935 a period of depression, and from this some, though not all, countries began to recover before 1939.

By 1925 the worst physical damage was repaired, production was restored, and currencies were stabilized. Demobilization in the victorious countries was rapid and easier than feared, because of a big demand for labour. The removal of governmental controls was eagerly demanded and quickly carried out; a short postwar boom ensued, during which depleted stocks were replenished. The Americans gave central Europe immediate loans to buy food, but the scrapping of the inter-Allied bodies which had controlled raw materials and shipping during the war removed agencies which might have been of greater help. The instability of the boom was first seen when a break in world prices began in 1920 in the United States. During the war, food production outside Europe had increased enormously.[2] By 1922, prices of many foodstuffs had halved, with disastrous effects on primary producers; a wave of tariff increases in central and east Europe opened an era of heavy protection in these areas.[3] Slump also revealed the weaknesses of the older and less competitive British industries. Finally, it touched off a wave of currency disasters. Inflation in the defeated countries and the succession states often went to unprecedented heights; the most spectacular examples

2 See, e.g., the extension of wheat acreages, in Canada from 10 to 15 million, in Australia from 6 to 12 million, in the Argentine from 14 to 16 million (R. J. Hammond, 'British Food Supplies, 1914–1939', *Econ. Hist. Rev.*, 1946).
3 For details, see Macartney and Palmer, *Independent Eastern Europe*, p. 237.

were Austria (where money prices were multiplied by 14,000), Hungary (by 23,000), Poland (by 2,500,000), Russia (by 400,000,000) and Germany (by 1,000,000,000).[4] To Austria and Hungary this brought League of Nations intervention and control of their finances until 1926, when drastic budget cuts and deflation made possible new stable currencies. The German inflation, the worst, stemmed from the prolongation of scarcity and the government's too-ready resort to the printing press. Its climax was only reached with the French occupation of the Ruhr in 1923. Germany had already been deprived of the chance to earn foreign currency by the seizure of her coal as reparations; the occupation now led the German government to print money almost unrestrainedly in order to support the Ruhr strikers against the French. The collapse of the mark which followed was complete. At some moments it disappeared altogether. Values were expressed locally in commodities or foreign currency. Recovery demanded more than the stiff budgetary control which had worked in Austria and Hungary. It started when, in 1924, Germany got its first postwar international loan and a flow of American capital to Europe began.

Meanwhile the illusion of reparations had led French governments to avoid unpopular taxation instead, they borrowed on the security of the German payments which were to come. But when the difficulties of exacting payment of reparations appeared, French investors abandoned government stock for other securities. Confidence in the currency sagged. Poincaré eventually produced a balanced budget, but it was only in 1928 that the slide of the franc was stopped and the French currency was restored to the gold standard. Only the Scandinavian states, Holland, Switzerland and the United Kingdom succeeded in maintaining parity with the dollar.

The currency stabilizations were part of a general economic recovery. It began with the international loan to Germany of 1924. In 1925 European production of food and raw materials for the first time passed the 1913 figure. A recovery was also beginning in manufacturing, although unevenly. Six countries were now surpassing their 1913 performances. Three of them, though Holland, Norway and Sweden, were former neutral nations and France's appearance in the list was misleading because of the

4 Lewis, p. 23.

return to her of Lorraine. Only Czechoslovakia and Italy showed really creditable advances. No other European nations had yet passed their 1913 level. Germany, the United Kingdom and Russia lagged well behind.

Nevertheless, a plateau of economic wellbeing was in sight. From 1925 to 1929 (the best year for European trade until 1954) economic recovery quickened over the whole world. World manufacturing output rose by 26 per cent, trade by 19 per cent, and Europe had a large share in both. One indicator was the resumption of the gold standard. The pound sterling went back on gold in 1925 and by 1928 all other European currencies had followed. In the previous year a conference at Geneva met to consider hindrances to international trade. There was a widespread hope that the time had come to resume the free flow of labour, capital and goods. It began to seem at last that the prewar economic system of multilateral exchanges might work once again. The new trend was sustained by a long boom in the United States which benefited Europe by increasing American purchases and making available a steady flow of American capital. Between 1925 and 1929 about $2,900 million was lent to European countries; it was the key to the reinvigoration of the European economy.

Unhappily this apparent prosperity was based on insecure foundations. The general resumption of the gold standard hid an important change in its machinery. London was the centre of the system. But London no longer held large enough reserves to cover foreign currencies with gold if required, as it had been able to do before 1914. Nor were the New York banks ready to take over this role. Thus there was danger in the dependence of many European countries on loans which might need to be repaid quickly. Events in the United States brought about just this calamity.

In 1928 it began to be more difficult to obtain short-term funds in the United States. There were also signs that the boom's long-expected close might be near. These two factors led to the repatriation of American money from Europe; short-term loans were called in more and more rapidly in 1929. A fall in American demand also took place; prices began to come down and it looked as if a severe slump was on the way. The notorious stock market collapse of October made it inevitable; it shattered business confidence, thus placing new barriers in the way of a restimulation of the American economy and although there was a brief rally in early 1930, American money for investment abroad finally dried up in that year. A world slump was now inevitable.

The fall in investment brought growth to an end. The United States itself, where the national income fell by 38 per cent between 1929 and 1932, suffered severely. Other countries were cut back by a smaller proportion, though they began with less. As debtor nations came under strain and sought to balance their accounts, it seemed an obvious step to cut imports. The result was further fall in world prices which, in turn, led to a further drop in the import demands of producer countries.[5] The result was the virtual collapse of world trade as tariffs rose. Finally, a European financial crisis swept away the last vestiges of confidence. It began with the failure of an important Austrian bank, provoked by France (see p. 506). It revealed the weaknesses of central European banks and their dependence on Germany, a run on whose reserves at once began. In a world in which internatinal lending had practically dried up, this meant a withdrawal of short-term funds invested in London. By August, a run began on London. The Bank of England had to make payment in gold, because much of the foreign exchange it commanded had already been committed to loans in Austria and Germany which were now blocked under a moratorium of interantional debt repayment which had been agreed the year before. In September the United Kingdom had to suspend payment in gold; by the end of 1932 twelve countries had followed. The dollar went off gold in 1933, the franc, at last, in 1936. The struggle to remain on gold had further prolonged the slump and had added to the hindrances placed in the way of international trade. As a result, at the lowest point, the world may well have had something like 30 million unemployed.

The disaster was not uniformly spread.[6] Russia's isolation from

---

5 Raw material prices fell by 56 per cent, foodstuffs by 48 per cent, manufactured goods by 38 per cent. This eased the position of a big raw material importer like Great Britain and intensified the difficulties of eastern European countries.

6 One indicator is the index of industrial production. This table takes 1929 = 100. 1932 was the worst year for all these countries.

	U.S.A.	Belgium	France	Germany	Italy	Sweden	U.K.
1932	52.7	69.1	72.2	53.3	66.9	89.0	83.5
1936	93.6	86.7	78.3	106.3	87.5	135.0	115.8

the depression was almost complete; foreign trade did not interest her except as a political instrument and her own problems were not much changed for better or worse by the world collapse. Among European countries, Sweden suffered least, and Great Britain less than many others. (British industry had, of course, benefited less from the boom of the 1920s and lost less ground comparatively.) Eastern Europe was driven into yet greater poverty; Polish farm incomes were cut by two-thirds.[7] The worst conditions in industrialized Europe were those of Germany. Her dependence on international credit had been the most complete and her setbacks at the beginning of the 1920s had been sharpest.

There followed only partial recovery, widespread political and social unrest, and a transformed economic scene. Attempts to seek recovery by cooperation came to an end when the World Economic Conference of 1933 broke down. Instead, each nation moved towards its own solutions, usually in tariffs, controls and attempts to achieve autarky. American tariffs made it impossible for her creditors to pay their debts to her. Even the United Kingdom at last abandoned free trade. Import quotas became common; bilateral agreements replaced an international market in commodities. Governments interfered more than ever before with the economy. Whatever psychological importance this had, it is not easy to say whether it did much to make recovery faster. It certainly helped to preserve inefficient industries. Recovery was helped more by the eventual picking-up of investment in the United States and preparation for war. Helped by redeployment of labour and resources inside the main industrial countries, this led to a partial recovery in production, but not in world trade by 1939.[8] The roots of its prolonged collapse lay in the depressed trade in primary products. Its failure to grow was persistent.

7 See N. Davies, *God's Playground: a history of Poland*, II (Oxford, 1981) pp. 411 for further detail.

8

	Exports		Imports	
	\(in millions of dollars: $4 = £1\)			
	1929	1938	1928	1939
World	33,024	13,318	35,595	14,231
W. Europe	15,649	6,100	19,410	7,960
U.S.A.	5,157	1,805	4,338	1,151
U.K.	3,549	1,358	5,407	2,478
U.S.S.R.	475	148	453	158

Manufacturing countries could not sell their goods, because they were buying too little food and raw materials from primary producers and at too low a price. By 1939, although the worst unemployment was over, this situation had not been repaired. It was beginning to be clear that the nineteenth century was gone for ever, in economics as well as in politics or culture. 'Throughout the whole of the postwar period', wrote a future British Prime Minister in 1938, 'there had been growing an uneasy consciousness of something radically wrong with the economic system . . . One of the consequences of the crisis was to confirm these suspicions and to liberate men's minds from a continued subservience to the economic orthodoxy of the prewar world.'[9] Since 1918 there had been only five years which could, by any stretching of terms, be called 'normal' in the pre-1914 sense. Russia had been throughout the period withdrawn from the old system of exchange, and after 1930 many other countries had withdrawn at least in part. The new economic isolation of other countries was to be intensified by political and ideological differences. International trade had dropped by more than half, but this demonstration of the real interdependence of nations led politicians to try to cut themselves off from world economic trends behind tariffs and discriminatory agreements. Together with the abandonment of the gold standard and the belief in noninterference, this marks the collapse of liberal bourgeois civilization in its economic dimension as strikingly as totalitarian régimes mark it in its political. Prolonged in appearance until 1929, the economics of the late nineteenth century had at last broken down.

STRUCTURAL CHANGE

Europe's population went on growing from 1918 to 1940 because the fall in mortality continued to outpace the fall in reproduction rates, but different nations experienced these two trends in different ways. The differing life-expectancies of rich and poor countries show that Europeans had less equal chances of life or death in 1940 than in 1880. The industrially advanced countries of the north and west had older populations and smaller families

9 H. Macmillan, *The Middle Way* (London 1938), p. 8.

than the backward east and south. This increased divergence was due in large measure to a marked slowing of the rate of growth in advanced countries after 1918, though some of them tried to encourage parenthood. To understand both of these new changes within the long-term trends, we must begin by trying to assess the demographic impact of the Great War.

The biological cost of the war is impossible to calculate precisely. Even the number of deaths caused by fighting, while it has been fairly accurately recorded for some states, remains uncertain. Also, a decision has to be made about what shall be considered the end of the war, whose aftermath in the east can be regarded as its prolongation. An estimate has to be made of the number of births which did not take place because of the war, by considering what would have happened if prewar demographic trends had continued, uninterrupted by the killing of potential fathers and the distortion of established patterns of marriage. Even deaths which occur after the fighting ended may be properly reckoned as part of its toll, if they came earlier than usual because of the weakening effect of wounds, malnutrition, or sickness, when that sickness was a consequence of the war – a factor which grows larger still if we include the famines and diseases of postwar Europe, or, all over the world, the victims of the Spanish 'flu epidemic.

Disagreement about figures is therefore easy, but whatever the basis of calculation, the results are always enormous. One estimate, limited to deaths directly caused by fighting from 1914 to 1918, is that nearly 10 million died; another, including the Russian civil war and disturbances down to 1920, reaches 13 million.[10] If we now include the losses of potential births in our calculations, we should consider the demographic 'cost' of the Great War as more than 20 million and probably not less than 24 million; this is the sort of figure by which we might have expected the population of Europe in 1920 to exceed that of 1914, had there been no war.

Of those who were killed, the great majority, of course, were young and mature men; France, for example, lost 10 per cent of her males, a proportion surpassed only by Rumania. Such losses led, after the war, to a disproportionate number of old people,

10 Woytinsky, p. 143, and Reinhard, *Histoire générale de la population mondiale*, p. 406.

and to surpluses of women for whom husbands could not be found.[11] It is also clear that although the Russian losses were huge, such losses were most damaging to the major western states, whose population growth was already slower than that of the still rapidly increasing peoples of the east. Their losses and deficiencies may be summed up as follows:

	Killed	*Population deficiency in 1919*
U.K.	0.75 m	1.78 m
France	1.4 m	3.07 m
Germany	3.0 m	5.43 m

Besides this demographic 'bite', three other new demographic forces can also be discerned after 1918. The first was a series of big migrations in the aftermath of the war which greatly changed the distribution of racial and national groups in some parts of Europe. The Russian revolution and civil war scattered about 2 million refugees over Europe, Asia and North America. About 800,000 Germans left Poland, the Baltic States and Alsace to live in Germany after the war; 400,000 Magyars flowed back to the shrunken rump of Hungary from other parts of the former Dual Monarchy; 200,000 Bulgarians left Macedonia and Thrace. It might have been hoped that displacements on such a scale would, by separating ethnic and national groups, help to allay the minorities problem but, big as they were, they still left large minorities in the new states. The biggest single exchange of all was the removal after 1922 of more than 1 million Greeks from Turkey and Thrace (350,000 Muslims went in the other direction). This move ended the history of Asia Minor as a part of Greek civilization, and was truly epoch-marking, but it created more bitterness for the future.

Another new force was an overall fall in European emigration. The 'Great Resettlement' was coming to an end. Europeans were no longer to play an important direct part in populating the known world outside Europe.[12] One important reason for this

11 In 1933, Germany had nearly 1 million more women than men aged 40–54. A rough comparison with France is possible; her 1931 census revealed a 'surplus' of 728,000 women aged 35–49.

12 *European emigration*

1901–10	14.9 m
1911–20	11.1 m
1921–30	8.7 m
1931–40	1.8 m

was the gradual restriction of immigration to the United States, until in 1928 a limit of 150,000 new entrants per year was imposed. Another important factor was the world economic depression of the early 1930s, which made other countries even less attractive than Europe. Among countries which had produced large numbers of emigrants before 1914, Italy suffered, and so did many eastern European countries which had sent large numbers to the United States; only Germany briefly increased her output of emigrants just after the war. Some countries, such as Spain and the United Kingdom in the 1930s, even showed net gains from immigration and repatriation, and foreign entrants were very important to France. Her gravely depleted labour force was able to recruit itself from foreigners who before 1914 would probably have gone to the United States. She also enjoyed the advantage of attracting, as she had always done, many political refugees, and she had a long-standing practice of using migrant agricultural labour. Immigration accounts for about three-quarters of the whole French population increase between 1920 and 1930. The peak was reached in 1931, when there were about half a million foreign-born residents in Paris alone and whole Polish villages in the northern mining districts. Even after 1936 an influx of more than 400,000 Spaniards was absorbed.

The economic depression of the 1930s also affected population history by discouraging parenthood. Economic depression usually presented itself to individual Europeans as unemployment. In an age of spreading contraceptive knowledge, this seems less to have affected the age of marriage then to have reduced the willingness of the married to have children. As employment began to pick up towards the end of the decade, natality again began to rise. The nutritional effects of the depression appear to be small (mortality rates continued to fall in most countries); its accentuation of the established trend towards smaller families may therefore have been its most important demographic effect.

The political effect of these influences was complicated by alterations of frontiers, but by 1940 the combined effects of political and demographic change had led to important differences in the relative ranking of the six great powers of 1880.[13] One great block of manpower, the Dual Monarchy, had disintegrated. Of the

13 See p. 26. For 1940, see the appendix (where the German and Russian figures do not include the populations of Poland or Czechoslovakia).

others, Russia and Germany occupied the same places at the top of the list, and France had gone to the bottom, being overtaken both by the United Kingdom and Italy. The losses of the Great War had fallen on a France whose population was already growing more slowly than those of other powers; she could repair losses less quickly than either her allies or her enemies. The gap between her military potential and Germany's had in 1880 not been apparent except to a very shrewd observer; by 1914 it was obvious and by 1939 it was irremediable. In that year, France had about 2.6 million men from twenty to twenty-nine years of age. Germany had about 5.5 million.[14] The building of the Maginot line was a logical insurance policy.

Most western European nations felt uneasy over the long-term drop in natality. Some of them attempted to remedy the decline in their rate of growth. Demographic thinking became 'populationist' again, as it had not been generally since the eighteenth century. The first signs of this change can be discerned before 1914, but war losses, new confidence in the powers of governments to interfere with social processes, and the rise of totalitarian regimes prepared to interfere vigorously with the individual now gave this thinking effect. In England, the debate still remained fairly open between those who feared overpopulation and those who feared underpopulation, and it is difficult not to connect this with a comparative freedom from the fear of land invasion. France, on the other hand, enacted laws forbidding abortion and the sale and supply of contraceptives and instituted a *médaille de la famille* for mothers of numerous children. These steps seem not to have been effective. By 1931 a fifth of French families had only one child. The next step was to introduce children's allowances and these were followed by greatly extended family benefits after the period of the Popular Front (see p. 404).

Totalitarian countries were better at encouraging larger families. Nazi Germany's policies were the most vigorous, but were complicated by a unique factor, the attempt to achieve and maintain racial purity. Propaganda supported the cult of the family. Loans were made to engaged couples, family allowances were generous, and abortion was discouraged. Provision was also made for illegitimate children; it was urged that no stigma rested on the

14 Reinhard (p. 417) makes the gap wider; these figures are based on the German census of 1939 and a French estimate of the following year.

unmarried mother who gave a child to the new Germany. A more sinister measure was the creation of an institute of racial marriage to promote the uniting of pure Aryan couples; marriage with Jews was forbidden. In July 1933, soon after the régime came to power, a law provided for the sterilization of incurably diseased or deranged persons; later, genetic considerations were alleged to justify the murder of these unhappy souls and many were killed. Nazi policy was in a measure efficacious. The marriage rate rose sharply and by 1940 natality was back to the level it had reached in the 1920s. But there was no sign of a fundamental reversal of the long-term trend to smaller families.

In Italy, Mussolini's ambition to preside over a great military power cut across the demographic pressures which burdened the Italian economy. Italy was less bled by the war than Germany; her population increasingly needed the outlet of emigration which disappeared in the 1920s and postwar economic conditions made it hard to create new employment by faster industrialization. Mussolini's remark in 1926, 'We are hungry because we are prolific', was true. As there was no racial policy to complicate Fascist population policy and Italy was still predominantly Roman Catholic (and therefore less open to modern ideas on contraception than France or Germany), a populationist policy was swimming with the tide. By 1936 prizes for large families, fiscal encouragements, loans and housing allowances had brought about a new increase in natality, although there were significant class and regional differences in family size. The other side of this policy, the encouragement of emigration to the Italian empire overseas, was notably less successful. Only 100,000 Italians in lived there in 1938.

Russian policy at first showed no concern for population. Early Bolsheviks, whatever their virtues as fathers and husbands, were disposed to regard the family as a bourgeois institution, and easier divorce was one of the first results of revolution. 'The Revolution is impotent', announced the Comintern in 1924, 'as long as the notion of family and of family relations continues to exist.'[15] The population, in spite of huge losses, grew rapidly; pressure on resources led to the legalization of abortion. A second severe famine in 1933–4 may have led to second thoughts. From 1935 until the outbreak of the second world war, changes in the law

15 See S. de Beauvoir, *The Second Sex* (London, 1953), p. 148.

progressively strengthened the structure of the family and in 1941 abortion became a crime against the state.

Although conscious policy had almost nothing to do with it, the difference between population growth in the advanced countries of the north and west, and the poor countries of the east and south had been intensified. The natality of the advanced countries continued to fall until the late 1930s while no east European country showed a rapid decline in its N.R.R. or crude birth rate, and some reached their highest points even after 1918.[16] The greatest demographic pressure between the wars fell, therefore, on just those areas where economic resources had been most damaged, and employment opportunities were smallest, because of the dominance of agriculture. Big populations accumulated in the countryside and further over-burdened inadequate resources.

In other countries, the shift of population to the cities continued. The density of settlement in some countries, indeed, seemed to be achieving the abolition of the distinction of town and country which the Communist Manifesto had proclaimed as the end of Communist society.[17] The spectacular growth of the largest cities went on. The seven cities of more than 1 milion inhabitants of 1910 were sixteen by 1940 and in that year about 19 per cent of Europeans outside Russia lived in 182 cities of more than 100,000 inhabitants each.[18] But they were not evenly spread. Their basic distribution had already been settled before 1914. Although occasional examples of very rapid growth could still occur,[19] in most urbanized countries change was a matter of size and nature, not location. This has been characterized, aptly, as the replacement of centripetal by centrifugal tendencies. Whereas at first more and more people had accumulated near industry in crowded city centres, in the second stage population and industry moved from the centres to the suburbs, and the built-up area spread into sprawling 'conurbations'. This was made possible by electricity and better transport. The first allowed factories to be

16 For these terms, see p. 23.
17 See translation in Karl Marx and Frederick Engels, *Selected Works* (Moscow, 1950), vol. 1, p. 51.
18 Dickinson, p. 448. Cities of more than a million: London, Berlin, Moscow, Leningrad, Paris, Vienna, Hamburg, Brussels, Warsaw, Rome, Barcelona, Glasgow, Milan, Budapest, Birmingham, Madrid.
19 Marseilles, for example, increased its size by 40 per cent between 1926 and 1936. Dickinson, p. 455.

sited away from city centres; the second made it possible to fill and empty the city of its working population quickly at the beginning and end of the day. The visible results are the brightly-lit and deserted streets of the business centres of great modern cities at night, and the sprawl of specialized residential and industrial suburbs around them.

Towns in Russia and eastern Europe were different. The absolute shift of population was often very great (in Russia, the town-dwelling population rose from 15.9 per cent to 31.6 per cent of the total between 1920 and 1940) but the new towns tended to be smaller than in the west. Many of them had between 20,000 and 100,000 inhabitants; the conurbation was a rarity and a big historic city like Warsaw or Budapest still stood out in semi-isolation against a background of overgrown villages. The great urban belt of Europe was still the old industrial area, running from Manchester across northern France and Belgium, and on across north Germany from the Rhine to Upper Silesia. Within it, the difference between town and country was much attenuated, and between it and the more agricultural south and east the contrast after 1918 grew even sharper. In the urban and industrial countries, although agriculture benefited from growing markets for its products, the proportion of the population engaged in farming continued to fall, even when its numbers remained fairly steady. In central, eastern and southern Europe, on the other hand, rural population grew so rapidly that it seems that more Europeans depended on agriculture in the 1930s than ever before or since.[20]

This implied a technical difference in agricultural activity. In north and west Europe, specialization and improved methods continued to increase productivity, though there was little further consolidation of holdings; over most of France and Germany they remained much as they had been and in Switzerland there may even have been a slight increase in their fragmentation. In Italy, on the other hand, there was a big increase in the number of peasant proprietors, and in eastern Europe something like an economic and social revolution.

20 In the U.K. in 1931, about 5½ per cent of the *employed* population were *engaged* in fishing or agriculture. At about he same time, Albania, Yugoslavia, Bulgaria, Rumania, Poland, Hungary and the Baltic States all had over half their *total* populations *dependent* on agriculture (see table in Macartney and Palmer, p. 243).

This was the breaking-up and distribution of many of the great estates which had been the main agricultural units since the seventeenth century. Where the former landlords were aliens, this sometimes implied national revolution, too. About 60 million acres in all changed hands – rather more than the whole area of the United Kingdom.[21] Rumania re-distributed an area bigger than Switzerland. The impact of such changes varied according to the size of the country. Huge as the acreage was, Rumania distributed only about 29 per cent of her agricultural land, while Latvia's smaller acreage represented 42 per cent of hers. In most countries, the state kept waste and woodland, and the remainder was divided between the former owners and the peasants. Generally, this meant much subdivision. The size of lots was usually small, except in the Baltic states. A lack of information about local differences makes it very difficult to say anything useful about this, but a very rough guide to the new patterns of distribution can be obtained by dividing the acreage distributed by the number of lots in each country. This shows that the biggest units went to the peasants in the Baltic states where the average acreage of new lots was in Estonia 170, in Latvia 118 and in Lithuania 36. Among the smallest were those of Hungary (2.5) where the change was insignificant,[22] Poland (11.8) and Rumania (18). As further subdivisions and sales almost certainly followed within a few years, these figures can only indicate very broad differences. The most important result, everywhere, was the entrenchment of millions of poor peasants, often on inadequate holdings, in areas of high population growth, where the resulting drop in productivity was bound to be severely felt. Nor did the depressed state of world prices encourage higher productivity. By

21 The main distributions were these:

	million acres
Rumania	14.8
Czechoslovakia	9.9
Latvia	9.1
Poland	6.4
Estonia	5.7
Yugoslavia	4.9
Finland	3.7
Bulgaria	0.5

22 See I. T. Berend and G. Ránki, *The Hungarian Economy in the Twentieth Century* (London, 1985), pp. 103–4.

1939 production per acre in Rumania was only a fifth of that of Switzerland.

Further east still, the agricultural history of Russia underwent an even more dramatic change. The success of the Stolypin reforms had been overtaken by the war, which took labour from the countryside and disrupted the transport system. Then, during the revolution, peasants took over many big estates and broke them up into smallholdings, thus accelerating the fall in grain delivery to the market. Requisitioning was difficult and only made the peasants recalcitrant. It had been abandoned by 1926 but the amount of grain delivered to feed the towns had still not risen so fast as production. This was the fundamental cause of the collectivization drive of the first Five Year Plan (1928–33). Collectivization was intended to eliminate the individual proprietor and to consolidate holdings in big collective farms, not merely to achieve technical improvement and economies of scale, but also to make it possible to get deliveries of food from the peasants at less than the true cost of production. The peasants were to provide (as Stalin believed the English worker had been made to provide in the Industrial Revolution) the savings needed for capital investment. But the beginning of the drive was determined by pragmatic and almost accidental factors, rather than by doctrine, and its momentum soon outran expectations. When the first Five Year Plan began, about half the Russian farms were between fifteen and twenty-seven acres in size; one-tenth were smaller, the rest larger. It envisaged the collectivizing of only a fifth of the land by 1933; but by 1930 about a third of Russia's sown area had already been taken over. In 1934, this had risen to 87 per cent and by 1937 the process was virtually complete, although peasants on collective farms were still allowed to own very small plots for personal exploitation and limited numbers of cattle and sheep.

The economic effect of this great change is hard to evaluate, although its social effect – the eradication of the peasant proprietor at great cost in bloodshed and violence – is easy to see. It seems likely that 2 million people died; the slaughter of their own livestock by the recalcitrant peasants halved the horse population, and almost halved the number of cows. This must have reduced output. As for grain, even if the proportion of the crop delivered to the public authorities increased, productivity did not do so at once, and output only benefited in the long run. The latest Soviet estimates claim only that in 1938 – a good year – gross agricultural output was 8 per cent above that of 1928. In every other year before 1940, it was lower. Moreover, the tiny plots left for private exploitation still in 1937 produced 21.5 per cent of Russia's agricultural output, although they formed so small a part of the total cultivated area. On the other hand, the growth of the Russian town population shows that more grain left the farms and that an increase of productivity released labour for other work.

In advanced agricultural societies, productivity continued to rise, that of England going up 20 per cent per worker in a decade. High labour costs spurred on farmers to improve their methods. One result was a still greater use of fertilizer, the heaviest use per acre in the 1930s being in the Netherlands, Belgium, Germany and the United Kingdom. The smallest consumption was recorded in Rumania, Yugoslavia, Hungary and Poland; Hungary used one-hundredth of the quantity per acre used in the Netherlands. Yet by 1939 Europe outside Russia used two-thirds of the world's fertilizers. Mechanization is another rough measure of progress. Advanced farm implements only began to be used in any quantity in the south and east after 1930; they had been familiar for decades in the west. Tractors were the most important innovation because they provided mobile sources of power; machine-driven implements no longer had to be linked to a static prime mover. In 1939 Russia had the enormous total of 480,000 tractors, Germany 60,000 and the United Kingdom 55,000; Hungary, on the other hand, had only 7,000. The numbers of horses employed in agriculture fell more slowly in the south and east than in the agriculturally advanced countries because the tractor replaced them more slowly. Electrification also began to change many farm operations, and by 1939 nearly all Swiss and Dutch farms had electric power. These changes all intensified the specialization of the most advanced agricultures and the decline of mixed farming. They made it possible for Europe in 1939 still to produce about 75 per cent of her main grain and meat needs, and although, of course, this was a smaller proportion than in 1880, many of her inhabitants were eating more of much higher quality foods. The increase in productivity had been enormous. But the overall picture still contained extremes which must not be lost to sight, in the near-subsistence farming of the peasant economies of the east and a United Kingdom whose highly productive farmers could not meet about 30 per cent of her food requirements in 1939.

The long-drawn-out and worldwide agricultural depression inevitably hurt the poorest countries most. They produced a few basic foods, mainly grains, and were badly hurt by the long fall in agricultural prices. The fall in grain prices was especially steep, some being more than halved in a decade. Unfortunately, agriculture is less flexible than industry and the adjustment of production to a falling market only came slowly.[23] Agrarian disturbance and political action through peasant political parties or pressure-groups was almost inevitable. Usually they sought protection; even English farmers got it at last. Governments also sponsored cheap farm finance, subsidies and marketing agreements in attempts to help. By 1939 agriculture had been in many respects removed from the brutal play of market forces.

This tended to happen to industry, too. Its problems were not new. Industrial growth had already slowed down before 1914 and Europe's share of world production had fallen. After 1918 the share of the pioneer industrial nations in Europe's activity declined relatively to that of Russia whose growth, after a sharp break, was resumed at a very high rate. Within these overall trends, the growth of older industries slowed down while new industries more closely dependent on scientific research, or providing consumer goods and services, expanded. Everywhere, too, the tendency for organization on a bigger scale seemed irreversible.

In the stagnating older and heavier industries, the impetus of the great nineteenth-century discoveries gradually ran out. Extra-European markets had often been disrupted during the war, when the United States and Japan had taken advantage of their opportunities.[24] Investment patterns turned against the metallurgical industries, once the postwar repair boom was over; the European railway network was virtually complete, and that of Russia was sealed off from its prewar suppliers. Shipbuilding fell off because of a surplus of wartime tonnage and the collapse of world trade

23 K. A. H. Murray, *Agriculture* (H.M.S.O., 1959), p. 19, points out that between 1929 and 1939, world industrial production contracted by 36 per cent, agricultural by only 2 per cent.
24 Japanese steel output rose from 255,000 tons in 1913 to 2,034,000 tons in 1929. G. C. Allen, *A Short Economic History of Modern Japan* (London, 1946), p. 177.

prolonged its depression. The cessation of international lending in the slump of the 1930s fell, therefore, on capital goods industries which were already badly handicapped; preparation for war, whose economic effect began to be felt from 1937 onwards in most countries, did not at once restore the old growth rates. In 1940 all the main European pig-iron producers except Russia were making less than in 1910. In the light industries, too, if they were old-established, the story was the same. Russia, Japan and India all had their textile industries greatly stimulated by the Great War; by 1930 there were for the first time more textile workers in Asian factories than in Europe.

Less traditional industries did much better. After 1929 they soon resumed their expansion and came to take up a much larger share of the labour force and loomed much larger as contributors to European manufactures than before. The chemically-based synthetic textile industries enjoyed fairly steady growth, benefiting from rising real wages in rich countries because they immediately fed a growing taste for a degree of comfort and luxury previously inaccessible. Rayon made cheap clothing more attractive than ever before; bicycles and small cars multiplied the consumption of other synthetics. The motor-car industry itself was very important, and one of the few to show rapid growth between the wars. In the United Kingdom, it began to seem a possible replacement for traditional big employers like textiles and ship-building.

Rapid expansion also occurred in energy production and consumption. Within Europe, the highest *per capita* consumption of power was in the United Kingdom, but energy demands rose steadily in all countries, although they lagged behind those of the United States. Paradoxically, this was coupled with depression in coal-mining, especially in the United Kingdom, although in 1937 about 70 per cent of Europe's energy requirements were still met by coal.[25] The reason why the absolute consumption of coal did not rise much was that less was being used at sea, as ships turned to oil-burning, and that improvements in fuel technology made

25 Woytinsky, p. 935. The remainder came from hydroelectric power (13 per cent), oil and gas (10.8 per cent) and wood and peat (5.3 per cent). It is interesting to compare this with India's energy consumption even decades later. In 1960–1, she was estimated to meet 60 per cent of her requirements by burning cattle-dung, wood and agricultural waste.

it possible to use coal more efficiently. Also, hydroelectric power and oil were steadily increasing their contribution to Europe's energy needs. One sign of the trend, affecting most strongly countries with small or no coal deposits, can be seen in a comparison of the extent of reliance on steam-engines for primary power in 1911 and 1925. Between these dates, the proportion of industrial power derived from steam-engines fell substantially in Italy and Switzerland, though hardly at all in Germany and the United Kingdom.

Electrical output grew everywhere.[26] Germany led in output, and France was overtaken by both Italy and Great Britain between 1930 and 1940. In almost all major countries, the indices of electrical power generation (or of combined gas and electricity output) show almost unfluctuating growth from 1929 to 1939, hardly affected by the general industrial and commercial depression. Here is another explanation of the continued importance of coal, much of which was burnt to produce this electrical power. Only a little generation derived from oil, which was mainly a source of power for cars. In 1938, Europe consumed only 15.4 per cent of the world's oil (the United States took 59.5 per cent). None the less, the demand for petrol was already very great.

This registered the fact that important changes in transport were based on the internal combustion engine. It did not much affect international communications: steam-driven trains and ships still dominated long-distance movement although their technical development and extent had reached something of a plateau and underwent no revolutionary change between the wars. In some respects, even, they declined. Railways suffered less from international depression than shipping – their main business was internal – but they expanded little and in some countries (above all Great Britain) suffered severely from the competition of road traffic. An enormous increase in the number of motor vehicles was the biggest change in transport before 1939. One of its side-

26 Electrical output in billion kilowatts:

	1930	1935	1940
Germany	29.1	36.7	63.0
U.K.	12.3	18.9	30.1
France	16.9	17.5	18.8
Italy	10.6	13.8	19.4

effects was the appearance of new motor roads, of which the German *Autobahnen* were the most celebrated.

The other great advances in transport came in the air. Between the wars there were still attempts to use the airship for long-distance passenger transport, but by 1939, after disasters which culminated in the tragic end of the *Hindenburg* at New York, it was clear that the future lay with the aeroplane. The first Atlantic crossing had been made in 1919 by two Englishmen, Alcock and Brown, and by 1939 a network of international and intercontinental air services had already been established. Their volume of traffic was still not great, and the aeroplane had only begun to show what it could do, but Europe was linked to the world more closely than ever before. The rapidity with which airlines had grown, and technical advances in design and construction, already foreshadowed possibilities to be realized by the enormous expansion of air transport during the second world war.[27]

In these widespread changes of emphasis and structure, nations with old-established industries had great difficulties. Among them the United Kingdom enjoyed an unhappy primacy. Doubly handicapped, as the greatest international trader, by the wartime disruption of normal trade and the onset of the depression, even her overseas earnings for services and from investments could not maintain a credit balance of payments after 1930. Her old staple industries – coal, steel, shipbuilding and textiles – were no longer competitive. Her shipyards had been great consumers of steel, and in 1920 still launched 2 million tons of new ships, but this figure was never reached again before the second world war. For four bad years in the 1930s, they launched less than half-a-million tons. Textiles declined; in 1938 India took only 300 million yards of

27 A rough guide to growth is provided by the total of kilometres flown: 35.7 m in 1931, 82.7 m in 1938. The League of Nations began to publish statistics of air navigation in 1937, and some of their series go back to 1928. Technical advance was most dramatically registered by the invention of helicopters and radar, but neither produced any commercial impact until after 1945. Nor did the jet engine, which came into use during the war. The major technical changes already absorbed before 1939 took the form of devices and improvements – more powerful engines, all-metal construction, retractable undercarriages, slots and flaps – all of which, although very important, only refined and made more efficient the basic tractor-propelled aeroplane whose fundamental shape had been settled before 1914.

English cotton goods – one-tenth of her consumption of 1913. Coal and pig-iron output never again reached 1913 levels, though heroic efforts brought about a recovery in steel production by 1939. Chronic unemployment dogged the older industries throughout the whole period, even before the onset of the world depression. To offset, this, there was progress in newer and lighter manufacturing industry, of which the most significant was motor-car and electrical engineering. Service industries, too, came to be a larger part of the industrial sector. And whatever the plight of the old industries and the unemployed, productivity and real wages rose.

Germany's more modern plant and organization imposed fewer handicaps on her old industries than those of Great Britain, though both countries lagged in industrial recovery.[28] Germany's interwar industrial history is so marked by special distortions that it is very difficult to characterize. Reparations disrupted the supply of her traditional markets, but kept the Ruhr mines working. Inflation threw capital investment into confusion but destroyed much of the indebtedness of big industrial firms. The collapse of world trade in 1929–31 hit Germany harder than any other European country and this was reflected in industrial output. Nor did rearmament begin to contribute to recovery until shortly before the outbreak of war. One of the few certainties seems to be that although total consumption was back to 1929 levels by the end of the next decade, productivity did not significantly increase and real wages did not rise as they did in Britain.[29]

France and Italy had to make a brutal readjustment to peace after wartime industrial expansion. The gap between north and south Italy was accentuated by the almost complete absence of industrial investment in the south between the wars. The greatest basic change in French industrial structure was the doubling of her metallurgical capacity by the territorial changes of the peace;

28 Indices of manufacturing production (1913 = 100):

	1925	1929
World	121	153
Germany	95	117
U.K.	86	100

29 See B. H. Klein, *Germany's Economic Preparations for War* (Cambridge, Mass., 1959), esp. pp. 76–82, and the criticisms of his views in *Past and Present*, Dec. 1964, pp. 77 ff.

the recovery of Lorraine gave her the second largest iron-field in the world. Yet because of financial and fiscal policy, France was actually less dependent on manufacturing in 1939 than in 1920. She lagged in new industries, such as car manufacture and rayon, and although her electrical output increased, it was at a slow rate. Production in 1939 was still only 80 per cent of that of 1929. The industrial worker was better off in that he had more leisure, but he had not won higher real wages. Economically as well as demographically, France could no longer be a great power.

The greatest industrial achievement between the wars was Russia's. Progress made under the *ancien régime* had been badly mauled by the war. Russian industrial production fell, largely because of the inadequacies of her transport and because of the calling-up of industrial workers to the army. Then came the dismemberment of the country, the loss of the Baltic and Polish industrial areas, and the destruction of the civil war. The Communists were unprepared for these disasters and although the formal nationalization of almost all Russia's remaining industry took place between 1918 and 1920, the years down to 1928 were a period of experiment and error, rather than of settled industrial policies. By 1928 industrial production had climbed back to the 1913 level and the foundations of a planning body had been laid.

The next ten years provide a heroic contrast. The first two Five Year Plans achieved the astonishing success of quadrupling Russian industrial production. The adoption of a deliberate policy of fostering heavy industry was the crucial decision for Russia's industrial future. It led to great expansion in metallurgy, electricity generation and transport. Geographically, it meant the appearance of new industrial areas and a big shift of Russian manufacturing towards the east and Siberia. The achievements were spectacular and convinced many people in western Europe that Russia had found the key to economic advance. The price was paid, as it had been paid during Witte's ministry, by the ordinary Russian. This was not merely a matter of forced labour, though much of it seems to have been employed, but of lower consumption. The second Plan gave more emphasis to consumer goods than the first, but performance in this sector fell far short of the performance of the basic capital goods industries. It has been calculated that heavier capital investment meant a drop in the share of consumption in the national income from 84 to 60 per cent between 1924 and 1940. Another estimate suggests that real wages fell 39 per cent during the first two Plans. The machinery of political terror made this possible.

The Russian example was remarkable both for its scale and because it was the most extreme instance in these years of political intervention with the economy. This was so general a trend between the wars, and has now become so commonplace, that it is important to stress the break it represented with prewar thinking. Tariffs and the regulation of working conditions had, of course, already encroached upon the virginal purity of a free market system – if such a thing had ever existed. But the assumption had always been that they needed special justification. The Great War heralded a much more profound change in thinking; its interferences with property went farther than ever before and many of them were permanent.[30] They were remembered after the war when four distinguishable forces pushed governments towards intervention in economic affairs. One was monetary: currency difficulties encouraged exchange control. Another was the plight of agriculture, which led to attempts to avoid surpluses by agreement or regulation. The third was unemployment, the main source of individual economic distress in the industrial countries, where governments strove the remedy it. Finally, in two or three countries, ideological and political motives came into play. Russia was the outstanding instance but Nazi Germany, which regulated dividends, wages and prices and, to a smaller extent, Fascist Italy, were others. Even in the democracies, economists sought for means to reconcile governmental intervention with democratic control as Keynes's work exemplifies.[31] Organizationally, British governments encouraged amalgamations and self-regulation.

Public interventions were undoubtedly helped by the continuing trend towards bigger and more highly integrated industrial

30 The United Kingdom, for example, has never been without rent control since 1915.

31 The doctrine of Keynes had little practical effect before 1939 because it was formulated decisively only in *The General Theory of Employment, Interest and Money* in 1936. His earlier writings on *The End of Laissez-Faire* (London, 1925) and *The Economic Consequences of Mr Churchill* (London, 1925), marked the beginning of his attempt to provide a theoretical replacement for the liberal economics of the self-regulating market which make him a major figure in the intellectual history of the era, although only the second world war was to see his ideas put into practice.

enterprises which had been observable before the war. The Dutch giants, Unilever, Shell and Phillips Lamps, brought about changes in Holland which almost amount to a new industrial revolution. In England, Imperial Chemical Industries (I.C.I.) was a portent of effective re-entry at last into the world market for chemicals, and in 1939, the three largest firms in metallurgy made 39 per cent of British iron and steel.[32] In German industry, too, the trend to concentration of ownership continued; in 1926 the *Vereinigte Stahlwerke* produced half of the Ruhr steel, while the whole of the smelting and most of the steel-making of the area was shared between only six firms. I.G. Farben became the biggest chemical complex in the world. The high concentration of German industry was to be important to Nazi economic policy, just as the comparatively large-scale average size of Russian industrial organization before 1917 had simplified the Bolshevik sequestrations. Everywhere, size and political influence and intervention seemed to wax side by side. It was in March 1939 that the English *Economist* noted: 'since 1932 the State has no longer appeared to industry solely in the guise of monitor or policeman; it has had favours to dispense . . . The policeman has turned Father Christmas.'[33]

EUROPE AND THE WORLD

The entanglement of Europe in the world economy before 1914 did not merely persist, it also changed. Although the pre-war economic relationship between Europe and other countries had been subtle and complicated, Europe's main role had been to supply capital and manufactures and to buy primary produce. She had been rivalled only by the United States as a concentration of wealth and industrial power. After 1918 these facts were still true, but less bluntly so. Interdependence was weakened with the decline of world trade in the 1930s and the appearance of new concentrations of economic power.

32 For examples in food processing and marketing, see R. J. Hammond, *op. cit.*
33 18 March 1939, see M. Dobb, *Studies in the Development of Capitalism* (London, 1959), p. 334.

Many indicators show the change. The share of western European nations in world manufacturing continued to fall. The United States remained top of the list; Japan moved into the sixth place. Among European nations, only Russia showed rapid growth, and then under such special conditions that few conclusions could be drawn about it. Europe's share of world trade, too, was falling. The United Kingdom was in 1939 the only important exporter of manufactures outside Europe and the only important European investor overseas (if we exclude colonial possessions). The war had dissipated European investments abroad and had interrupted the export of capital to nourish them. The United Kingdom lost a quarter of hers, France a half, and Germany almost everything. Although the resumption of British lending overseas rebuilt by 1939 an investment even bigger than that of 1914, it grew at a slower rate than before, and after 1930, the United Kingdom had always an unfavourable balance of payments which meant, in effect, reimporting capital.[34]

The economic roots of European dominance had therefore suffered gravely by 1939, and were to be further damaged during the second world war. Meanwhile, although the more impalpable influence of culture and technique remained strong, it, too, was affected by the war. Europe's prestige suffered gravely from the contrast between the humanitarian ideals professed before and during the war and the ruthlessness and *realpolitik* displayed in waging it and in the peace settlement. The wish to westernize began to be qualified; non-Europeans sought to acquire European technique, without losing their own cultural identity.

Yet some values and assumptions continued to be exported with the institutions and techniques. The most obvious example came in Turkey, where Kemal set up a secular and national state

---

[34] See Woytinsky, pp. 1003–4, and P. L. Yates, *Forty Years of Foreign Trade* (London, 1959). The shares of European exports and imports in world totals at different periods are, *per cent,*

	1896–1900	1913	1928	1937
Exports	69	65.1	56.2	55.8
Imports	63.8	58.9	48.0	47.0

Investments abroad (in millions of dollars at $4 = £1):

	U.K.	France	Germany
1914	18,351	8,686	5,593
1938	22,905	3,859	676

at the heart of the old Ottoman Empire, and as a symbol of progress, abolished the fez and the veil. Two other agencies in the diffusion of 'modern' and 'western' ideas in a vivid form were the cinema and radio – which communicated not only European ideas but European quarrels. Italian broadcasting fostered Arab feeling against the British in the 1930s and the Indian government was always sensitive to Russian wireless propaganda.

This illustration raises another question. The anticolonial tendency of Russian policy since 1917 has been much remarked, but it is sometimes overlooked that Bolshevism was not the first Russian revolutionary influence in Asia. The 1905 revolution had excited interest and admiration in Iran, Turkey, India and China, where nationalists and reformers felt they had much to learn from attempts to transform a great multinational agrarian empire.[35] But the 1905 revolutionaries had not embarked upon deliberate propaganda and subversion abroad. Here the Bolsheviks were innovators. In 1920 a Congress of Peoples of the East met at Baku and the Comintern was far more attentive to the non-European world than the Second International had ever been. To what has been called 'the heady wine of Western political thought'[36] was added the corrosive power of Marxist analysis. Yet the spread of Marxist ideas and language was in itself a subtle reinforcement of European cultural dominance. Just as the non-European world had already absorbed constitutional and political ideas from civil servants, journalists and missionaries who took for granted the European national state as the highest achievement of politics, so did an ideology elaborated to grapple with European industrial society on a basis of European materialist philosophy now affect Asia. Marx and Lenin added their voices to those of Paine and Mazzini, but the message remained European.

Obviously, important indigenous sources also fed the wave of mounting anti-European sentiment. But it is impossible not to see in the dialectical effects of European politics and culture a major solvent of Europe's political domination. They created the men and the instruments to remove European control after 1945. After 1914 their rapid development was always stimulated by the divisions and self-destructiveness displayed by Europe itself. The

35 See I. Spector, *The First Russian Revolution: Its Impact on Asia* (Englewood Cliffs, N.J.), 1962.
36 D. G. E. Hall, *A History of South-East Asia* (London, 1955), p. 617.

isolation of Russia by the Anglo-Japanese treaty had been a portent. The Great War eliminated one colonial power, Germany, had focussed the attention of the others on Europe (where it was to remain pinned down by the German problem). Japan had taken advantage of this to resume pressure on a China no longer propped up by European powers. The *Entente* was anxious to placate Japan in order that she should not make peace with Germany, while Germany strove to encourage her ambitions even across the Pacific.

The Great War weakened European world domination in other ways. Indian industrialization was accelerated by the expansion of Indian production to provide a base for operations in the Persian Gulf and Mesopotamia. China and Siam also benefited economically, and were able to use their formal entry into the war to obtain reductions of the extraterritorial rights enjoyed by Europeans.[37] In the Middle East, the changes were more dramatic. An Arab revolt against the Turks had been deliberately fostered there by British agents who encouraged hopes of independence in the future. Ideologically, too, the propaganda made for the Fourteen Points was an important reinforcement of the desire for political self-determination among non-European peoples and sometimes fell on ground prepared by the central powers, who had encouraged local nationalism during the war for their own ends.[38]

Many expectations were to be disappointed. Nevertheless, the Peace Conference itself registered a great change in world relationships. Most of the nations represented at it were non-European, it was dominated by the President of the United States and the British Dominions attended as independent nations. Its decisions, too, were a break with the past. Instead of a simple distribution of colonial spoils as in 1763 or 1815, the doctrine of trusteeship was given institutional expression in the Mandate system. Mandates from the League of Nations were intended to provide – and did – tutelage for what would now be called 'new nations'. Although the United States declined any, non-European nations were given some of these mandates; Japan was the most

---

37 The Anglo-Japanese treaty had been the first surrender of these rights by a European power enjoying them in Japan; other nations had soon followed.

38 N. Ziadeh, *Origins of Nationalism in Tunisia* (Beirut, 1962), pp. 89–90.

significant example, and Australia, New Zealand and South Africa were others.

Asia was one of the two areas where European domination was most seriously strained. For China this meant a change of bullies rather than true independence. Although she joined the *Entente* in the Great War and sent labour to France (thus obtaining the abolition of the extraterritorial rights of Germans and Austro-Hungarians and a suspension of the payment of the Boxer indemnity), she began again during the war to experience severe pressure from Japan, and after the war faced a new threat in Russian Communism. The results are less a part of European than of Asian history but both forces were bound to reduce British and French influence in China. In 1919 the Allies had to concede Japan's claims to Shantung; after 1931 nothing could be done to restrain the Japanese in China (even by the United States). England and France could only hope to hold on to such territory and privileges as they possessed. These, too, had been further reduced because of the ability of the Chinese nationalist government to use the Russian danger to get concessions from the British (in agreements signed in 1927, and in 1930, when Wei-hai-wei was surrendered).

It was the advance of Japan to world power status which was the greatest danger to European influence in Asia. At the Peace Conference, she had not only pressed large claims against China, but had obtained the Mandates for the former German Pacific islands. The Japanese government, however, was deeply offended at the refusal of the Peace Conference to write into the Covenant of the League any declaration of racial equality. Wilson favoured such a declaration and supported the Japanese, but it was defeated by the pressure of another non-European state, Australia, on the British government. The Japanese intervention in Siberia had also to be liquidated, and the Russian government's resumption of its far eastern territories was a setback to Japanese ambitions. During the 1920s the Japanese suspiciously watched Russian intrigues in China, but when these culminated in the victory of the Kuomintang and the massacre of the Nanking Communists, the Russian withdrew from active participation in Chinese affairs and did not come into open conflict with the Japanese until 1938. Then the movement of large Japanese armies up to the borders of Russia provoked an outburst of heavy fighting, in which the Japanese seem to have been discomfited. By this time the old rivalry of competing aggressive tendencies in China had been overtaken by the change of political situation in Europe, the anti-Comintern pact of 1936, and the increasing paralysis of British and French policy towards Japan. They could not hope to contain Japanese ambitions alone and without the Russians and Americans the reconstitution of a system such as that of the 1890s was impossible. China could not be protected from her vigorous neighbour, whose entry to world politics had originally been made under British patronage.[39] In 1939, the British government could do no more than protest formally when the Japanese shelled a British gunboat in 1937 and blockaded the British concession in Tientsin in 1939.

Meanwhile imperial power in Asia was troubled elsewhere, too. The example of Gandhi in India had repercussions throughout south-east Asia. The British government committed itself in principle to a gradual advance to self-government as early as 1917. Later, growing nationalist pressure forced a quicker pace; in 1935 a large measure of representative government was conceded. Events followed a similar course in Burma. One reason for these concessions was that it was impossible for a British government to rely simply upon superior physical power to hold its possessions. This was not true of France, in whose colonies the policy of assimilation of colonial peoples by turning them into Frenchmen was vigorously pursued. During the Great War 100,000 Viet-Namese were taken to Europe for military service but many went home imbued both with western ideas and contempt for France. An Indo-Chinese revolutionary movement was ruthlessly repressed with hundreds of executions in 1930, and the Communists, who had now begun to interest themselves in Indo-China, went underground under the leadership of Ho Chi Minh.[40] The Dutch in Indonesia also had to deal with a nationalist movement but had shown signs of wishing to make moderate concessions. In 1917, a carefully controlled *Volksrad* of racially mixed composition was set up. Soon the Comintern was taking a special interest in Indonesia, adding its influence to that of Islam and the Indian example in shaping Indonesian nationalism. But the Communist movement was broken up after abortive revolts

39 See p. 480, also, on Japan's Manchuria intervention in 1931. In 1934 she denounced the 1922 naval agreements.
40 In 1939 his movement was renamed Viet-Minh.

in 1926–7 and from that time until the outbreak of war, the Dutch remained firmly in control.[41]

The other great area of challenge to European supremacy was the Islamic Middle East and North Africa. Here, new pressures were at work. Two or three generations of intellectuals had been shaped by western education and national selfconsciousness had spread beyond them to the masses.[42] This made the course of events between the wars very disturbed and complicated. A widespread sense of Muslim and Arab unity favoured nationalist agitators in different areas. This tendency was strengthened at the end of the 1930s by Arab opposition to a British plan for the establishment of a Jewish National Home in Palestine, a scheme pregnant with trouble for the future. But the example of Ataturk and the nationalism of westernized politicians also cut across the old unity of the Faith. The *Jehad* proclaimed in 1914 had been largely disregarded. Later, when in 1931 an Islamic conventioin met at Jerusalem, the Arab delegates held an independent assembly to sign a declaration that the Arab countries were an indivisible whole whose goal should be independence and unification. On the whole, the Pan-Arab movement did not achieve much and Great Britain and France, the two major powers interested in the area, were able to act without interference until Italian and German propaganda and intrigue began to be important in the late 1930s.[43]

France, for example, checked nationalists in Tunis and made only a few minor administrative concessions. In Morocco the story is more complicated and the maintenance of French supremacy was harder. The old Moroccan resistance to Europe achieved the destruction of a Spanish army at Annual by the Moroccan leader, Abd-el-Krim, in 1921 and only ended in 1926 when a joint Franco-Spanish campaign forced him to surrender; he was sent into exile. A modern nationalist movement appeared

41 See, for further information, D. G. E. Hall, *op.cit.*, and G. M. Kahin, *Nationalism and Revolution in Indonesia* (Ithaca, N.Y., 1952), pp. 64–100.
42 See H. A. Gibb, *Modern Trends in Islam* (Chicago, 1947), p. 119, and by the same author, *Studies in the civilisation of Islam* (1962).
43 Mussolini's attempt to pose as 'Protector of Islam' was unsuccessful, although it was taken seriously in London. His harsh treatment of the Arabs of Libya may explain this. His own African Empire, however, was fairly immune from internal subversion until 1940 made it possible for the British to exploit Abyssinian resentment with money and arms.

in the 1930s; unlike the rebellion of Abd-el-Krim, it owed much to the general agitation of the Arab world at this time, and in 1937 led to fighting with the French. In Algeria there was a similar movement. But the most violent resistance to French rule came in Syria. A Syrian congress at Damascus in 1919 petitioned the Peace Conference for independence. The appeal was ignored because of promises made to France during the war. The next Syrian request, for a British or American mandate, was also set aside. The French were then awarded the mandate, and imposed their rule by force and a period of very rough government. In 1925 an insurrection was followed by a French bombardment of Damascus, a step repeated the following year. No progress was made towards self-government and in 1936 there was again heavy street-fighting and a general strike in Damascus.

The gravest British problem was Egypt. Egyptian nationalism had been one of the first to appear as an anti-European force. Because of the preoccupation of the British strategists with the Suez canal, it seemed especially dangerous. Yet the deposition of the khedive and the proclamation of a British protectorate in 1914 was another step in the revolutionizing of Egypt and created the first succession problem to arise from the Great War. British control during the war fed the flames and in 1919 there appeared a new nationalist force, the Wafd, which was for twenty years a bitter opponent of British control. Its leaders were not allowed to go to Versailles to ask for independence in 1919, but were shipped off to Malta to keep them out of the way. From this time trouble was more or less continuous. Passive resistance, riots, sabotage, were all tried. The ending of the protectorate in 1922 made no difference because Great Britain still retained controls over the nominally independent Egyptian monarchy. Every opportunity to appeal to world sentiment was used; in 1927, for example, the Egyptian government appealed to the League Economic Conference at Geneva for the abolition of the capitulations. Finally, in 1936, an Anglo-Egyptian treaty made important concessions to the Egyptians and the violence of the nationalist movement began to decline. The British garrison remained. That in Iraq, where a British Mandate had been set up in 1920, also retained its grip on the country – a remarkable instance of policing by air-power – and was not threatened until 1941, and then only briefly. The government of Iran, where Reza Khan was carrying out a programme of modernization like that of Ataturk may also be mentioned among Muslim countries which showed no love for Great Britain.

Colonial powers were much less troubled in trans-Saharan and tropical Africa than in the north. Although a Pan-African congress first met in Paris in 1919 (and was to be followed by others), European techniques and culture had not gone far enough to create important nationalist movements there. Great Britain set up more representative and consultative institutions in her territories, and Southern Rhodesia took its first steps towards practical self-government by its white settler population, but no great threat to European supremacy could be seen. Only Portugal, among European colonial powers, expressed concern at the repercussions on African sentiment which might be expected from the Italian attack on Abyssinia in 1935.

Nor is there much to say about Central and South America. One tiny surrender of European territory occurred there when Denmark handed the Virgin Islands over to the United States in 1917. Elsewhere, European economic influence declined as American trade and investment outpaced British. Germany, an important economic force in the hemisphere before 1914, had ceased to count. The Mexican Revolution brought about the sequestration of British oil interests. Those of the United States, too, were taken over. None the less, United States policies, unpopular as they sometimes were in South and Central America, always reinforced the tendency towards a reduction of European influence – as they had done since the promulgation of the Monroe Doctrine – and President Roosevelt warmly advocated inter-American consultation and cooperation as the international situation grew more tense. The Declaration of Lima in 1938 set up machinery for this.

The interwar years are confusing, and it is not easy to arrive at a balance-sheet of European influence overseas. But some facts stand out. Direct political supremacy was now being challenged almost everywhere in Asia and the Muslim world. This challenge was felt both in European colonies and in areas where European political direction had been strong because of the weakness of the local authorities. It was in one instance a challenge from a very self-confident and aggressive state, Japan. It was a challenge which was more difficult to resist because of the divisions of European powers among themselves, first in the Great War, then in the new circumstances produced by the Russian Revolution, then in the approach march to the war of 1939. Nor was European economic strength faring any better than political supremacy. Only the domination of Europe's nineteenth-century ideas and of its twentieth-century technology were more evident than ever.

12

DEMOCRATIC EUROPE

DEMOCRACY BETWEEN THE WARS

Before 1914 the advance of formal democracy, measured by such institutions as a wide franchise and representative government, seemed increasingly assured. When the century began, liberals had everywhere assumed that the triumph of democracy was inevitable. The Great War reinforced this confidence. Autocracy and aristocracy were, it was believed, responsible for the disasters into which Europe had been misled. Their discredit was final and, indeed, was accompanied by the collapse of the great dynastic and authoritarian empires which had been their citadels. Allied propaganda and the fastidiousness of President Wilson transformed the war officially into a struggle for democracy. Their success was reflected in the speed with which those European states without them (outside Russia) adopted or at least pretended to adopt democratic and constitutional forms of government soon after the armistices. Not all were to last for long, but by 1920, formally democratic government was more widespread in Europe than ever before. Some were monarchies, but republics had been set up in the Baltic states, Poland, Czechoslovakia, Germany and Austria. The erection of a republic in Germany was, indeed, a startling achievement. Under the Weimar Republic (as it came to be called), Germany, potentially the strongest European power, had one of the most advanced constitutions in Europe. Even in democratic England an extension of the franchise in 1918 almost trebled the electorate and gave women the vote.

Yet, by 1939, whatever the lip service still paid to constitutional principle, no government that Wilson could conceivably have commended existed anywhere in Europe outside Scandinavia, the Low Countries, Switzerland and the two Allied states he had so distrusted, Great Britain and France. This recession of constitutional government by no means always meant that its successors lacked popularity, but it always brought the destruction of many of the institutions of traditional liberal democracy, such as liberty of the press, freedom from arbitrary arrest, the struggle of parties and free and secret elections. In some states democracy gave way to old-fashioned authoritarianism. In others, above all Germany and Italy, it was destroyed by a new political radicalism with popular support (see next chapter). In these countries, the extreme left, too, contributed to the overthrow of democracy. Propaganda against democratic institutions as the camouflage of class-oppression and the revolutionary violence which some on the left urged helped to sap the liberal principles which gave them protection. Even in the democracies which survived, Communism often divided the resistance to Fascism. Left-wing dogmatism found fuel, of course, in the apparent inability of capitalists to prevent the economic disasters of the interwar years. These disasters (above all by creating unemployment) provided material for the new anti-democratic forces. They sometimes helped to revive the traditional right, too. But the deepest sources of the weakness of democracy in these years were cultural. It had always been seen by its defenders as the logical development of the liberal political values of the nineteenth century. Though it had quickly been pointed out that individual freedom, and not the popular will, was the supreme value of liberalism and that the two might conflict, the potential disjunction of democracy and liberalism had been concealed by the continued recruiting of politicians from men bred in the traditions of liberal culture. After 1918 not only was this tradition weaker, but attempts were made to extend democracy to countries which had never known it, and even where liberal civilization was established, it was often fiercely attacked by its own children. The deepest roots of democratic failures are finally to be sought in the cultural weakness which glorified unreason and emotion – a glorification sometimes undiscerningly indulged by liberals themselves – as well as in the reassertion of more traditional anti-liberal values. *Pas d'ennemis à la Gauche!* was not a very sensible political judgment; its extension to the intellect in the muddled form of adulation of the critical and experimental at all costs was disastrous.

The smaller democracies were, on the whole, less troubled than the large by these ills. Quasi-Fascist movements appeared in both Belgium and the Netherlands and something like a Fascist terror briefly in Finland in 1930. But by 1939 the Belgian and Dutch Fascist movements had already begun to ebb, and in Finland in 1936 a left-wing coalition government which included Social Democrats took office. Some of the explanation of the relative healthiness of the smaller democracies must be sought in deep-rooted factors, such as their patterns of land-holding (in almost all of them, ownership had been widely spread for a long time). Unfortunately, there is no space to give even an adequate sketch of such foundations. More immediate factors were the preservation of the neutrality of all these states except Belgium and Finland in the Great War and their consequent freedom from destruction and disruption. Nor, although Swedish-speaking Finns were unpopular, did any of these countries have big minorities of foreign nationals. Even in Belgium a compromise was reached in 1932 over the use of French and Flemish, which for the time being took most of the heat out of that issue.

Against the background of such facts all these states continued to democratize the constitutional governments they had all (except Finland) enjoyed in 1914. By 1939 Socialists sat in the governments of all the Scandinavian countries, whose industrial unions also showed an unusual lack of militancy. The sustained development of social services and the large measure of social and economic equality attained in these countries commanded much admiration elsewhere and Scandinavia became something of a myth to the non-Communist and progressive left. The smaller democracies even seemed better able than the large to protect their citizens from the world depression; by 1939 Sweden had enjoyed a greater rise in average real wages since 1900 than any other European country.

FRANCE

After 1918 France proved less and less able to play her traditional role as the leader and patron of European liberalism. In 1914 the institutions of the Republic had proved adequate to the burdens laid upon them; in 1940 they were to show that they were not. France had been unable to meet new challenges. If, therefore, history is the story of significant change, France has little history between the wars; the problem is to decide why significant change did not occur. Social stagnation and political stalemate seemed to dog one of the most vigorous of prewar cultures, although it still showed astonishing intellectual and artistic fertility.

One source of this was the losses of the Great War which so accentuated the military disparity between France and Germany. Although a smaller population protected Frenchmen to some degree against the blight of unemployment, it was a psychological handicap. It led also to new political strains (through immigration) and helps to explain the lack of important growth in the economy. The motorcar industry showed that it could maintain the expanded production which the war had evoked, but soon reached a production plateau of about 200,000 vehicles a year and rested there. Frenchmen remained warier of investment in equities than Englishmen or Germans. None the less, France was at last an urbanized country; by the mid-twenties, more than half her population lived in towns, though most of them in towns of less than 10,000. Much of the countryside, though drained of labour and suffering from the world-wide agricultural depression, remained trapped in backward techniques and heavily subdivided holdings. Three-quarters of French peasants were proprietors. Only one great economic achievement marks the period, the rehabilitation of north-western France, the terribly devastated area of the heaviest fighting.

There is a connexion between this uninteresting story and the dominance of currency questions in French politics. Inflation had taken its toll in France as elsewhere during the war. The absence of effective income tax and the unwillingness of politicians to impose heavier indirect taxation had led to a great reliance on government borrowing, sustained by the belief that German reparations would be forthcoming to pay off the holders of government stock. Meanwhile French prices continued to rise and French external earnings were sustained by little except tourist traffic. One devaluation took place in 1928 and good times restored confidence, but when pressure on the franc began again it had become a dogma of French politicians at all costs to avoid another devaluation and its damage to middle-class savings. The cost of the obsessive concern with the maintenance of the franc was among other things the stagnation of national income which, at adjusted prices, shows no visible gain in 1936 over that of 1913.

The dangerous obsession with the currency was encouraged by the state of French politics. The electoral system itself encouraged electoral compromises and an absence of clearcut issues. In the interwar years, there was a bewildering multiplicity of party distinctions and fractional groupings, but three main tendencies were important. The left was split soon after the war when at the Congress of Tours, 1920, the majority of delegates voted to join the Comintern; this founded the *Parti Communiste Française* (*P.C.F.*). The right contained many factions united largely about resistance to social reform and support for a strongly nationalist foreign policy. The centre ground was occupied by the Radicals, the preponderant party of the Third Republic, without whose support, after 1924, no one else could govern. Radicals were dominant in the Senate and sat in every government after 1922. But radicalism was no longer a progressive force. It was deeply rooted in sections of French society which clung to the past, the independent peasantry and lower bourgeoisie.[1]

The war had at first overridden party divisions but the *union sacrée* had crumbled as misgivings arose about the conduct of the war. In 1917 the Chamber again turned to Clemenceau who ran a parliamentary dictatorship for the last year of the war. Acting like a *commissaire* of the Revolution, he lashed out ruthlessly to left and right, imprisoning and shooting traitors and defeatists and adding to his already long list of enemies. The Russian revolution envenomed further his bad relations with the Socialists; he imprisoned Caillaux – who had, after all, pushed through the acceptance of income tax – and thus offended many radicals. Victory gave his enemies their chance. The right *Bloc National*, of which he was a member, had a great electoral success in November 1919, and Clemenceau remained head of the government until the election of a new president. He was a candidate but the politicians rejected him. They feared that he would be a strong president; he had shown too much vigour during the war. They could use the excuse of popular disappointment with the peace terms. They wanted to be back in the saddle, intimidating a weak executive and chose as president a man who shortly afterwards went mad.

---

1 The word 'socialist' was now a part of the official name of the radical party, but meant nothing.

Clemenceau at once retired, normal political life was resumed, and with it political stagnation. Yet there were important issues before the French electorate in foreign policy and social policy, and quarrels over them largely replaced the issue of anti-clericalism, in which most Frenchmen had lost interest.

Nothing much in the way of social policy was to be expected in 1919 of the most right-wing Chamber since 1871, but the gap between socialists and radicals also delayed attention to it. In 1906, reforming governments with high ambitions had taken office on both sides of the channel. Clemenceau's had fizzled out in bitterness and violence, its social programme almost unopened; in England, the advance begun then was to steadily go forward under all governments. The contrast of the two democracies was flagrant and after the war, legislation was demanded more strongly than ever before. France experienced the same wave of strikes as other countries in 1919–20, and there were now 2 million trade unionists, many of whom found their official leaders far too moderate. The prestige of the Bolshevik revolution was immense. But the socialist movement was divided and the government was determined (as the failure of a general strike in 1920 showed). Soon, in 1921, the Communists split the painfully achieved unity of the C.G.T., even cooperating with Catholics against its leaders, and setting up a rival C.G.U.T. The worker had won an important concession in 1919, the eight-hour day, but had to wait until 1930 for the next instalment of social reform – national insurance against sickness and old age.

The victory of a *Cartel des Gauches* in the 1924 elections did not meet France's need for social reform, though it brought a change in foreign policy (see p. 353). The radicals dominated the *Cartel* and in domestic policy they were better at winning elections than knowing what to do with their victories. Formed in a tradition of distrust of government, they knew better how to obstruct policy than to realize one. Their victory in 1924 was really an expression of a longing to go back to 1914. The socialists, led by Léon Blum, had to compete against the P.C.F. for working-class votes; they were not going to risk discredit by joining radicals in governments which were bound to be ineffective. The sterility of the government of the *Cartel* is, therefore, hardly surprising. In addition, it came to power when the financial problem was reaching its height. Inflation defeated a succession of fleeting governments; when Caillaux failed, Poincaré had again to be sent for. His government of National Union restored confidence and the franc rose to about a fifth of its nominal value. It was officially stabilized at this level. France had, in effect, repudiated four-fifths of her debts, but investors were glad to have saved a fifth and to have escaped the nightmare of a German inflation.

Recovery was maintained by the economic upswing of the later 1920s and was to dissolve only by the world economic crisis. This affected France in two ways. One was by damaging France at first less than her neighbours, above all, Germany. That meant the recrudescence of German nationalism and the degeneration of German politics to their nadir at the beginning of 1933. This galvanized the French right, alarmed by the apparent failure of French foreign policy as one after another of its expedients proved useless and such security as France had possessed against Germany was swept away, but did not prevent an electoral victory for the left in 1932. Just then, the second effect of the economic crisis was about to be felt. Heavily protected, without a large dependence on industrial exports, attractive to immigrant labour, France took longer to feel the effects of the collapse than other countries. In 1932 she was still on gold, but the pressure had begun. Unemployment was mounting. It provided fuel for the growing xenophobia of some right-wing groups, who denounced the *métèques* who were working in France when Frenchmen were beginning to have to look for jobs. Immigration was restricted. It also fed the demands for more social reform. The best the radicals could do was to cut civil service salaries. The quarrels of politicians over this gave more ammunition to the new right.

This new right was to play an important part in the remainder of the history of the Republic. It had some Fascist, or semi-Fascist traits. Some of its roots went back to the prewar *Action Française* of Maurras. This had undergone something of an eclipse; royalism had become an increasingly ludicrous programme. The movement had incurred a papal condemnation in the 1920s and in 1937 the Pretender to the throne said it was not royalist, either. But its anti-parliamentarianism and dynamism now made it seem relevant. The physical strength of the new right came from the humdrum dissatisfactions of ex-servicemen and lower middle-class workers of the kind recruited by Fascism in Italy and Nazism in Germany. Their Leagues and associations made up a more or less coordinated though loose opposition to the régime in the early 1930s, which blamed it and its institutions for the plight of French society and foreign policy.

They were presented with a great opportunity by the bursting in 1933 of the Stavisky affair. In itself this exposure of frauds perpetrated by a notorious swindler was less remarkable than preceding scandals, but the Panama scandal is the closest parallel, because the effect of the Stavisky revelations and his mysterious death was to give force to the argument that his protectors were high in the service of the Republic and that their responsibility implicated the whole régime. The scandal justified attacks on the Republic as the inevitable embodiment of corruption. This also discredited the radicals who were above all identified with the régime and formed its government. Rioting and street-fighting in Paris by right-wing organizations followed. The climax came on 6 February 1934, the most celebrated day in French political history between the wars, when the security forces for some hours fought right-wing demonstrators around the Chamber of Deputies and succeeded in holding them at bay only with much bloodshed. The origins of the demonstrations are still not completely known. They were believed to be part of a deliberate and organized attempt to stage a *coup d'état*. This belief at last rallied the forces of the Left.

A *rassemblement populaire* was not easy to bring about. The communists' feud with the socialists was bitter. Down to 6 February the tight discipline of the P.C.F. had bound it to the Moscow 'line' which had already destroyed the German Communists. Soon afterwards, there were signs of uneasiness among the rank-and-file, who began to respond to overtures from left-wing socialists who saw danger on the right, but the communists' leaders went on abusing the Socialist party as before. Nor was Blum anxious for an alliance with the P.C.F., and he had always been unwilling to cooperate with the radicals. He was, however, now prepared to envisage entering a government of Republican Defence; 'when the Republic is threatened', he wrote, 'the word republican changes its meaning'.[2] The situation was not unlike that of the Dreyfus era, but the radicals needed more frightening before they would believe that the Fascist League actually threatened the *république des copains*.

2 *Le Populaire*, 11 February 1934.

This began to be provided during 1935, when the leading Fascist organization, the *Croix de Feu*, attracted great public attention. Meanwhile, orders from Moscow were making the communists more conciliatory. The first agreements between them and the socialists were made in July 1934, but they still seemed more tolerant of the radicals than of Blum. Then, in May 1935, came a Franco-Russian pact.[3] Socialists and radicals were already negotiating; now the P.C.F. suddenly came out in support of French rearmament (which it had previously bitterly opposed) and covered Paris with posters proclaiming '*Staline a raison*' to steady those made dizzy by a 180° turn. Real progress towards a *Front Populaire* could at last be made. A huge demonstration on 14 July was followed by discussion to hammer out the programme of the new electoral alliance.

The complicated negotiations of the politicians were only one side of the Popular Front's history. There was also a great mass impulse behind it. Though the economic depression came later to France than other countries, times were getting harder by 1934. Economic conditions worsened in the next two years and reawoke the militancy of the industrial workers. Between 1934 and 1937, the membership of trade unions rose from less than 800,000 to nearly 4 million. It was this swing of mass opinion as well as electoral discipline which gave the Popular Front a sweeping majority of 380 radical, socialist and communist deputies in the Chamber elected in May 1936. By then, the financial situation had deteriorated and Germany had reoccupied the demilitarized Rhineland. More money would be needed for national defence, but the banks were insisting on deflation to reinvigorate public credit. In these circumstances, the social reforms demanded by the Popular Front had an added bite. They were advocated as an attack on the '200 families' who were supposed to govern France through their control of industry and the banks. Almost at once the Popular Front found itself in difficulties. It was, in the first place, again taking power, as the left had done in 1924, when the franc was dropping rapidly. Blum dared not devalue and endanger his radical support. This was important to him because the communists, although supporting the Popular Front, had not joined the government and were enjoying the credit for supporting it without any responsibility for what it did. Worse

3 For the background of international affairs to this section, See Chapter xv, below.

still, the installation of the government was soon followed by the outbreak of a Spanish Civil War, which divided the government. Blum wished to support the Spanish Republic, but the radicals did not. Nor did he wish to endanger improving relations with England (which he had hoped to rescue from the doldrums because of the danger from Germany), whose government favoured non-intervention. Blum fell back on that policy, hoping it would be a reality and that an isolated Spain would make victory for the loyalists possible. When non-intervention worked only in favour of the insurgents, Blum was increasingly attacked from the left for allowing Fascism to triumph in Spain.

Meanwhile he had achieved one great success. The election had been accompanied by the spontaneous occupation of factories and department stores by workers. The panic this caused enabled Blum to summon employers and workers to conferences which gave the workers most of what they wanted, above all, the forty-hour week. This was very popular, yet France could hardly afford these 'Matignon agreements' against a background of stagnating industrial production and accelerating inflation. Gold poured out of the country; in the end, Blum had a carry out the devaluation he resisted and France went off gold. This completed the disillusionment of much of the bourgeoisie with his policies, which included the reorganization of the Bank of France, nationalization of the armaments industry and holidays with pay. By the beginning of 1937 the economic strain was producing political danger in the Chamber; social reform had put up production costs when new defence expenditure was needed. Blum had to announce a 'pause' in the social reforms of the Popular Front; this was at once exploited by the communists. Their charges that Blum was the captive of the bourgeoisie seemed to be justified when in June 1937 the Senate refused him special powers to stop the export of capital. The only alternative to acquiescence was force and this, although some socialists would have supported it, was not a risk Blum could afford to take in the presence of the Spanish example. He resigned. After another short attempt to form a Popular Front government in 1938, he again withdrew and the socialists supported a radical government under Daladier which was given the powers refused to Blum and carried out yet another devaluation. Shortly afterwards, the radical party itself split over the German annexation of Austria, and Daladier lost his support on the left at Munich.

The failure of the Popular Front should not be exaggerated. With the exception of the forty-hour week, its labour and social legislation remained intact until after 1940. But partly because of the circumstances in which it ended, partly because of communist propaganda, and partly because of disappointment over Spain, it had not overcome the forces which alienated the masses from the régime. The failure of another attempt at a general strike, in 1938, and the growth of the communist influence were symptoms of this. At the same time, the Popular Front had reinforced the right by carrying the fear of communism into foreign policy. In the 1920s the right had asked for a tougher line towards Germany; now it sought accommodation with Hitler to prevent social reform at home and to avert war. On both wings intellectuals were by 1939 taking refuge in a spiritual emigration from the Republic. They looked to Moscow or to Berlin for the models for France's future, thus consummating politically a *trahison des clercs* which had begun long before in the abandonment of reason and the liberal ideals of 1789.

These things made France's health precarious on the eve of another great war. In the test, she failed, not merely because of the deep psychological wounds of the Great War, of a falling population, of the conduct of the British at Munich, or because of faulty military doctrine, but also because none of her governments between the wars generated the respect which leadership commands even from its opponents. The *Front Populaire* had briefly done so. But the circumstances of its fall revealed the inappropriateness of the attitudes of French politicians to French problems. The political institutions of France had long before lost touch with the changing realities of society and this was the politicians' fault. Under the leadership they gave, it is hardly surprising that the *volte-face* of the communist party over a Nazi-Soviet pact should have knocked the bottom out of the hope of a new popular resistance to Hitler when the war came. In the twilit war which followed the destruction of Poland, the French war effort was sapped by a defeatism on the right which preferred Hitler to Blum, and by pro-German propaganda from the communists. It was hardly surprising that the onslaught of 1940, once it had punctured the myth of a defensive war, should have opened the way for men some of whom at least thought that the whole of the Republic's history since Dreyfus had been one great apostasy from the ideal of France. Others thought that the

Republic had condemned itself by the failure of its foreign policy since 1924. In 1940, France had no general will.

THE UNITED KINGDOM

In England, the Great War wrought enormous psychological damage. The postwar world had to carry the burden of cynicism about the culture which produced such disaster.[4] Patriotism seemed to have cloaked the interests of profiteers and the vanity of soldiers; quarrels between politicians and generals made Englishmen cynical about their leaders. Other certainties had been threatened. England had contemplated famine, and the first bombs dropped from the air revealed that it was no longer enough to be an island. Government had broken its traditional bounds. Real wages and expectations had risen (thus resuming a briefly interrupted prewar trend) but the pound lost half its purchasing power in the sharpest inflation Englishmen could remember. Reliance on borrowing did not prevent the quadrupling of income tax; such heavy taxation was startling and implied a significant redistribution of wealth.[5]

This would not have been altogether discordant with the principles of the government in office in 1914. Its collapse and the shattering of the Liberal party was an important political effect of the war at home. Both had always had internal problems. Lloyd George, the chancellor of the exchequer in 1914, deserved his reputation as a radical reformer, but had ambitions and a liking for coalition. These traits became more important in the circumstances of war. A bad shell shortage early in 1915 showed that the demands and duration of the war had been under-rated and that a long struggle was ahead. Some people distrusted Asquith's view that the war was a matter for the soldiers and sailors and that he and his ministers should interfere as little as possible. There had also been a quick revival of party feeling over the Home Rule Bill for Ireland passed in September 1914 (its oper-

---

4 Lytton Strachey's *Eminent Victorians* (London, 1918) is a famous example.

5 A bachelor earning £10,000 p.a. in 1914 paid about £750 income and supertax; in 1918 he paid £3,250.

ation was suspended until the end of the war). In May 1915 the Dardanelles failures brought a political crisis. Law, the Conservative leader, told Lloyd George that unless Churchill, an advocate of the Dardanelles expedition, was removed, the Conservatives would fall on the government (which depended on Irish and Labour votes for its majority) and the resultant outcry would shatter a national unity so far precariously preserved. Lloyd George agreed; Asquith consented. Churchill went and the Conservatives joined a coalition government, still under Asquith. It was the end of the Liberal monopoly of power, though not of Liberal preponderance. The first minister from the Labour party now took up office,[6] and Lloyd George became the first minister of munitions. His successes in expanding the supply of weapons and materials and in handling labour problems were well publicized. He achieved, in passing, a lasting social revolution by restricting the sale of drink. As import duties on luxuries showed, the war's demands would be more revolutionary than had been anticipated. In a world of changing ideas and dissolving certainties, Lloyd George would be more at ease than his colleagues or opponents.

In January 1916 England adopted compulsory military service; she was becoming a great landpower, soon to have seventy divisions in France. The voluntary system, which had already provided 2,500,000 men, was no longer thought adequate. This was another blow to Liberal principles. At Easter there was a rising in Dublin; Lloyd George seemed to hit upon an emollient solution by negotiating with Redmond and Carson to grant Home Rule, excluding Ulster, immediately, but this agreement was watered down by Asquith and came to nothing. In the summer there was the bloody failure on the Somme. Obviously, things were going badly and Lloyd George used dissatisfaction with Asquith's conduct of the war to provoke a crisis. From it, he emerged on 7 December as prime minister. He had captured the public imagination as (in words he applied to the businessmen he had brought into the ministry of munitions) a 'man of push and go' and he was indispensable to the Conservatives as the only man who could keep the Liberals in the Coalition.

This was the turning-point of British political history in the

---

6 Arthur Henderson, as president of the Board of Education. He had replaced MacDonald as leader of the parliamentary Labour party in 1914.

twentieth century. The split in the Liberal party was deepened by later events and the general election of 1918. Lloyd George was to be increasingly bound to the Conservatives, who were now the dominant partners in the Coalition. He had left the way open to the Labour party. A Labour minister entered the War Cabinet (the small body of ministers engaged in the higher direction of the war). The collapse of the broadly based and progressive Liberal party which had come to power in 1906 meant that the myth of class warfare was for years institutionalized in British politics by the existence of one party formally committed to it and another which all but monopolized the support of property. The war brought no other political change of comparable importance, though the revolutionizing of society and the economy went steadily ahead.

Immediately after the armistice, the Coalition government won an overwhelming majority in the House of Commons (478 seats out of 707).[7] Eighty of the other members were Irish nationalists and Sinn Feiners, and the Asquith Liberals who opposed Lloyd George were routed. There were only twenty-eight of them but sixty-three Labour members. This parliament faced the complicated problems of adjusting the economy and demobilizing 5 million men. It was assumed that the simple removal of wartime controls would restore prewar conditions. This combined with the collapse of a shortlived boom in 1920 to produce widespread industrial unrest.

The trade unions had nearly doubled their numbers during the war and had almost 8 million members in 1919. Many of them shared the militant feelings which swept through all European countries after the Russian revolution. There was talk of industrial action for political purposes; the threat of a general strike in 1920 seemed to stop British intervention in the Russo–Polish war. Economic dislocation and depression in these circumstances was bound to mean unrest. 1919–21 brought the worst period of industrial disturbance in this century. Lloyd George's conciliatory skills were deployed in setting up machinery for investigation. A

7 This was the biggest House of Commons in history, elected by an electorate nearly three times as big as in 1910. The 1918 Representation of the People Act had lowered residence qualifications. It gave votes to some men who had not previously had them and to some women over thirty; it also created new seats.

notable example was the Coal Mines (Sankey) Commission, whose recommendation that 'the present system of ownership and working in the coal industry stands condemned, and some other system must be substituted for it' was accepted by the government. When nothing was done, relations between masters and men in this old industry were further poisoned. Yet the moment when strike action might have been effective really passed by the end of 1919. Thereafter, the ebbing of working-class militancy and the slump carried the country past the postwar crisis with its economic structure more or less unchanged, although a general strike again briefly seemed possible in 1922. Almost unnoticed, the Coalition passed two important measures. One was a Housing Act of 1919, which took the government into the housing business with subsidies and laid obligations on local authorities to meet housing needs. Under this Act and its many successors, the 'council house' became a permanent feature of the English urban landscape and of the mythology of English class warfare. The Unemployment Insurance Act of 1920 was even more farreaching, extending the restricted benefits of 1911 to nearly everyone earning less than £250 a year; it was to be almost immediately swamped by applications for the 'dole' when heavy unemployment came back in 1921.

Almost unnoticed, Victorian politics had crumbled away. Even the Irish question was at last laid to rest, though far from imperceptibly. The blunder of shooting some of the Easter rebels gave Irish nationalism its final intransigent twist. By 1921 an Irish rebellion was only being mastered by violence unacceptable to British public opinion, which condemned the undisciplined violence of the 'Black and Tans' and 'Auxis' recruited from restless ex-servicemen. A truce in July 1921 led to long, complicated and interrupted negotiation until it was agreed (6 December) that Ireland should be partitioned. Ulster was to be part of the United Kingdom, the south a self-governing Dominion within the Empire. Disagreements about this settlement led to a bloody civil war (in which the new Free State government executed three times as many Irishmen as the British had done in 1920–21), but the Irish question at last passed out of English politics, to be replaced, in due course, by the Ulster question.

Ireland was almost the end of the Coalition. Another dubious success proved its undoing. A danger of war with Turkey revealed that the Dominions were, after all, truly independent;

only New Zealand was likely to help out the 'mother country' it appeared, when invited to send troops to resist the Kemalists. In the end, the British gained the point at issue, but war had seemed near over Chanak and the Conservatives had had enough. Many of the rank-and-file had seen the threat of electoral rout in the danger of war and felt they had to cut loose from Lloyd George. Their leaders who still supported him, men like Balfour and Birkenhead, no longer spoke for the back-benchers. Chanak also came after the failure of the Genoa economic conference and two years of slump and unemployment.

Law was unhappy, but decided to end the Coalition; the Conservative ministers supported their official leader, Austen Chamberlain, against him, but a party meeting voted against them (19 October). The Conservative ministers resigned and Lloyd George had to do the same. No one believed it was the end of his career as a minister; the great improviser would surely soon find his way back to power. He never did, yet he had been the greatest prime minister since Gladstone, though always, for all his consummate skill in handling the English public, something of an alien, in more than one sense an outsider. His wizardry in improvising solutions and reducing complex issues to crucial decisions had been the fruit of a certain lack of consistency, some said of principle. He inflicted one grave wound on the national life by his treatment of Asquith; this, by leaving the Labour party as the only credible alternative to the Conservative between the wars, condemned the country to unimaginative government. But this was what democracy wanted, apparently. His positive services to his country were immense. He provided the leadership which enabled it to endure its greatest war and with the assistance of the only other man of comparable stature in twentieth-century British politics, Winston Churchill, he founded the welfare state.

Law won a comfortable majority in a general election in November 1922 but was a dying man. The Labour party was now the official Opposition; it had won 142 seats and over 4 million votes and the Liberals were split. The postwar generation of political leaders was appearing. Law's government could not include the Conservatives who had wanted to maintain the Coalition, the old guard, and had to make do with the 'second-class brains' of junior and untried men.[8] One of them was Stanley

8 F. E. Smith's phrase.

Baldwin, chancellor of the exchequer, who became prime minister when Law resigned in May 1923. He was prime minister or second-in-command for ten out of the next sixteen years. Complicated and emotional, he was astonishingly successful at presenting himself to the electorate as a guileless, pipe-smoking country-lover who was all that many Englishmen wished to be. It was very hard to distrust him, and he undoubtedly abhorred sharp practice and duplicity. This was one reason for his implacable dislike of Lloyd George. In 1922, he had made a decisive speech at the party meeting which ended the Coalition, basing his opposition to Lloyd George, characteristically, on the Welshman's 'dynamism'. Other, personal, judgments no doubt also influenced Baldwin, but he always distrusted men who stirred things up and troubled the state.[9] He was the main author of the exclusion of Lloyd George from power after 1922, and of the good and bad consequences of this. In 1924, 1931 and 1935 he gave his party a bigger share of the popular vote than that of any party since 1900, and in the last two elections he achieved an absolute majority of the total votes cast – thus making the Conservatives of 1931 and 1935 the only British politicians in this century to have a serious claim to represent the expressed will of a majority of the voters. If government in this period became a matter of routine discharge of duties in a complacent and unimaginative manner, that is what the electorate wanted. Baldwin owed much to his very reassuring personal aspect and demeanour. It was also important that he was the first English politician to realize the possibilities (and new stylistic demands) of 'wireless' broadcasting. There was something of an artist about him. Some of his popularity he also owed to real achievements.

None the less, his sudden announcement that the remedy for unemployment was Protection seemed precipitate, even rash. Whatever his motives, Conservatives now had a new principle around which to rally after the strains of 1922. The Liberals reunited to defend free trade. An election in December left the Conservatives the biggest party in the House, but outnumbered by its opponents; Liberals had 159 seats, and Labour 191. No

9 Towards Winston Churchill, another dangerously dynamic politician, he acted with great astuteness; by offering him the Treasury in 1924 he cut off the possibility of a revived alliance between Churchill and Lloyd George.

Conservative government was possible. The first Labour government, therefore, took office with Liberal support and for ten months Ramsay MacDonald was prime minister. He could do little to put through Labour policies, but this did not greatly matter. The government's importance was its inoculation of the voters with the idea that Labour was a conceivable and responsible alternative government. In foreign affairs, it had some success until it ran into trouble over Russia. Treaties were signed, but were never to be ratified. At home a new Housing Act expanded municipal housing schemes. Meanwhile, the Conservatives ceremonially dropped Protection from their programme, the reuniting of the party having been achieved. The Labour government came to an end when MacDonald, tired of the complications of minority rule, resigned in October over an enquiry into an allegation of political interference with a prosecution.

Baldwin's successful years began with the 1924 election. It does not now seem that he owed many of the 419 Conservative seats to the publication of an alleged letter from Zinoviev linking the Russian treaties with the provocation of class war in England. His own promise of moderate, safe government was the real vote-catcher. Until 1929 he held office on this basis, helped by economic recovery and the 'Locarno spirit' in international affairs. The symbol of the resumption of 'normal' prewar life was the return to the gold standard in 1925. There was only one great crisis, and it immeasurably strengthened Baldwin. This was the 'General' Strike.

This took place because of renewed trouble in the coalfields. In 1925 the end of the French occupation of the Ruhr brought the collapse of British coal exports and the disappearance of the profits which had led mine-owners to concede higher wages. An immediate stoppage was avoided by setting up another enquiry. Its report in March 1926 recommended the nationalization of coal royalties, substantial reorganization of the industry and, immediately, reduction in wages. Both miners and owners rejected the Report. A member of the government wrote that 'it would be possible to say without exaggeration that the miners' leaders were the stupidest men in England if we had not had frequent occasion to meet the owners'.[10] Complicated negotiations petered out in a lock-out of miners which began on 1 May. The T.U.C. now

10 See C. L. Mowat, *Britain between the Wars, 1918–40* (London, 1955), p. 300.

prepared half-heartedly to strike in their support; on 3 May, the government broke off negotiations with the T.U.C. and the General Strike began the next day.

In spite of its conventional name, it was not strictly general; those who were called out, came out, almost to a man, but not all industries struck. The strike lasted only nine days. It showed that careful preparation (under way for several months) and plentiful volunteer help could maintain essential services. It showed that both sides were deeply imbued with a wish to avoid violence, in spite of some hotheads in the government. It showed the solidarity of the Labour movement. But it also demonstrated that unless the T.U.C. really wanted a revolution, they could not win. Baldwin's case was that a sympathetic general strike was a challenge to the constitution, since what was at issue was a domestic problem of a particular industry to be settled by itself. The surrender of the T.U.C. accepted the fact that victory was impossible and what should have been the greatest demonstration of the reality of class war, was a reassuring demonstration that the trade unions recognized that violent class warfare was a thing of the past. Whatever their temporary enthusiasm for Russian visitors or their violent language, they had come of age during the Great War. They were now a great national interest, committed to the preservation of the national structures of politics and industry, anxious to win benefits for their members by conciliation and agreement. They had drifted into a position whose implications were directly opposed to these realities. They had to surrender, putting the best face on it that they could.

Baldwin helped by his conciliatory manner. The miners felt let down and abandoned – as, indeed, they were – and as did other workers who were victimized when they went back to work. The miners' strike dragged on before petering out in agreements which meant victory for the owners on all counts. The government passed a Trade Disputes and Trade Unions Act to prevent sympathetic strikes in the future. Plenty of bitterness, therefore, was left by the General Strike, but it was the end of the most militant phase of the Labour movement. Experience of government had already began to sober the Labour Party. The impalpable pressure of responsibility and the need to organize a mass party to seize the opportunities presented by the Liberal disarray helped to restrain the lunatic fringe. Baldwin helped too; amongst other ways by being the first prime minister to give honours to trade union leaders. Good times in the later 1920s also helped to allay discontent.

As the credibility of a Labour government grew, a feedback effect appeared. More votes meant more moderate leadership in order to keep them, and as the party attracted more middle-class voters of the kind it had to win to be a national party, a repeat performance became more likely. It came in 1929, when Ramsay MacDonald again took office as prime minister. Although without an absolute majority in the Commons (288 seats), and with fewer votes cast for it than the Conservatives, the Labour party had Liberal support, and 3 million more votes than in 1924. Since 1910 the votes cast for Labour had steadily risen and the party's optimism was high on the eve of its greatest disappointment.

Ramsay MacDonald had done much for his party. He had given it confidence in foreign affairs, respectability at home. His vague, windy idealism admirably suited the coalition of working-class aspiration and middle-class Nonconformist conscience. Unfortunately, his government ended in a way which damned him in the eyes of many of his followers. This was largely because it listened to expert advice (the Conservatives would probably have done the same, had they been in office). The contemporary belief in orthodox finance and balanced budgets forced the government in 1931 to make a choice between maintaining government expenditure (in which the most important symbolic element was relief to the rising numbers of unemployed) and showing a budget deficit, or of cutting expenditure and balancing the budget. Agreement about the correct course was made more difficult by the European financial crisis which had begun to drain British reserves. A pessimistic report on British finance and industry had predicted a further rise in unemployment. The crisis came with the publication of another report just after Parliament dispersed in August, in which a committee set up by the chancellor of the exchequer recommended drastic cuts in government expenditure; this destroyed such confidence as foreign investors yet retained. At the centre of this storm, MacDonald seems to have been, in any case, tired of governing without full power. In the confusing comings-and-goings of three weeks the crucial question was the degree of economy in government expenditure which would recover the confidence of foreign investors. It divided the cabinet on 23 August. MacDonald then left his colleagues with the impression that the Labour government was about to resign. So it was. What they had not expected was that MacDonald would remain in office as prime minister of a coalition. This 'betrayal', as many Labour men saw it, distracted attention from the fact that the government had already been incapable of meeting the challenge of unemployment posed by the collapse of world trade. Nor was its successor; within a month, England had to go off the gold standard.

MacDonald's personal responsibility now seems an unimportant issue except to the hagiographers. The effects of the crisis were to give power to the Conservatives. Labour was hardly split, but it was discredited and stunned. By bad luck, Lloyd George was absent from the scene, ill. In an October election the Conservatives won 473 seats (the Coalition in all had 554). This preponderance led directly to protection, now again proclaimed the salvation of the economy. The Liberals were rent again over this and MacDonald was trapped by his majority. A more or less complete tariff on imports was capped by imperial preference agreements in August 1932. This led to the resignation of the Liberal ministers and the former Labour chancellor of the exchequer. The last Victorian political issue was settled.

The National government which ruled until 1935, and then renewed its mandate, still with a Conservative majority of the popular vote, deservedly enjoys low repute. But there is a danger of exaggerating its failures. A black legend has grown up that England experienced unprecedented economic disaster and social injustice in the 1930s. This is too simple. The first thing to remark is that the slump, however severely felt in some places and however vivid in hunger-marches and dole-queues, was an intensification of an economic malaise which lay over the whole interwar period, not just these years. Its roots lay in the dislocation of the traditional export industries and no government before or after 1931 showed itself able to do much about this. The economics of sustaining demand by expenditure had found their way into one party programme, that of the Liberals, but, not for the last time, they paid the price of being up to date; no one else believed in them. Another qualification to be made is that the effects of the slump were neither absolutely nor relatively so bad as in other countries and were mitigated by important regional and occupational differences.

Some immediate distress may have been alleviated by national economic policy, but it is difficult to be sure about this. What is clear is that changes were made which had important long-term effects on economic structure. The housing acts, for example, contributed to the maintenance of building, and until 1939, an abnormal year of prewar alarms, the number of completions per year showed a steady upward trend, with only minor annual fluctuations downwards. The reorganization of agriculture's economics which followed 1931 was also important for the long term. By 1939 the organized markets and guaranteed prices of post-1945 England already existed and the landed interest was again showing its teeth as a pressure-group.

Economic depression did little to halt the steady advance in living standards which has been so marked a feature of twentieth-century British life. Only in 1931–2 was there no rise in real income *per capita*. Figures are important here, but it is also permissible to use more impressionistic but vivid evidence, such as photographs.[11] Expectation of life at birth still rose and so did the number of deaths from the diseases of old age. The stock of houses increased faster than the population, and more Englishmen owned their homes than ever before, thanks to the building societies. The purchasing power of the pound benefited from lower world commodity prices and although cash benefits to the unemployed were cut, the years from 1918 to 1939 were full of legislation bringing real benefits in welfare and social services to large numbers of people.[12] There were six Housing Acts;[13] subsidies for slum clearance were increased in 1933, and rent control, established in 1914, was never removed, several amending Acts being passed until one in 1939 extended restriction again to many decontrolled houses. The origins of the National Health Service go back to the provision of free treatment for V.D. in 1918. Local authorities were empowered to set up maternity clinics in that year. Widows', Orphans' and Old Age Contributory Pensions Acts[14] greatly enlarged the pensionable population.

11 One easily accessible comparison is the pair of photographs of boys of the same age at a Bermondsey school in 1894 and 1924 printed in Phelps Brown, pp. 42–3.
12 Unemployment Insurance was the subject of legislation in 1920, 1927, 1930, 1934, 1936. 'An unemployed man with a family was better off in the thirties than the unskilled labourer in full work in 1913', Mowat, p. 492.
13 1919, 1923, 1924, 1930, 1933, 1938.
14 1925, 1929, 1937.

Blind people were given special old age pensions in 1920, and an entitlement to them at forty in 1938. The old Poor Law structure was abolished by two great statutes in 1929 and 1930. In 1918 compulsory attendance at school was made universal up to fourteen and in 1936 provision was made for this to be raised to fifteen (this was not done until after the war). These facts are not very informative without exposition of their detailed meaning but they give an authentic impression of steady change for the better. So does the pattern of public expenditure. Between 1913 and 1935, expenditure on social services rose from £74 million to £382 million.[15] This was a big redistribution of income, for all the contrasts of rich and poor life. Taxes were lowered in the 1920s, but in the following decade they again began to rise (rearmament was to put them up further). By 1935 the working class received £91 million more in social services than it paid in taxation.

These continuing changes were great achievements. Many of them were due to Neville Chamberlain, whose record as a reformer is in danger of oblivion because of his failure in foreign policy. Yet his foreign policy was in many ways only the logical outcome both of the work of his predecessors and of the expressed will of the electorate.[16]

The important break in the history of British foreign policy between the wars came in 1922. The Labour party aspired to Gladstonian rectitude, used more idealistic language and was emotionally attracted by the idea of reconciliation with Russia. The Conservatives were emotionally repelled by it. On the more important issues of western Europe and Asia, both parties followed more or less the same line, avoiding the reconstitution of an *entente* with France and 'adventures' such as those of the Coalition. They differed importantly only over means, in that the Labour party favoured the League and the Geneva Protocol, the Conservatives the traditional structure of agreements between major powers which made Locarno.

Ramsay MacDonald's interest in these matters suited Baldwin, who gave them little attention during the first years of the National Government. Insular in his own tastes, unresponsive to the political forces loose in Europe, he was representative of many

15 The buying power of the pound fell by about a quarter between these dates.
16 For what follows, see also ch. 15.

of his countrymen who felt vaguely that France made most of the fuss in Europe and that Germany had been somehow victimized. Yet in 1932, the government abandoned the rule that war need not be expected for ten years. In 1934, after violent criticism by Winston Churchill, the enlarging of the R.A.F. was begun, in the truth of Liberal and Labour opposition. In the following year came almost the last act of MacDonald's prime ministership, the White Paper on Defence. A departmental committee was set up to consider food supplies in case of war. In 1935 Baldwin again became prime minister, and, for the remainder of his life, foreign affairs was to dwarf domestic politics.

The two mingled, of course. The general line of the Opposition was to oppose the rearmament which would allow the British government to take a firm line abroad. The Labour party did not make up its mind about sanctions until 1935. Baldwin was, in any case, over-susceptible to the generally peaceful mood of his countrymen. In the election campaign of 1935, he told a meeting 'I give you my word that there will be no great armaments.' This helped to give him the name of a conscious deceiver of the electorate, but he won the election with 387 seats. There followed the Hoare-Laval 'pact' which further discredited Baldwin (see p. 513) and left the uneasy feeling that the country had been too weak to stand up even to Italy, and the shock of the Rhineland (see p. 519). Rearmament was accelerated; the Labour party voted against it. The Spanish Civil War muddied the political waters still further and widened divisions over foreign policy. They came to be related to familiar conflicts at home and were translated into the language of left and right, and of class.[17] Baldwin must share the responsibility for this deterioration, since he was prime minister, but he was distracted by the crisis which led to the abdication of Edward VIII, who had come to the throne in January 1936. The survival of the impalpable prestige of the monarchy, scarcely strained, owed much to Baldwin's handling of affairs. In December, George VI ascended the throne. It was Baldwin's last success. He retired in May 1937, with an earldom.

His successor, Neville Chamberlain, sought to pursue a personal foreign policy. Its popularity is Chamberlain's best

17 For interesting comments see C. Bright, 'Class interest and state policy in the British response to Hitler', in *German nationalism and the European response, 1890–1945*, ed. C. Fink *et al.* (London, 1985).

justification, as it is Baldwin's. He remains responsible, nevertheless, for the encouragement of a dangerous state of confusion in the public mind by his inflexibility and vanity. His mistakes of judgment led in the end not only to distrust of the government's integrity (Munich deepened the divisions over Spain), but to Great Britain at last going to war at the wrong time, on the wrong issue, and with the wrong ally.

The country that went to war had undergone revolution in the preceding half-century no less than many states which had more spectacular breaks in their development. In 1939 the British had the highest *per capita* national income in Europe and though great poverty still existed in their cities and depressed industrial areas, the world of Rowntree and Booth had almost gone. Someone who was an adult in 1880 could have lived to see industrialization advance so far that by 1939 only one workman in twenty-five was engaged in agriculture. Political democracy, still dreaded in 1880 by many Englishmen, was by 1939 triumphant; yet the monarchy and the Lords, their powers reduced, were still there. There was less violence in politics and industrial life, yet the trade unions had nearly 6 million members. Obscured though it might be by the survival of the Liberals and the overwhelming success of the Conservatives in the 1930s, England still had a two-party political system, though one partner in it had not existed in 1880. Yet a shrewd observer would see a deeper continuity, too, for the Labour party was already well on the way to turning itself into that sort of coalition of progressives which the Liberal party had been in its great days. Adamant on the danger of contamination by the tiny British Communist movement, the Labour party was recovering steadily from the *débâcle* of 1931 and would inevitably be again one day a party of government.[18] The lack of success of the extreme Left was significant, but Fascism did not much tempt Englishmen, either. It might be able to provoke street brawls in Jewish districts but it was never electorally important. The traditionalism of the Conservative party saved it from the errors of continental conservatives. It continued to believe in parliament (anti-parliamentarianism had a history in twentieth-century England, but it was only of political mavericks, like Rosebery and Milner). It continued its policy of slow concession by passing

18 In 1931 Labour membership of the Commons sank to 46, but in 1935 rose again to 154.

welfare legislation and condoning the gradual loosening of imperial ties. It was not obvious, but the brief age of the third British Empire was already ebbing. Winston Churchill hoped to prolong it and quarrelled again with his party over it, but his dogmatism only irritated the Conservatives who passed the India Act of 1935. Although the Act left unsatisfied the Indian nationalists, its logical end was Dominion status – the ultimate that could then be envisaged.

The most remarkable fact of all modern British history is the growing acquiescence in such major changes. The agencies making agreement easier were more evident after 1918 than before. The towns began to sprawl more into the indistinguishable and dull wastes of suburbia; but these were places where life was gentler, opinion more likely to gravitate to a mean than in the turmoil of the Victorian cities. Education was all the time doing its work, creating intermediate groups of clerical and technical workers who blurred the lines of class conflict by their ambiguous status. It stimulated some able children to take advantage of the receptivity of the existing social order to talent. Everywhere it created readers for the new mass newspapers. Some of them, the better off, would also listen to the B.B.C., probably the most important single cultural force created (1926) between the wars. Many would have cars, which were beginning to crowd the roads (there were still horses to be seen in towns, but usually only between the shafts of milk-floats or coal-carts).

Such agencies worked within a slowly but steadily enriched material culture. Now and then it could be discerned that behind the new rayon dresses of shop-assistants and the motor-bikes of the young clerks, there were still the relics of an older, poorer, harsher life in the depressed colliery towns of Yorkshire or the ship-building towns of the Clyde. The pattern of the English future, nevertheless, could be seen. In 1941 one observer pinned it down:

The place to look for the germs of the future England [he wrote] is in the light-industry areas and along the arterial roads. . . . There are wide gradations of income, but it is the same kind of life that is being lived at different levels, in labour-saving flats or Council houses, along the concrete roads and in the naked democracy of the swimming-pools. It is a rather restless, cultureless life, centring around tinned food, *Picture Post*, the radio and the internal combustion engine. It is a civilization where children grow up with an intimate knowledge of magnetoes and in complete ignorance of the Bible.[19]

The change, he thought, was great, but not to be feared, and when he wrote, 1940 had already saved England from the doubts of the previous decade.

19 George Orwell, *The Lion and the Unicorn* (London, 1941), pp. 53–4.

13

TOTALITARIANISM AND DICTATORSHIP

RUSSIA

No totalitarian state has seemed so successfully to centralize political, social and economic control as the Soviet Union. It developed to a high degree the dominance of a single party of devotees, the central direction of the economy, the eradication of other foci of loyalty and the machinery of a police Terror. But it was a special case in more than its completeness. Whatever the illusions of monolithic doctrinal identity, the vagaries of its behaviour, the moral relativism of its official theory, the corruption of its rulers by power, the theoretical and moral justification of the Soviet state system was a belief in social progress which stemmed ultimately from the Enlightenment. However brutal their methods, and however blind Russian rulers may sometimes have been to the evil they did, or to the disjunction between their principles and their practice, they could never abandon rationality and a belief in progress as the Nazis were to do.

Nonetheless, the demands of Marxist orthodoxy have made it easy to exaggerate the debt of the modern Russian state to theory. It is more important that in 1917 revolution came to the most backward of the great powers – the one least ready for revolution, according to Marxist teaching – and that it was as much a collapse of an old as an insurrection of a new order.

In the end, imperial Russia had at last outrun even her own giant's strength. From the outset, the war had been a terrible strain, given Russia's inadequate arms and transport. The Brusilov offensive was to be the last effort. By the end of 1916, the game was up; the German army had damaged the régime so much that only a slight shaking would now bring it down. War-weariness grew not only because of Russia's enormous casualties, but because the Russian cities were starving. The greatest prewar grain exporter in the world could no longer feed herself; transport had broken down so that food could often not be got to market. Mobilization of the huge Russian armies had carried millions of men from the farms, where they had been fed at the source of production, to faraway battle fronts. The railways were the keys to Russian survival. With more track and rolling-stock, Russia's allies could have saved her, but in 1917 it would have taken the trans-Siberian line a year simply to carry the supplies already at Vladivostok to western Russia.[1] By the end of 1916, the morale of the peasant-soldiers was cracking. Scandals undermined confidence in the autocracy. The industrial workers were infected with socialist doctrine and were beginning to riot for food. It was not surprising, therefore, that 1917 should bring collapse, yet few were ready for it.

Although Russian constitutionalism had lost ground after its first triumphs, the Duma had throughout the war heard criticism and denunciations of 'dark forces' in ruling circles. But the constitutional politicians were neither preparing nor prepared for a revolution at the beginning of 1917. Nor were the socialists, divided as they were. Among them the Bolsheviks were at loggerheads with the 'social patriots' or 'defensists' who supported the war. Lenin, the most uncompromising of the Bolshevik leaders, was in Switzerland. The real author of the revolution was the German army.

The February revolution,[2] therefore, was an extemporization. In a mounting wave of food riots and strikes it became obvious that the troops were not reliable. On 27 February, when nearly 100,000 workers were on strike in Petrograd, the garrison mutinied and the Duma, which reopened that day, refused to dissolve. Within a few days, there were more strikes and the Duma set up a provisional government. On 15 March the tsar abdicated for

1 *League of Nations Report on Economic Conditions in Russia* (Geneva, 1922), pp. 7, 12.
2 The Russian calendar was out of step with the western, hence the references to the 'February' and 'October' revolution, although they took place in March and November according to western dating.

himself and his son and the crown passed to the Grand Duke Michael; he, too, abdicated the next day. This was the end of the régime. It collapsed when pushed by war-weary peasants, soldiers and townspeople acting almost without leadership. All over Russia they elected Soviets, or councils, which began to act as executive bodies in the general breakdown of government.

The Mensheviks saw the need to mobilize and lead the people. Remembering 1905 they set up a Soviet in Petrograd before the tsar's abdication; the Bolsheviks would not act with them and for the moment, therefore, the Mensheviks led the people. The Provisional Government sought popularity by including a socialist in its numbers and by announcing reforms. National independence was granted to Poland, and autonomy to Finland and Estonia. The government also promised a Constituent Assembly. But it wanted to go on with the war. This was likely to bring the government into conflict with the masses and the army, and thus to give the Bolsheviks the chance to bid for popular support. Menshevik and Bolshevik attitudes to the provisional government were theoretically divergent. The Mensheviks believed that a period of bourgeois rule was indispensable in the transition to proletarian government which would come about when Russian society had been transformed by capitalism. The Bolsheviks almost from the start would have nothing to do with this idea. Here, Lenin's personal influence was very important. When his fellow-Bolsheviks seemed to waver, he at once, from exile, recalled them to intransigent opposition to the war and a demand for immediate socialism. He succinctly defined his programme in a telegram: 'Our tactics: absolute distrust, no support of new government. Kerensky particularly suspect; to arm proletariat only guarantee; no *rapprochement* with other parties. The last is *conditio sine quo non*.[2]

Lenin and some other Bolsheviks went back to Russia with

---

2 See in L. Schapiro, *The Communist Party of the Soviet Union* (London, 1960), pp. 162–3. Kerensky was at this time the only socialist member of the Provisional Government; in May, he became minister of war and in July, prime minister. See also, 'The task of the proletariat in the present revolution', an article printed in *Pravda*, 20 April (*Lenin: Selected Works*, vol II, pp. 17–21). In this article the need to change the name of the Russian party from Social Democrat to Communist is first announced. In March 1919, the Bolshevik party was renamed the Communist party.

German help in April. His contribution to the Revolution was above all one of character and morale; unswervingly he sought power, never flagging in his pursuit of it, intent on capturing it without compromise or obligations. He was ruthless; he was to be the first socialist leader to unleash a Terror as harsh on fellow-socialists as on class enemies. He was also a masterly tactician, extraordinarily skilled in exploiting opportunities. Grasping at once that the Revolution had been made by the peasants and soldiers, Lenin knew they had to be kept loyal to it; the slogan 'Land to the peasants' hardly fitted Marxist theory but embarrassed the government and won the respect of the Social Revolutionaries, while attacks on the war won over the soldiers. When a last abortive Russian offensive led to a remodelling of the government, the Bolsheviks thought the time propitious for a *coup*: they failed, and Lenin again went into exile (though only as far as Finland). The belief now became widespread that the Bolsheviks were, in fact, German agents.[3]

Kerensky was now the head of the gravely weakened government. When, in September, General Kornilov (acting in connivance with the Allied military missions who wanted, above all, to keep Russia in the war) attempted to occupy Petrograd in order to overthrow the Soviet, Kerensky had to turn to the Bolshevik 'Red Guards' and the Soviets (which the Bolsheviks were now winning over) to save the Provisional Government. From this time the movement to the second, 'October', revolution was almost uninterrupted. The Provisional Government was less and less able to rely on the army and had done little to remedy the economic hardships of the townspeople, who faced another winter at war. Under attack from both S.R.s and Bolsheviks, it lost influence in the Petrograd Soviet. In September, fearing the forthcoming Constituent Assembly, Lenin urged his colleagues to attempt a *coup*. After obtaining a majority in the Petrograd Soviet, the Bolsheviks decided to act. On the night of the 6–7 November soldiers, sailors and Red Guards seized the main government offices in Petrograd. The *coup* was successful because the Bolsheviks controlled sufficient force in the capital, the decisive spot; it was acceptable because the Provisional Government's fall promised the end of the war. On the following day, a

3 This was an over-simplification, though they undoubtedly received German money. See ch. 9.

Congress of Soviets met and although only 300 of its 650 delegates were Bolsheviks, it at once announced that 'the Soviet government' would seek peace, confiscation of estates and their distribution, control of industry by the workers, and that the promised constituent Assembly should meet.

The Council of People's Commissars which was set up by the Congress was, in fact, entirely Bolshevik. Yet although it stood at the levers of government, the party as a whole faced powerful opposition. It could rely only upon about 200,000 members, scattered throughout Russia, but most numerous near Petrograd and Moscow (to which the government moved in March 1918). Almost its first problem was the forthcoming Constituent Assembly. The Bolsheviks' main electoral rivals were bound to be the S.R.s, who commanded wide support among the peasants. The elections to the Constituent showed this – and also provide the only numerical evidence we have about support for Bolshevism in a democratic election. The S.R.s won 370 of the 707 seats, the Bolsheviks 175. They were now certain to be embarrassed by the Constituent which they had demanded so urgently from Kerensky. When it met (18 January 1918) and rejected a Bolshevik resolution, the Bolshevik delegates withdrew, and on the following day soldiers prevented the Constituent meeting again. A little later, a Congress of Soviets elected under heavy Bolshevik pressure approved of this action.

This was the second division within the revolution. The Bolsheviks had overthrown the Provisional Government: now the uneasy alliance with the S.R.s was destroyed. Civil war had really begun. Lenin's tactics had, it is true, been made easier because some 'Left S.R.s' supported the Bolsheviks. But the Revolution was from this time the property of one party. Former promises of freedom of speech were ignored, censorship was tightened and non-Bolsheviks were not allowed to publish newspapers. In December, even before the Constituent met, the *Cheka* had been set up to replace the old tsarist secret police. Some felt misgivings: 'We had never thought that the idea of revolution could be separated from that of freedom.'[4] This drift to dictatorship was none the less fairly bloodless down to the middle of 1918, when

4 V. Serge, *Memoirs of a Revolutionary, 1901–1941* (Oxford, 1963), p. 69. Gorky, he says, at this time thought the Bolsheviks 'drunk with authority', 'starting bloody despotism all over again' (p. 73).

capital punishment (abolished the previous year) was restored. The first Soviet constitution, promulgated in July, disfranchised the 'non-toiling' classes and provided for open elections without a secret ballot.

The coming of peace also produced new strains, throwing up the first important divisions among the Bolsheviks themselves. One sign of this was the so-called 'Left Communism' of Bukharin and others who wished to refuse the German terms and trust to a revolutionary guerrilla war. Lenin was determined to make peace because he was sure that without it the government would lose control of the army. The strain within the party was great; the peace terms also estranged the left S.R.s, to say nothing of more tradition-minded patriots, and thus accelerated the drift towards civil war.

Thus began the crisis of the régime which lasted from 1918 to 1921, an unrolling succession of dangers, in which civil war and factions within the régime were accompanied by steadily increasing economic strain. The civil war is too complicated to describe briefly. It was a series of local wars against separation and reaction, confused by the intervention first of the Germans (in the Ukraine) then that of Russia's former allies and a war with Poland. The Russian government long hoped vainly for the European revolution; it was in the end saved by its opponents' divisions, and the energy and ruthlessness of Trotsky, the organizer of the October *coup*. 1919 saw the worst moment; in the following year, peace was made with Poland and the civil war ended.[5]

Differences among supporters of the revolution crystallized in open divisions when the civil war ended. Broadly speaking, the most important were between those communists, often in the trade unions, who distrusted the growing authority of the party's Central Committee and sought to give workers the direct management of industry, and the party officials who sought efficient use of resources, even if this meant, for example, employing non-proletarian experts, or disciplining the trade unions. (The Soviets had already lost their independence to the party: 'As the governing party', said Lenin in 1921, 'we could not help fusing Soviet authorities with party authorities.') In hard times, with

5 On the Civil War, see D. Footman, *Civil War in Russia* (London, 1961). On the Polish war N. Davies, *God's playground*, pp. 394–399.

Mensheviks and Social Revolutionaries still able to compete for the allegiance of the masses, such differences could be dangerous, especially when, as in 1921, they were expressed in an open struggle between two members of the Central Committee – Zinoviev, who attacked party dictatorship, and Trotsky, who advocated it. Lenin temporized, but appeared to be more sympathetic to Zinoviev than to Trotsky.

The issue still hung in the balance when a mutiny broke out at the Baltic naval base at Kronstadt (2 March 1921). For fifteen days a Provisional Revolutionary Committee ruled there, demanding, in essence, the ending of the communist party's privileged position and the satisfaction of the demands of peasants and trade unionists. It was the last expression in Russia of the proletarian idealism which had sustained so many European revolutionaries since 1848. The Kronstadt programme asked for freedom of speech and the press, secret ballots, and the release of all political prisoners. 'Objectively', such a programme was incompatible with the new régime. Trotsky directed operations from Moscow and on 18 March the resistance of the sailors was overcome. No public trial of the mutineers was held, they were simply massacred on the spot. Almost incidentally, Trotsky had also triumphed over Zinoviev.[6]

At the Party Congress which met in the middle of these events Lenin admitted that the Communists had 'failed to convince the broad masses'.[7] But the sailors were vilified as counter-revolutionaries; the rule of the party was to be the only admitted path to socialism. The abuse heaped on the men at Kronstadt showed the tragic intensification of Bolshevik suspiciousness by the crisis years. The Terror mentality grew out of xenophobic distrust of the outside world and an obsession with counter-revolutionary danger. It fed on its own progress; after a time it became dangerous to be merciful to the opponents who had been terrorized. The first important outbreak of terror had come after an attempt on Lenin's life in 1918. Many people believed to be opponents of the Communists were then murdered more or less spontaneously in a widespread panic. After this, and above all

6 See I. Getzler, *Kronstadt 1917–1921: the fate of a Soviet Democracy* (Cambridge, 1983), and for an excellent description of the atmosphere at Petrograd, Serge, pp. 115–30, and especially his *apologia*, pp. 128–9.
7 See Schapiro, p. 204.

after Kronstadt, terror became more systematic and it was extended to critics on the left. By 1922 Anarchist and S.R. leaders had been put on trial, and the first Party purge (of about 130,000, or about a fifth, of its members) had taken place. Like the beleaguered Jacobins of 1793, the Communists felt that only Terror could save them. The *Cheka* (renamed the G.P.U. in 1922) was confirmed in its discretionary repressive powers and the Criminal Code of 1922 forbade *any* political activity which might help the 'international bourgeoisie'. In this drift towards totalitarianism, circumstance was playing as big a part as Marxist doctrine. Lenin's pre-October vision of a rapid withering away of the revolutionary state, and the creation of a society in which there would be no 'special apparatus of repression' and in which 'all take part in the administration of the state' was forgotten;[8] the dictatorship of the proletariat came to be that of the party, which used violence against the workers and peasants as unhesitatingly as against the bourgeoisie. Not all Bolsheviks could silence their misgivings. But there did not seem to be a practical alternative.[9]

Political opposition would not have seemed as threatening had the country not been plunged in economic disaster. The revolutions had accelerated the breakdown of the economy by prompting the spontaneous seizure of large estates by the peasants and the institution of 'workers' control' in the factories. A further drop in food deliveries to the city markets and in industrial production had resulted.

	Pig-iron output (million poods)	Coal output (million poods)	Locomotives in service
1913	1,536	256	16,866
1917	1,510	185	17,012
1918	552	31	14,519
1919	310	7	4,577
1920	271	7	3,969
1921	329	7	7,683

8 V. I. Lenin, *State and Revolution* (Engl. trans., London, 1933), pp. 69, 77.

9 'They say that the English Parliament can do everything except change a man into a woman. Our Central Committee is far more powerful than that. It has already changed more than one not very revolutionary man into an old woman, and the number of these old women is increasing daily.' Ryazanoff, see Schapiro, p. 214. See also, Serge, pp. 73–6, 80–3.

The Bolshevik response was coercion: 'War communism' meant rationing and requisitioning to stop peasants keeping back more grain than they needed for their own consumption and seed. This was popular with the 'Left Communists' because it deliberately exploited the class feelings of the poor against the richer peasants in domiciliary visits and searches, intimidation and Terror. It also meant increased power for the *Cheka* and the Party bureaucracy, since only physical force could maintain 'war communism'. Yet these methods, it soon appeared, were economically inept and politically dangerous. The militants might be pleased, but as the economic situation worsened, so Menshevism revived. The figures of production tell the story.[10]

Behind this statistical collapse, it is true, lies the loss of industrial areas at Brest-Litovsk and the destruction of the civil war, but much of it must be attributed to the running down of the whole economy as trade collapsed, transport ceased to be able to supply materials and, above all, workers went short of food. People were deserting the towns in 1919; soon millions had left. Strikes and food riots became more frequent and serious. They had brought down the tsarist régime; those in Petrograd just before the Kronstadt revolt were the danger signal.

In spite of the raids of 'Food Detachments' from the towns, the peasants were not making deliveries. Nearly half the arable area of Russia was out of cultivation in 1921, cereal deliveries were less than two-fifths of those of 1916 and the livestock population had declined by between a quarter and a third. This collapse combined with the Kronstadt outbreak, led the government to adopt the New Economic Policy (N.E.P.). Lenin, in October 1921, candidly described

the defeat we have suffered on the economic front at the beginning of 1921, in our attempt to make a transition to communism [as . . .] much more serious than any we have suffered at the hands of Kolchak, Denikin or Pilsudski. . . . The requisitions in the villages and the direct application of communist principles in the towns have hindered the revival and become the main cause of the tremendous economic and political crisis which descended upon us in the spring of 1921.[11]

N.E.P. was designed to make it profitable again for the peasant to grow and market grain. It restored freedom of trade, legalized

10 For the table, see League *Report*, p. 15. A *pood* = approx. 36 lb.
11 See League *Report*, p. 16.

individual landholding, and re-admitted private enterprise to industry and commerce. The party militants disliked it, but it worked. Immediately, its announcement stiffened the Red Army so that its peasant soldiers were persuaded to go into action against the Kronstadt mutineers. But another disaster had to be weathered before N.E.P. could produce results. In 1921 a bad drought led to an appalling famine over most of the Ukraine, Crimea, Donetz basin and the Tartar republics. Between 2 million and 3 million died. Observers reported people eating acorns, the straw from roofs and leather harness, and even cannibalism. Foreign aid (mainly from the United States) prevented even greater tragedy, but it was not until 1922 that N.E.P. began to deliver more food.

Emergence from this crises brought a partial relaxation of the political atmosphere. Combined with N.E.P. and the thaw in Russia's relations with other countries, this made some Bolsheviks fear the onset of a creeping reaction. But there was no fundamental change. The leaders of the Revolution had been too deeply shaped by the traditions of the struggle against despotism, too corrupted by power, and were too confident of their possession of the truth to envisage compromise as anything but a tactical expedient. They only disagreed about tactics. Lenin was in poor health from the end of 1921 and a period of confusion and evolution within the party was likely. When he died in January 1924, this confusion was deepened by the question of succession. The period from 1924 to 1927 was taken up with the struggles within the party which settled this. They are too complicated to summarize, but roughly speaking two views were in conflict. One emphasized dependence on peasants, the makers of the Revolution, and therefore the continuation of N.E.P. Another stressed the need to exploit the peasants in the interest of the revolutionary militants of the towns, and looked to rapid industrialization and the spread of the revolution to other countries as the road to the future. Personal rivalries were mixed up with this. Trotsky, intellectually the most able of the leaders and the advocate of the second course, was distrusted. His expulsion from the party in December 1927 was the climax of the debate. But the outcome, the ascendancy of Stalin, was not what all Trotsky's opponents had expected.[12]

12 On the confusion within the Party at this period, see Serge, pp. 209–43.

In retrospect less attractive than Lenin and Trotsky, Stalin was to prove of greater historical importance than either. Only sycophants found him likeable. He was cunning and secretive; with a peasant's patience, he knew how to wait for his moment. His rivals had not realized the danger until too late; Trotsky always thought him a mediocrity. But by 1922 he already had great power. A member of the five-man Politburo which had appeared in 1919 as an inner cabinet, he was also a member of the Party Secretariat exercising influence and patronage through its organizations. Intellectually he could be subtle;. he had a seminarist's ability to dissimulate. He had already shown his ability – and some of his limitations – as chairman of the Commissariat of Nationalities, a post in which his Georgian background helped him.[13] But it was in the Party bureaucracy that his real power lay and as this bureaucracy entrenched itself (in spite of Lenin's misgivings) it came to be more and more his personal creation and instrument. When Lenin died, Stalin had shrewdly assumed the leadership of the cult of 'Leninism' which established itself; thus, establishing by implication a claim to be the orthodox heir to the master, he put his opponents at a disadvantage. Lenin would have disliked idolization of his own role and had in fact seen dangers in Stalin's growing powers, but too late. His preparations to attack Stalin at a party congress had been silenced by his final relapse and his misgivings were known only to a few.[14]

From the Trotskyists Stalin took over the programme of intensive industrialization, supported by collectivism in the countryside, and from their opponents the subordination of international revolution to the needs of Russia. 'Socialism in one country' was the slogan embodying this synthesis of socialist and Russian ideals. The price paid was prolonged economic privation at home and the disillusionment of many Communists abroad. The Chinese and German communist parties were in effect destroyed by being subordinated to Russian interests and leadership; the Spanish Republic was sapped from within by Stalin's refusal to treat Anarchists and Trotskyists as allies against Fascism. The

13 One of his first ministerial acts in 1917 had been to go to Helsinki to proclaim the independence of Finland.
14 On Lenin's misgivings, see Schapiro, pp. 228–9, 271–2, Serge pp. 113–14. Stalin delivered a lecture on 'Foundations of Leninism', in 1924, which established the theory of the new orthodoxy.

Comintern became the mere spokesman of Russian diplomacy, reflecting every twist and turn of circumstance with fresh rationalizations and explanations. Some of this caused deep disillusionment. But Stalin's vilification of his opponents as traitors to socialism was always remarkably successful; indeed, it became grotesquely so in the confessions and self-incriminating statements produced in the great show trials of the 1930s. His opponents themselves endorsed the verdicts passed on them. The explanation of this lies not only in torture or intimidation, but in the overriding loyalty of many of them to socialism. The state of mind has been brilliantly described in one work of fiction,[15] but it can also be seen in Trotsky. In spite of the abuse and persecution by which he was harried by Stalin's agents, Trotsky always remained reluctant to criticize Russia. There were several reasons for this. One was vanity, his own commitment to much of what had been done; another was a doctrinal orthodoxy which still made Russia in his eyes the best hope for the future of the world, whatever its temporary errors. Only after the crowning disillusionment of the Spanish war did he go so far as to try to organize a 'fourth International'. Such an attitude was not peculiar to Trotksy; it explains both the intellectual trapeze-artistry displayed by Communists who accommodated themselves to each rewriting of the history of the Revolution and to the sombre self-incrimination of the victims of the purges.[16] The refusal of the opponents of Stalin in the 1920s to challenge (until the last moment) the authority of the corrupt Party Congresses which silenced them, already embodied this attitude. It has been summed up in a phrase by Trotsky in 1924: 'I know one cannot be right against the party.'[17]

A fresh obstacle was later placed in the way of a just assessment of Stalin's achievement by the wish to dissociate Communism

15 A. Koestler, *Darkness at Noon* (London, 1940). See also L. Trotsky, *The Revolution Betrayed* (London, 1937), and Koestler's autobiography *The Invisible Writing* (London, 1954).

16 The gradual removal of Trotsky from the official version of the October Revolution began in 1924. During the Moscow trials he was denounced by Vyshinsky as an agent of the German *Gestapo*.

17 See Schapiro, p. 303. See also the views of Piatakov (expelled the Party 1927, then readmitted after public recantation, subsequently a Deputy Commissioner for Heavy Industry, arrested 1936, confessed to treason, shot in 1937), *idem*, pp. 380–1.

from his excesses. In the 1930s no such need was felt by the communists in any part of the world. The crimes were either denied, or accepted as necessary means to the end of building a just society. Fortunately, Stalin's place in history rests on more secure foundations than his own propaganda or the hysterical adulation of his foreign admirers in the 1930s.[18] He made Russia again a great power. The evidence of his success was that by 1941, in spite of his cruelties, most Russians identified themselves with the régime sufficiently to survive the greatest onslaught they ever suffered. It was a paradoxical achievement for a Marxist, for it stood the theoretical primacy of economics over politics on its head. The cost was the consolidation of the totalitarian system and an intensified Terror. One way of describing what began in 1928 is to call it a 'third Revolution'; another is as the conquest by Bolshevism of the rural Russia it had never controlled. For the peasant, it meant the wiping out of all the gains he had made since 1917.

This was because an old choice still faced Stalin as it had faced Witte. The tsarist statesman had seen as the alternative to industrialization the political abdication of the autocracy to the more vigorous powers of western Europe; Stalin reminded Russians how often they had been beaten in the past 'because to do so was profitable and could be done with impunity . . . Do you want our socialist fatherland to be beaten and lose its independence? If you don't want this, you must liquidate our backwardness and develop a real Bolshevik tempo in building our socialist economy. There is no other road.'[19] But this road was blocked unless the peasants gave up the grain they would rather have eaten. This is why collectivization was the starting point of the transformation of the Russian economy.

By 1927 both industrial and agricultural production were getting back to prewar levels and there had been some improvement in the supply of consumer goods. Most factories and businesses were still formally nationalized and there existed a rudimentary planning organization. From 1928 two Five Year Plans transformed this picture. By 1937, although the Plans were

18 Much praise was given to the meaningless civic and political rights of a formally very democratic Soviet constitution adopted in 1936.
19 See T. H. von Laue, *Sergei Witte and the Industralization of Russia* (New York, 1963), p. 3, and H. Schwartz, *The Soviet Economy since Stalin* (New York, 1965), p. 14.

not wholly successful, a spectacular increase of production had occurred. It was based on very high investment and a rapid growth of the labour force. Capital investment rose from 13 to 26 per cent of national income during the Plans. By 1937, 80 per cent of Russian industrial output came from plant built since 1928.

This was done by using a police apparatus to enforce low consumption. Estimates of real wages make it clear that there was a substantial fall between 1928 and 1937, though there was some compensation in better communal services.[20] What is certainly true is that the greatest hardships fell on the peasants. Collectivization made possible enforced grain deliveries. The economic effects of this have been described (see pp. 376–7). Its political and social dimensions are equally important. The Party had been weak in the countryside, where the *Kulaks*, or rich peasants, often had some influence over their neighbours. Now, not only the *Kulaks*, but millions of poorer peasants were killed or transported in what was virtually a new Civil War. Five million families disappeared from European Russia in seven years. The new grain levies brought back famine to the countryside. Stalin later said it was a more severe trial than the second world war.[21]

Russia became a great industrial power; Stalin succeeded where Witte had failed. Although adulation heaped on Stalin at the height of his dictatorship produces scepticism today, this was a great achievement. He ruthlessly swept aside opposition to collectivization and industrialization. The disciplining of the Party continued after Trotsky's expulsion. Bukharin, having first been removed from the Politburo, joined others who had wanted to retain N.E.P. in recanting his errors publicly and promising not to deviate from the Party – that is to say, Stalinist – line in future. At this time, Stalin still had to take account of Party feeling and in 1930 he showed he was sensitive to the alarm of some of his colleagues at the state of the countryside by accusing local officials of being 'dizzy with success'. Now that this essential work had been done and they were compromised by their violence, these useful agents could be rebuked and abused for carrying out their

20 Janet C. Chapman, *Real Wages in Soviet Russia since 1928* (Cambridge, Mass., 1963), suggests at worst a fall of 39 per cent in real wages, at best, one of 14 per cent.
21 Churchill, *The Second World War*, IV, pp. 447–8. For material from O.G.P.U. archives, see M. Fainsod, *Smolensk under Soviet Rule* (London, 1959), pp. 142–4, 185–8, 238–64.

orders. Meanwhile, deportations, forced labour and shootings went on. The police control of society was enormously increased by the new economic activity of the state. The trade unions were reformed and purged in 1929. Official hostility to religion was intensified (not that the Russian Orthodox tradition could much embarrass an autocracy) and the Communist youth movement undermined the family structure. But it was very difficult for foreign observers to see or understand what was going on. Only the great show trials of the late 1930s revealed what was happening.

Although the Terror had, so to speak, come above the surface in 1930–31, when technicians, intellectuals and civil servants were tried for sabotage, and a pretended 'Menshevik centre' was destroyed, Stalin seems to have met opposition in the Politburo to the unleashing of the Terror against members of the Party itself.[22] For the moment it was confined to 'saboteurs' on whom the shortcomings of the first Five Year Plan could be blamed, or to 'counter-revolutionaries'. In 1933, some 'oppositionists', including Zinoviev and Kamenev, were exiled. It was only in 1934 that the assassination of a Leningrad Communist provided an excuse for what was to be a bloody purge of the Party itself. In 1935 Zinoviev and other Old Bolsheviks were brought to trial and condemnation. There was a pause, and the abolition of bread rationing brought the régime some popularity until 1936, just after the outbreak of the Spanish War, when sixteen old leaders were convicted: Zinoviev and other old Bolsheviks were shot. In 1937 thirteen more were convicted and shot (among them Radek). Eight generals were shot, too. In March 1938 eighteen more Old Bolsheviks were sentenced to death, and Bukharin died after a year in prison. And this was only the top of the iceberg. Hundreds of thousands of Party official and administrative officers were shot, deported, or simply replaced. Half the officer corps were removed.[23] Five years after the Seventeenth Party Congress of 1934 more than half the delegates who had attended it had been arrested on charges of counter-revolutionary crimes. The generation which carried out the crimes of collectivization had quickly

22 For a description of one of the early trials, see E. Lyons, *Assignment in Utopia* (London, 1938), pp. 114–7.
23 Schapiro, p. 420, using Japanese intelligence estimates. On the purge in the Smolensk region, see Fainsod, pp. 232–7.

reaped what it had sown. It was a great personal victory over the Party for Stalin, capped by carrying the purge even into the N.K.V.D. itself, characteristically by saying that 'excesses' had been committed by it at the instigation of traitors and enemies of the state.[24] The Terror came suddenly, quietly, to an end, having removed all the critics or potential critics of the régime who might have provided an alternative government in the international crisis opened by the Spanish War.

That there was more to the Terror than industrialization was shown when the Revolution devoured its own makers. Some weight must be given to Stalin's personal pathology, some to the background of international affairs and the fears roused by the rise of Germany. It may be argued that the obsession of the régime with secrecy was justified by the surprise of the German army at the resistance it encountered in 1941. Nevertheless, it is hard to believe that Russia was much strengthened by the purging of nine in ten of her generals. The Purges were also in part a conflict of generations. One of Stalin's achievements had been the creation of a new governing class and the virtual elimination of the leaders of the Revolution and the Civil War. By 1939 70 per cent of the Party had joined since 1929. Many new vested interests had been created. The search for talent and the provision of educational and economic privileges for experts had created a new intelligentsia, to which Stalin proudly referred in 1936. In society this meant the emergence of a new functional élite, in government, the assumption of power by young men and women who knew nothing of the outside world, for whom pre-revolutionary Russia was only a childhood memory of privation, and the history of the Revolution only what the official Stalinist historians told them. They were given in 1938 a new ideological handbook, Stalin's *History of the Communist Party of the Soviet Union (Short Course)*. The possibility of opposition was remote. Stalin had obliterated possible alternative governments and no social group or institution existed outside the party which could give opposition a firm base. Crime, perhaps, was the only way to protest against the new order.

This social transformation was the other great change of the Stalinist era. In twenty years, the old élite had followed the insti-

24 The G.P.U. had become the O.G.P.U. in 1923; in 1934, this became part of the N.K.V.D., the People's Commissariat of Internal Affairs.

tutions of tsarism into oblivion and had been replaced by a new one of great talent and much more disciplined mentality. The promotions of the purges accelerated this. An Old Bolshevik looking back on the eve of the German invasion could hardly have failed to believe that whatever might have been lost in this process, the total gain far outweighed the cost because of its implications for the future. Even by 1939, too, the gain was enormous. Effective government had for the first time been made a reality over one sixth of the world's surface. It had transformed a barbaric continent, provided universal education on an undreamed of scale, emancipated women and spawned great scientific and academic institutions. The peasant mentality was in retreat and a huge industrial labour force had been created. Moreover, the power necessary to defend these gains had also been created. True, Russia's potential was vast; had she not been defeated and plunged into revolution, would she not in any case have been transformed by capitalism to become the dominant European power of the second half of this century? It is at least conceivable: Tocqueville had discerned Russia's potential a hundred years before and German generals and statesman had feared that outcome before 1914.

It does not diminish Stalin's achievement to make this point, nor to remember that Witte had anticipated him in his will to industrialize, if not in his police powers. Stalin put Russia back on the historical highroad after she had been diverted by war and revolution. For all the Marxist jargon he used, this is likely to define his place in history. Although a Georgian by birth, he became increasingly a Russian ruler, a new tsar of Muscovy or Peter the Great, seizing and exploiting ruthlessly the possibilities inherent in Russian history. The novelist Alexei Tolstoy had to rewrite his vilification of Peter the Great to stress his resemblance to Stalin. In the last years before the war and invasion, indeed, much more was heard in Russia about the great national heroes of the past. One work of art which this produced was Eisenstein's great trilogy *Ivan the Terrible*. The film of Ivan's struggle against the intriguing Boyars was given wide circulation, but the last part, which depicted Ivan's madness, was not completed.

AUTHORITARIANS AND FASCISTS: SOME DISTINCTIONS

Strenuous efforts were made after 1918 to ensure that the new states emerging from the wreckage of the empires enjoyed the benefits of democracy and constitutional rule. Yet by 1939 all had abandoned these principles, willingly or unwillingly, and one of the victors of 1918, Italy, set up the first Fascist dictatorship. In central and eastern Europe only Czechoslovakia had been able to maintain a democratic constitution until the eve of its absorption by Germany; by then, all other states in these areas had régimes which may be described as authoritarian or dictatorial, and most of them had long had right-wing governments. A *coup* established a dictatorship in Lithuania in 1926; Latvia and Estonia followed suit in 1934. Of the new constitutional monarchies, Yugoslavia became a dictatorship in 1929 (the formal ending of this two years later meant very little); Greece turned itself into a republic (1924) but then reverted to a monarchy in 1935 before Metaxas's *coup* in the following year set up a dictatorship there. The Polish Repubic was ruled more or less dictatorially and often harshly from 1926 by Pilsudski. There were other states, too, where, even if forms did not alter startlingly, the conduct of government was from the first markedly illiberal. The régime of Stamboulisky in Bulgaria (1919–23) was something of a special interlude of government in the interests of the peasants against the bourgeoisie, but it was certainly not liberal. The constitution left great powers in the hands of the king himself (although it was to pass into the hands of soldiers from 1934 to 1936) and in this respect, Bulgaria resembled the superficially constitutional Rumania. Hungary, briefly a republic, formally became again a monarchy in 1920, when Admiral Horthy assumed power as regent and head of state, and was governed by a succession of conservative administrations which enjoyed wide support because of the popularity of revisionism but ensured their stability by carefully managed elections. The Austrian Republic was dominated by Catholic conservatives who used their police unflinchingly against the Social Democrats.

This shows the overall trend; its sources, too, are fairly easy to see. During the upheavals following the end of the war, many countries ran the risk of revolution. Soviet governments appeared briefly in Budapest and Munich, and Vienna and Berlin looked as if they might follow suit. The Baltic States and Poland were threatened with invasion by the Red Army; as late as 1924 a Communist *coup* was attempted in Estonia. The first stimulus to the abandonment of democracy was the Bolshevik threat. Though all the Bolshevik attempts to revolutionize eastern Europe failed dismally, the danger continued to be feared. Some new states also had alien minorities which they felt able to control only by firm government. Others sought (or feared) revisions of the 1918 settlement which defined their borders. In some states, traditionally dominant groups were being asked to make a transition from the Middle Ages to the twentieth century in one jump and resented it. Others had bureaucracies which were inadequate or corrupt. In such settings, the absence of a tradition of constitutional politics reduced democracy to a sterile bickering between parties which ignored national interests.

All these things helped the drift to authoritarianism. Their operation was intensified by the world economic crisis. Even where great land reforms had removed some of the social and national divisions of the countryside, most of these countries remained poor and essentially agrarian (Czechoslovakia was economically the most advanced and politically the most stable). They were hard hit by the collapse in world prices. The blows of the depression were followed rapidly by the deterioration of international affairs. Many of these countries found themselves drawn towards the governments of Germany and Italy, not because of sympathy, but because France was weak and trade with a Germany anxious to expand her markets and purchases in the south-east was attractive.

In these circumstances, it is not surprising that what we may call 'right-wing' governments became common. Often this was the obvious reflex of societies looking for any means to keep themselves in being. But because there were also movements of a new kind struggling for power in these years, it is important to make distinctions within this general trend; some movements sought to do more than conserve. Here, the old terminology of left and right is inadequate. These terms are rooted in the division of European opinion by the French Revolution; they become confusing if we seek to apply them to all political movements, as if they all formed part of the same spectrum.

Between the wars, the confusion was deepened and thickened by some other factors. International changes, especially after the advent to power of Hitler, led central and eastern European governments to court the German Nazis and Italian Fascists and to ape their language and manners. Everywhere, too, the depression accentuated an old and deeply rooted antisemitism just at a time when Nazi racialism was giving it a new and more beastly emphasis. The anti-Bolshevism of the Nazis was another confusing fact, because of the obsession of many more traditional and conservative governments with the Communist danger. This bred up in response an undiscriminating anti-anti-Communism, which confused political language further by lumping together all sorts of right-wing régimes as 'Fascist'. Fascism was treated as an international phenomenon which was the right-wing equivalent of the Popular Front. This obscured important differences between traditional conservatives and Fascists.[25]

The most obvious novelty of Fascist movements is their revolutionary dynamic. Self-conscious Fascists were uninhibited by respect for tradition, institutions or ideas, and had an ambivalent relationship with traditional forces and groups. The social sources of Fascism's energy, in any case, were to be found outside the established hierarchies of market or status society. It courted the mob. It opposed Bolshevism by seeking mass support through the exploitation of the same grievances that favoured Bolshevism. It appealed to the masses with talk of national socialism and to the uncertain, uneasy middle classes, torn from their usual loyalties by inflation and fear of revolution, with the promise of national regeneration. To do this, it sketched big, vague historical aims, although always setting these within a national framework. In so doing, it was drawing on the uncertainty and anxiety bred by the increasing atomization of bourgeois civilization; it offered the security of the herd to the lonely individual. For some, this was precisely and personally true; one frequent characteristic of the individual Fascist is an inability to distinguish myth from

25 One of the earliest examples of the treatment of Fascism as a supra-national movement of this kind can be found in the Comintern's denunciations of the 'victorious Bulgarian Fascist clique' in 1923 (see Nolte, *Three faces of Fascism* p. 12). But Macartney and Palmer, *Independent Eastern Europe*, have no entry for 'Fascism' or 'Fascist' in their index. The whole subject has been much obscured by scholarship but some useful guidance can be obtained from Nolte, and the essays in *European Fascism* (edited by S. J. Woolf) and *The European Right* (edited by Rogger and Weber). Full citations are given in the bibliographical note at the end of this book.

reality. The emotional relationship between Fascist movements and their members was strongly marked and reached its heights in the adulation accorded to Hitler. In this, there was a plentiful dash of élitist ideas, but Fascism was more than a simple belief in élites: as Rosa Luxemburg pointed out, Lenin had that, and so did the Webbs. Nor was it just authoritarian, or Stalin would be properly called a Fascist.

The fundamental distinction between Fascism and other right-wing movements was its total rejection of bourgeois civilization. Here we are talking of model characteristics; in practice, of course, both the Nazis and the Italian Fascists often made tactical concessions to existing interests. Fascists believed that bourgeois civilization had failed; they were not merely attempting to stave off its arrival or prevent its replacement by socialism, but to put something in its place. They rejected the whole of liberal civilization – capitalism and the market system, individualism and rationality, the belief in progress and the faith in politics as a way of meeting society's needs without violence.[26] The demand of Fascism for allegiance went far beyond that of traditional authorities or conventional military 'strong men'.

Fascist movements sought, and, where successful, won, popular support, but as this characterization shows, they are essentially post-liberal phenomena. It was only in Germany and Italy, both, by comparison with eastern Europe, advanced countries with large rootless urban populations, that they were really popular successes. In other countries Fascism appeared only sporadically. Hungary's government between the wars, for example, was undoubtedly in the interest of the traditional ruling class, but the proto-Fascist 'right radicals' who thrived on the distress of the middle class just after the war were gradually tamed by being given jobs by Bethlen, a great aristocrat. He presided over a sort of Magyar Whig oligarchy, ruling by a judicious mixture of political corruption, electoral management and violence, while getting the economy back on its feet. Only after the depression of 1931 did this system change and a right radical government come to power under Gombos. It lasted until 1936, Gömbös pursuing strong antisemitic and anti-Habsburg policies and looking for ideological support to Hitler and Mussolini. But the

26 Cf. Henlein, the Sudeten German leader (see Gilbert, *Britain and Germany between the Wars*, p. 106): 'We declare war to the death upon liberalism . . . men wish to be led in manly fashion.'

regent, Horthy, retained much of the reality of power, and Gombos found he could do little. He died in 1936 and this 'half turn' to Fascism came to an end.[27] The old conservative interests resumed control (although the changing European scene meant they had to pay increasing attention to Nazi demands).

A similar continuation of traditional authority and absence of a victorious popular Fascist movement makes it impossible to regard Poland as more than a military dictatorship, although some of the 'Colonels' Party', which governed the country after Pilsudski's death in 1936, undoubtedly had Fascist views. Even Austria, where both the *Heimwehr* and Nazi movements were strong, did not have a Fascist government. Dollfuss set up a government which was, rather, an intensification of the clerical dominance of Austria in the 1920s. It crushed the Austrian social-ists with the aid of the *Heimwehr* in February 1934, but the new constitution of that year drew its inspiration from Papal Encyc-licals and the government violently harried the Austrian Nazis.

This suggests similarities with the other Catholic states, Spain and Portugal. Both moved towards authoritarian government between the wars and did so from somewhat similar back-grounds. In 1880 Portugal, like Spain, was an old state ruled by a constitutional monarchy. Her politics down to the Great War showed the classical pattern of European constitutionalism in a poor and largely illiterate country, being in the main a matter of ins and outs. The 'Regenerator' and 'Progressive' parties split, reformed and split again, producing ministerial changes about once a year. The monarchy, discredited by court extravagance and humiliations brought upon it by England in colonial disputes in the 1880s, could not appeal to the people against the politicians. It survived a republican rising in 1891 and politics relapsed again into moribundity until the arrival of a French queen, soon followed by French clergy, revived Portuguese anticlericalism. This may have been one reason for the attempt of a king, Carlos I, to break out of the system in 1906 by appointing a minister to govern without the parliament. The repressive measures of Joao Franco bred conspiracy and disorder and in 1908 the king and the

27 The phrase is from C. A. Macartney, *Hungary. A short history* (Edin-burgh, 1962), p. 223. A very full and authoritative treatment of Hungarian history between the wars is to be found in the same author's *October fifteenth: a history of modern Hungary, 1929–1945* (Edinburgh, 1957).

crown prince were assassinated. Manuel II restored the politicians to their seats and Franco fled, but this could not stabilize the system.

In October 1910 a revolution in Lisbon forced Manuel to go into exile and the Republic was proclaimed. The new régime fell upon the Church, separating it from the State in 1911, and set up a liberal constitution. But it did little to please the mass of the people. In 1912 a general strike in Lisbon, the most important centre of population, led to military rule and the Republic entered a stormy period which lasted until 1928. Portugal committed itself to the Allied side in the Great War (23 November 1914) but this only led to the appearance of yet another factious opposition. Between 1914 and 1928 there were six successful insurrections and counter-insurrections, nine presidents or dictators (one of them assassinated) and a large number of bloody strikes, *coups* and uprisings from left, right and centre. In the latter year, a military clique took power and appointed as minister of finance the man who was to govern Portugal until 1968, Antonio de Oliviera Salazar. In 1932 he became prime minister, and in effect dictator. Only one party was permitted and a new constitution in 1932 reduced the representative role in government to an advisory one. The national assembly (which consisted of heads of families with certain educational qualifications) did not, in fact, meet until 1935. Portugal was a Catholic dictatorship lucky enough to have found a ruler of great ability at the price of delayed modernisation.

Spanish politics were less obviously affected by the Great War than those of Portugal, but they were already complicated by even deeper divisive forces (see ch. V), some of which were accentuated indirectly. As a neutral supplier of minerals, food and manufactured goods to the Allies, Spain did well. Coal and textile exports shot up, though the results were not all beneficial. The prosperity which was brought to Catalonia not only strengthened Catalan nationalism, but intensified the bitterness of class warfare, since the profits of prosperity went to the rich. When the postwar slump brought unemployment in Barcelona, the situation there again became as dangerous as it had become when the loss of Cuba ended an artificially protected market and brought about a crisis of overproduction. In 1920 Spanish industry had fewer workers than in 1910.[28] The political system of the Restoration

28 Vicens Vives, p. 307.

almost gave way under these strains. It was further compromised by the Moroccan involvement which culminated in 1921 in the disaster of Annual, where a Spanish army was wiped out by the Moors. This was too much even for the *Cortes*, which appointed an investigating commission. Its report was never published because in 1923 Spain acquiesced in the end of the Restoration compromise and reverted to military dictatorship.

The politicians having failed to provide a régime which could command widespread support and preserve order, General Primo de Rivera seized power with the approval of the king, dissolving the *Cortes* and silencing the press. His aim, he said, was 'a brief parenthesis' in constitutional government, but its formal resumption in 1925, with Primo as prime minister and a cabinet of generals, did not signify much. This régime for some years looked surprisingly successful. Even the socialists came to an understanding with it against the anarchists and there was an unprecedented era of industrial peace. This owed much to Primo's good luck; he took power just before the general improvement in world economic conditions in the later 1920s from which Spain benefited. The dictatorship was successful (in alliance with France) in overthowing Abd-el-Krim in Morocco. Primo was popular, too; his legendary drinking bouts were the sort of indulgence that the man in the street could understand. It was the liberals and middle-class intellectuals who remained opposed to the régime and were harried by it. Political tension survived because the dictatorship produced no institutional answer to the problems of Spain; rural poverty and class-warfare. Primo de Rivera's attempts to found both a political party and a National Assembly proved unsuccessful.

The lack of consensus which underlay the régime was soon shown when Primo, ill and weary, retired in 1930. His successor announced conciliatory measures, the restoration of political freedom and new elections, but this only removed a check on intransigent criticism of the government and, now, the monarchy. The army was beginning to show republican sympathies. In February the constitution was restored. Elections for the municipalities took place in April and were a great republican victory. Alfonso did not abdicate, but at once left Spain, announcing he would await abroad the expression of the people's will. The republican leader, Alcalá Zamora, became president of a provisional government (14 April) which was endorsed by a large majority in the elections of June. The constituent assembly which now drew up the constitution of the Spanish Republic was to become its first parliament; it had come to power after an unambiguous expression of Spanish sentiment.

Both the constitution and the first acts of the Republic showed advanced liberalism. One symbol of its attitude to the Spanish past was its dissolution of the ancient military Orders whose origins lay in the Reconquest. Precisely because of this attitude, the collapse of the Republic began with its foundation. The removal of the monarchy revealed that Spain was without a general will; the republican majority in the *Cortes* masked important disagreements on principle and the landowners who dominated the economy distrusted a regime which might threaten their wealth and the power it gave them. Two great institutions, the Church and the Army, waited suspiciously for signs that the Republic would undermine their authority. Meanwhile, the anarchist syndicates and the Catalan national movement were overtly hostile to the democratic but centralised state.

The Church had consolidated its connexion with the monarchy during the Regency, thereby reviving the anticlericalism of Spanish Liberalism. The twentieth century had brought to Spain its first major experience of dechristianizing and paganizing forces which were already operating elsewhere. Against this background, the separation of church and state in the Constitution is understandable. But the Republicans went on to secularize education and to nationalize church property. In 1932, they dissolved the Jesuit order. Such acts might be possible in France and even, in principle, desirable in a perfected and regenerated Spain, but they were precipitate and unrealistic. Whatever the reason, the Church had wide support. It was a profoundly native institution, intimately linked to Spanish attitudes and culture. When, in 1933, a Law of Association imposed further disabilities on the Church, an important section of Spanish opinion had been alienated, and this showed in the elections of November, when the first *Cortes* of the Republic contained twice as many right-wing deputies.

Anarchism and Catalan separatism were tangled together and were also complicated by the failure of the Republicans to carry out effective land reform. The Republic was as unlucky in the trend of the world economy as Primo had been lucky. As conditions in the countryside grew worse, violence increased.

Police brutality at Casas Viejas in Andalucia in 1933 lost the government the support of the socialists. Meanwhile, a grant of home rule to Catalonia had not met the social demands of the Barcelona workers (though it had provoked other demands for regional autonomy and had displeased traditionalists). In January 1933 there was a rising in Barcelona and yet another, which took ten days to suppress, occurred in the following December.

The swing of opinion against the government was shown by elections in 1933 and a succession of shaky coalitions. One anti-republican factor was that women were voting for the first time in Spain and were doing so in an atmosphere poisoned by the régime's anticlericalism. A new right-wing party appeared, supported by the Church and landowners which joined with the so-called radicals (led by Lerroux, the hero of the *Semana Tragica*) to govern Spain during what came to be called the *Bienio Negro*. Reaction in education and land reform led to more violence. It broke out in a general strike in March 1934, called by the parties of the left in protest against the drift to the right, and in a proclamation of Catalan independence. The Catalan rising was crushed and the autonomy statute suspended. In October the miners of the Asturias rose and proclaimed a communist régime. This, too, was crushed with great brutality. Governing harshly and with increasing difficulty, Lerroux held on until September 1935. His successors could not manage a right-wing *Cortes*, and obtained a dissolution. New elections, the last of the Republic, were held in February and resulted in a sweeping victory for a Popular Front of republicans, socialists, communists and anarchists and the elimination of 'centre' parties such as the radicals. The government which emerged under Azaña, at once resumed social reform, promising land reform and a restoration of Catalan autonomy. But its supporters wanted more. Peasants began to divide up estates for themselves. Churches and convents were attacked and burned. Political murder and gang warfare in the streets seemed to be carrying Spain towards anarchy. A Spanish Fascist party, the *Falange*, led the forces of the right and on 12 July one of its leaders, José Calvo Sotelo, who had been Primo de Rivera's finance minister, was found murdered.

The army, although it had accepted the overthrow of the monarchy, had watched with growing dislike the decline of the Republic into disorder. It was led by men of whom many were temperamentally and economically opposed to social reform. In

1932 an attempt by a general to seize Seville had been suppressed, but it indicated that all was not well with the loyalty of the soldiers. The spread of disorder and the dislocation of historic Spain by the autonomy statute alienated them even more. A *coup* had several times been contemplated, but the soldiers remained quiet during the Lerroux government, until the elections of February 1936 announced the end of the road for many of them. The murder of Calvo Sotelo provided an opportunity. Calculating that the new government would not arm the people to resist, three generals, Franco, Mola and Sanjurjo, launched a new *pronunciamiento* in Spanish Morocco on 18 July.[29] The *coup* failed in that not all the garrisons rose and that anarchist and socialist militias rallied to the government. This meant civil war.

It was not only the technical and military assistance of Germany and Mussolini which enabled Franco to beat the Republican forces by March 1938. To the defeat of the Republic there also contributed the policies of England and France – which made the purchase of arms abroad all but impossible – and of Russia, whose policy in Spain was to assert the domination of the Spanish communist party on the Republican side. This meant, paradoxically, protection of the Republican middle classes against the social and revolutionary aims of the anarchists in Catalonia. In Spain the issue of the war could not be simple; too many historic forces were represented on each side. Hostility between the Anarchists and the Spanish Socialists, for example, was in one light a twentieth-century version of the old contest between the regions and the centralizing pressure of Castile, where the strength of Spanish Marxism lay. The same force of regionalism took the Basque provinces, the most fervently Catholic of Spain, into battle on the side of the Republic which guaranteed their *fueros*.

The cost of the war was appalling. Three-quarters of a million Spaniards were killed. Ruthless political purges followed the victory and hundreds of thousands went into exile. Reaction was in the saddle and turned on Protestants and freemasons as enthusiastically as on Marxists and Anarchists. Physical destruction was enormous, given the poverty of Spain, and makes it hard to disentangle the effects of the fighting from the social and economic backwardness which already existed in 1936.

29 Both Mola and Sanjurjo were shortly to die in aeroplane crashes.

At the time, Franco's association with Hitler and Mussolini in the anti-Comintern pact led many foreigners to label his régime Fascist. Republican propaganda made much of this theme and colour was given to it by the adherence to the nationalist cause of the *Falange*. But as early as 1937 Franco combined the *Falange* with the Carlist *Requetes*, in a new organization significantly named the *Falange Española Traditionalista* and little more was heard of the radical and sometimes anti-clerical demands of the Falangists, some of whose leaders were imprisoned. Franco's Spain was to prove in victory as well as in war a brutally authoritarian one, but this only attests that it was Spanish, and does not stamp it as Fascist. When Spain's isolation was artificially prolonged by the outbreak of the second world war, it appeared that Franco did not take his debts to Hitler and Mussolini very seriously after all, and certainly did not intend to subordinate Spanish national interests to ideological fraternity. A Spanish division was sent to Russia and this was the limit of Franco's implementation of the anti-Comintern pact. Meanwhile, in Spain, the old Falangists showed increasing irritation at the power of the two great traditional forces of the army and the Church. Anti-Communism and anti-anarchism were religious and nationalist, rather than Fascist in Spain. As in Portugal, the régime is best understood not in terms of Fascism, with its associations with the disturbed middle classes of Germany and Italy, but in terms of traditional authoritarianism. Both were backward countries superficially constitutionalized in the nineteenth century, and in both conservatism was based on the enduring local forces of Church, army and landholders.

THE FAILURE OF DEMOCRACY: ITALY

The establishment of Fascism in Italy was far less important than the victory of Communism in Russia. It had less potential strength behind it and was to prove far less efficient. Yet it looked impressive and led statesmen to continue to treat Italy as a great power. It also provided the only example of a member of the victorious coalition of constitutional states turning totalitarian and as the first Fascist state, it was an important example and influence. Finally, it left a mark on Italy's national history.

Italian Fascism had deep roots. Its extreme nationalism went back to the *Risorgimento*. The violent social struggles after unification in part explain the shallowness of constitutionalism and the strength of anti-parliamentarianism in Italy. The Great War precipitated a crisis in Italian politics and society which made these facts more important. Economically weaker than her allies, Italy had in comparison with them undergone a much greater financial and economic strain. War budgets had brought heavy taxation, but also heavy government borrowing; after the war, middle-class investors found that inflation had depreciated their government stock. Wages during the war did not lag far behind prices; the working class had a worse grievance in conscription, which fell too heavily on the peasants. The military record itself was disillusioning and helped to turn the masses against their leaders. This accentuated the divorce between patriotism and the left which had lain in the teachings of prewar Socialism. Patriotism, unhappily for Italy, became something to be distrusted by the majority of the population and even a sectional interest. This, in its turn, made nationalists anti-socialist; too many respectable middle-class patriots tolerated the ex-service roughnecks with nothing to do who gathered round d'Annunzio – or later Mussolini. Even the army's discipline was not safe, as the Fiume episode showed (see p. 341).

Such men could exploit the bitterness felt by Italians over the peace, especially when the principle of national self-determination was applied to Italy's disadvantage. A truculent popular revisionism could be exploited, and Nitti's underhand behaviour towards d'Annunzio, whom he abetted in secret, demonstrates the unwillingness of Italy's politicians to affront it. Their problems were made worse by the postwar economic slump. The highly inflated industrial demand of wartime fell off rapidly after 1918. Unemployment grew as demobilization took place. At the same time, inflation continued; prices rose more quickly than ever.[30] Strikes and industrial violence became common. As Italy imported much of her grain, the loss of confidence in the *lira* only

30 Prices (1938 = 100)   1914–21
1918–52
1919–65
1920–92
1921–93
1922–95

raised the cost of imports still more. For the man in work, a rise in the cost of living was tolerable, because a strong trade union movement ensured his wages some degree of protection, but for the out-of-work, the salaried, and the small *rentier*, the effects were very harsh.

The alarm and outraged feelings of middle-class people who saw nationalism derided at home and thwarted abroad, and whose standard of living was eaten into by inflation, explains much of the behaviour of Italian politicians when confronted with Fascist competition. Five governments came and went between the armistice and the Fascist *coup* of October 1922. None of them seemed able to stabilize the economy, or to banish the threat of revolution. The postwar wave of industrial disturbance was general throughout Europe, but in Italy it seemed especially bad. Lenin's prestige was great among the workers and there appeared within the Socialist party a Communist movement which weakened the influence of the moderates (and finally broke away completely in 1921). There was also disturbance in the country-side where, in some regions, peasants had seized waste, and even cultivated, lands in 1919. This produced an atmosphere of tension and fear; it also bred exasperation with politicians who seemed unable to maintain order and might be opening the door to revolution. Giolitti, who again became prime minister in June 1920, was one of the few to see further than this. When in August a sensation was caused by industrial workers occupying factories illegally, he remained calm, knowing that there was no danger in the situation so long as he remained firmly in control of the police and administration. Yet people believed he was not doing enough and did not feel more confident when the crisis evaporated (as Giolitti said it would) or even when, in the following February, his abolition of grain subsidies opened the way to the stabilization of prices.

There was some justice in criticism of Giolitti (though not for his handling of disorder). What was to happen in 1921 and 1922 was to show that he had misjudged not the danger of revolution, but the viability of the old political system. Essentially this had depended on the absence of parties representing big interests and principles, and on the continual adjustment in parliament of the competing claims of deputies lightly bound by party ties. The emergence of the Socialists had been a blow to this system and in 1920, the introduction of proportional representation gave them

156 deputies (they also controlled nearly a quarter of the municipal administrations). Largely in response to the challenge on the left, the papacy removed the last restraints on Roman Catholic politicians. A new, Catholic, *Partito Popolare*, ably led by a priest, Sturzo, who saw it as a genuine instrument of social reform, now appeared in the electoral lists. The old politicians were thus faced with popular contenders who stood for important principles and interests and were intransigent competitors. Both had the ear of the masses. The mistake of Giolitti and those who thought like him was to believe it possible to use another new force, Fascism, against them, while taming and controlling it by letting it participate in power. This was to treat Fascism as he had hoped to treat Socialism in 1904. The nature of Fascism, and the context in which it appeared, made this impossible.

The first organization of Fascism was a fighting body, the *Fascio di combattimento* founded by Mussolini in March 1919; the new political movement was to be a struggle for power by any means, but primarily by violence. By the end of 1920 there were about 300,000 Fascists, mainly in industrial Lombardy and in the countryside of the Romagna and Tuscany. Their brawls with socialists and attempts to intimidate them were already notorious. In early 1921 several people were killed in riots in Florence and Pisa in which Fascists and communists came into conflict, but Fascism fed on the growing atmosphere of violence. In the general election of May, they secured thirty-five seats, thanks to an electoral alliance with Giolitti, who had made available to them police protection and governmental influence. He had hoped they would support him, but they at once opposed him in the Chamber. Although the liberal *bloc* still had 275, and the socialists and communists 139 (they had lost some seats), the Fascists now had to be taken seriously by the politicians as an electoral and parliamentary force.[31] Some groups opened negotiations with Mussolini with an eye to future coalitions. The Fascist squads were already developing a systematic use of terror against socialist unions, cooperatives and municipal officers. At this stage, Giolitti stepped off the stage, as he had done in 1914, to leave others to discover they could not do without him.

31 The *Partito Popolare* had 108 seats. They would not, however, support the liberals because of their wish to maintain intact their agrarian and educational programmes. They later refused an alliance with the socialists.

Violence continued. At Modena in September the Fascists were in action against the security forces and five people were killed. But it was obvious that they often enjoyed official connivance when their activities were directed against the left. 1922 opened with the fall of Bonomi's government and its replacement by one under Facta which, like its predecessor, was unable to maintain public order. When a general strike took place in May, Fascists drove out the Communist administration in Bologna. In August they installed their own municipality at Milan. The crisis came on October 24, when Mussolini reviewed some 40,000 Fascists at Naples and challenged the government to solve the country's problems or to make way for the Fascists. Two days later, the Fascists announced that they were about to march on Rome 'to cut the Gordian knot and hand over to the King and Army a renewed Italy'.[32] Some members of the government wished the king to declare martial law, but Facta advised against this at first. When he came round to the idea, it was too late. The king refused to support him. After an attempt to form a right-wing government under a conservative, the king turned to Mussolini. His government contained representatives of the moderates and the *Partito Popolare*, and was sworn in on 31 October. Disorder and violence came to an end almost at once. The Chamber gave the new government wide powers and thus consummated the Fascist revolution.

Mussolini owed his final success to the king and the politicians. The king would not commit the army, the only force capable of imposing order in the deteriorated circumstances of 1922, when local administrations everywhere were terrorized by the Fascist militia. Some politicians were willing to use Fascism against the socialists (as Sturzo was at first) and others were hoping to tame them with a share of office. This was unimaginative, but it must be remembered that Fascism was new: nothing like it had yet been seen. In any case, the 'revolution' was the affair of a minority of Italians: the majority acquiesced because they wished to have the threat of social revolution removed and because it did not seem, at first, that a fundamental change was implied. Italian governments had always been responsible to the Chamber: even the concession of special powers was limited in time, and the presence of non-Fascists in the government was reassuring. It was clear that

32 See *AR*, p. 159.

Italy was to have vigorous, strong government; it was not yet clear that the constitutional state had been set aside.

The imposition of dictatorship was gradual. Although the *Partito Popolare* was ejected from the government in May 1923, Liberals remained members until the end of 1924. During this period the Fascists secured control of local administration and continued to bully and intimidate their opponents. A new electoral law provided that the leading party at the polls should automatically receive two-thirds of the seats in the Chamber. In April 1924 an election under these conditions gave the Fascists 374 seats and 64 per cent of the votes cast. Armed with this majority Mussolini could move faster. Press censorship and a ban on political meetings by opponents of the régime followed. In 1925 a fundamental law ended the constitution based on the *Statuto* and made the 'head of government' responsible only to the king. In 1928, the Fascist Grand Council was given the nomination of the head of government and was formally charged with the oversight of the constitution. This made the Party an official organ of state. Meanwhile, government by decree had been authorized (31 January 1926), provincial and municipal elections indefinitely postponed, and, finally, parliamentary elections were replaced by a choice of candidates from a single list by the Fascist Grand Council.

The lack of successful opposition seems extraordinary, but it was inherent in the conditions of Italian politics. Mussolini's opponents were divided, lacked widespread support embracing all classes, and were frightened. Terror did not play in Italy the part it played in Russia or Nazi Germany, but it was important. It had been a part of Fascism from the start at a local level. In 1923, the 'squads' were turned into a militia which gave the new régime its own armed force and made it independent of the army. In June 1924 violence was carried into parliament, when a socialist member, Matteotti, was murdered in circumstances which made it overwhelmingly likely that his murderers were Fascists. This temporarily galvanized the opposition: unfortunately, their action was to withdraw from parliament. This 'Aventine secession' (27 June 1924) was morally impressive, but politically disastrous. It gave the king an excuse to ignore pleas to act against Mussolini in that the Chamber gave him no lead. Meanwhile, opposition in the press was stifled by the violence of the Fascist militia and by new censorhip provisions. Anti-Fascists began to go into exile. Giolitti (who had not 'seceded' in 1924) took up an outright stance of opposition, but it was too late and he was too old. He died in 1928. By the end of that year, the only opposition left was a few senators, the philosopher Croce among them, whom Mussolini felt unable to touch.

To understand Fascism one must begin with Mussolini. A British foreign secretary thought him 'a patriot and sincere man'.[33] Fascism begins with his temperament and character, rather than with his principles. He needed to feel himself to be in action. 'I do not love the hesitant and conventional style', he once said, 'I affirm.'[34] His drive for self-expression, a manifestation of the degeneracy of European Romanticism, was the mainspring of Mussolini's politics. 'Everyone wants to realize himself, but only I have the power to do so.'[35] The politics which stemmed from this were strikingly negative. He was profoundly anti-bourgeois in youth (this was why he had turned to socialism) and remained so. The objects of his scorn and rejection might vary – at one time or another the Roman Catholic Church, capitalism, Great Britain and the Italian people were all objects of his violent praise or abuse – but he had consistent admiration for little but success. He was a *condottiere* of politics. He was also a political aesthete who strove to create a satisfying atmosphere about himself, rather than a statesman. As he was an accomplished demagogue with a journalist's responsiveness to his audience, Fascism never presented any real ideological coherence. It was always in large measure the projection on a public screen of the monstrous, semi-comic, gesticulating figure of Mussolini. Just this also kept it from the vileness of Nazism.

Fascist rule was important in Italian foreign policy, yet effected no substantial changes at home. This may be related to the lack of positive content in Fascism. When the movement began, Mussolini later asserted 'there was no specific doctrinal plan in my mind'. His earlier declarations, too, were stamped with a negative, critical character which clearly identify him as an expression of the anti-liberal tendencies of his age (he called attention to the common opposition of the Fascists and the Bolsheviks to 'liberals, democrats, and parliaments') and the main theoretical document

33 Austen Chamberlain; see Gilbert, p. 85.
34 See M. Oakeshott, *The Social and Political Doctrines of Contemporary Europe* (Cambridge, 1939), p. 168.
35 See Mack Smith, p. 447. Georges Sorel admired this side of Mussolini.

of the movement, an encyclopaedia article which appeared in 1932, is very vague. It spoke of 'the general reaction of modern times against the flatly materialistic positivism of the nineteenth century'. The Fascist, it said, disdained the 'comfortable' life; he was serious, austere, religious. At the same time, austere conviction had to operate within a tradition; 'outside history man is nothing', and the nation was the vehicle of the tradition which the Fascist protected. 'For the Fascist, everythng is in the State, and nothing human or spiritual exists, much less has value, outside the State,' 'Fascism . . . wants to remake, not the form of human life, but its content, man, character, faith.'[36] Unfortunately, a quasi-aesthetic rejection of utilitarian criteria in favour of 'holiness and heroism, that is . . . acts in which no economic motive – remote or immediate – plays a part' went ill with rational planning, however typical of a widely shared mood in early twentieth-century European culture. Only foreign policy was to bring together – disastrously – Fascist theory and practice.

Mussolini's rise had shown this subordination of political thought to impulse and emotion clearly enough. He abandoned extreme socialism to support the war because of his compulsive need to act and because the despised Giolitti was against it. Caporetto, a great shock, intensifed his hatred of the opponents of the war and his distrust of parliamentary government. After the armistice there were to be no further changes (though Mussolini expressed admiration for Lenin as a successful tactician) and time was to reveal that although he might be temperamentally well equipped for the seizure of power, he was not a man for constructive government. Fascism turned out to be a compromise of totalitarian aspiration with Italian social and economic reality, decked out in rhetorical flourishes.

As a totalitarian system Fascism was far less impressive than Bolshevism. This could be seen in its treatment of two of the traditional powers in Italian life, the monarchy and the Church. Although Mussolini was personally irritated by the king and unsympathetic to monarchy, he owed much to royal acquiescence in his assumption of power: the army, loyal to the king, could have stopped him. On his side, Victor Emmanuel disliked Mussolini as an individual and despised the antics of the Fascist hierarchy, but supported the régime so long as it seemed strong

36 See Oakeshott, p. 164.

enough to threaten the House of Savoy. In tolerating the Fascist seizure of power, the king had been influenced by the reactionary views of the queen mother and by worries about the ambitions of another member of the royal family to the throne. Only military defeat was to shatter this uneasy alliance of interests; both monarchy and Fascism had by then so long tolerated one another that one soon followed the other into oblivion.

The Church remained more independent of Fascism and dissociated itself from the régime just enough to escape any fatal compromise. Catholics had been sympathetic to Fascism as an anti-socialist force before it came to power; members of the hierarchy were glad to see the troublesome Sturzo silenced, and the secretary of the *Partito Popolare* driven to take refuge in the Vatican.[37] A general disposition to think well of an authoritarian régime which had replaced the constitutional state whose very foundation was rooted in the humiliation of the Papacy made many Italian Catholics, clerical and lay, ignore the gulf between Fascist ideas and their own. As Mussolini was anxious above all to settle the question which had bedevilled Italian politics since the *Risorgimento*, such conflicts as soon occurred (over, for instance, the rivalries of youth organizations) did not prevent the signing in 1929 of the Lateran treaties.

These agreements were the major event of Italy's domestic history under Fascism and they have survived the régime. They created a new idependent state, the Vatican city, provided the Papacy with a large endowment by way of indemnity for its losses, embodied a Concordat with the Italian state and acknowledged the end of the temporal power. In return for this last, empty concession, the Papacy received far more than it gave. The Concordat was a great stroke of prestige and embodied important concessions by the state, for instance in the surrender of civil marriage and the guarantee that the army would not be secularized. 'We have given back God to Italy and Italy to God', said the Pope, adding that 'perhaps the times called for a man such as he whom Providence has ordained we should meet.'[38]

To the régime, the Lateran Pacts were an important tactical gain. But they disappointed some Fascists and did not prevent

37 Alcide De Gasperi, later prime minister.
38 See A. C. Jemolo, *Church and State in Italy 1850–1950* (Oxford, 1960), p. 232.

later conflicts. Indeed, these soon began. The two main issues were education and the activities of Catholic Action, an organization founded in 1931. There was a flurry of polemics during which the pope asserted that the Church could not admit the state's exclusive claim to the direction of youth. This blew over because Mussolini was alarmed by the resignation of several members of the party, and until the end of the 1930s, conservatives and Roman Catholics abroad looked with pleasure on a régime which appeared to show that two authoritarian systems could cooperate peacefully for the protection of the social and the moral order. The suspicions on both sides were usually concealed, though Mussolini grumbled to a German emissary in 1936 that 'the Catholic Church is like a rubber ball; pressure must be constantly exercised in order to maintain the results of pressure, otherwise the ball resumes its original shape'.[39]

If its compromises with traditional forces is one illustration of Fascism's weakness as a totalitarian system so is its grasp of the economy. Italy was specially dependent on external conditions. She needed emigration outlets to reduce unemployment at home and to provide foreign currency in the form of remittances to the families of emigrants. She needed to buy grain abroad but had few exports except agricultural produce to sell in return. In responding to these circumstances, Fascist economic policy down to 1925 was orthodox and traditional. Mussolini strove to preserve the value of the *lira* by deflationary measures. This was followed by a period of much more decisive interventionism. One of its most publicized aspects was the experiment of 'corporatism', which grew out of limitations laid on trade unions in the early years of the régime. The Fascists ran their own trade union movement, and in 1925 the back of the socialist unions was broken when the Fascist unions were declared to be the only ones recognized as the legitimate representatives of labour in industry. In 1926 the 'Rocco law' on corporations set up six workers' organizations, six employers', and one for intellectual and professional men. Over them was placed a minister of corporations, at first Mussolini himself. Through this machinery the state was to negotiate collective contracts between employers and employees which would remove the need for strikes and lockouts, now officially prohibited. In the face of this competition, the Catholics dissolved their

39 *Ciano's Diplomatic Papers* (London, 1948), p. 48.

unions and the socialists in effect disbanded theirs by moving their executive abroad.

This structure was not simply a means of exploiting the working class. This may have been one major effect: it was not the whole intention. A 1927 Labour Charter subordinated the individual interest of the capitalist to those of the state. Further changes followed which, on paper at least, appeared to extend the corporative structure beyond the purely economic sphere to become a new form of political and social control. This, indeed, seems in retrospect to have been the main significance of the corporative experiment. It was a way of giving the party power over more and more of the nation's life. As an economic measure, its results were insignificant, although one institution, the *Istituto per la Ricostruzione Industriale* (I.R.I.), founded in 1933, was to play an important part in Italian recovery after the fall of Fascism.

In the 1930s Fascist economic policy had to grapple with the double strain imposed by the world economic collapse and the Abyssinian war. By 1939, Mussolini's drive for autarchy had improved agricultural production, notably of grain, so that Italy was able to feed herself, but her balance of payments remained obstinately in deficit. Some land improvement and reclamation schemes were launched and the number of peasant landholders increased. But agricultural policy was the only area of important success. The Abyssinian war showed how fragile the economy really was and led to the devaluation of the *lira*. Nevertheless, although no conspicuous economic improvement came to the Italian under Fascism, it cannot be said that his life changed for the worse in material terms.

The moral factor is more difficult to evaluate. Terror had been a weapon of Fascism from the start. The murder of Mateotti was only a conspicuous instance. The members of the Fascist Youth organization, the *Ballila*, were encouraged to spy upon their families for anti-Fascist sentiment or opinion and, apart from the Church, few independent organizations were left outside the corporative structure to provide a forum for even discreet protest. Fascism, too, had its secret political police, the O.V.R.A. Yet, when all is said and done, it is difficult to see terror as Fascism's mainspring in Italy. The régime was never able to command unquestioning obedience by fear. An instance of this was the response to the anti-Jewish racial laws of 1938. These were evaded with great ease – and with popular and official connivance – until military defeat brought German occupation.

Such a failure seems to show that Fascism did not have wide-spread support. This could be an exaggeration. Except for the liberal bourgeoisie, of whom there were relatively few, Fascism did not provoke much more than individual opposition until the economic crisis brought on by the Abyssinian war. No savage terror was needed. Even after defeat, it took action by the crown and the Fascist Grand Council itself to bring about the end of the régime. The political regeneration of Italian constitutionalism only began after Mussolini's fall, with the resistance to the Germans.

THE FAILURE OF DEMOCRACY: GERMANY

United Germany's experience of democracy began on 9 November 1918, just before the armistice. On that day the majority Socialists under Ebert took over the government in Berlin and were soon joined by the independent socialists from whom they had been divided during the war. The new republic began, therefore, in the hands of politicians believed by many Germans to be anti-national and unpatriotic. It was born of defeat, mutiny and revolution, and almost its first act was the acceptance of a humiliating armistice. That the old imperial régime and the High Command were actually responsible for this went almost unnoticed; the leadership of the traditional right had for the moment disappeared from view. The socialists assumed the task not of carrying out a revolution but of bringing the ship of state safely to port when the officers had deserted.

Almost at once, a split appeared inside the new régime. The S.P.D. wanted to move forward by means of a constituent assembly to a liberal, democratic republic. This would reassure the Allies (and perhaps persuade them to relax the blockade), and would unite a wide range of liberals and socialists in support of an orthodox democratic demand. By the end of November this view had prevailed; the representatives of the different states agreed to summon a constituent assembly. This was opposed by other socialists and by some of the shop stewards and workers' leaders who had achieved the revolutionizing of many towns in early November by setting up workers' and soldiers' councils. Fearing there would be no place for them if a constituent assembly were elected, they sought to cash in on enthusiasm for the Bolshevik Revolution and push ahead with a real social revolution. A minority of 'Spartacists' refused to participate in the elections at all and turned themselves into the German Communist Party (K.P.D.) at the end of December. The first episode in the history of the Republic was, therefore, a struggle between two groups on the Left to decide what direction it should take. Already in December a clash between left-wing radicals and soldiers had led to the resignation of half the coalition government. In January 1919 a minor civil war began. Spartacist demonstrations led to an attack on their strongholds in Berlin by the regular army and the *Freikorps*, a right-wing volunteer force of ex-soldiers. These men murdered Rosa Luxemburg and Liebknecht, the Spartacist leaders, and crushed the left in Berlin. More fighting took place in the next two months in other parts of Germany and the climax of this abortive 'revolution' came when a Soviet Republic was set up in Bavaria in April; a division which was to prove permanent had been made in the German working class.

The victory of the armed forces of the state over the revolution saved the new Republic. Elections in January had given no decisive majority to one party, but a coalition of socialists, Catholic centrists and democrats formed a government which accepted the peace terms. In July the blockade was brought to an end, the Weimar constitution was inaugurated in August,[40] and a new phase of the new Republic's history began. It had grave weaknesses. The large minority vote against accepting the peace terms (138 to 237) showed the strength of the irreconcilables on the Right. On the left, another irreconcilable movement, the K.P.D., looking to the Comintern for direction, had emerged from the civil war and had drawn to itself many Independent Social Democrats; when, in 1922, the independents agreed to merge with the majority socialists of the S.P.D., more of their rank-and-file joined the K.P.D. The S.P.D. meanwhile had been thrown back into dependence on the army, a profoundly conservative and undemocratic force, because of the threat presented by revolution at the end of 1918. A repetition of the Russian Revolution in Germany, Ebert knew, would mean prompt Allied invasion and the break-up of Germany as separatism fed on fears of Bolshe-

40 It was drawn up at Weimar, where the constituent assembly met.

vism. Inevitably he leant on the army, greeting soldiers returning to Berlin with the significant words 'I salute you, who return *unvanquished* . . .'[41] Weimar democracy, therefore, had weak roots. It had to build on the traditional discipline of the S.P.D. voters and the eroded traditions of German liberalism. From the right, its parliamentarianism looked like an affront to the nation, from the left, like a mask for social conservatism.

As a democratic republic, sustained by universal adult suffrage and safeguarded by a supreme court and guarantees of fundamental rights, it had a very liberal constitution. Unfortunately, institutional changes had not led to a change of personnel. The imperial régime bequeathed to its successor its civil servants and its judges. The first proved fairly loyal, but the second were to show by their tolerance of political crime that they were sympathetic to the enemies of the new state. Above all, the army remained wedded in sympathy to the past and aspired to a restoration of a strongly nationalist Germany. Its numbers were restricted by Versailles, but it was a force of unrivalled quality. It could insist on high educational qualifications for its officers and N.C.O.s, and also on their moral and political suitability. By 1921 a higher percentage of the officer corps came of aristocratic lineage than in 1913. To prepare this force it was necessary to evade the terms of Versailles: thus duplicity, even towards the political leaders of the Republic, became a patriotic virtue for the soldier who was encouraged in his belief that he somehow owed allegiance to a State above and beyond the here-and-now arrangements of particular constitutions. The General Staff continued in disguise; private industry carried out military research; factories were built in Russia beyond the reach of Allied inspectors, and 'police' units carried out basic training. The cadres were prepared for a future army: at one time there were 40,000 N.C.O.s in a rank-and-file of only 96,000.

These social and institutional weaknesses in the foundation of the Republic were made more dangerous by its shallow roots in popular culture and ideology. The dominant themes of German political mythology in the 1920s were not democracy, tolerance and peacefulness, but nationalism, antisemitism and intransigent violence. These had roots which went back to Imperial Germany. Now they thrived on new postwar tendencies which achieved a

41 See G. A. F. Scheele, *The Weimar Republic* (London, 1946), p. 81.

special intensity in Germany (see also p. 491). A general cultural irrationalism, manifesting itself in attacks on what was alleged to be the 'cold', 'stiff', 'dead' rationalism of liberal civilization, led to the spread of ideas like those of a 'life philosophy' which stressed the 'living', 'organic', 'vital' values of acts of pure will or emotion. Ernst Jünger's enjoyment of what he termed high treason against the intellect epitomized this atmosphere. Socially, it favoured an anti-individualism which was expressed in the search for the *völkisch* community, the comforting reassurance of the wordless communion of the herd. Harmless enough when expressed in youth movements and folk-dancing, it was dangerous when it fed beliefs that parliamentary democracy was a foreign importation, and that Germany needed native political forms drawn from its own tradition and history. When such criticisms were voiced by thinkers of great prestige, such as Spengler, the Republic became emotionally unacceptable to many Germans.

Other states, though, have survived this kind of criticism. It was more vicious in Germany because of the character of German nationalism. The old, conservative nationalism which dreamed of a restoration of the Bismarckian era, was represented by Hugenberg's *Deutschnationale Volkspartei*. But the irrationalism of Weimar culture fed a new sort of nationalism which looked back to the heroic days of the 'war experience' and forward to the achievement of a mass, total democracy which would sweep away parties and embody the unity of the *Volk*. Such ideas boiled down into policy recommendations only in the most vague and general way. Antisemitism was the commonest manifestation; it was not new in Germany, but drew now on the association of Jews with monopoly capitalism during the postwar depression. Another nationalist symptom was the legend, quickly established, that Germany, like Wagner's Siegfried, had not been defeated but stabbed in the back. The consequence was inescapable: Versailles was not only brutal and unjust, it was the fruit of treason; it had to be overthrown. Such propaganda was doing Hitler's work for him, long before he became a serious contender for power.

The instability of Weimar was also fostered by the anxiety of the German middle classes. After social advance and increasing prosperity down to 1914, the postwar inflation swept away middle-class savings and raised the spectre of 'proletarianization'. White-collar workers and professional men observed bitterly that in Weimar it was big business which benefited from the devalu-

ation of the *mark* and shared the direction of affairs with the
leaders of Social Democracy. At the same time, the old-fashioned
parties of the right did not appeal to middle-class voters. They
looked to the new authoritarians who might produce a heroic
leader to save Germany from Bolshevism and Big Business.

In these circumstances, the violence of German politics was
particularly dangerous but also explicable. In March 1920, Kapp,
a former civil servant, attempted to set up a rival government in
Berlin. The Kapp *Putsch* seemed for a few days successful: the
government left Berlin. But the movement collapsed after a
general strike in Berlin which had demonstrated the loyalty of the
S.P.D. rank-and-file to the Republic. Its most sinister feature had
been the unreliability of the army, which had told the government
that soldiers could not be expected to fire on their own comrades
who took part in the *Putsch*. Afterwards, these participants were
not severely punished, and the indiscipline of the soldiers was not
checked. It was the civilian minister of defence who resigned, not
the commanders of the army. In the same month, a communist
rising took place in the Ruhr. Another catastrophically unsuccessful communist revolt was attempted the following March.
Meanwhile, political intimidation and assassination grew more
common. In 1921 Erzberger, the proposer of the 1917 peace
resolution, and in 1922, Rathenau, the organizer of German
industry during the war, were murdered by nationalists. Nine-
teen-twenty-three saw the height of the crisis of violence. There
were abortive communist attempts to overthrow the state governments (in which communists had a place) in Saxony and
Thuringia. In Hamburg, too, a communist rising failed. The
climax of this disturbed period was a *Putsch* in Munich mounted
by a German National Socialist Workers' Party which involved
Ludendorff in its attempt. Its failure ended a dangerous period
during which the Bavarian state government had itself plotted to
take over power from Berlin. The government survived the crisis
by using the emergency powers conferred on the president by the
constitution and with the mastering of inflation the stormy foundation era of the Republic came to an end.

The parties in the coalition which sustained the Republic were
ill-fitted to deal with such dangers. The centre, although its
ministers participated in every government from 1919 to 1932,
seemed to drift slowly into a more and more authoritarian posture
and a more and more rigid ideology. The democrats lost their

support in the depression of the early 1920s and never regained it. The new People's Party, led by Stresemann (who died in 1929), was an anomaly of non-republican principle and parliamentary practice. Only the social democrats provided a solid basis for the republic. Even in March 1933 the S.P.D. could still poll 7 million votes. But its leadership was conservative and unimaginative, fatally handicapped by the mythology of a 'Marxist' and 'revolutionary' party, enjoying an 'inevitable' success. The movement had become an end in itself which justified passivity and the avoidance of risks. It must also be said that it is to the credit of the S.P.D. that its leaders' humanitarianism and respect for reason also handicapped it in a nation so many of whose members looked to irrationalism and emotion for evidence of political leadership.

This shaky *bloc* of parliamentarian parties had to compete with far more dynamic forces. The K.P.D. was by 1925 thoroughly purged and subservient to Russian direction. Soon uncompromisingly Stalinist it would devote more energy to attacking the social democrats – stigmatized as 'Social Fascists' – than to resisting the threat from the right. This explains the replacement in 1925 of the socialist Ebert by Hindenburg in the presidency. In the first round, a right-wing candidate polled 10.5 million votes and the socialist centre and communist candidates together about 14 million. The Republicans then selected a joint candidate to run against Hindenburg, the new right-wing candidate, but the communists still chose to run one of their own. He received nearly 2 million votes, and Hindenburg beat his republican opponent by less than 1 million. Thus began the presidency under which the Nazis came to power.

The attractiveness of a war hero, nationalist candidate was shown by Hindenburg's 13.6 million votes. This followed nationalist entry to the government for the first time in 1925. Much of the enthusiasm for the nationalists rested on the assiduously cultivated legends of the Great War. Great efforts were made to deny Germany's 'war guilt'. In a measure, these had a practical aim: many Germans saw it as the premise of the reparations clauses of Versailles and thought that its expunging would lead to the destruction of the machinery of reparations itself. But there was also a hysterical, inward-looking preoccupation which kept the issue alive. When, in September 1927, the new president repudiated Germany's responsibility for the war, he was not only arguing a brief, he was responding to a deep emotional need of

Europe 1880–1945

many Germans. Extremes met on the common ground of nationalism. The Kapp movement had hoped to draw support from left and right and even in 1930, the K.P.D. programme talked of Russia helping a 'disarmed and isolated' Germany back to her 'national liberties', via the abrogation of Versailles and the Young Plan.

Yet there were signs in the later 1920s that Weimar might, after all, be emerging into a healthier era. In May 1928 the socialists did well in the elections and in the following year, in a referendum on the Young Plan, the nationalists were heavily defeated. But optimism was wiped out by the second great economic collapse. In March 1930, when Brüning took office, the worst was about to come. In the September elections, a party which had only recently become important, the Nazi party, won 107 seats. The communists had 77, so that the extremists now held a substantial segment of power in the *Reichstag*. By the end of 1931, governments having persisted in attempts to deflate by compulsory wage and price cuts, in order to avoid another inflation, Germany had 6 million unemployed and was looking for a new saviour.

She was to find him in Hitler. Personally, his appeal is incomprehensible. In 1914 he was only a half-educated lounger with aesthetic aspirations which outran his talent (he wanted to be a painter) and a heart stuffed full of lower middle-class resentment of the Slavs, Jews and labourers among whom he had lived in poverty in Vienna. The war offered him, as it offered so many, a release from frustration and a simplifying challenge. He was a good N.C.O., was gassed, and decorated. Defeat settled the pattern of his life; it was to be dedicated to undoing the verdict of 1918. Passionately interested in politics, he was employed by the army as a political agent and in 1919 was ordered to investigate a small 'German Workers' Party'. When he joined it, it was about fifty strong, containing a fair number of former *Freikorps* men, and did nothing much except hold meetings at which antisemitic speeches were made. Hitler quickly moved to the front of its meetings, drew up a programme for it in 1920, and became leader of the National Socialist German Workers' Party in the following year. In 1922 it numbered 6,000. Backers were found to buy a newspaper. Two other institutions of great significance for the future also made their appearance: special groups of thugs were set up to prevent interruption of Nazi meetings which were to grow into the 'stormtroops' of S.A., and a personal bodyguard was given to Hitler which was to evolve into the S.S.[42]

In spite of a modest initial success, Hitler's next step seemed to show it would be shortlived. When in 1923 inflation and the Ruhr occupation stirred up all the nationalists, he and his colleagues sought the help of the Bavarian state government to mount a march on Berlin (they had Mussolini's *coup* of the previous year in mind). The result was the bungled *Putsch* of 9 November. Hitler was imprisoned, the party proscribed and its newspaper closed down. But the failure was important for the future: it persuaded Hitler to adopt the machinery of elections as the way to power.

In fact, the Republic was about to enter a phase of stabilization and economic boom. Until 1929, Hitler could do little except hold the party together and wait. It emerged to win fourteen *Reichstag* seats in 1924 but lay thereafter in the doldrums, troubled by internal divisions. Hitler spent some of his time writing *Mein Kampf*, the political bible of the Nazi movement. Displaying neither ordered exposition nor clear analysis, it is a rambling mixture of diatribe and autobiography whose central messages establish themselves by repetition: a strident nationalism, looking to the overthrow of Versailles and the replacement of the republican régime which depended from it by one more conscious of Germany's racial needs – above all, for living-space in the east – and a virulent antisemitism. Nevertheless, the very simplicity and hysteria of this message give it its success. Preached from the rostrum by Hitler, an increasingly successful mass orator, it awoke a response in many Germans. Moreover, Nazism had extra-political dimensions which made it appealing. It was, its leaders often pointed out, a 'movement' not a 'party' like other political parties. Indeed, it implied the abolition of other parties – a suggestion which awoke response in a country where the idea of the state as a moral entity whose claims overrode those of factions had always been strong.

It was only the onset of the 1929 economic crisis that gave Nazism its opportunity. Communists and Nazis alike gained votes in 1930. This happened at a crucial juncture of Weimar parliamentarianism. As the economic crisis deepened, the S.P.D. set its face against reductions of welfare benefits. On this issue it

42 On Hitler's basic notions, see E. Jäckel, *Hitler's Weltanschauung. A blueprint for power* (Connecticut, 1972).

finally left the coalition which had sustained governments since 1919. The withdrawal was unwise. The Social Democrats had no fresh policy to offer the electorate but simply relied on riding out the storm until capitalism recovered. Meanwhile, they had abandoned their effective positions of power to rely on parliamentary opposition.

On 30 March, the leader of the centre party, Brüning, was installed as Reich chancellor by the president. He had no *Reichstag* majority and was the first of the chancellors who depended on the president's confidence and ruled by special decree. Brüning hoped that a final settlement of the reparations question would be the foreign policy success needed to steal the nationalists' thunder. The preliminary, he thought, had to be financial stability and therefore deflation and the protection of the *mark* from another collapse.

Unfortunately, the economic crisis deepened. The Nazis and the Communists both thrived on unemployment. The S.A. was 100,000 strong by 1931. The Communists, loyal to their orders from Moscow, hailed the rise of Nazi strength as evidence that Germany was moving quickly towards the revolution which must follow Fascism, the last kick of capitalism. Traditional nationalists began to court the Nazis as a way to winning mass support for themselves. When Brüning called a general election in September, the Nazis had 6 million votes and won 107 seats. Their appeal was strong in rural areas, and they were now the second largest party in the country, having left their Nationalist rivals far behind. The Communists also gained. Clearly, it was not Brüning who was benefiting from his economic policies.

The banning of the S.A. now followed, but events continued to run against Brüning; the Austrian Customs Union scheme collapsed. By 1932 unemployment had risen to over 5 million. There are signs that Brüning now began to consider new economic policies, but he was overtaken by events. In March a presidential election confirmed Hindenburg in his office (he had 19.3 million votes, outstripping Hitler and the Communist candidate combined). Strengthened by this vote, Hindenburg now forced Brüning to resign. A combination of landlords, soldiers and industrialists were behind this and the government now installed under von Papen (31 May). It was a turning-point. Germany's rulers were now men who wanted to work with the Nazis and so to tame them.

This government hoped to use the Nazis and lifted the ban on the S.A. It went on to do more of Hitler's work for him. One of the centres of administrative power still left in hands loyal to Weimar was the government of Prussia (which made up about half of post-Versailles Germany). Here, on 20 July, von Papen carried out a *coup d'état*, removing from office the Social Democrats who had been the government since 1921. The pretext was the failure of the Prussian government to maintain order; a state of siege was proclaimed. This was the great test of the S.P.D., and the socialists failed. Backed by the 'Iron Front' of socialist organizations and the para-military *Reichsbanner*, and still in control of the Prussian police, they could have tried to resist. But they did nothing, preferring to wait for the elections at the end of July. It was perhaps too much to ask that the Social Democrats should, overnight, live up to their own revolutionary pretensions, and their resistance would undoubtedly have been crushed by the army, but it was an ironic conclusion to the story of the party Bismarck had feared.

In July, the Nazis became the biggest party in the *Reichstag*, with 230 seats (nearly 14 million votes were cast for them). The Communists had 89, the S.P.D. 133, and the Centre 97. The communists applauded the Prussian *coup* but were not going to support von Papen's government. nor were the Nazis; in August Hitler refused to enter a coalition. The manoeuvres of the winter which followed are obscure but led, at the beginning of December, to the appointment of General von Schleicher as chancellor. He hoped to conciliate the Centre and S.P.D., while winning over the Nazi left wing under Gregor Strasser. This was made impossible when Hitler ejected Strasser from the party. Schleicher now contemplated a military dictatorship to break the Nazis, but was refused Hindenburg's support. The 'wooden Titan' had decided he had to accept Hitler as chancellor. Elections in November had reduced Nazi seats to 196 and had increased the Communist total to 100. It may be that Hindenburg thought the tide had turned against Hitler. Certainly he was reassured by the knowledge that other right-wing groups would be represented in the cabinet, and on 30 January 1933, Hitler became chancellor, called to office legally and constitutionally by the elected head of the Republic. There could hardly be resistance and there was none. The new chancellor asked for a dissolution for new elections and this was granted.

Perhaps overlooking the declaration of the Nazi newspaper, the *Völkischer Beobachter*, that the forthcoming elections would be Germany's last, the nationalists in the cabinet acquiesced in the dissolution. The Nazis could now deploy their propaganda with police and radio on their side. Helped by emergency decrees to which Hindenburg's consent gave legality, they began to terrorize their opponents. A few days before polling, a mysterious fire destroyed the *Reichstag*: it was blamed on the communists and was used as an excuse for a decree abrogating constitutional guarantees of freedom of expression and property. On 5 March, the electoral returns came in. With 17 million votes the Nazis had 288 seats. This was only 43.9 per cent of the electorate. But the nationalists had 8 per cent of the votes, so that a majority of those voting plumped for the governing coalition. This made Hitler the first chancellor with a parliamentary majority for three years. It introduced an Enabling Act conferring sweeping powers on the cabinet, in effect suspending the constitution. The Centre party's votes produced the two-thirds majority such a measure legally required. Only the Social Democrats showed themselves at their best by defying the threats hurled at them to speak and vote against it. It passed (23 March) and the revolution could now proceed, every step having been authenticated by the appropriate legal mechanism. A few days later, the German Roman Catholic bishops put their moral weight behind the government by withdrawing their previous warnings about Nazism. A concordat followed in July.

Hitler had successfully gulled all those whose cooperation he had needed with understandings which now vanished. Firmly in control of the police, with the S.A. and S.S. acting under official sanction, he could eliminate the opposition at leisure. The Communist party had already been banned and its eighty-one deputies imprisoned. Now the Nationalists were squeezed out of the government and the Centre forced to dissolve. The Social Democrats were banned. In July, the Nazi party was declared the only tolerated political party and in December, a law established the unity of Party and State. Like the Italian Fascists before them, the Nazis were at once able, through a sophisticated machinery of state, to take a firm grip of society. A propaganda ministry was one of the earliest creations of the régime. Strikes were forbidden in May 1933 and the trade unions were dissolved; in the following year, a Nazi Labour Front was set up.

But behind the legal and formal changes lay the reality of an unrestrained use of physical force to consolidate the position of the Party. Although thousands of arrests were carried out in 1933 and the new 'concentration camps' first made their appearance, and though there were hundreds of political murders, the full brutality of Nazism only appeared in 1934 in a great purge. (30 June–1 July) of the Party itself.

The S.A. contained a core of potential opposition to Hitler; it had always supplied the violence, but also much of the dynamism and twisted idealism of the movement. Its leader was Röhm, an intimate friend of Hitler, who sought to have the S.A. taken into the army *en bloc* – thus transforming the *Reichswehr* into the Praetorian Guard. As the *Reichswehr* alone in Germany had the power to stop Hitler if it wished, he was bound to take notice of its dislike of Röhm and his ideas. The generals began during 1934 to hint that Hitler should control his S.A. friends who were talking of the need for a 'second revolution'. The purge was the result. The leadership of the S.A., including Röhm, was eliminated. So were many others who could conveniently be got rid of. Gregor Strasser was murdered, along with von Schleicher and scores of other victims of revenge, personal vendetta and pure accident. The purge stabilized the dictatorship and guaranteed the future of the S.S. (which provided the gunmen). Hitler received a congratulatory telegram from Hindenburg. Much more important, when the old man died, the *Reichswehr* transferred its loyalty to the new regime by taking a personal oath of loyalty to Hitler, now both President and Chancellor. Most Germans approved. In a plebiscite on the merger of the two offices, 38.3 million voted for Hitler; just over 5 million were brave enough to vote 'no', or cast invalid ballots.

It was not clear at first what use the Nazis wished to make of their power. Their success had been based on the failure of Weimar to generate the interests needed to entrench it, on an appeal to youngsters tired of older and more reputable parties, and on the mistakes of their opponents. Their own contribution has been technical – superb propaganda was its heart – and nihilistic; they and their supporters had always known much more clearly what they did not want than what they did. It is revealing that the Nazis never had a constitution: Germany was ruled for twelve years under the emergency decrees of 1933. The purge suggested that what revolutionary impetus there had been in the movement was now gone. There was something to this, in that Strasser and his friends had urged radical social and economic changes, but the nature of Nazism as a revolutionary movement is more complicated than this suggests.

It had contained, for example, some left-wing elements. The first (1920) programme of the party had set out an appeal to the peasants, farmers and anti-capitalist lower middle classes and artisans. It demanded the abolition of unearned incomes, a share for the state of the profits of large industrial concerns, and the control of the large shops which seemed to threaten the small man. The anti-capitalist note continued to be sounded in Nazi propaganda and, as one Nazi leader was later to declare, 'at no time did the party cease to consider industry a political and foreign body'.[43] Moreover, the ranks of the party hierarchy were conspicuously filled with persons who enjoyed no, or very inferior, status outside it. It offered power and success to men who could get it in no other way and were therefore ostentatiously contemptuous of the *ancien régime* which was forced to accept them after 1933.

On the other hand, this bias found little expression in policy. Gregor Strasser, the main publicist of left-wing Nazism, was murdered in the 1934 purge. A law on homesteads which was supposed to give the peasant security in fact gave him something like the old status of villeinage. Industrial capitalism was little interfered with although profits and wages were controlled more and more brusquely down to 1939 to drive up output and employment. This meant no effective rise in real wages after 1936. The high degree of centralization of industrial management was inherited by the Nazis and maintained by them. Nor were there important innovations in the methods of directing the economy, except in the brutality of the police measures employed. The much-advertised public works programme had been initiated before the Nazis took power and the power of financial orthodoxy was such that Dr Schacht insisted on balanced budgets right down to 1938. Throwing open the membership of bowling-clubs was a mere sop to class envy.

It is a mistake, then, to think of the Nazi revolution as the embodiment of a clear class interest, whether that of exploiters or exploited. Nazism was not greatly interested in questions of

43 Funk, see Pounds, *Ruhr*, p. 249.

economic privilege except as tactical devices. Nazi society was focussed in the possession of political power, not in the possession of economic goods or the exercise of economic function. The Labour Front organization showed this. It was only a piece of window-dressing to replace the 'coordinated' trade unions and to demonstrate by its inclusion of employers that the class war was over. It did nothing. When indiscipline began to lead to decline in productivity just before the war, outright police measures were used to coerce the working force. A 'service decree' of February 1939 provided for conscription of labour to meet certain essential needs, and in the following September, a war economy decree imposed in principle a complete direction of labour. Such arrangements, enforced by the secret police, were tempered by special workers' holiday schemes, public housing and the programme for a *Volkswagen*.

It was in a deeper sense than the economic or social that Nazism was revolutionary. Its deliberate irrationalism was one sign. Its rejection of liberal culture was embodied in the ritual book-burnings of the works of 'decadent' authors and the pseudo-romantic sentimentalities of the Hitler Youth. The Boy Scouts were banned (as they were in Russia and Italy). In the more lunatic recesses of the Party, this irrationalism was consciously fostered by grubbing among the folklore and mythology of the Germanic past for symbols, allegories and evocative legends. The S.S., for example, were solemnly instructed that the origin of the Nazi salute was to be sought in the resistance of a primitive Germanic tribe to Christian baptism at the hands of Charlemagne. When immersed in a river for the ceremony, it was said, many of the barbarians raised their sword-arm so that it should escape baptism and thus preserve its heathen power.

Such rubbish was taken seriously by many Nazis and there were other examples far more vicious. So conscious a rejection of the civilized past was bound to have revolutionary implications for traditional and conservative institutions. Nazism being irrational and incoherent, this was not always a simple matter. To the family, for example, Nazism had an ambiguous attitude. On the one hand it conducted propaganda to promote its solidarity and to encourage the production of children. On the other, it enlisted more women in the labour force and struck at the traditional authority of parents by encouraging illegitimate births and eugenic experiments with state support.

The major traditional institutions proved quite unable to resist once the Nazis felt secure. The symbol of the break with the past came with the abolition of the historic subdivisions of Germany in 1933. With this, the foci of local loyalties in the administration were practically destroyed. The churches, too, were treated high-handedly. Many Protestant pastors were taken off to imprisonment and, later, to execution for their temerity in protesting against the acts of the régime, but the Lutheran church had an erastian tradition and could not provide an organizational focus for opposition. The Roman Catholic church agreed upon a Concordat in 1933, but was later to see some of its clergy persecuted and its educational and youth work thwarted. Little notice was taken of papal protests. Neither Protestant nor Catholic denominations, however, lost much ground among believers to the extreme racialist sects associated with the Nazis.

There was only one major traditional force which Hitler feared. This was the army, which alone had the power, if it wished, to crush the S.A. and S.S. The attitude of the *Reichswehr* to the new régime was predetermined in two ways. It saw itself as the custodian of the interests of a state which transcended particular governments and constitutions (and saw its oath of loyalty as a symbol of this) and it kept constantly in mind the need to destroy the Polish state which had emerged from 1918. At first, it was inclined to patronize the Nazis because it did not fear them and saw them as instruments to be used in the interests of Germany. The soldiers were pleased when Hitler bid from the start for their support with a promise of 'everything for the armed forces'.[44] In 1934, its misgivings over the S.A. were removed by the purge. Later, the calling to order of the Austrian Nazis also pleased it. On the other hand, the army also found it was being pushed into policies it did not like. Accelerated rearmament was one, the remilitarization of the Rhineland another. As Hitler's successes grew his prestige and popularity were enhanced and it became progressively more difficult to resist him. Moreover, younger officers looked to the rising sun and sought professional advancement through political reliability. In 1937 the crisis took place, when the generals Blomberg and Fritsch were ousted. Afterwards resistance to Hitler by the army was minimal and was always

44 See E. M. Robertson, *Hitler's Pre-war Policy and Military Plans 1933–9* (London, 1963), p. 9.

qualified morally by the fact that generals who had misgivings about Hitler (as did some at the time of Munich) had them because they feared he would be unsuccessful, not because they disagreed with his aims, and never had them strongly enough to contemplate independent action on their own part.

Nazism thus tamed the traditional and conservative forces in German life as Fascism was never able to do in Italian. Only in 1944 were some soldiers and a few relics of the Centre party to act against Hitler. Nazism was not, as wartime propaganda often asserted, the same thing as old-fashioned Prussian militarism, bedfellows though they might be. What the Nazis did was to break the Prussian hegemony which had been stabilized by Bismarck and had survived into Weimar through the army. This was a genuine revolutionary achievement. It reversed the verdicts of 1848 and 1866: *Grossdeutschland* became a reality under Hitler and no doubt many Germans liked that. Hitler won his mass support by being a democratic politician; he then used his mass support to castrate the forces which had resisted democracy and might now resist dictatorship.

The most radical and revolutionary break with the past was Nazism's racial policy. Its eventual extension is an extraordinary phenomenon and the most terrible story in modern history. The Nazi contribution to this was one of power and technique. Always, in Germany, a certain vision of the *Volk* had implied the inferiority of those who were not of it. Hitler turned the ideology of a minority into a movement of racial persecution – predominantly, but not solely, of Jews – which was accepted, at least passively, by the whole nation. His own convictions were sincere, as, indeed, were those of many of his *entourage*; their appeal to many Germans in the 1920s, on the other hand, was one of class jealousy and envy among the middle classes. After the installation of the Nazis in power, antisemitism appeared more clearly than ever as a substitute for class war. The Nuremberg laws of 1935 were the first great announcement that the new régime looked beyond the traditional programme. A decree of December 1938 went much further. Before the war it was already known to the British government that Hitler intended to pursue policies of racial extermination in Poland. The war removed the brake on genocide (see p. 565).

Much has been said since the war about the responsibility for these abominations. The debate is tangled: it is at any rate clear that millions of Germans sensed something of what was going on. It is also clear that some of these were terrorized into silence and acquiescence by fears of what might happen to them. For Germany, though somewhat inefficiently, became very rapidly a state based on terror, depending ultimately on the S.S., which became an élite army within the army, and the secret state police, the *Gestapo*. The second-rate qualities of Himmler, who ran the machinery of terror, are an astonishing commentary on its efficacy. It was also backed by a continuous effort of propaganda and indoctrination which was so effective that sudden reversals of direction such as the Nazi-Soviet agreement of 1939 were taken by public opinion in its stride.

This particular change was only a temporary abandonment of the anti-Bolshevism which was always one of Hitler's most powerful appeals. It struck a response in his hearers, as did his diatribes against Versailles. His own magnetism, the appeal of success, low taxation, the cushion of full employment and the traditional docility of Germans before authority explain much of the lack of opposition in prewar Germany without it being necessary to invoke the argument of terrorization. The régime, after all, gave most Germans what they wanted. It had enormous successes in foreign policy before 1939, and from 1939 to 1941 an apparently unbroken series of military victories achieved at virtually no cost to German standards of living or safety.

Many foreigners had better reason to oppose Hitler, since they saw their national interests crumbling in his hands, refugees flying from the *Gestapo*, foreign correspondents who told the truth about Germany expelled. Yet they appeased him, too. The charisma of success was all-persuasive. Unhappily for Germany and Europe, it blotted out not only the wickedness of Nazism but the essential incoherence and nihilism behind its dynamism. For Germany this was in the end to mean defeat and division; more disastrously, for Europe it meant rule by a man on whose obsessive personality there played a chaos of unrelated and irrational forces. Because he was an unbalanced crank, Hitler made a Germany which in every way represented a retrogression not only from Weimar but from the second Reich, too. He was the least creative, though not the least influential, of the dictators. Stalin's monument was the great industrial and military strength which destroyed the German army and set up Communist governments all over eastern Europe. Even Mussolini's I.R.I. remains in being, and the Lateran treaties closed a long-running wound. Hitler is commemorated only by destruction, degradation, and the extirpation of whole peoples. Most ironic of all, he gave east Germany her first taste of Slav occupation since 1813, and for many years the most unyielding communist régime in Europe outside Albania.

14

SOCIAL AND CULTURAL CHANGE, 1918–1939

WAYS OF LIFE

In 1919 a young English official at the Peace Conference was talking to a great Polish aristocrat when the name of Paderewski, the first president of the new Polish Republic, was mentioned. 'A very remarkable man', said Count Potocki. 'Do you realize that he was born in one of my own villages? And yet, when I speak to him, I have absolutely the impression of conversing with an equal.'[1] The count's surprise was natural. He, like many of his generation in eastern Europe, still accepted almost unquestioningly the assumptions and values of a hierarchical and agrarian order which the upheavals of the war had violently disturbed; by 1939 they would have been replaced almost everywhere by the assumptions of that market society which had already made such great strides before 1914 in 'advanced' countries.[2]

The continuance of this movement from status to market society, while general, was, nevertheless, uneven in its pace and extent during these years. Setting Russia aside because of her special history, we can from this point of view roughly divide the rest of Europe in two: rich and poor. The distinction must not be pressed too far, or made too neatly. It is evident, nevertheless, in many specific indices. On the whole, after 1918 northern and western Europe and Czechoslovakia enjoyed high *per capita*

1 Harold Nicolson, *Peacemaking 1919* (London, 1945), p. 176.
2 See pp. 60–1. For a contemporary judgement, see W. McDougall, *The Group Mind* (London, 1920), pp. 287–8.

incomes and levels of consumption, general literacy and a susceptibility to the diseases of old age. Eastern Europe and the Mediterranean coasts had low *per capita* incomes, consumed less, had
large illiterate populations and a high infant mortality. Distinctions already present in 1914 were now exaggerated further. The
poorer societies tended to stagnate. They were in the most disadvantageous economic position to begin with, they suffered most
damage in economic depression, and they were burdened with
fast-growing populations. Because of this, the rich countries show
most clearly the main social and cultural changes of these years.

The big social trends already remarked in rich countries before
1914 continued after the war. The share of agriculture in the
economy declined, service industries took more labour, and the
proportion of women in the labour force went down. The power
station, motor-car and tractor became familiar objects: they were
the most obvious signs of an industry increasingly organized to
take advantage of large-scale, continuous-flow production and the
research of the laboratory. More people lived in big towns and
town and country were brought closer together by large-scale
distribution and marketing, telephones and radios, motor-cars and
bicycles.

Cultural communications also became easier with the spread of
mass education. For the first time in history, almost all Europeans
in the major states had received some form of full-time primary
education and many were also at secondary schools.[3] One result
was an immeasurable spread of common attitudes; another was
the statistically more accessible fact of greater mass literacy.
Several newspapers between the wars achieved circulations of
more than 2 million among this new audience; the apogee of their
influence was reached before 1939. Partly because of this, public
affairs became a matter of mass concern as never before. The journalists were not to lose their ascendancy until the coming of mass
television after 1945 (there were regular television transmissions
in England before 1939, but few sets to receive them), but two
other cultural agents were already shaping public attitudes: the
cinema and radio.

3 *Pupils receiving secondary education.*

France	1913:	138,000	1940:	218,000
Germany	1911:	640,000	1937:	670,000
Italy	1911–12:	226,000	1937–8:	602,000
U.K.	1912–13:	214,000	1937–8:	659,000

The European cinema did not recover ground lost during the Great War. Its output had grown rapidly between 1911 and 1914, but Hollywood had by 1918 established a lead it never lost. Most films shown in European cinemas between the wars were American and through them mass entertainment rapidly acquired a transatlantic flavour. Attempts to impose quotas of domestic films on cinemas did not help much. This was important (especially after the introduction of sound), because the cinema was a great educational force, diffusing notions of the desirable life which were often at variance with tradition, accepted practice and even, at times, economic possibility. It was a great standardizer of attitudes and manners. So powerful an engine inevitably attracted politicians. Some of the first examples of films in support of a political campaign were sponsored by the Greek delegation at the Peace Conference in 1919.[4] Later, the Nazis presented to the world a picture of a new, united and irresistible Germany through films of massed storm-troopers and great party rallies. The Russians quickly saw the importance of the cinema to a mainly illiterate population and set up a special Cinema Commission only a few weeks after the October Revolution. Great use was made of non-theatrical outlets and throughout the villages of Russia films were shown which depicted the threats facing the Revolution from abroad, and the strength and cohesion of the Russian masses. Such themes lent themselves well to dramatic visual presentation, and were adapted to changes in official orthodoxy as required; in *Ten Days that Shook the World*, a film about the October revolution, Trotsky's part in events was ignored. Russian films enjoyed an excellent reception abroad and did much to enhance the prestige of the Soviet state. Towards the end of the 1930s, their international appeal began to diminish, as social and revolutionary themes gave way to patriotic spectacles which stressed the contribution of great national heroes of the past to Russian history.[5]

In radio, the other great force in mass communication, England led the way. As the price of receiving sets fell, their numbers rose; by 1926 there were 2 million British sets. Other countries quickly

4 See D. Kitsikis, *Propagande et pressions en politique internationale; la Grèce et ses revendications à la Conférence de la Paix* (Paris, 1963).
5 On the artistic achievement of the cinema, see p. 494.

followed. The effects, like those of the cinema, were in part unanticipated, in part contrived. In England the monopoly enjoyed by the B.B.C. led to a consciously educational choice of programmes. Less expectedly, it also led to an homogenizing of speech; Gladstone naturally spoke with a Lancashire accent, but his twentieth-century successors had to cultivate regional affiliation if they wanted it. The political use of broadcasting was soon important, though not all politicians were at once aware of it. Baldwin was one of the first English politicians to use the radio effectively and it contributed much to the maintenance of order during the General Strike. In Russia the state's monopoly of the radio system was a great instrument of government in so large and backward a country. The Russians also made great use of radio propaganda abroad, especially in the Middle East and India. Hitler, too, used the medium to bring to bear his great demagogic gifts on a nationwide audience.

Greater material prosperity and a more rapid diffusion of ideas and information implied mental changes. It is very hard to be precise about such things in the present state of our knowledge, and there are also two important preliminary qualifications to be made. One is that the rate of change since 1945 has been so fast that we are in danger of under-rating the earlier transformations of this century. We must keep in mind that our reference is 1880, not today. The second is that overall growth and improvement were often less obvious than was particular and local deterioration. Additionally, in rich and poor societies alike, the countryside lagged behind in the rise of standards.

None the less, material betterment reached many people. Greater productivity permitted the continuing fall in the average working week; the sixty-nine hours of 1890 had fallen by 1930 to fifty-six. Real wages and consumption rose in most countries. Wages and salaries took more of national income, interest on capital less, while taxation began to redistribute wealth through welfare and insurance arrangements. Technology brought more immediate improvements; millions of people had their lives made a little easier by cheap soap, electricity and sewing-machines. Rayon and cheap cosmetics gave women a faint taste of the luxury which they saw on the cinema screen. Such changes led to a reshaping of family budgets and a diversion of a much larger proportion of income to nonessentials – to something more than the mere business of staying alive, warm, and housed.[6] A new industry arose to provide mass entertainment through cinema, newspaper and professional sportsmanship.[7] An international musical idiom, transatlantic in origin, expressed itself in, successively, ragtime, jazz and swing.

People were coming to expect more of life. At a moment when a cultural élite had already lost faith in material progress as the solvent of social and moral problems, the masses came to take material progress and its fruits for granted. One sign was a new preoccupation with speed and 'records'.[8] It marked another triumph of man over his environment, in this case, over time. Such an extension of the control exercised by men over the rhythms of their lives had far-reaching implications. Because a belief grew up that things *could* be changed, men said more readily that they *should* be. There was an erosion of the acquiescence in the here-and-now which had provided so much of the social cement of the past. More was to be expected of society and of its servant, government. A rise in tolerable *minima* was one aspect of a 'revolt of the masses' which began to attract attention after 1918.[9]

Changed attitudes affected the family. At least since the seventeenth century, many forces had been limiting and breaking up the traditional omnibus functions of the family as the primary organizing, disciplining and educational agency of society; increasingly, what a man did or owned came to define his rights and duties rather than did the group into which he was born. Material forces accelerated this change by dissolving traditional work patterns and increasing social mobility. The factory system deprived old and experienced men of the authority and prestige they had in an era of individual craftsmanship and sucked women and children into work outside the home. One authority has said

6 An English working-class budget of 1937 allocated 40 per cent to food, 13 per cent to rent, 11 per cent to clothes, 7 per cent to heat and light, and 29 per cent to 'various' expenditures.
7 Its scale can be seen in two figures: by 1939 a major English film cost over £100,000, whereas the great success of 1905, *Rescued by Rover*, had cost £7 13s 9d. (R. Manvell, *Film*, (London, 1944), p. 13).
8 1883 is the earliest date given in the *New. Eng. Dict.* for an example of 'record' in the sense of an outstanding performance.
9 The phrase provided the title for a famous book by J. Ortega y Gasset, *La Rebelión de las Masas* (Madrid, 1930).

that industrialization 'put the family on the defensive',[10] but other forces helped. The Great War strained marriages by long separations. More efficient contraception modified the life of the family; by changing, in particular, the role of the mother, it led to changes in the use of the family income and strengthened a new idea of marriage as primarily a partnership of two people. This was congenial to a culture long bombarded with the literary notion that the only valid moral basis for marriage was romantic love.

The dissociation of sexuality from biological reproduction was another expression of man's growing control of his environment and, as such, an extension of personality. But there are great local and social differences to be borne in mind. Religious and legal regulation, for example, variously affected the opportunities of finding out about contraceptive methods. The papal encyclical *Casta Connubii* of 1931 rejected all save 'natural' methods of family limitation as sinful. Some countries had laws against contraception. Even in Sweden, a law of 1911 had prohibited the diffusion of knowledge about contraception, though the subsequent history of that country seems to show that its effect was to give publicity to the fact that effective techniques existed. Countries also differed widely in the general degree of relaxation and permissiveness towards sexual behaviour. The most ostentatious tolerance of a wide variety of discussion on sexual matters was shown in Weimar Germany (where there appeared a notable Institute of Sexual Science in Berlin) and in Scandinavia. Sweden began to provide public finance for contraceptive clinics in 1936 and legalized abortion in 1938. Such steps not only had immediate positive effects, but announced a de-mythologizing of sex which heralded a cultural revolution.

Material changes also affected the family in less obvious ways. As such household processes as clothes-making and laundering were increasingly done outside the home, and as standardized products and prepared foods were more frequently used inside it, the family's role as a provider came to be seen in a new way. The complicated associations of dependence and affection built round provision and nourishment began to break up. Like the complex effect of contraception, material changes affecting the family had

10 R. M. Titmuss, 'Industrialisation and the family', p. 117, in *Essays on 'The Welfare State'* (London , 1958).

more than a simple material significance. They also changed mentality by changing assumptions long taken for granted.

Conscious legal and political interference also had a complex effect. The collective rights of the family were increasingly set aside; it was coming to be dealt with as a group of individuals whose personal interests needed protection. This fitted the general individualist trend of liberal bourgeois civilization. Increasingly, too, it was the smallest biologically significant unit, the married couple and their children, which was regarded as a 'family'. The tentacular, multi-generation family of the past was giving way, its continuum dissolving into a series of independent couples which was linked by little except sentiment. Interferences with property, such as restrictions on entail, had already clearly announced this trend. The small family itself was forced to make concessions to its individual members. The feminists had always sought to give married women control of their own property and it was frequently safeguarded by the law. In 1938 the French removed the obligation of obedience to the husband which had been laid upon the wife by the Napoleonic code. The right to freedom from an intolerable tie was more widely recognized by the extension of divorce. This did not exist in some countries and nowhere except in Sweden was its incidence high before 1939, but there was a growing acceptance of the idea. Children, too, had greater protection given them by laws assuring their nurture and education against parental neglect.

Such legal interventions to protect individuals were typical of much social action to fill gaps left by the weakening of the family as a whole. As the family had less and less control over its economic security and was less and less able to support its members against hardship, the provision of public welfare services became more common. Before 1939 this had gone furthest in Scandinavia. It could also be seen in the totalitarian states, but their attitudes to the family had roots other than simple social concern. Real ideological suspiciousness faced the family in Soviet Russia or Nazi Germany.

In other countries, traditionalists, often with strong religious views confidently advocated the resurrection of the family's authority as a cure of social and moral ills. They were faced with a difficult task, not only because so many material and political factors were weakening the family, but because twentieth-century culture was often hostile to it. Many writers attacked it. Denunciation came not only from anarchists and socialists, but in much bourgeois writing about heroes and heroines in conflict with family ties. Admiration for what one novelist cuttingly called *la solidarité de la tripe* was waning.[11] The diffusion of anti-authoritarian ideas undermined the paternal authority which, at least in theory, stabilized the traditional family. After 1918 the vulgarization of the ideas of Freud was much more rapid, and those whose business it was to traffic in ideas began to present to a wide public an alarming picture of what might lurk behind the façade of parental love and filial piety. Names like Oedipus and Elektra became charged with meaning for people who had not the slightest interest in the drama of ancient Greece. Only in the mid 1930s did the tide which had so long run against the family begin to show signs of a turn. Perhaps the life of the family had been made more attractive by the harsh workings of political and economic change. The signs were clearest at the level of state action. The Russians, for example, set about enhancing the family's stability and prestige.[12] In France the fiscal benefits which the Popular Front brought to individual workers were increasingly adjusted so as to discriminate in favour of those with families, a change greatly accelerated and developed by the government of Pétain after 1940.

In many ways changes in family life affected women more immediately (though not necessarily more profoundly) than men. Accurate assessments are difficult and generalization is almost impossible because of great variations. It can be seen that the 'emancipation' of women was much more than a merely legal and political matter in this period. The whole female personality was involved. In all countries the Great War made a huge difference, whether by involving women in men's work they had not previously attempted (so that it was impossible later to believe they could ever have been thought unable to do it), or by producing such an imbalance of population that big changes in sexual behaviour, marriage patterns and creative activity followed in the next two decades. The home became slightly less materially confining as less time was occupied in child-rearing – or at the

11 Jules Romains, see R. Prigent, *Renonveau des idées sur la famille* (Paris, 1934), p. 199.
12 See p. 356. It seems possible that a huge increase in juvenile crime and vagabondage played a part in this.

wash-tub, thanks to cheap soap powders. Formal political rights were widely extended after 1918; the assertion of the principle of equal pay in article 427 of the Treaty of Versailles was less enthusiastically taken up.[13] Meanwhile, apart from exceptional periods such as the Great War, the effect of trade union pressure, rapid population growth and growing sophistication of machinery and industrial organization was to drive women out of manufacturing employment in the long run. On the whole the effect of this was beneficial; it largely eliminated, for example, the 'sweating' domestic workshops of the Paris attics and the East End of London. It was accompanied by some increase of female employment in other industries as clerks, secretaries and shop assistants, but the overall proportion of women in the labour force of most fairly advanced countries, none the less, was dropping before 1939.

One social institution which hardly changed at all was prostitution. During the nineteenth century, the growth of cities had been matched by a rise in the number of prostitutes. Most European countries (England was the only important exception) adopted some sort of *police des moeurs* to regulate the conditions of their trade. This usually meant the designation of certain streets or the licensing of authorized brothels as places where prostitution could legally be carried on. It was an important – and often very visible – factor in the cultural and social history of most continental countries, but it has been largely unstudied by historians. The system was still established in most countries in 1939, though the international movement of prostitutes after 1918 was increasingly interfered with. The League of Nations took the lead in this, seeking to prohibit traffic in women deceived or coerced into prostitution, and to protect children from exploitation.

As we approach the end of this story, it is tempting to remember the promise of the future in 1880, and assess what had been achieved sixty years later. The question can be posed in terms of happiness, though it can hardly be answered precisely. Great efforts had been made by 1939 to secure the wellbeing which had more and more seemed to be an achievable goal. Informally it had been sought through rising material standards

13 Women received the vote in the following years: 1915, Denmark; 1917, Russia; 1918, U.K.; 1919, Austria, Germany, Czechoslovakia, Luxemburg, Holland, Poland; 1920, Bulgaria; 1921, Sweden.

and a hedonistic liberalization from the restraints of the past. Formally it had been sought by social and political experiment, of which the most successful examples seemed to be the Scandinavian democracies. While such attempts did not fit inside the traditional liberal pattern, they were clearly related to it; they did not reject its goals, though its means might seem inadequate. To this extent, a belief in material progress was still an important force among the masses in 1939. A general economic *malaise* and the political insecurities which followed 1914 nevertheless had done much to undermine it and whatever advantages had been won, they can hardly be said to have satisfied the majority.

Moreover there were new dissatisfactions abroad. Industrial society seems to deprive the individual of much of the nourishment of his self-respect which is necessary to happiness. Work, as the great René Clair film, *A nous la liberté* (1930), showed, was often anonymous and monotonous, demanding nothing except regularity. Uncertainty about future employment grew as industrial operations became larger and more complex. Events occurring the other side of the world might unexpectedly involve European cities in ruin. The relationships of young and old were revolutionized by the decline in the older worker's value to the employer, who now might prize experience and skill less than strength and reliability. It is still hard to assess such facts, as it is to explain such phenomena as the increase of suicide. 'We cannot so easily measure the complex sicknesses of a complex society; the prevalence of the stress diseases of modern civilization, the instabilities of family relationships or the extent of mental ill-health', we are told, as we can the simpler physical toll of bad drains and undernourishment.[14] Much of our data is lacking, too. But neither this nor uncertainty about technique permits the historian to ignore such themes. They represent, in fact, some of the most promising areas for research in recent history.

We do not even know enough about religious practice, traditionally a great source of comfort to the distressed. The progress of the ecumenical movement gladdened some Christians, but there is no reason to believe that the general weakening of reliance on belief in a supernatural order was reversed after 1914. Even when baptisms remained numerous, the formal adherents

14 Titmuss, p. 33.

of a faith often never went near a church. Much more information is needed before we can speak with confidence, but it is hard to believe in the nominal Christianity of many Germans who took part in the beastly policies of racial extermination (denounced by some of their clergy). The experience of French priests called up for military service in 1939 or later working as forced labour deportees in Germany was that the French workers among whom they found themselves were not simply estranged from a particular form of belief but had no sense of a religious dimension to their lives at all.[15] Unfortunately it is really only since 1945 that the systematic study of religious sociology has begun to provide us with some quantitative measurement of the decline of religious practice.[16] There is still much more to do before we can speak confidently about belief.

SELF-CONSCIOUS EUROPE

The importance of the Great War in the evolution of conscious art and articulated ideas can easily be exaggerated. Once, almost everything that was startling or unpleasant in postwar culture was attributed to the terrible experiences of that struggle. It is now clear that explanation must start before 1914. The accentuation of the minority nature of advanced ideas and art, and their fragmentation so that even educated persons could hardly come to terms with them, were already discernible then. So was the rejection of traditional aesthetics and morals part of an already established trend away from liberal bourgeois standards. After 1918 there continued an evolution already begun.

This is very clear in the natural sciences. Their increasing complication had already begun to confine an understanding of them to highly trained minorities. Few educated men, for example, could even dimly sense the significance of the huge extension of knowledge of the universe provided by twentieth-century astronomy. Of course, the scientific elite itself grew rapidly in numbers; it became truly international, extending well

15 See E Poulet, *Naissance des prêtres-ouvriers* (Paris, 1965).
16 A notable example is G. Le Bras, *Études de sociologie religieuse* (Paris, 1955–6).

beyond Europe. Its increasing integration and ease of communication contributed to the enormous acceleration of its discoveries. This was so great that it is difficult to single out moments of outstanding importance without losing sight of the continuum of new knowledge which gave individual achievements their significance; more and more, the interaction of scientific work in hitherto unconnected fields provided research with its dynamism.

Nevertheless it was clear by 1939 that the greatest advances made since 1918 had been in biochemistry and physics. Those in physics were the most spectacular. They continued the revolution begun at the end of the nineteenth century by the exploration of the basic nature of matter as revealed in the atomic nucleus. The disintegration and manipulation of that nucleus was the heart of postwar physics. In 1919 Rutherford brought about the first experimental transmutation of an element, by bombarding nitrogen with alpha particles. This opened two decades of astonishingly fertile work as physicists sought to absorb the importance of Rutherford's practical work and the theoretical contributions of Einstein and Planck. Many distinguished men contributed to this; it is no disparagement of them to say that the fundamental steps had now all been taken. The production of elements some of which did not occur in nature was now in sight. In 1932 a new particle which was called the 'neutron' was discovered and in 1939 it was used to split the uranium atom. With this, the way was open to the production of the nuclear power reactor and the atomic bomb.

This was the most important achievement of science between the wars, and the full outcome was not to be seen until after 1945. The same was true of many other of the material results of prewar scientific research. One reason for the lag was their dependence for effective deployment on technological resources which were not at once available. Before 1939, the great discoveries of nuclear physics had hardly touched the ordinary man's life, except in the form of medical X-rays. Radar, a by-product of research, only began to affect many people's lives in 1940, when it made possible the effective air defence of Great Britian. Biochemical discoveries had been diffused rather more rapidly. 'Vitamins', which had begun to be discovered in 1901, were commonly spoken of by 1939. Several had by then been identified, studied, and synthesized; the result was a revolution in nutrition – and therefore indirectly in clinical medicine and public health. New drugs had continued to appear. The doctors of 1900 had little but quinine, mercury and digitalis to rely upon; by 1939 Salvarsan had been joined by insulin and then by penicillin, discovered in 1928 in a London hospital. Work on penicillin at Oxford in the 1930s meant that it was ready for mass-production and use in the closing years of the Second World War. By then, too, streptomycin was available. The needs of warfare greatly accelerated the application of science in medicine (as in other ways), but again it is necessary to recall that advance was unevenly distributed. For all the huge advances in medicine before 1945, neurophysiology, for instance, was still working with a model of the mind as a vast network of connections in a huge switchboard; in the 1930s it was clear that this would no longer do, but a better model was not to be forthcoming until after 1945. The work which most obviously and visibly transformed the ordinary man's world before 1939 was the chemistry of the first plastics, the physics of radio and electricity, the technology of the internal combustion engine. These, all basically done by 1914, maintained the popular faith – the 'scientism' – which saw science still as the wonder-working magic of nineteenth-century materialism. This favoured a crude determinism. Professional scientists and philosophers were faced with more complicated problems than those raised by this kind of faith.[17] The success of scientific method in reaching its goals seemed to endorse practically the value-free conceptual world of the scientist. From this it was a short step for some to the exclusion of any objective value or meaning from life. The difficulty of maintaining at once the assumptions of advanced science and the values of liberal civilization was posed, although many scientists were to go on ignoring it. For philosophers, fundamental uncertainties and misgivings about the nature of reality and the profitability of such traditional enquiries as metaphysics followed from contemplation of the revolutionary implications of Relativity and Quantum theory.

Not many of Europe's intellectuals knew enough about science to get so far. This may have been in part because of the traditional bias of education in most countries. Scientists themselves found

17 This interesting and growing divergence between the layman's and the scientist's view of 'science' cannot be explored here. For some contemporary reflexions, see W. McDougall, *World Chaos: The Responsibility of Science* (London, 1931), esp. pp. 14–19.

their conclusions difficult to state in ordinary language and its implications hard to discern; it was not surprising that laymen should find it impossible to keep up. One of the reasons why psychoanalysis quickly established itself as an intellectual fashion was that it provided an unusual instance of what purported to be science having an immediate and comprehensible relevance to daily life. With this exception, intellectual Europe did not show much awareness of truly contemporary science between the wars. Old-fashioned materialism still satisfied many people and the élite was still dominated by ideas derived from the distinguished thinkers active towards the end of the nineteenth century.

Such men as Nietzsche, Bergson and Weber had undermined many of the assumptions on which the intellectual culture of liberal civilization had been built (see p. 236–7). More important still was Freud, whose influence was as generalized as that of Darwin a generation before. By 1919 a writer could use the phrase a 'Freudian complex' and expect to be understood in a book about economic affairs.[18] Freud's message was the most destructive of all, for it was believed to expose the fictions of reason itself. This background explains the ferment of ideas among European intellectuals after 1918. By then the unprecedented horrors of the war had bred cynicism and disillusionment and had tainted the social order and the ideas that had produced it. The language of idealism was devalued everywhere and the language of reason seemed inadequate.

In Germany, defeat and political and economic upheaval developed this trend of postwar culture with special intensity. To this extent, Germany was the cultural centre of the new Europe rather as France had been before 1914. In Germany were to be seen more extreme developments than elsewhere, both in ideas and politics.[19] The ferment there produced a cultural anarchy which was in the end self-destructive; one of its creations triumphed in 1933. Nothing so extreme marked England, where traditional patterns both of behaviour and thought were little disturbed before 1939, as both the insularity of culture and the weakness of political extremism was to show.

18 J. M. Keynes, *The Economic Consequences of the Peace*, p. 50.
19 For an interesting discussion of one aspect of this, see S. Kracauer, *From Caligari to Hitler* (London, 1947), a study of the German cinema of the Weimar era.

Philosophy provides a good example of this cultural divergence. Bergson was the most celebrated continental philosopher, Croce and Husserl among the most important, yet none of them had much impact in England. There, classical empiricism was still the most important element shaping the work of professional philosophers; no first-rate English philosophers of these years had anything like the audience and influence among the laity of the great Europeans. In part this was because of a difference of tradition; in part it was because of a European anxiety to relate philosophical teaching immediately to the personal and social problems of life in the ruins of a crumbling civilization. The irrigation of philosophy by such external influences as the work of Freud kept European philosophy in a state of muddled concern. In so far as a trend can be discerned in it, academic philosophy in Europe was by 1939 producing its widest impact through the spread of what were to be identified as 'existentialist' ideas. As the main doctrines of existentialism have never been clearly and coherently stated – and as (some existentialists would say) they cannot be – it is hard for the non-philosopher to do more than recognize their symptomatic quality. Predominantly a German phenomenon before 1939, existentialism embodied reiterated criticisms of contemporary society and civilisation.[20] Heidegger condemned the 'flight from Existence' – from human reality – as the characteristic evil of his times; existentialism was an assertion that life was more than logic, that engagement in it was more important than the motive or nature of the engagement, that the subjective and personal must be more highly valued and the objective and intellectualized must be depreciated. Here can be seen its character as a product of its age. In so far as it had a formal enemy, it was liberal bourgeois civilization and the Enlightenment from which it sprang.[21]

It is difficult to draw so chaotic a picture together. Obviously, philosophy was fragmented by the irruption of irrational and subjective considerations which often denied, explicitly or im-

20 Sartre produced an important novel in 1938, but his identification as an existentialist and his acceptance as its spokesman dates from 1943.
21 The political consequences were sometimes extremist; Sartre, as is well known, pursued his own activities in occupied France after 1940 without concerning himself with his country's plight, and then took up with the communists after 1945. Heidegger found no difficulty in coming to terms with the Nazis.

plicitly, the bases on which discussions between philosophers had hitherto proceeded. To this extent philosophy shared the weakness of the traditional culture which had formed it. This cultural weakness could be seen also in the growing prestige of a vulgarized historicism. Academic historians, who as a clan had enjoyed great esteem in the nineteenth century, seemed to have little to offer an intellectual public more excited by the ideas of Spengler or A. J. Toynbee.[22] In this, they expressed a growing distinction between the mandarin specialist and the lay intellectual. Specialists and scholars had always been remote from ordinary men because of the technicality of their own studies (the scientists were the best example of this); the gap was now accentuated by a difference of concern. However radical their conclusions might be, most university teachers continued to act and argue as if the whole tradition of assumptions in which they had been formed, with its emphasis on rational, orderly procedures and civilized argument, was still intact. More and more lay intellectuals abandoned this tradition.

Anti-intellectualism and irrationalism were fed from many sources but they always led to illiberalism. Pessimism about the future was one response; even liberals were not immune from it. Another was to turn to historicist or irrationalist politics, to find in action a release from decision and uncertainty, and both communists and fascists benefited from this. The title of a popular German book, *Mind as Enemy of the Soul*, indicates another reaction. This was the exaltation of the vital and instinctual, of blood, Mother Earth and all the other claptrap of the anti-industrial, back-to-nature movements which proliferated in the 1920s and which made the 'spiritual' concern of early Nazism seem so attractive. Some intellectuals, too, turned to religion. What seems clear in retrospect was that one form of the *trahison des clercs* of the age was the specialist's abandonment of cultural leadership to the charlatans. The hungry sheep looked up and were not fed. In place of doctrine they were given yet more grounds for uncertainty. It was significant that by 1939 the one country in which intellectuals upheld the idea of progress, the great nineteenth-century idol, was Soviet Russia. There, preserved in the deep-

---

22 It is another interesting symptom of English cultural insularity that Toynbee's *Study of History* (London, 1934–54) has been received much more enthusiastically abroad than at home.

freeze of Marxist jargon along with its twin, materialistic determinism, the idea of progress was still potent; it was one reason why so many European intellectuals admired the Stalinist régime.

Like the world of ideas, art was deeply marked by irrationalism, anti-objectivism and introspection. Only the cinema and the new architecture seemed still to have something to say to the man in the street. In spite of the commercial dominance of Hollywood, the European film had great artistic achievements to its credit between 1918 and 1939. The first was the German expressionist cinema of the early 1920s. By the use of non-naturalistic lighting, acting and setting, it produced a series of claustrophobic films of great artistic merit, of which an outstanding example was *The Cabinet of Dr Caligari* (1920). The movement failed to sustain its first impetus, possibly because of the temporary ebbing of the popular tide of disillusionment and bitterness with which it was intimately linked. The closeness of the cinema to popular mood and its dependence on a mass audience was also reflected in the work of the great Russian directors of the silent film. Their work produced the first important statement of an aesthetic of the cinema, Pudovkin's *Film Technique* of 1929 which launched the idea of 'montage'. The British contribution to this new art lay mainly in the production of documentary, and was often the work of the General Post Office film unit, which showed remarkable imagination and appreciation of the possibilities of the new medium. From *Drifters* (1925) to *Nightmail* (1935), a film which imaginatively linked visual images to a verse script by W. H. Auden, the British documentary consistently pursued social purpose. The film was the least aesthetically fragmented and least coterie-ridden of the arts, expressing positive values when other artists were demolishing them.

For architecture, too, the twentieth century has been a great creative period. The origins of this lay in the nineteenth century, in the invention of new materials and methods – of which the most important was reinforced concrete in 1889 – and in the diffusion of the ideals of workmanship and functional beauty embodied in the English arts and crafts movement which derived from William Morris. These influences set the stage for a revolution. Since the Renaissance, European architecture had been a succession of recoveries, reminiscences and adaptations of past styles, some of them brilliantly successful. The twentieth century saw the creation of a new aesthetic and technique based on the whole-hearted acceptance of the possibilities inherent in industrial civilization and its materials. The great creative centres of this revolution were Germany and Austria; its greatest period began about 1907. Among pioneer names, two stand out: Loos and Gropius. One institution above all stood for the new architecture, the *Bauhaus* at Dessau. From the mid-twenties, the new architecture spread fairly rapidly in a new phase of consolidation and extension of the original principles, helped by, among other things, the general exodus of many of Germany's leading architects after 1933. It would be untrue to say that by 1939 the lives of the majority had been greatly changed by the new architecture. Some housing developments in Holland and Germany were widely admired, but most urban Europeans in 1939 were still living in buildings put up before 1914, whether they were Victorian terraces in Leeds, or the airless and lightless tenements of central Europe. The new architecture left a greater mark in public and industrial building; schools, chemical factories, aircraft hangars were the first and most visible embodiments of the revolution.

There were close ties between the cinema and architecture and the other arts. A painter like Klee was a member of the *Bauhaus*, and the cinema produced surrealist experiments such as Buñuel's *Le chien anadalou*. Nevertheless, experimentalism in them was disciplined by the need for a technique for dealing with new materials. Painting and literature presented a far more anarchic spectacle.

In 1900 Paris was still the artistic capital of Europe. The Impressionists and post-Impressionists were by then accounted respectable. Just before 1880 Cézanne, the greatest painter of his day, had broken with the Impressionists. From his determination to seek an authentic view of the world, a vision of the object with no interposition by emotion or even the senses, and no interpretation, stems the Modern movement in painting. (*Art nouveau* may be ignored, a mere decorators' whim.) The doctrine of the Modernists was to be condensed by Matisse: '*l'exactitude n'est pas la verité*'.[23] The multitude of artists then in Paris formed a movement only in the negative sense of this proposition. Derain, Picasso, Braque, Utrillo, Matisse, Léger, Arp, Rousseau, Chagall,

23 See Read, p. 44. Matisse did not write these words until 1951.

Klee, Kandinsky, Brancusi, Modigliani, Nolde, all worked there between 1900 and 1914 and contributed to a rich confusion of influences and ideas. This makes it hard to isolate 'schools' or even significant moments in these years. The general tendency, however, is unmistakable. Pictorial art rapidly exhausted one approach after another in its pursuit of a truthful rendering of reality. In Cubism it sought totality, in Futurism the illusion of simultaneity. Each experiment broke down more and more of the traditional canons; abstraction flooded in as first form and then meaning were broken up. By 1914 painting had left behind the merely visual, and the work of, for example, Picasso, had passed beyond Cubism to a phase in which the free mental association of images constituted the raw material of the canvas.[24]

The experimentalism of Paris – to employ an inadequate short-hand expression – was not the only source of fragmentation and loss of direction. Before 1914, in Dresden and Munich, the first German Expressionists were at work. They produced a greater literary documentation than the Parisian painters and were increasingly preoccupied with art as an access to the unconscious and non-rational. This awoke sympathy in a culture aware of the writings of Jung and Freud. The Expressionists tended to be lonely and isolated men, emphatically rejecting traditional themes and canons. Some of them, too (an example is the near-caricaturist painter, Grosz) deliberately harnessed their art to an anti-bourgeois ethic. At least, however, such work retained the idea of an objective standpoint. With Surrealism, the objective itself disappeared.

Surrealism is of great symptomatic interest. Its exponents cut across all art forms, moving rapidly from one expression to another, seeking by representation, chance, symbolism, shock, suggestion and violence to reach a truer reality beyond not only the sense but consciousness itself. They sought to tap the unconscious. The word (invented in 1917) was defined in André Breton's *Manifeste du Surréalisme* of 1924 as 'pure psychic auto-mation . . . thought dictated in the absence of all control exerted by reason, and outside all aesthetic or moral preoccupations'.[25] It

24 e.g. his *Aficionado*, 1912.
25 P. Waldberg, *Surrealism* (London, 1965), p. 72. The whole manifesto is printed in translation in this book.

was not wholly destructive in intent, in that Surrealists sought to liberate a human personality said to be oppressed, crushed and stunted by state, church and the formalism of conscious logic. Some of them tried to attach themselves to the Communist party, but not very successfully. 'We were possessed by a will to total subversion', said Breton,[26] and this hardly suited Stalinist discipline. Their revolutionary efforts were most successful in the arts where they pressed the assault on traditional form, the programme of so many artists in this century, to unprecedented lengths. They sought the beautiful in the surprising, whether in words or design, in fur teacups or in the productions of the insane. In their rejection of conventional 'meaning' they are the purest distillation of that dialectical criticism of liberal culture by its own creations which is the story of this century.[27]

When the composer Schönberg read Kandinsky's manifesto, *Über das Geistige in der Kunst*, he praised it warmly for giving him the hope 'that those who ask for a text and thematic content will soon have asked their last'.[28] Certainly music shared the fragmentation and experiment which marked other arts after 1918. Many professional musicians admitted themselves unable to understand the work of a Webern or a Schönberg. Yet this impression is somewhat superficial. The most important musical figures of the period – Stravinsky, Bartók – won increasing audiences once the novelty of their idiom had been assimilated, and this was more rapid in the age of the gramophone than it had ever been before. An older tradition, too, was still genuinely alive, as its exploitation by Richard Strauss showed. Lesser figures, such as Weil, were able to use music as a vehicle for a social commentary which by its nature implied accessibility to a wide audience. The esoteric and inaccessible were connected with anti-liberalism, in music as well as art (as Mann showed in *Dr Faustus*) but it is less easy to trace than in painting.

Literature provides good evidence of the decay of liberal culture. In Mann's novel *The Magic Mountain* (1924) the central

26 See R. S. Short, 'The Politics of Surrealism, 1920–36', *JCH, 1966*, no. 2, p. 3.
27 For an exemplary statement, see the 'Letter to the Buddhist Schools', Waldberg, p. 60.
28 See 'Peter Theone', *Modern German Art* (London, 1938), p. 79.

issue became explicit in a debate between two of its characters about the Enlightenment origins of liberal civilization. A symptom was the retirement of such poets as Rilke or Stefan George into private concerns, of Kafka into allegory, of Proust into the world of things remembered or of Eliot into the feature-less landscape of *The Waste Land*. This sort of withdrawal had its antecendents in the privacies of romantic literature. A new and more jarring note came from conscious attack upon the analytical, self-regarding tendency of bourgeois culture. D. H. Lawrence had already by 1918 produced his best work, but his novels embodied the plea of the era to be allowed to escape self-consciousness and the restraint of objective rules. In the literature of futurism or Dada a plunge was made into complete incomprehensibility in search of spontaneity. One reason why American writers were eagerly taken up by Paris in the 1930s was the freshness and vitality they seemed to show by comparison with the tiredness of Europeans.

It is difficult to assess the literature of the period without exaggeration and distortion. While the alienation of the writer from society which had marked bourgeois culture for decades was carried to a new pitch, great numbers of educated people went on reading poetry and novels, and seeing plays which were recognizably within the older tradition. The novel was still the dominant literary form. Publishing for mass markets underwent a huge expansion. But advanced literature had become inaccessible to the ordinary reader in quite a new way. Prévert and Joyce seemed beyond comprehension, Eliot and Breton beyond enjoyment, in a way Swinburne or Verlaine had not been.

The strange fertility and variety of art between the wars sprang from the very disintegration of tradition which makes it hard to make a general judgement about it. It may be too soon for one which will stand any hard scrutiny. Some characteristics which run through all its manifestations can be detected and it is probably wisest simply to state them, and to leave the matter there. In the first place, culture became much more a matter of *coteries* and fashions; the possibility of comprehension was less than ever before. It was a related fact that art became much more individual and private in its expressions, its social purpose usually much harder to see. It was also more than ever alienated from traditional culture and traditional society and it manifested this above all in its irrational and destructive nature. If there was one great intellectual influence which pervaded it, it was that of Freud.[29] Finally, it is impossible not to feel that it expresses not merely alienation from bourgeois society but a loss of nerve by that society and that culture itself. Never was there a time when intellectual élites with an important stake in the preservation of a privileged culture so readily tolerated even contributed to its abuse. They often refused to admit and sometimes actually denied their own debt to the taming of violence and the dominance of reason.

THE SHAKING OF LIBERAL SOCIETY

Changes in culture and ways of life affect social stability, though it is not easy to say how. When we observe that, say, political institutions are easily overthrown in some countries, we must not be too anxious to accept any one explanation. Economic distress may have something to do with it, but so may the presence of genuine political grievance or the decline of the prestige of old assumptions. And there may be reciprocal effects; we should not rush to plump for chickens or eggs.

Great damage was done to social cohesion by the two great physical and psychlogical blows of the Great War and chronic economic *malaise* after 1918. The gap of generations was suddenly widened by millions of deaths and a difference of experience between those who had been in the trenches and those who had not. Similarly, economic disaster had different effects in different sectors of society. The unemployed underwent a demoralizing experience of idleness; the confidence of the saving class was sapped by inflation. These experiences did much to break up the 'cake of custom', to use a Victorian phrase. Old habits had to be discarded, and traditional standards and authorities were weakened. Changes ran right through the social order, sometimes enlarging individual freedom, but this did not always happen. It became clear, for example, that the movement from status to contract which had run through European history since the

29 One of the best summaries of the illumination which Freud's work brought to intellectuals and artists is the speech made by Mann on Freud's eightieth birthday in Vienna, 1936, reprinted in *Essays of Three Decades* (London, 1947).

French Revolution was no longer accepted by the masses or endorsed by intellectuals as it had been.

This shift in the deepest currents of European history was not easily discernible, because many of the social developments of the interwar years still seemed logically continuous with what had gone before. The ruling élites, for example, continued to evolve as they had been evolving before 1914. The Great War did great damage to the hereditary principle which lay at the basis of status society; it nowhere any longer seemed by itself a sufficient justification of authority.[30] Nevertheless, criticisms that this was not enough were now coming to be heard, and not only from the traditional Left. Europe was still divided effectively into minorities and masses. The prestige of the new ruling élites was being undermined, too; it was asserted that they could not grapple with economic and social problems as the times demanded. It was urged that the persistence of social divisions was wrong in societies whose official mythologies were democratic and egalitarian. Some critics of the existing order admired efficiency, and would have liked a shift of real power to managers and technocrats which liberal political institutions seemed to resist. Other critics, disliking market society, equally disliked the socialism they believed to be its child and the prospect of rule by economic experts; they were prepared to assent in the rule of new élites which justified themselves by the simple ability to govern and hold power by force. Still others attacked market society in the name of criteria which had confessedly irrationalist grounds, such as racial purity, or because they believed it to be in some vague but alarming sense, 'decadent'.

All these criticisms of the general tendency of European society towards rational and contractual arrangements found some support after 1918. Almost no thinker, writer, poet or artist of stature who could be termed 'modern' had much good to say of the society which had produced him. Almost all bitterly attacked the social and political institutions they saw around them. Meanwhile the masses were profoundly alienated from market society both by its economic inefficiency and by the subtler pressures of uncertainty, fear and pointlessness which arose from urbanization

30 For a contemporary and characteristically optimistic assessment of the trend sketched here, and its intimate connexion with the belief in progress, see W. McDougall, *The Group Mind* (Cambridge, 1920), especially its last chapter, 'The progress of nations in their maturity'.

and industry. Men were left without guidance to face incomprehensible challenges. Church, family and locality had been so battered by liberal civilization that they were weaker than ever as steadying forces. Europeans were rootless as never before, and less moved by custom and tradition. They were ready to follow men who promised security and a sense of purpose. Capitalism had been unprecedentedly successful in meeting material needs (though even that was not easy to see unless the observer was sophisticated enough to take a long view), but it appeared to have been unable to generate spiritual and intelletual purpose in any but a few.

The comprehensiveness of these criticisms and the shaking of the foundations in the war and slumps is somehow linked to the greater irruption of violence and irrationalism in political behaviour between the wars. In many places this helped authoritarian and even fascist régimes. Another beneficiary was communism.

After the Great War, Europe was obsessed with communism and it was often very difficult to see it in perspective. In 1939 communism was feared in many countries as socialism, with its evolution towards moderation and practical revision, had not been in 1914. In retrospect, it is not easy to see why, because communism had a long record of failure. Its greatest achievement, the seizure of power in Russia, was a by-product of military defeat. None of the brief communist revolutions in central and eastern Europe, in the postwar period, took root. Communist parties proved as helpless as democratic organizations in dealing with dictatorships. Often their only achievement was negative, the emasculation of the Left by their bitter attacks on liberals and socialists.

Some of this is to be explained by the roots of the Comintern in the determination of the Bolsheviks to prevent a revival of a socialist International by the Social Democrats of the great western countries (who accepted a parliamentary framework for their activity). Affiliation to the Comintern became the test of communist parties. By 1922 the prewar socialist parties and, in some cases, the trade unions, of the main western countries had settled on one side or another of the line, or had split. The German independent socialists who had opposed the majority view on the war were shattered and some of them driven back into the S.P.D. The French socialist party was taken over and the minority left it to rebuild a new non-communist party. The Italian

socialists were completely disorganized. These were ill consequences for the Left. In England, on the other hand, the
communist party was insignificant, and the Labour party's
strength steadily grew.

Socialist history for the next two decades is the story of the
consequences of Comintern mistakes in these years. Rightly, a
socialist historian has commented that 'judged by the standard of
its early hopes and aspirations, the Communist International was
an egregious failure.'[31] It drove many socialists back into the arms
of the right-wing party bureaucracies, it delivered others to
destruction at the hands of reactionaries by encouraging the illusion of an imminent world revolution, and it smoothed the path
for Fascism and Nazism. Later, it was to sap the democracies'
will and power to resist Hitler. All these unhappy consequences
sprang from the original differences of culture and historical
circumstance between the Russian revolutionaries and the socialists of western Europe. These differences were sharpened and
deepened by Russian national policy; its extreme of cynicism was
reached after the Nazi-Soviet pact of 1939, when the N.K.V.D.
and *Gestapo* cooperated in the return of political refugees to one
another's prisons. Although the Comintern itself did not meet for
several years after 1928, the national communist parties continued
the vilification of other socialists which made cooperation with
them impossible except during the brief period of the Popular
Front.

The Bolsheviks' attacks on their opponents promoted the
barbarizing of European politics which is so marked after 1918.
Their extremism, which made them incapable of assessing a
political situation in any but intransigently revolutionary terms,
was, of course, matched by that of irreconcilably anti-democratic
movements on the right. Both favoured the increasing use of violence in politics. The treatment of political opponents sharply
deteriorated. Conduct which had previously been regarded as an
unhappy legacy of Turkish rule in the more backward corners of
the Balkans, was generalized over much of eastern Europe. The
worst horrors were not the appalling massacres carried out in the
name of collectivization in Russia, or even the huge slave-labour
camps of Siberia, but the deliberate resumption of racial and
political persecution by the Nazis; often they had no conceivable

31 G. D. H. Cole, *A History of Socialist Thought* (London, 1953–60),
vol. IV, p. 855.

object except the infliction of pain but the torture chambers and concentration camps of Nazi Germany seem never to have been short of staff. In some sense they met a psychological demand of German society. Worse was to be seen after 1939.

It was a perverse triumph of the European liberal conscience that so many people found it impossible to believe in the horrors of Stalin's Russia and Nazi Germany; although disbelief gradually weakened, there were still some people who could not credit the truth even in 1939. It was undeniable, however, that nineteenth-century standards had crumbled in the conduct of formal warfare. In 1914, exaggerated and inflated reports of German atrocities against civilians in Belgium had caused great disgust. No one had worried about the way in which Napoleon's Grand Army had behaved: this disgust was the marker of a century's humanizing of opinion and warfare. The conduct of the war which followed began to undermine it. The drowning of civilians without warning or attempts at rescue, and the first air raids on civilian targets showed what was happening. People became readier to accept lower standards. The use of poison gas in Abyssinia and the bombing of the Spanish Civil War were dramatic announcements of the new way in which war was likely to be waged. By 1939 everyone in the west expected mass bombing and were surprised in fact when it did not occur, although the fate of the Polish cities was to show that its absence was not due to any moral scruple.

Such facts make it tempting to forget the strength which humanitarian sentiment could still display in such fields as the relief of the Russian famine of 1922, or the pursuit of disarmament, or the work of the ancillary agencies of the League. Important though these things were, they had their dangerous side, too, in that they distracted some people's attention from the danger and violence of the postwar world and encouraged the illusion of a return to the old certainties. This was never to happen. Some people blamed the Enlightenment for devouring itself. Science, it was said, had swept away the restraints of transcendental ethics and traditional codes and in a value-free universe man had to abandon moral restraint to survive. It was merely ironic that the Nazis should burn the books of Freud and display the works of the Expressionists in an exhibition of Decadent Art; persecutors and persecuted were, after all, symptoms of the same disorder.

15

THE APPROACH TO THE SECOND WORLD WAR

POWER POLITICS 1930–36

'Power politics' were discredited in the later 1920s, but never vanished: Locarno was founded only on agreement between the major states. At Geneva, their representatives held their own, private, meetings during the Assembly, and these 'Locarno tea-parties' (as they were called) were a little like the old 'Concert of Europe', in which large states settled Europe's affairs over the heads of smaller ones. The growing international security of the years before 1930 was therefore something of a façade. A coincidence of interests among the major states and personal ties between their statesmen were safety-valves for the antagonisms of international life, but they were fragile and temporary safeguards. German revisionism had been appeased at Locarno but remained as alive as that of Hungary or Italy. Russia might take part in the practical work of the League, but she stayed outside. Anglo-French antagonism was always liable to break out when disarmament negotiations revealed the inevitable differences of interests between a continental state which faced her only likely enemy across a land frontier, and the insular centre of a world-wide empire, increasingly vulnerable to air attack and dependent on sea communications. Finally, however many non-European states might join the League, the United States did not.

Such facts were given new meaning by economic disaster after 1930. Tariffs rose everywhere as European states began the search for autarky which characterized the 1930s. The goodwill which had sustained international cooperation in the past evaporated;

economically at least, it was each nation for itself. This made remedies even more difficult while unemployment and insecurity were feeding political extremism. Nationalist and social demagogy flared up and soon the psychological oppression of fears of war was added to the obstacles to economic recovery.

Because not all countries suffered in the same degree, international politics was further embittered by a widening of the gap between countries satisfied by Versailles and those which were not. France, for example, was slow to feel the effects of recession and her economic self-confidence encouraged her statesmen to drag their feet over remedial proposals and made them insensitive to the dangers of America's economic troubles. The United Kingdom underwent a change of government and the abandonment of the gold standard and free trade, but began soon to shake off the worst of the depression. Germany suffered most. Before the 1931 election, the communists and the Nazis had considerable success in polarizing the political struggle there as the clash of two extremisms. German governments sought support by pursuing a strong nationalist line in foreign affairs. The crisis settled the reparations question, because it was manifestly impossible for Germany to pay. When Brüning said so in 1932, France could do nothing about this breach of Versailles, though there were rumours that the government considered mobilization and even the bombing of the Rhineland. Finally, in June 1933 Germany stopped payments on all her foreign debts. This was at least a clarification, in that the vexed and complicated question of reparation and debt repayment now disappeared, but the French felt cheated. Germany had shed the economic burdens which were to Frenchmen so important a part of Versailles. It was the gravest blow to French security since the end of the war. The Americans, too, felt cheated; their European debtors persisted in linking reparations to the settlement of Allied war debts. American isolationism was strengthened by the spectacle of former Allies welshing on their creditors.[1]

Economic and political troubles flowed together in one small state, Austria, where pan-German sentiment combined with the economic crisis in 1931 to lead her government to begin nego-

---

1 The Americans in the end received (in round figures) $3,000 million of the $10,000 million they had lent, $2,000 million of it from Great Britain.

tiations for an Austro-German Customs Union. France was at once alarmed by the spectre of an *Anschluss*. She protested that this would contravene the Versailles stipulation that the two countries should not be united. The Bank of France refused to give support to the Viennese *Kredit-Anstalt*, by way of bringing pressure to bear on the Austrians, thus contributing materially to the failure of that bank in May, and the beginnings of the most intense phase of the European crisis (see p. 365). The scheme was abandoned amid great nationalist resentment in Germany and Austria.

There now followed a much greater shock. The Manchurian crisis belongs to Asian history, and here it is enough to say that Japan had long regarded the Chinese province of Manchuria as one in which her vital interests gave her real moral claims. The consolidation of the Chinese national state after the revolution and an influx of Chinese immigrants to Manchuria made some Japanese think that their claims, if not asserted, would go by default. In September 1931 the Japanese army forced the issue by acting independently. It quickly conquered Manchuria and set up there a puppet state, Manchukuo. The League sent out a Commission of Inquiry which criticized the Japanese. No formal condemnation followed, but Japan left the League (27 March 1933).

This was a major step in the long course of revisionism in the Far East which Japan had followed since European intervention had forced her to abandon the gains of Shimonoseki. Insured by alliance with Great Britain, she had first defeated her major rival in the Yellow Sea area. German interests in China had then been eliminated in the Great War, from which Japan had emerged as the third largest naval power in the world. Soviet Russia was weak and blundered in China. The Japanese seizure of Manchuria was only the latest of many demonstrations of the power of the first Asian nation to challenge European supremacy in the Far East.

In 1931 most of this was overlooked in the uproar over the affront to the League. Japan had ignored the Covenant. If no one was prepared to use force to uphold it, the League counted for nothing. The issue was confused, but the Covenant bound League members not to go to war to support their claims (rightfully or wrongly based though they might be) until the League had undertaken arbitration or enquiry. Japan had simply ignored this.[2] The lesson was not lost on Germany and Italy, and smaller

European states felt alarmed by the League's failure in its first confrontation with a major power. Worse still, the United States did nothing, although the Far East was an area in which she was traditionally interested. What, then, could be expected of her in places where her direct interest was smaller?

The League's failure to achieve international disarmament was the next great disappointment. The Covenant laid on it the obligation of bringing about a reduction of armaments. Humanitarian idealism, the horrors of the Great War and dismay over the heavy cost of military preparedness made electorates and governments responsive. In Britain the security provided by the Channel and the Royal Navy made it easy to feel that it was unfair to penalize Germany in the matter of land armaments when other states did not reduce theirs. This view was unpopular in France, where security came before disarmament as a goal of foreign policy. French governments, nevertheless, were by no means wholly negative and unconstructive; they several times made it clear that an international armed force to police the Versailles settlement under League control would have their support.

In this setting, the belief had prospered that international disarmament was possible. But it proved much harder than expected. British maritime and imperial commitments complicated discussions on aircraft and shipping.[3] The French grew suspicious of further reduction of their strength after the reduction of Germany's reparations burden. Locarno left them alone with commitments in eastern Europe where, beside German revisionism, the Russian army, potentially the greatest in Europe, might one day threaten Poland. And all the time, German resentment at unequal treatment was mounting, and strengthening the German nationalists who demanded treaty revision. When the occupation of Germany ended in 1930, Germans demanded from the League equality of treatment with England and France, who had not disarmed. 1930 brought a great outburst of nationalist clamour in Germany; election troubles in Upper Silesia had led to German complaints to the League of Polish brutality (though the only people who actually *died* in these incidents were, in fact,

---

2 Though, strictly, she was not in a state of war with China.
3 But an extension of the Washington Agreements limiting the size of navies was achieved in 1930; smaller vessels were then controlled as capital ships had been by the 1922 treaties.

Poles). The German election of September 1930 was startlingly bitter. From it emerged the alarming spectacle of the Nazis as the second largest party in the *Reichstag*. This was followed by more nationalist agitation in April, when quarrels at Danzig led to the withdrawal of the Polish minister from the city because his safety could not be guaranteed. This background explains the German delegates' growing truculence at Geneva. It was made worse by French suspicions that Germany had already achieved an important degree of secret rearmament.

The work of the League in disarmament was therefore coming to a head at a bad moment, when the confidence of Locarno had been dissipated and people were again beginning to speak of the danger of war. A Disarmament Conference which had at last assembled sat during most of 1932 and 1933, but achieved nothing. Technical arguments and divergences between British and French policy hampered it from the start, and the situation in Germany steadily worsened. Her delegates uncompromisingly demanded equality of armaments. When Hitler became chancellor, the attitude of the French further stiffened; they pointed out that such trained quasi-military forces as the Stormtroops should now be taken into account in assessing Germany's military strength. Hitler refused to admit this, on one occasion drawing an unconvincing parallel between the S.A. and the Salvation Army. Unfortunately, the logic of the French position left unsolved the problem of power: the only solution of the French dilemma was a punitive and preventive war to destroy German military strength while there was still time, but this was unthinkable. Instead, France offered, as a last concession, equality for Germany after four years. This was rejected by Hitler, who insisted that Germany should at once be allowed to possess 'defensive' weapons.[4] On October 14 Germany announced her withdrawal both from the Disarmament Conference and the League, and effectively ended the story of disarmament.

This did not stop efforts to achieve it. The British government already believed that Hitler was preparing to build military aircraft in large numbers, but hoped that German rearmament might at least be limited by an agreement freely negotiated by

4 At this time, there was a real fear in Berlin of a Polish attack on Germany, E. M. Robertson, *Hitler's Pre-war Policy and Military Plans 1933–9* (London, 1963), pp. 10–11.

Germany. Hitler encouraged such hopes by what was to become a familiar technique of conciliatory and moderate language. Yet more odium therefore fell on a distrustful France, whose government was at this time distracted by domestic troubles and badly placed to negotiate effectively. In April 1934 France finally rejected further disarmament negotiations on the grounds that Germany had already broken the Treaty's limits on her military strength. The Disarmament Conference fizzled out in June, one of its last sessions hearing renewed assurances of goodwill from the United States delegate while he repeated that his country could not in any circumstances commit itself to military obligations in Europe.

In fact, no power, in or out of the League, was prepared to go to war to enforce the Treaty of Versailles strictly. Nor was anyone willing to give the French convincing guarantees if a disarmament convention were to be agreed. Neither England nor the United States wanted to quarrel with Germany, although the British ambassador at Berlin was already advising that Hitler could best be handled by firmness, and attention began to be paid to the military problem he posed. The German military estimates for 1934 were twice those of 1933 and Hitler's withdrawal from the conference was very popular at home. Such facts lay behind a British White Paper of 1 March 1935, which justified British rearmament. This provoked much public and official indignation in Germany, where it put paid to another British attempt to start negotiations on disarmament. The existence of the *Luftwaffe* was made public, and on 16 March, a law reintroducing conscription set the German army's peacetime strength at thirty-six divisions (about 600,000 men). The figures and timing of this step were decided by Hitler without consulting his startled generals. In a conversation with the British foreign secretary at the end of the month, he also made the alarming claim that Germany had already achieved parity in the air with the Royal Air Force.[5]

---

5 The evaluation of these and similar statements was complicated but on any interpretation they were bound to cause the British government grave disquiet. Exaggeration, however, was not all on one side. The German generals were arguing at the beginning of 1935 that a long time was needed to build up their forces, in part because their intelligence assessments indicated a great increase in French, Czech and Russian strength since 1933. The defensive power of the Maginot line was said to have tripled in two years.

These German acts dealt the League a harder blow than had Japan, and were much more ominous for the future peace of Europe. It was beginning to appear that the power relationships on which Versailles had rested had been so eroded that the settlement was no longer viable. Its foundation had been the power of a victorious coalition which had dissolved almost at once. Later, the Disarmament Conference had encouraged an atmosphere which made resistance to aggression difficult, and had helped to make France appear responsible for international tension. Other states could now denounce the disarmament clauses of their peace treaties; on 1 April Austria set aside the Treaty of Saint-Germain by reintroducing conscription.

Diplomacy had already begun to take account of the new violence of German nationalism and tacitly set aside the League machinery. In February 1933 the '*Little Entente*' had reorganized itself with the aim of conducting a common foreign policy. In 1934, Turkey, Greece, Rumania and Yugoslavia signed a Balkan pact and France made treaties with Italy and Russia. The British government, on the other hand, further weakened collective resistance to revisionism by negotiating an Anglo-German naval agreement which gave Germany the right to build a fleet of 35 per cent of the strength of the Royal Navy. The arguments for this were that German rearmament was going ahead in any case, and Versailles was ignored; why not, therefore, settle terms which Germany would keep because she had freely negotiated them? Unfortunately, this resumption of bilateral agreements was implicitly a repudiation of Versailles; it disregarded the interests of other signatories of that Treaty (France would now have to increase her navy) and made nonsense of the condemnation of the German Army Law which Britain, together with France and Italy, had forced on the League.

In this adjustment of European politics, Italy was now temporarily to attract the limelight as a disturbing force, and to draw attention away from Germany. Fascist foreign policy had always been confused, but its basic revisionism and violence had been tempered in practice by awareness of the dangers of isolation. Mussolini was worried both by French influence in the Balkans and the Mediterranean, and by a possible German threat to the weak Austrian Republic. Roughly speaking, this had encouraged good relations with an oddly-assorted trio: Britain, Hungary and Russia, with whom Italy signed a non-aggression treaty in

September 1933. Mussolini had already tried to safeguard Austria by a Four Power pact (15 July 1933) whose signatories only confirmed their existing commitments under Locarno and the Covenant; its chief importance was its demonstration of Mussolini's willingness to set aside League procedures in favour of old-fashioned 'power politics'. He acted much more effectively in July 1934, when the murder of Dolfuss led him to mobilize forces on the Austrian frontier to resist a possible German *coup*. This improved his relations with France.

Unfortunately, Italo-French friendship was shattered by what have been called by one observer 'the first shots of the second world war',[6] those that killed the French foreign minister and his guest, King Alexander of Yugoslavia, at Marseilles in October. It was believed that Mussolini had known what was planned. Because the murder set Hungary and Yugoslavia at loggerheads (it had been encouraged by a Croat group operating from Hungary), Italy and France had to support their respective *protégés*. In 1935 Laval, the new French foreign minister, visited Rome and signed an agreement with Italy which seemed to repair the damage (7 January). It tidied up some African questions left over from 1919, confirmed the intention of the two countries that Austria should remain independent and expressed readiness for future consultations. Much cordial coming-and-going followed, the Italians sending an art exhibition to Paris, and the French a squadron of ships to Naples. Consequently, at a conference at Stresa in April 1935 between Britain, France and Italy, it was possible for the three powers to look united in face of the German threat, though no one had any positive steps to propose against Germany. This made discussion easy, and Stresa resulted only in a communiqué which said the powers were in complete agreement on every matter they had considered. Austria was one of these; Ethiopia was not.

Ethiopia had long interested Mussolini and since 1932 he had intended to have a war with it. His main motive seems to have been the desire for war itself, which would give him the chance to play the role of war leader, and would also provide, he believed, an easy and spectacular success for Fascism. It would appeal to the frustrated colonial ambitions of the Italians, and avenge the long-rankling defeat of 1896. In 1934 the moment had

6 Avon, p. 408.

seemed propitious. Austria looked safe for the foreseeable future. The British and French were anxious to cooperate with Italy and impressed by her strength. Britain had no special sympathy for Ethiopia, whose entry to the League, indeed, she had opposed. France and Italy were about to sign the Rome agreement.

On 5 December 1934 Italian and Ethiopian forces came into conflict at an oasis in Ethiopian territory where Italy claimed certain rights. The legal situation was not clear, but several men were killed on both sides. Within a few days the Ethiopian government drew the attention of the League to the grave situation resulting from Italian claims for reparation and reassurance for the future. The League was slow to act, but sought to decide first where lay the responsibility for the clash. Meanwhile the Italian government raised its demands and assembled reinforcements in its East African colonies. The existence of a treaty of friendship between Italy and Ethiopia, signed in 1928, and the concern of Britain and France (who had joined Italy in 1906 in defining their interests in Ethiopia), encouraged hopes of a peaceful settlement and made it plausible for the League to delay. But by the summer of 1935, Mussolini's extravagant demands were beginning to be recognized as sinister and criticism of Italy's action was growing. In June Britain attempted a solution by proposing that territory in British Somaliland should be accepted by Ethiopia as a corridor to the sea to compensate her for concessions to Italy elsewhere. Mussolini at once refused (and it offended France, which had no wish to see Ethiopia's external trade rerouted away from Djibuti). It was soon clear that Mussolini was not interested in a solution other than war. At the League Council, the Italian representative announced Italy's refusal to negotiate with Ethiopia. This made it necessary to face the question which Britain and France had been anxious to avoid: what should they do if the League condemned Italy as an aggressor?

When the Assembly met (11 September), the British foreign secretary, Hoare, strongly supported collective action against a disturber of the peace. It seemed that Britain was prepared to uphold the League's authority even at the cost of war. In spite of Laval's misgivings and attempts to weaken it behind the scenes, France held the same language. The reinforcement of the British Mediterranean Fleet also made a strong impression. Nevertheless it did not deter Mussolini, who launched a full-scale invasion on 3 October, when the rainy season in Ethiopia at last came to an end. An attack upon a fellow-member of the League was a clear breach of the Covenant. It now remained to be seen what the League's authority meant.

On 6 October the Council of the League formally declared Italy to have resorted to war in breach of the Covenant, a conclusion endorsed by the Assembly. This meant that Italy had committed an act of war against all members of the League, which now set up machinery to devise 'sanctions' against her. Italy could be refused financial services or aid, imports of her goods could be rejected, and exports to her could be stopped. Although Laval at Geneva and the British cabinet in London showed no anxiety to pursue this policy very actively,[7] the formal step was very important. It looked as though the League was at last to be what its admirers had said it could be, an effective instrument for peace. Many must have shared the thankfulness of a member of the House of Commons that 'the League has passed from shadow into substance'.[8]

Unfortunately, French policy, with the support of French public opinion, sapped the vitality of the British stand. Sanctions could hardly be effective unless they were quickly applied to war-making materials, above all, oil. Yet pressed this far they might bring about a military clash with Italy. Although by the end of the month Rumania and Russia had agreed to apply oil sanctions if other countries did the same,[9] the League delayed in deciding whether to instruct its members to cut off Italy's oil. Laval strove to prevent resolution of the question. By the beginning of December, he had so worked upon the fears of the British foreign secretary that he obtained his agreement to a set of proposals for a settlement which would have truncated Ethiopia. It made nonsense of the League's stand on principle.

The Hoare-Laval 'pact' leaked out in Paris. The outcry in Britain (where the government had just won an election on a programme of support for the League and sanctions) was so strong that the government disavowed it.[10] Hoare was replaced

7 One British minister who *was* very keen on effective sanctions was Neville Chamberlain.
8 Winston Churchill, 23 October 1935.
9 Between them they supplied over half Italy's needs. India, Iraq and the Netherlands gave the same undertaking in November.
10 None of Hoare's colleagues had had any idea that Hoare's holiday trip to Switzerland would result in such an agreement.

as foreign secretary by Eden, a man believed to be wholeheartedly in favour of effective sanctions. Laval's government broke up in January. But the damage to international confidence was irreparable. Nor did the British government now prove any more inclined to risk armed conflict with Italy, although in February it decided to apply oil sanctions if other countries did. The new French government declined to act. The Italian armies meanwhile went ahead more quickly (with a widespread use of poison gas). In May Addis Ababa fell, and the Ethiopian war ended with annexation to Italy (May 9). The emperor, Haile Selassie, began a five-year exile with a dignified and moving protest before the Assembly of the League.[11]

This story of failure is complicated, but its structure is clear. The first facts which matter are Mussolini's determination and the simple passage of time. The only aim of Italian policy, whatever misgivings might arise along the way, was a war, and every delay in procedure was exploited by Mussolini to this end. This suited the British and French governments in so far as it put off the unpleasant dilemma of a choice between Italy and the League. As two great powers, as two Mediterranean powers, and as two East African powers, England and France had to take the lead. But they were also the two Stresa powers, who saw Italy as a potential ally against Germany. Both wished for most of the time not to alienate Mussolini so violently that his troops would be unavailable on the Brenner. When Japan and Germany had already left the League, would it help world peace to drive Italy out too?

Unfortunately Mussolini did leave the League, and this alienation did take place. But this does not mean that the inconsistency at the heart of the British and French policy could have been recognized and eliminated at the start. Other complications made that difficult. One was timing: the Ethiopian crisis was for a long time not the major preoccupation of statesmen. Ethiopia's appeal to the League, for example, had to compete for attention with the German reintroduction of conscription on the same day. Nor was Anglo-French cooperation assured. It seems likely that Laval communicated his doubts about it to Mussolini long before the dramatic 'pact' of December. (The British government, after all, had set him an example of disregard for collective agreements in

---

11 He next stood on Ethiopian soil, 20 January 1941, after the reconquest of Ethiopia had begun.

the Anglo-German naval agreement.) The British government was unsure about public reactions to a threat of war and was not confident that the Mediterranean fleet could stand up to Italian air attack. And always, in the background, there was doubt whether, if sanctions were extended to oil, United States producers would not continue to meet Italy's needs.

Yet in spite of these complications, it is difficult to envisage any outcome worse than that which actually resulted. The League was fatally damaged. Henceforth, it was all but ignored by the great powers, and the last phase of European power politics began. The Stresa front was moribund, too. Laval had told Eden so at the time of the Anglo-German naval agreement, though there were attempts to apply artificial respiration even after the Italian invasion began. But the outcry over the Hoare-Laval pact began to turn Mussolini towards Hitler. It also embittered Anglo-French relations, many Britons being persuaded that Laval had pursued a policy approved by all his countrymen.

Mussolini's prestige and self-confidence benefited enormously, though Italy had suffered economically from the war and had given hostages to fortune for the future. Hitler observed the hollowness of sanctions even against a country far more vulnerable to them than Germany could ever be. He noted the indecision and divisions of the democracies in an international crisis. He was quick to profit. Meanwhile, the collapse of respect for the Covenant, the revelation that it would not be supported in arms, and the new violence of German policy meant, inevitably, that European states would now seek new methods of achieving security. Only two seemed available in 1936, the traditional system of alliances of major powers, or the creation of ideological *blocs*. The difficulties of both were quickly to be shown.

THE GERMAN PROBLEM, 1935–38

By 1938 Germany dominated Europe diplomatically as it had never done before. The rebuilding of her military power was central to this; even in 1914 Germany was less feared. The origins of rearmament went back into the secret preparations of the *Reichswehr* under the Weimar Republic, long before its formal acknowledgment in March 1935. But rearmament was only the last of many steps which, one by one, made possible the renewal of Germany's claim to European pre-eminence. By 1935 little of the structure set up to contain Germany was intact except the territorial settlements of Versailles. In spite of Hitler's acceptance of the engagements of Locarno, these were to be shattered by him in the next four years. Cumulatively, that run of success enormously enhanced his power to commit his countrymen to more grandiose and fantastic schemes than the revision of the 1919 settlement.

Circumstances were peculiarly favourable to him. One essential pre-condition of his success was the disarray of his potential opponents. Although the contrast between the 'democracies' of Britain and France and the 'dictatorships' of Germany and Italy grew sharper, the democracies' defence of their interests was inept and confused; a democratic crusade along ideological lines was never a practical policy. Even the earlier French stand against German resurgence gave way from 1934 to division. Some Frenchmen of the Right thought Hitler a lesser threat than left-wing governments. Others felt disillusioned and discouraged by past failures. The check to the proposed Austro-German Customs Union of 1931 had been, after all, the only successful effort among all those made by France since 1919 to maintain the German clauses of the treaty. It was tempting to relapse into passivity, to recall the terrible butcher's bills of the Great War and France's demographic inferiority, and to rely upon the Maginot fortifications to inflict unbearable losses in the event of another German attack.

Other states were even less likely to resist a resurgent Germany. Italy, although she feared for Austria, had no love for much of the Versailles settlement. Mussolini patronized Hungarian revisionism (which endangered its neighbours as much as did Germany's), and was alienated from Britain and France by Ethiopia (see above). As for British slowness in reacting to Germany's new stance, it had deeper and more tenacious sources and had always been influenced by the view that Versailles was both morally and practically questionable. Anglo-French relations had long suffered from the belief that the French were acting harshly and unjustly in trying to maintain the full rigour of the peace settlement and that it was in any case impractical to seek to restrain forever a nation with a population of 65 million. There was also a broad current of humanitarianism, hatred of war, and fear of what a new war would be like in an age of poison gas and incendiary bombs, which made it hard for British statesmen to take up uncompromising positions, or to win credence abroad when they did.[12] The presence of experts in the foreign office who clearly discerned the German danger could not offset these forces. Finally, British policy was dominated by an unrealistic and exaggerated sense of military and air inferiority. The rearmament announced by Hitler, it is now clear, was taken far too seriously. It was true that immediately after taking office as chancellor, Hitler had assured the *Reichswehr* that it could expect soon to train with real tanks instead of motor-cars and in 1934 the first tank battalion was formed. But production of the *Pzkw* III – the 'Mark III' medium tank which was to be the backbone of the armoured divisions of 1941 – did not begin until 1938. Serious armament only began after Germany left the League. Moreover, the prospect of dissolving the *Reichswehr*'s highly trained cadres into the enormous mass of thirty-six divisions envisaged by Hitler, had appalled the professional soldiers. They feared, rightly, that Germany's preparedness for war would actually be lessened by the rearmament programme. Between 1935 and 1937, the German army was really weaker than at any time in the decade. Yet its strength, and that of the German air force, was continually overestimated abroad. Russia was potentially the best military counter-weight to Germany, but no one could be sure what she counted for in the era of the project while she could only act against Germany with the cooperation of Poland and the Baltic countries whose very existence was a reminder of Russian defeat in 1918–20. In 1914 Germany and Russia had a common frontier; now at their closest point, between Minsk and East Prussia, they were separated by two hundred miles of Polish territory. Czechoslovakia was a hundred miles from Russia, across Polish territory and the Carpathians (which blocked any effective communications). Russian policy was, in any case, suspect because of the revolutionary propaganda of the Comintern.

Any German nationalist leader could have exploited such a situation. At home, conservative and military circles would provide

---

12 The effects of editorial opinion expressed in *The Times* are notorious; for an early specific example, see Avon, pp. 176–8; the most celebrated is the leader of 7 September 1938. On the whole question, see *The History of the Times* (London, 1935–52).

support from the right for further attacks on Versailles; the blanket charge that reparations had been the cause of all Germany's economic ills was a powerful rallying force for the masses. Nor had Germans lost the self-indulgent racialism which had made them think it intolerable that a German should ever be governed by a Slav, by, for example, a Polish official in Silesia. All the resources and commonplaces of German nationalism were at work in his favour before Hitler came to power.

The individual contribution of Hitler to what followed, therefore, may be and has been much debated.[13] His first concern was internal consolidation; successes in foreign policy were sought with this aim. His demands did not seem very unusual; their danger lay in a limitlessness not then apparent. Although he stressed *Grossdeutsch* themes, he added to the revisionism, rearmament and the restoration of lost territory sought by many Germans only a vague dream of a racialist policy of *Lebensraum* in the east and a sentimental respect for the British Empire. His decisive contribution to German diplomacy was, in spite of his growing pursuit of irrational goals, not one of content, but of technique. It was shown in Germany's departure from the League and avowal of rearmament. This announced a coming change in the balance of military power, but one at that moment unachieved. Hitler brought to policy great daring and dexterity. Once engaged in action, he seldom looked beyond the next move. He acted boldly, pushing further and harder than others who shared his aims would have done, but he chose his moment and his issue carefully, uttering conciliatory language to confuse his opponents at home and abroad even while he acted. He was thus able to exploit the almost universal popular desire for peace in France and Britain, and the weaknesses of their governments.[14] At the outset his audacity had elements of bluff in it, because he could not have afforded a war. This is why his generals were frightened.[15] When he no longer feared war – apparently from late 1937 – he became more dangerous still. His claims posed a

13 See I. Kershaw, *The Nazi dictatorship*, pp. 106–129 for an admirable summary.
14 The British government long pursued the will-o'-the-wisp of placating Hitler by a restoration of German colonies, in which he had little interest.
15 Even to the point of resisting his diversion of men and weapons to help Franco.

dilemma to his opponents. Either they could resist, accepting the risk of war and its unknown horrors with divided councils and unappealingly negative aims, or they could try to stabilize the situation by recognizing the new realities of power and negotiating limits to them which would be viable because freely negotiated. The Rhineland soon provided the opportunity for an exercise in this problem.

The Treaty of Versailles forbade German armed forces or fortifications on the left bank of the Rhine or within a fifty-kilometre deep zone on the right bank. The Locarno treaties guaranteed this 'demilitarization'. When the Saar was returned to Germany in 1935 after a plebiscite, the German government specifically recognized that it formed part of the Rhineland and demilitarized zone, and in this way again appeared to acquiesce in its existence. Hitler had also said that he would respect freely negotiated treaties (as Locarno had been). Nevertheless, during 1935 misgivings began to be felt that a reoccupation of the Rhineland was intended. The return of the Saar had given Hitler more freedom of action. Violations of the demilitarization conditions were noticed and it was later alleged that as many as 20,000 German soldiers had been introduced into the zone in a clandestine manner. The irritation and alarm which the German government expressed over the signing of a Franco-Russian treaty in May 1935 increased apprehension. It was not, therefore, from a completely clear sky that there fell the *coup* of reoccupation.

On 3 March 1936 German troops began to reoccupy the demilitarized zone. An announcement that this was taking place was made to the British and French governments, accompanied by a repudiation of Locarno, on the grounds that the Franco-Russian pact (ratified the previous month) was incompatible with it. At the same time, Germany offered to make a new, comprehensive agreement and held out the prospect of her re-entry to the League, a concession calculated to confuse opinion and to exploit differences between the guarantors of Locarno. This action was taken on a Saturday, the onset of the weekend making it difficult for officials and politicians to confer quickly and react decisively.

France was the power most affected: the demilitarized Rhineland had been her guarantee that she could, if the need arose, strike at Germany without fear. But her government was hesitant and indecisive. When the blow fell, France was on the eve of a general election; only three ministers were prepared to resist. Neither troops nor plans for a counter-occupation existed. Nor was Britain prepared to fight to uphold Locarno. It did not seem reasonable in London for the French, who had resisted the imposition of sanctions on Italy for making war on another League member, now to demand that sanctions should be enforced on Germany for action taken bloodlessly on her own soil. Public opinion in Britain was unprepared to support France, even had she tried to act.

As a result, Hitler won his first major diplomatic success and great popularity at home. The Council of the League formally condemned the breach of Versailles, and the Locarno powers invited Germany to lay her case against the Franco-Russian Treaty before the Hague Court, but this was all. In April the British and French governments, at the request of the Belgian, declared that Belgium was relieved of her obligations under the Locarno treaties, while their own remained in force. The only hopeful development was that Anglo-French relations began to improve when Blum became prime minister, but a British minister could still cause a sensation by a speech in Paris asserting that Anglo-French friendship was a matter of life and death to both countries.[16] New impetus was given to British rearmament, and official attitudes towards Hitler began almost imperceptibly to harden, though this did not silence criticisms of the Anglo-French staff talks which began in April about the new military situation. The change had, in fact, been grave. France's sally-port was closed and it was clear that, whatever they wished, France and England were militarily unable to prevent the unilateral repudiation of a treaty freely negotiated.

The revived Franco-British cooperation was soon to be tested by the Spanish Civil War. This episode, overwhelmingly important in the domestic history of Spain, to which it brought appalling destruction, cruelty and trauma, should not be given exaggerated international importance.[17] There was less danger of a general war than Ethiopia had seemed to threaten. Its significance was that it conditioned diplomacy in other parts of Europe for nearly three years.

In Spain the military revolt of 1936 produced within two or

16 Duff Cooper, 26 June 1936.
17 On its domestic significance, see pp. 447–8.

three weeks two contending and fairly clearly defined sides both
of which were helped by foreign states.[18] The insurgent
'Nationalists' were helped by Italy, Germany and Portugal, the
government forces ('Loyalists' or 'Republicans') by the Russians.
Such support became more important as the battle-line solidified
and it became clear that there was a long struggle ahead. Germany
and Italy both supplied Franco, the Nationalist leader, with arms
and men (in the guise of 'volunteers') and recognized him as chief
of the Spanish state in November 1936. The Republicans received
less from the Russians (though what they received may have been
decisive in saving the Republic in 1936), and found it difficult to
buy arms elsewhere because of the policy of 'non-intervention'
adopted by France and Britain. Germany, Italy and Russia paid
lip service to this principle, but ignored it in practice, as heavy
Italian casualties made plain. As a result the Nationalists slowly
wore down the Republic, while Britain and France looked on. In
January 1939 the end of the war came in sight when Barcelona
fell to Franco. In February Britain and France at last recognized
the Nationalists as *de jure* belligerents, and in March the war ended
with the fall of Madrid.

These events had great psychological and moral impact. Yet
although the *rapprochement* of Italy and Germany was consummated and France was caused some strategic anxiety by the establishment of their client on her western frontier, there was no
significant change in the balance of European power. Spain, whatever the value of her territory to others, was so ravaged by the
war that she was militarily negligible for the foreseeable future.
The war's most important effects were less tangible: the intense
embitterment of the international atmosphere, the prolongation
of British and French misgivings and confusion, the increased
confidence of the dictators, and the frustration of hopes that
Russia might be brought into European affairs as a restraining
force.

18 An appendix to Hugh Thomas, *The Spanish Civil War* (London,
1961), pp. 634–8, summarizes the available information. It appears that
the Italians and Russians both gave support valued at about £80 million
(1939 values) to their friends. Germany put up about £43 million worth.
Italy had most men in Spain (about 50,000 at their maximum); the
Germans are unlikely to have had more than 10,000, and the Russians
more than 500, at any one time. About 20,000 Portuguese fought for
Franco, and 40,000 foreigners of various nationalities for the Republicans.

The Spanish war destroyed the hopes of reducing international tension and created new bitterness. After Ethiopia and the Rhineland, there had been hopes in England and France of a general improvement. Sanctions against Italy were wound up; the British Home Fleet was recalled from Gibraltar, and assurances given by England and France to smaller Mediterranean countries at the height of the Ethiopian crisis were announced to have lapsed. There were even hopes of a new Locarno and Germany's re-entry to the League. Optimism was kept alive for a little by Italy's adhesion (belatedly, and with qualifications) to the non-intervention agreement on 21 August, but by the end of the year the atmosphere was poisoned by bitterness and distrust, and by deliberate attempts to distort the nature of the Spanish struggle and give it more international and ideological significance. The conduct of Germany and Italy in sending 'volunteers' to Spain quickly showed a cynicism and duplicity which destroyed confidence in their words. Another cause of ill-feeling was the character of the fighting itself, which was from the start marked by ferocious atrocities on both sides. This was characteristic of Spanish civil strife, but as the two sides won supporters abroad, it became a source of international recrimination.[19] The conduct of formal warfare, on the other hand, deteriorated in a way which seemed to owe more to foreign influences. Opinion outside Italy and Germany was especially antagonized by the bombing of civilians from the air which provided a grim continuation and intensification of the Italian methods in Ethiopia.[20] Something of a climax of horror came on 26 April 1937, when the Basque town of Guernica was heavily bombed by the Nationalists, 1,600 people being killed. It quickly became known that this had been done by German aircraft.

Acts like these made it easier to accept propaganda depicting the struggle as a clearcut one of 'Reds' against 'Fascists'. Russian propaganda on this theme began two or three weeks after the start of the war, and leaders of the Popular Front in France had quickly identified themselves with the Republic as an anti-Fascist cause. As Italian and German participation grew, the more plausible this blanket identification of all Franco's supporters as 'Fascists' became. For their part, Franco's propagandists and those of

19 The worst atrocities were carried out by Spaniards on Spaniards.
20 Though mustard gas was not used in Spain.

Germany and Italy blurred all distinctions between their opponents by calling them 'Reds'.

Propaganda of this sort, and confusion over what was happening in Spain, gravely weakened the unity and self-confidence of the 'democracies'.[21] Opinions were divided. There were sympathizers with each side, some of whom went to Spain to fight. There were also those who felt strongly that the victory of either side in Spain would be a disaster as German and Italian interests appeared more nakedly and unabashedly on one side, and the Spanish Communist Party more and more brutally dominated the Republican coalition. But failure to take sides, it was also alleged, was bound to help the 'Fascists', since the Republic could not obtain material support from abroad. This, in turn, led to charges that the Republic was unsympathetically regarded in England and France because of social and political antipathies.

Unhappily, all these views had something to be said for them. None took account of the dilemma set to English and French statesmen by their awareness that Spain was only an apparent issue. What mattered was policy towards Germany and Italy; Spain's future, if this were solved, was irrelevant. Two attitudes were possible, and pointed much the same way in practice. One was appeasement of the dictators so as to win their goodwill for future European peace; this meant non-intervention so that they could do what they liked in Spain. The other was to stand up to the dictators and thwart them in Spain; this, too, meant non-intervention, but backed with effective policing so that Spain could be sealed off. Roughly speaking, Great Britain and France began by half-heartedly pursuing the second and ended by reluctantly accepting the first.

Domestic politics further complicated matters. Blum's government was hated by many at home who thought it crypto-communist. Although his enemies and supporters harped on parallels with the *Frente Popular* in Spain, he dared not goad the right too far. After a few gestures of help to the Spanish Republic, he plumped for non-intervention. The British were relieved by this; above all they feared any action which would give the Italians an excuse to install themselves in the Balearics and thus disturb the strategic balance in the Mediterranean. Non-intervention

21 It was from the beginning of this war that German and Italian official documents began to use this term.

caused great bitterness in British domestic politics, but critics of the government found it hard to accept that effective action of any other sort implied in the end Anglo-French cooperation in military and naval measures. The alternative of 'collective security' preached by Russia since 1934 only intensified misinterpretation of the war as a clearcut struggle between left and right. To all these complicating currents must be added the genuine belief of many British politicians that an agreement with Hitler might have been arrived at (he had said that the Rhineland reoccupation was the last territorial change he contemplated in the west) had it not been so irritatingly cut across by the Spanish war. People who thought like this deplored Eden's attempts to move closer to France. Finally, in the background of British policy were the grave distractions of Japanese pressure in Asia and the abdication crisis.

It seems likely that the Spanish war strengthened the arguments for British appeasement. There was no way in which England could bring pressure effectively to bear on either Germany or Italy because neither needed her support. The only, and slight, leverage she possessed was the power to withhold recognition of Italy's conquest of Ethiopia. Otherwise, only when force could actually be employed to defend British interests could she act effectively. This happened in one connexion only during the Spanish war, when it seemed that British shipping was in danger from attacks by unidentified submarines, strongly suspected to be Italian. Early British proposals for policing the dangerous areas had no success. Finally, at Nyon in September 1937, a conference of Mediterranean states was held which led to the creation of patrol zones within which policing naval forces were to attack suspected submarines without further identification. Sixty British and French destroyers were at once made available in the western Mediterranean. Italy had not attended the Conference, but to save her face, had been allocated a patrol zone. This exercise of force was completely effective. The attacks stopped at once.

But this was a unique instance; British policy never again operated in so favourable a context during the Spanish war. Mussolini's intervention could not be prevented so long as British policy was anchored to the wish to conciliate him as a possible ally against Hitler; because of this, Italy was not to be publicly affronted or humiliated. British policy was to try to get a workable non-intervention agreement and then to hold that line. In

October 1936 Eden assured Mussolini of Britain's wish to resume friendly relations, and some agreements followed which meant little. Eden, however, still held in reserve his one low trump, recognition of the conquest of Ethiopia.

Eden's lack of success also had domestic sources. There had always been strong opposition to his policies within the government. Hoare's return was a step in its consolidation. When Hitler, in an otherwise conciliatory speech (30 January 1937), singled out Eden for special attack, there were renewed grumblings that he was endangering good relations with Germany by clinging too closely to the French alliance. The replacement of Baldwin as prime minister by Neville Chamberlain in May at first caused Eden no alarm, but Chamberlain was soon behaving in an underhand and equivocal way towards his foreign secretary. Convinced that he could handle foreign affairs better than Eden, he came to believe that a basis for friendly relations with Hitler could be found in meeting his demands half way and obliging him to use methods of negotiation. The first sign of change came in November, when Halifax visited Hitler. Chamberlain hoped much from this meeting. It was not, in fact, a very easy one (possibly because Halifax did not at first recognize Hitler and walked straight past him). But Hitler was left assured that Britain was not opposed to *agreed* and *peaceful* change in central Europe; Austria, Czechoslovakia and Danzig were specifically mentioned.

It was soon clear to Eden that policy was moving in a direction contrary to his wishes. He was gravely perturbed when, in January, Chamberlain dealt a serious rebuff to President Roosevelt, who made a proposal for American diplomatic intervention. The final break came in the following month. Chamberlain was anxious to concede *de jure* recognition of the Italian conquest of Ethiopia to avoid driving Italy into the arms of Germany. Eden refused to believe that Mussolini would give anything substantial in return and insisted on the withdrawal of Italian forces from Spain as a minimum. On 20 February Eden resigned. 'Now we shall be able to get on terms with the Germans', observed Henderson, the delighted ambassador in Berlin.[22] This was not to be true, but an Anglo-Italian treaty was signed in April, and marks the climax of Mussolini's successes in foreign affairs. It gave him a propaganda triumph in British recognition of Italy's

22 Avon, p. 504.

sovereignty in Ethiopia, and Chamberlain saw it as the preliminary to a similar arrangement with Hitler. This was as unrealistic
as the lingering hopes of the old policy of using Mussolini against
Hitler. The Spanish war had consolidated a partnership between
the dictators. In July 1936 German-Italian discussions on the
possibility of replacing Locarno revealed, the Italian minister
thought, a 'complete parallelism'.[23] In the same month, an agreement between Germany and Austria allayed Italian misgivings
about Hitler's policy. The Spanish war then brought a consciousness of a common ideological alignment, helped by Mussolini's
communication to Hitler of secret British documents on the
'German Peril'. Agreements reached in October, when Ciano
visited Berlin, were the basis of a 'Rome-Berlin Axis', revealed
by Mussolini on 2 November. Within a few weeks it was
followed by the signature of the anti-Comintern pact (25
November) between Germany and Japan; Italy adhered to it a year
later.[24]

Although the history of this new alignment is complicated, it
is clear that the dictators arrived at a common position from
different starting-points, and that it was largely Spain which
brought this about. Hitler's ideological reaction to the struggle
there may have been at first more fundamental than Mussolini's.
Italy's treaty with Russia in 1933 had, after all, been greeted
warmly in the Fascist press in an article said to be by Mussolini
himself which spoke of 'two great revolutions, the Fascist and the
Bolshevist', meeting and joining hands.[25] At this stage, Hitler had
long been a committed anti-Bolshevik. Yet his practical caution
was greater than Mussolini's. He quickly decided to help the
Nationalists, but not to grant them official recognition until they
had captured Madrid. Mussolini acted more vigorously. Attracted
by strategic and territorial prospects (above all, in the Balearic
Islands) and the chance of discomfiting France by establishing a
government friendly to Italy at Madrid, and given his fondness
for violence, Mussolini's speedy decision (25 July) to send aircraft
to Morocco is understandable. Once the Russians announced
support for the Republic, it became easy to cover the policy of
both Mussolini and Hitler towards Spain with the ideological flag

23 *Ciano's Diplomatic Papers*, p. 20.
24 Franco signed it 7 April 1939.
25 See G. Tabouis, *Blackmail or War* (London, 1938), p. 53.

of anti-communism. In April 1937 Mussolini told Schuschnigg that although he had reservations about Germany's racial policies, the relationship between Rome and Berlin which was born of the Bolshevik Peril in Spain was being consolidated by the attitude of democracies. The Axis was still far from solid at that moment, but by September, when Mussolini visited Hitler, he was ready to adhere to the anti-Comintern pact.

The consolidation of the Axis was accompanied by a crumbling of confidence in eastern Europe. The process had begun in 1934 when Poland made a treaty with Germany which greatly dismayed France. In the following year, a visit by Eden to Warsaw revealed that Poland was too concerned about Russia to enter any arrangement to contain Germany in the east. Nor did Poland want an eastern Locarno which would petrify her frontiers, and she resented the Franco-Russian treaty. Attempts in 1936 to reactivate Poland were again unsuccessful, and when the French foreign minister visited Poland in December 1937, it was clear that France's former ally only wanted a free hand. The same visit revealed the virtual disintegration of the *Little Entente*. The blow dealt to French influence in Yugoslavia by Alexander's murder had been followed by the fall of Titolescu in Rumania (29 August 1936). King Carol, a Hohenzollern by descent, was disposed to look to the dictators rather than France in the future, not only because of personal taste, but because of his fears of Russian designs on Bessarabia. Yugoslavia had broken its commitments to the *Little Entente* by a treaty with Bulgaria in January 1937, followed in March by an Italo-Yugoslav pact. Stoyadinovitch was soon freely expressing his sympathies for Fascist aims and Yugoslav participation in anti-Communist policies. The authoritarian régime in Hungary was also sympathetic to the dictators, seeing them as co-revisionists. In eastern Europe, the democracies could find little support by the end of 1937, except in Czechoslovakia.

The only possible counterweight was Russia. But the whole tenor of Russian policy since 1930 made this difficult. After a disastrous misreading of the German situation before 1933, Russian foreign policy had begun to adjust to the situation with which it was confronted by the rise of Hitler. The clandestine arrangements for military and technical cooperation which had gone on right down to the end of Weimar were cancelled. A non-aggression pact was made in July 1933 with the *Little Entente* and another in September with Italy. Russian policy then received another jolt from the German-Polish treaty of 1934; the Poles had previously turned down a Russian offer of a Baltic security pact. The Russian response was to turn to collective security and the League. This policy was advocated by Litvinov at Geneva; he seems to have been in some sense its personal exponent in the Kremlin. Its aim was to organize a collective confrontation of powers to restrain Hitler. In effect, this meant that France and Britain were to draw the German threat away from Russia. Russia's entry to the League of Nations (9 September 1934), inaugurated the new line.

In March 1935 Eden had travelled to Moscow to meet Litvinov and Stalin; some revealing exchanges took place. It became clear that the Russians, closer readers of *Mein Kampf* than the British, took seriously Hitler's dream of expansion in the east, and were obviously afraid that England and France might attempt to turn Hitler towards Russia. In these circumstances, British coolness towards the idea of a Baltic pact disappointed them. Two months later, in May, a treaty was signed between France and Russia which at first sight looked important. Yet it was not the revival of the old pre-1914 alliance and only envisaged mutual help in the face of aggression until the League could act. The French were more concerned to prevent a revival of Rapallo than to draw actively on Russian fighting-power, which, in any case, would be hard to deploy.

In spite of its modest terms, though, the treaty caused a stir. German pressure appears to have combined with Laval's dislike of French communists and the misgivings of French generals about Russian secrecy to prevent the military consultations which would have given it more substance. It had also caused alarm in England, both to those who believed that alliances had caused the disaster of 1914, and to those who feared communism. Confusion grew when the Comintern began to stress unity of interest among socialists and democrats to meet the danger of 'international fascism', and, in July 1935, to support the French domestic equivalent of collective security, the Popular Front.

The outbreak of the Spanish war therefore found Russia to some extent already opposing the dictators. Yet, like Hitler, Stalin was cautious. Although the Comintern urged support for the Republicans on 24 July, it was only on 3 August that spontaneous popular demonstrations in favour of help to the Republic, and widespread voluntary subscriptions to funds to help Spain were reported from Russia. It does not seem that Stalin felt any great concern about what happened in Spain. He was only concerned to keep the pot boiling so long as this involved Italy and Germany in expensive commitments. This could be done on the cheap by Comintern propaganda and the activities of communist militants in the democracies who would drum up support for the Republic. Russia's own direct help to the Republic appears not to have begun until September, then to have continued only so long as it was necessary to keep the Republicans in the field, and to have tapered off after the early months of 1937. (The Russians also took the opportunity, not available to the Germans or the Italians, of obtaining cash for their help by carrying off the gold reserve of the Republic.) Whatever equivocations and qualifications surrounded Russian help to the Republic, the fact that it was given at all undercut Russia's official support for non-intervention but awoke popular admiration and enthusiasm in England and France. At the same time Russian distrust grew because British and French support of non-intervention told only against the Republicans. Thus Spain drove still further apart the potential components of a coalition against the dictators.

Disappointment with Litvinov's policy was, in any case, not long in appearing in Russia. Internal developments in that country in 1936 and 1937 remain mysterious, but such evidence as is available about the purges and the formal diplomatic action of the Russians make it seem likely that the Spanish war was a catalyst assisting another major shift of policy. Russian aid to Spain fell off in 1937, probably because it was becoming clear that sufficient aid would cost too much. From this time Russian action in Spain was increasingly limited to eliminating non-Stalinists, while in Russia, too, the great purges removed most of the important Russian agents who had served in Spain. (They also struck down soldiers who had formerly worked with the Germans.) Litvinov's continued advocacy of collective security seemed less and less convincing against this background. Perhaps Stalin had already decided that Russian policy should turn back towards an attempt to cooperate with Germany. It is certain that his first approaches to Hitler were made in January 1937, and were at the time rebuffed. Meanwhile, by the end of that year the communists' behaviour in Spain confirmed the suspicions of those who had always said that the Russians could not be trusted. The purges caused grave doubts about Russia's military effectiveness, too. 'Collective security' remained a suspicious phrase to the countries on Russia's borders. The same suspicions showed themselves at Nyon, where the eastern Mediterranean countries resisted Russian participation in the naval patrol scheme. The Russians did nothing to reassure their potential friends. In their treason trials no distinction was made between the democracies and the dictatorships when allegations were made of plots with foreign powers. In early 1938, too, the Russian government took the mysterious step of closing down all foreign consulates outside Moscow and Leningrad. There were few grounds by then for believing that Russia was still available as an effective ally against Germany.

THE *ANSCHLUSS* AND MUNICH

From 1937 to 1941, although Great Britain made one great diplomatic effort to turn the tide of events by appeasement and Italy provided a minor distraction by seizing Albania (7 April 1939), European history is, in the main, the story of German initiative and triumph. Even in eastern Europe, where Russia helped to demolish the order set up in 1918–20, the great changes flowed from German decisions. Europe in these years responded to impulses from Berlin as never since the days of Bismarck; to the rest of the world, she responded hardly at all. Only England was much troubled by Japanese policy, and the United States hardly mattered until 1941. These were the last years of European political autonomy.

1938 brought two great German successes, the *Anschluss* with Austria and the breaking up of Czechoslovakia. The first caused less of a stir than had the Rhineland reoccupation. Austria had been handicapped since 1918 by the difficulties of trying to run as a national state part of the Germanic rump of the Dual Monarchy (Bohemia had been separated from the German-speaking state that had begun to organize itself in 1918, and had been given to Czechoslovakia). Not all Austrians believed their state was economically or politically viable. Some of them hankered after the union with Germany which was forbidden by Versailles, and the popularity of *Mitteleuropa* ideas after the war favoured them. Other Austrians felt the simple tug of racial and ideological affinity; often they joined the Austrian Nazi party. In 1933, when Hitler took power, the Austrian Nazis thought more about an *Anschluss* than did the German foreign office which, said the German foreign minister, 'had other and bigger matters to be concerned with'.[26] Hitler, although he had always preached the reunion of all Germans in one state, was only just beginning rearmament. Nevertheless, the Austrian Nazis made the running. When their violence and clamour led the Austrian government to act against them, they won increasing sympathy in Germany. Charges and countercharges began to be exchanged between the two governments. Each complained of illegitimate interference with its internal affairs. Hitler cut off the German tourist trade to Austria and arrested an Austrian diplomat; Dollfuss banned and dissolved the Austrian Nazi party. Radio and leaflet propaganda from Germany was intensified. The first climax came when Austrian Nazis attempted to assassinate Dollfuss in October and failed.

In February 1934, Dollfuss's suppression of the Austrian socialists indirectly weakened his position; they had been a force which might have defended the republic against Nazi subversion. Many former Social Democrats now joined the Nazis. Dollfuss preferred to rely on external support from Hungary, and more important, Italy. On the initiative of Italy, they signed the 'Rome protocols' on economic matters (17 March 1934), agreements which also affirmed respect for the independence of each of the signatory states. It helped that the dictatorial régime of Dollfuss comfortably fitted the ideological as well as the strategic requirements of Fascist Italy.

At his first meeting with Mussolini, in June 1934, Hitler declared that an *Anschluss* was of no interest to him, although he wanted Dollfuss removed. Italy's importance was seen when Dollfuss was murdered in an abortive Nazi *coup* (25 July). Italian troops were at once mobilized on the frontier; German intervention, if contemplated, was impossible unless Hitler was willing to go to war with Italy, and the Austrian government was able to deal with the internal threat. The episode showed that the Austrian Nazis could not, unsupported, bring about an *Anschluss* with Germany and that support from outside would not be available so long as Italy stood by Austria. This had been recognized

26 *Documents on German Foreign Policy 1918–1945*, Series C, I, p. 351.

in Berlin, where overt attacks on the Dollfuss régime had already been given up. Hitler had abandoned immediate violence for slow infiltration and for the diplomatic isolation of Austria.

Ostentatious visits to Mussolini by Schuschnigg, the successor to Dollfuss, showed that friendship with Italy was now his dominant concern. In 1935 it was successfully maintained. Hitler was preoccupied elsewhere and did little more than grumble from time to time about the danger of Habsburg restoration in Austria. The Austrian Nazi party had been dissolved. During 1936 Mussolini sought to use this lull to urge Schuschnigg to try to stabilize Austro-German relations on a more friendly basis. He was anxious at that moment to have free hands for Ethiopia. The result was a German-Austrian agreement (11 July) by which Germany acknowledged Austrian sovereignty as an independent state, and Austria promised to conduct a policy suited to her nature as a 'German state'.[27] The Austrian Nazis were promised an amnesty and two of them were shortly afterwards taken into Schuschnigg's cabinet.

Schuschnigg was at this time pursuing his predecessor's attack on the left, while balancing the other Austrian party of the right, the *Heimwehr*, by his new tolerance of the Nazis. He strove not to commit himself too far and was soon irritating Hitler by speculative remarks about the Habsburgs. In November 1936, in order to reassure his supporters, he made a speech in which he spoke of Austrian Nazism as an 'enemy' to the state. But the foundations of his position were shifting. Ethiopia was proving expensive to Italy and Spain entangled Mussolini further. Then came the alarming news of the Axis.

In January 1937 Goering reminded Mussolini that the Austrian government 'is neither Fascist nor National Socialist, but clerical'.[28] He asked Mussolini to press Schuschnigg to be more favourable to the Austrian Nazis and harped on the dangers which Austria might present to the new alignment of Italy and Germany. Mussolini began to waver; in April he told Schuschnigg that he still supported Austrian independence but accompanied this by the significant rider that it should be in harmony with the Axis. In September Mussolini's visit to Hitler

27 *Documents on German Foreign Policy 1918–1945*, Series D, I, pp. 278–81.
28 *Ciano's Diplomatic Papers*, p. 88.

caused great alarm in Vienna. Others, too, were showing signs of abandoning Austria. Stoyadinovitch told Ciano in March that he considered an *Anschluss* inevitable; as Yugoslavia was the other state which had mobilized its army when Dollfuss was murdered, this was a significant recognition of the new power of Germany. More important, England was not very concerned about Austria. The régime there did not appeal much to English public opinion and the argument for national self-determination still seemed strong. At the end of 1937 Eden told Ribbentrop that 'people in England recognize that a closer connection between Germany and Austria would have to come about sometime'.[29]

Schuschnigg could not do much. A visit to Italy in April 1937 had been followed by unpleasantly chilly gestures from his patrons. Nevertheless, even in November Hitler told his military leaders that it was impossible to estimate Italy's attitude over Austria, which together with Czechoslovakia, was to solve the problem of Germany's need for living-space.[30] His own attitude to Austria was deeply tinged by his early life in Vienna. Anti-Habsburg and anti-Catholic, he saw an *Anschluss* only in racial and opportunist terms. It was to be part of the consolidation of German strength not only by absorbing territory from which non-Germans would be removed, but by mobilizing at home the *Grossdeutsch* sentiment thwarted for nearly a century. Greater Germany was to become a reality, in spite of Bismarck and the statesmen of Versailles.

Only a few days after Hitler's conference with his commanders, Mussolini announced to Ribbentrop that he was 'tired of mounting guard over Austrian independence'.[31] The actual timing of what followed may have been accidental. In January 1938 a raid by the Austrian police on the headquarters of the Austrian Nazis revealed plans for terrorist activity on a scale sufficient to provoke a German invasion. Schuschnigg did not publish this evidence, but seems to have believed it would be possible to use it to resist Hitler's demands to end the uncertainties of the situation. He was given no time to do this. On February 12 he met Hitler at Berchtesgaden and was submitted to abuse, bullying, and finally an ultimatum. Under the threat of invasion Schuschnigg gave

29 See L.B. Namier, *In the Nazi Era* (London, 1952), p. 127.
30 *Documents . . . Series D.* I, p. 36.
31 *Ciano's Diplomatic Papers*, p. 146.

way. He admitted Seyss-Inquart, the Austrian Nazi leader, to his cabinet as minister of the interior with control of the police and another Nazi as foreign minister. A complete amnesty for Nazis arrested for criminal and terrorist activity was also announced. This effectively destroyed the power of the Austrian government. Encouraged by a speech by Hitler on 20 February, the Austrian Nazis almost at once began street demonstrations which the government could not control. There was no force to use against them; the socialists were gone and the police under their new head co-operated with the Nazis against the Fatherland Front and the *Heimwehr*. At the beginning of March, huge demonstrations of Nazis took place at Graz and Linz in the presence of Seyss-Inquart. Schuschnigg played his last card by announcing on 9 March that a plebiscite would be held on the question of whether or not Austria should remain independent. This was calling Hitler's bluff; it was a desperate attempt to use against him the weapon of self-determination he had himself flourished. This decided Hitler. On 10 March the German generals were told to be ready to act on 12 March. An ultimatum was sent to Austria demanding the postponement of the plebiscite; when this was accepted, Schuschnigg's resignation was demanded. That night the German invasion began, officially at the invitation of a Nazi government under Seyss-Inquart appointed by the Austrian president. On the following day the *Anschluss* was proclaimed and the German army entered Vienna. Hitler arrived on 13 March. A terror against Jews, Socialists and Catholics had already been launched by the Austrian Nazis. It was intensified by the arrival of the *Gestapo*. Thousands of the Nazis' political opponents and suspects were killed, beaten up or imprisoned. Not surprisingly, the plebiscite (which was eventually held on 10 April) produced a 99 per cent favourable vote. But some of its success was due also to the sudden change of front by the only great force left intact by the Dollfuss and Schuschnigg régimes, the Catholic Church, hitherto anti-Nazi. Under the leadership of the Cardinal-Archbishop of Vienna, Innitzer, it advised its flock to vote for the *Anschluss*.

The *Anschluss* was the greatest achievement of German nationalism since Versailles and a crucial personal success for Hitler. With it began his liberation from professional advice in diplomatic and military matters which was to lead first to German domination of Europe and then to disaster. The immediate benefits were almost entirely psychological. The bitter and violent persecution of opponents and imagined opponents of the Nazis in Austria (now renamed the *Ostmark*) was terrible, but unnecessary and provocative; Germany's grip on Austria would have been tight enough without it, and foreign opinion was startled by the public humiliation of Jews. Demographically, 8 million people were added to the German population, but it does not seem likely that this was an economic advantage. Germany's international standing, on the other hand, greatly benefited. The *Anschluss* showed the emptiness of the Anglo-French dream of Italian opposition to Hitler. On 16 March, Halifax deplored to the House of Lords the fact of revision unsanctioned by the League, but this was as far as Britain would go.[32] France was again in the middle of a ministerial crisis, although she had proposed to Italy a joint *démarche* with Great Britain (11 March) which had been turned down by Mussolini.

The British government had already embarked upon the first major initiative of British policy since the Peace Conference. Mistakenly or not, Chamberlain was determined to make a serious attempt to provide European leadership and break with the drift of British foreign policy under Baldwin. Of the strength of Chamberlain's fundamental convictions his actions provide ample evidence. He believed that another great war would shatter civilization (a belief shared by many of his critics who were less clear than he about what action should be taken to avoid a disaster). He believed also that the best hope of avoiding another war would be to persuade Hitler that many of his claims could be sustained by negotiation and orderly diplomacy, rather than force. To bring Hitler to accept that view, Chamberlain sought direct contact with him. In this there was no consciousness of weakness. Chamberlain was tough and hard-headed, rational in his appreciation of what was required to deal with genuine grievances. His gravest error was to attribute his own kind of rationality to his opponent; Chamberlain was, after all, a Victorian, already 45 years old in 1914. Yet his aim was similar to that of Mussolini, when he had proposed a four-power pact five years before. The League machinery had failed to meet the real problem of Germany's appetites and the resurrection of the policy of agree-

32 Ribbentrop seems to have watered down earlier warnings from Halifax before conveying them to Berlin. See Robertson, p. 117.

ment between the great powers was indicated.

Besides the convictions of the prime minister, two other factors entered into the making of British policy. One was British public opinion, still unprepared to envisage armed opposition to Germany for a number of reasons. The other was the state of British armaments, only belatedly understood, and then given exaggerated emphasis. The scale of effort required was slowly realized; the government's announcement in March 1937 that re-armament could no longer be financed from current revenue was a shock. British policy was still haunted by the fear of being too weak to fight. In May 1937 the United Kingdom had forty-eight long-range bombers; intelligence estimates credited Germany with 800. This was an exaggeration, but British planning had to go ahead in the knowledge that no up-to-date monoplane fighters would be in squadron service until the end of 1938, and that the army would have no new medium tanks until 1939. Eden had spoken for more of his colleagues than usual when, in October 1937, he minuted that 'we must keep Germany guessing as to our attitude on Austria and Czechoslovakia. It is all we can do until we are strong enough to talk to Germany.'[33]

Chamberlain's policy had begun to unfold with Halifax's visit to Hitler in November 1937 and its clear indication that he was willing to envisage change in central Europe, but wished it to come about by agreement, not by force. There was no response before the *Anschluss*. This should have been a warning, it came after the resignation of Eden – who had always been alleged to be a great obstacle to Anglo-German understanding – and at a time when the British government was well disposed to the Axis. But the British government, although it received advice to do otherwise, persisted in analysing German policy in terms of a statesmanlike calculation of interest. Hitler was not thinking in these terms. He was not afraid of any war except one which might be lost; victorious war would be a positively valuable experience, he thought. Consequently, confronted with oppo-nents who genuinely believed that any war would be disastrous, he was always able to raise his stakes. His lack of restraint fright-ened his own generals, but it made nonsense of his opponents' calculations. Their lack of readiness for the next German move is summed up in a message from the British ambassador to Berlin

33 Avon, p. 509. See also, on the question of armaments, p. 491.

to Halifax within a month of the *Anschluss*. 'I do believe', wrote Henderson, 'that, once the Sudeten question is satisfactorily settled, Hitler would be quite willing to talk seriously about disarmament.'[34]

'The Sudeten question' was one part of the complex of problems entailed by the creation of Czechoslovakia in 1918. Whatever the Allies might have hoped, they then stood god-parents to a new multi-national state. Its main constituents were 10 million Czechs, Slovaks, Magyars, Poles, Ruthenes and 3 million Germans. Most of these Germans lived in the Sudetenland frontier areas, traditionally racialist, and many of them had enjoyed life more under the old Empire. The new state could not, therefore, command the loyalty of all its citizens, and even in the immediate aftermath of the Great War it faced the hostility of Hungary and Poland. However, it also included something like four-fifths of the industrial areas of the old Empire and had no grave social problems. Even national minorities, though they might be a danger, were a price paid for excellent strategic frontiers, and these were defended by one of the best armies in Europe, and the most powerful in central Europe until Germany was rearmed. To support it, Czech diplomacy and the interest of other states had given her allies. The *Little Entente* with Yugoslavia and Rumania had originally been a guarantee against Hungarian revisionism. The patronage and protection of France stood behind this and was embodied in the 1924 alliance. Finally, in 1936, Czechoslovakia had signed a mutual assistance treaty with Russia by which that state was obliged to come to the assistance of Czechoslovakia if she were attacked, subject only to the rider that France would do the same.

This understanding with Russia was only a pretext for Hitler's excitement about Czechoslovakia; to anyone envisaging European policy in anti-Bolshevik terms, it undoubtedly might appear a strategic threat to Germany. But Czechoslovakia was also abhorrent to Hitler as the one stable democracy and capitalist society in central Europe. And the Czechs were Slavs. The Sudeten question gave Hitler the opportunity to bring latent enmity to a head. It was the supreme example of the perversion of principle which was latent in the idolization of nationality in 1918.

The Versailles guarantees for the German-speaking minorities

34 7 April 1938.

of Czechoslovakia had been observed legalistically, though not enthusiastically, by the new state. The Sudeten Germans, aggrieved by their status, boycotted Czech politics for a time, but eventually began to use the democratic machinery available to them. Some of their leaders became ministers. But they were unable to rid themselves of their psychological burdens. They no longer enjoyed their old privileges as the civil servants of the Empire and, unfortunately, because they lived in the most industrialized regions of Czechoslovakia they felt the economic depression of the early 1930s particularly acutely. Among the Sudeten politicians who were willing to use these grievances to make more radical demands than the politicians who had led the minority since 1918 was Konrad Henlein. Helped by radio propaganda from Germany and the excitement aroused by Hitler's success, he had by 1935 won over more than half the Sudeten voters. The Sudeten German party now began to receive subsidies from Germany. Soon Henlein began to demand autonomy for the Sudetenland within Czechoslovakia. The first rumbles of the Sudeten question were noticed in the British foreign office in the autumn of 1936.

By then Hitler already wanted to eliminate Czechoslovakia, if possible, by force. Simply to give the German minority what they were asking fell short of his design. At the beginning of 1937 German propaganda in support of the Sudetenlanders rose in intensity. It also accused the Czechs of providing bases for Russian aircraft. Hitler's conference with his advisers on 5 November revealed that his mind was made up, and they were startled to learn he was preparing to act. Military support to Franco was to be cancelled. To the *Reichstag*, on 20 February 1938, he declared his intentions that the Germans of Austria and Czechoslovakia should achieve the right of self-determination.

The *Anschluss* opened the way to Czechoslovakia. There had already been signs that France was beginning to regret her commitments to her *protégé*. The new strategical situation increased the doubts of her former friends that Czechoslovakia could survive, menaced from the south as well as from the north by German forces. The British prime minister had no doubts of the preponderance of German military power. Moreover, the success of the *Anschluss* aroused great excitement in the Sudetenland, and thus increased Henlein's appeal and further weakened the Czech government at home.

Henlein now demanded (24 April) full autonomy for the German areas and other changes in Czech government and foreign policy. He then went to Berlin and London to win support. Big concessions were in fact made by the draft of a nationality statute which the Czech government produced in July, but even if this had been acceptable to Henlein, it was not to Hitler. Nazi propaganda and agitation strove to keep the Sudetenland pot boiling, to excite conflicts with the Czech authorities and police, and to make it impossible for Henlein to accept the Czech proposals. In the middle of May there were rumours of German movements to which the Czechs showed so determined a front that it seemed that the Germans had lost their nerve and called off an intended attack. On 30 May Hitler told his general staff that it was his intention to smash Czechoslovakia by military action in the near future. Some German generals feared that France and Great Britain would fight; they knew themselves unprepared. Beck, the Chief of Staff, resigned. In the event, Hitler was proved right. The British government had already decided to do all it could to avoid war over Czechoslovakia and the French were to be only too glad of an excuse to get out of its undertakings. The Yugoslavs and Italians had agreed that German annexation was inevitable soon after the *Anschluss*.

The diplomacy of September was determined by Neville Chamberlain's conviction that a war with Germany would be folly. The only British interest in the Czechoslovak question, he thought, was the preservation of the practice of orderly and civilized diplomatic intercourse; if Hitler could be made to observe civilized standards and to accept the principle that revision of Versailles was acceptable if carried out by agreement, then peace would be safe. Seeking as he did to stabilize Europe for the foreseeable future, he saw Czechoslovakia only as a tiresome obstacle. He had consistently urged the Czechs to make concessions to Henlein. He did not believe that Hitler was out to destroy Czechoslovakia, but that the main problem was to get both sides to accept autonomy for the Sudeten areas. At the beginning of August, he felt optimistic. It seemed as if the question of foreign troops in Spain might soon be settled and a British mission to Prague held out hopes of resolving the differences between Henlein and the Czech government which, under pressure, eventually accepted almost all his demands. Unfortunately this atmosphere was soon clouded by German provocation and propaganda.

Few people doubted that the British government, earnestly though it sought to avoid war, would stand by France were Czechoslovakia actually attacked by Germany. When, on 12 September, Hitler demanded self-determination for the Sudeten Germans and promised them German armed support the crisis broke. Henlein had already broken off negotiations with the Czech government on the grounds that violence and intimidation were being used against his followers, who were in revolt. Disorder spread rapidly, twenty-three persons were killed, martial law was proclaimed in some areas, and Henlein left the country. The Czechs began a secret mobilization. Meanwhile Chamberlain had taken the initiative. He suggested that he should meet Hitler (but not the Czech government) and on 15 September flew to Germany to do so. In conversations at Berchtesgaden, Hitler reiterated his demand that the Sudetenland should be given self-determination at once, making it clear that this was to be the prelude to annexation to Germany. Chamberlain was prepared to accept this; he believed it to be the limit of the German aims and sought only to have them conceded in an orderly manner by agreement between Germany, Czechoslovakia and the powers. He obtained from Hitler a promise to hold his hand for a week while Chamberlain consulted his colleagues and the French. As the German army's timetable did not permit action at once, the promise was no concession. Threatened with invasion from Poland and Hungary, as well as Germany, the Czechs agreed to concede the right of self-determination to the Sudetenland in return for guarantees for the future from France and Britain.

Many people who had, until this moment, believed that the Berchtesgaden meeting had made plain to Hitler the determination of the British and French governments to protect Czechoslovakia, experienced a great shock when these terms were published. Ignoring criticism, Chamberlain returned to Germany with these terms, meeting Hitler again at Godesberg on 22–23 September. To his distress and amazement he found that he had not offered enough. Hitler now asked for more. The Sudeten areas were to be surrendered immediately, plebiscites were to be held in other areas where there were large German minorities, and Polish and Hungarian claims were also to be satisfied; these terms were to be accepted by 28 September. They meant, in effect, the ending of the authority of the Czechoslovak state. Chamberlain would not accept them and returned to England, angry and exasperated. A new Czech government, now confident of British support, rejected Hitler's terms. War now seemed very close. The British fleet was mobilized (28 September) and millions of gas-masks were issued to the civilian population. But in both Britain and France there was a consciousness of military unreadiness. In each country, too, large numbers of people were emotionally against war, especially over a seemingly remote issue such as that of Sudetenlanders' rights of self-determination. *Veux-tu mourir pour le Tchechoslovaquie?* one French newspaper asked readers. Years of antiwar propaganda and of idolization of the specious doctrine of national self-determination helped to disorganize resistance to Hitler.

Chamberlain himself was outraged not by what was proposed but by its manner. He was not upset by the transfer of territory, which he had already accepted, but by Hitler's abandonment of peaceful negotiation for threats and violence. He wished to disci-pline Hitler by making him accept negotiation as a solution to his problems. He appealed to Mussolini to help him by persuading Hitler to attempt one more conference. Hitler agreed to meet Chamberlain, Daladier and Mussolini at Munich (29 September).[35] At this conference, terms ostensibly drawn up by Mussolini were agreed by the four powers. They were far harsher than those settled at Berchtesgaden. They provided for German occupation of the Sudetenland by 10 October, for plebiscites elsewhere and concessions to Polish and Hungarian minorities. The British and French guaranteed the new frontiers of Czechoslovakia. These terms were presented to the Czech government with the assurance that if they did not accept them the Czechs would have to fight the Germans alone. On 30 September the terms were accepted. Thus Hitler obtained most of what he had asked for, and Cham-berlain had maintained the forms of peaceful agreement. The only other outcome of the Munich conference was a meaningless declaration of Anglo-German friendship, to which Chamberlain attached great importance because of his conviction that the important thing to do with Hitler was to tie him down with written words and precise statements. In a longer perspective, what had happened was that, for the last time, a Concert of

35 Italy's main interest throughout was to secure a share of the spoils for Hungary and Poland as a partial off-setting of German influence in central Europe.

Europe had briefly appeared. The price of getting it working again, of replacing by direct agreement between major states the machinery of European intercourse which had collapsed at Geneva, was paid by Czechoslovakia. And one great power, Russia, had not been consulted.

HITLER'S EUROPE 1938–41

In England and France, relief was quickly followed by recrimination. Hitler had won a great victory. The one army in central Europe which could have put up serious resistance to the German, was now stripped of its fortifications, many of its arms, and its munitions works. It now had to defend a poor frontier behind which cowered a demoralized government and disillusioned people. Germany had made great economic gains and had 3 million new subjects. The last trace of the *Little Entente* had vanished. Yugoslavia was busily courting Mussolini; Rumania trembled. The Poles joined in the pillage in October, taking Teschen; the Hungarians took some of Slovakia and Ruthenia (more, indeed, than Hitler had intended, thanks to Italian support). A great step had been taken towards the eventual realization of Hitler's dreams of expansion in the east.

Paradoxically, Hitler now began to squander his advantages. The successors to President Benes attempted to anticipate future dangers by cooperating with Germany and by granting autonomy to Slovakia and Ruthenia. This was not enough for Hitler. Using as a pretext a Slovak demand for independence, he announced that the post-Munich 'Czecho-Slovakia' had ceased to exist. German forces occupied Prague (15 March 1939), Bohemia and Moravia being declared German protectorates and German troops entered Slovakia. Ruthenia was taken by Hungary. The British government declared that collapse by internal dissolution rendered inoperative the guarantee promised at Munich. Yet an important change was about to occur. Down to the seizure of Prague, British and French governments had still tried to follow a policy of appeasement. The revolution of public feeling which now occurred swept even Chamberlain into the conviction that Hitler's words could not be relied on unless he faced a clear threat of war. Rumours of a German intention to fall on Rumania (and Mussolini's occupation of Albania in April) now led the British government to proliferate guarantees and treaties to small countries in eastern and south-eastern Europe. Poland, Rumania and Greece were the first; Turkey followed.[36] During the summer, England accepted peacetime conscription for the first time, largely to convince the French that she meant what she said. Most significant of all, the British government began to consider Russia as a possible ally and asked for information about her attitude if Rumania were attacked.

British and French policy towards Russia at the time of Munich and after has been much discussed. There were strong arguments for caution in seeking her cooperation against Germany. There was the strategic problem of bringing Russia into action without the cooperation of Poland and Rumania. There was the fact of the purges and the belief that they had made a disastrous impact on the personnel and morale of the Russian army. There was the risk of replacing German hegemony with Russian. And, when all was said and done, there was an emotional reluctance to ask for the help of a declared enemy of the capitalist democracies, a police state whose methods had provided models for the Nazis.

Nevertheless, for a little while an alliance seemed possible. The British government treated Russian approaches in April 1939 with caution (the French responded more warmly). There were suspicions that the Russians were only trying to make themselves seem more formidable to the Germans. By 23 July discussions had produced a draft treaty but its military details remained to be settled. They never were, because England and France were always held back by the Poles, who refused to allow Russian forces to cross their territory to attack Germany. A military mission to Moscow in August could do nothing. The Russian case for the failure of these negotiations boils down to asserting that England and France wished to turn Hitler against Russia, that they therefore dragged their feet, and that as a result, Russia had to turn to Germany in self-defence. Chamberlain may not have liked the idea of an alliance, but the first assertion is untrue. It had some plausibility, however, in the aftermath of Munich. It was then that the Russian deputy foreign minister said to the French ambassador in Moscow: '*Mon pauvre ami, qu'avez-vous fait? Pour*

36 Poland was guaranteed 30 March, and a treaty was signed 6 April. Greece and Rumania signed treaties 13 April, and Turkey 12 May.

nous, je n'aperçois plus d'autre issue qu'une quatrième partage de Pologne.[37] It is also true that British diplomacy still sought to find out what Hitler really would accept as a final appeasement. But the Russians were in a much less responsive frame of mind than some of their admirers thought. On 10 March Stalin had warned the Party that its task in foreign policy was 'to observe caution and not to permit our country to be drawn into a conflict by the *provocateurs* of war, who are accustomed to having others pull the chestnuts out of the fire for them.'[38] In the previous year, negotiations to renew an agreement on credits with Germany had only been cancelled on Hitler's orders.

Whether the Russians wished to improve their relations with Germany or not, the end of Czecho-Slovakia brought to a head the Polish question. After Munich, the Germans had offered Poland more territory in Slovakia (to offset Polish fears of Ruthenian nationalism) in return for extraterritorial communication with East Prussia and Danzig. The Poles declined. They went further, reaffirming their non-aggression treaty with Russia and refusing to adhere to the Anti-Comintern pact. Hitler was sure that a Franco-German declaration of non-aggression on 6 December was a tacit writing-off of eastern Europe by France, and felt confident he could intimidate Poland at leisure. His occupation of Slovakia in March showed that he no longer cared to pretend to consider Polish susceptibilities. On 23 March, he caused a crisis by seizing Memel. Believing a *coup* against Danzig to be imminent, the Poles mobilized. The Anglo-French guarantee and Anglo-Polish treaty soon followed. Hitler now began to make plans to deal with Poland by force. September 1 was laid down as the date for an invasion, and the 1934 treaty was denounced on the grounds of Polish participation in a British 'encirclement' of Germany.

The British guarantee made an insurance policy against Russian hostility attractive to Germany. The Russians, too, had been offended by the guarantee, which had underwritten the 1921 frontiers of Poland as Locarno never had, and, in spite of the hopes of the English and French Left, there were plenty of signs that Russian policy might have other aims than simple opposition to German aggression. Litvinov, the advocate of collective security,

37 R. Coulondre, *De Staline à Hitler* (Paris, 1950), p. 165.
38 G. Kennan, *Soviet Foreign Policy*, p. 176.

was finally removed from office (3 May) and a new Russian ambassador was sent to Berlin. Reports appeared in the French press of a German offer to Russia of a new partition of Poland. On 31 May, Molotov reproached the democracies publicly for trying to turn Germany's aggressiveness against others. From the German side, there came a proposal in June for a joint German–Russian guarantee to the Baltic states. When the Anglo–French military mission arrived in Moscow, the chance of a successful negotiation between Russia and the democracies had already almost disappeared – if it had ever existed.

At the same moment, the last prewar crisis was coming to a head. From May onwards tales of violence and intimidation against Germans in the Polish corridor multiplied as they had done in Austria before the *Anschluss* or in the Sudetenland before Munich. A Polish terror of castration, killing and rape was alleged by Hitler. When he decided that the simple incorporation of Danzig in Germany would not be enough, his hesitation towards Russia finally disappeared. Agreement with Moscow would insure against a two-front war, and he seems to have believed that the democracies would not dare to fight in the west alone. A non-aggression treaty was signed on 23 August; it also provided for the allocation of Estonia and Latvia to the Russian sphere of influence, of Lithuania to the German, and for an approximate division of Poland. The Germans declared themselves uninterested in the fate of Bessarabia.

This was the most startling diplomatic stroke of the interwar years. Japan announced that she resumed her freedom of action. Italy had been alarmed by the news that negotiations were in progress. Great Britain, oddly, rushed now to ratify her treaty with Poland. In the democracies, though, Right and Left alike were flung into disarray by this defiance of ideology. Russia's benefit was enormous. She had averted the danger of a German attack and had taken a big step towards the recovery of the glacis she had possessed in 1914. Stalin's motive was probably fear, not aggressiveness, for he knew Russia to be weak. Germany's gain also seemed great. Hitler was able to pursue his designs on Poland sure that he would face her alone.

He was almost right. The order for an attack on Poland was issued by Hitler on 25 August. It was postponed that evening, after Mussolini had made it clear that he could not enter the war at once. At the same time, the British government reiterated its guarantee to Poland. Yet there were signs that some British ministers still hoped to avoid war by persuading Poland to make concessions, and their efforts continued to the last moment. Hitler was contemptuous of English and French statesmen since Munich – 'little worms', he called them[39] – and at the end of August was convinced that he could prise England away from Poland. On 29 August he demanded that a Polish negotiator should come to Berlin. When his 'final' demands were read to the British ambassador at midnight 30–31 August, Hitler did not intend to accept any check to the plan for an attack on 1 September and refused to see the Polish ambassador. At 6.30 a.m. on 1 September, the German invasion began, its ostensible justification being a faked attack on a German radio station by Germans dressed in Polish uniforms. At the news, the British and French began to mobilize but still made it clear that they would welcome the chance of negotiation, if the German forces withdrew. Only on 2 September was it agreed to send a British ultimatum to Germany. It was sent the next morning and expired at 11 a.m. The French declared war at five o'clock in the afternoon. Thus began the second world war. Britain and France entered it unwillingly, believing themselves weaker than they really were, and with the enormous strategic disadvantage (as compared with 1914) that Russia was not at war. There was no likelihood that they would receive much help from the United States. Italy declared her neutrality.

In these circumstances, the destruction of Poland was not surprising. The Russians, it is true, do not seem to have expected it would take so little time. They had to move quickly, and on 17 September, using arguments of racial affinity which would have been appropriate to the tsarist Empire, they invaded Poland, deploring the unfortunate war into which the Polish people had been dragged by unwise leaders. By the end of the month, Poland was prostrate. A new Russo-German settlement was worked out which divided Poland on a roughly ethnic basis, Germany receiving purely Polish areas, and Russia getting White Russia and the Ukraine. Lithuania, previously allocated to the German sphere, now went to Russia. It was clear that Russia was able to put a higher price on her neutrality because Britain and France were actually at war. While Germany's attention was turned to

39 See Nolte, p. 526.

the west, the Russians began the business of political and social purification in occupied Poland.

Hitler had not expected to fight England and France in 1939. In October he offered to make peace, and there seems to be no reason to doubt his sincerity. A settlement would have fitted his conception of a series of piecemeal victories and further justified his strategy. At this stage, he would have accepted a truncated Polish satellite as a neighbour. But the Allies were already asking for the restoration of Austria and Czechoslovakia. Nevertheless, in spite of Hitler's fears, they were not prepared to mount a big land offensive in the west to obtain this. Haunted by the memory of the Somme and Verdun, allied planning envisaged only an economic offensive. It was this, a threat to Germany's Scandinavian ore supplies, together with Hitler's growing conviction that another victory would be necessary before peace could be made, that led to the end of the 'phoney war'. On 9 April 1940 a German attack on Norway and Denmark quickly overran them.

The Norwegian campaign was prolonged by the arrival of French and British forces, but the disasters which followed the British landings brought about a parliamentary crisis in England. Its consequence was Churchill's assumption of office as Prime Minister on the evening of 9 May. The next morning, the Germans attacked Holland and Belgium. German planning always feared that the Allies would seize the Low Countries in order to bring the Ruhr under air and land bombardment; the other motive of the invasion was a victory which could lead to negotiated peace. A succession of allied defeats led to the withdrawal of the bulk of the British army, at the cost of its equipment, from the beaches of Dunkirk, and to the despatch of a second expeditionary force which had almost immediately to return when the French government asked for an armistice (17 June). In just over two and a half months, German arms had achieved victories far greater than any in the first world war. Geographically, they controlled the northern European coast from the Pyrenees to the North Cape. They had destroyed the war-making capacity of one of the two great powers opposed to them. England was left with no ally, and Gibraltar as is only foothold, on the European continent. The end, it seemed, was in sight; the British had only to recognize the fact. Once again, Hitler was ready to make peace and said so in a speech on 19 July.

That a strategical disaster had overtaken the Allies was true, but it could not be fatal so long as the British will to fight was intact. The advantages of being *poissons* (see p. 88) were suddenly apparent. Further, the significance of two new developments soon became clear. One was the outcome of a great air battle which raged over southern England from mid-July to the end of September. The British won it and were unlikely therefore to be overcome by air bombardment alone, or exposed to invasion by losing command of the air. The other development was Italy's entry into the war.

Soon after Munich, Mussolini thought war between the Axis and the democracies inevitable. The seizure of Albania (7 April 1939) showed a recovery of appetite after the strains of Ethiopia and Spain. Nevertheless, in spite of the military alliance he made with Germany in May – the 'Pact of Steel' – Ciano was horrified to hear in August that Hitler had decided to bring the Polish crisis to a head. When war came Italy was still too weak for Mussolini to join in. Only the prospect of cheap pickings decided him. But by entering the war (10 June 1940), Italy ceased to be useful to Hitler and became a nuisance. An entirely new strategic theatre was opened – the Mediterranean and Africa – and it was of no importance to Germany. A quick Italian occupation of British Somaliland was the limit of Mussolini's success. There followed two great Italian defeats, one in the western deserts of Egypt and Cyrenaica (December 1940–February 1941), where an Italian army of 300,000 was shattered and 113,000 prisoners and 1,300 guns captured at a cost of 438 British dead, and the other in East Africa, where by November 1941 the whole of Italy's possessions were taken from her and the Emperor of Ethiopia re-established on his throne. These victories could not win the war for England, but they were of great moral importance and led to the diversion of German forces to the Mediterranean. Another Italian initiative ended in just as humiliating a failure, when an attack launched on Greece on 28 October 1940 (without consulting the Germans) bogged down in the winter and was followed by Italian retreat. The arrival of British air forces in Greece was a potential threat to the German-controlled Rumanian oilfields.

Just after its greatest successes, therefore, German strategy had to take account of an ally in trouble, and one whose economic weakness was increasingly evident. Confronted with stalemate in the west, Germany's best course would have been to rely on the immensely favourable geographical position she had won to weaken her enemy by blockade. This course was only half-heartedly followed; dangerous though submarine and air warfare against her shipping was to prove for England, a comparatively small part of Germany's strength was applied to it in the first two years of the war.

Immediately, there was something of a German diplomatic offensive. A pact between the two Axis powers and Japan (28 September) was meant to discourage the United States from further such gestures of sympathy and support to England as her sale of fifty destroyers earlier that month. German diplomacy also turned to eastern Europe. Great changes there followed the victory over France. Rumania renounced the Anglo-French guarantee in July; in September a pro-German dictatorship was set up and German forces soon began to arrive to protect the oilfields. In November Hungary formally recognized the three-power pact of September. Now Hitler decided to settle accounts with Russia. Yet just at this moment he was distracted by the need to send forces to help Italy. Plans were made for a German attack on Greece, but another event now complicated this operation. At the end of March 1941 a *coup d'état* in Belgrade overthrew the pro-German government of the regent and led to the assumption of government by the young king. Ten days later, the German attack was launched on both Yugoslavia and Greece. It was wholly successful, as the other *blitzkrieg* operations had all been, but it took time and led to new commitments.

From the British point of view, the situation was grave. Driven from Crete by a spectacular airborne invasion after evacuating the Greek mainland, England was also on the defensive in Cyrenaica, after a bad defeat through over-extension. In a wider perspective, it was encouraging that a pro-German *coup* in Iraq had been contained and that President Roosevelt had been re-elected in the United States in November 1940. The authorization of 'lend-lease' in March removed the danger that the British government would be unable to buy the supplies it needed. Nevertheless, the advantage lay with Germany. Only the first of Hitler's two greatest mistakes, the invasion of Russia, changed this. Since August 1939 Russian diplomacy had won huge successes. By 1941 much of the geographical position of 1914 was restored. Poland had been partitioned. The Baltic states obediently accepted Russian garrisons, became virtual protectorates, and then, in July 1940, asked for admission to the U.S.S.R. It was not, of course, refused.

Before this, a war had been fought with Finland (30 November 1939–12 March 1940) to obtain a naval base and a more defensible frontier. The performance of the Russian army was at first deplorable and bore out the misgivings felt about it in the west. There was almost an Anglo–French intervention on the Finnish side. Fortunately this was avoided, and the Russians were able to impose their will at the peace. Finally, an ultimatum to Rumania (29 June 1940) had obtained the cession of Bessarabia and north Bukovina.[40]

This impressive record was marred only by uneasiness about Germany. The Russians had duly congratulated Hitler on the successes of the Scandinavian campaign. The rapidity of the next victory in the west had been a shock; the Russians seem to have expected a repetition of 1914. Then came the three-power pact of September between Germany, Italy and Japan. Still confident of their bargaining position, Molotov went to Berlin in November to negotiate Russian adherence to the pact. In a note of November 25 he set a high price. He asked that Germany should withdraw support from Finland, should put pressure on Japan to be more accommodating to Russian interests in the Far East and should recognize a Russian sphere of influence south of Batum and Baku. He also asked for Russian bases in the Dardanelles and the recognition that Bulgaria was a Russian dependency. These terms were ill-received. Hitler had already been irritated by the absorption of Bessarabia and the north Bukovina (which was not part of the agreement of 29 September) and had decided to deal with Russia by war. Molotov went away empty-handed.

Hitler was convinced he could defeat Russia. Indeed, if he was not to launch a seaborne invasion of England, no other strategical employment for the German army existed; that it should not be allowed to idle and lose its tone was an element in his decision. But the central motive was the old dream of living-space in the east and the exploitation of the wealth of the Ukraine. On 18 December formal orders were issued for operation Barbarossa, the

---

40 The Bulgarians and Hungarians promptly presented their demands, too. The first obtained the south Dobrudja (7 September 1940) by agreement. The Germans arbitrated the other demand (30 August), awarding northern Transylvania to Hungary. The Rumanian foreign minister fainted on hearing the terms.

invasion of Russia. German intelligence estimates of Russia's strength were based on the performance of the Russian army in Finland; another *blitzkrieg*, over in eight weeks, was envisaged. By March the British government was sure that an attack on Russia would come in May and soon told the Russians so. In spite of signs of alarm, Stalin clung to a policy of appeasement. On the eve of the attack, Russia was almost paralysed into non-resistance.

On 22 June the blow fell.[41] The German army rapidly won great successes, penetrating Russian territory deeply, breaking up Russian formations and taking huge numbers of prisoners. After a month, Hitler was contemplating measures of demobilization. But in December, after great defeats, the Russians were still in the field. They were about to launch their first victorious counter-offensive. The early onset of winter, faulty intelligence appreciation, seven or eight weeks lost in the Balkan campaigns, the destruction of the German airborne army in Crete, and the diversion of a small but crack force to Africa had helped to save Moscow. More important, Hitler's strategic assumption that he could continue to fight a victorious series of short wars was finally destroyed. This had been implicit in the summer of 1940, but not evident. From June 1941 German strategy lost the initiative. The Russians had only to be kept in the field and German military strength was inextricably tied down.

Hitler made one more fatal decision. After the Japanese attack on Pearl Harbour and the launching of the first Russian offensive on 6 December, there was a chance of the Pacific war distracting the United States from Europe. Hitler's declaration of war on the United States (11 December) threw it away. Under the defensive alliance concluded in 1940, there was no need for Germany to act. The irrational origins of Hitler's diplomacy were never more strikingly shown. Lend-lease, the expulsion of many German consuls from American cities, an Atlantic meeting of Churchill and Roosevelt had made a growing contribution to the Allied cause. Yet America was not at war with Germany and might well have turned her back on Europe to fight Japan. This possibility was destroyed by Hitler. Few acts so decisively mark the end of

41 Mussolini was only told when the attack had actually begun, though for some weeks he had suspected what was coming. His relations with Hitler were irritated at the time by rivalry for influence within the new Croatian state set up after Yugoslavia's overthrow.

an epoch and the eclipse of the European balance of power through which Germany had played so great a world role. The fate of Europe was now to be settled by the two world powers on her flanks.

16

EUROPE AND THE SECOND WORLD WAR

THE NATURE OF THE WAR IN EUROPE

Although truly worldwide, the war which began in 1939 had at its heart the same struggle as that of 1914–18, the overcoming of Germany. Her preponderance was greater than in 1914 because her opponents were weaker. Even though she was not to develop her full strength until 1943, Germany achieved a series of victories so complete that by the summer of 1941 there was a small likelihood that blockade could sap her strength in the short run. Only the entry of Russia and the United States to the war made it possible to envisage a military defeat of Germany by forcing her to fight on more than one major front. It was not, therefore, until 1941 that the war entered its major phase.

The victories of the first two years owed much to the disarray of Germany's opponents. The 'phoney war' which lasted until April 1940 sprang from the wish of French and British soldiers to avoid the slaughter of Passchendaele and Verdun. Nor were German generals at first happy to risk its repetition. Nevertheless, when ordered to attack, they brought to bear superior skill, thinking, training and technology in a successful effort to reassert the power of the offensive over the defensive strength of modern armies. The doctrine of the *Blitzkrieg* was the condensation of their efforts. Owing much to British military thinking which was neglected or ignored at home, it exploited the powers of rapid movement and concentration made possible by the internal combustion engine. It used them in close coordination with aerial bombing to achieve a successful break in the enemy lines which was then exploited to the uttermost by penetration as far-ranging and deep as possible. This left defending forces outflanked and insecure before they had ever come into action. Great play was made with the moral and tactical possibilities of attacks on civilians so as to create an atmosphere of panic and block lines of communication. Campaigns of this sort were successful as late as the autumn of 1941, when the forward Russian armies were cut up and trapped by German armoured formations. They finally came to an end because the Russians had space and numbers enough to endure these attacks but, while they lasted, they provided Germany with victory without the economic and social strains of the Great War.[1].

The military technology behind these victories was based on the innovations of the Great War; what was new was the much greater use of devices first seen twenty-five years before, above all, the tank, the lorry and the aeroplane. These sustained the new mechanized war, but they could not suffice alone; infantry and artillery were still the backbone of the battle. Radar, pilotless and rocket missiles and jet-propelled aircraft were major innovations, but only the first produced a decisive effect by making possible British victory in the 'Battle of Britain' of 1940. The great change in methods of fighting was the restoration of mobility to land warfare, and the extension of the effective area of battle by the use of aircraft for reconnaissance, bombing and supply. This change had been implicit in the innovations of 1914–18.

The war on land, therefore, had a recognizable, though transformed shape. It was in the air that strategic innovation went furthest. Apart from its helpfulness in providing extra mobility, the aeroplane had long attracted military thinkers as a new kind of weapon. Between the wars, extravagant claims were made for it. Bombing attacks, it was alleged, would cripple economic resources and break civilian morale. Such claims were tested in Europe between 1940 and 1945. The German attempts to bomb London into submission in 1940 and later attacks with unmanned aircraft and rockets both failed (though this may have been because of the relative lightness of the first efforts, and because of the quick over-running of the flying bomb and rocket bases by the allied armies in 1945). More difficult to assess is the value

1 On the wider implications of the *Blitzkrieg*, see A. Milward, *The German Economy at War* (London, 1965), esp. pp. 7–14.

of the Anglo-American bombing of Germany. Roughly speaking, the British night attacks after February 1942 aimed chiefly at the obliteration of big urban areas and the smashing of civilian morale. They seem to have had little direct impact on Germany's war-making power although, of course, indirectly weakening it by the demands they made on the German labour force and by diverting into air defence resources which might have been used in Russia. The American day attacks (at first costly, but feasible as soon as long-range fighter escorts could be provided) had greater direct economic effect. They could inflict damage upon precise and important targets; the selective destruction of oil installations, for example, in the last months of the war had grave effects on the German air defence system, which finally collapsed completely for lack of fuel, and on the movement of land forces.

The Russians all but ignored the bomber as a strategic weapon and concentrated on its tactical use. The German air force had always assumed that its main role would be cooperation with ground forces and showed great tactical expertise in the *Blitzkrieg* campaigns of the first two years of the war. From 1942 onwards the R.A.F. and American Air Forces showed that they, too, had learned this lesson, and after the North African campaigns of that year the German army rarely had the help of local air superiority. The tactical employment of air power was the most striking change in the nature of land warfare since 1918 and may be thought more important than strategic bombing. Certainly the fear of damage to civilian morale proved exaggerated; if anything, heavy bombing created a sense of shared danger and national unity in both Germany and England. But the arguments about the bombing offensive are complicated and it should not be assumed immediately that it was a wasted effort.

Mechanized warfare on such an overwhelming scale as air and land operations now demanded had quickly brought about big internal changes in the main combatant nations. England and Russia achieved the greatest subordination of economy and society to the war effort. About Russia's adaptations of her economic and social structure we do not know very much. It is certain that there were great changes, for example in the distribution of her industries, as a result of the evacuation of her western areas and the removal of plant to the east. It is also certain that the 'scorched earth' tactics of 1941 and 1942 – the relentless destruction by the retreating armies of anything which might be of value to the Germans – brought great suffering and hardship to the populations who were unable to withdraw. But sheer hardship was probably the most marked difference between life in Russia before and after 1941, and the centralization of the Russian state machinery must have made the formal transition from peace to war government much less significant than in a constitutional state such as England.

Although critics of the British government from time to time demanded much greater discipline and direction of public life, an intensive and efficient mobilization of the country's resources took place, on a scale unmatched and for a duration unequalled by any of the other major states. The experience of the Great War was there to be drawn on, and from the start the necessary legislation was available. At the top, the War Cabinet system of 1916 was set up at once. Private property was interfered with more than ever before, especially when the defeat of England's continental allies, the possibility of invasion, and siege warfare by sea and air placed the islands in greater danger than ever before. By the end of the war, in spite of the great economies obtained by ruthless controls of manpower in a manpower 'budget', the strain was proving too much. British military and economic power was past its peak in 1944. At its height it had been an impressive demonstration of the efficacy of central controls which convinced many Englishmen that it might have lessons for peacetime, too. Interesting social changes made this seem plausible. After 1942 public health improved markedly (even the suicide rate fell). Real earnings rose more than the cost of living and a larger share of personal incomes was received in wages and salaries than in rent, dividends or interest on capital. The redistribution of income was carried further by high personal taxation; income tax and surtax were producing nearly four times as much revenue in 1945 as in 1939, and indirect taxes only about two and a half times as much.[2]

It seems likely that Great Britain was more successful than Germany in mobilizing science behind her war effort. One success of British science was the continuing exploitation of its lead in radar and its deployment both behind the bomber offensive and against the submarine menace. Another was the perfection of

2 The official *History of the Second World War. United Kingdom Civil Series*, under the editorship of W. K. Hancock has more than twenty volumes on various aspects of the war's domestic effects.

ultra-secret techniques for the decoding of German signals traffic, the so-called 'Enigma' operations which, among other things, led to the building of the first electronic computer at Bletchley. This machine, 'Colossus', so secret that its existence was not acknowledged until thirty years after the war, when American historical primacy in the field was already taken for granted, represented a radical break with the improvements in mechanical calculating machines which had been the story of the twentieth century until then and it launched the electronic and information technology revolution in which we are still living. The other major European contribution to the allied war effort through British science brought to a culmination the work of applying the revolution in nuclear physics. This was the work which opened the way to making an 'atomic bomb'. In 1940 two European physicists working in the United Kingdom showed that the isotope 235 of uranium could be separated industrially. In the following year, the Maud committee reported that an atomic bomb was possible. Two years later, British work on the project was transferred to the American 'Manhattan Project' and the development which ended at Hiroshima and Nagasaki two years later was under way.

Germany achieved neither scientific nor economic mobilization with such success as Great Britain. She was able to put jet aircraft into service before her enemy, had a lead in the applied science of rocketry, and showed great technological superiority in the improvement of conventional weapons. But fundamental science did not contribute much to her war effort. Yet Nazi propaganda had always made much of German's preparedness for 'total' war. This preparedness was real in so far as one particular sort of war was envisaged. Until the Russian recapture of Rostov at the end of 1941, German planning assumed a series of short *Blitzkrieg* campaigns which would not require violent adaptation of the economy. The machinery for efficient planning and allocation of resources did not exist because it had always been assumed that a long struggle which would really tax Germany's strength would not be needed. Although there had been a paper system of control of employment and wages since the beginning of the war, there was inadequate statistical information available about many sides of the war effort. To make matters worse, Nazi government at the top had always been a matter of court-politics and favouritism, an incoherent structure in which vested interests of all sorts, political, military and economic, struggled as best they could for the resources they required.[3] Nor did things improve as the war went on. After 1942, Hitler was himself almost always absent from Berlin and the public eye, preferring to brood over a world of increasing unreality in his East Prussian field headquarters. This left his chief lieutenants to run their rival empires unchecked.

In these circumstances, Germany's survival from 1942 to 1945 appears remarkable. Apart from the outstanding fighting skills of the German army, the explanation must be sought first in the existence of huge untapped reserves in the economy even in 1942. Reserve capacity was there largely because of Hitler's wish not to reduce the production of consumer goods and because it was easy to loot occupied countries for resources. Yet even after the decision to plan for a long struggle had been taken in January 1942, adaptation was slow and inefficient.[4] Although armaments production was tripled by the summer of 1944, a totally controlled economy never existed except in theory. The nature of the regime militated against rationality. Hitler insisted, for instance, that to employ more women in armaments production would be biologically harmful to the race, while the armed services continued to take from the labour force many of its skilled workers. The gaps were partly filled by over 7 million foreign deportees and prisoners of war. But rivalries and divisions within the régime continued to militate against efficiency; S.S., for example, maintained all through the war a growing and independent industrial structure of its own, often run by officials with a fiercely anti-capitalist distrust of the policies of the armaments minister, Speer. Such experiences did something to account for the fact that by the end of 1944 the economic administration of Germany was no longer loyal to the régime. When, in March 1945, Hitler ordered the total destruction of German economic resources before they fell into foreign hands, Speer ordered his managers to disobey and save what they could for the future.

This was an unusual instance of dissent. One of the most striking features of the last two years of the war was the moral

3 For what this implied see Milward, pp. 49–52, and 131–61.
4 A. Milward, *The German Economy at War* (London, 1965), p. 6. Indices of consumer goods production (1939 = 100)

	1943	1944
UK	54	54
Germany	91	85

solidity of the German resistance to land and air attack. This owed much to the skilful conduct of propaganda of Goebbels, who made much of the gloomy fate awaiting Germany in the event of an Allied victory. One major attempt was made to overthrow the régime by combining a military *coup* with the assassination of Hitler. It misfired, and thousands of those concerned or suspected were rounded up and murdered. Apart from this, there were few signs of disloyalty, defeatism or opposition. In October 1944 civilian status for men was practically abolished by the creation of a *Volksturm* in which every male between sixteen and sixty was enlisted under the direct command of the *Wehrmacht* for what was obviously a hopeless fight to the death. Some of Germany's endurance was sustained by terror, but it is difficult to believe that this is the whole story.

Germany had one organizational advantage: she had no allies who had to be consulted. Her opponents, on the other hand, had to coordinate the efforts of three major states of very different geographical and social character. In spite of the acrimony which has since been generated by discussion of the conduct of the war, these difficulties were surmounted to a remarkable degree. Much of the credit must go to Winston Churchill, who tirelessly travelled about the world to confer with Stalin and Roosevelt, and whose views, whatever their strategic shortcomings, were all the time subordinated to a realistic grasp of the two essentials: that the Russians would for a long time have to bear the brunt of the land war against Germany and that Anglo-American agreement was the heart of the matter anywhere except on the Russian front. Smaller states therefore played little part in the calculations of the three great powers, except as counters in their quarrels.

The main business of inter-allied consultation was done at the highest level, at a series of conferences. The first took place before the entry of America to the war, when Churchill and Roosevelt met on a British battleship in August 1941; the next at Christmas, in Washington. Churchill first visited Moscow in August 1942. At the end of 1943 Stalin left Russia to meet Churchill and Roosevelt at Teheran. The three met again at Yalta in February 1945, after Churchill had again gone to Moscow. The last of the great conferences took place at Potsdam in July 1945, after the defeat of Germany. None of these meetings of statesmen, it may be observed, took place in England; after 1941 the two larger partners in the Grand Alliance inevitably and slowly showed their preponderance within it and it was the British prime minister who had to join his colleagues as it suited them.[5]

The personal tie between Churchill and Roosevelt, although it was to weaken as the war progressed, was the apex of a complicated system of Anglo-American coordination at every level. The mingling of their armed services under Combined Chiefs of Staff was unprecedented and effective; it led to much more genuine cooperation between allies than in the first Great War. It weathered the clashes of interest and outlook which arose more and more pressingly towards the end of the war. The vital decision was taken at the first conference between Roosevelt and Churchill, at Washington in December 1941: that Germany should be defeated before Japan. This was never shaken and culminated in agreement in Teheran to launch 'Overlord', the Anglo-American assault on western Europe so long asked for by the Russians, in 1944. The deployment of American strength in the European theatre to prepare for this operation was all the more important because the entry of the United States into the war made it certain that even the huge potential of the American factories would not satisfy the sudden expansion of American military needs and those of her allies before the end of 1942. Nevertheless, Anglo-American planning and cooperation in the use of scarce resources reached a far higher degree of efficiency than anything achieved within the apparently unitary Germany state.

It was decisive for the allied victory that British and Russian industry could be reinforced by the arsenals of the United States. This gave the allies a quantitative supremacy so great that any official discussion of it was actually forbidden in Germany. But the accessibility of American support depended on winning the 'Battle of the Atlantic' and the maintenance of overland supply to Russia *via* Persia and, at first, by the expensive convoys to the northern Russian ports.[6] The worst month for merchant ship losses in both world wars was March 1943, when nearly half a million tons of shipping were sunk in the North Atlantic, but by the end of the year, the battle of the Atlantic was won.

---

5 Perhaps we should not exaggerate this; Roosevelt's health was not good and Stalin cannot have wished to have been far from the levers of power in Russia at moments of danger.
6 Persia was occupied by British and Russian forces in August 1941.

The fighting itself can be described simply in outline, not because it was without interest or drama, but because the development of strategy was fairly straightforward and simple. From 1941, the enormous reserves of Russian strength on land and the retention of air and sea supremacy by the British and Americans imposed upon Germany a two-front war. Its 'western' front was at first limited to the Mediterranean and the air space over northern Europe and was then extended from 1944 onwards by land warfare in France.

Hitler had squandered his earlier successes by his attack on Russia, but this did not appear at once. At the beginning of December, when the German offensive belatedly came to an end, Russia had lost about half her industrial area, the Germans had broken into the Crimea and crossed the Don at Rostov, and Leningrad was besieged. The domes of the Kremlin itself could be seen by the German advance guards before Moscow. A successful counter-offensive was launched by the Russians on 6 December, and the entry of the United States to the war was good for Russian and British morale, but at the end of the year it was by no means certain that the tide had turned. The British were soon weighed down by new defeats in the Far East. The battle of the Atlantic was a grievous strain and they had little to encourage them in North Africa, where failures obliterated the brilliance of Wavell's early victories. Yet, unobserved, the Germans had lost the war.

In spite of their huge losses and further retreats in 1942 the Russian armies were obviously going to stay in the field. Moscow was safe, and its communications with the rest of Russia intact. The German armies still were able to advance deep into the Caucasus and reach the Volga at Stalingrad in 1942. They again ejected the British and 'Free French' forces from Libya and came closer to Suez than ever before. But at the end of 1942 came two great German defeats. The battle of El Alamein (23–30 October) finally erased the danger to Suez. It launched an advance soon followed by Anglo-American landings in French North Africa (8 November) whose outcome, the following May, was the surrender at Tunis of all the German and Italian forces in Africa. This freed the Mediterranean to Allied shipping and exposed southern Europe to assault. The other great German defeat began when Hitler ignored the advice of his soldiers to disentangle his forces from the savage street-fighting which had begun at Stalingrad in September. A Russian offensive began in mid-November and soon cut off many of his best units. Had they been allowed to do so, they had still for a few weeks a chance of breaking out, but they were ordered not to give ground. On 2 February 1943 the German commander at Stalingrad surrendered, after his army group of nearly 250,000 men had been destroyed.

The turning of the tide raised many problems, political and strategic, to embarrass the relations between the allies. The conference between Roosevelt and Churchill at Casablanca in January 1943 defined allied war aims as the unconditional surrender of Germany. It was made much use of by Goebbels' propaganda machine and the failure to distinguish between the German people and the Nazi régime was subsequently much critcized, but it is difficult to see how such a distinction was to be sustained when there was no sign of significant German opposition to Hitler.

In spite of this declaration and of repeated Anglo-American assurances, Stalin was always suspicious of his allies, believing that they were delaying in their own interests the sea-borne invasion of Europe which he wanted to remove pressure on the Russian armies. After further experience gained by the successful invasion of Sicily and Italy, and the assembly of huge quantities of shipping and materials, the enormous operation of a cross-channel invasion of France was finally launched on 6 June 1944. The last German offensive in Russian had collapsed nearly a year before and since then the Russian armies had pressed forward with little rest. Kiev and Smolensk had been recaptured in 1943; in July 1944 the Russians entered Poland. In France, the Anglo-American armies followed up their landings by defeating the main German armies in northern France and capturing Paris and Brussels (25 August and 5 September). Meanwhile, the Russians invaded Rumania and Bulgaria. A briefly successful German attack in the Ardennes at the end of the year could not stem the tide. Early in 1945 the Russians entered Warsaw, Cracow and Budapest. In March the Anglo-American forces crossed the Rhine. In April the Russians reached Berlin, amid whose ruins Hitler committed suicide (30 April) and the last flicker of German resistance in the east was soon suppressed, although Doenitz, the last head of the Third *Reich*, briefly tried to continue the struggle. The final German capitulation came on 7 May, and with it the end of the European, though not the Asian, war.

WARTIME EUROPE

Only Spain, Portugal, Ireland, Switzerland and Sweden remained neutral throughout the war, and even they were troubled. Spain, in particular, was held back in her recovery from the disasters of her civil war. None the less, these states escaped the revolutionary changes that came to many others on whom battle and occupation left deep scars. Defeat was the lot of most continental countries, whether at the hands of Germany or the Grand Alliance,[7] and by 1945 this had swept away the Europe of 1939.

Great Britain was unique among European great powers in that she was undefeated and uninvaded. Her political constitution survived almost unchanged, its vigour shown best by a willingness to accept encroachments on traditional liberties and a discipline more complete than that of any other state except, perhaps, Russia. The crisis of 1940 brought to power (by a revolt within the Conservative ranks) Winston Churchill, indisputably the greatest leader of his people in this century. This made possible the entry of the Labour party to a coalition government of historic significance. It not only expressed successfully the country's general will to win the war, but also gave the Labour party the cabinet experience which again made it a convincing alternative government. In 1945, to the surprise and shock of many Conservatives who had expected Churchill's popularity to carry his party to victory, a general election held after the defeat of Germany returned to office for the first time a Labour government with a safe working majority.

The mood which produced this result is now easier to understand than many found it at the time. British electors distinguished between their war leader and his party, which had so belatedly recognized his claims to office. Voting for the first time for ten years, they could show what they thought of the policies which had led to the defeats and disasters of 1939, 1940 and 1941. And they voted in an atmosphere transformed by the war. The prewar erosion of *laissez-faire* ideas had been carried much further by wartime regulations. The experience of directing a siege economy and of shared collective purpose – for the British people, war aims were a simple matter of destroying the Nazi régime – were subtly influential in preparing the electorate for the

7 Or, as it was called after 2 January 1942, the United Nations.

Labour campaign of 1945, with its promise that a directed peace economy could remove the spectre of unemployment and poverty and maintained the sense of a common enterprise. This was to prove harder than expected because the war impoverished Britain. Whatever the economic difficulties of the inter-war years, in 1939 she had been still a rich nation. The war cut deeply into her wealth. British exports fell to less than a third of their 1939 figure. Balances of dollars and foreign currencies abroad were swept away and replaced by £2,000 million of sterling balances held by other countries. In the first postwar year, a deficit of £750 million in the balance of payments was expected. 'Invisible' income from abroad had been halved, and the subordination of industry to the demands of war had gravely distorted it and left it ill-equipped to win back foreign markets. In 1945, although the only 1939 European great power other than Russia to survive, the foundations of Britain's political and military role were crumbling beneath her.

But she had escaped the horrifying and demoralizing experiences known by almost every continental country as a result of German domination. Its greatest extent was not reached until after the invasion of Russia, but it was probably firmest at the beginning of 1941. Then, half of France, all Belgium, Holland, Denmark, Norway and half Poland had been occupied. Most of this territory was under direct military rule, though Poland had been divided, a part of its western lands being incoporated in Germany, while the large tracts remaining constituted a 'General Government' in the east. To it were driven the Poles from the western areas. The Third *Reich* itself had also enlarged its boundaries by annexing the territories in the west lost at Versailles (Alsace, Lorraine, Eupen and Malmédy) together with Luxemburg (August 1942) and Slovenia (September 1942). Around it clustered the occupied territories, Germany's allies and puppets, and the neutrals. An 'independent' Croatia had been set up after the occupation of Yugoslavia and Greece (shared by the Germans with their Italian allies), and in 1942 the southern half of France, seized after the Anglo-American landings in North Africa. When Mussolini was overthrown in July 1943, and his successors sought an armistice from the allies, Italy, too, or, at least its northern half, became an occupied area (we may disregard the formally independent 'republic of Salo' which was Musolini's last refuge). The attack on Russia added enormous tracts of land to those already occupied, and also brought new allies to the German side. Finland resumed the war of 1939–40. Hungary struggled to retain some freedom of action but had a puppet pro-German government imposed in March 1943. Slovakia, throughout, remained a curious satellite, too small to be of great importance to the German war effort. Rumania was occupied by protecting forces and was obliged to send troops to the Russian front. (Later, defeated, she was obliged to declare war on Germany.) Thus many countries found themselves tied to the German chariot wheels and involved eventually in a common ruin. But they at least escaped the full weight of German government as it was felt in the occupied lands.

German government of occupied territories was appalling and was often meant to be. Unlike the civilian chancellors of the Wilhelmine *Reich*, Hitler held his generals firmly in his grasp; immediate military necessity therefore plays only a small part in justifying German behaviour. Policy, indeed, sometimes conflicted with the demands of military prudence; Russians who had welcomed the German armies in 1941 were quickly and irrevocably alienated by the savagery of German behaviour. This made occupation duties much more burdensome to the army. Even the use of forced labour had more than a utilitarian dimension and was only a step in an unrolling design, the realization of fantasies about the expansion of the German race in the east and the extirpation and expulsion of the races already established there whose roots went back to German policy in the first world war. At its widest, this programme threatened the national existence of the Poles, Czechs and Russians; it was carried furthest in the case of the Jews.

Nazi racial policy was sustained by the S.S., whose leader, Himmler, had been given, in October 1939, the duty of resettling populations to achieve a racially pure German nation. All over Europe, his minions in the *Gestapo* and *Waffen S.S.* units revived the brutalities of the Middle Ages without the excuse of ignorance in the pursuit of the myth of racial purity.[8] It was the most bizarre as well as the most iniquitous example of the abuse of German power. It also provides the most striking example in modern history of the recession of liberal bourgeois standards.

8 The *Waffen S.S.* were full-scale military units organized in formations as large as a division for normal warfare.

The most atrocious phase of racial policy began with the authorization of the 'Final Solution' which had been long contemplated. This was the extermination by shooting and gassing of the Jewish populations of central Europe, many of whom had already been concentrated in the Polish General Government area. The man in charge of this operation, Heydrich, was assassinated by agents flown from England in June 1942, but this did not affect the extermination policy, which proceeded all the more terribly because it might never be named. In its course, starvation and exposure, deliberately imposed, carried off many Jews deported to the east. In April 1943, the Jews herded to starve in the Warsaw ghetto rose and killed about a thousand Germans before they were overcome. But for the most part the extermination proceeded efficiently and systematically in the gas-chambers and crematoria. Perhaps a million Jews died in the extermination camps at Auschwitz, another million in shootings and exterminations on the spot in the Ukraine and Bessarabia, and another million from overwork, hunger, disease and neglect. The Polish Jews were almost obliterated, and the Dutch Jews also suffered heavily in proportion to their numbers. But the crime is so great that distinctions within it seem almost meaningless. Altogether, something like six million Jews seem to have perished.[9]

It must not be forgotten, too, that although it was the most terrible feature of German rule, the 'Final Solution' was only one of many crimes. The treatment of prisoners of war and forced labour deportees, especially those from the east, provides much evidence of this. Some Germans protested, but in vain. The head of the *Abwehr* (the military intelligence service), Canaris, objected to maltreatment of Russian soldiers, to whom the conventional protection of prisoners of war was not extended; when his protests were brushed aside, it was not by the *Gestapo* but by the German army. It is the conscious brutality of German Europe which provokes disgust. Even if the atrocities committed by the German army in the field – such as the shooting of American prisoners in France in 1944 – or by the S.S. against civilian populations believed to require intimidation – such as the massacre of the inhabitants of Oradour soon after the Allied landings in

9 See Reitlinger, pp. 489–500, on the problems of estimating the extent of the killings; the rough total is taken from M. Gilbert, *The Holocaust* (London, 1986).

France, or the wiping out of Lidice in Czechoslovakia – or even the harsh exploitation of foreign labour have all been discounted on grounds of panic, provocation and economic necessity, there remain to this day the terrible monuments of the extermination camps. Auschwitz and Treblinka and the photographs which revealed to a horrified world what greeted the allied troops who entered Belsen and Buchenwald, are the evidence of deliberate, orderly policy, with the cooperation of thousands of civil servants, soldiers and professional men and women, of all ranks of society and of varying degrees of attachment to the régime. It is inconceivable that such things could have been done in the Germany of Bismarck; its explanation is the central problem of German social and cultural history during the years discussed in this book.

Extermination policy influenced the great demographic effects of the war. Outside Russia, one estimate is that about 16 million Europeans died, although the fighting was never as bloody as that of the Great War except in the east, where the German and Russian armies suffered and inflicted terrible losses.[10] The German army lost more men than in 1914–18, while the British armed forces lost far fewer (even when the war against Japan is taken into account). The Germans also suffered more civilian deaths.[11] The high mortality among civilians was striking in many countries. A fifth of the Polish population died. Yugoslavia lost four times as many civilians as soldiers; Greek losses were in the same proportion unless Jews are included, in which case the ratio is seven to one. German occupation policy and starvation explain many of the civilian deaths. But the total demographic loss to Europe remains hard to establish because of uncertain data, and because of complications arising from population movement. In the first year of the war, for example, a great repatriation of Germans took place, while Russia shifted more than a million people from her newly acquired territories to the east. Later, German occupation brought about even greater displacements.

10 See *Population* (1953), p. 373, which breaks down overall, European losses outside Russia as (in rounded figures) 5.8 m servicemen, 4.9 m civilians and 4.3 m Jews.
11 Approximately 264,000 British servicemen and 30,000 merchant seamen were killed, most of them in the war against Germany. 96,000 British civilians died as the result of operations of war; 600,000 Germans were killed by Allied bombing, and about 3.5 m servicemen in all.

Many people who died as a result should be counted as a part of the toll of the war which made their deaths possible. Health, too, deteriorated in most occupied countries because of starvation and the lack of essential medical supplies, although neither England nor Germany suffered in this way. Certainly eastern Europe suffered most in all respects. It has been suggested that Russia alone may have experienced a population deficiency of about 30 million as a result of the war.[12]

The privations of the occupied territories often arose from conscious economic exploitation. Hitler's wish to use the European economy in the interests of Germany led to outright requisition, currency-rigging and forced labour, which ensured that Germans for a long time had a high standard of living. But there were many disappointments, of which the greatest came in the Ukraine and the Russian industrial areas which had been devastated before German occupation. Moreover, the much-talked-of 'New Order' was from an economic point of view meaningless. There was no European planning and no attempt to rule the conquered territories as an economic whole. The defects of German domestic government were magnified on a continental scale. Germany never did as well out of her conquests as she should have done.

Economic exploitation of Germany's conquests also bred resistance, especially where there was recruitment of forced labour. This fed the local resistance movements with recruits. Their extent, strength and military importance varied from country to country. Resistance was affected by the local intensity of anti-German feeling, by the nature of the terrain, by the availability (or lack) of allied support, and by the state of local politics. It merits the attention of the historian not only because of its achievements against the Germans, but because of its political legacy after the war. Strategically, resistance probably mattered most in France and Yugoslavia, where it pinned down large numbers of German troops. The most remarkable achievement was that of the Poles, whose national record was a glorious one; their country was ill-suited to partisan activity, but they maintained a large 'Home Army' in readiness for use when the Russians were near enough. They also produced no politicians

---

12 Reinhard, p. 494. But estimates have gone as high as 40 m (*Population, loc. cit.*)

who collaborated with the Germans. In Norway, Denmark, Belgium and Holland there were resistance movements which rendered great services to the Allied cause by carrying out sabotage, obtaining information and by helping allied prisoners to escape, and Italian partisans appeared after the fall of Mussolini. All such potential help led the British and exiled governments to organize subversive and clandestine organizations to cooperate with resistance networks.[13] The Russians seem to have trusted less to this kind of warfare (outside Russia), though they awoke the loyalty of the remnants of west European Communist parties. These brought into the Resistance many working-class organizations which before 1941 had been taught that the war was an anti-imperialist one in which the Allies were as much their enemy as Germany.

In the occupied countries, resistance was an important political influence both before and after the collapse of German rule. Another was the existence or non-existence of governments in exile. What mattered most for the future in most cases, nevertheless, was the identity of the allied forces which carried out the campaigns of liberation. Together, all these influences produced in 1945 a Europe utterly transformed since 1939 and the foundation of the Europe of today. Arguably, the appearance of this political structure is the most important result of the European war.

So much time has been spent bemoaning this outcome, a divided Europe, that it is important to remember the rewards of victory, for they were very great, above all in the destruction of German power. That destruction was a means to the end which came to be sought without qualification by all the allies: the overthrow of the Nazi régime and its dependent despotisms. This was an unambiguously great and noble goal, and it was successfully achieved. Nazism was the worst challenge ever presented to liberal civilization and its conception of the humane society. The horrors of the Final Solution, the lunacies of racialism and the brutalities of German occupation threatened all that had been laboriously built up since the eighteenth century – perhaps since the coming of Christianity. This challenge was the great justification of the war, though it was not why the war began. To meet it success-

13 For one of the most celebrated examples, see M. R. D. Foot, *SOE in France* (London, 1966).

fully was a great positive achievement. But it had required greater strength than Europe alone could muster.

EUROPE AND THE WORLD IN 1945

By 1945, the power system of 1880 was in ruins. Many people even doubted if the historic states of Europe, so many of which had been laid low by the war, could survive. Only England had entered the war with an aim successfully achieved, the destruction of German hegemony; this experience and the memory of her successful stand alone in 1940–41 kept confidence in her state structure high. Russian nationalism had revived under the German attack, too, but elsewhere the re-established governments of the allied nations sat shakily in their saddles. Europe, moreover, would obviously be impeded in the work of recovery by the rough division established between east and west Europe by the fighting.[14] It was not, of course, certain that this division might be permanent; nor that the gap which had suddenly and inexplicably opened across the middle of Europe might widen further. Yet conditions on the one side of this gap already looked much more fixed than on the other. The régimes set up in the wake of the Russian advance were all, except for Finland and Austria, either in the hands of communists, or shared with them. The Comintern had been dissolved as a wartime gesture of solidarity with Russia's allies; the Russian army had proved a far more effective missionary of revolution.

In the balance of power alone, this was a great change. Russia had nothing to fear from any of her neighbours, nor from the prostrate Germany of 1945. She had recovered all and more of the strategical advantages of tsars; her glacis was now the regained Polish lands, the Baltic states, the Karelian isthmus (though not tsarist Finland as a whole) and Bessarabia. Beyond this protective

14 The positions reached by the Allied armies were slightly different from the lines along which Germany was divided into occupation zones; in the interests of getting Russian help against Japan, the Americans not only held back the British and their own forces (which could, for example, have reached Prague), but also actually withdrew bridgeheads across the Elbe.

curtain stretched the Russian satellites. The most important, Czechoslovakia, was, it is true, governed in 1945 by a coalition, but the Czechs felt deep gratitude to the Russians for their liberation, had sided with them against the Poles, and still looked back on Munich as a betrayal by the western powers. Finally, the Russian armies, enormously powerful, with no other significant strategic commitment, garrisoned the centre of Europe and held Germany's second greatest industrial area.

Below this obvious political and strategic transformation, other big changes had occurred within Russian Europe. The prewar minority problems which had plagued the area had been reduced by the brutal surgery of expulsions, removals and exterminations. Further population movements were to carry the process further. Economic problems, nevertheless, had been if anything intensified by the destruction of the fighting. As this was the 'poor' Europe of over-population and under-industrialization, reconstruction would be hard.

That Russia would long seek to hold it in thrall was not obvious in 1945. Only the Poles had by then experienced the intransigence of Russian power. Stalin, in 1941, had been as much of an aggressor as Hitler in the eyes of the exiled Polish government in London. Nevertheless, something like cooperation between Poland and Russia had been achieved by 1943, when the relations of the two states received a bad setback when what were said to be the bodies of thousands of Polish officers murdered by the Russians were found near Smolensk. There followed the appearance in Russia of a Polish committee which challenged the right of Poles in London to speak for their countrymen. With much English goodwill on its side (thanks to the gallantry of Polish airmen, soldiers and sailors who had escaped to England in 1940), the London government was by no means powerless. Moreover, in Poland itself it controlled the 'Home Army' which could take control immediately if the Germans withdrew. Unfortunately the Russians had concluded that the London government was irreconcilable. When their armies advanced on Warsaw in August 1944, and the Home Army rose against the Germans, the Russian advance suddenly came to a halt for two months. While the Germans crushed the Poles, Stalin refused to help Warsaw, even by cooperating with the R.A.F. in dropping supplies. Meanwhile the 'Lublin Committee', as the Russian-sponsored Polish group was called, agreed to accept the 1920 'Curzon line' for Poland's postwar frontier in the east, thus identifying themselves with the Russian search for security.

These events sowed mistrust of Russia in England and the United States. Suspicion clogged the discussion of a Polish settlement in Yalta the following February but to prevent the unilateral assumption of authority in Poland by the Lublin group, Churchill, under pressure from Roosevelt, conceded that the western frontier of Poland should run along the Oder and the western Neisse, the German populations to the east of them being removed. A government of National Unity set up in June contained representatives of the major parties, but already many exiled Poles chose to remain in exile rather than return to a régime whose future they distrusted. Poland thus provided the first instance of what a changed balance of power meant, although, like Hungary and Czechoslovakia, in 1945 she was still ruled by a coalition. Elsewhere, Bulgaria and Rumania had communist governments. Only Austria among the nations of central Europe seemed by the end of 1945 to be truly independent, her first elections having produced a government under social democratic leadership.

Two other states had been the subject of bargaining between the great powers. In Moscow in 1944 Churchill and Stalin had agreed that Russia should have a 90 per cent say in the postwar affairs of Rumania, and England the same share in those of Greece. In Yugoslavia their interest was agreed to be equal. This agreement became operative when the withdrawal of the Germans from Greece and the restoration of the monarchy led to a communist rebellion. It was put down by the Greek and British armies, with the connivance of the Russians and the help of the strategic errors of the Greek communists. Yugoslavia, on the other hand, settled her own fate. In 1943 the communist-led partisan movement of Marshal Tito had crushed its monarchist opponents and was fighting the Germans hard enough for the British to give them strong support; the political colour of Tito's movement was disregarded. This enabled the Yugoslavs, uniquely among European peoples, to liberate themselves in 1945. There were no significant allied forces on the spot, and Tito set up the only communist régime in Europe established without the aid of the Russian army.

Though a coolness between Russia and her allies had by the end of 1945 begun to alarm some observers, not many people then despaired of the distinction between east and west Europe. For one thing, the liberated countries of the west certainly had no settled future ahead; they might throw up governments which would enjoy good relations with Russia. The two most important examples were Italy and France. Italy changed sides after the overthrow of Mussolini.[15] Surrender in September 1943 was the culmination of negotiation during which the Allies had regarded with suspicion the Badoglio government which succeeded Mussolini; the outcome was muddle and misunderstanding, which allowed the Germans to occupy much of Italy immediately after the armistice. Although British and American forces landed in south Italy, the chance of drawing a rapid dividend from the surrender was thrown away. As the Allies would not subsequently regard Italy as a major theatre, the fighting dragged on there for another year and a half.

This prolongation brought destruction to an enfeebled economy and suffering to the Italians. The monarchy was further discredited by the results of its policies, and political divisions were exacerbated by a neo-Fascist movement which appeared in the north under German sponsorship. Mussolini, rescued from his Italian captors by the Germans, nominally presided over this but was a broken man; its masters were extreme Fascists who now acted without the restraint imposed on them in the old days. There also appeared in the north a strong resistance movement in which communists took a leading part. The south experienced neither.

There were hopeful signs that a recovery from Fascism would be rapid. The clandestine communist party came to life, and the leaders of the old *Partito Popolare* reconstituted themselves as the new *Democrazia Christiana*. The left wanted to avoid the errors of the past and soft-pedalled anticlericalism; the church, for its part, was less outspokenly anticommunist. No one suggested the abrogation of the Lateran treaties, and communists and socialists turned up with their red flags to cheer the Pope in St Peter's Square the day after Rome had been liberated.[16] The preoccupations of struggle against the Germans and economic hardship for a while sustained agreement among Italians.

15 For events leading to this, see F. W. Deakin, *The Brutal Friendship* (London, 1962).
16 See Jemolo, pp. 278–80.

One sign of reviving political life was congress of the main parties at Bari in January 1944 which condemned the monarchy. None of the allied states was willing to accept this. The Russians told the Communists to maintain the monarchy (which, to the surprise of their allies, they had recognized as the legal government of Italy), and to participate in a coalition formed in April 1944. The liberation of Rome was followed by the cession of his constitutional powers by the king to Prince Umberto, and Italy once more had its own government at Rome.

In the north, divergencies appeared between the communist and non-communist partisans. The allied command feared a repetition of the Greek troubles, and took steps to assert control of the resistance before the Germans collapsed. In the end, the German surrender only shortly anticipated that in Germany itself, and although the northern partisans rose and seized the cities, the revolutionary tide ebbed rapidly as the allied forces arrived. Elsewhere the bureaucracy had already assumed its temporarily shaken hold on the country and the Church was beginning to make itself felt as the focus of conservative sentiment in the country. In December de Gasperi, the former secretary of the *Partito Popolare*, took office as the first prime minister of Italy who led an avowedly Catholic party. His coalition cabinet (which included communists) presided over a ravaged, starving and increasingly divided country. The monarchy was compromised, Italy had lost her fleet and her colonies, and even Trieste was under international control after being fought over by Italian and Yugoslav partisans. Italy's future was uncertain and ominous. Her assets were the claims to Allied goodwill of nearly 100,000 Italians killed fighting Germans, and large sterling balances built up by British purchasing of local supplies.

By the end of 1945, France had long been mistress of her own territory. The regime which had emerged could trace its origins back to a broadcast made from London, on 18 June (Waterloo Day) 1940, by the French soldier, General de Gaulle, announcing that he was not going to abandon the struggle and calling on his countrymen everywhere to follow him. This was an act of revolution, or at least of insubordination; the legal government of France, in the eyes of most Frenchmen, was in Bordeaux and led by de Gaulle's old commander, Marshal Pétain, defender of Verdun and restorer of the French army's morale in 1917. That government had surrendered to the Germans. It subsequently set itself up at Vichy, from which it ruled the unoccupied south of France (and, technically, the occupied north) until the whole country was occupied by the Germans in 1943. Frenchmen were divided, not only by self-interest but by views of where their duty lay. Nevertheless, some in the French colonies had at once responded to de Gaulle's call, and many French soldiers, sailors and airmen made their way to England to join him.

Only Clemenceau can in this century rival de Gaulle as a servant of France. In spite of his difficulties in dealing with his allies – some self-imposed, though the Americans treated him with special distrust and dislike – his obstinacy maintained France's moral independence as an allied nation and won back her recognition as a major European power in 1945. The crisis of de Gaulle's Free France came after the Anglo-American landings in North Africa and the American decision to cooperate with the Vichy officials on the spot. At the same time, the German occupation of the whole of France and the scuttling of the French fleet at Toulon to prevent its capture did much to expunge from the record the misgivings felt in England about France since 1940. An attempt was made to patch up agreement between de Gaulle and Giraud, a prickly but patriotic soldier much favoured by the Americans and put up by them as a candidate to lead the French war effort, now based on North Africa. This was, it was thought, achieved at Casablanca in January 1943. There followed the formation of the *Comité Français de Liberation Nationale*, from which de Gaulle gradually excluded Giraud's men; it was recognized in August as the representative of the French Republic by the Russians, and the British and Americans followed suit.

From this time, de Gaulle dominated the French national revival. He was already cooperating with the communists, who, since the invasion of Russia, had ceased to oppose the war and had begun resistance activity. Other groups were also in action, and a *Conseil Nationale de la Résistance* had been set up to coordinate their activity under a representative of de Gaulle in the spring of 1943.[17] Thus, on the eve of the invasion of France, the despised Free French leader of 1940 was the *de facto* ruler of much of the French empire and one director and co-ordinator of the Resistance movement in France. Resistance was greatly strength-

---

17 This brave man, Jean Moulin, was tortured to death by the *Gestapo* the same year, but the organization remained in existence.

ened by the extension of the German occupation to the whole of France and the imposition of forced labour, and large quantities of arms were supplied to it by the British. Although de Gaulle was angered by the severance of his communications with France on the eve of the invasion and the refusal of the Americans to allow him to proceed at once to France, his organization gave invaluable help to the allied armies. The general's next great stroke was to ignore his allies and go at once to Paris after its abandonment by the Germans on 26 August. There exists a memorable film of this; it may have been his happiest day.

France was re-established. Significantly, her first alliance was made with Russia in December. De Gaulle, head of the Provisional Government, was not invited to Yalta or Potsdam, but France was admitted to the Allied Control Commission which was to govern Germany. At home there were terrible problems. Liberation had released pent-up hatreds; it seems likely that some 9,000 people were summarily shot or lynched, mostly before fighting came to an end. Courts condemned 767 of the guilty to death. But the figures are still debatable and say nothing about thousands of acts of vindictiveness which led to head-shaving, beatings, detention and deprivation of civic rights as old scores were settled, bad men were punished and late-comers to the Resistance sought to obliterate earlier caution by belated patriotic zeal. Re-establishing law and order was not easy. There was a grave problem of disarming the Resistance, many of whom were communists. Pétain was condemned to death for treason (though the sentence was not carried out), and Laval, another ritual victim, was tried and executed.

In October, elections to a Constituent Assembly made the communists the largest party in the Assembly, closely followed by the socialists: the Gaullist *Mouvement Républicain Populaire* had only a few seats less, but came third. The General was ceasing to be the leader of the nation and becoming only the leader of a party. Nevertheless, the Assembly unanimously elected him president of a provisional government, and France ended the year, like Italy, ruled by a coalition which included communists.

The other great power of 1939 had disappeared. This was almost physically true; battles had raged across Germany, and her towns had received 315 tons of bombs for every one dropped on England. The death-throes of the Third *Reich* had been appalling. Germans who had moved east away from the bombing flooded back again into central Germany as the Russians drew nearer. Macabre and terrible episodes stood out even among the horrors. In February 1945 the allies bombed Dresden, thus saving the Russians some street-fighting, but killing 20,000 people. At the end the Nazi party itself began to break up and its leaders sought to negotiate individually with the allies. On 25 April the Russian and American armies met; on the same day the Russians surrounded Berlin. There, in the atmosphere of a madhouse (which well reflected the lunacies still going on outside as S.S. guards strove to kill off the inmates of concentration camps before they could be rescued) Hitler handed over the *Reich* to Admiral Doenitz and committed suicide. Two days earlier Mussolini had been shot by Italian partisans. On 12 April Roosevelt had died. Soon, Churchill was to be dismissed by the British electorate. At the end of the year, of all the major combatant states, only Russia was ruled by the man under whom it had entered the war.

Europe's self-inflicted wounds had all but destroyed her. Two great extra-European armies were camped in her heart lands. Only in England and the smaller states did constitutional government seem secure; countries which had never known it had passed directly from right-wing authoritarianism to Stalinist totalitarianism. Those which had constitutional governments in the past now faced dangers which made them look fragile. Starvation, industrial destruction, the devastation of towns and crowds of 'displaced persons' (as refugees had come to be called) seemed more threatening to governments based on liberal principles than even the conditions which had sometimes proved fatal to them before 1939. It could not be seen in 1945 that the danger of popular revolution in industrialized societies was still, as it has always been since 1880, remote, nor that super-power rivalries would make it even more so. In the middle of Europe lay the most ruined area of all, Germany, and there revolution was impossible. To extend to her the privileges of the Atlantic Charter was unthinkable; memories of occupation were too recent and bitter. One tie between Europeans in 1945 was a deep determination to contain Germany against a recurrence of her aggressiveness in the future. Unwittingly, they were thus to divide Germany in two, and to give Bismarck's Prussia a government which looked to Moscow for its direction.

At the moment, it was hard even to detect a glow in the ashes; the economic resurgence of the next quarter-century could no more be anticipated than the shape of new political structures which was to accompany it. All that was certain was that a dream which had haunted the interwar years had been blown to the winds; there could be no return to 1914. It was at last clearly impossible. In this sense, European history enters a new historical phase. The next was to make explicit what had already been implied by such facts as American participation in the two great wars and the Japanese successes of 1905–41: the European world domination of 1880 was now inconceivable, its foundations stricken in the first world war and pulverised in the second. It was replaced by that of two world powers, one of them equipped with a more powerful weapon than any yet known. Both enjoyed immense prestige round the globe.

It hardly mattered that the colonial powers of 1939, except for Italy, formally resumed their sway (indeed, there were parts of the world where it had hardly been disturbed). Russia was the only power vigorous and willing enough to extend her frontiers in the old way (she took back the tsarist territories lost to Japan in 1905), though. The United States was not interested, though she had the strength to do it. Elsewhere the older colonial states felt that 800 million people still under their rule in 1945 were trouble enough, without acquiring more. What had happened since 1939 could not be erased. Japanese victories in Asia had irremediably damaged European prestige in countries where 'face' was supremely important. Sixty thousand British and Commonwealth troops had surrendered at Singapore in 1942 in the most humiliating disaster to British arms since Yorktown, and the greatest capitulation in their history. The replacement of colonial by Japanese rule had not always been a pleasant experience for the nationalists who had at first warmly greeted their fellow Asiatics, but they had benefited from it in several ways. Where resistance movements against Japanese had been encouraged from the outside, arms and advice had been supplied and organizations set up which could later be used against the colonial powers. The Japanese collapse, too, in many places presented stores of arms to the nationalists before European forces could resume control.

The European powers had already been forced to make concessions. The French had to admit Japanese forces to Indo-China in 1940. The presence of China among the allied nations led to the abandonment of their extraterritorial rights in China by the

British in 1942. The British Empire was then already an association of independent states so far as its white Dominions were concerned, and although this conception had been brilliantly vindicated by the assistance given to England in her lone European struggle, the Japanese war had revealed that Australia and New Zealand must for the future look to the United States for their main defence in the Pacific. On the other side of the world, another symbol of a passing pattern of world power was the lease of British bases to the United States in 1940 for the defence of the Atlantic seaboard and Caribbean. The long dependence of the Monroe doctrine on the Royal Navy was over. Hemisphere defence was now to be an American responsibility.

The most portentous change came in India. Self-government, though bitterly opposed by Churchill, had long been asserted to be the ultimate goal of British rule in the subcontinent. The appearance of a Japanese army in Burma and a Japanese fleet in the Bay of Bengal in 1942 led to an offer of self-government immediately after the war if asked for by a Constituent Assembly. The offer was refused (and most of the nationalist leaders were then locked up) but the meaning of the step was not lost. British policy in India was in retreat. It was clear in 1945, when a party took power in England which had long had self-government for India and Burma as a part of its programme, that further British concession would soon take place.

Churchill was often under pressure from Roosevelt over India. The American president, in spite of Churchill's explicit disclaimers that only a European reference had been intended, always insisted that the Atlantic Charter's respect for the 'rights of all peoples to choose the government under which they will live' extended to colonial peoples. Great expectations were aroused by these words in the United States, so great, indeed, that Churchill was provoked into his most celebrated pronouncement on colonial policy in November 1942: 'I have not become the King's First Minister to preside over the liquidation of the British Empire.' The collapse of the eastern empires before the Japanese strengthened American policy because only American power could restore them. Roosevelt tirelessly sought to influence his allies' postwar settlement of colonial issues. He strove to persuade the British to grant immediate self-government to India. He courted the Russians (who had not hitherto shown much awareness of colonial issues as a possible source of postwar difficulty), to get some kind of postwar trusteeship under international control.[18] He urged an allied declaration promising independence to colonies as soon as possible. At Teheran, Roosevelt spoke alone to Stalin about the need to prepare for Indian, Burmese and Malayan independence, warning him at the same time against talking to Churchill about. He also sought international trusteeship for French Indo-China. When, in 1944, the shape of a future world organization was being decided, the Americans were disappointed that international trusteeship was only envisaged for former League mandates and territories acquired from the enemy.

The publicity given to American disagreements with England and France over colonial issues, and the suggestive overtures of American policy towards Russia which resulted from this, helped to sap the old empires. Morally, their prestige waned; politically, trouble was being laid up for the future. But in 1945 the rapidity with which they would disappear could hardly have been envisaged; we must beware of the distorting effects of hindsight in assessing the damage already done. Only in retrospect can it be seen to have been fatal. In any case, there was more to the collapse of the European hegemony than the waning of empire. Colonial possessions had only been its glittering façade.

The world can hardly be said to have profited from Europe's suicidal disasters. Even before 1939, Japanese aggressiveness had showed what the world had lost with the disappearance of the old European balance of power. When the policemen of the world fell out, there was bound to be uncertainty and disorder until new policemen appeared and could agree. Only in one respect did the European hegemony survive, yet it was crucial. As the men of 1945 looked round for guidance and landmarks in a world of new possibilities, they discerned two sources of hope and enlightenment. One was the tradition of liberal nationalism, the other, Marxist communism; both were European. Inspired by them, and armed with inventions and practical knowledge from the same source, the men of the post-European age faced an alarming future in 1945. Yet in some perspectives, that future now seems likely to be regarded as the most European age of all: *Graecia capta ferum victorem cepit.*

18 R. E. Sherwood, *Roosevelt and Hopkins: an intimate history* (New York, 1948), pp. 572–3.

APPENDIX

1. Estimated populations of European countries, 1880–1940

(in millions)

	1880	1890	1900	1910	1920	1930	1940
Austria-Hungary	37.8	—	47.0	51.4			
Austria					6.5	6.7	6.7
Hungary					8.0	8.6	9.3
Belgium	5.5	6.1	6.7	7.4	7.6	8.1	8.3
Bulgaria	2.8	3.3	3.7	4.3	4.8	5.7	6.7
Czechoslovakia					13.0	14.0	14.7
Denmark	2.1	2.3	2.6	2.9	3.2	3.5	3.8
Finland	2.0	2.4	2.7	3.1	3.4	3.4	3.7
France	39.2	40.0	40.7	41.5	39.0	41.2	39.8
Germany	40.2	44.2	50.6	58.5	61.8	65.1	69.8
Holland	4.0	4.5	5.1	5.9	6.8	7.9	8.9
Italy	29.6	31.7	33.9	36.2	37.0	40.3	43.8
Norway	1.8	2.0	2.2	2.4	2.6	2.8	3.0
Poland					26.8	31.5	34.6
Portugal	4.6	5.1	5.4	6.0	6.0	6.8	7.7
Rumania	4.7	6.3	7.3	15.5	18.0	15.5	16.5
Russia	97.7	—	131.7	153.8	158.0	176.0	192.0
Spain	16.6	17.6	18.6	19.9	21.2	23.4	25.8
Sweden	4.6	4.8	5.1	5.5	5.9	6.1	6.4
Switzerland	2.8	2.9	3.3	3.8	3.9	4.1	4.2
U.K.	31.1	34.3	38.2	42.1	43.7	45.9	48.2
Yugoslavia					11.9	13.8	15.8

Most of this table is drawn from that in *The Cambridge Economic History of Europe*, vol. VI, p. 61. Supplementary material has been added from other sources. Different bases of estimation, reliance in some instances on figures drawn from censuses taken in years nearest to those shown, boundary changes, and the paucity of information about Russia mean that such a table as this can only be used as an approximate guide. It is certainly more accurate for some countries than for others. Nevertheless the table gives a general impression of comparative population movement. The Austro–Hungarian figure for 1910 includes Bosnia and Herzegovina; those of Belgium, Italy, Rumania, Russia and Bulgaria for 1920 take account of boundary changes at the end of the Great War. The Second World War produced large population movements and boundary changes which often do not make 1945 population figures usefully comparable with pre-war figures, even where there is agreement about the figures themselves.

2. Production of basic industrial materials

(i) *Coal output*

Annual Averages for quinquennia. Production in million tons

	1880–84	1885–9	1890–94	1895–9	1900–04	1905–9
U.K.	159	168	183	205	230	260
France	20	22	26	31	33	36
Belgium	17	18	20	22	23	24
Germany	66	78	94	121	157	203
Russia	4	5	7	11	17	23
World	374	442	533	643	827	1,048
U.S.A.	85	117	156	192	286	393

	1910–14	1915–19	1920–24	1925–9	1930–34	1935–9
U.K.	274	247	240	227	223	233
France	40	24	34	52	50	47
Belgium	23	15	23	26	25	29
Germany	247	244	249	316	265	351
Russia	27	28	11	31	73	133
World	1,232	1,269	1,280	1,448	1,251	1,488
U.S.A.	474	545	521	548	388	408

Source: W. S. and E. S. Woytinsky, *World population and production* (New York, 1953), p. 868.

(ii) *Pig-iron output*

Annual production in million tons

	1880	1890	1900	1910	1918	1930	1940
U.K.	7.9	8.0	9.1	10.2	9.2	6.3	8.3
France	1.7	2.0	2.7	4.0	1.3	10.1	3.7
Belgium	0.6	0.8	1.0	1.9	—	3.4	1.8
Germany	2.7	4.6	8.5	14.8	11.9	9.7	13.9
Luxemburg	0.3	0.6	1.0	1.7	1.3	2.5	1.0
Italy	—	—	—	0.3	0.3	0.5	1.0
Russia	0.4	0.9	2.9	3.0	0.5	5.0	15.2
World	18.5	27.6	41.0	66.3	67.0	79.6	103.2
U.S.A.	3.9	9.4	14.0	27.7	39.7	32.3	43.0

Source: Woytinsky, p. 1, 117 and Romeo, pp. 170–1.

(iii) *Steel output*

Annual production in million tons

	1880	1890	1900	1910	1918	1930	1940
U.K.	1.3	3.6	5.0	6.5	9.7	7.4	13.4
France	0.4	0.7	1.6	3.4	1.8	9.4	4.4
Belgium	0.1	0.2	0.7	1.9	—	3.4	1.9
Germany	0.7	2.2	6.6	13.7	15.0	11.5	19.0
Italy	—	0.1	0.1	0.7	0.3	0.5	1.0
Russia	0.3	0.4	2.2	3.5	0.4	5.8	18.0
World	4.4	12.4	28.3	60.5	78.6	95.0	142.0
U.S.A.	1.3	4.3	10.4	26.5	45.2	41.4	60.8

Source: Woytinsky, p. 1, 118, with Italian figures from R. Romeo, *Breve storia della grande industria in Italia* (Bologna, 1961), pp. 170–1.

NOTE ON FURTHER AND REFERENCE READING

Footnotes to the foregoing text provide references to sources for quotations and particular facts, and some indications of discussions of special topics. Here, I wish also to mention some publications which the reader is often likely to find useful, a few suggestive contemporary books which can be used as 'documents', some specialist studies of particular value not yet mentioned and, finally, a few collections of sources which are helpful ways into basic data. This brief selection is a very personal choice from an immense literature, tempered by a wish to stick as far as possible to writing in English. It is arranged so as to follow the sequence of chapters in this book.

Some easily accessible general books provide much more information than can this short survey, but (unfortunately for monoglot English and American readers and for my wish to stick to English) there is nothing in our language on this period which is so continuously and comprehensively useful as the relevant volumes in the French series called *Peuples et Civilisations*. These volumes are M. Baumont, *L'essor industriel et l'imperiálisme colonial (1878–1904)* (Paris 1949), P. Renouvin, *La crise européenne et la première guerre mondiale* (Paris 1948), and M. Baumont, *La faillite de la paix (1918–1939)* (2 vols, 5th edn, Paris 1967 and 1968). Three volumes in *The New Cambridge Modern History* (hereinafter *NCMH*) span the years 1880 to 1945. Volume XI, *Material Progress and World-wide Problems 1870–1898*, ed. F. H. Hinsley (Cambridge 1962) is good, but its chronological successor, vol. XIII, *The Era of Violence*, ed. D. Thomson (Cambridge 1960), was unsatisfactory and has been replaced by a new Volume

XII, *The shifting balance of world forces1898–1945*, edited by C. L. Mowat (Cambridge 1968). None of these has a bibliography, unlike the volumes of the old *Cambridge Modern History*, the last of which, XIII, *The Latest Age*, edited by A. W. Ward and others (Cambridge 1910), is a mine of useful information and in some respects itself a historical document. Its bibliographies should be consulted; they mention much contemporary material lost to sight in more modern books. Another collective work, which also exploits the pictorial and visual record of much that is covered by this book, is the part-work *History of the Twentieth Century* (London 1968–70), edited by A. J. P. Taylor and J. M. Roberts.

The best introductions to the topics of Chapter 2 are to be found in two collective works of economic history. Volume VI of *The Cambridge Economic History of Europe, The Industrial Revolution and After*, was edited (in two parts) by H. J. Habakkuk and M. Postan (Cambridge 1965, bibl.). In the *Fontana Economic History of Europe*, edited by C. M. Cipolla, Volumes 4, *The Emergence of Industrial Societies* (London 1973) and 5, *The Twentieth Century* (London 1976), are full of relevant and helpful material. On population, C. McEvedy and R. Jones, *Atlas of World Population History* (London 1978) is concise and valuable; less well-organized but useful is the *Histoire générale de la population mondiale* by M. R. Reinhard and A. Armengand (Paris 1961). The old book by J. H. Clapham, *The Economic Development of France and Germany 1815–1914* (Cambridge 1921) is a classic account organized around national economic history but there are now numerous other excellent national studies. One which importantly qualifies the apparent primacy of Great Britain is A. L. Levine, *Industrial retardation in Britain 1880–1914* (London 1967). Among others are G. P. Palmade, *French Capitalism in the Nineteenth Century (1961)*, (Newton Abbot 1972); H. Böhme, *An Introduction to the Social and Economic History of Germany* (Oxford 1978); S. Clough, *The Economic History of Modern Italy* (New York 1964), supplemented by R. F. Neufield, *Italy; School for Awakening Countries* (New York 1961) and the convenient statistical tables in R. Romeo, *Breve storia della grande industria in Italia* (Bologna 1961). A further important study of France which goes beyond economic history is E. Weber's *Peasants into Frenchmen, the Modernization of Rural France* (London 1977). For an international perspective, see W. Ashworth, *A Short History of the International Economy since 1850* (4th edn, London 1986) and W. A.

Lewis, *Growth and Fluctuation 1870–1913* (London 1978). Several topics touched on in the section of this chapter entitled 'Europe and the World' can be followed up through the ideas and references contained in G. Barraclough, *An Introduction to Contemporary History* (London 1964) and J. M. Roberts, *The Triumph of the West* (London 1985). R. E. Dickinson, *The West European City* (2nd edn, London 1961) is helpful on urbanization, but the veteran A. F. Weber, *The Growth of Cities in the Nineteenth Century* (1899, repr. Ithaca, N.Y., 1963) is better. For a fine synthesis of one country's experience, see P. J. Waller, *Town, City, and Nation: England 1850–1914* (Oxford 1982).

Initial guidance on topics in Chapter 3 can be found in some of the chapters in *NCMH* Vol. XI. An old book by A. L. Lowell, *Governments and Parties in Continental Europe* (5th edn, London 1900) should not be overlooked on political assumptions and institutions. E. Kedourie's essay, *Nationalism* (London, 1960), remains outstanding; A. Cobban's *The Nation State and National Self-Determination* (New Edition, London 1969) is also valuable, while long shadows are cast by W. W. Hagan's book on *Germans, Poles and Jews. The Nationality Conflict in the Polish East 1772–1914* (Chicago 1980). A useful pre-war collection of documents edited by M. Oakeshott, *The Social and Political Doctrines of Contemporary Europe* (Cambridge 1939) is mainly concerned with the period after 1918, but has some earlier material. L. L. Snyder, *Race: a History of Modern Theories* (London 1939) and P. Pulzer, *The Rise of Political Antisemitism in Germany and Austria* (London 1963) open other themes of importance. On one important country see S. Wilson, *Ideology and Experience: Antisemitism in France at the time of the Dreyfus Affair* (London 1982). The immense bibliography of Christianity can be approached through K. S. Latourette's *Christanity in a Revolutionary Age* (5 vols, London 1959–63), of which volumes I, II, and IV deal with Europe; H. McLeod, *Religion and the people of Western Europe 1789–1970* (Oxford 1981), brief and confined to Christianity in spite of its title, nonetheless contains much to stimulate thought and further reading.

The best short guide to printed sources for the international relations dealt with in chapter IV is still to be found in A. J. P. Taylor, *The Struggle for Mastery in Europe 1848–1919* (Oxford 1954). Ampler narratives are to be found in, among older books, W. L. Langer's *European Alliances and Alignments, 1871–1890* (2nd edn, New York 1951) and *The Diplomacy of Imperialism, 1890–1902* (2nd edn, New York 1952). More recent and very perceptive is N. Stone, *Europe Transformed 1878–1919* (London 1978). One helpful monograph on international relations is G. F. Kennan, *The Decline of Bismarck's European Order* (Princeton 1979). For a continuing guide through the affairs of south-eastern Europe, see C. and B. Jelavich, *The Establishment of the Balkan National States, 1804–1920* (Seattle 1977). On military and naval matters, B. Bond, *War and Society in Europe, 1870–1970* (London 1984) is thought-provoking and A. J. Marder, *The Anatomy of British Sea Power* (New York 1940) is a classical monograph. Its subject can be pursued chronologically further in the same author's history of the Royal Navy in the early twentieth century, *From the Dreadnought to Scapa Flow* (5 vols, London 1961–1970).

Imperialism and colonialism in this period are huge subjects. The first major literary and polemical landmark was J. A. Hobson, *Imperialism: A Study* (London 1902); D. Fieldhouse's *Colonialism 1870–1945* (London 1981) and W. J. Mossman's *Theories of Imperialism* (London 1981) should provide as much as anyone needs for a summary view of a fertile debate so far as major shifts of interpretation are concerned. Also useful are *Imperialism in the Twentieth Century* by A. P. Thornton (London 1977) and a collection edited by W. Mommsen and J. Oster-hammel, *Imperialism and after. Continuities and discontinuities* (London 1986). There is also much useful information in volume III of *The Cambridge History of the British Empire, The Empire Commonwealth, 1870–1919* ed. E. A. Benians *et al.* (Cambridge 1959).

On the Constitutional states before 1914 see R.C.K. Ensor, *England 1870–1914* (Oxford 1936), the earlier chapters of T. O. Lloyd, *From Empire To Welfare State* (3rd edn, Oxford 1985), the old but still helpful *Democracy in France*, by D. Thomson (London 1946), J. M. Mayeur and M. Rébérioux, *The Third French Republic from its Origins to the Great War 1871–1914* (Cambridge 1984), C. Seton-Watson, *Italy from Liberalism to Fascism 1870–1925* (London 1967), G. Brenan, *The Spanish Labyrinth* (new edn, Cambridge 1960), and Raymond Carr, *Spain 1808–1939* (2nd edn, Oxford 1980). Among books contemporary with events discussed in this chapter, see J. E. C. Bodley, *France* (London 1898) and G. Sorel, *La Révolution Dreyfusienne*, (Paris 1909), A. V. Dicey, *Law and*

Opinion in England during the Nineteenth Century (new edn, London 1963), and L. T. Hobhouse, *Democracy and Reaction* (new edn, Brighton 1972).

Among the conservative empires, the fundamental work on Russia is H. Seton-Watson, *The Russian Empire 1801–1917* (Oxford 1967). One interesting Russian source in translation is C. Pobedonostev, *Reflections of a Russian Statesman* (London, 1898). Bernard Pares, *Russia and Reform* (London 1907) is also a contemporary account by a fine observer; another 'document' (and a classic of interpretative history in that it long did much to define the terms of debate over the events of 1904–5) is L. Trotsky, *History of the Russian Revolution* (new edn, London 1965). Useful special studies are two books by P. A. Zaionochkovsky, *The Russian Autocracy under Alexander III* (Gulf Breeze 1976) and *The Russian Autocracy in Crisis 1878–1882* (Gulf Breeze 1979). J. Blum, *Lord and Peasant in Russia* (Princeton 1961), T. H. von Laue, *Sergei Witte and the Industrialization in Russia* (New York 1963), J. L. H. Keep, *The Rise of Social Democracy of Russia* (Oxford 1963), and the readable book by B. D. Wolfe, *Three who made a Revolution* (London 1956) are all excellent. Finally, a brief pamphlet by R. B. McKean, *The Russian Constitutional Monarchy 1907–1917* (the Historical Association, London 1977) is a good survey of what can be said about the political alternatives to revolution at the end of the *ancien régime*. Polish history from the years covered in this book can best be taken up via N. Davies' magnificent two-volume study, *God's Playground – A History of Poland* (Oxford 1981). On the Dual Monarchy, the classic contemporary work remains H. Wickham Steed's polemic *The Habsburg Monarchy* (London 1913); it can be supplemented by another old interpretative book, O. Jászi's, already cited in the text. The best modern comprehensive account is C. A. Macartney, *The Habsburg Empire* (London 1969). On the nationality questions, see the general study by C. and B. Jelavich already cited, A. C. Janos, *The Politics of Backwardness in Hungary 1825–1945* (Princeton 1982) and two striking books by British observers, R. W. Seton-Watson, *Racial Problems in Hungary* (London 1908) and Rebecca West, *Black Lamb and Grey Falcon* (London 1941). Social history in south-eastern Europe is helpfully opened up by a collection of documents edited by Doreen Warriner, *Contrasts in Emerging Societies* (London, 1965). A. Ramm's *Germany 1789–1919, a political History* (London 1967) is a good starting point for the German empire. The whole of the history of imperial Germany has been debated vigorously in the last twenty years and there is now much more important material in English than when the first edition of this book appeared in 1967. See, on the issues, A. U. Wehler, *The German Empire 1871–1914* (Leamington Spa 1984), for comments on (*inter alia*) his views, G. Eley and D. Blackbourn, *The Peculiarities of German History* (Oxford 1984) and Eley's collection of articles, *From unification to Nazism* (London 1986). For what followed the Bismarckian era, *Germany without Bismarck* by J. C. G. Röhl (London 1967) is still helpful, but the best starting point is a collection of papers *Society and Politics in Wilhelmine Germany* (London 1978) edited by R. J. Evans, whose own introductory essay is a splendid summary of a couple of decades of historiographical debate. W. Z. Laqueur, *Young Germany* (2nd edn, London 1962) and H. C. Meyer, *Mitteleuropa in German thought and Action 1815–1945* (The Hague 1955), are still suggestive on special topics; for another important aspect of the interplay of ideas and politics in Germany before 1914, see G. Eley, *Reshaping the German Right* (London 1980). G. Masur, *Imperial Berlin* (London 1974) is an attractive essay illuminating some aspects of German social history.

The best way into the rich and complex intellectual history touched on in chapter VII is still probably H. Stuart Hughes, *Consciousness and Society* (London 1959). K. W. Swart, *The Sense of Decadence in Nineteenth Century France* (The Hague 1964) is something of a catalogue, but useful over a wider field than its title suggests. F. Stern, *The Politics of Cultural Despair* (Berkeley 1961) remains stimulating on Germany. H. Read, *A Concise History of Modern Painting* (London 1959), is as helpful as any other summary book on the subject, though that is not saying much; catalogues of some major exhibitions (e.g. *Les Réalismes 1919–1939*, Centre Georges Pompidou, Paris, 1981 or P. Vergo's *Vienna 1900*, National Museum of Antiquities of Scotland, Edinburgh, 1983) are likely to be more useful, though (or perhaps because) more narrowly-focussed. Two other valuable specialized collections of papers which illuminate more than their titles would indicate are John Rewald's *Studies in Post-Impressionism* (London 1986) and *Homage to Barcelona: The City and its Art 1888–1936* (London 1986). The pervasiveness of Nietzsche's influence makes some acquaintance with his ideas indispensable; W. Kaufmann, *Nietzsche* (Princeton 1950) is a good start. On anarchism see J.

Joll, *The Anarchists* (London 1964); on socialism the same author's excellent and brief study of *The Second International* (rev. edn, London 1975) and, flat-toned but comprehensive, G. D. H. Cole, *A History of Socialist Thought* (5 vols, London 1953–60), Vols II–III. G. Lichtheim, *Marxism: an Historical and Critical Study* (London 1961) ably introduces the theoretical debates, but the outstanding heavyweight discussion is L. Kolakowski, *Main Currents of Marxism* (3 vols, Oxford 1978). J. P. Nettl's *Rosa Luxemburg* (Oxford 1966) and C. E. Schorske's *German Social Democracy 1905–1917* (Cambridge, Mass. 1955) remain valuable monographs, but should now be supplemented by W. L. Guttsman, *The German Social Democratic Party, 1875–1933* (London 1981). Feminist issues are at this stage of historical writing best approached through monographs rather than general books. One such is S. C. Hanse and A. R. Kenney, *Women's Suffrage and Social Policy in the Third French Republic* (Princeton 1984).

The literature on the origins of the Great War long dominated the discussion of international relations before 1914. The best introduction is James Joll, *The Origins of the First World War* (London 1984). Old, but still valuable studies are B. E. Schmitt, *The Coming of the War* (New York 1930) and, because of its perspective (its author was editor of the Milan newspaper, *Il Corriere della Sera*), L. Albertini, *The Origins of the War of 1914* (3 vols, London 1952–7). For the main diplomatic documents see a collection dealing with the final crisis edited by I. Geiss under the title *July 1914* (London 1967). On other related topics see *German nationalism and the European response, 1890–1945*, edited by C. Fink and others (London 1986); G. F. Hudson, *The Far East in World Politics* (Oxford 1937); B. E. Schmitt, *The Annexation of Bosnia* (Cambridge 1937); J. A. White, *The Diplomacy of the Russo-Japanese War* (Princeton 1964); and the first part of F. Fischer, *Germany's aims in the First World War* (London 1967) a book whose (longer) German first edition of 1961 detonated a noisy debate among Germans both about Germany's responsibility for war in 1914, and about the continuity of cultural and political factors in twentieth-century German history. On the first topic, Fischer's views have since been developed further in another book, *War of Illusions: German Policies from 1911 to 1914* (London 1975). On the war itself, his first book was truly pioneering. No comparable study exists for any of the other great powers, though there is a huge list of publications on Europe at war. One of the most enjoyable, plunging the reader into the heart of affairs as they were seen from London, is Winston Churchill's semi-autobiographical *The World Crisis*, (6 vols, London 1923, single-volume abridgement 1941). R. Haigh, *The Great War at Sea 1914–18* (Oxford 1983), K. Robbins, *The First World War* (Oxford 1984) and *War Aims and Strategic Policy in the Great War 1914–18*, edited by B. Hunt and A. Preston (London 1977) are all very helpful. J. Kocka, *Facing Total War: German Society 1914–1918* (Leamington Spa 1985) is suggestive and goes further than Fischer in exploring the degeneration of political culture in the German middle class and its 'radicalization'. Of a vast number of books on operations, one which is among the best introductions to the nature of large-scale warfare on the Western Front is about the end of fighting there: H. Essame, *The Battle for Europe 1918* (London 1972).

In pursuing topics introduced in Chapter X, H. W. V. Temperley, *The History of the Peace Conference* (6 vols, London 1920–24) should be supplemented as a documentary source by D. Lloyd George's self-justifying *The Truth about the Peace Treaties* (2 vols, London 1938) and by *Papers relating to the Foreign Relations of the United States 1919* (2 vols, Washington D.C. 1942–3). The first series of *Documents on British Foreign Policy 1919–1939* also deals with this period. Keynes' comments on Versailles were first seriously criticized by E. Mantoux in *The Carthaginian Peace* (Oxford 1946). See, further, Arno J. Mayer, *Politics and Diplomacy of Peacemaking* (London 1968) on the background. G. Kennan, *Russia and the West* (Boston 1961) is the best introduction to Russian foreign policy. For the origins of later Russian attitudes and policy J. W. Wheeler-Bennett, *Brest Litovsk: The Forgotten Peace* (London 1938) remains definitive and Kennan's volumes on Soviet-American relations, *Russia Leaves the War* and *The Decision to Intervene* (Princeton 1956 and 1958), are outstanding. Also on the interventions, see R. H. Ullman's fine trilogy, *Anglo-Soviet Relations 1917–1921* (3 vols, London 1961–1972). The League is still a neglected topic, but F. P. Walters, *History of the League of Nations* (2 vols, Oxford, R.I.I.A. 1951) is useful. On Eastern Europe, see C. A. Macartney and A. W. Palmer, *Independent Eastern Europe* (London 1982). For a narrative guide to the interwar years, Baumont, *op. cit.*, can be supplemented by an interpretative essay by E. H. Carr, *The Twenty Years' Crisis* (London 1939, 2nd edn, 1946).

On post-war economic and social history several books already cited for chapter 11 are helpful. So is the League of Nations *International Statistical Yearbook*, published from 1927 onwards (later re-titled the *Statistical Yearbook of the League of Nations*). There is an admirable selection of original materials in the third volume of *Documents of European Economic History, The End of the Old Europe 1914–1939* edited by S. Pollard and C. Holmes (London 1973). W. A. Lewis's *Economic Survey 1919–1939* (London 1948) is old, short but good. There is a useful chapter on 'Economic interdependence and planned economies' by Asa Briggs in NCMH, XII. L. Robbins, *The Great Depression* (London 1934) is interesting contemporary observation. On one important and neglected topic, peasant central and eastern Europe, see the authentic but dated *Agricultural Systems of Middle Europe* (New York 1933) edited by O. S. Morgan, D. Mitrany's *Marx Against the Peasant* (New York 1961) and I. T. Berend and G. Ránki, *Economic Development in East-Central Europe* (New York 1974).

For chapter XII some of the books recommended in chapter V are relevant: Spain and Italy are dealt with later, but on other individual countries see: E. H. Kossman, *The Low Countries 1780–1940* (Oxford 1978); E. D. Simon, *The Smaller Democracies* (London 1939); T. K. Derry, *A short History of Norway* (London 1957; bibl.); D. A. Ruston, *The Politics of Compromise* (Princeton, N. J. 1955); A. Werth, *The Twilight of France* (London 1942); G. Lefranc, *Histoire du Front Populaire* (Paris 1965); E. Weber, *Action Française* (Stanford 1962); P. J. Larmour, *The French Radical Party in the 1930's* (Stanford 1964). T. O. Lloyd's *Empire to Welfare State* has excellent up-to-date bibliographical references for Great Britain.

There is plentiful translated material in topics dealt with in chapter XIII. Readers might begin with the two-volume *Lenin; Selected Works* (Moscow 1947), Trotsky's *History of the Russian Revolution* (already cited), N. H. Baynes (ed.), *The Speeches of Adolf Hitler 1922–1939* (London 1942), and the seven volumes of selected materials on *Nazi Conspiracy and Aggression* (Washington D.C. 1946), which contain material not in the 42 volumes of evidence printed after the Nuremberg Trials. From a mass of contemporary comment see, on Russia, N. N. Sukhanov, *The*

Russian Revolution 1917 (Oxford 1955), E. Lyons, *Assignment in Utopia* (London 1938), A. Gide, *Retour de l'URSS* (Paris 1936), and V. Serge, *Memories of a Revolutionary 1901–1941* (Oxford 1963). A useful collection of documents is edited by M. McCauley, *The Russian Revolution and the Soviet State 1917–1921* (London 1975); it has some interesting maps. Among secondary books, the enormous work of E. H. Carr, *A History of Soviet Russia* (14 vols, some with R. W. Davies, London 1950–1978) dominates the landscape down to 1929, but those coming fresh to the subject (if there be any among readers of the this book) may prefer to begin with J. P. Nettl's brief illustrated essay on *The Soviet Achievement* (London 1967) and *Stalinism: Essays in Historical Interpretation*, ed. R. C. Tucker (New York 1977). On Germany, one contemporary account of great interest (though to be used with caution) is H. Rauschning's *Germany's Revolution of Destruction* (London 1939). A. J. Nicholls' *Weimar and the rise of Hitler* (2nd edn, London 1979) and I. Kershaw, *The Nazi Dictatorship: Problems and Perspectives of Interpretation* (London 1985) are sure-footed and clear guides in much-debated areas. On particular topics, see M. Broszat, *The Hitler State* (London 1981), on the chaotic nature of Nazi administration, J. Overy, *The Nazi Economic Recovery 1932–1938* (London 1982) on what was and was not achieved with the economy, W. S. Allen, *The Nazi Seizure of Power. The Experience of a Single German Town 1930–1935* (London, 1966), and (wide-ranging and suggestive) P. Gay, *Freud, Jews and other Germans* (Oxford 1978). G. Salvemini set out in *The Fascist Dictatorship in Italy* (London 1928) the view of a committed observer. Among many biographies, D. Mack Smith, *Mussolini* (London 1981) is outstanding, and A. J. Gregor, *Italian Fascism and Developmental Dictatorship* (Princeton 1980) is a valuable supplement to Clough and Noether (see above). See A. Lyttelton, *The Seizure of Power* (London 1973) on the establishment of the regime. For other authoritarian regimes in the east, start with A. Polonsky, *The Little Dictators* (London 1975). On Spain, besides Carr's revised Oxford history, see also *The Spanish Tragedy* (London 1977) by him, R. A. H. Robinson, *The Right, The Republic and Revolution, 1931–1936* (Newton Abbot 1970) and B. Bolloten, *The Spanish Revolution: The Left and the Struggle for Power during the Civil War* (Chapel Hill 1979). Many of the essays contained in *European Fascism*, edited by S. J. Woolf (London

1968) and in *The European Right: a historical profile*, edited by H. Rogger and E. Weber (London 1965), are also helpful and particularly relevant to chapter XIII's subject-matter.

Several books recommended in chapter XI will be found relevant to chapter XIV. See also the useful collection of essays edited by R. Prigent, *Renouveau des idées sur la famille* (Paris 1954). The best introductions to the cinema of the period are films. A selection should include an 'escapist' American piece such as *Top Hat* (1935), a 'western' such as *Stagecoach* (1939), German classics like *Metropolis* (1926) and *M* (1932), Russian classics of such different styles as *The Battleship Potemkin* (1925), *The General Line* (1929) and *Alexander Nevsky* (1938), Nazi propaganda exemplified in the significantly-titled *Triumph of the Will* (1937) or *Olympiad*, the film of the Olympic games of 1936, and the British documentaries mentioned in the text. For a good introductory bibliography, see Paul Rotha, *The Film Till Now* (rev. edn. with additional material by R. Griffith, London 1949); *The Politics of the Soviet Cinema 1917–1929*, by R. Taylor (Cambridge 1979), is interesting. On broadcasting, Asa Briggs, *The History of Broadcasting in the United Kingdom* (4 vols, Oxford 1961–1979). For painting, Herbert Read, *op. cit.*, and for architecture, N. Pevsner, *Pioneers of the Modern Movement*, (London 1936). About literature it is difficult to know where to begin, but C. Connolly, in *The Modern Movement* (London 1965) provided an interesting if idiosyncratic 'list of books with outstanding originality and richness of texture and with the spark of rebellion alight' (p. 6), though one limited to England, France and America. One first-class work of popularizing criticism was Edmund Wilson, *Axel's Castle* (London 1931). The topics touched on in the last section of chapter XIV are not easy to annotate but two works of contemporary reflexion are very suggestive: P. Drucker, *The End of Economic Man* (London 1939) and L. Schwarzschild, *World in Trance* (London 1943). On political irrationalism E. Nolte, *Three Faces of Facism* (London 1965), is tough going, but good. On socialism, see Cole and Kolakowski. Some of the books recommended in chapter X are relevant to the subject of chapter XV. The most useful introductory bibliography (with comments) is in A. J. P. Taylor, *The Origins of the Second World War* (2nd edn, with 'Second Thoughts', London 1963), a book possibly over-praised when it appeared but also one certainly over-condemned later. Its bibliography was completed before the official *Documents Diplomatiques Francaises 1932–1939*, began to appear in 1963, or *Facing the Dictators* (London 1962), a justificatory but interesting volume of Lord Avon's memoirs, or W. Carr's excellent *Arms, Autarky and Aggression* (London, 2nd edn, 1979). Elizabeth Wiskemann's brief and somewhat dated *Europe of the Dictators 1919–45* (London 1966) is good on the neglected topic of connexions between foreign and domestic politics in the smaller states. G. C. Peden, *British Rearmament and The Treasury: 1932–1939* (Edinburgh 1979) is a way into the debates on one great power's policies, a collection of papers edited by W. J. Mommsen on *The Fascist Challenge and the Policy of Appeasement* (London 1983), and K. Robbins, *Munich 1938* (London 1968), are also helpful on the crisis era. Finally, see the collection edited by G. Martel, *The origins of the Second World War reconsidered* (London 1986).

On the vast literature of the Second World War comment must be even more selective. Up-to-date when published, and still the best comprehensive single volume account, is G. Wright's *The Ordeal of Total War 1939–1945* (New York 1968). In *The Second World War* (London 1948–54) Winston Churchill provided what is for all its defects the outstanding account by a man at the centre of the struggle: it is now easier to aim off for suppression and bias since we have available Volumes VI and VII of Martin Gilbert's meticulous biography *Winston Churchill* (London 1983 and 1986). General de Gaulle, too, wrote important *Mémoires de guerre* (Paris 1954–9). Below the level of the war leaders there are too many other personal accounts even to select examples. Some other stimulating books are A. Dallin, *German Rule in Russia 1941–45* (London 1957), A. Werth, *Russia at War* (London 1963), J. Erickson's two volumes, *The Road to Stalingrad* and *The Road to Berlin* (London 1975 and 1983), E. Kogon, *The Theory and Practice of Hell* (London 1950, an abbreviated translation of a German work on the concentration camps), and A. Milward, *The German Economy at War* (London 1965). The real meaning of a new dimension in strategy is brought out by R. J. Overy, in *The Air War, 1939–45* (London 1980). On one terrible subject M. Gilbert, *The Holocaust* (London 1986) supplants all other narratives. An unrivalled selection of pictorial evidence as well as some excellent articles can be found in the weekly *History of the Second World War* (London 1967–1969). One important film is the French *Nuit et brouillard,* produced by the *Commission d'histoire de la déportation* of the *Comité d'histoire de la deuxième guerre mondiale.* Very different, but equally revealing, films are the German (*Feldzug in Polen* (1939) and the British *Desert Victory* (1942).

MAPS

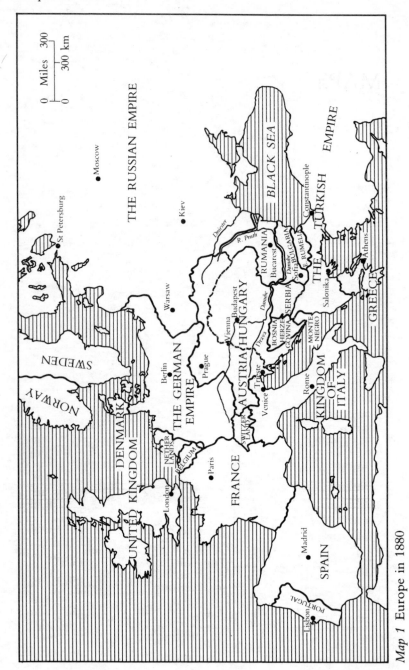

Map 1 Europe in 1880

Map 2 The Balkans, 1880–1914

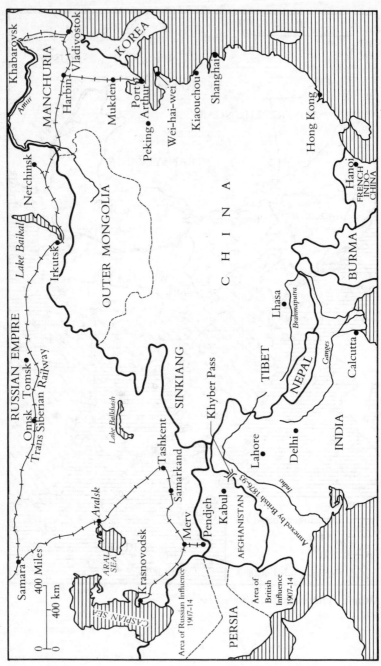

Map 3 Russia's interests in Asia, 1880–1914

Map 4 The Great War: Western and Italian Fronts

Map 5 The Great War: Eastern Front

Map 6 The Settlement of Central and Eastern Europe, 1917–1922

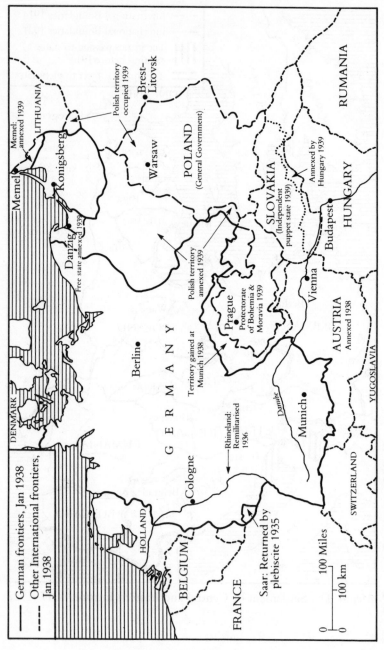

Map 7 Greater Germany, 1933–40

Map 8 Russian Recovery: 1939–1941 and the German Invasion

Index

627